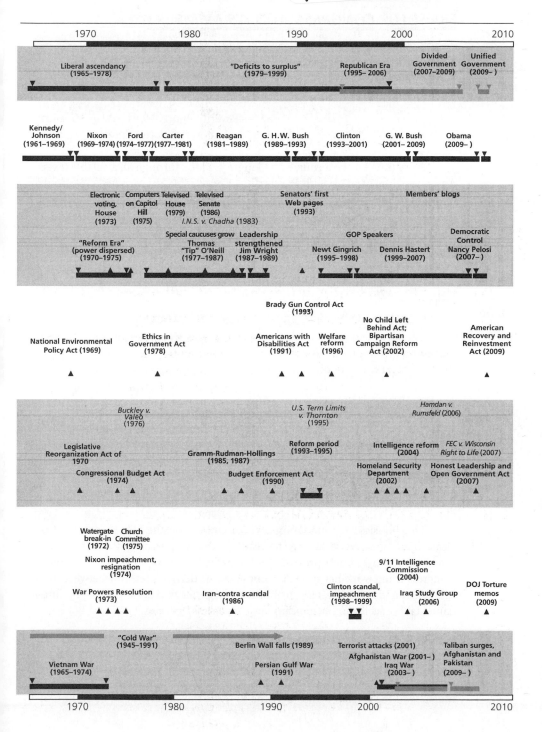

1970   1980   1990   2000   2010

Liberal ascendancy
(1965–1978)

"Deficits to surplus"
(1979–1999)

Republican Era
(1995– 2006)

Divided
Government
(2007–2009)

Unified
Government
(2009–)

Kennedy/
Johnson
(1961–1969)

Nixon
(1969–1974)

Ford
(1974–1977)

Carter
(1977–1981)

Reagan
(1981–1989)

G. H.W. Bush
(1989–1993)

Clinton
(1993–2001)

G. W. Bush
(2001– 2009)

Obama
(2009–)

Electronic
voting,
House
(1973)

Computers
on Capitol
Hill
(1975)

Televised
House
(1979)

Televised
Senate
(1986)

Senators' first
Web pages
(1993)

Members' blogs

I.N.S. v. Chadha (1983)

"Reform Era"
(power dispersed)
(1970–1975)

Special caucuses grow
Thomas
"Tip" O'Neill
(1977–1987)

Leadership
strengthened
Jim Wright
(1987–1989)

GOP Speakers

Newt Gingrich
(1995–1998)

Dennis Hastert
(1999–2007)

Democratic
Control
Nancy Pelosi
(2007–)

Brady Gun Control Act
(1993)

National Environmental
Policy Act (1969)

Ethics in
Government Act
(1978)

Americans with
Disabilities Act
(1991)

Welfare
reform
(1996)

No Child Left
Behind Act;
Bipartisan
Campaign Reform
Act (2002)

American
Recovery and
Reinvestment
Act (2009)

Buckley v.
Valeo
(1976)

U.S. Term Limits
v. Thornton
(1995)

Hamdan v.
Rumsfeld (2006)

Legislative
Reorganization Act of
1970

Gramm-Rudman-Hollings
(1985, 1987)

Reform period
(1993–1995)

Intelligence reform
(2004)

FEC v. Wisconsin
Right to Life (2007)

Congressional Budget Act
(1974)

Budget Enforcement Act
(1990)

Homeland Security
Department
(2002)

Honest Leadership and
Open Government Act
(2007)

Watergate
break-in
(1972)

Church
Committee
(1975)

Nixon impeachment,
resignation
(1974)

9/11 Intelligence
Commission
(2004)

DOJ Torture
memos
(2009)

War Powers Resolution
(1973)

Iran-contra scandal
(1986)

Clinton scandal,
impeachment
(1998–1999)

Iraq Study Group
(2006)

"Cold War"
(1945–1991)

Berlin Wall falls (1989)

Terrorist attacks (2001)

Taliban surges,
Afghanistan and
Pakistan
(2009–)

Vietnam War
(1965–1974)

Persian Gulf War
(1991)

Afghanistan War (2001–)
Iraq War
(2003–)

1970   1980   1990   2000   2010

PRAISE FOR *CONGRESS AND ITS MEMBERS*

"Books don't make it to a twelfth edition by accident. *Congress and Its Members* is the standard work on the subject because it is engaging, comprehensive, and always current. It is the rare book that is relied on by both students and faculty."

—Peverill Squire, *University of Missouri*
and Co-Editor, *Legislative Studies Quarterly*

"Every time I teach a course on Congress, I look through all available texts. And every time I end up with the classic—*Congress and Its Members*. The book manages to incorporate the latest scholarship, have a theme that can spark class discussion, and engage students at the same time. I have used the book in a summer course with combined undergraduate and MA students, and frequently find the students read even some chapters that I have not assigned, because the book engages their interest."

—Clyde Wilcox, *Georgetown University*

"I assign *Congress and Its Members* because of its reliably high quality. It is accessible to undergraduate students yet manages to introduce sophisticated ideas. And it combines classic theories and examples with timely material from the most recent session of Congress."

—Barry C. Burden, *University of Wisconsin–Madison*

"I have used *Congress and Its Members* for more than twenty years. The book is clear, comprehensive, and extremely useful for classroom use. It represents a nice balance of the contemporary and historical, the theoretical and the practical. I look forward to using it again."

—John J. Pitney Jr., *Claremont McKenna College*

"This book is *the* foundation text for courses on the U.S. Congress. It is clear, comprehensive, and easy to read. Students appreciate the up-to-date examples and the clearly presented information. The authors' use of the dual Congress framework helps to illuminate the underlying tension between the individual and collective responsibilities of legislators. This is one of the fundamental books for understanding how Congress operates."

—Pam Camerra-Rowe, *Kenyon College*

"Written in clear, direct prose, *Congress and Its Members* provides students with a central theme—the two Congresses—that enables them to organize and understand the myriad details that characterize the structure and operation of a very complex institution. I particularly value the fact that by following that theme through the many dimensions of Congress, students learn to think analytically as they learn about Congress itself."

—Dennis J. Goldford, *Drake University*

"I have used *Congress and Its Members* for many years now. Although I look at the alternatives, I have never seriously considered changing texts. Students generally resist textbooks, but mine have never complained about this one. The authors appreciate the importance of political life and the welter of difficulties in representative and legislative politics. They present the lows without cynicism, and the highs receive appropriate attention. The presentation of each topic is accessible, clear, and engaging; social science analysis is used only as a means to the end of understanding political life."

—Stephen Wirls, *Rhodes College*

"*Congress and Its Members* is the classic text for teaching and learning about Congress. It is written by the authoritative giants in the field of congressional scholarship. Readers will find it well written and comprehensive."

—Janet M. Box-Steffensmeier, *Ohio State University*

F *our Pivotal Events in Congressional History.* British troops burn the Capitol and capture Washington, D.C., in 1814 (top left). Inflamed sectional passions caused violence on the Senate floor in 1856 (top right): An enraged Rep. Preston Brooks (S.C.), right, raises his cane against an unsuspecting Sen. Charles Sumner (Mass.), beating him senseless. Laurence M. Keitt, a fellow South Carolinian, at left, raises his cane and holds a pistol behind his back to keep other northerners from interfering. In the televised Army-McCarthy hearings of 1954 (bottom), Sen. Joseph McCarthy (R-Wis.) is chastened by U.S. Army counsel Joseph Welsh (left) during the Senate inquiry into McCarthy's reckless charges about communists in government. "At long last, sir, have you no sense of decency?" Welsh exclaimed after McCarthy attacked one of the lawyer's young aides. The dramatic exchange was a turning point in McCarthy's career; eventually he was censured by his Senate colleagues. Finally (center), Senate Majority Leader Lyndon B. Johnson (D-Texas) gives "the treatment"—prolonged persuasion at very close range—to Sen. Theodore Francis Green (D-R.I.).

TWELFTH EDITION

Congress and Its Members

Roger H. Davidson
University of Maryland

Walter J. Oleszek
Congressional Research Service

Frances E. Lee
University of Maryland

CQ PRESS

A Division of SAGE
Washington, D.C.

CQ Press
2300 N Street, NW, Suite 800
Washington, DC 20037

Phone: 202-729-1900; toll-free, 1-866-4CQ-PRESS (1-866-427-7737)

Web: www.cqpress.com

Cover design: Anne C. Kerns, Anne Likes Red, Inc.
Composition: C&M Digitals (P) Ltd.

♾ The paper used in this publication exceeds the requirements of the American National Standard for Information Sciences—Permanence of Paper for Printed Library Materials, ANSI Z39.48-1992.

Printed and bound in the United States of America

13   12   11   10   09   1   2   3   4   5

ISBN: 978-0-87289-967-4
ISSN: 1539-1779

FOR *Nancy; Douglas, Victoria, Elizabeth, Thomas, James, Alexander; Chris, Teddy, Emily, and Olivia*

—*R.H.D.*

FOR *Janet, Mark, and Eric*

—*W.J.O.*

FOR *Emery and Beverly*

—*F.E.L.*

Roger H. Davidson is professor emeritus of government and politics at the University of Maryland, and has served as visiting professor of political science at the University of California, Santa Barbara. He is a Fellow of the National Academy of Public Administration. For the 2001–2002 academic year, he served as the John Marshall Chair in political science at the University of Debrecen, Hungary. His books include *Remaking Congress: Change and Stability in the 1990s,* co-edited with James A. Thurber (1995), and *Understanding the Presidency,* 3rd ed., co-edited with James P. Pfiffner (2003). Davidson is co-editor with Donald C. Bacon and Morton Keller of *The Encyclopedia of the United States Congress* (1995).

Walter J. Oleszek is a senior specialist in the legislative process at the Congressional Research Service. He has served as either a full-time professional staff aide or consultant to every major House and Senate congressional reorganization effort beginning with the passage of the Legislative Reorganization Act of 1970. In 1993, he served as Policy Director of the Joint Committee on the Organization of Congress. A longtime adjunct faculty member at American University, Oleszek is a frequent lecturer before various academic, governmental, and business groups. He is the author or co-author of several books, including *Congressional Procedures and the Policy Process,* 7th ed. (2007), and *Congress under Fire: Reform Politics and the Republican Majority,* with C. Lawrence Evans (1997).

Frances E. Lee is associate professor of government and politics at the University of Maryland. She has been a Research Fellow at the Brookings Institution and an APSA Congressional Fellow. She is the author of *Beyond Ideology: Politics, Principles, and Partisanship in the U.S. Senate* and co-author, with Bruce I. Oppenheimer, of *Sizing Up the Senate: The Unequal Consequences of Equal Representation* (1999). Her articles have appeared in *American Political Science Review, Journal of Politics, Legislative Studies Quarterly,* and *American Journal of Political Science,* among others.

BRIEF CONTENTS

CONTENTS

PART V Conclusion

Reference Materials

TABLES, FIGURES, AND BOXES

Boxes

A s authors of the twelfth edition of a book that first appeared in 1981, we are perforce believers in the maxim that in politics six months is a long time and four years practically a lifetime. Events of recent years surely bear out this wisdom.

George W. Bush entered the presidency after a 2000 presidential contest that ended in the political equivalent of a tied score resolved by a judicial coin toss. His presidency was dramatically transformed by the terrorist attacks of September 11, 2001, which led him to reinvent himself as a wartime leader. This image helped him in 2004, when voters narrowly reelected him over Democratic candidate John Kerry, a Massachusetts senator and Vietnam War hero.

As with many second-term presidents, Bush's support plummeted amid vocal opposition from Democrats and Independents, and eventual ruptures within his own Republican ranks. Disapproval of the administration—especially over the Iraq war and the failure to cope with the devastation of Hurricane Katrina in 2005—led to election losses in 2006 and 2008. Democrats now control both chambers of Congress (2007–2011).

The remarkable rise of first-term Illinois senator Barack Obama underscores the unpredictability of politics. No one rated him a front-runner in the presidential race; but his campaign—innovatively designed, skillfully managed, and lavishly financed—won him the Democratic nomination over New York senator Hillary Clinton, followed by his defeat of Republican senator John McCain of Arizona, arguably the GOP's most credible candidate. But, alas, Obama, who expected to win for his opposition to the Iraq war, found that the threat of national and global economic collapse topped his ambitious agenda.

The roller-coaster fortunes of recent presidents and congressional majorities remind us of the pervasive pluralism of the American political system, with its diverse viewpoints and interests. Presidents and congressional leaders see their mandates sooner or later bump against the Founders' intricate "auxiliary precautions" for preventing majorities from winning quick or total victories. Not the least of the system's attributes is what we call the "two Congresses" dilemma: Congress is both a conduit for localized interests and a maker of national policy.

In this edition we discuss new developments and fresh research findings regarding nearly every aspect of Congress. The wartime context—thus far embracing two wars and reconstruction efforts in Afghanistan and Iraq and ongoing offensives against terrorism—has placed extreme pressures on Congress. Deliberative legislative processes can seem out of place when people demand immediate, concerted actions. But hasty responses invariably were regretted, and sober reflections demanded legislative oversight and remediation.

The strength of partisanship and party leadership is probably the leading Capitol Hill story. Congress is a vortex of so-called permanent campaigns, in which electioneering goals and techniques are routinely interlocked with the process and content of lawmaking. We record changes in party leadership, the committee system, floor procedures, and the Capitol Hill community. Shifting relationships with presidents, the bureaucracy, and the courts illustrate the centrality of Congress to the entire federal government apparatus.

Amid all these global and political changes, there are underlying constants in Congress's character and behavior. Most important is the dual nature of Congress as a collection of career-minded politicians, and also as a forum for shaping and refining national policy. We employ the two Congresses theme to explain the details of congressional life as well as the scholarly findings about legislators' behavior. Colorful personalities and practical examples illustrate the enduring topics essential for understanding Capitol Hill. We strive to describe recent events and trends precisely and perceptively; more than that, we try to place these developments in the broader historical and conceptual frameworks necessary for understanding how Congress and its members function.

These are troubling times for those of us who believe in representative democracy. True, Congress has, with varying levels of success, absorbed astonishing changes in its membership, partisan control, structural and procedural arrangements, and policy agendas. Yet Congress has all too often retreated from its constitutional mandate to initiate national policy and oversee government operations. Its prerogatives are under siege from executive decision makers, federal judges, and elite opinion makers, who constantly belittle its capacities, ignore its authority, and evade its scrutiny. Yet lawmakers themselves must accept blame for yielding too often to the initiatives of others, for failing to ask hard questions and to insist upon straight answers, and for at times substituting partisan allegiance for independent judgment. Today's Congress all too often falls short of the Founders' vision that it is the "first branch of government" for reasons that this book explains.

This edition, like its predecessors, is written for general readers seeking an introduction to the modern Congress as well as for college or university students taking courses on the legislative process or national policymaking. We try to present accurate, timely, and readable information, along with thoughtful and influential insights from scholars and practitioners alike. Although wrapped around our core theme, the book's chapters are long on analysis. We make no apologies for this. Lawmaking is an arduous and complicated business that demands special skills; those who would understand it must master its details and nuances. At the same time, we hope to convey the energy and excitement of the place. After all, our journalist friends are right: Capitol Hill is the best beat in town.

We have incurred more debts to friends and fellow scholars than we could ever recount. We thank especially our colleagues at the Congressional Research Service and elsewhere: Mildred Amer, Richard Beth, Ida Brudnick, Kevin Coleman, Curtis Copeland, Royce Crocker, Christopher Davis, C. Lawrence Evans, Louis Fisher, Sam Garrett, Richard Grimmett, Valerie Heitshusen, William Heniff Jr., Henry Hogue, Frederick Kaiser, Robert Keith, Michael Koempel, Emery Lee, Betsy Palmer, Harold Relyea, Morton Rosenberg, Steve Rutkus, Elizabeth Rybicki, James Saturno, Wendy Schiller, Judy Schneider, Barbara Schwemle, Stephen W. Stathis, Sean M. Theriault, Jim Thurber, and Donald Wolfensberger. The views and interpretations expressed in this book are in no way attributable to the Congressional Research Service.

We also wish to thank our reviewers, Carol Dwyer, Syracuse University; Kristin Kanthak, University of Pittsburgh; Sean M. Theriault, University of Texas at Austin; and Charles E. Walcott, Virginia Tech. The thoughtful comments of these valued colleagues provoked us to consider new questions and revisit enduring ones, and helped us to shape the current edition.

Our friends at CQ Press deserve special appreciation. Brenda Carter, director of the college division, has inspired and prodded us over the last eight editions. Charisse Kiino, our editor, capably reviewed the book's overall structure and helped us tighten this edition. Anna Socrates, Allyson Rudolph, and Jason McMann offered skilled and probing editorial assistance. Allyson supervised the book's production and gave invaluable advice on photo research.

Our deep appreciation for our families, for their love and support, cannot be fully expressed in words. As a measure of our affection, this book is dedicated to them.

—Roger H. Davidson
Santa Barbara, California

—Walter J. Oleszek
Fairfax, Virginia

—Frances E. Lee
Washington, D.C.

May 2009

TWELFTH EDITION

Congress and Its Members

Rep. Thaddeus McCotter's Two Congresses. As a voice in national affairs, Representative McCotter (R-Mich.) addresses the domestic auto industry crisis during a cable news interview (top left), and fires tough questions at the CEO of insurance giant AIG concerning the firm's debts from sub-prime lending (top right). At home in his Michigan district, he visits a senior glee club (center) and reads to local elementary school students (bottom).

The Two Congresses

Representative Thaddeus McCotter, R-Mich., took to the House floor to denounce President George W. Bush's proposed $700-billion bailout of the financial industry. "We will not walk out of this room after a forced vote waving a piece of paper in our hands claiming 'fleeced in our time,'" he declared.[1] In September 2008 the Bush administration sought to forestall further financial panic after credit markets seized up following the collapse of the Lehman Brothers investment bank. The plan proposed that the United States Treasury would purchase troubled assets from financial institutions, freeing capital for lending and investment. But McCotter, the first of many conservative lawmakers, loudly decried the bailout plan as a betrayal of basic free-market principles. Blogging on the House Republican Policy Committee's Web site, McCotter put the matter even more starkly: "We were not elected to abet American socialism."[2]

Less than a month later, McCotter faced another bailout proposal. This time, the chief executives of the Big Three automakers flew to Capitol Hill, each in his own company's private jet, to ask for $25 billion in loans to help their companies survive the economic downturn.[3] "Forces beyond our control have pushed us to the brink," the CEO of General Motors told Congress, with the firm's bankruptcy looming within a matter of weeks.[4] A large majority of Republicans in Congress opposed the auto bailout, just as they had opposed the rescue package for financial institutions.

For McCotter, representing a suburban Detroit constituency, this policy decision would hit very close to home. A Detroit native and graduate of both its Catholic Central High School and the University of Detroit, McCotter had watched Michigan's manufacturing base steadily deteriorate over the preceding thirty years.[5] Even as the national economy grew between 2000 and 2005, Michigan's economy hemorrhaged nearly a quarter million manufacturing jobs—more than any other state.[6] McCotter's district—home to many automotive suppliers and manufacturers, including a General Motors powertrain plant and the headquarters of TRW Automotive—would suffer widespread losses of both white- and blue-collar jobs, along with increased home foreclosures and personal bankruptcies.

As a conservative Republican and a Detroit-area representative, McCotter had to weigh his economic ideals against local political and economic realities.

Thus McCotter now characterized the issue as a "question of equity."[7] If Congress was willing to appropriate hundreds of billions of dollars for financial institutions, why shouldn't it also spend a much smaller sum for "the very hard-working men and people whose taxes have gone into the $700 billion bailout?"[8] "In the district," he explained, "people feel that this is clearly Congress caring more about people who wear Guccis than people who wear Levi's."[9] Advancing this equity argument, along with concerns about the national security importance of maintaining a domestic manufacturing capability, McCotter forcefully advocated the auto bailout—not only in the House, but also before a variety of audiences, including talk shows on Fox News and CNN. In the end, Congress refused to provide assistance to the automakers, but the Bush administration intervened at the last minute with a short-term bridge loan to help the automakers avoid bankruptcy.

McCotter navigates a difficult political landscape representing a competitive district in rust-belt Michigan. In a district closely divided between Republicans and Democrats, McCotter has faced strong Democratic opposition since winning the seat in 2002; he was reelected in 2008 with 51.4 percent of the vote.

McCotter's experiences illustrate the themes in this book. The work of Congress is conducted not only on Capitol Hill but also in states and districts hundreds or thousands of miles away. A congressman whose immediate and extended family resides in the district, a man who first achieved notice performing in rock bands as part of Detroit's club scene, McCotter remains firmly committed to his constituents. But he is certainly more than a ward heeler or a "Republican in name only." He currently chairs the Republican Policy Committee, a stepping-stone to higher leadership in Congress. And he views his party as a "transformational political movement,"[10] not a mere personal affiliation. With national ambitions and local ties, McCotter must balance his party's positions with constituency sentiment on many policy issues, including extending unemployment benefits, the State Children's Health Insurance Program, and the auto bailout.

THE DUAL NATURE OF CONGRESS

Thaddeus McCotter's representational dilemmas underscore the dual nature of Congress. Like all members of Congress, McCotter inhabits two very different but closely linked worlds. As a representative of a district suffering economic hardship, McCotter needs to prove that he can be an effective local advocate— that he understands his constituents' needs and will act on their behalf. At the same time, McCotter also endeavors to be a national policymaker and party leader. In the wake of Republicans' congressional losses in the 2008 elections, McCotter perceived an imperative to think big. "We're rock bottom," he said. "We are now free to start thinking again, acting again, and doing the right thing by what our constituents and our country need."[11] He advised Republicans to respond to Democratic policies by "craft[ing] an alternative that hits real people and frames the debate,"[12] and to that end he contributes to his party's internal conversation by regularly posting "thinking points" on the Republican Policy Committee's Web site. McCotter's various goals and activities highlight the dual character of the national legislature—Congress as a lawmaking institution and also an assembly of local representatives.

In this sense, there are two Congresses. One is the Congress of textbooks, of "how a bill becomes a law." It is Congress acting as a collegial body, performing constitutional duties and debating legislative issues that affect the entire nation. This Congress is a fascinating arena where all the forces of American political life converge—presidents, cabinet members, career bureaucrats, activists, lobbyists both powerful and weak, all of them ambitious political entrepreneurs. This Congress is more than a collection of its members at any given time. It is a mature institution with a complex network of rules, organizations, and traditions. Norms mark the boundaries of the legislative playing field and define the rules of the game. Individual members generally must accept Congress on its own terms and conform to its established ways of doing things.

A second Congress also exists, and it is every bit as important as the Congress portrayed in textbooks. This is the representative assembly of 541 individuals (100 senators, 435 representatives, 5 delegates, and 1 resident commissioner). This Congress includes men and women of diverse ages, backgrounds, and routes to office, with each doing what is necessary to maintain the support of their local constituencies. Their electoral fortunes depend less upon what Congress produces as a national institution than upon the policy positions they take individually and the local ties they build and maintain. "As locally elected officials who make national policy," asserts Paul S. Herrnson, "members of Congress almost lead double lives."[13]

The two Congresses are in many ways separated by a wide gulf. The complex, often insular world of Capitol Hill is far removed from most constituencies, in perspective and outlook, as well as in miles. Lawmaking and representing are separate tasks, and members of Congress recognize them as such. Yet these two Congresses are bound together. What affects one affects the other—sooner or later.

Legislators' Tasks

The duality between institutional and individual duties surfaces in legislators' daily activities and roles. As Speaker Sam Rayburn, D-Texas, once remarked: "A congressman has two constituencies—he has his constituents at home, and his colleagues here in the House. To serve his constituents at home, he must also serve his colleagues here in the House."[14]

No problem vexes members more than that of juggling constituency and legislative tasks. The pull of constituency business is relentless. To maintain their local connections, Congress schedules lengthy recesses, termed "district work periods," and many short Tuesday-to-Thursday legislative weeks. On average between 2000 and 2009, Congress was in session for less than

40 percent of every calendar year. Members largely spent the rest of their time at home in their constituencies. Even when members are in Washington, one study found that they spend less than 40 percent of their time on lawmaking duties on the floor of the House or in committee.[15]

Reelection is the paramount operational goal of members of Congress. As a former representative put it: "All members of Congress have a primary interest in getting reelected. Some members have no other interest."[16] After all, politicians must win elections before they can achieve any long-range political goals. "[Reelection] has to be the *proximate* goal of everyone, the goal that must be achieved over and over if other ends are to be entertained," David R. Mayhew observed in *Congress: The Electoral Connection*.[17]

Individual legislators vary in how they balance the twin roles of legislator and representative. Some legislators devote more time and resources to lawmaking, while others focus almost entirely on constituency tending. With their longer terms, some senators stress voter outreach and fence mending during the year or two before reelection and focus on legislative activities at other times. Yet senatorial contests normally are more competitive and costly than House races, and many senators now run for reelection all the time—like most of their House colleagues.[18] Across the board, most senators and representatives would like to devote more time to lawmaking and other Capitol Hill duties instead of to constituency demands, according to the results of a congressionally sponsored survey of members.[19]

Popular Images

The two Congresses notion also conforms to the average citizen's perceptions. Opinion studies reveal that people view the U.S. Congress differently from the way they see their individual senators and representatives. Congress as an institution is perceived primarily as a lawmaking body. It is judged mainly on the basis of citizens' overall attitudes about politics, policy processes, and the state of the union. Do people like the way things are going, or not? Do they feel that Congress is carrying out its duties equitably and efficiently? Are they optimistic or pessimistic about the nation's future? Do they subscribe to Mark Twain's cynical view that Congress is "a distinctly native criminal class"?

Citizens view their own legislators as agents of local concerns. People judge their legislators by such yardsticks as service to the district, communication with constituents, and home style (the way officeholders present themselves in their districts or states). In judging their senators or representatives, voters are likely to ponder questions such as these: Is the legislator trustworthy? Does the legislator communicate well with the state (or district) by answering mail promptly and offering timely help to constituents? Does the legislator listen to the state (or district) and its concerns?[20]

The public's divergent expectations of Congress and its members send conflicting signals to senators and representatives. Congress as a whole is judged by the processes it uses and the policies it adopts (or fails to adopt), however vaguely voters understand them.[21] But individual legislators are more apt to be elected, and returned to office, because of personal qualities and constituent service. This incongruity leads some officeholders to adopt a strategy of opening as much space as possible between themselves and those other politicians back in Washington—even sometimes their own party's leaders.

The Constitutional Basis

Congress's dual nature—the dichotomy between its lawmaking and representative functions—is dictated by the U.S. Constitution. Congress's mandate to write the nation's laws is found in Article I of the Constitution. By contrast, Congress's representational functions are not specified in the Constitution; rather these duties flow from the constitutional provisions for electing senators and House members.

It is no accident that the Constitution's drafters devoted the first article to establishing the legislature and enumerating most of the government's powers. Familiar with the British Parliament's prolonged struggles with the Crown, the authors assumed the legislature would be the chief policymaking body and the bulwark against arbitrary executives. "In republican government, the legislative authority necessarily predominates," observed James Madison in *The Federalist Papers.*[22]

Although in the ensuing years the initiative for policymaking has shifted many times between the legislative and executive branches, the U.S. Congress remains virtually the only national assembly in the world that drafts in detail the laws it passes, instead of simply debating and ratifying measures prepared by the government in power.

The House of Representatives was intended to be the most representative element of the U.S. government. Representatives are elected directly by the people for two-year terms to ensure that they do not stray too far from popular opinion. As Madison explained, the House should have "an immediate dependence on, and an intimate sympathy with, the people."[23] For most members of the House, this two-year cycle means nonstop campaigning, visiting, looking after constituents, and errand running.

The Senate was originally one step removed from popular voting: State legislatures selected senators. Some of the Constitution's Framers hoped the Senate would temper the popular passions expressed in the House. But they were ultimately overruled in favor of a Senate that, like the House, directly expresses the people's voice. In 1913 the Seventeenth Amendment to the Constitution was adopted, providing for direct popular election of senators. Although elected for six-year terms, senators must stay in close touch with the electorate. Like their House colleagues, senators typically regard themselves as constituency servants. Most have transformed their office staffs into veritable cottage industries for generating publicity and handling constituents' inquiries.

Thus the Constitution and subsequent historical developments affirm Congress's dual functions of lawmaker and representative assembly. Although the roles are tightly bound together, they nonetheless impose separate duties and functions.

Back to Burke

On November 3, 1774, in Bristol, England, the British statesman and philosopher Edmund Burke set forth the dual character of a national legislature. The constituent-oriented parliament, or Congress, he described as

> a Congress of ambassadors from different and hostile interests, which interests each must maintain, as an agent and advocate, against other agents and advocates.

The parliament of substantive lawmaking he portrayed in different terms. It is

> a deliberative assembly of one nation, with one interest, that of the whole—where not local purposes, not local prejudices, ought to guide, but the general good, resulting from the general reason of the whole.[24]

Burke preferred the second concept and did not hesitate to let his voters know it. He would give local opinion a hearing, but his judgment and conscience would prevail in all cases. "Your faithful friend, your devoted servant, I shall be to the end of my life," he declared; "a flatterer you do not wish for."[25]

Burke's Bristol speech is an enduring statement of the dilemma legislators face in balancing their two roles. Burke was a brilliant lawmaker. (He even sympathized with the cause of the American colonists.) But, as might be said today, he suffered from an inept home style. His candor earned him no thanks from his constituents, who turned him out of office at the first opportunity.

Burke's dilemma applies equally on this side of the Atlantic. American voters tend to prefer their lawmakers to be delegates who listen carefully to constituents and follow their guidance. During an encounter in Borger, Texas, an irate Baptist minister shouted at then-representative Bill Sarpalius, D-Texas, "We didn't send you to Washington to make intelligent decisions. We sent you to represent us."[26] Sarpalius subsequently was defeated for reelection.

Representing local constituents is not the whole story, of course. Burke's idea that legislators are trustees of the nation's common good is still extolled. In a 1995 decision, U.S. Supreme Court justice John Paul Stevens noted that, once elected, members of Congress become "servants of the people of the United States. They are not merely delegates appointed by separate, sovereign states; they occupy offices that are integral and essential components of a single national Government."[27]

Many talented individuals seek public office, often forgoing more lucrative opportunities in the private sector, precisely because they believe strongly in a vision of what government should do and how it should do it. For such legislators, winning office is simply a means to a larger end. It is reasonable to assume that elected officials "make an honest effort to achieve good public policy."[28]

Burke posed the tension between the two Congresses so vividly that we have adopted his language to describe the conceptual distinction that forms the crux of this book. From Burke, we have also drawn the titles for Part 2, "A Congress of Ambassadors," and Part 3, "A Deliberative Assembly of One

Nation." Every member of Congress sooner or later must come to terms with Burke's dichotomy; citizens and voters will have to form their own answers.

THE TWO CONGRESSES IN COMPARATIVE CONTEXT

Looking around the world, most democracies do not elect legislators in the manner used in the United States. Members of Congress are selected via the oldest form of democratic representation involving elections: a plurality vote within geographic constituencies. By contrast, most other advanced democracies around the world elect legislative representatives under systems of proportional representation (PR), a more recent innovation in democratic institutions. There are many varieties of PR; but compared to the United States, these systems tend to tie legislators more closely to their political parties than to local constituencies. As such, PR systems alleviate somewhat the difficult trade-offs that members of Congress face as they attempt to balance national lawmaking with attention to local constituencies.

PR systems rest on the basic principle that the number of seats a political party wins in the legislature should be proportional to the level of support it receives from voters. If a political party wins 40 percent of the vote overall, then it should receive about 40 percent of the seats. In other words, these systems explicitly assume that political parties are more important than geographic locales to voters' values and political interests.[29] Most commonly in these systems, the parties put lists of candidates before the electorate; the number of a party's candidates to be seated in the legislature from those lists then depends on the percentage of voters supporting that party in legislative elections. To a greater extent than members of the U.S. Congress, candidates elected in PR systems thus serve as representatives of their party's interests and ideological commitments.

Legislators in PR systems face fewer dilemmas about how to balance local constituency politics with national party platforms. Indeed, some PR systems, such as those in Israel and the Netherlands, do not tie representatives to local geographic constituencies at all; all legislators represent the entire nation. Other countries, such as Austria and Sweden, elect multiple representatives from regional districts. Unlike the U.S. districts, such districts are not captured by a single party on a winner-take-all basis, with only one representative for each constituency. Districts where more than one political party enjoys a meaningful level of voter support will elect representatives from more than one party, with each legislator representing those voters who supported his or her party. Some countries, such as Italy, Germany, and New Zealand, use a mixed system, with some representatives elected in individual geographic constituencies and others drawn from party lists to ensure proportionality. In all cases, citizens and legislators alike recognize that the system is primarily designed to ensure that voters' party preferences are proportionally represented.

Members of the U.S. Congress, by contrast, must represent all residents of their geographic constituency, a very difficult task. Constituents grouped together in congressional districts often have little in common. Constituencies can be very diverse in terms of race, class, ethnicity, religion, economic interests, and urbanization. The largest states are microcosms of the nation. Like McCotter's 11th district of Michigan, constituencies may also be narrowly divided in terms of partisanship and ideology. Some members of Congress even face the challenge of representing a constituency that leans towards the opposing party. In attempting to represent their whole state or district at once, House members and senators often employ a "lowest common denominator" form of representation, deemphasizing their party affiliation and their opinions on controversial national issues. Instead, they advertise their personal accessibility to constituents and focus on narrow, localized concerns.[30]

To an important extent, the U.S. system of representation ensures parochialism on the part of lawmakers. All members see themselves as attorneys for their constituencies. They must constantly cultivate the local roots of their power as national legislators. Yet Congress is one body, not two. The same members who shape bills in committee and vote on the floor must rush to catch planes back to their districts, where they are plunged into a different world of local problems and personalities. The same candidates who must sell themselves at shopping centers must shape the federal budget or military weapons systems in Washington, D.C. The unique character of Congress arises directly from its dual role as a representative assembly and a lawmaking body.

DIVERGENT VIEWS OF CONGRESS

Congress has been the subject of a huge array of books, monographs, and articles. Many of its features make Congress a favorite object of scholarly scrutiny. It is relatively open and accessible. It can be approached by traditional means—journalistic stories, case studies, normative assessments, and historical accounts. It is also amenable to the analytic techniques of social science. Indeed, the availability of quantitative indicators of congressional work (floor votes, for example) permits elaborate statistical analyses. Its rule-governed processes allow it to be studied with increasingly sophisticated theoretical formal models. And Congress is, above all, a fascinating place—the very best site from which to view the varied actors in the American political drama.

Writers of an interpretive book on the U.S. Congress thus can draw on a multitude of sources, an embarrassment of riches. Studies of Congress constitute a vast literature. This is a mixed blessing because all this information must be integrated into a coherent whole. Moreover, the scholarly writing is often highly detailed, technical, or theoretical. We have tried to put such material into perspective, make it accessible to all interested readers, and use illustrative examples wherever possible.

A gaping chasm exists between this rich scholarly literature and the caricature of Congress prevalent in the popular culture. Humorists from Mark Twain and Will Rogers to Jay Leno, Stephen Colbert, and Jon Stewart have found Congress an inexhaustible source of raw material. Citizens tend to share this disdain toward the legislative branch—especially at moments of furor over, say, congressional pay raises or ethics scandals or difficult legislative fights like that over the 2009 economic stimulus package. When they are at home with constituents, legislators themselves often reinforce Congress's poor image by portraying themselves as escapees from the funny farm on Capitol Hill. As Richard F. Fenno Jr. puts it, members "run *for* Congress by running *against* Congress."[31]

The picture of Congress conveyed in the media is scarcely more flattering. Journalistic hit-and-run specialists perpetuate a cartoon-like stereotype of Congress as "a place where good ideas go to die in a maelstrom of bureaucratic hedging and rank favor-trading."[32] Newsmagazines, editorial writers, comedians, and nightly news broadcasts regularly portray Congress as an irresponsible and somewhat disreputable gang resembling Woodrow Wilson's caustic description of the House as "a disintegrated mass of jarring elements."[33]

To comprehend how the two Congresses function—both the institution and individual members—popular stereotypes must be abandoned and the complex realities examined. Citizens' ambivalence toward the popular branch of government—which, by the way, goes back to the beginnings of the Republic—says something of the milieu in which public policy is made. We believe we know our subject well enough to appreciate Congress's foibles and understand why it works the way it does. Yet we try to maintain a professional— yes, scholarly—distance from it.

According to an old saying, two things should never be viewed up close: making sausages and making laws. Despite this warning, we urge readers to take a good look at the workings of Congress and form their own opinions about Congress's effectiveness. Some may recoil from what they discover. Numerous flaws can be identified in members' personal or public behavior, in their priorities, incentive structures, and in lawmaking processes generally. Recent Congresses, especially, have displayed troubling tendencies, including rushed legislation, extreme partisanship, burgeoning earmarks, minimal executive oversight, and abdication of legislative power to the executive branch.[34]

Yet careful observers will also discover much behavior in Congress that is purposeful and principled, many policies that are reasonable and workable. We invite students and colleagues to examine with us what Congress does, and why, and ponder its values and its prospects.

SUGGESTED READINGS

Bianco, William, ed. *Congress on Display, Congress at Work.* Ann Arbor: University of Michigan Press, 2000.

Hamilton, Lee H. *How Congress Works, and Why You Should Care.* Bloomington: Indiana University Press, 2004.

Hibbing, John R., and Elizabeth Theiss-Morse. *Congress as Public Enemy.* Cambridge: Cambridge University Press, 1995.

_____. *Stealth Democracy: Americans' Beliefs about How Government Should Work.* Cambridge: Cambridge University Press, 2002.

Mayhew, David R. *Congress: The Electoral Connection.* 2d ed. New Haven: Yale University Press, 2004.

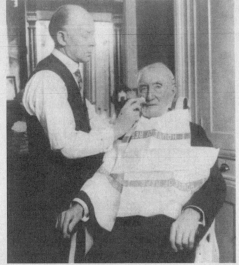

Changing Gender Demography on Capitol Hill. Former Speaker "Uncle Joe" Cannon (R-Ill.), the last of the strong post–Civil War House leaders, gets a shave from his barber (top). Challenging male domination on Capitol Hill, the women of the 71st Congress (1929–1931) pose on the Capitol steps (center). In 2009 (bottom), the Congressional Women's Caucus gathers in the White House's East Room to witness President Obama signing legislation creating a White House Council on Women and Girls.

Evolution of the
Modern Congress

The first Congress met in New York City, the seat of government, in the spring of 1789. Business was delayed until April 1 when a majority of members arrived to make a quorum. Once the thirtieth of the fifty-nine elected representatives reached New York, members chose Frederick A. C. Muhlenberg of Pennsylvania as Speaker of the House. Five days later the Senate achieved its first quorum, although its presiding officer, Vice President John Adams, did not arrive for another two weeks.

New York City was then a bustling port on the southern tip of Manhattan Island. Congress met in Federal Hall at the corner of Broad and Wall Streets. The House of Representatives occupied a large chamber on the first floor and the Senate a more intimate chamber upstairs. The new chief executive, George Washington, was still en route from Mount Vernon, his trip having become a triumphal procession with crowds and celebrations at every stop. To most of his countrymen, Washington—austere, dignified, the soul of propriety—embodied a government that was otherwise no more than a plan on paper.

The two houses of Congress did not wait for Washington's arrival. The House began debating tariffs, a perennial legislative topic. In the Senate, Vice President Adams, a brilliant but self-important man, prodded his colleagues to decide upon proper titles for addressing the president and himself. Adams was dubbed "His Rotundity" by a colleague who thought the whole discussion absurd.

On inaugural day, April 30, Adams was still worrying about how to address the president when the representatives, led by Speaker Muhlenberg, burst into the Senate chamber and seated themselves. Meanwhile, a special committee was dispatched to escort Washington to the chamber for the ceremony. The swearing-in was conducted on an outside balcony in front of thousands of assembled citizens.[1] Then the nervous Washington re-entered the Senate chamber and haltingly read his inaugural address. Following the speech, everyone adjourned to St. Paul's Chapel for a special prayer service. Thus the U.S. Congress became part of a functioning government.[2]

ANTECEDENTS OF CONGRESS

The legislative branch of the new government was untried and unknown, searching for procedures and precedents. And yet it grew out of a rich history of development—stretching back more than five hundred years in Great Britain and no less than a century and a half in North America. If the architects of the U.S. Constitution of 1787 were unsure how well their new design would work, they had firm ideas about what they intended.

The English Heritage

From the eleventh century reign of Edward the Confessor, a central problem of political theory and practice was the Crown's relationship to its subjects. Out of prolonged struggles, a strong, representative parliament emerged that rivaled and eventually eclipsed the power of the Crown. The evolution of representative institutions on a national scale began in medieval Europe. Monarchs gained power over large territories where inhabitants were divided into social groupings, called "estates of the realm"—among them the nobility, clergy, landed gentry, and town officials. The monarchs brought together leaders of these estates, not to create representative government but to fill the royal coffers.

These assemblies later came to be called parliaments, from the French *parler*, "to speak." Historians and political scientists have identified four distinct stages in the evolution of the assemblies of estates into the representative legislatures of today. At first the assemblies representing the various estates gathered merely to vote taxes for the royal treasury, and they engaged in little discussion. Next, these tax-voting bodies evolved into bodies that presented the king with petitions for redressing grievances. Third, by a gradual process that culminated in the revolutions of the seventeenth and eighteenth centuries, parliaments wrested lawmaking and tax-levying powers from the king, transforming themselves into truly sovereign bodies. Finally, in the nineteenth and twentieth centuries parliamentary representation expanded beyond the older privileged groups to embrace all adult men and women.[3]

By the time the New World colonies were founded in the 1600s, the struggle for parliamentary rights was well advanced into the third stage, at least in England. Bloody conflicts, culminating in the beheading of Charles I in 1649 and the dethroning of James II in the Glorious Revolution of 1688, established parliamentary influence over the Crown.

Out of struggles between the Crown and parliament flowed a remarkable body of political and philosophic writings. By the eighteenth century, works by James Harrington (1611–1677), John Locke (1632–1704), William Blackstone (1723–1780), and the Frenchman Baron de Montesquieu (1689–1755) were the common heritage of educated leaders in North America as well as in Europe.

The Colonial Experience

European settlers in the New World brought this tradition of representative government with them. As early as 1619 the thousand or so Virginia colonists elected twenty-two burgesses, or delegates, to a General Assembly. In 1630 the Massachusetts Bay Company established itself as the governing body for the Bay Colony, subject to annual elections. The other colonies, some of them virtually self-governing, followed suit.

Representative government took firm root in the colonies. The broad expanse of ocean shielding America fostered self-reliance and autonomy on the part of colonial assemblies. Claiming prerogatives similar to those of the British House of Commons, these assemblies exercised the full range of law-making powers—levying taxes, issuing money, and providing for colonial defense. Legislation could be vetoed by colonial governors (appointed by the Crown in the eight royal colonies), but the governors, cut off from the home government and dependent on local assemblies for revenues and even for their own salaries, usually preferred to reach agreement with the locals. Royal vetoes could emanate from London, but these took time and were infrequent.[4]

Other elements nourished the growth of democratic institutions. Many of the colonists were free-spirited dissidents set on resisting traditional forms of authority, especially that of the Crown. Readily available land, harsh frontier life, and—by the eighteenth century—a robust economy expanded the colonists' self-confidence. The town meeting form of government in New England and the separatists' church assemblies helped cultivate habits of self-government. Newspapers, unfettered by royal licenses or government taxes, stimulated lively exchanges of opinions.

When Britain decided in the 1760s, following the ruinous French and Indian War, to tighten its rein upon the American colonies, it met with stubborn opposition. Did not the colonists enjoy the same rights as Englishmen? Were not the colonial assemblies legitimate governments, with authority derived from popular elections? As British enactments grew increasingly unpopular, along with the governors who tried to enforce them, the locally based legislatures took up the cause of their constituents.

The colonists especially resented the Stamp Act of 1765, which provoked delegates from nine colonies to meet in New York City. There, the Stamp Act Congress adopted a fourteen-point *Declaration of Rights and Grievances*—mainly written by John Dickinson, who called himself a Pennsylvania farmer but who had studied law in London. The Stamp Act was later repealed. But new import duties levied in 1767 brought inflated customs receipts that enabled the Crown to begin directly paying the salaries of royal governors and other officials, thus freeing those officials from the influence of colonial assemblies. The crisis worsened in the winter of 1773–1774, when a group of colonists staged a revolt, the Boston Tea Party, to protest the Tea Act's taxes. In retaliation, the House of Commons closed the port of Boston and passed a series of so-called Intolerable Acts, further tightening royal control.

National representative assemblies in America were born on September 5, 1774, when the First Continental Congress convened in Philadelphia, Pennsylvania. Every colony except Georgia sent delegates—a varied group that included peaceable souls loyal to the Crown, moderates such as Pennsylvania's Dickinson, and firebrands such as Samuel Adams and Paul Revere. Gradually anti–British sentiment congealed, and Congress passed a series of declarations and resolutions (each colony casting one vote) amounting to a declaration of war against the mother country.[5] After Congress adjourned on October 22, King George III declared that the colonies were "now in a state of rebellion; blows must decide whether they are to be subject to this country or independent."[6]

If the First Continental Congress gave colonists a taste of collective decision making, the Second Continental Congress proclaimed their independence from Britain. When this second Congress convened on May 10, 1775, many still thought war might be avoided. A petition to King George asking for "happy and permanent reconciliation" was even approved. The British responded by proclaiming a state of rebellion and launching efforts to crush it. Sentiment in the colonies swung increasingly toward independence, and by the middle of 1776 Congress was debating Thomas Jefferson's draft resolution that "these united colonies are, and of right ought to be, free and independent states."[7]

The two Continental Congresses gave birth to national politics in America. Riding the wave of patriotism unleashed by the British indignities of 1773–1774, the Congresses succeeded in pushing the sentiments of leaders and much of the general public toward confrontation and away from reconciliation with the mother country. They did so by defining issues one by one and by reaching compromises acceptable to both moderates and radicals—no small accomplishment. Shared legislative experience, in other words, moved the delegates to the threshold of independence. Their achievement was all the more remarkable in light of what historian Jack N. Rakove describes as the "peculiar status" of the Continental Congress, "an extra-legal body whose authority would obviously depend on its ability to maintain a broad range of support."[8]

More than five years of bloody conflict ensued before the colonies won their independence. Meanwhile, the former colonies hastened to form new governments and draft constitutions. Unlike the English constitution, these charters were written documents. All included some sort of bill of rights, and all paid lip service to the doctrine of separating powers among legislative, executive, and judicial branches of government. But past conflicts with the Crown and the royal governors had instilled a fear of all forms of executive authority. So nearly all the constitutions gave the bulk of powers to their legislatures, effectively creating what one historian termed "legislative omnipotence."[9]

The national government was likewise, as James Sterling Young put it, "born with a legislative body and no head."[10] Strictly speaking, no national executive existed between 1776 and 1789—the years of the Revolutionary War and the Articles of Confederation (adopted in 1781). On its own, Congress struggled to wage war against the world's most powerful nation, enlist diplomatic allies, and manage internal affairs. As the war progressed and legislative direction proved unwieldy, Congress tended to delegate authority to its own committees and to permanent (executive) agencies. Strictly military affairs were placed in the hands of George Washington, who at the war's end returned his commission to Congress in a public ceremony. Considering the obstacles it faced, congressional government was far from a failure. Yet the mounting inability of all-powerful legislative bodies, state and national, to deal with postwar problems spurred demands for change.

At the state level, Massachusetts and New York rewrote their constitutions, adding provisions for stronger executives. At the national level, the Confederation's frailty led many to advocate what Alexander Hamilton called a more "energetic" government—one with enough authority to implement laws, control currency, levy taxes, dispose of war debts, and, if necessary, put down rebellion. Legislative prerogatives, Hamilton and others argued, should be counterbalanced with a vigorous, independent executive.

In this spirit, delegates from the states convened in Philadelphia on May 25, 1787, intending to strengthen the Articles of Confederation. Instead, they drew up a wholly new governmental charter.

CONGRESS IN THE CONSTITUTION

The structure and powers of Congress formed the core of the Constitutional Convention's deliberations. The delegates broadly agreed that a stronger central government was needed.[11] But the fifty-five delegates in Philadelphia that summer were deeply divided on issues of representation, and more than three months passed before they completed their work. The plan, agreed upon and signed September 17, 1787, was a bundle of compromises. In structuring the representational system, divergent interests—those of large and small states, northern and southern (i.e., slave-holding) states—had to be placated. The final result was an energetic central government that could function independently of the states, but with power limited to specific purposes and divided among three branches.

Powers of Congress

The federal government's powers are shared by three separate branches: legislative, executive, and judicial. Separation of powers was not a new idea. Philosophers revered by the Framers of the Constitution, including Harrington, Locke, and especially Montesquieu, had advocated the principle. But the U.S. Constitution's elaborate system of checks and balances is considered one of its most innovative features. The Articles of Confederation's failure to separate governmental functions was widely regarded as a serious defect, as were the all-powerful legislatures created by the first state constitutions. Thus the Framers sought to create a federal government that would avoid the excesses and instabilities that had marked policymaking at both national and state levels.

Article I of the Constitution embraces many provisions to buttress congressional authority and independence. Legislators have unfettered authority to organize the chambers as they see fit and are accorded latitude in performing their duties. To prevent intimidation, they cannot be arrested during sessions or while traveling to and from sessions (except for treason, felony, or breach of the peace). In their deliberations, members enjoy immunity from any punitive action: For their speech and debate, "they shall not be questioned in any other place" (Article I, Section 6).

Despite their worries over all-powerful legislatures, the Framers laid down an expansive mandate for the new Congress. Mindful of the achievements of

New World assemblies, not to mention the British Parliament's struggles with the Crown, the Framers viewed the legislature as the chief repository of governmental powers. Locke had observed that "the legislative is not only the supreme power, but is sacred and unalterable in the hands where the community have placed it."[12] Locke's doctrine found expression in Article I, Section 8, which enumerates Congress's impressive array of powers and sets out virtually the entire scope of governmental authority as the eighteenth-century Founders understood it. This portion of the Constitution clearly envisions a vigorous legislature as the engine of a powerful government.

Raising and spending money for governmental purposes lie at the heart of Congress's prerogatives. The power of the purse was historically the lever by which parliaments gained bargaining advantages over kings and queens. The Constitution's authors, well aware of this, gave Congress full powers over taxing and spending.

Financing the government is carried out under Congress's broad mandate to "lay and collect taxes, duties, imposts and excises, to pay the debts and provide for the common defense and general welfare of the United States" (Article 1, Section 8). Although this wording covered almost all known forms of taxation, there were limitations. Taxes had to be uniform throughout the country; duties were prohibited on goods traveling between states; and "capitation…or other direct" taxes were prohibited, unless levied according to population (Article I, Section 9). This last provision proved troublesome when the U.S. Supreme Court held in 1895 (*Pollock v. Farmers' Loan and Trust Co.*) that it applied to taxes on incomes. To overcome this obstacle, the Sixteenth Amendment, ratified eighteen years later, explicitly conferred the power to levy income taxes.

Congressional power over government spending is no less sweeping. Congress is to provide for the "common defense and general welfare" of the country (Article I, Section 8). Furthermore, "No money shall be drawn from the Treasury, but in consequence of appropriations made by law" (Article I, Section 9). This funding provision is one of the legislature's most potent weapons in overseeing the executive branch.

Congress possesses broad powers to promote the nation's economic well-being and political security. It has the power to regulate interstate and foreign commerce, which it has used to regulate not only trade, but also transportation, communications, and such disparate subjects as civil rights and violent crime. The exact limits of the commerce power have been the subject of numerous political and legal battles. Congress may also coin money, incur debts, establish post offices, build post roads, issue patents and copyrights, provide for the armed forces, and call forth the militia to repel invasions or suppress rebellions.

Although the three branches supposedly are coequal, the legislature was given the initiative in formulating the structure and duties of the other two. The Constitution mentions executive departments and officers, but it does not specify their structure or duties, aside from those of the president. Thus the design of the executive branch, including cabinet departments and other agencies, is spelled out in laws passed by Congress and signed by the president.

The judiciary, too, is a statutory creation. The Constitution provides for a federal judicial system consisting of a Supreme Court and "such inferior courts as the Congress may from time to time ordain and establish" (Article III, Section 1). Congress determines the number of justices on the Supreme Court, and the number and types of lower federal courts. The outer limits of the federal courts' jurisdiction are delineated in Article III, but Congress must also define their jurisdictions through statute. (It is worth noting that Congress has never extended the federal courts' jurisdiction as far as the Constitution would presumably allow.) Moreover, the Supreme Court's appellate jurisdiction is subject to "such exceptions" and "such regulations as the Congress shall make" (Article III, Section 2).

Congress can also limit the federal courts' discretion in ways other than altering their jurisdiction. Mandatory minimum sentences imposed by statute, for example, limit judges' discretion in imposing prison sentences.

Congress's powers within the federal system were greatly enlarged by the Civil War amendments—the Thirteenth (ratified 1865), Fourteenth (ratified 1868), and Fifteenth (ratified 1870). The Radical Republicans, who had supported the war and controlled Congress in its aftermath, feared that former Confederate states would ignore the rights of former slaves—the cause over which the war had ultimately been waged. The Civil War amendments were intended to ensure former slaves' rights to vote, to be accorded due process, and to receive equal protection of the laws. The amendments also authorized Congress to enforce these rights with "appropriate legislation." In so doing, these amendments (and subsequent legislation) greatly expanded the federal government's role. In protecting the civil rights of all persons, the Civil War amendments effectively nationalized key rights of citizenship throughout the United States. Through a long series of Court rulings applying the rights guaranteed in these amendments, state governments were eventually required to respect many of the Bill of Rights guarantees that originally applied only to the federal government.

Congress can also be an active partner in foreign relations and national defense. It has the power to declare war, ratify treaties, raise and support armies, provide and maintain a navy, and make rules governing the military forces—including those governing "captures on land and water." Finally, Congress is vested with the power "to make all laws which shall be necessary and proper for carrying into execution the foregoing powers" (Article I, Section 8).

Limits on Legislative Power

The very act of enumerating these powers was intended to limit government, for by implication those powers not listed are prohibited. The Tenth Amendment reserves to the states or to the people all those powers neither delegated nor prohibited by the Constitution. This guarantee has long been a rallying point for those who take exception to particular federal policies or who wish broadly to curtail federal powers.

Eight specific limitations on Congress's powers are noted in Article I, Section 9. The most important bans are against bills of attainder, which pronounce a particular individual guilty of a crime without trial or conviction and impose a sentence, and ex post facto laws, which make an action a crime after it has been committed or otherwise alter the legal consequences of some past action. Such laws are traditional tools of authoritarian regimes.

The original Constitution contained no bill of rights. Pressed by opponents during the ratification debate, supporters of the Constitution promised early enactment of amendments to remedy this omission. The resulting ten amendments, drawn up by the First Congress (James Madison was their main author) and ratified December 15, 1791, are a basic charter of liberties that limit the reach of government. The First Amendment prohibits Congress from establishing a national religion, preventing the free exercise of religion, or abridging the freedoms of speech, press, peaceable assembly, and petition. Other amendments secure the rights of personal property and fair trials and prohibit arbitrary arrest, questioning, or punishment.

Rights not enumerated in the Bill of Rights are not necessarily denied (Ninth Amendment). In fact, subsequent amendments, legislative enactments, judicial rulings, and states' actions have enlarged citizens' rights to include the rights of citizenship, of voting, of privacy, and of "equal protection of the laws."

Separate Branches, Shared Powers

The Constitution not only lists Congress's powers but also sets them apart from those of the other two branches. Senators and representatives, while in office, are prohibited from serving in other federal posts; those who serve in such posts are, in turn, forbidden from serving in Congress (Article I, Section 6). This restriction forecloses any form of parliamentary government, in which leading members of the dominant party or coalition form a cabinet to direct the ministries and other executive agencies.

Because the branches are separated, some people presume that their powers should be isolated from one another. In practice, however, governmental powers are interwoven, even if the branches are separate. Madison explained that the Constitution created not a system of separate institutions performing separate functions but separate institutions that share functions so that "these departments be so far connected and blended as to give each a constitutional control over the others."[13]

Historically, presidents and Congresses (and the courts) have reached accommodations to exercise the powers they share. As Justice Joseph Story once wrote, the authors of the Constitution sought to "prove that rigid adherence to [separation of powers] in all cases would be subversive to the efficiency of government and result in the destruction of the public liberties." Justice Robert Jackson noted in 1952 that "while the Constitution diffuses power the better to secure liberty, it also contemplates that practice will integrate the dispersed powers into a workable government."[14]

Legislative-Executive Interdependence. Each branch of American government needs cooperation from its counterparts. Although the Constitution vests Congress with "all legislative powers," these powers cannot be exercised without involvement of the president and the courts. This same interdependency applies to executive and judicial powers.

The president is a key figure in lawmaking. According to Article II, the president "shall from time to time give to the Congress information on the state of the Union, and recommend to their consideration such measures as he shall judge necessary and expedient." Although Congress is not required to consider the president's legislative initiatives, the president's State of the Union Address profoundly shapes the nation's political agenda. In the modern era, Congress has "enacted in some form roughly six in ten presidential initiatives."[15] The Constitution also grants the president the power to convene one or both houses of Congress in a special session.

The president's ability to veto congressional enactments is a seemingly blunt weapon that influences the outcome and content of legislation. After a bill or resolution has passed both houses of Congress and been delivered to the White House, the president must sign it or return it within ten days (excluding Sundays). Overruling a presidential veto requires a two-thirds vote in each house. Presidential review might seem to be an all-or-nothing affair. In the words of George Washington, a president "must approve all the parts of a bill, or reject it in toto." Veto messages, however, often suggest revisions that would make the measure more likely to win the president's approval. Furthermore, veto threats allow the president to intervene in the legislative process by letting members of Congress know in advance what measures will and will not receive presidential support. Considering the extreme difficulty of overriding a president's veto, members of Congress know that White House support for legislation is almost always necessary.

Carrying out laws is the duty of the president, who is directed by the Constitution to "take care that the laws be faithfully executed" (Article II, Section 3). To this end, as chief executive, the president has the power to appoint "officers of the United States." However, the president's appointment power is limited by the requirement to obtain the Senate's advice and consent for his nominees, which has been interpreted as requiring a majority vote in the Senate. The president's executive power is further constrained by Congress's role in establishing and overseeing executive departments and agencies. Because these agencies are subject to Congress's broad-ranging influence, modern presidents have struggled to force them to march to a single common cadence.

Even in the realms of diplomacy and national defense—traditional domains of royal prerogative—the Constitution apportions powers between the executive and legislative branches. Following tradition, presidents are given wide discretion in such matters. They appoint ambassadors and other envoys, they negotiate treaties, and they command the country's armed forces. However, like other high-ranking presidential appointees, ambassadors and envoys must be approved by the Senate. Treaties do not become the law of the land until they are ratified by a two-thirds vote of the Senate. Although the president may dispatch troops through executive order, only Congress may formally declare war. Reacting to the Vietnam War, Congress in 1973 passed the War Powers Resolution, intended to restrain presidents from making war without congressional approval. The next year it refused further funding for the war. Even in time of war, Congress wields formidable powers—but only if it chooses to employ them (see Chapter 15).

The constitutional division of power between the executive and legislative branches is, as we have seen, somewhat fluid. It became a subject of debate during the presidency of George W. Bush, whose advisers sometimes relied on the so-called unitary executive theory in order to rebuff congressional oversight and judicial review of executive branch actions. This controversial theory—rejected by most constitutional scholars—holds that the president, by virtue of Article II, should have complete (and sole) control over the executive branch. President Obama and the Democratic majorities in the House and Senate will be challenged in the 111th Congress to fashion a different interbranch working relationship.

Impeachment. Congress has the power to impeach and remove the president, the vice president, and other "civil officers of the United States" for serious breaches of the public trust: treason, bribery, or "other high crimes and misdemeanors." The House of Representatives has the sole authority to draw up and adopt (by majority vote) articles of impeachment, which are charges that the individual has engaged in one of the named forms of misconduct. The Senate is the final judge of whether to convict on any of the articles of impeachment. A two-thirds majority is required to remove the individual from office, or to remove and also bar the individual from any future "offices of public trust."

Three attributes of impeachment fix it within the separation of powers framework. First, it is exclusively the domain of Congress. (The chief justice presides over Senate trials of the president, but his rulings may be overturned by majority vote.) The two chambers are free to devise their own procedures for reaching their decisions. The Supreme Court refused to review the Senate's procedures when a former federal judge, Walter L. Nixon Jr., objected that although he had been convicted by a vote of the full Senate, the evidence in his case had been taken by one of the chamber's committees.[16]

Second, impeachment is essentially political in character. The structure may appear judicial—with the House resembling a grand jury and the Senate a trial court—but lawmakers decide whether and how to proceed, which evidence to consider, and even what constitutes an impeachable offense. Treason is defined by the Constitution, and bribery by statute; but the words "high crimes and misdemeanors" are open to interpretation. They are usually defined (in Alexander Hamilton's words) as "abuse or violation of some public trust"— on-the-job offenses against the state, the political order, or the society at large.[17] This means they can be either more or less than garden-variety criminal offenses. Both presidential impeachment trials (Andrew Johnson, 1868; Bill Clinton, 1998–1999) were fiercely partisan affairs, in which combatants disputed not only the facts but also the appropriate grounds for impeachment.

Finally, impeachment is a clumsy instrument for punishing officials for the gravest of offenses. Congress has many lesser ways of reining in wayward officials. As for presidents and vice presidents, their terms are already limited. Although impeachments are often threatened, only fifteen Senate trials have taken place, and only seven individuals have been convicted. Significantly, all seven who were removed from office were judges—who, unlike executive officers, enjoy open-ended terms of office.[18]

Interbranch "No-Fly Zones." Although the constitutional system requires that the separate branches share powers, each branch normally honors the integrity of the others' internal operations. Communications between the president and his advisors are mostly (though not entirely) exempt from legislative or judicial review under the doctrine of "executive privilege."

Similarly, Article I places congressional organization and procedures beyond the scrutiny of the other branches. In 2006 House leaders of both parties protested when FBI agents staged a Saturday-night raid of the office of Rep. William J. Jefferson, D-La., who was under investigation for accepting illegal payments for supporting certain legislation. (In a separate raid of Jefferson's home, agents had found a stash of money in his freezer.) Then-majority leader John A. Boehner, R-Ohio, called the office search "an invasion of the legislative branch." Then-minority whip Steny H. Hoyer, D-Md., asserted, "The institution has a right to protect itself against the executive branch going into our offices and violating the Speech and Debate Clause that essentially says, 'That's none of your business, executive branch.'"[19] Jefferson filed suit in federal court challenging the constitutionality of the search and demanding the return of material seized. Although initially rebuffed, Jefferson's claim was ultimately successful.[20] The U.S. Court of Appeals for the District of Columbia Circuit held that the FBI's search of Jefferson's office did, in fact, violate the Constitution's Speech and Debate clause,[21] a ruling that the Supreme Court declined to review.[22] The case establishes a precedent that members of Congress be provided advance notice and the right to review materials before the execution of a search warrant on their congressional offices.

Judicial Review

The third of the separated branches, the judiciary, takes a leading role in interpreting laws and determining their constitutionality. Whether the Framers anticipated this function of judicial review is open to question. Perhaps they expected each branch to reach its own judgments on constitutional questions, especially those pertaining to its own powers. Whatever the original intent, Chief Justice John Marshall soon preempted the other two branches with his Court's unanimous assertion of judicial review in *Marbury v. Madison* (1803). Judicial review involves both interpretation and judgment. First, "it is emphatically the province and duty of the judicial department to say what the law is." Second, the Supreme Court has the duty of weighing laws against the Constitution, the "supreme law of the land," and invalidating those that are inconsistent—in *Marbury,* a minor provision of the Judiciary Act of 1789.[23]

Until the Civil War, Congress—not the Court—was the primary forum for weighty constitutional debates. Prior to 1860, only one other law (the Missouri Compromise of 1820) had been declared unconstitutional by the Court (*Dred Scott v. Sandford*, 1857). Since the Civil War, the Court has been more aggressive in interpreting and judging congressional handiwork. For the record, the Supreme Court has invalidated 163 congressional statutes, in whole or in part—the vast majority of these during the twentieth century.[24] This count does not include lower court holdings that have not been reviewed by the Supreme Court. Nor does it cover laws whose validity has been impaired because a similar law was struck down.

Who Is the Final Arbiter? Congress's two most common reactions to judicial review of its enactments are not responding at all (38 percent of the cases, 1954–1997) or amending the statute to comply with the Court's holding (36 percent of cases).[25] Other responses are repealing the law, repealing the law to pass new legislation, or even seeking a constitutional amendment.

The Supreme Court does not necessarily have the last word in saying what the law is. Its interpretations of laws may be questioned and even reversed. One study found that 121 of the Court's interpretive decisions had been overridden between 1967 and 1990, an average of ten per Congress. The author of the study concluded that "congressional committees in fact carefully monitor Supreme Court decisions." Congress was most apt to override decisions of a closely divided Court, decisions that rely on the law's plain meaning, and decisions that clash with positions taken by federal, state, and local governments.[26]

The Lilly Ledbetter Fair Pay Act offers a recent example of Congress overturning the Supreme Court's interpretation of a congressional law. In 2007 a conservative 5–4 majority of the Supreme Court made it more difficult for plaintiffs to sue employers for pay discrimination.[27] Lilly Ledbetter was a longtime supervisor at a Goodyear tire plant in Gadsden, Alabama, who received an anonymous tip that she had been earning less than similarly situated male supervisors at her company for many years. After learning of these longstanding pay discrepancies, she successfully sued the company for discrimination under Title VII of the Civil Rights Act of 1964, and a jury awarded her back pay and damages. Hearing the case on appeal, the Supreme Court threw out Ledbetter's complaint. The Court held that the statute of limitations had expired, because Ledbetter had not sued within 180 days of the intentionally discriminatory pay decisions that had occurred early in her career. The 111th Congress made it one of their first orders of business to reverse the Court's ruling. The legislation passed by Congress and signed by President Obama, among other provisions, revises the relevant statute of limitations to ensure that a new 180-day statute of limitations begins with every paycheck, reversing the Supreme Court's narrow reading of the statute.

Nor are the courts the sole judges of what is or is not constitutional. Courts routinely accept customs and practices developed by the other two branches. Likewise, they usually decline to decide sensitive political questions within the province of Congress and the executive.

When courts do strike down an enactment, Congress may turn around and pass laws that meet the courts' objections or achieve the same goal by different means. However, Congress sometimes reacts to judicial holdings by trying to impede, modify, or reverse them or by simply ignoring them. Reconstruction laws and constitutional amendments after the Civil War explicitly nullified the Court's 1867 holding in *Dred Scott v. Sandford*.[28] And even though legislative veto provisions were largely outlawed by the Court's decision in *Immigration and Naturalization Service v. Chadha* (1983),[29] Congress continues to enact them, and administrators nevertheless feel obliged to honor them out of political prudence.

The courts play a leading but not exclusive role in interpreting laws and the regulations implementing them. When Congress passes a law, the policy-making process has just begun. Courts and administrative agencies then assume the task of refining the policy, but they do so under Congress's watchful eye. "What is 'final' at one stage of our political development," Louis Fisher observes, "may be reopened at some later date, leading to revisions, fresh interpretations, and reversals of Court doctrines. Through this never-ending dialogue, all three branches are able to expose weaknesses, hold excesses in check, and gradually forge a consensus on constitutional issues."[30]

Bicameralism

Although "the Congress" is discussed as if it were a single entity, Congress is divided internally into two very different, virtually autonomous, chambers. Following the pattern initiated by the British Parliament and imitated by most of the states, the Constitution created a bicameral legislature. If tradition recommended the two-house formula, the politics of the early Republic commanded it. Large states with greater populations preferred popularly based representation, but the smaller states insisted on retaining the equal representation they enjoyed under the Articles of Confederation.

The first branch—as the House was called by Madison and Gouverneur Morris, among others—rests on the idea that the legislature should represent "the many," the people of the United States. As George Mason put it, the House "was to be the grand depository of the democratic principles of the government."[31]

In contrast, the Senate's composition reflected the Framers' concerns about controlling excessive popular pressures. Senators were chosen by the state legislatures and not by popular vote. The Senate—insulated in theory— would curb the excesses of popular government. "The use of the Senate," explained Madison, "is to consist in its proceeding with more coolness, with more system, and with more wisdom, than the popular branch."[32]

Senate behavior did not necessarily match up with the Framers' theories. Even though senators were chosen by state legislatures, they were not insulated from democratic pressures. In order to be selected, Senate candidates "had to cultivate local party officials in different parts of the state and appeal directly to constituents in order to bolster their electoral chances."[33] Once in office, senators voiced their state's dominant economic interests. They also sponsored private bills for pensions and other relief for individual constituents, doled out federal patronage, and sought committee assignments that would enable them to bring home their state's share of federal money. Recent research has shown that senators selected by state legislators were not substantially different from modern, directly elected senators.[34]

Historical evolution finally overran the Founders' intentions. Direct election of senators came with the Seventeenth Amendment, ratified in 1913. A by-product of the Progressive movement, the new arrangement was designed to broaden citizens' participation and blunt the power of shadowy special interests, such as party bosses and business trusts. Thus the Senate became directly subject to popular will.

Bicameralism is the most obvious organizational feature of the U.S. Congress. Each chamber has distinct processes for handling legislation. According to the Constitution, each house sets its own rules, keeps a journal of its proceedings, and serves as final judge of its members' elections and qualifications. In addition, the Constitution assigns unique duties to each of the two chambers. The Senate ratifies treaties and approves presidential appointments. The House must originate all revenue measures; by tradition, it also originates appropriations bills.

The two houses jealously guard their prerogatives and resist intrusions by the other body. Despite claims that one or the other chamber is more important—for instance, that the Senate has more prestige or that the House pays more attention to legislative details—the two houses staunchly defend their equal places. On Capitol Hill there is no "upper" or "lower" chamber.

INSTITUTIONAL EVOLUTION

Written constitutions go only a short way toward explaining how real-life governmental institutions work. On many questions such documents are inevitably silent or ambiguous. Important issues of both power and process emerge and develop only in the course of later events. Political institutions continually change under pressures from public demands, shifting political contexts, and the policy and electoral goals of officeholders.

Congress has evolved dramatically over time. Early on, Congress had little formal structure. When the first Congress convened, there were no standing committees. Deliberation about policy issues occurred directly on the floors of the House and Senate, where any interested members could participate. After chamber-wide debate had taken place on the broad issue, members would create temporary ad hoc committees to draft bills. The early Congress also had no formal party leadership organization.[35] Prior to the 1830s, the Federalist and Republican coalitions that existed in Congress were "no more than proto-parties"[36] There was almost no professional staff. Even by 1891 a grand total of 142 clerks, 62 for the House and 80 for the Senate, were on hand to serve members of Congress. Many senators and all representatives handled their own correspondence. Compared to the present, the early Congress was informal, fluid, and unstructured.

Today's Congress is a mature institution characterized by complex internal structures and procedures. It is led by a well-defined party apparatus, with each party organized according to established rules and led by a hierarchy of leaders and whips, elected and appointed. Party organization extends to policy committees, campaign committees, research committees, and numerous task forces. Minority and majority party leaders command considerable resources in terms of budgets and staff. Taken together, they employ some four hundred staff aides, and the various party committees employ approximately an equal number.[37]

The contemporary Congress also has an elaborate committee system bolstered by a vast body of rules and precedents regulating their jurisdictions and operations.[38] The Senate has sixteen standing committees and the House has twenty. These committees are only the tip of the iceberg. House committees have about one hundred subcommittees; Senate committees, nearly seventy subcommittees. Four joint House–Senate committees have been retained. This adds up to some two hundred work groups, plus an abundance of informal caucuses.

In addition, every member heads up a well-staffed personal office with employees to handle mail, appointments, policy research, speechwriting, and constituent service. Employing nearly 30,000 staff members housed in nearly a dozen Capitol Hill buildings, Congress now sustains a distinct Washington subculture.

A basic concept scholars use to analyze the development of Congress's growth and adaptation is *institutionalization*. Political scientist Nelson Polsby applied this concept to track the institution's professionalization of the legislative career; its increasing organizational complexity—the growth of more component parts (committees, subcommittees, caucuses, leadership organizations) within the institution; and its elaboration and observance of formal rules governing its internal business.[39] Scholars have identified a number of important factors that have driven institutionalization. Among these are legislative workload, institutional size, conflict with the executive branch, and members' partisan interests.

Workload

Congress's workload—once limited in scope, small in volume, and simple in content—has burgeoned since 1789. Today's Congress grapples with many issues that were once considered entirely outside the purview of governmental activity or were left to states or localities. From eight to ten thousand bills and joint resolutions are introduced in the span of each two-year Congress; from four to eight hundred of them are enacted into law. By most measures—hours in session, committee meetings, floor votes—the congressional workload doubled between the 1950s and the late 1970s. Legislative business expanded in scope and complexity as well as in sheer volume. The average public bill of the late 1940s was two-and-a-half pages long; by the late 1990s it ran to more than eighteen pages.[40]

Changes in workload have been an important driver of institutional change over the course of congressional history. Many of the earliest committees were established to help Congress manage a growing volume of constituent requests. "Congress was confronted with thousands of petitions requesting benefits of various sorts," writes Eric Schickler; committees such as Claims, Pensions, and Public Lands "facilitated the processing of such requests."[41] Similarly, the creation and, occasionally, abolition of committees parallel shifting perceptions of public problems. As novel policy problems arose, new committees were added.[42] The House, for example, established Commerce and Manufactures in 1795, Public Lands in 1805, Freedmen's Affairs in 1866, Roads in 1913, Science and Astronautics in 1958, Standards of Official Conduct in 1967, Small Business in 1975, and Homeland Security in 2003. An extensive system of committees allows the contemporary Congress to benefit from division of labor as it strives to manage a far-reaching governmental agenda and the press of public business.

Congress's growing workload does not come only from outside the institution. From the earliest days to the present, members themselves have contributed to their collective burden. Seeking to make names for themselves, members champion causes, deliver speeches on various subjects, offer floor amendments, refer matters to committees for consideration, and engage in much policy entrepreneurship. All these activities raise the congressional workload.

At regular intervals over congressional history, the crush of business, combined with a widespread sense that Congress is unable to manage its responsibilities, leads members to experiment with institutional reforms.[43] Under workload pressure, Congress has often adopted measures to streamline procedures and to limit the participation of individual members. Such reforms are ongoing, with congressional innovators devising new "unorthodox" procedures to cope with the workload challenges of today.[44]

The Size of Congress

Like workload, a legislative institution's size profoundly affects its work. From a study of fifty-five legislatures worldwide, Andrew J. Taylor found that "legislators in large chambers are willing to trade away procedural rights for centralized procedures…[in order to] prevent gridlock and cut the costs of forging cooperation."[45] Legislatures with more members face greater problems of agenda control and time management, unless they adopt mechanisms to manage the participation of their members. The United States Congress has grown dramatically over time, and this growth created pressure for institutional adaptation.

Looking at the government of 1789 through modern lenses, one is struck by the relatively small circles of people involved. The House of Representatives, that "impetuous council," was composed of sixty-five members—when all of them showed up. The aristocratic Senate boasted only twenty-six members, two from each of the thirteen original states.

As new states were added, the Senate grew. There were thirty-two senators in 1800, sixty-two in 1850, ninety by 1900, and one hundred today. (Since 1912 only the states of Alaska and Hawaii have been added.)

For much of the nation's history, the House grew along with the nation's growing population. The House was raised to 104 members after the first census, and there were steady enlargements throughout the nineteenth century. The 1910 census, which counted ninety-two million people, led to a final expansion to 435 members. Following the 1920 census Congress declined to enlarge the House further. And that is the way things stand to this day. (However, Congress has recently considered adding two House seats to award a voting member for the District of Columbia and a fourth House seat for Utah.

Growth impelled House members to empower strong leaders, to rely on committees, to impose strict limits on floor debate, and to devise elaborate ways of channeling the flow of floor business. It is probably no accident that strong leaders emerged during the House's periods of most rapid growth. After the initial growth spurt in the first two decades of the Republic, vigorous leadership appeared in the person of Henry Clay (1811–1814, 1815–1820, and 1823–1825). Similarly, the House's post–Civil War expansion was met with an era of forceful Speakers that lasted from the 1870s until 1910.

In the smaller and more intimate Senate, vigorous leadership has been the exception rather than the rule. The relative informality of Senate procedures, not to mention the long-cherished right of unlimited debate, testifies to looser reins of leadership. Compared with the House's complex rules and voluminous precedents, the Senate's rules are relatively brief and simple. Informal negotiations among senators interested in a given measure prevail on most matters. Although too large for its members to draw their chairs around the fireplace on a chilly winter morning—as they did in the early years—the Senate today retains a clubby atmosphere that the House lacks.

Conflict with the Executive Branch

Conflict with the president is a perennial impetus for institutional reform. When Congress cannot collaborate effectively with the executive branch to develop policy, members seek out ways to increase their capacity for independent action. During such confrontations, Congress creates new institutions and procedures that often endure long beyond the specific contexts that gave rise to them.

One of the most important standing House committees, Ways and Means, was first established to provide a source of financial information independent of the controversial and divisive Treasury secretary Alexander Hamilton. "Members understood that the alternative to a standing committee would be continued reliance on Hamilton and his department for information about such issues as tariffs and economic development," observes Eric Schickler.[46]

Similarly, the landmark Legislative Reorganization Act of 1946 was adopted in the midst of members' growing concern about congressional power. Following massive growth of the administrative state during the New Deal and World War II, members feared that Congress simply could no longer compete with the executive branch. Reformers saw "a reorganized Congress as a way to redress the imbalance of power that had developed between the branches."[47] The Act streamlined the legislative process by dramatically reducing the number of committees and regularizing their jurisdictions. Sen. Owen Brewster (R-Maine) argued at the time that the reforms were necessary "if we are to retain any semblance of the ancient division of functions under our constitution."[48] The Act was adopted by a sizeable bipartisan majority, with both Republicans and Democrats expressing hope that reform would strengthen Congress's power and prestige.

Another major institutional innovation, Congress's budget process, was fashioned in an environment of intense interbranch warfare between President Richard Nixon and a Democratic Congress.[49] President Nixon's unprecedented assertion of authority not to spend funds that Congress had appropriated was a major stimulus for passage of the Congressional Budget and Impoundment Control Act of 1974. Without the power of the purse, Sen. John Tunney (D-Calif.) remarked, "we may as well go out of business."[50] However, the Act addressed an array of structural issues that went far beyond the particulars of the dispute over the president's impoundment powers. It established a new internal congressional budget process, new Budget committees in both chambers, and a new congressional agency, the nonpartisan Congressional Budget Office (CBO). The goal was to allow Congress on its own to formulate a comprehensive national budget, backed by appropriate estimates and forecasts, without relying on the president's budget or the executive branch's Office of Management and Budget.

In *Federalist* No. 51 Madison justified the Constitution as a system to "divide and arrange the several offices in such a manner as that each may be a check on the other." Congress's institutional development bears the indelible stamp of this checking and balancing, as Congress has repeatedly reformed itself to meet challenges from the executive branch.

Partisan Interests

Political parties had no place in the original constitutional blueprint. However, no account of institutional development in Congress can ignore the vital role of political parties. Everything about the organization and operation of the Congress is shaped by political parties. Indeed, the first thing a visitor to the House or Senate chamber notices is that the seats or desks are divided along partisan lines—Democrats to the left facing the dais, Republicans to the right. Although today's congressional parties are particularly cohesive and energetic, their importance is by no means unique to the present day. The goals and capacities of the political parties have been a major engine of change throughout congressional history.

Parties began to develop in Congress during the first presidential administration. When Treasury secretary Alexander Hamilton unveiled his financial program in 1790, a genuine partisan spirit swept Capitol Hill. The Federalists, with Hamilton as their intellectual leader, espoused energetic government to deal forcefully with national problems and foster economic growth. The rival Republicans, who looked to Thomas Jefferson and James Madison for leadership, rallied opponents of Federalist policies and championed local autonomy, weaker national government, and programs favoring rural, lower-class, or debtor interests. By 1794 Sen. John Taylor of Virginia could write:

> The existence of two parties in Congress is apparent. The fact is disclosed almost upon every important question. Whether the subject be foreign or domestic—relative to war or peace—navigation or commerce—the magnetism of opposite views draws them wide as the poles asunder.[51]

Parties flourished in the years following the Civil War. Regional conflicts, along with the economic upheavals produced by rapid industrialization, nurtured partisan differences. The Civil War and World War I mark the boundaries of the first era of militant partisanship on Capitol Hill and in the country at large. At the grassroots level the parties were divided along class, occupational, and regional lines. Grassroots party organizations were massive and militant. Strong Speakers tamed the unruly House, and a coterie of statewide party bosses dominated the Senate. However, even after the end of this partisan era, parties never became irrelevant. During periods of party weakness after the demise of the strong speakership (1910) and direct election of senators (1913), the parties were still able to organize the Congress.[52] The Speaker of the House has always been the leader of the majority party. House and Senate members receive and retain their committee assignments through their parties. Likewise, members of the majority party always chair all the standing committees of Congress. (An exception of sorts in the 111th Congress is Independent— formerly Democrat—Sen. Joe Lieberman of Connecticut, who chairs the Homeland Security and Governmental Affairs Committee, though only with the acquiescence of the Democratic Caucus.)

The political parties have profoundly influenced the development of the legislative process. Party politics have impelled the development of floor procedure, the parliamentary rights of members, the powers of leaders, and processes of agenda control. The rules of the legislative process at any given time are, in Sarah A. Binder's words, a "result of hard-nosed partisan battles— fought, of course, under a particular set of inherited institutional rules."[53]

A watershed moment in the development of the House of Representatives, the adoption of Reed's Rules in 1890, offers one of the clearest examples of partisan influence on institutional procedure. Prior to 1890 the minority party in the House of Representatives possessed an arsenal of dilatory tactics to obstruct the majority party's agenda. Reed's Rules, named for then-House Speaker Thomas Brackett Reed, R-Maine, revolutionized House procedure by granting the Speaker secure control over the order of business and strictly curbing the minority party's ability to obstruct the majority party's floor agenda. Republicans, the majority party, fought for the adoption of Reed's Rules over strong opposition from the Democrats. At that time, Republicans had just won unified party control of the government for the first time in more than a decade, and they had an ambitious and controversial agenda. Knowing that Democrats would use their resources to obstruct their agenda, Republicans changed the rules of the House to permit majority party control over the institution, a fact of life in the House of Representatives ever since. In procedural terms, Reed's Rules permanently transformed the House of Representatives.

The circumstances surrounding the adoption of Reed's Rules offers a blueprint for many partisan rules changes over the course of House history. Based on a study of all procedural rules changes that benefited the majority party at the expense of the minority party between 1789 and 1990, Binder finds that "crucial procedural choices have been shaped not by members' collective concerns about the institution, but by calculations of partisan advantage."[54] When majority parties are cohesive in their policy preferences, but narrow enough that the minority party's resistance has the potential to obstruct their agenda, majority parties will be inclined to change the institution's rules to ensure the passage of their agenda. Majority parties are especially likely to do this when the minority party makes aggressive use of its procedural powers of obstruction.

Members' Individual Interests

Institutional development has been driven by more than members' partisan and institutional goals. Members are not just concerned whether Congress can manage its workload and the party agenda can be enacted. Members have individual as well as collective goals. As individuals, members want to build a reputation as effective lawmakers and representatives for their constituencies. To do so, they need to be able to point to achievements of their own. When congressional rules or structures inhibit their ability to do so, pressure builds for institutional reform.

In addition to its value as institutional division of labor, the elaborate committee system in Congress serves members' individual political needs and policy goals. The multitude of leadership positions created by numerous committees and subcommittees gives nearly every member an opportunity to make an individual contribution. "Whatever else it may be, the quest for specialization in Congress is a quest for credit," observes David Mayhew. "Every member can aspire to occupy a part of at least one piece of policy turf small enough that he can claim personal responsibility for some of the things that happen on it."[55]

The congressional reforms of the 1970s offer one example of the ways members' individual goals have affected institutional development. Over that decade, the two chambers extensively reworked their committee systems through a series of measures designed to allow more input from rank-and-file members. The streamlined committee systems put in place after the Legislative Reorganization Act of 1946 had offered relatively few committee leadership positions, which were gained on the basis of seniority. Each committee was led by its longest-serving members, who retained their positions until death, defeat, or retirement. The large classes of new members elected in the 1970s, feeling themselves thwarted by this system, began to press for change.[56] Out of this ferment emerged a variety of reforms that opened up new opportunities for junior members. Subcommittees within the committees gained greater authority and independence as they were granted specific jurisdictions, staffs, budgets, and leaders no longer chosen by the full committee chairs. The seniority system was weakened as committee chairs were forced to stand for election in their party caucus, making them accountable to the party's rank and file.

The persistence of Senate rules that permit unlimited debate provides another example of the way individual goals shape institutional rules.[57] Despite the many frustrations unlimited debate has caused for Senate majority parties over the years, senators have been unwilling to embrace changes that would allow for simple majority rule. Senators realize that a great part of their own institutional power derives from their ability to take advantage of unlimited debate to block votes on matters that have majority support. Senate leaders are forced to negotiate with senators who obstruct Senate action via unlimited debate. Reforms that would make it possible for a Senate majority to force a vote have long been in the interest of the Senate's majority party. But such reforms would come at direct, substantial cost to senators' individual power. Not surprisingly, senators have proven very reluctant to trade off so much of their individual influence in favor of collective party goals.

As with everything else about Congress, the institution's rules and procedures can only be fully understood in light of the two Congresses. Members want rules and processes to serve them as individual lawmakers and representatives, as well as to facilitate the functioning of the legislature as a whole.

Changing pressure on the institution, congressional-executive conflicts, partisan agendas, and members' individual goals have all been important drivers of Congress's institutional development. Indeed, significant reforms are almost always the result of several of these forces simultaneously buffeting the institution. In his broad-ranging survey of forty-two major institutional innovations, Schickler finds that institutional reforms are typically brought about through "common carriers," reform initiatives that are at once supported by several different groups of legislators for different sets of reasons.[58] The Legislative Reorganization Act of 1946, for example, was espoused by many legislators who wanted to enhance the power and effectiveness of the legislative branch, but it was also supported by members who valued the new pay and pension benefits included in the legislation.[59] Similarly, many members favored the 1970s reforms reducing the power of committee chairmen because they wanted access to more policy turf of their own, but many liberal members backed the reforms because they wanted to reduce the influence of the disproportionately conservative committee chairs.[60]

Because the same reforms are so often backed for several different reasons, no single theory can explain congressional change. "[L]egislative institutions are historical composites, full of tensions and contradictions."[61] Furthermore, reforms inevitably fall short of their sponsors' objectives. Instead of achieving stable, effective arrangements, what often results is "a set of institutions that often work at cross-purposes."[62] Also, innovations usually have unanticipated consequences, which may lead to yet another round of reform. In broadest terms, change is always a product of the dual Congress—driven by both electoral and institutional goals.

EVOLUTION OF THE LEGISLATOR'S JOB

What is it like to be a member of Congress? The legislator's job, like the institution of Congress, has evolved since 1789. During the early Congresses being a senator or representative was a part-time occupation. Few members regarded congressional service as a career, and from most accounts the rewards were slim. Since then the lawmakers' exposure to constituents' demands and their career expectations have changed dramatically. Electoral units, too, have grown very large. With the nation's population estimated at some 306 million citizens, the average House constituency contains more than 700,000 people and the average state, more than six million.

The Congressional Career

During its early years Congress was an institution composed of transients. The nation's capital was an unsightly place, and its culture was provincial. Members remained in Washington only a few months, spending their unpleasant sojourns in boardinghouses. "While there were a few for whom the Hill was more than a way station in the pursuit of a career," James Sterling Young observes, "affiliation with the congressional community tended to be brief."[63]

The early Congresses failed to command the loyalty needed to keep members in office. Congressional service was regarded more as odious duty than as rewarding work. "My dear friend," wrote a North Carolina representative to his constituents in 1796, "there is nothing in this service, exclusive of the confidence and gratitude of my constituents, worth the sacrifice....Having secured this, I could freely give place to any fellow citizen, that others too might obtain the consolation due to faithful service."[64] Of the ninety-four senators who served between 1789 and 1801, thirty-three resigned before completing their terms, only six to take other federal posts.[65] In the House almost 6 percent of all early nineteenth-century members resigned during each Congress. Citizen legislators, not professional politicians, characterized that era.

Careerism mounted toward the end of the nineteenth century. As late as the 1870s more than half the House members at any given time were freshmen, and the mean length of service was barely two terms. By the end of the century, however, the proportion of newcomers had fallen to 30 percent, and average House tenure reached three terms, or six years. About the same time, senators' mean term of service topped seven years, in excess of one full term.[66]

Today the average senator and House member has served more than twelve years. The data in Table 2-1 show changes since 1789 in the percentages of new and veteran members and the mean number of terms claimed by incumbents. In both the House and Senate, members' average length of service has increased over time, and the proportion of first-termers is substantially lower than it was during the first 200 years of the nation's history.

Rising careerism had a number of causes. The increase in one-party states and districts following the Civil War, and especially after the partisan

TABLE 2-1 **Length of Service in House and Senate, 1789–2009**

	Congress			
Chamber and terms	*1st–56th* *(1789–1901)*	*57th–103d* *(1901–1995)*	*104th–110th* *(1995–2007)*	*111th* *(2009–2011)*
House				
One (up to 2 years)	44.0%	23.3%	13.4%	12.9%
Two to six (3–12 years)	53.4	49.7	54.6	44.2
Seven or more (12+ years)	2.6	27.0	32.1	42.9
Mean number of terms[a]	2.1	4.8	5.4	6.2
Senate				
One (up to 6 years)	65.6%	45.6%	33.2%	30.0%
Two (7–12 years)	23.4	22.4	27.0	25.0
Three or more (12+ years)	11.0	32.0	39.8	45.0
Mean number of terms[a]	1.5	2.2	2.6	2.8

Sources: Adapted from David C. Huckabee, *Length of Service for Representatives and Senators: 1st–103d Congresses,* Congressional Research Service Report No. 95–426GOV, March 27, 1995. Authors' calculations for the 104th through 111th Congresses. See also: Mildred Amer, *Average Years of Service for Members of the Senate and House of Representatives, First–109th Congresses,* Congressional Research Service Report RL32648, November 9, 2005.

[a] Figures are derived from the total number of terms claimed by members whether or not those terms were served out. For example, members in their initial year of service are counted as having one full term, and so on. Thus the figures cannot be equated precisely with years of service.

realignment of 1896, made possible repeated reelection of a dominant party's candidates—Democrats in the core cities and the South, Republicans in the Midwest and the rural Northeast. Vigorous state and local party organizations dominated the recruitment process and tended to select party careerists to fill these safe seats.[67] Members themselves also began to find congressional service more rewarding. The growth of national government during the twentieth century enhanced the excitement and glamour of the Washington political scene, especially compared with state or local politics.

The seniority rule further rewarded lengthy service. Seniority triumphed in both chambers at about the same time. In the Senate there was no decisive event. Senate seniority was largely unchallenged after 1877.[68] In the House, strong post–Civil War Speakers, struggling to control the unruly chamber, sometimes bypassed seniority to appoint loyal lieutenants to major committees. But in 1910, when Speaker Joseph G. Cannon passed over senior members for assignments and behaved arbitrarily in other ways, the House revolted, divesting the Speaker of committee assignment power. With the Speaker's clout diminished, David W. Brady relates, "seniority came to be the most important criterion for committee assignments and chairmanships."[69]

Although the seniority system unquestionably increased the returns on long service in Congress, recent changes to the seniority system have not affected members' inclination to seek long careers. Seniority norms saw significant challenge during the 1990s. After taking over the House in 1995, Republican leaders passed over several senior members in naming committee chairs. At the same time, the GOP Conference limited chairs' terms to six years—a provision initially extended when Democrats organized the House in 2007, but repealed two years later. Seniority is no longer the unquestioned norm it once was, but all would-be chairs are still experienced members. Despite changes to the seniority system, extended service remains a prerequisite for top party and committee posts.

Professionalization

During the Republic's early days, lawmaking was not a full-time occupation. As President John F. Kennedy was fond of remarking, the Clays, Calhouns, and Websters of the nineteenth century could afford to devote a whole generation or more to debating and refining the few great controversies at hand. Rep. Joseph W. Martin, R-Mass., who entered the House in 1925 and went on to become Speaker (1947–1949, 1953–1955), described the leisurely atmosphere of earlier days and the workload changes during his service.

> From one end of a session to another Congress would scarcely have three or four issues of consequence besides appropriations bills. And the issues themselves were fundamentally simpler than those that surge in upon us today in such a torrent that the individual member cannot analyze all of them adequately before he is compelled to vote. In my early years in Congress the main issues were few enough so that almost any conscientious member could with application make himself a quasi-expert at least. In the complexity and volume of today's legislation, however, most members have to trust somebody else's word or the recommendation of a committee. Nowadays bills, which thirty years ago would have been thrashed out for hours or days, go through in ten minutes.[70]

The most pressing issue considered by the Foreign Affairs Committee during one session, Martin related, was a $20,000 authorization for an international poultry show in Tulsa, Oklahoma.

For most of its history Congress was a part-time institution. Well into the twentieth century Congress remained in session for only nine of every twenty-four months, the members spending the rest of their time at home attending to private business. As Representative Martin related:

> The installation of air conditioning in the 1930s did more, I believe, than cool the Capitol: it prolonged the session. The members were no longer in such a hurry to flee Washington in July. The southerners especially had no place else to go that was half as comfortable.[71]

In recent decades legislative business has kept the House and Senate almost perpetually in session—punctuated by constituency work periods. The average senator or representative works an eleven-hour day when Congress is in session.[72] Members of the contemporary Congress are—and must be—full-time professional politicians.

Constituency Demands

From the start, American legislators have been expected to remain close to their voters. Early representatives reported to their constituents through circular letters, communications passed around throughout their districts.[73] In an era of limited government, however, there was less constituent errand running. "It was a pretty nice job that a member of Congress had in those days," recalled Rep. Robert Ramspeck, D-Ga. (1929–1945), describing the Washington of 1911, when he came to take a staff job:

> At that time the government affected the people directly in only a minor way....It was an entirely different job from the job we have to do today. It was primarily a legislative job, as the Constitution intended it to be.[74]

In those days a member's business on behalf of constituents was confined mainly to awarding rural mail routes, arranging for Spanish War pensions, sending out free seed, and only occasionally explaining legislation. At most, a single clerk was required to handle correspondence. Members from one-party areas often did little personal constituency work. It was said that Democratic Speaker John Nance Garner, who entered the House in 1903 and ended his career as vice president (1933–1941), "for thirty years did not canvass his [south Texas] district and franked no speeches home."[75] His major constituency outreach consisted of the barbecues he gave at his home in Uvalde, Texas.

This unhurried pace has long since vanished. Reflecting on his forty years on Capitol Hill, Representative Martin remarked on the dramatic upsurge of constituent awareness.

> Today the federal government is far more complex, as is every phase of national life. People have to turn to their Representative for aid. I used to think ten letters a day was a big batch; now I get several hundred a day. In earlier times, constituents didn't know their Congressman's views. With better communications, their knowledge has increased along with their expectations of what he must know.[76]

Even people of Martin's era (he left the House in 1967) would be astonished at the volume of constituency work now handled by House and Senate offices. Not only are constituents more numerous than ever before, but they are also better educated, served by faster communication and transportation, and mobilized by lobby organizations. Public opinion surveys show that voters expect legislators to dispense federal services and to communicate frequently with the home folks. Even though the more flagrant forms of pork-barrel politics are denounced, constituents' demands are unlikely to ebb in the future.

CONCLUSION

Although the Founders understood the guiding principles of representative assemblies, they could not have foreseen what sort of institution they had created. They wrote into the Constitution legislative powers as they understood them and left the details to future generations.

Just as physical anthropologists believe the earth's history is marked by periods of intense, even cataclysmic, change—punctuated equilibrium—so historians of Congress have identified several eras of extensive institutional change. "Reconstitutive change" is what Elaine K. Swift calls these instances of "rapid, marked, and enduring shift[s] in the fundamental dimensions of the institution."[77] During one such period—1809–1829—Swift argues, the Senate was transformed from an elitist, insulated "American House of Lords" into an active, powerful institution whose debates stirred the public and attracted the most talented politicians of the time. Major reform efforts in Congress have also periodically resulted in bold new departures in process and structure.

Institutional change is not necessarily dramatic. Incremental changes of one kind or another are also always unfolding. For example, the House in 1999 streamlined and codified its rules, and hardly anyone noticed. In a detailed examination of changes in committee jurisdictions, David C. King showed that periodic, large-scale jurisdictional "reform acts" were mainly compilations of gradually accumulated precedents created as novel bills were introduced.[78]

Over time, as a result of changes large and small, Congress became the mature institution of today. The contemporary Congress bristles with norms and traditions, rules and procedures, committees and subcommittees. In short, the modern Congress is highly institutionalized. How different from the First Congress, personified by fussy John Adams worrying about what forms of address to use.

The institutionalization of the contemporary Congress must be taken into account by anyone who seeks to understand it today. Capitol Hill newcomers—even those who vow to shake things up—confront not an unformed, pliable institution but an established, traditional one that must be approached largely on its own terms. This institutionalization has a number of important consequences, some good and some bad.

Institutionalization enables Congress to cope with its extensive workload. Division of labor, primarily through standing committees, permits the two houses to process a wide variety of issues simultaneously. In tandem with staff resources, this specialization allows Congress to compete with the executive branch in absorbing information and applying expertise to public issues. Division of labor also serves the personal and political diversity of Congress. At the same time, careerism encourages legislators to develop skills and expertise in specific areas. Procedures and traditions can contain and channel the political conflicts that converge upon the lawmaking process.

The danger of institutionalization is organizational rigidity. Institutions that are too rigid can frustrate policymaking, especially in periods of rapid social or political change. Structures that are too complex can tie people in knots, producing inaction, delays, and confusion. Despite its size and complexity, however, today's Congress continues to adapt and change.

SUGGESTED READINGS

Binder, Sarah A. *Minority Rights, Majority Rule: Partisanship and the Development of Congress.* Cambridge: Cambridge University Press, 1997.

Devins, Neal, and Keith E. Whittington, eds. *Congress and the Constitution.* Durham and London: Duke University Press, 2005.

Polsby, Nelson W. *How Congress Evolves: Social Bases of Institutional Change.* New York: Oxford University Press, 2004.

Rakove, Jack N. *Original Meanings: Politics and Ideas in the Making of the Constitution.* New York: Vintage, 1997.

Remini, Robert V. *The House: The History of the House of Representatives.* Washington/New York: Smithsonian Books/Harper Collins Publishers, 2006.

Schickler, Eric. *Disjointed Pluralism: Institutional Innovation and the Development of the U.S. Congress.* Princeton: Princeton University Press, 2001.

Swift, Elaine K. *The Making of an American Senate: Reconstitutive Change in Congress, 1787–1841.* Ann Arbor: University of Michigan Press, 1996.

Wirls, Daniel, and Stephen Wirls. *The Invention of the United States Senate.* Baltimore: Johns Hopkins University Press, 2004.

***E**lectoral Triumphs and Stalemate*
Rep. Anh "Joseph" Cao (R-La.), t
first Vietnamese elected to Congres
walks with his daughters—who we
traditional clothing—to the House chan
ber to be sworn in as a member of th
111th Congress (top left). After one
the closest Senate contests in histo
Al Franken (D-Minn.) passes a pre
gauntlet in the Capitol (top right). His fc
incumbent Norm Coleman (bottom), po
ders his fate after a three-judge pan
determined that he had lost to Franke
by 312 votes out of nearly 3 millic
cast. The litigation dragged on throug
mid-2009, when the state's Suprem
Court rejected Coleman's case and h
conceded to Franken.

chapter 3

Going for It: Recruitment and Candidacy

The 111th Congress (2009–2011) has made electoral history in several respects. First, after winning thirty House seats in the 2006 election, the Democrats won an additional twenty-one House and eight Senate seats (the Minnesota seat remained contested after Congress was sworn in) in the 2008 election. In the post–World War II period only once before had either major party "followed a gain of more than twenty House seats with another double-digit gain" two years later. The last instance of a comparable back-to-back triumph occurred more than five decades ago.[1]

Second, the exact makeup of the Senate was still unsettled even after the swearing-in of senators. Several changes were directly linked to the presidential election of Illinois senator Barack Obama, the first sitting senator since John F. Kennedy to win the White House. Obama resigned his Senate seat shortly after winning the presidency. Senators Hillary Rodham Clinton, N.Y., and Kenneth Salazar, Colo., who were nominated by Obama to be Secretary of State and Secretary of the Interior, respectively, did not resign their seats until after they were confirmed for their new positions. All three states had Democratic governors, so the replacements were Democrats.[2] Colorado's governor named the superintendent of Denver's public schools, Michael Bennet, as Salazar's replacement. New York's governor, David Paterson, appointed Rep. Kirsten Gillibrand to fill Clinton's vacant seat. Sen. Joe Biden of Delaware, who was reelected to the 111th Senate, resigned that position to assume his duties as vice president of the United States. Delaware's Democratic governor named Biden's longtime aide, Edward Kaufman, to fill Biden's seat.

The major controversy erupted over the appointment process in Illinois. Gov. Rod Blagojevich was arrested for allegedly trying to sell the Senate post vacated by President-elect Obama to the highest bidder for personal and political profit. Despite the arrest and the loss of confidence in his leadership, the governor, in a bold move, reasserted his authority to make the appointment. He named seventy-one-year-old African American Roland W. Burris, the state's former attorney general, to fill Obama's seat. Senate leaders initially said they would prevent Burris from taking the seat, objecting that anyone appointed by a tainted governor could not be an effective representative for the people of Illinois. (Democratic leaders also had a political motive to resist Burris's appointment because he seemed a weak contestant to defend the seat in 2010.) The Senate's position raised major legal and constitutional issues. "[W]e absolutely contend that the Constitution gives the Senate the sole power to seat, or not to seat, the members of the body," a spokesperson for Majority Leader Harry Reid of Nevada insisted.[3] But legal scholars asked: "By what authority can [Senate Majority Leader Reid] deny a governor carrying out his constitutional duties?" In the end, Burris was seated. Denying the seat to Burris, who would be the chamber's only African American, became politically untenable.

The other uncertainty, not directly related to Obama's election, involved Minnesota's Senate seat. On January 5, 2009, the day before the 111th Congress officially began, Minnesota's Canvassing Board declared Democrat Al Franken the victor over incumbent GOP senator Norm Coleman. In a bitterly fought recount battle involving numerous legal challenges and controversies, Franken defeated Coleman by 312 votes out of more than 2.4 million cast. Even so, the Minnesota outcome was subject to further legal challenges. Senate Republicans announced that they would act to delay the seating of Franken "until all legal matters are settled, even if it takes months."[4] (Franken was declared the winner after an eight-month legal battle.) Thus, the 111th Senate began with four appointed members and one unresolved contest.

A third historical milestone occurred in the House chamber where the first Vietnamese-American took the oath of office. Rep. Joseph Cao, R-La., who first arrived in the United States as a Vietnamese refugee at the age of eight, defeated nine-term Democratic incumbent William Jefferson. The outcome surprised political pundits, because Jefferson seemed like a sure bet to win again, as he had two years earlier, despite being under indictment on federal corruption charges. (FBI agents famously found $90,000 stashed in Jefferson's freezer at his home.) New Orleans voters, said Charles Cook, a well-known election analyst and Louisiana native, "don't usually turn out candidates with ethics problems."[5] (Worth a brief mention is that the Northern Mariana Islands elected a delegate to serve in the 111th Congress for the first time ever.[6])

How did these people get to Congress? The question has no simple answer. In the broadest sense all legislators are products of recruitment—the social and political process through which people achieve leadership posts. Recruitment is a key to the effective functioning of all institutions, including legislatures. Ideally, the recruitment process should secure the ablest individuals to lead their community, a subject addressed in the first great book about politics, Plato's *Republic*. Sociologists, however, have long observed that recruitment reflects a society's class structure, with the most privileged disproportionately represented in the power structure. Contemporary political scientists, whatever their normative concerns, have charted the paths individuals travel to posts in Congress and other institutions of government.

Any recruitment process has both formal and informal elements. For Congress, the formal elements include the Constitution and state and federal laws governing nominations and elections. Equally important are the informal, often unwritten, rules of the game. Ambitions, skills, and resources favor certain aspirants over others; popular attitudes lead citizens to support some candidates and reject others. Taken together, such elements add up to a series of filters or screens. The recruitment process is a mix of rules, probabilities, chance events, and timing. Its biases, both overt and hidden, affect the day-to-day operation of the House and Senate, not to mention the quality of representation and decision making.

FORMAL RULES OF THE GAME

The constitutional qualifications for holding congressional office are few and simple, though specific. The three specifically mentioned are age (twenty-five years of age for the House, thirty for the Senate); citizenship (seven years for the House, nine years for the Senate); and residency (in the state from which the officeholder is elected). Thus the constitutional gateways to congressional officeholding are fairly wide.

These qualifications cannot be augmented by the states or by Congress. In 1995 the Supreme Court held these qualifications could only be changed through constitutional amendment.[7] Advocates of term limits had campaigned to impose limits on the number of terms that members of Congress could serve. By the early 1990s, twenty-three states had adopted restrictions on the number of terms their members of Congress could serve. The state of Arkansas, whose law the Court reviewed (*U.S. Term Limits, Inc. v. Thornton*, 1995) argued that its scheme did not create an additional "qualification" for holding office (Article I, Sections 2 and 3), but had been written as a ballot-access measure within the state's power to regulate the "times, places, and manner of holding elections" (Article I, Section 4). Speaking for the Court, Justice John Paul Stevens spurned this subterfuge as "an indirect attempt to accomplish what the Constitution prohibits Arkansas from accomplishing directly." (Laws enacted by states or localities limiting terms for their state officeholders were unaffected by the ruling.)

As the term-limits controversy showed, even the three simple requirements for holding congressional office can arouse controversy. The authors of the Constitution considered but eventually rejected term limits. According to the Framers (especially the authors of *The Federalist Papers*), reelection of senators and representatives was left unrestricted for three reasons. First, the Framers did not wish to limit electors' choices. Second, they regarded the reelection option as a powerful incentive for faithful service by officeholders: Gouverneur Morris (speaking of the presidency) called the opportunity of reelection "the great motive to good behavior." Finally, they valued the expertise that experienced lawmakers—much like themselves—could bring to legislative deliberations.

The residency requirement is traditionally stricter in practice than the Constitution prescribes. Voters tend to prefer candidates with long-standing ties to their states or districts and to shun outsiders who move into a state primarily to seek public office (so-called carpetbaggers). The issue is sure to be raised whenever the candidate is an outsider. For example, when the Illinois-born and Connecticut-raised Hillary Clinton first ran for the Senate in New York State, the carpetbagger charge was leveled at her. Only by crisscrossing the Empire State, learning about the issues, and meeting voters was Clinton able to prove her qualifications.

Americans' geographical mobility has swollen the "carpetbagger caucus" on Capitol Hill. A congressional inventory found that some 37 percent of all House members were born within the districts they represented.[8] On the other hand, about a third of the members of both chambers in recent congresses were born outside the states they represent. (In the 111th Congress, twelve House members and one senator were born outside the United States.) Especially in the more populous, faster-growing areas, shrewd candidates can overcome objections to their outsider status. Barely a year after he settled in Arizona, Sen. John McCain, R-Ariz., a career navy officer, war hero, and six-year prisoner of war in North Vietnam, beat three established politicians for a congressional nomination. He stifled carpetbagging charges by explaining that, as the son of a navy officer and one himself, he had never been able to put down roots: "The longest place I ever lived was Hanoi."

Senate Apportionment

The Framers envisioned that the Senate would add stability and wisdom to the actions of the popularly elected House, so they provided that senators would be chosen by the respective state legislatures, not directly by the voters themselves. This distinction between the two houses was put to rest by the Seventeenth Amendment, which, in 1913, mandated the direct popular election of senators.

Small states' delegates at the Constitutional Convention demanded equal representation in the Senate as the price for their support of the Constitution. The arrangement is virtually unamendable, because Article V assures that no state can be deprived of its equal voice in the Senate without its own consent. Because states vary wildly in population, the Senate is the one legislative body in the nation where "one person, one vote" emphatically does not apply. By this measure the Senate is one of the most malapportioned legislatures in the world.[9] As various scholars have noted, "The nine largest states are home to 51 percent of the population but elect only 18 percent of the Senate; the twenty-six smallest states control 52 percent of the Senate but hold only 18 percent of the population."[10]

The Senate's representative character has been further undermined by widening disparities in state populations. After the first census in 1790, the spread between the most populous state (Virginia) and the least populous one (Delaware) was nineteen to one. Today the spread between the most populous state (California) and each of the seven least populous states (Alaska, Delaware, Montana, North Dakota, South Dakota, Vermont, and Wyoming) is fifty-three to one. Nearly a third of U.S. citizens live in four megastates (California, Texas, New York, and Florida), represented by only eight senators. Populous states complain that they are shortchanged in the federal bargain. Compared with lightly populated states, they contribute more revenue and receive fewer benefits.[11] In spite of the constitutional barriers, the late senator Daniel Patrick Moynihan, D-N.Y. (1977–2001), warned that "sometime in the twenty-first century the United States is going to have to address the question of apportionment in the Senate."[12]

In a recent study using attitudinal, electoral, and demographic data, John D. Griffin concludes that the Senate's malapportionment, in combination with state boundaries, "has increasingly come to underweight the preferences of ideological liberals, Democrats, African Americans, and Latinos." Although such biases may not affect all issues, Griffin finds that they come into play when issues important to minorities are voted upon—because "racial minorities tend to reside in states with less [Senate] voting weight."[13]

House Apportionment

The 435 House seats are apportioned among the states by population—now averaging nearly 700,000 people per district. This apportionment process excludes the five delegates (American Samoa, the District of Columbia, Guam, the Virgin Islands, and the Northern Mariana Islands) and one resident commissioner (Puerto Rico). These nonapportioned seats represent populations ranging from around 217,000 (Samoa) to 4 million (Puerto Rico).

To allocate House seats among the states, the Constitution requires a census of population every ten years. Once the census figures are gathered by the Commerce Department's Bureau of Census, apportionment is derived by a mathematical formula called the method of equal proportions.[14] The idea is that proportional differences in the number of persons per representative for any pair of states should be kept to a minimum. The first fifty House seats are taken because the Constitution assures each state at least one representative. The question then becomes: Which state deserves the fifty-first seat, the fifty-second, and so forth? The mathematical formula yields a priority value for each seat, up to any desired number. The bottom line is to ensure that states are "entitled to a percentage of representatives equal to [their] portion of the national population."[15]

Because congressional districts cannot cross state lines, however, reapportionment does not yield equal districts. After the 2001 apportionment, for example, the entire state of Montana, with one representative-at-large for nearly a million people, was the nation's most populous district. Neighboring Wyoming, with barely half a million represented by its single seat, was the least populous.

People on the Move. Because the House's size has remained fixed since 1911, one state's gain means another's loss.[16] This reality provoked sharp controversy in the aftermath of the 1920 census. For the first time ever, the results indicated that most people lived in urban instead of rural areas. With the size of the House fixed, this meant that rural states and lawmakers would lose their House seats to urban areas. The clash between the two sides was so fierce that

FIGURE 3-1   **House Apportionment in the 2000s and Estimates for the 2010s**

Sources: "The 2010 Seating Plan," *National Journal,* July 21, 2007, 31–28

Note: Numbers in parentheses show estimated gains and losses following the 2010 census, based on Census Bureau population projections. These projections mirror states' gain-and-loss trends over recent decades, although the numbers may not all be borne out by the 2010 count.

Congress failed to enact a reapportionment bill setting the number of House seats per state. Finally, in 1929, a law was enacted that "established a permanent system for apportioning the 435 House seats following each census."[17] Thus, the reapportionment of House seats occurred after the 1930 census.

For some decades now, older industrial and farm states of the Northeast and Midwest have lost ground to fast-growing states in the South and West—the declining Rust Belt versus the booming Sun Belt. Following the 1940 census, eastern and midwestern states commanded 58 percent of all House seats, compared to 42 percent for the South and West; with the 2000 census, the ratio was exactly reversed. Over two generations, "a huge shift in political power" had occurred between the geographic regions.[18] In that same time frame, moreover, people shifted within states—from rural areas to cities and then to suburbs.

The nation's population continues to move from the Northeast and Midwest to the South and West. The Census Bureau is expected to announce in December 2010 the actual population shift among the states and the number of

House seats allocated to each state. Then those states with two or more House seats will engage in an often-contentious redistricting process prior to the November 2012 elections.

Census Politics. Because population figures determine seats and affect power, controversy surrounds nearly every aspect of apportionment and districting. The Census Bureau's statisticians are able and nonpartisan civil servants, but their political managers in the Commerce Department respond to White House pressures. And following the last two counts, diverse political forces—among them lawmakers, state and local officials, party strategists, minority groups, and the courts—have waged battles over census numbers. Three of these battles merit mention, because they reflect the kinds of issues usually raised regarding the decennial census.

As background to the first census battle, the decennial census is described as an "actual enumeration" (Article I, Section 2) of persons. The Fourteenth Amendment adds: "Representatives shall be apportioned among the several States according to their respective numbers, counting the whole number of persons in each State, excluding Indians not taxed." But counting such a large and diverse population is logistically and methodologically daunting. Certain hard-to-contact groups—transients, the homeless, renters, immigrants (legal or not), children, and poorer people generally—elude census takers and are undercounted. College students or others temporarily living away from home are sometimes double-counted (an overcount, in effect). Meanwhile, as the Census Bureau gears up for the first post-9/11 count, projected to cost over $14 billion, it faces a number of obstacles: people concerned about their privacy in the wake of increased government surveillance authority, home foreclosures that have scattered families into temporary facilities, and natural disasters like Hurricane Katrina that have displaced scores of people from their residences.[19]

The so-called "tri-caucus" in the House—the Black Caucus, the Hispanic Caucus, and the Asian Caucus—has long been concerned about getting accurate counts of these hard-to-reach minorities. These ad hoc House groups are working together to ensure that the Census Bureau receives adequate resources to conduct an accurate head count for the 2010 census. The Census Bureau "estimated that its 2000 head count might have failed to count 1 percent of white and Asian residents, as many as 3.17 percent of Hispanics, and as many as 1.8 percent of blacks."[20]

In the second battle, the issue of statistical sampling became the pivot for partisan conflict over the 2000 census. The Census Bureau planned to use statistical sampling to augment their traditional methods for counting people—mailing questionnaires to households, sending 500,000 enumerators door-to-door, and following up nonresponses with multiple telephone calls—with statistical sampling to minimize the undercount of minority populations. Because minorities tend to vote Democratic, congressional Republicans feared "that sampling would overestimate minority populations and thereby cause Republicans to lose seats to Democrats."[21] Legal challenges to the sampling plan eventually ended up in the Supreme Court. The Court ruled (*Department of Commerce v. House of*

Representatives, 1999) that sampling cannot be used to apportion seats among the states; however, the decision kept open the possibility that sampling could be used for other purposes, such as in the redistricting of House seats within a state.

In the third battle, the lead-up to the 2010 census witnessed further legislative debate about the national population count. Two examples make the point. Lobby groups working on behalf of Americans who live abroad worked with sympathetic lawmakers to encourage the Census Bureau to include the several million American expatriates in its count. (Following the 2000 census, Utah lost a House seat to North Carolina because it had about a thousand fewer inhabitants. The Census Bureau did not take into account the approximately 11,000 Mormon missionaries living abroad when determining Utah's total.) The Census Bureau agreed to conduct a feasibility study, but determined that it had no effective way to reach the scores of Americans (exclusive of military personnel and government workers) living in different parts of the world.[22]

Today, the national debate on immigration adds yet another dimension to the controversy over apportionment. Immigration is politically charged because it affects which states gain or lose House seats, in addition to a host of other public concerns, including border security, jobs, citizenship, education, health care, and even recession-fueled "economic stimulus" funds doled out state by state. The so-called Sun Belt states (Arizona and Texas, for instance) with large numbers of undocumented workers will gain House seats at the expense of Rust Belt states (Michigan and Pennsylvania, for example). This development has aroused the ire of some lawmakers. "It's one thing if we lose seats simply because of population loss, but it's another thing if we lose this seat because of illegal immigration, and that's exactly what is happening," stated Rep. Candice Miller, R-Mich.[23] (She introduced a constitutional amendment requiring only citizens to be counted for apportionment purposes.) Census figures show that Latinos are the fastest growing group in the United States because of immigration and higher birth rates, which will translate eventually into increasing numbers of Hispanics in the House of Representatives. For example, a scholar who studies African American political power pointed out that "Hispanics outnumber blacks in five districts now represented by blacks."[24]

DISTRICTING IN THE HOUSE

Redistricting is fundamentally a state responsibility. Today, congressional districting is regulated by only two statutes, but federal courts increasingly govern the process through their interpretation of constitutional rights (see below).[25] The federal laws affecting redistricting come into play in two ways. Once congressional seats are apportioned, those states entitled to more than one seat must create districts—each represented by a single member. A 1967 statute prohibits at-large or multimember elections in these states. Districts must be nearly equal in population within states—a standard rigorously enforced by the courts—and they must not dilute representation of racial minorities, an outgrowth of amendments to the Voting Rights Act of 1965.

Redistricting is a fiercely political process that affects the fortunes of many people—state legislators, governors, incumbent House members, congressional leadership, lobbyists, and leaders of racial and ethnic causes. To insulate the process from politics, seven states have turned the job over to some form of independent commission.[26] In most states, however, redistricting is done by the legislature, with the governor able to approve or veto the plan. Political considerations of all kinds affect redistricting. In California, where Democrats controlled the state in 2001, the party and its consultants were buffeted by clashing interests: nervous incumbents who sought safer reelection margins; term-limited state legislators, with their sights set on Washington, D.C.; minority groups demanding more representation (especially Latinos, who account for much of the state's population growth); and national party leaders counting on California to help Democrats keep control of the House in 2008—which did happen—by offsetting GOP districting gains elsewhere.

In the redistricting wars no weapons are left untouched. Both political parties pour money into state legislative and gubernatorial elections and into post-census lobbying efforts, so they can control the mapmaking process. The shift of only a few seats in the legislative chambers of various states, for example, can determine not only which party dominates their congressional delegation, but which party achieves majority control of the House itself. For example, state legislatures and governorships controlled by Democrats following the 2010 census will enjoy large advantages in the redrawing of House district boundaries. If those states lose seats per the census, the legislature might simply eliminate a number of GOP-held seats, place Republicans into Democratic areas, or put two Republican incumbents in the same district. If the states gain House seats, the legislatures might decide to carve out generally safe seats for members of both parties. As a GOP consultant said about his role in drawing House seats for Republicans, "As a mapmaker, I can have more of an impact on an election than a campaign, than a candidate."[27]

If a state's politicians become deadlocked on redistricting, or if they fail to observe legal guidelines, judges may need to finish the job—sometimes awarding victory to parties that lost out earlier in the political fracas. Both parties engage in "forum shopping," seeking the court friendliest to their side. Republicans during both Bush administrations could rely on the Justice Department and a federal bench composed of mostly GOP appointees. State courts can also become engaged in these battles. The Supreme Court has ruled that state courts should normally be preferred over federal courts in redistricting cases.[28]

Because congressional seats are political prizes, districting is a tool for partisan, factional, or even personal advantage. Two potential problems of districting are malapportionment and gerrymandering.

Malapportionment

Before 1964 districts of grossly unequal populations often existed side by side. Within a single state, districts varied by as much as eight to one. As metropolitan areas grew in population, their representation lagged in Congress and even more so in state legislatures. Sometimes malapportionment resulted from explicit actions. More often rurally dominated legislatures simply refused to redistrict, holding on to power regardless of population movements and demographic trends—the "silent gerrymander."

The courts were slow to venture into this "political thicket." By the 1960s, however, the problem of unequal representation cried out for resolution. The Supreme Court ruled that state districting schemes that fell short of standards of equality violated the Fourteenth Amendment's Equal Protection Clause (*Reynolds v. Sims,* 1964). Writing for the Court, Chief Justice Earl Warren held that all state legislative seats must be apportioned "substantially on population."[29]

That same year, the Court also applied the "one person, one vote" principle to the U.S. House of Representatives. An Atlantan who served in the Georgia senate, James P. Wesberry Jr., charged that the state's congressional districting violated equal protection of the laws. The Supreme Court upheld his challenge (*Wesberry v. Sanders,* 1964). The decision was based not on the Fourteenth Amendment but on Article I, Section 2, of the Constitution, which directs that representatives be apportioned among the states according to their respective numbers and chosen by the people of the several states. This language, argued Justice Hugo Black, means that "as nearly as is practicable, one person's vote in a congressional election is to be worth as much as another's."

How much equality of population is "practicable" within the states? The Supreme Court has adopted rigid mathematical equality as the underlying standard. In a 1983 case (*Karcher v. Daggett*), a 5–4 majority voided a New Jersey plan in which districts varied by no more than one-seventh of 1 percent. "Adopting any standard other than population equality would subtly erode the Constitution's ideal of equal representation," wrote Justice William J. Brennan for the majority.[30]

Other goals are sometimes sacrificed to achieve population equality. District mapmakers must often ignore existing political divisions and cross city and county lines. It is often not feasible to follow other economic, social, or geographic boundaries in drawing districts of equal population in more populous states. The congressional district, therefore, tends to be an artificial creation, often bearing little relationship to real communities of interest—economic, geographic, or political. "The main casualty of the tortuous redistricting process now under way," remarked journalist Alan Ehrenhalt, "is the erosion of geographical community—of place—as the basis of political representation."[31]

The typical congressional district's isolation from other natural or political boundaries forces candidates to forge their own unique factions and alliances. It also aids candidates, especially incumbents, who have ways of reaching voters beyond relying on costly commercial media.

Traditional Gerrymandering

Most districting is gerrymandering in the sense that single-member, winner-take-all districts normally favor the local majority party. But the term

BOX 3-1   **Origins of the Gerrymander**

The practice of "gerrymandering"—the excessive manipulation of the shape of a legislative district to benefit certain persons or groups—is probably as old as the Republic, but the name for the practice originated in 1812.

In that year the Massachusetts Legislature carved out of Essex County a district which historian John Fiske described as having a "dragon-like contour." When the painter Gilbert Stuart saw the misshapen district, he penciled in a head, wings, and claws and exclaimed: "That will do for a salamander!"—to which editor Benjamin Russell replied: "Better say a Gerrymander"—after Elbridge Gerry, then-governor of Massachusetts.

By the 1990s the term had broadened to include the modern-day practice of drawing maps to benefit racial and ethnic groups. In the past the term was applied largely to districts drawn to benefit incumbents or political parties.

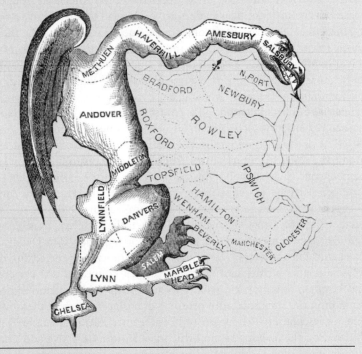

Source: CQ's Guide to Congress, 5th edition, Vol. III (Washington, DC: CQ Press, 2007).

gerrymander usually refers to line drawing that purposefully maximizes seats for one party or voting bloc at the expense of another party or bloc. The gerrymander takes its name from Gov. Elbridge Gerry of Massachusetts, who in 1812 created a peculiar salamander-shaped district north of Boston to benefit his Democratic Party (see Box 3-1). Gerrymandering is used not only to gain partisan advantage but also to protect (and occasionally punish) incumbents, boost aspirants' political prospects, and help or hinder racial or ethnic groups. For most of its history, Congress has regarded gerrymandering as part of the spoils of partisan warfare.

Two common gerrymandering techniques are cracking and packing. Cracking a district splits an area of partisan strength among two or more districts, thus diluting that party's voting leverage. Packing a district draws the lines to include as many of one party's voters as possible, thus rendering the district safe—either to make one party's representatives more secure or to confine its opponents' seats. Whatever the motivation, packed districts waste votes because the majority party wins with more votes than it needs.

Today, gerrymandering is much easier to accomplish than in the past. Computer technology and software make it feasible for knowledgeable individuals and groups to use census and other data to match peoples' voting patterns to where they live, even street-by-street. Alternative plans can be devised easily until political leaders are convinced that they have a redistricting map that achieves their objectives, such as advantaging their party. Reasonable estimates can even be made of the partisan affiliation of people who are moving into or out of a district. "Reinforcing predictability has been the increased polarization of American politics," which promotes straight-ticket voting.[32]

Partisan Gerrymandering. The most common form of gerrymandering, partisan redistricting, occurs in states in which one political party controls the process. A noteworthy and unusual example involved the Texas legislature following the 2002 elections. Texas Republicans—controlling both legislative chambers and the state house for the first time since Reconstruction—pushed through a partisan "re-redistricting" plan over frantic Democratic opposition. (Democratic lawmakers even staged quorum-busting walkouts to Oklahoma and then New Mexico.) The new map "reflects the fact that Texas is an increasingly Republican state," argued House majority leader Tom DeLay, R-Texas, who instigated the plan.[33] Several House Democrats targeted for defeat by DeLay, along with black and Latino advocates, countered that a second post-census remap was impermissible (though such mid-decade revisions were common in the late nineteenth century) and that it deprived them of fair and equal representation. Relying on approval from a federal court, the DeLay plan was used for the 2004 balloting, which yielded the GOP five additional seats, four from defeated Democratic incumbents. Subsequently, the U.S. Supreme Court upheld the DeLay-initiated 2003 Texas redistricting scheme by a 7–2 margin (*League of United Latin American Citizens v. Perry*, 2006).[34] Despite finding that the Texas GOP appeared to have acted "with the sole purpose of achieving a Republican majority," Justice Anthony M. Kennedy—speaking for the Court—found that the case did not provide a "workable test" for deciding "how much partisan dominance is too much."

On the issue of partisan gerrymandering the Supreme Court, like Congress, has thus far chosen to look the other way. In a 1986 case involving Indiana state legislative districts, a Court majority held that gerrymandering was a justiciable issue—that is, it could be properly raised in court (*Davis v. Bandemer*).[35] If the gerrymandering were substantial, long-standing, and truly harmful to a political minority, it could violate the Constitution's Equal Protection Clause. At the same time, the Court's majority was not convinced that the Indiana gerrymander met those tests.

Partisan gerrymandering continued for almost two decades more before the Supreme Court revisited the issue in the Pennsylvania case of *Vieth v. Jubelirer* (2004).[36] The GOP-controlled state legislature drew a congressional districting plan for the 2002 elections that produced Republican victories in twelve of the nineteen House districts. Democrats brought suit noting, among other things, that their party outnumbered Republicans by voter registration in the state.[37] In the end, as a law professor noted, "a badly divided Court [5 to 4] was unable to reach agreement on any new [judicial] standard" for determining permissible from impermissible partisan gerrymandering. He concluded that *Vieth* resolved nothing except to invite more legal suits until the Court could establish workable standards for determining unconstitutional partisan gerrymandering.[38]

A two-Congresses consequence of partisan gerrymandering, according to various House members, is that it inhibits the construction of cross-party coalitions. As Rep. John Tanner, D-Tenn., stated:

> When Members come here from these [partisan] districts that have been Gerrymandered..., they have little incentive really to work across party lines in order to reach solutions. As a matter of fact, they have a disincentive because if their district is skewed so heavily one way or the other, then the election is really in the party primaries, where barely more than a third of the people, in most instances, are the highly charged partisans, either Democrat or Republican. And so if one comes here wanting to work across the aisle, one has to...watch one's back, because the highly charged partisans don't like that.[39]

Some scholarly research, however, undermines Tanner's linkage of partisan gerrymanders with the dearth of bipartisan cooperation in the House. Several scholars conclude that "gerrymandering has not contributed to [party] polarization in the House." Instead, "most of the increase [in partisanship] came unaided by redistricting."[40]

Pro-Incumbent Gerrymandering. Bipartisan or "sweetheart" gerrymanders are those with lines drawn to protect incumbents. Any gains or losses in the number of seats are shared by the two parties. These gerrymanders are often by-products of divided party control—within the legislature or between the legislature and the governor. In the wake of the 2000 census, several populous states—California, Illinois, Michigan, and New York—chose to hoard their parties' existing assets. In New York, which lost two seats in the count, two pairs of incumbents (one from each party) were eventually thrown together, resulting in two retirements. The remaining twenty-seven districts were drawn for incumbents. "Neither party [wanted] to lose its hard-won gains," election analyst Rhodes Cook explained. "With the partisan balance almost even, every seat counts." Further,

> Incumbent protection [was] the path of least resistance for state legislatures redrawing the lines...And there were fewer districts that [were] competitive by virtue of their internal contradictions—for example, voting for one party's candidate for president and the other party's for Congress. In 2000, the number of such "split-ticket" districts was at its lowest level in nearly 50 years.[41]

Less than 10 percent of the post-2000 House races were truly competitive. In California, home of 12 percent of all House members, the dominant Democrats opted to play it safe and claim only the added seat awarded by the census. This minimalist approach dismayed the party's national strategists and angered Latino leaders who had counted on gaining more seats. The redrawn map eliminated one swing district in Los Angeles County (when its Republican incumbent retired) to craft a new Latino district, created a new GOP seat in the Central Valley, and shored up several swing-district members. The result was that, in 153 races involving incumbents over three elections (2002–2006), only one was defeated, and in all but fourteen instances incumbents drew 60 percent or more of the vote.

Debates about Gerrymandering. Political analysts are almost as divided as judges in assessing the consequences of gerrymandering. Some commentators blame incumbent-protective line drawing for producing noncompetitive elections—which dilutes the voting experience and leads to lower turnout. "Already the House...has become virtually safe for most incumbents and in recent elections experienced less turnover than the Senate, which has far fewer members and only one-third of its members up for reelection," Charles Backstrom and his colleagues observe in urging the courts to step in.[42] Yet partisan gerrymandering (defined as maximizing a party's number of seats) ought in theory to counteract the phenomenon of incumbent "safe" seats, as the party seeks to expand its number of winnable—but not necessarily "safe"—seats.

Other analysts deny that gerrymandering is the main cause of noncompetitive elections. Incumbents enjoy multiple advantages, even when they do not have the luxury (as critics put it) of choosing their own constituents. More visible and better financed than most challengers, incumbents tend to be as successful in unredistricted areas as in redistricted ones. As an example, Iowa's five districts were drawn in 2001 by a nonpartisan panel to be competitive. Over the next two elections, all of the incumbents, even those considered vulnerable, were returned to office.

But demography also matters. "The problem is not who draws the legislative lines, it's where people live," one observer notes.[43] As Bruce Oppenheimer of Vanderbilt University puts it, "Democrats tend to live next to Democrats. Republicans tend to live next to Republicans."[44] Emory University's Alan Abramowitz tested the strength of demographic changes by measuring the post-redistricting jump in noncompetitive districts (those that were more than ten percentage points above or below the presidential margin in the nation as a whole). He confirmed that imbalances occurred not so much from newly redrawn districts as from population shifts over the intervening years.[45]

The state of California illustrates this insight. Although regarded as a "blue" (Democratic) state, California has a deep political fault line readily visible on electoral maps. Democratic voters tend to center in populous and mainly coastal counties, whereas Republicans are strongest in inland counties. Creating truly competitive districts would mean, to put it simply, linking together disparate coastal and inland communities—an exercise that could itself require extensive gerrymandering. Such highly differentiated geographic patterns are by no means peculiar to this one state.

Combating partisan and incumbent-friendly districting has nonetheless become a reformist cause. California governor Arnold Schwarzenegger, for example, unsuccessfully pushed a ballot initiative that would have shifted districting from the legislature to a panel of retired judges. A number of other states are considering such proposals. A bipartisan duo in the House (Tanner and Zack Wamp, R-Tenn.) introduced legislation (H. Res. 1365, 110th Congress) urging the states to establish independent redistricting commissions that would have as their goals the discouragement of gerrymanders and the promotion of competitive House districts. Whether such remedies can address the root causes of safe districts is another matter. Some reformers hold that the ultimate solution lies in some form of proportional representation, involving multimember districts—a system at this time prohibited in federal elections.[46]

Racial Gerrymandering

Another form of gerrymandering is intended to promote the election of racial minorities. The Voting Rights Act, enacted in 1965 to ensure the right of blacks to vote in elections, drastically curtailed voting discrimination. Coverage of linguistic minorities was added in 1975. Amendments in 1982 barred election laws having the intent or effect of reducing minority voting power (Section 2). Sixteen states (mainly southern) that historically discriminated against minorities are required (under Section 5 of the act) to "pre-clear" with either the U.S. District Court for the District of Columbia or the U.S. Attorney General changes in election rules to ensure that the changes do not have the purpose or effect of "denying or abridging the right to vote on account of race or color." The pre-clearance of changes to election rules depends on whether the rules "would lead to a retrogression in the position of racial minorities with respect to their effective exercise of the electoral franchise" (*Beer v. U.S.*, 1976).

Under the 1982 provisions, states were not only restrained from diluting (cracking) minority votes, but they were also encouraged to pack districts to elect minority officeholders (majority-minority districts). After the 1990 census a number of states set about creating majority-minority black or Latino districts. The decade thus saw the creation of fifteen new African American districts, thirteen of them in the South (for a total of thirty-two nationwide, seventeen of them in the South), and nine new Latino districts (totaling twenty). Many of these were artfully contrived to concentrate minority voters, making Governor Gerry's 1812 creation look amateurish by comparison.

Racial redistricting contributed to the Democratic Party's southern meltdown in the 1990s. Republican Party strategists quickly learned that confining minority (mostly Democratic) voters into safe (mainly urban) districts would strengthen the GOP in outlying suburban and rural areas. The combination of African Americans, who wanted more representation in the House, and Republicans, who supported that goal because it served their political purposes, was dubbed the "unholy alliance." Charles S. Bullock of the University of Georgia summarized the impact of racial gerrymandering in the South:

> After 1994, Republicans received handsome rewards while black Democrats were becoming an increasing numerical force within the minority party. The replacement of moderate white Democrats with conservative Republicans, even with the addition of a few African American legislative seats, bodes ill for the ability of African American legislators to find the allies they need to achieve their policy goals.[47]

Another scholar, David Lublin, described the outcome as a "paradox of representation" in which packed districts yielded more minority lawmakers but also led to a more conservative House that reduced minorities' leverage and influence over legislative outcomes.[48] Of course, between 1995 and 2006, these majority-minority representatives were in the political minority in the House, as well. However, in the 110th (2007–2009) and 111th (2009–2011) Congresses, with a Democratic House majority, the presence of so many majority-minority representatives in the majority party elevated the political power of racial and ethnic minorities to unprecedented levels. For example, the third–highest ranking Democrat in the chamber, Democratic House whip James Clyburn, represents a majority-minority district in South Carolina.

Proponents of majority-minority districts view them as "the political equivalent to the ethnically homogeneous neighborhood," in the words of law professor Lani Guinier. "They are a safe haven for members of that group, a bit of turf that one ethnic grouping controls, a place where their voice is preeminent."[49] But opponents are troubled by categorizing voters by race and ethnicity. "Racial districting is a vision of America deeply at odds with that upon which the civil rights revolution was built," warns Abigail M. Thernstrom, a leading critic. "Race-based districting has been unprincipled, unnecessary— and (to top it off) a gross distortion of the law."[50] As former Supreme Court Justice Sandra Day O'Connor noted, racial districting conveys "the belief … that individuals should be judged by the color of their skin."[51]

Others doubt that packing districts is the best way to advance minorities' interests. Concentrating minorities in their own districts wastes their votes by producing outsized electoral majorities for the winning candidates. It also bleaches surrounding nonminority districts. Minority voters, along with whatever leverage they have, are drained from areas surrounding the new districts. Even if the number of minority officeholders rises, "the number of white legislators who have any political need to respond to minority concerns goes down as their minority constituents are peeled off to form the new black and Hispanic districts."[52]

Another strategy for maximizing the political influence of minorities would thus be to maintain substantial minorities of racial and ethnic minority voters, say 40 percent or so, in a larger number of districts (termed "influence districts") to expand the ranks of officeholders responsive to minority needs.[53] It was no surprise that in the wake of the 2000 census, many Democrats concluded that racial gerrymandering had hurt their party and set about unpacking some of the minority districts. "For 20 years I've been arguing against the stacking of black voters in districts that has the overall effect of diluting the voting strength of black people," stated representative Clyburn. "It's better to maintain a 35 to 40 percent black district where [blacks] would have a tremendous influence on elections. I don't think you need 75 percent in order for a black to be elected. That's kind of insulting to me."[54] The unpacking effort appears in the main to be unsuccessful.[55] This effort has an ironic twist: Republicans support minority districts while many Democrats want to dismantle them.

The Court Enters the Quagmire

Since the 1960s the Supreme Court has repeatedly ruled against districts drawn deliberately to disadvantage a racial or ethnic group. In 1960 the Court declared unconstitutional the "obscene, 28-sided" boundaries of Tuskegee, Alabama, that disfranchised blacks by excluding them from the city (*Gomillion v. Lightfoot*).[56] Courts upheld the Voting Rights Act of 1965 and its later amendments, which forbid electoral arrangements that dilute the voting power of racial or linguistic minorities.

After the 1990 redistricting, the Court initially ruled against districts drawn deliberately to advantage minority representation as well. In *Shaw v. Reno* (1993), the Court rejected two oddly shaped North Carolina congressional districts, the First and Twelfth. Although conceding that race-conscious districting might be permissible, the Court's majority expressed shock at the bizarre boundaries of the Twelfth District. Writing for a 5–4 majority, Justice O'Connor questioned "districting so highly irregular that, on its face, it rationally cannot be understood as anything other than an effort to segregate voters…on the basis of race."[57]

In *Miller v. Johnson* (1995), the Supreme Court similarly rejected two Georgia districts drawn with race as the "predominant factor."[58] "To challenge a districting scheme as violating the equal protection clause," wrote Justice Kennedy for a 5–4 majority, a plaintiff must prove that "race was the predominant factor motivating the legislature's decision to place a significant number of voters within or without a particular district." To prove racial predominance, it must be shown that "the legislature subordinated to racial considerations traditional race-neutral districting principles, including but not limited to

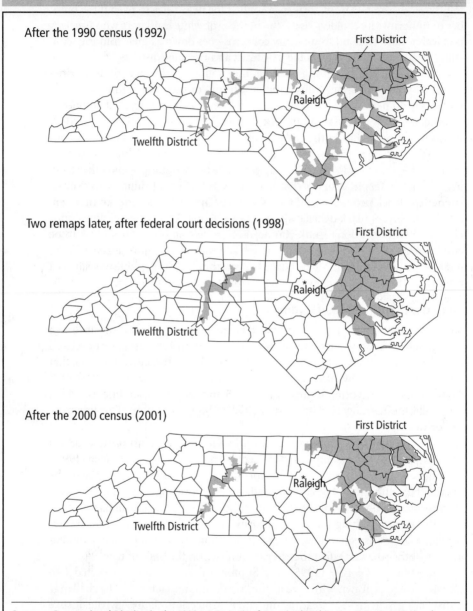

After the 1990 census (1992)

First District

*Raleigh

Twelfth District

Two remaps later, after federal court decisions (1998)

First District

*Raleigh

Twelfth District

After the 2000 census (2001)

First District

*Raleigh

Twelfth District

Sources: Congressional Districts in the 1990s: A Portrait of America (Washington, D.C.: Congressional
Quarterly, 1993), 548. *Congressional Districts in the 2000s: A Portrait of America* (Washington, D.C.: CQ
Press, 2003), 673.

Note: North Carolina's First and Twelfth Districts were drawn to give the state its first black representatives
in ninety-three years. First elected in 1992, the two African American representatives were subsequently
reelected; after the First District representative retired in 2003, she was replaced by another African American.

compactness, contiguity, and respect for political subdivisions of communities defined by actual shared interests."

Over the ensuing years federal courts ruled on districting plans in a number of states—not all of them in the South. By 2000 five southern states had drawn new district maps in response to the Court's rulings. North Carolina's shoestring Twelfth District remained under a legal cloud after four remappings (see Figure 3-2).

Virtually all the minority members running in their new districts won subsequent elections, some with widened margins. Foes of racial gerrymandering seized on the results as vindication. "The idea that minorities have to have a super-majority of black voters to win in their districts, that's history now," declared the lawyer who had challenged the Georgia districts. Black officeholders credited their success to incumbency, which they argued was made possible by racial gerrymandering. They won reelection by combining overwhelming black support with 20 percent or more of the white vote.[59]

At the same time that conservative members of the Supreme Court have taken a hard-line against majority-minority districts, the Court's more liberal members have charted a different course. Dissenting in *Miller*, Justice Ruth Bader Ginsburg noted that "legislative districting is a highly political business" and that "apportionment schemes, by their very nature, assemble people in groups." Historically, many ethnic groups sought and gained power through their own voting districts. "Until now, no constitutional infirmity has been seen in districting Irish or Italian voters together, for example." Why, Ginsburg asked, shouldn't African Americans be accorded the same right? Courts, she explained, should intervene only to protect the rights of minorities: "Special circumstances justify vigilant judicial inspection to protect minority voters—circumstances that do not apply to majority voters."

Ginsburg's argument offered a way for the Court to retreat strategically from its hard-line stance on racial gerrymandering. The final decisions on 1990s redistricting involved the much-litigated North Carolina Twelfth District, whose black population had been whittled from 57 to 47 percent after two remappings. A group of the district's white voters had persuaded a lower court that the newly remapped district was still racially gerrymandered. The state, for its part, argued that it simply wanted to create a district of loyal Democrats, many of whom happened to be black. A unanimous Court sent the case back to the district court, which was instructed to take into account the state's point of view (*Hunt v. Cromartie*, 1999). Writing for the Court, Justice Clarence Thomas declared:

> A jurisdiction may engage in constitutional political gerrymandering, even if it so happens that the most loyal Democrats happen to be black Democrats and even if the state were conscious of that fact. Evidence that blacks constitute even a supermajority in one Congressional district while amounting to less than a plurality in a neighboring district will not, by itself, suffice to prove that a jurisdiction was motivated by race in drawing its district lines when the evidence also shows a high correlation between race and party preference.[60]

All nine judges agreed with the decision, although the four liberal dissenters from earlier cases declined to join Justice Thomas's opinion. In a concurring opinion written by Justice Stevens, they argued that the evidence of race-based districting in this instance was weak. At the very least, the guideposts erected in *Hunt* gave the states "very significant breathing room" in the post-2000 round of redistricting.

Two years later—just as states were beginning their next round of redistricting—the Court followed the less hard-line approach of *Hunt* (*Easley v. Cromartie,* 2001). Weighing another challenge to North Carolina's redrawn Twelfth District (held by Rep. Melvin Watt), a three-judge district court had ruled that the districting was driven by race. By yet another 5–4 vote, the Court disagreed, describing as "clearly erroneous" the district court's findings. "The evidence taken together," wrote Justice Breyer, "does not show that racial considerations predominated in the drawing of District 12's boundaries. That is because race closely correlates with political behavior."[61] Justice Thomas, now in the minority, did not dispute the facts but simply held that the Court should have deferred to the lower court's factual findings.

In another 5 to 4 decision, the Court in 2003 (*Georgia v. Ashcroft*) addressed the issue of retrogression (weakening a minority electorate's political power), which involved the Georgia legislature's unpacking of several majority-minority senate districts. The Supreme Court held that an earlier district court ruling focused too heavily on whether black candidates could be elected only in "safe" black districts. States can consider a variety of factors to promote minority influence, such as creating minority "influence districts" instead of "packed" districts. Second, the district court failed to consider a number of factors relevant to a determination of retrogression, such as whether black lawmakers backed the creation of additional "minority-influenced" districts. For example, Rep. John Lewis, D-Ga., the civil rights hero, supported the plan as did every black state legislator. The Supreme Court's decision, however, left the state legislature with the complex issue of determining "how many influence districts are necessary to balance the loss of majority-minority districts."[62]

More to Come. Race-conscious districting is likely to be contested well beyond 2010. As a North Carolina state senator in charge of his chamber's redistricting efforts quipped to a reporter: "If the Lord God Almighty threw down lightning bolts and carved plans into the side of Mount Mitchell, and we adopted them, there would still be challenges to redistricting under every legal theory devised."[63]

The leading question is whether the Supreme Court will ever attempt to provide clear guidelines as to what racial (even partisan) redistricting the Constitution will permit. In the quest for a workable standard, the justices have adopted a version of the late Justice Potter Stewart's test for identifying obscenity: They seem to "know it when they see it." And given the closeness of its past decisions on majority-minority districts—every major case on this question has turned on a 5–4 vote—the Court could again shift its direction as a result of further changes in its membership.

BECOMING A CANDIDATE

Very few of those who are eligible for Congress vie for a seat. Candidates who meet the legal qualifications must weigh a variety of considerations—some practical and rational, others personal and emotional. Candidacy decisions are often the pivotal moments in the entire recruitment process, although students of politics have only recently given them the attention they deserve. "The decision to run obviously structures everything else that goes on in the primary process," writes political scientist L. Sandy Maisel. "Who runs, who does not run, how many candidates run. These questions set the stage for the campaigns themselves."[64]

Called or Chosen?

From their Jacksonian heyday in the 1830s to the decline of big-city machines in the 1960s, local party organizations customarily enlisted and sponsored candidates. When such organizations withered, the initiative passed to the candidates themselves: self-starters who pulled their own bandwagons. "The boys in the back room aren't going to decide who stays in this race," one representative remarked. "There are no boys anymore."[65] "The skills that work in American politics at this point in history," wrote Alan Ehrenhalt, "are those of entrepreneurship. At all levels of the political system, from local boards and councils up to and including the presidency, it is unusual for parties to nominate people. People nominate themselves."[66]

After self-starting, however, congressional aspirants quickly encounter national networks of party committees and their allied interest groups. At the heart of these networks are the two major parties' House and Senate campaign committees, now active in nearly all phases of congressional elections.[67] They seek out and encourage promising candidates at the local level, sometimes even taking sides to help ensure their nomination. Once nominated, candidates receive help for nearly every phase of the campaign, from fundraising to finding seasoned campaign managers to researching the backgrounds of their opponents. Filing deadlines must be met, backers lined up, and financing sought. Candidates may be free to keep their national party at arm's length, but few nonincumbents can turn their backs on party sponsorship.

During the recruiting season (beginning in early 2009 for the 2010 contests, for example), the two major parties' leaders and campaign committee staffs "reach out across the country in search of political talent. Like college football coaching staffs in hot pursuit of high-school prospects, they are…putting together the lineups of the future."[68] Prospects can expect calls from the president, former presidents, governors, high-profile financial backers, and other notables. The run-ups to recent elections all began with fierce recruiting seasons, as both parties sought lineups that could win House and Senate majorities.

Not all recruiting takes place on the road. Because open seats—newly created districts or those in which incumbents have died or retired—are less secure, party leaders strive also to discourage their incumbent colleagues from retiring.

Nonparty groups also sponsor congressional candidates. The leading small business lobby, the National Federation of Independent Business (NFIB), has been a major contributor to the GOP cause. In the mid-1990s the NFIB began to pick potential candidates from its own membership, train them, and help them run for office. "We're trying to develop a farm team for down the road," explained the federation's national political director, "so we can work in more of a proactive instead of a reactive way," fielding, not just endorsing, candidates who support the small business agenda.[69] Other organizations with strong grassroots networks now pursue a similar course.

Most would-be officeholders seek advancement within the two major parties, which boast not only the brand loyalties of a huge majority of voters but also extensive financial and logistical resources. Still, independents and minor-party candidates enter congressional contests. Some twenty-three party labels appeared on ballots somewhere in 2008. Seldom do these contenders win a sizable number of votes, although they do provide alternatives where only one major party fields a candidate. Sometimes they add something unusual to a campaign, as happened in Idaho's 2008 senatorial race, which was easily won by Republican Jim Risch, the state's lieutenant governor. An independent candidate legally changed his name to "Pro-Life" so it would appear that way on the November ballot in Idaho, "along with a brief aside identifying him as a person, not a position."[70] Only two Independents currently serve in Congress: Vermont senator Bernard Sanders, a self-styled "democratic socialist," and Connecticut senator Joseph I. Lieberman.

Ambitious Amateurs and Professionals

How do would-be candidates, whether self-starters or anointed by party leaders, make up their minds to run? The answer depends on whether the individual is an amateur or a strategic politician.

Amateurs. Amateur candidates are defined by their lack of previous political experience. Despite inexperience and nonexistent name recognition, many amateurs run for Congress. A few even run to bring a specific issue to public attention and are less interested in winning than in advancing their cause. Most amateurs are what David T. Canon calls "hopeless amateurs"— people with little or no chance of winning.[71] A long-shot bid is their only way of becoming a candidate. They run because "it was something they knew they were going to do sometime and for whatever reasons it appeared to be the right time."[72] "I think his chances have gone from absolutely out of the question to extremely remote," remarked the wife of one hopeless contender. "But he's learning a lot, and I think he has enjoyed it."[73] Many such amateurs indulge in self-delusion about their prospects. Maisel, a political scientist who wrote candidly of his unsuccessful congressional primary campaign, described politicians as possessing an "incredible ability to delude themselves about their own chances."[74]

There is, however, one group of amateurs who sometimes prove to be the exception—those with highly visible nonpolitical careers. Astronauts, war heroes, entertainers, and athletes are in big demand as candidates. Local or statewide television personalities also make attractive contenders. Only occasionally do other nonpolitical careers have such visibility. First elected to the Senate in 1988, Democrat Herb Kohl was familiar throughout Wisconsin from his family's food stores long before he wrote an $18.5 million check to keep the Milwaukee Bucks basketball team from moving elsewhere—not a bad advertisement for a would-be senator. And in 2000 Republican Tom Osborne captured 80 percent of the vote in Nebraska's open Third District even though he wholly lacked political experience. Everyone in the state knew him as the longtime football coach of the University of Nebraska Cornhuskers.[75] Al Franken's status as a nationally-known comedian, writer, and commentator helped to launch his political career as a candidate in 2008 for Minnesota's U.S. Senate seat.

Strategic Politicians. Like the savviest amateurs, strategic contenders are ambitious individuals who have decided to run for a seat in Congress. They have concluded that the rewards of office exceed the drawbacks, especially compared with their current status.

Strategically-minded individuals, however, move to a second decision stage—determining when (not simply whether) they should run. This decision hinges on "the not-so-simple calculus of winning."[76] Strategic contenders weigh the chances of getting the party's nomination, considering the party's ideological bent, leadership, and nominating procedures. They consider what it will cost to succeed. If there is an incumbent, they identify the incumbent's weaknesses. Personal strengths and weaknesses in campaigning, voter appeal, fundraising, and local or national trends that could boost or impede one's chances—all of these concerns enter the calculations of the strategic politician, as opposed to the political amateur.

Most successful candidates are seasoned politicians long before they run for Congress. Grassroots organizations and movements are a breeding ground for candidates—for example, environmental activists in the 1970s, religious conservatives and antiregulation businesspeople in the 1990s, and antiwar activists in the 2000s. More often, elective office is the springboard: mayors, district attorneys, or state legislators for the House; and governors, lieutenant governors, and attorneys general—who have already faced a statewide electorate—for the Senate. House members, especially from smaller states, are also strategically positioned. A majority of senators in the 111th Congress had "moved up" from the House.

The circle of people pondering a candidacy (the challenger pool) may be large or small, depending on the office and the circumstances.[77] Any number of elected officials—state legislators (especially if subject to term limits), county officers, mayors, city council members, even governors—are weighing a race for Congress at any given time. In Ohio, for example, a number of term-limited state lawmakers regularly contemplate when they should run for the Congress. "The people who have been successful in the political world are people who know when to strike at the right time," remarked a veteran state legislator contemplating a run against an incumbent House member.[78]

Finding the Quality Candidates

Candidate quality and campaign strength are critical factors in many battles for congressional seats.[79] A party's success in November hinges on its efforts during the recruitment season. Often races turn on bids that are not made.

According to Maisel and his colleagues, candidate quality is measured in terms of strategic resources and personal attributes.[80] Quality candidates are people who are skilled in presenting themselves as candidates and attractive to voters. Attractiveness typically means having gained experience in public office, which implies visibility and credibility to voters. However, the importance of visibility means that simply having a familiar political name can be a ticket to candidacy. Fame or notoriety may even overcome lack of relevant background or experience. Attributes of quality candidates include physical appearance, personality, speaking ability, and a talent for organizing or motivating others. Fundraising ability or potential is also an essential. Ambition and a keen desire for public life lead people to become candidates and help them to succeed.[81]

Stamina is also important. No matter how talented, principled, or well-funded, aspirants for public office must be ready, physically and emotionally, to face the rigors of campaigning. They must be willing to hit the road nonstop, meet new people, attend gatherings, sell themselves, ask for money, and endure verbal abuse—all the while appearing to enjoy it. "People who do not like to knock on strangers' doors or who find it tedious to repeat the same 30-second introduction thousands of times," explains Alan Ehrenhalt, "are at a severe disadvantage in running for office."[82]

No-Shows. High-caliber potential candidates apparently abound in America's communities—even among minority-party circles within non-competitive districts.[83] But all too often these individuals prefer to remain on the sidelines. The road to public office is increasingly arduous and costly. The odds are often long, especially when running against a dominant party or an entrenched incumbent. Therefore, quality challengers often fail to step forward. Low-quality challengers raise less money and are less successful than the handful of blue-ribbon contenders. This dynamic works in Senate as well as House elections and depresses competition in congressional elections across the board.

Raising the money needed to run an effective race is a major deterrent to would-be candidates. This stumbling block was cited twice as often as any other factor by the potential contenders in two hundred districts surveyed by Maisel and Walter J. Stone.[84] Other candidates reject campaigns because of the cost to their personal lives, incomes, careers, and families. The benefits side of the ledger may not outweigh the costs of gaining and holding public office. Rep. Thomas M. Davis III, R-Va., a former House GOP campaign chair who chose not to seek reelection to the 111th Congress, describes the drill:

> We'd get them here under the Capitol dome, have their wife take a
> picture, have the Speaker of the House tell how important they'll be.
> You're not selling the lifestyle. You're not selling the salary. You're
> selling relevance.[85]

All too often, prospective candidates decide that their destinies lie elsewhere—in state or local politics, in nonprofit community service, or in family
and profession.

The Incumbency Factor

Of all the inducements for launching a candidacy, the odds of winning stand
at the top. A clearly winnable seat seldom lacks for eager quality candidates.
Open seats, those without an incumbent running, are especially attractive. As
a result, open-seat races are more likely to be competitive and to shift in party
control than those with an incumbent. Party strategies thus often pinpoint
those races.

In most House and Senate contests, however, incumbents will be running,
and most of them will be reelected. As Gary C. Jacobson writes, "Nearly everything pertaining to candidates and campaigns for Congress is profoundly influenced by whether the candidate is an incumbent, challenging an incumbent, or
pursuing an open seat."[86] With somewhat less force, the same could be said of
the Senate.

Anyone contemplating a congressional race would do well to study Table
3-1 carefully. Since World War II, on average, 93 percent of all incumbent representatives and 80 percent of incumbent senators running for reelection have
been returned to office. Historically, incumbents' reelection rates have always
been robust, whereas voluntary turnover declined in the late nineteenth century and has remained low ever since. Even in 2006, a year when the party
control of Congress shifted to the Democrats, incumbent winners included 94
percent of all representatives and 79 percent of senators who ran for reelection.
Comparable percentages from the unusually contentious 2008 races were 95
percent and 87 percent; the Democrats' gains occurred as often by winning
seats opened up by GOP retirements as by defeating incumbents.

Higher than normal casualty rates occur periodically: for example, a post–
World War II generational shift (1946–1948), a midterm recession (1958),
Barry Goldwater's failed presidential candidacy (1964), the Watergate burglary
fallout (1974), and a combination of a generational shift and partisan realignment (1978–1980). During the early 1990s, the largest turnover in two generations was produced by political unrest, Capitol Hill scandals, the 1992
economic recession, and voter anger at those in charge (the Democrats and
President Bill Clinton in 1994). In 2006 the Bush administration's plummeting
popularity led to Democratic gains of thirty House seats and six in the Senate.
Two years later Bush's continued low popular approval, along with the financial meltdown on Wall Street and an economic recession, contributed to
Democrats expanding their numbers in the House and Senate.

TABLE 3-1 Reelection Rates in the House and Senate, by Decade, 1950s–2000s, plus 2008

Decade	House					Senate				
	Sought reelection	Faced no opponent	Lost primary	Lost general election	Percent reelected	Sought reelection	Faced no opponent	Lost primary	Lost general election	Percent reelected
1950s	402	85	6	25	93.2%	30	4	1	6	77.3%
1960s	404	52	8	26	91.5	32	1	2	4	80.8
1970s	389	57	2	23	92.3	27	1	2	6	67.7
1980s	403	67	13	15	95.7	29	1	0	3	88.0
1990s	385	36	8	18	93.6	26	0	0	3	87.4
Fifty-year average	376.6	59.4	7.4	21.4	93.3	28.9	1.4	1.0	4.4	80.2
2000s avg.	395	46.4	3.3	16	95.2	27.9	1	0.4	4.2	89.7
2008	391	32	3	17	94.9	30	0	0	4	86.7

Source: CQ Weekly Report, April 5, 1980, 908; November 8, 1980, 3302, 3320–3321; July 31, 1982, 1870; November 6, 1982, 2781; November 12, 1988, 3264, 3270; November 10, 1990, 3796–3805; November 7, 1992, 3557–3564, 3570–3576; November 12, 1994, 329ff; February 15, 1997, 447–455; November 7, 1998, 3027–3035; November 11, 2000, 2694–2706; December 14, 2002, 2694–2706; November 6, 2004, 2653–2660; November 13, 2006, 3068–3075; and November 10, 2008, 3043–3052.

Note: Statistics for each decade are election-year averages for the five elections conducted under that decade's apportionment of House districts. For example, the 1950s include the five elections 1952 through 1960. "Percent reelected" takes into account both primary and general election defeats. "Faced no opponent" means no major-party opponent. Figures for the 2000s are derived from the 2002, 2004, 2006, and 2008 elections.

Defeating a House incumbent is nonetheless an uphill struggle, absent a major scandal or misstep. Senate races tend to be closer, and so challengers—more often well-known and generously financed—have a stronger chance of unseating incumbents than do those seeking House seats. More than four of five Senate incumbents win the contests they enter. About half of all winning Senate candidates receive more than 60 percent of the votes.

In Senate contests, the size of the state affects all elections, not just those in which an incumbent is running. Frances E. Lee and Bruce I. Oppenheimer find that "Senate elections in more populous states tend to be decided by much closer margins than Senate elections in less populous states"—mainly because larger states are more diverse and contests tend to be more competitive.[87] Yet small-state senators reap no real incumbency advantage. Although they are better known and tend to enjoy higher public approval than their big-state colleagues, their challengers, too, can more easily win visibility and support. Two recent Senate casualties occurred in such states: South Dakota (2004), where former representative John Thune toppled the Senate's Democratic leader, Tom Daschle (President Obama's nominee for Secretary of Health and Human Services, who then had to withdraw for tax problems); and New Hampshire (2008), where former governor Jeanne Shaheen defeated one-term GOP Senator John Sununu.

Why are incumbents so formidable? Political scientists have launched a veritable cottage industry to answer this question. It is no secret that incumbents have built-in methods of promoting support—through speeches, press coverage, newsletters, staff assistance, and constituent service. The average House member enjoys perquisites valued at between $2 to $3 million over a two-year term; senators, with six-year terms, command between $17 and $27 million in resources.

Everyone concedes the value of incumbents' perquisites, but scholars differ sharply on how they affect electoral success. One view is that incumbents exploit their resources to ensure reelection, seizing upon their ability to assist constituents in dealing with the bureaucracy to build electoral credit. Others counter that legislators are simply responding to constituents' demands, aided by advances in communication technology. Still others question whether incumbents' resources are directly translatable into votes. However these questions are resolved, incumbents and their staffs spend much of their time and effort forging links with their voters, and these links typically hold fast on election day.[88]

An incumbent's most effective electoral strategy is to scare off serious opposition. "If an incumbent can convince potentially formidable opponents and people who control campaign resources that he or she is invincible," Jacobson observes, "he or she is very likely to avoid a serious challenge and so will be invincible—as long as the impression lasts."[89] Any sign of weakness may encourage opponents in the next election. That is why incumbents try to sustain wide electoral margins, show unbroken strength, keep up constituency ties, and build giant war chests of reelection money.

NOMINATING POLITICS

Nominating procedures, set forth in state laws and conditioned by party customs, further shape the potential pool of candidates. Historically, they have expanded to ever wider circles of participants—a development that has diminished party leaders' power and thrust more initiative upon the candidates themselves. In most states the direct primary—allowing party voters to choose their party's nominees—is the formal mechanism for selecting congressional candidates.

Rules of the Nominating Game

Every state has election laws that provide for primary elections for House and Senate candidates, but they exhibit wide variety.[90] The critical question is who should be permitted to vote in a party's primary. The states have adopted varying answers. Party leaders naturally prefer strict rules that reward party loyalty, discourage outsider candidates, and maximize the leaders' influence upon the outcome. States with strong party traditions therefore tend to have closed primaries. This arrangement, found in twenty-six states, requires voters to declare party affiliation in order to vote in the primary. (Their affiliation is considered permanent until they take steps to change it.) In open primaries, conducted in twenty states, voters can vote in the primary of either party (but not in both) simply by requesting the party's ballot at the polling place.

Several states have experimented with schemes that diminish the parties' role even further. In blanket primaries (politicians call them "jungle primaries"), voters receive a single ballot listing all candidates running for office, regardless of party affiliation. People vote for one candidate for each office, moving back and forth between parties as they wish. Californians overwhelmingly adopted such a scheme by voter initiative in 1996. The Democratic, Republican, Libertarian, and Peace and Freedom parties challenged the initiative in court as a violation of their First Amendment right to free association. The U.S. Supreme Court struck down the scheme by a 7-2 vote.[91] Calling the blanket primary a "stark repudiation of freedom of political association," Justice Antonin Scalia argued that it invited nonparty members to raid the primary and select a candidate who did not share the party's core beliefs. "In no area is the political association's right to exclude more important than in the process of selecting its candidates." In dissent, Justice Stevens noted that, while a party's internal governance was a private matter, "an election, unlike a convention or a caucus, is a public affair." The 2000 ruling invalidated blanket primaries in Alaska and Washington, as well as in California.

Few primaries are competitive races. The level of competition depends on the party's prospects in the general election. "If a district party is without an incumbent, and has a fighting chance in November," Harvey L. Schantz writes, "there is a strong possibility of a public contest for the U.S. House nomination."[92] In one-party areas the dominant party's nomination is tantamount to election. Within that party, open seats are virtually certain to be contested, and states hold runoff primaries when no candidate receives a majority. Contests also are likely in two-party competitive areas.

Parties and Nominations

Despite the prevalence of primaries, party organizations at all levels are not without leverage in nominations. Party organizations play no formal role in the primary process in the majority of states.[93] But in nine states, parties have conventions that influence candidates' access to the primary ballot—for example, by conferring pre-primary endorsements.

Party organizations mostly influence nominations indirectly—by contacting promising prospects, offering support, endorsing them, and assisting in other ways. Of the hundreds of prospective candidates identified in recent canvassing, about two out of five had been contacted by one or more party organizations—local, state, or national.[94] Parties are most active in districts regarded as winnable, and the people they seek out are the "usual suspects"—officeholders, prominent figures, and the wealthy. "They go after the obvious candidates and leave some of the less obvious ones alone."[95] The obvious candidate also may be someone who has run for the seat before. For example, fifty-five Democratic and Republican challengers who ran unsuccessfully in 2006 made a second try for the House two years later. National parties increasingly assert themselves in nominating contests. In the run-up to 2008, both parties struggled to gain a recruiting advantage. Given the state of public opinion, the Democrats had little trouble finding quality candidates. The party's seasoned pair of campaign chairs (Sen. Charles E. Schumer of New York and Rep. Chris Van Hollen of Maryland) cast their nets widely and tried to "clear the field" for their preferred candidates. Democratic Congressional Campaign Committee (DCCC) Chairman Van Hollen worked actively and behind the scenes "to back selected candidates and push others from key races around the country."[96] For example, Van Hollen's preferred candidate in Nevada's Second District was state senator and political science professor Dina Titus. She won the Democratic primary against several other contenders and went on to topple the three-term GOP incumbent in November. Worth noting is that every successful Democratic newcomer recruited to run for the House, like Titus, had political or public service experience. Rep. Tom Cole, Okla., the GOP's campaign chair for 2008, was not reluctant to get involved in specific primary contests, but he did not imitate his Democratic counterpart's large involvement in primary contests. "There's some arrogance in always thinking you know who the right nominee is," Cole said. "Sometimes these candidates have to be produced locally and the process has to play out."[97]

Intraparty rivalries often mark nomination contests. Perhaps the biggest primary upset in recent years occurred in 2006 when Connecticut Democrats rejected three-term senator Joseph Lieberman, the party's 2000 vice presidential candidate. Lieberman's steadfast support of the Iraq war and his coziness with the Bush administration had angered many party loyalists in an increasingly Democratic state. Although most of the party's national figures initially backed

Lieberman, his antiwar opponent, multimillionaire businessman Ned Lamont, won the backing of large numbers of Internet-connected supporters and volunteers. Lamont won the primary (52 percent to Lieberman's 48 percent). Prior to the primary vote, however, Lieberman had also filed to run as an Independent candidate in the general election in November (as Connecticut law allows). In this guise he was reelected with support from some Democrats and a majority of Republicans. The hapless GOP candidate received only ten percent of the vote.

Intraparty conflicts in 2008 led to three primary defeats for Republicans (David Davis, Tenn., Chris Cannon, Nev., and Wayne Gilchrest, Md.) and one for Democrats (Albert Wynn, Md.). Take the Maryland cases as examples of why these two members lost their primaries. The ultra-right Club for Growth successfully backed a conservative state senator against Gilchrest, a moderate portrayed as out of step with party principles. After his primary loss, Gilchrest endorsed the Democratic candidate, county prosecutor Frank Kratovil, who went on to win narrowly in November. On the Democratic side, eight-term incumbent Albert Wynn was defeated by his primary opponent, Donna Edwards, for "being too moderate for his liberal constituents on issues including the economy and the Iraq war."[98] Edwards went on to win a special election to fill the remainder of Wynn's term (who resigned from the House following his primary defeat) and then the general election.

The bottom line is that party leaders tend to be pragmatists—above all, bent upon finding winners. Thus, Democrats deliberately embarked on a strategy in 2006 and 2008 to recruit anti-abortion, pro–gun rights candidates in conservative areas, such as the South. In 2008, for example, the staunchly anti-abortion mayor of Montgomery, Alabama, Bobby Bright, received extensive assistance from the national party. In fact, as one account noted, "Mr. Bright is one of a dozen anti-abortion Democratic challengers the party has recruited to run for the House [in 2008] and has aggressively supported with millions of dollars and other resources in culturally conservative districts long unfriendly to the party."[99] Republican leaders, too, will lean toward moderates over extremists in swing states or districts.

Sizing Up the Primary System

The direct primary was one of the reforms adopted early in the twentieth century to overcome corrupt, boss-dominated conventions. It has certainly permitted more participation in selecting candidates. Yet primaries normally attract a narrower segment of voters than do general elections (except in one-party areas, where primaries dictate the outcomes). Primary contests have drawn less than 20 percent of eligible voters in recent years—less than half the number who voted in the general elections.[100] Less publicized than general elections, primaries tend to attract voters who are somewhat older, wealthier, better educated, more politically aware, and more ideologically committed than the electorate as a whole.[101]

Primaries also have hampered the political parties by encouraging would-be officeholders to appeal directly to the public and construct support networks apart from the party machinery. Still, leaders strive to influence who enters their primaries and who wins them. Displaying impressive resilience and adaptability, party organizations at all levels have recast themselves into organizations "'in service' to [their] candidates and officeholders but not in control of them."[102]

Finally, primaries are a costly way of choosing candidates. Unless candidates begin with overwhelming advantages (such as incumbency), they must mount virtually the same kind of campaign in the primary that they must repeat later in the general election.

THE MONEY FACTOR

"Money is the mother's milk of politics," declared California's legendary Assembly Speaker Jess Unruh. Money is not everything in politics, but many candidates falter for lack of it, and many others squander valuable time and energy struggling to get it. Money attracts backers (who in turn give more money), it can frighten away rivals, and it can augment or lessen the gap between incumbents and challengers. Every candidate, writes Paul S. Herrnson, wages not one but two campaigns—a campaign for resources (the so-called "money primary") that precedes, and underwrites, the more visible campaign for votes.[103]

Campaigns in the United States are very costly. In the 2007–2008 electoral cycle, congressional candidates raised $1.4 billion and spent most of it. The average winning Senate races cost $5.6 million. House contests averaged $1.1 million.[104] Thirty years ago (when modern record keeping began), no House candidate spent half that much.[105] Even controlling for inflation, expenditures for congressional campaigns have more than doubled over the last thirty years. And beyond what candidates spend, interest groups of all stripes pour untold millions of dollars into independent efforts aimed at changing election outcomes.

No mystery surrounds these skyrocketing costs. Population growth and new campaign technologies—electronic media, polling, and consultants of all kinds—account for much of the increase. Moreover, long-term changes in the campaign process itself have escalated costs. In old-style campaigns, party-anointed candidates could rely upon the party's legions of volunteers to mobilize loyal voters and to canvass precincts. Contrast that process with modern campaigns, in which candidates must win their party's nominating primary and then face general election voters who can be reached most easily through direct mail, phone banks, or electronic media. Many campaign services once provided by well-oiled local parties must now be purchased on the open market. That is much of the reason for today's high costs of reaching voters.

Campaign price tags also depend on the level of competition and other characteristics of the electoral unit. "Candidates for open seats tend to raise and spend the most money because when neither candidate enjoys the benefits of incumbency, both parties normally field strong candidates, and the election is usually close."[106] Costs in competitive races can be astronomical. In the top three House races considered "hot" in 2008 by election analysts, the candidates raised, respectively, $11.7 million (New York's Twentieth District), $10 million (Illinois's Eleventh), and $9 million (Illinois's Tenth). Senate candidates in such races raised $43 million in Minnesota, $31.6 million in Kentucky, and $28 million in North Carolina.

A district's demography also affects campaign costs. One study showed that suburban districts have the most expensive campaigns and urban districts the least expensive, with rural districts somewhere in between.[107] In the suburbs partisan loyalties are shifting and contests are volatile. Where stable party organizations are lacking, candidates must advertise through paid media. In rural districts wide-open spaces keep costs high. Candidates must travel farther and advertise in many small media markets to get their messages across. In cities, despite the greater compactness, candidates shun media contests because of the huge cost and wasted effort of covering adjoining districts. Here, too, party organizations are strongest.

The Haves and Have-Nots

Although incumbents need less money than do challengers, they receive more—a double-barreled financial advantage (see Figure 3-3). Because they are better known and have government-subsidized ways of reaching constituents, incumbents usually can get their message across more cheaply than challengers can. Incumbents of both parties tend to attract more money than challengers because contributors see them as better investments. As Jacobson points out, "Incumbents can raise whatever they think they need. They are very likely to win, and even when they lose, it is almost always in a close contest."[108]

Senate incumbents running in 2008 raised an average of $8.6 million compared to the $1.1 million raised by their challengers. For House races the figures were $1.3 million and $333,000, respectively. Senate candidates for open seats in 2008 raised on average $2.3 million; House candidates $578,000. The challengers who raised the most money in 2008 were Democrats: Al Franken for Minnesota's Senate seat ($20.5 million) and Colorado's Jared Polis, who ran for Rep. Mark Udall's House seat in Boulder and northwest Denver ($7.3 million). The incumbents (both reelected) who raised the least were Rep. Bill Delahunt, D-Mass. ($93,956), and Sen. (now vice president) Joseph R. Biden Jr. ($786,523).

The electoral reality is that challengers must raise a great deal of money to defeat an incumbent; the more they can raise, the more votes they are likely to receive, especially crucial in close elections. As Jacobson points out, "the minimum price tag for a competitive House campaign under average conditions today is probably [around] $800,000; sixty-two of the sixty-four challengers who defeated incumbents from 1996 through 2006 spent more than that amount."[109] In 2008, the importance of money is underscored by the fact that the better funded candidate won 93 percent of the House seats. Further,

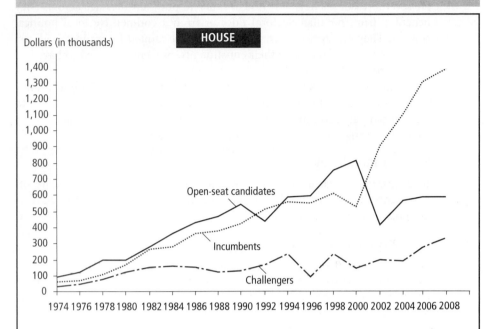

Dollars (in thousands)

HOUSE

Open-seat candidates

Incumbents

Challengers

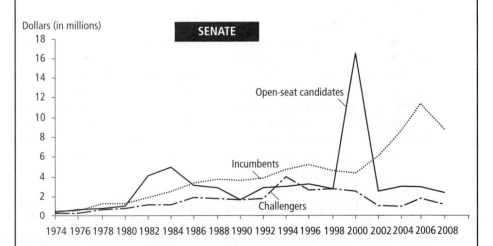

Dollars (in millions)

SENATE

Open-seat candidates

Incumbents

Challengers

Sources: Federal Election Commission figures for campaigns through 2000 are compiled in Norman J. Ornstein, Thomas E. Mann, and Michael J. Malbin, *Vital Statistics on Congress 2001–2002* (Washington D.C.: AEI Press, 2002), 87–98. Figures through 2008, also derived from the FEC, are found in Center for Responsive Politics, "Election Overview, Incumbent Advantage," accessed at www.opensecrets.org.

"93.5 percent of those elected or reelected [to the Senate] spent more than their opponent."[110] Challengers who prevail against incumbents typically do so for several reasons. They had enough funds to put their message across. They benefited from popular electoral tides or from a competitive local political context. They ran against incumbents who were tainted by scandal, had cast tough votes that upset many their constituents, or were perceived to have lost touch with the folks back home.

Many incumbents finish their campaigns with a surplus. Surplus money can be hoarded for future races, dispensed to needier candidates, donated to the Hill campaign committees to cover their debts, or used to buy constituency goodwill through outreach projects or charitable donations.

Shaking the Money Tree

Raising money preoccupies all candidates. Incumbents need it to scare off opponents, challengers need it to gain visibility, and contenders for open seats need it to gain an edge. Fundraising is time-consuming, odious, and demeaning. "I'd rather wrestle a gorilla than ask anybody for another fifty cents," grumbled John Glenn, D-Ohio, as he retired after twenty-four years in the Senate.[111]

Funding sources can be individuals (including the candidates and their families), party committees, and political action committees (PACs). The motivations of contributors fall into two major categories: consumers and investors. Consumers, usually individuals, want simply to show their support for a candidate or a cause, often responding to candidates most in need of funds. Investors—interest groups and PACs, typically—give with an eye on a return on the investment. Because they seek access or support from winning candidates, they tend to disregard the candidates' needs and support those (mainly incumbents) most likely to win.[112]

Individuals. More than half of the money raised by House and Senate candidates comes from individuals. Individuals may lawfully contribute up to $2,000 per candidate for primaries and $2,000 per candidate in the general elections (the figure, adjusted for inflation, was $2,300 in 2008), totaling no more than $37,500 in any given year. Primary, runoff, and general contests are regarded as separate elections. Individuals may contribute up to $20,000 a year to a political party committee and $5,000 to any PAC, and they may spend an unlimited amount independently to promote parties, causes, or candidates. Contributions greater than $200 must be reported, and the individual must declare that the money was not spent in collusion with the candidate. Individual party fundraisers called "bundlers" solicit many donations. Although federal law limits the amount that an individual can contribute to a candidate or party, bundlers understand that "there is no limit on how much an individual can round up in small contributions from friends and associates, and then deliver to a favored politician or party as a 'bundle.'"[113] Under the Honest Leadership and Open Government Act of 2007 (P.L. 110-81), registered lobbyists—but not other fundraisers—must disclose their bundling activities if they have made two bundled contributions totaling more than $15,000 during the specified six-month reporting period.

Congressional candidates can spend as much of their own money as they want on their own cause. Donations and loans from family members also are unrestricted. The hope is that heavy spending may boost an underdog's chances of winning (usually futile in the absence of other resources) or help pad a front-runner's margin of victory. Especially in long-shot races, a candidate's ability to shoulder the financial burden may attract support from party or group leaders. The biggest self-investor in congressional history was New Jersey Democrat Jon S. Corzine, a former Goldman Sachs partner who used $63 million of his own money in 2000 to capture New Jersey's open Senate seat. (He soon tired of the job, however, and resigned in five years after spending another $2.6 million to win the state's governorship.) Sen. John D. Rockefeller IV, D-W.Va., spent about $10 million of his fortune to win his Senate seat in 1984—more than $27 for every vote he received. The Bipartisan Campaign Reform Act of 2002, discussed below, had a provision to aid candidates who run against such wealthy opponents.

Party Committees. National, congressional, and state party campaign committees may contribute $5,000 apiece to each House candidate at each stage of the electoral process—primary, runoff, and general election. The party campaign committees augment the resources amassed by individual candidates. The national and senatorial committees can give a combined total of $39,900 to each Senate candidate in an election cycle, whereas state committees can give $5,000. As these amounts make clear, party funds cannot begin to cover the costs of campaigns today. Party organizations of all types account for a relatively small portion of individual candidates' funding. More significant are the parties' coordinated and independent expenditures.

Regarding *coordinated expenditures*, parties may pay for services (polling, producing ads, or buying media time, for example) requested by a candidate, who has a say in how they are spent. Coordinated funds apply to general elections but not to primaries. Dollar limits restrict spending for House and Senate races under guidelines set by the Federal Election Commission. "In the 2008 election cycle, national parties can spend $81,800 in coordination with House candidates in states with only one Representative. For the majority of states with two House members, national parties can spend $40,900 and, in some cases, up to $2.2 million in certain Senate races."[114]

Party committees also sponsor their own campaigns, run media ads, and underwrite GOTV (get-out-the-vote) drives—*independent expenditures*, with no formal connections with the individual candidates' own efforts. In 2008, the House DCCC spent over $75 million in independent expenditures on behalf of their candidates; the GOP counterpart (the National Republican Congressional Committee) spent $22.8 million. The Democratic Senatorial Campaign Committee had nearly a two-to-one advantage ($70 million to $36 million) in independent expenditures over the National Republican Senatorial Committee. Especially in Senate contests, parties can pump in huge sums of money by means of cooperative arrangements among state committees and the several national committees. To be sure, the party campaign committees will abandon what they view as losing races and shift their efforts and resources to races perceived as winnable.

A major source of the four Hill committees' funds are the contributions they require from flush incumbents—with such "dues" varying by the members' seniority and public stature. Republicans began this practice in the 1990s, but the Democrats caught on quickly. During the 2008 election cycle, the dues of selected House Democrats were as follows: (1) $800,000 each for the Speaker, majority leader, majority whip, and caucus chair; (2) $300,000 for the chief deputy whips; (3) $500,000 for each chair of an exclusive (lawmakers may serve only on this panel) committee: Appropriations, Energy and Commerce, Financial Services, Rules, and Ways and Means; (4) $250,000 for subcommittee chairs; and (5) $125,000 for rank-and-file members.[115]

Interest Groups. Under existing law, corporations, federal contractors, and labor unions may not contribute funds directly to candidates, though individuals within those entities may do so on their own. Such groups may indulge in independent spending for or against candidates without the candidates' cooperation or consent. Corporations, labor unions, and membership organizations may recommend to their stockholders, employees, or members the election or defeat of a candidate. Unions and corporations also may pay for nonpartisan voter registration or participation drives directed at their members, stockholders, or employees.

Other kinds of groups are embraced by existing finance laws. Multicandidate committees may give no more than $5,000 per election to a candidate. These committees must have more than fifty members and must support five or more candidates. Such committees also may contribute up to $15,000 per year to a political party.

PACs. Corporations, labor unions, membership groups, and even individuals may sponsor PACs and underwrite their administrative or fundraising costs. Currently, PACs are the preferred method of channeling corporate or union energies into campaign war chests. Corporate executives contribute to PACs with such names as the Good Government Fund. Industry associations such as the National Association of Realtors and the American Medical Association donate millions of dollars, mostly through their PACs. Labor unions—both large and small—have PACs, most of which favor Democrats. Ostensibly, such donations are voluntary. However, it does not take a confirmed cynic to believe that subtle coercion and social pressure help pump money into the coffers.

Political action committees are thriving, in part because the finance laws encourage them. At the end of 1974 there were 608 PACs; by 2008, more than 4,200. All types of PACs grew in numbers, but business-related PACs grew most of all (now numbering 1,600). The growth of PACs has changed the way campaigns are run. Candidates are forced to make the rounds of PACs to beg for funds. Nonincumbents win support by knocking on doors, filling out forms, being interviewed, and proving the viability of their candidacy.[116]

Incumbents attract PAC support by gaining a lucrative congressional committee assignment and compiling a favorable voting record.

The PACs also have grown in financial clout. In 1972 they contributed $8.5
million to House and Senate candidates; in 2008 their contributions nearly
topped $400 million. PAC donations are especially significant in House races:
They accounted for a third of House candidates' receipts in 2008 but only
about a fifth for Senate candidates.

Because they are campaign investors, PACs tend to favor incumbents and
shun all but the most promising nonincumbents. For the same reason, PACs
are more attracted to leaders and members who are in power on Capitol Hill.
Majority-party assets are more attractive to donors; majority-party leaders—
who have more rewards to give out—insist that these donors spread their
wealth among their neediest colleagues—in order to retain their majority status. After the GOP takeover in 1994, PAC giving naturally flowed to the victors.
Still, as long as control of the House was in doubt, many PACs hedged their
bets in post-1994 campaigns. Even before the Democratic victories of 2006
were recorded, funds began to flow in their direction.

Many PACs tend to support the party that most closely endorses their
objectives or interests. "Our PAC endorsement typically comes with significant financial support," remarked the right-wing Club for Growth's president,
former Rep. Pat Toomey, R-Pa.[117] On the opposite end of the spectrum,
EMILY's List in 2008 gave over $33 million to candidates, including the two
female Democratic Senate winners (to Kay Hagan of North Carolina,
$580,244; and to Jeanne Shaheen of New Hampshire, $950,000). Business and
banking interests traditionally support Republicans, whereas labor, law firms
(especially trial lawyers), and the entertainment industry generally lean the
opposite way.

Members themselves increasingly create so-called leadership PACs to
exploit their prominence and fundraising prowess. Rep. Heath Shuler, D-N.C.,
a former pro quarterback for the Washington Redskins, created a PAC and
named it the "3rd and Long PAC."[118] Although they trade on the name of their
sponsors, such PACs are separate from their sponsors' own war chests. They are
normally used to contribute to other candidates' campaigns as a way of gaining
a party majority and earning their colleagues' gratitude and later support,
perhaps for a presidential bid. During the 2006 cycle, for example, Senator
Obama, gave $770,000 to party candidates and committees from Hopefund,
his leadership PAC. Sen. Hillary Rodham Clinton, D-N.Y., who raised a record
$51.5 million for her reelection race, transferred some $15 million to about
fifty candidates and a number of party committees—most from her own campaign funds, but also from her Hill (for Hillary) PAC. The two presidential
hopefuls were careful to support candidates and committees in such early primary states as Iowa and New Hampshire.[119] (See Box 3-2, "Some Questions
and Answers about Leadership PACs.")

Pressure on PACs comes from both givers and recipients. PAC officers
complain that they are dogged by incumbents, most of whom do not need the

Q. What is a "leadership" political action committee (PAC)?
A. It is a PAC affiliated with a politician that is separate from his or her official campaign committee. Leadership PACs are subject to the same contribution and expenditure limits as PACs organized by businesses, unions, and others.

Campaign finance watchdogs have long criticized leadership PACs because they allow candidates to get around contribution limits. Many of the same donors to lawmakers' leadership PACs have also donated to their campaign committees. Many lawmakers also use them for large outside expenses.

Q. Who uses leadership PACs?
A. They are most commonly used by members of Congress to collect contributions from their political supporters to pay for donations to party organizations or other candidates for federal, state, and local offices, as well as for travel and expenses incurred in pursuit of those party-building activities.

Governors and other municipal- and state-level officeholders seeking to build their national profile have become more inclined to start leadership PACs in recent years. Former New York mayor Rudy Giuliani, former Massachusetts governor Mitt Romney, and former Virginia governor, now Senator, Mark Warner have all raised and spent significant sums of money through leadership PACs in recent years.

Former members of Congress also use them to influence the political process through donations to their one-time colleagues.

Q. If politicians routinely use their leadership PACs to donate to candidates in other races, why has Senator Obama been accused of violating election law?
A. Under federal election law, a candidate may not use a political action committee to spend more than $5,000 to help his or her own campaign. Opponents of Obama might argue

contributions, and that members keep mental accounts of contributors. "I've had congressmen open up the drawer and look down a list to see if we have contributed," one of them said. "And I've had them say, 'Well, I like your organization but you haven't given me a contribution.'"[120]

Candidate Funding: A Regulated Industry?

The burdens of campaign fundraising, as well as the financial inequalities—between incumbents and nonincumbents and between wealthy donors and average citizens—have led to demands for legal ways of monitoring or even controlling campaign finance. Laws have been passed not only to clean up campaigns but also to shift political influence from those who rely on financial contributions to those who depend on other resources. Several techniques have been employed. The primary ones thus far have been disclosure of campaign contributions and expenditures, limits on campaign contributions and expenditures, and (in presidential races) public financing of campaigns.

that Obama's purpose in spending more than that in support of other candidates was to benefit his own presidential campaign.

Q. How does a politician benefit from operating a leadership PAC?

A. Traditionally, a handful of high-level lawmakers—mostly party leaders and senior members of top committees—have used leadership PACs to collect money from their own donors for redistribution to their parties' candidates in other districts and states.

The political giving is seen as a way to have a positive effect on the party's political fortunes and to curry favor with candidates who receive the money. Fundraising prowess has long been a factor in party leadership elections and, more recently, in determining who becomes a committee chair.

Money can be raised more easily by leadership PACs because individual donors can give up to $10,000 ($5,000 for the general election) every two years to a leadership PAC, whereas they are limited to $4,600 per two-year cycle ($2,300 for the primary and $2,300 for the general) to another candidate. However, like other PACs, a leadership PAC can give up to $10,000 ($5,000 per election) to each candidate it supports.

Q. How does a donor benefit from giving to a leadership PAC?

A. Because the donor can give to the leadership PAC more than double what he or she can give to the official campaign committee, the donor can have greater influence by contributing to the PAC. It is a second, bigger bite at the apple of traditional campaign giving, allowing a donor to give a total of $14,600 to a federal candidate he or she supports in an election cycle through two committees.

Source: Jonathan Allen and Alex Knott, *CQToday,* December 4, 2007.

FECA, 1974, 1976. Reacting to campaign scandals of the early 1970s, Congress decided to erect regulatory standards for financing federal election campaigns. A broad-gauged campaign finance law, the Federal Election Campaign Act (FECA) Amendments of 1974, was signed into law by President Gerald R. Ford. Major features of the act included limits on individual contributions, limits on party and nonparty group contributions, and reporting requirements for all contributions.

The Supreme Court subsequently held that Congress may limit contributions to congressional candidates but that it may not limit expenditures by candidates themselves, their campaign committees, or individuals or organizations independent of the candidate (*Buckley v. Valeo,* 1976). The reasoning was that spending to influence elections is a form of free expression protected by the First Amendment and that Congress did not have a sufficient compelling interest in regulating campaign spending to overcome that protection. In the case of campaign contributions, which the Court also concluded were protected speech, Congress's interest in protecting the integrity of the democratic system was held sufficient to overcome the First Amendment. To end the confusion and meet the Court's constitutional objections, Congress passed a revised act (P. L. 93-443) to reconcile the Court's rulings with the original congressional intent.[121]

Experience has shown that *Buckley* undercut Congress's intentions and ultimately rendered the law unworkable. Many critics have found the Court's reasoning to be faulty, even wrongheaded. First, it stretched the First Amendment to treat campaign contributions as protected speech. Such giving might better be treated as, say, economic activity—which can be regulated. As dissenting Justice Stevens put it: "Money is property; it is not speech."[122] "In fact," writes lawyer-novelist Scott Turow, "given *Buckley*'s rationale, I've never figured out why outright vote-buying isn't also protected by the First Amendment."[123]

Second, with no enforceable restrictions on campaign spending, politicians and interested groups were free to exploit creative ways of maximizing their financial leverage, in the process stripping from the law the one element the Court sanctioned: contribution limits. The free-for-all system that resulted, critics charge, has replaced the principle of "one person–one vote" with a "regime of one dollar–one vote," which "distorts the fundamental principle of political equality underlying the First Amendment itself."[124]

The law is enforced by the bipartisan Federal Election Commission (FEC), its members appointed by the president and confirmed by the Senate. The commission issues regulations and advisory opinions, conducts investigations, and prosecutes violations of the law. Most important, the FEC compiles and disseminates campaign finance data from the reports it receives. Federal law requires strict accounting by candidates and political committees. All contributions of $50 or more must be recorded; donors of more than $200 must be identified. Accounting of funds must be made by a single committee for each candidate, and receipts and expenditures must be reported regularly. Disclosure of the sources and uses of campaign money is the one aspect of current regulations that everyone agrees is a success.

Campaign Finance Politics. Campaign financing laws have failed to limit the influence of money in politics. Big money is alive and well in American elections, although now it flows through more issue and candidate groups than in the past. The best that can be said is that many of the best-funded PACs depend on large numbers of mail-solicited donations rather than checks from a few fat cats. The 1976 act, moreover, failed utterly to reduce inequalities between incumbents and challengers. The changes may even have helped incumbents and kept challengers from raising the money they need to win.[125] Finally, the reforms have blurred the distinction between interest groups and political parties. Labor unions, business and industry associations, consumer and environmental organizations, ideological movements, and a host of special issue groups have invaded the electoral arena as never before. By boosting and even recruiting candidates—and hindering others—they hope to win favorable treatment for their causes on Capitol Hill.

Campaign finance laws are so loosely drawn that money pours freely into congressional elections. Parties and PACs use tax-exempt foundations to take donations in excess of legal limits. Creative accounting and independent spending on behalf of candidates are used to skirt legal limits on what PACs can give directly to candidates. Bankers and other moneyed people can lend money or extend credit to candidates under permissive rules. And money is being raised in new ways, thwarting federal enforcement and disclosure efforts. For example, the legal limit on individual contributions (in 2008, $2,300 to a candidate per election) is easily circumvented when parties establish "joint fund-raising committees" that are technically not part of the candidate's campaign "war chest, but that nonetheless are spent on his or her behalf."[126] These joint committees can raise tens of thousands of dollars from individuals which are then disbursed to various campaign accounts, such as the candidate's, congressional campaign committees, or the home state's political party.

BCRA, 2002. The Bipartisan Campaign Reform Act (BCRA) of 2002 was something of a political miracle, given the opposition to reform from across the political spectrum (see Box 3-3). The drive for reform began in the mid-1980s and raged through four presidencies, multiple floor votes, a 1992 veto by President George H. W. Bush, and repeated parliamentary setbacks. In the mid-1990s the cause was taken up in the Senate by John McCain, R-Ariz., and Russell D. Feingold, D-Wis., and in the House by Christopher Shays, R-Conn., and Martin T. Meehan, D-Mass. The growth of unregulated "soft money" and scandals associated with the 1996 and 2000 elections kept the issue alive. And a final scandal in 2002—involving Enron, an energy firm whose political connections kept it in business despite its economic collapse—pushed the bill over the top. "What McCain said repeatedly was right," Senator Feingold remarked. "It would take a scandal—might take more than one scandal—but we would prevail."[127]

Court challenges to BCRA quickly surfaced. When the act reached the Supreme Court, a 5–4 majority (*McConnell v. Federal Election Commission,* 2003) upheld the act's core provision (Title I), which prohibited national parties and their committees from soliciting or accepting "soft money"—the large, unlimited contributions that corporations, labor unions, and individuals gave to lawmakers and party committees outside of "hard-money" limits set by law. The opinion, coauthored by Justices O'Connor and Stevens, accepted Congress's judgment on the issue:

> As the record demonstrates, it is the manner in which parties have sold access to federal candidates and officeholders that has given rise to the appearance of undue influence. It was not unwarranted for Congress to conclude that the selling of access gives rise to the appearance of corruption.[128]

The act's more problematic Title II, regulating "electioneering communications," limits nonparty or candidate groups' broadcast ads within thirty days of primary elections or sixty days of a general election that mention a "clearly

BOX 3-3   **The Bipartisan Campaign Reform Act of 2002**

The Bipartisan Campaign Reform Act (BCRA) of 2002, which took effect on November 6 of that year, was the first major enactment since the advent of modern campaign finance regulations in 1974. More than ninety pages long, BCRA has a variety of provisions but was touted mainly for its ban on soft money and for regulating election-time issue advertising on radio and television by corporations, unions, and interest groups. Following are the major provisions of the law, known as McCain-Feingold for its principal Senate sponsors, John McCain, R-Ariz., and Russell D. Feingold, D-Wis.

Hard-Money Contribution Limits. Individual contribution limits for House and Senate candidates are doubled to $2,000 per election, indexed to grow with inflation; aggregate contribution limits for individuals are $95,000—$37,500 to candidates and $57,500 to parties and political action committees (PACs). Contribution limits for PACs are unchanged: $5,000 per candidate per election, plus $15,000 to a national party committee and $5,000 combined to state and local party committees.

Soft Money. National party committees cannot accept or spend soft money—unregulated contributions from corporations, labor unions, and wealthy individuals ostensibly intended for party-building activities, such as voter registration, but often used for campaign-related purposes.

State and Local Parties. Non-national political parties cannot spend soft money on federal election activities. They may spend soft money for voter registration and mobilization under certain conditions.

identified" candidate for federal office. (Those ads, however, could be paid for with hard money; i.e., funds raised and spent according to the requirements of campaign finance laws.) Although Title II was upheld by the Court majority—with but a brief discussion—this section has aroused criticism because it protects incumbents from last-minute attacks and may violate the principle of free speech.[129] The issue soon reappeared on the Supreme Court's docket.

On June 25, 2007, the Supreme Court ruled 5 to 4 in *Federal Election Commission v. Wisconsin Right to Life, Inc.* that the electioneering communication provision was unconstitutional as applied to the anti-abortion group's ads. (Worth notice is the change in the majority that upheld the core provisions of BCRA in the McConnell case. Justice Samuel Alito had replaced Justice Sandra Day O'Connor.) The Wisconsin case involved ads the group wanted to run in 2004 urging voters to contact their two senators—Russell Feingold and Herb Kohl—and ask them to stop blocking confirmation votes on President Bush's judicial nominees. Feingold was up for reelection and, given the communications provision in the BCRA, the anti-abortion group dropped its planned radio and television ad campaign specifically referring to the two senators. The group then brought suit in federal court, and the case reached the Supreme Court.

Independent and Coordinated Expenditures. The Federal Election Commission (FEC) must issue new rules covering coordination between candidates or parties and outside groups. The rules cannot require formal evidence of coordination to treat spending by outside groups as a regulated contribution instead of an unregulated independent expenditure.

Tax-Exempt Organizations. National, state, and local parties may neither solicit money from nor contribute to any nonprofit group that spends money on federal elections. They also may not contribute to or solicit money from so-called 527 organizations that intervene in campaigns but do not expressly advocate any candidate's election or directly subsidize federal campaigns.

Electioneering Communications. Broadcast, cable, or satellite communications that name candidates for federal office or show their likeness and are targeted at candidates' states or districts—known as electioneering communications—may not be issued within sixty days of a general election or thirty days of a primary.

Unions and Corporations. Labor unions and corporations remain banned from directly funding electioneering communications and can pay for such advertising only through political action committees with regulated hard money.

Nonprofits and 527s. Tax-exempt groups, including those covered under Section 527 of the Internal Revenue Code, raise unregulated (soft) money for political activities: voter registration, issue advocacy, and the like. They may operate through PACs, and they may even contribute to candidates (under hard-money rules).

Sources: Revised and reprinted from *CQ Researcher,* November 22, 2002, 974; and Center for Responsive Politics, "Types of Advocacy Groups," www.opensecrets.org.

Chief Justice John Roberts wrote the majority opinion and carved out a major exception to the BCRA's prohibition on corporate and union soft money funding of campaign advertisements in the weeks before an election. Roberts concluded that the ads of the Wisconsin group were genuine issue ads designed to influence a legislator's vote and not his or her election. The test Roberts devised to distinguish genuine from phony (banned under the BCRA) issue ads is whether the ads are "susceptible of no reasonable interpretation other than an appeal to vote for or against a specific candidate." He added: "Where the First Amendment is implicated, the tie goes to the speaker, not the censor."[130] Although the test articulated by Roberts is somewhat vague, it appears that electioneering communication can only be banned if it is, as Roberts said, "the functional equivalent of express advocacy" for a candidate.

A year later, in another 5-4 decision (*Davis v. Federal Election Commission*), the Court struck down as unconstitutional another provision of BCRA: the so-called "millionaire's amendment." BCRA provided that House or Senate candidates running against wealthy opponents who significantly self-finance their campaigns will be able "to solicit three times the normal limit of $2,300 per contributor and grants greater spending by the [candidate's] party on the candidate's behalf."[131] BCRA provides that a financially well-off House candidate would have to spend more than $350,000 of his or her personal funds before the contribution limits would be increased for his or her opponent. For Senate candidates, the threshold amount required to raise the contribution limits varies based on the number of eligible voters in a state. It is interesting to note that Barack Obama was able to take advantage of the millionaire provision and "collect increased campaign money in his 2004 Senate race because he faced a self-financed opponent in a primary."[132] Writing for the majority in *Davis,* Justice Alito said the law "imposes an unprecedented penalty on any candidate who robustly exercises [his or her] First Amendment rights."

When BCRA was enacted, skeptics argued that the new law would do little to halt the overall flow of money into political campaigns. "This law will not remove one dime from politics," predicted Sen. Mitch McConnell, R-Ky., the leading GOP opponent of the measure.[133] His prediction was borne out by political scientist David Magleby, who has recorded "a surge in individual giving to the political parties and the candidates, which more than replaced the old soft money."[134] The $5.3 billion spent by federal candidates in the 2008 election cycle underscores Magleby's point. Still, the soft-money ban does favor those who are best equipped to attract hard-money donations—including national party committees and individual candidates with hordes of dedicated followers, volunteers, and small donors, as in Obama's presidential campaign.

The other growth sector in campaign finance is the explosion in third-party nonprofit advocacy groups (that is, not formally associated with either parties or candidates). Many register as PACs; others are so-called 527 or 501(c)4 groups (the names come from the relevant tax code sections; see Box 3-4). They are free to collect money—much of it unlimited soft money—and, ironically, may contribute a portion to parties or candidates according to hard-money limits. But their energies are typically devoted to influencing elections through voter mobilization and issue ads, often with strong partisan or candidate messages.

Reformers and Skeptics. Some critics advocate public funding of Senate and House campaigns. For example, Democratic representatives David Obey, Wis., Barney Frank, Mass., and Tom Udall, N. M. (elected to the 111th Senate) recommended a public financing system for House general election races.[135] Congress has declined to enact such legislation because it runs afoul of public antipathy of spending more tax dollars on politicians. As an editorial in *USA Today* opposing public financing proclaimed: "No Welfare for Politicians."[136]

As for presidential campaigns, the 1974 act included an optional public financing scheme that was intended to provide sufficient resources for presidential candidates who agreed to use it. However, only "about 10 percent of taxpayers check off the box designating $3 of their tax payment for the presidential campaigns."[137] But that has not stopped candidates and parties from raising money over and above the public funds, in violation of both the spirit and the letter of the law. Presidential candidates simply opt out of the system and raise sums that exceed the statutory limits imposed by the 1974 law, such as the record-setting $750 million raised by Obama for his presidential race.

The most common categories of organizations permitted to raise and spend money to influence federal elections all come with important restrictions, and some strategic benefits for fundraisers looking to work around Federal Election Commission restrictions.

Legal Classification	Restrictions	Disclosure	Total Raised[a]
Political Action Committee Examples: • MoveOn.org Political Action • Club for Growth PAC • VoteVets PAC • SEIU Political Education and Action Fund	• PACs connected to member-based organizations may accept contributions only from the group's members. • Non-connected PACs (those run by politicians, for example) may take donations from the general public • They may donate directly to candidates and may sponsor broadcast advertising that advocates explicitly for or against a candidate. • Donations to them are subject to federal contribution limits.	• Periodic reports to the FEC are required. • Must report all their contributions and spending.	$1.2 billion
527 Examples: • Club for Growth.net • Republicans Who Care • The Fund for America • Progressive Media Action	• Their primary purpose must be to raise and spend money to influence the outcome of federal, state, or local elections. • They may accept unlimited donations from individuals, corporations, and unions. • They may not advocate for or against any candidate. • They may not donate directly to candidates or political parties.	• Periodic reports (more frequently in election years) to the IRS are required. • Must report all their contributions and spending.	$162.7 million
501(c)4 Examples: • MoveOn.org Civic Action • Freedom's Watch • Americans United for Change • Progressive Media USA	• Their primary purpose must be civic engagement. • They may accept unlimited donations from individuals, corporations, and unions. • They may not advocate for or against any candidate. • They may not donate directly to candidates or parties.	• Must file annual reports with the IRS. • Must report all income and spending, but not individual contributors.	2008 totals not available

Source: CQ Weekly, May 5, 2008.

[a] Between Jan. 1, 2007, and March 31, according to the FEC and IRS. The FEC reported that PACs raised $1.2 billion in 2008.

Through sophisticated use of the Internet, Obama may even have created a new model for raising money and, in the process, triggered a reexamination of campaign finance laws by the 111th Congress. The old model emphasized raising money from special interests and wealthy individuals. Obama's use of technology to raise large sums of money from millions of small contributors (less than $200) avoided the need to make thousands of telephone calls to potential contributors and attend scores of fundraising events. Whether congressional and other presidential candidates can be as successful as Obama in raising huge sums in this way is uncertain. Obama, after all, had unique abilities and rhetorical gifts to galvanize people in support of his campaign motto: "change we can believe in."[138]

Perhaps the most promising way to level the playing field, at least for incumbents and challengers, would be to provide the latter with subsidized mailings and free radio and TV time. This option, predictably, is fiercely opposed by broadcasters—a potent lobby because politicians crave the exposure their outlets provide. Even the innocuous provision that broadcasters offer time for political messages at the lowest prevailing rates has drawn opposition.

Reform commands public support, but for voters it rarely seems a salient issue—a fact not lost on those who benefit from the current state of affairs. The Court's notion that campaign spending is protected speech is another huge obstacle. That interpretation has its critics, but few public figures dare to campaign publicly for a narrower reading of the First Amendment.

Conceding that further controls are desirable, a majority of political scientists nonetheless are very skeptical about the benefits of many of the proposed changes in campaign financing. Overall spending limits must be approached cautiously. Challengers need to be able to spend money to offset incumbents' advantages, and because they start from behind they get more value for every dollar they spend. As for PAC contributions, they are easily stigmatized, but they are nonetheless a lawful way for interested groups to give money—gifts that at least are recorded and scrutinized. Independent campaign activities of individuals or groups are forms of free expression that should be accorded wide latitude. Even the much-maligned soft money, in part, underwrote party activities. Abolishing it forced interest groups to shun parties and spend the money on their own.

Finally, there is what journalist Chuck Alston calls the "whack-a-mole" problem. In the arcade game "the mole pops up in one hole, and you whack him down. But then he pops up somewhere else. Likewise, campaign spending, whenever it is suppressed in one form, always pops up elsewhere."[139] That fate will surely confound any reform that is adopted.

CONCLUSION

The rules of the game that narrow the potential field of congressional contenders can be thought of as a series of gates, each narrower than the one before. First are the constitutional qualifications for holding office. Far more restrictive are the personal attributes associated with a successful public career. Next are the complex rules of apportionment and districting. Beyond these are nominating procedures (usually primaries) and financial demands. These successive gates cut down sharply the number of people who are likely to become real contenders.

Equally important, individuals must make up their own minds about running for the House or Senate. Such choices embrace a range of considerations—many personal and emotional but all based on some estimate of the likely benefits and costs of their candidacy. This winnowing process presents voters with a limited choice on election day: two, sometimes more, preselected (or self-selected) candidates. From this tiny circle senators and representatives are chosen.

SUGGESTED READINGS

Bickerstaff, Steve. *Lines in the Sand: Congressional Redistricting in Texas and the Downfall of Tom DeLay.* Austin: University of Texas Press, 2007.

Brunell, Thomas L. *Redistricting and Representation: Why Competitive Elections are Bad for America.* New York and London: Routledge, 2008.

Canon, David T. *Race, Redistricting, and Representation.* Chicago: University of Chicago Press, 1999.

Ehrenhalt, Alan. *The United States of Ambition.* New York: Random House, 1991.

Fowler, Linda L., and Robert D. McClure. *Political Ambition: Who Decides to Run for Congress.* New Haven: Yale University Press, 1989.

Jacobsen, Gary. *The Politics of Congressional Elections,* 7th ed. New York: Pearson Longman, 2009.

Kazee, Thomas A., ed. *Who Runs for Congress? Ambition, Context, and Candidate Emergence.* Washington, D.C.: Congressional Quarterly, 1994.

Magleby, David B., and J. Quin Monson, eds. *The Last Hurrah?* Washington D.C.: Brookings Institution Press, 2004.

Samples, John. *The Fallacy of Campaign Finance Reform.* Chicago: University of Chicago Press, 2006.

Stonecash, Jeffrey M. *Reassessing the Incumbency Effect.* New York: Cambridge University Press, 2008.

***C*ampaigning and Voting.** A citizen ponders her vote in Cleveland, Ohio (top left). A compelling Senate campaign in North Carolina in 2008 pitted incumbent Elizabeth Dole, who addresses the news media in Morrisville, N.C. (top right) against Democratic state senator Kay Hagen (center), who greets voters outside a polling place in Raleigh, North Carolina. Door-to-door campaigning still marks most successful congressional races: candidate Earl Perlmutter (D-Colo.) (bottom) talks to a voter in 2006. Perlmutter won his House seat in 2006 and was reelected in 2008.

Making It:
The Electoral Game

The 2008 North Carolina Senate race initially looked like not much of a contest.[1] Sen. Elizabeth Dole, running for reelection, claimed many assets: she was a skilled Washington fundraiser, a seasoned policymaker who had served in two presidents' cabinets, and a mainstream Republican in a traditionally Republican state. The wife of a former Republican presidential nominee, she enjoyed a famous name and considerable personal wealth. Given Dole's apparent strengths, Democratic Party officials had failed in their efforts to recruit a prominent challenger, having been turned down by outgoing governor Michael F. Easley, former governor Jim Hunt, and Rep. Brad Miller.

State senator Kay R. Hagan, a comparatively unknown state senator from Greensboro, initially declined to enter the race. But when the Democrats' only willing candidate seemed to be an openly gay candidate lacking any significant political experience, Hagan finally agreed to run for the seat.[2] However improbable, the North Carolina Senate race turned out to be one of the most hotly contested Senate races in the country. And at its end, the low-profile Hagan prevailed over the high-profile Dole.

The political context undoubtedly boosted Hagan's chances, as it did for Democratic candidates nearly everywhere. President George W. Bush's unpopularity damaged the Republican Party's prospects throughout the country, and a sharp economic downturn starting in 2008 produced an issue environment favorable to Democrats generally. At the same time, the Democratic presidential nominee, Barack Obama, had launched an unprecedented drive to organize and register Democratic voters in North Carolina.[3] But the national story alone cannot explain the outcome in North Carolina. While Obama carried the state by a mere 0.4 percentage point margin, Hagan defeated Dole by a resounding eight percentage points.

Despite her seeming liabilities, Hagan proved to be an energetic, disciplined campaigner. "Hagan campaigned about as aggressively as anyone I have ever seen," said North Carolina's Democratic chairman, Jerry Meek. "She was everywhere, at event after event."[4] With the physical stamina of "an exercise junkie," Hagan crisscrossed the state, cultivating a ground organization.[5] Hagan also possessed self-assurance earned through political experience, having served for ten years in the state Senate where she co-chaired the powerful appropriations committee. Coming from a politically ambitious family (she was the niece of former Florida governor Lawton Chiles), Hagan had been day-dreaming about a political career since a Capitol Hill internship in the 1970s.

To defeat Elizabeth Dole would be no mean feat. Dole had grown up in Salisbury, one of the state's small towns, and her accent and genteel demeanor were a comfortable fit for many of her constituents. "Her style is still very much 1950s North Carolina," observed journalist Rob Christensen, "She's always smartly dressed and displays a get-more-bees-with-honey style of graciousness."[6] On the campaign trail, she talked about her Christian faith often and easily. In an election year where the watchword was "change," Dole was able to "remind voters that she once personified change" herself: "I've had to break a few [glass ceilings] as I came along," she reminisced.[7]

Nevertheless, Dole had vulnerabilities that Hagan effectively exploited. One difficulty was a widespread sense in the state that she had been an absentee sena-tor. A study of Senate records and news clippings by the *Winston-Salem Journal* found that she had spent only thirteen days in the state in 2006 and just two months there between 2004 and 2006.[8] Dole had many Washington obligations during that time, having been elected chair of the National Republican Senatorial Committee by her colleagues. "No one disputes the charge that she didn't spend enough time in the state during the first four years of her term," noted election analyst Jennifer Duffy.[9] In addition, Hagan also criticized Dole as "ineffective," pointing to a "power rankings survey" compiled by a nonpartisan political Web site (www.Congress.org) that rated Dole as ninety-third in the Senate.

Hagan's campaign gained momentum after the airing of a television ad by the national Democratic senate campaign organization, The Democratic Senatorial Campaign Committee (DSCC). When the ad was launched in August 2008, Dole was still strongly favored to win. But "the DSCC's targeted investment produced an impressive and immediate return," writes veteran journalist Bob Benenson, "Polling showed such a pronounced downturn for Dole that she decided to stay home and campaign rather than attend the Republican National Convention."[10] The ad featured two elderly men seated in rocking chairs on the front porch of a country store:[11]

"I'm telling you," says the first good old boy, "Liddy Dole is 93."

"Ninety-three?" replies the second.

"Yup, she ranks 93rd in effectiveness."

"After 40 years in Washington?"

"After 40 years in Washington, Dole is 93rd in effectiveness, right near the bottom."

"I've read she's 92," says the second old man.

"Didn't I just tell you she's 93?" says the first.

"No, 92 percent of the time she votes with Bush," says number two.

"What happened to the Liddy Dole I knew?"

"She's just not a go-getter like you and me," says number two as both rock in their rockers.

Using gentle humor, this ad leveled three powerful charges against Dole: that she was ineffective despite her long Washington tenure, that she rubber-stamped unpopular Bush policies, and that she was not the "Liddy Dole" she once was. The ad also not so subtly raised the issue of Dole's age (she was 72).

Idiosyncratic as it may be in many respects, the North Carolina Senate battle illustrates several elements of congressional campaigns. It highlights how even seemingly secure incumbents can become vulnerable if they are perceived as being out of touch with constituents. It shows the challenge faced by party leaders intent upon recruiting high-profile challengers to run against incumbents. It points to the importance of campaigns, especially candidates' dynamism, personal accessibility, and the effective use of media. Finally, it exemplifies how national party politics—including the broader political environment and the national parties' use of funds—reverberates down to local races.

CAMPAIGN STRATEGIES

Campaigns are volatile mixtures of personal contacts, fundraising, speechmaking, advertising, and symbolic appeals. As acts of communication, campaigns are designed to convey messages to potential voters. The overriding goal is to win over a plurality of those who cast ballots on election day.

Asking the Right Questions

Whether incumbents or challengers, candidates for Congress strive to map out a successful campaign strategy. To that end, each potential candidate must consider: What sort of constituency do I have? Are my name, face, and career familiar to voters, or am I relatively unknown? What resources—money, group support, volunteers—can I attract? What leaders and groups are pivotal to a winning campaign? What issues or feelings are uppermost in potential voters' minds? How can I reach those voters most effectively with my message? When should my campaign begin and how should it be paced? And, perhaps most importantly, what are my chances for victory? The answers to such questions define the campaign strategy.

The constituency shapes candidates' campaign strategies. In populous states, Senate aspirants must appeal to diverse economic and social groups, scattered over wide areas and many media markets. In fast-growing states, even Senate incumbents must introduce themselves to new voters who have arrived since the last election. Only small-state Senate candidates can know their constituents as intimately as House candidates know theirs. But unlike states, House districts often fit within no natural geographic, community, media market, or existing political divisions.[12] In such situations, candidates and their managers must find the most suitable forums, media outlets, and local organizations to reach voters with potentially little in common except being enclosed within the same district boundaries.

Because incumbents are typically hard to defeat, the incumbent's decision to seek reelection colors the entire electoral undertaking. The partisan leanings of the electorate are also critical. The dominant party's candidates stress party loyalty, underscore long-standing partisan values, and sponsor get-out-the-vote (GOTV) drives, because high voter turnout usually aids their cause. Minority-party campaigns highlight personalities, downplay partisan differences, and exploit factional splits within the majority party, perhaps by invoking "wedge issues" designed to pry voters away from their majority-party home.

The perceptions and attitudes of voters, finally, must be reflected in campaign planning. Through surveys, focus groups, or old-fashioned informal pulse taking, strategists take account of what is on voters' minds and what, if anything, they know or think about the candidate. Well-known candidates try to capitalize on their visibility; lesser-known ones run ads that repeat their names over and over again. Candidates with a reputation for openness and geniality highlight those qualities in ads. Those who are more introverted (yes, there are such politicians) stress experience and competence, at the same time displaying photos or film clips reminding voters that they, too, are human. Candidates who have made tough, unpopular decisions are touted as courageous leaders.

Candidates' appearances, speeches, advertising, and appeals are designed to exploit changing voter preferences. In the wake of scandals, honesty and openness are on display. In 2008, candidates of both parties sought to capitalize on public dissatisfaction with the status quo by portraying themselves as agents of change.

Choosing the Message

The average citizen is barraged with media messages of all kinds—an hour of television commercials per day, among other things. The candidate's overarching challenge is to project an image through this cacophony of media appeals, including those from other candidates. "The only way to cut through this communication clutter," a political marketing executive points out, "is to adopt the strategy proven effective by successful businesses. Create a brand. And manage the message with discipline and impact."[13] In other words, forge a message that will stand out from all the competing messages in the media marketplace.

Framing the Voters' Choice. A candidate's message is usually distilled into a single theme or slogan that is repeated on radio, TV, billboards, and in campaign literature. "A good message … is a credible statement that can be summed up in a few sentences and frequently ends with a kicker slogan.… In most races, messages define campaigns."[14]

Strategists use these messages to frame the campaign: to set the election's agenda—not by changing people's attitudes, but by shifting their attention to issues that favor their candidate or diminish the opponent. "There's only three or four plots," explained Carter Eskew, a Democratic consultant. "Plots for incumbents are Representative X is different from the rest; X can deliver; X stands with you. And the perennial plot for challengers is (fill in the blank) years are long enough; it's time for a change."[15]

Campaign messages usually appear in the form of slogans attempting to frame the voter's choice. In her 2004 race for the South Carolina Senate seat, Democrat Inez Tenenbaum relentlessly repeated a theme that arose from her party's minority status in the state: "It's not whose team you're on, it's whose side you're on." The message of her victorious opponent, Republican representative Jim DeMint, was expressed by the shouts of his backers: "Jim DeMint, George Bush!"[16]

Vulnerable Incumbents. Incumbency can be a liability. An extensive public record gives enterprising opponents many potential openings to exploit. Past votes or positions may be highlighted to discredit the officeholder, sometimes fairly and sometimes unfairly. Incumbents may be shackled to unpopular issues, such as nuclear waste dumps, Medicare premium hikes, unresolved wars, economic crises, or to disliked personalities on the national scene.

Or incumbents, like Elizabeth Dole, can take voters' support for granted, a major political mistake. One campaign consultant summed up the lesson of such races: "You have to earn that support every two years. A lot of members of Congress forget how to run."[17]

CAMPAIGN RESOURCES

Even the best campaign strategy will fail if the candidate cannot muster the resources necessary to implement it. The chief resources in congressional elections are money and organization.

Allocating Resources

Money's importance in campaigns cannot be overemphasized. A well-funded campaign can reach voters through paid media and campaign professionals hired to craft a message and poll the electorate. Less well-funded campaigns have a much harder time reaching voters. To be sure, old-fashioned campaigns based on canvassing door-to-door, and relying on armies of volunteers, can be effective in some contests. But candidates raise as much money as they can for good reason. Especially useful is early money—funds on hand at the outset of the campaign, or even before the campaign officially begins. EMILY's List— Early Money Is Like Yeast ("It makes the 'dough' rise")—a group begun in 1985, was formed on this premise. EMILY's List collects (bundles) individuals' donations for Democratic women candidates who support abortion rights. The Republican counterpart is Women in the Senate and House (WISH).

Late blitz money also can turn the tide, although money alone rarely makes the difference at the end of a race. The final weeks of a hard-fought race are tough because both sides are trying to reach undecided voters. "You've got to move that 10 or 15 percent, many of whom are not paying much attention," a Democratic consultant explained. "Unfortunately, the way to do that is with negative or comparative ads."[18] Late in the game, opponents frantically attack and—despite the scant time—counterattack.

Another question of timing involves candidates facing tough contests in both primary and general elections. In this situation, candidates lacking personal wealth have an especially vexing dilemma. Should they ration their outflow of funds and risk losing the primary, or should they wage an expensive primary campaign and risk running out of money later on?

Incumbents' Money. Incumbents raise more money and also spend more on their campaigns than challengers do. House incumbents in 2008 raised $1.3 million on average to defend their seats—two and a half times what their opponents could muster. Senate incumbents outpaced their challengers in 2008 by an even wider margin, raising on average 3.6 times as much as their opponents.[19]

Because incumbents are better known than challengers, their spending often has strategic purposes. Preemptive fundraising can dissuade serious opponents. "If you look like a 900-pound gorilla, people won't want to take you on," remarked a GOP campaign aide.[20] This was the strategy of Illinois Sen. Dick Durbin in 2008. With no Republican opponent in sight, Durbin kicked off his fundraising drive early. More than a year and a half before the 2008 elections, Chicago columnist Lynn Sweet observed, "Durbin wants millions of dollars in his war chest as soon as possible to make any GOP multimillionaire think twice about the cost of challenging him. Durbin wants to raise the financial bar so high no one but a rookie, long shot or no-name Republican will bother to run."[21] Durbin eventually raised more than $11 million, nearly twice as much as the typical senator running for reelection that cycle, despite facing a low-profile Republican challenger who had never held elective office.

If a strong, well-financed challenger surfaces, incumbents can also spend reactively to stave off defeat. New incumbents tend to invest heavily in both preemptive and reactive spending because they are more likely than longtime veterans to face vigorous challenges. More senior members tend to raise and spend less than junior members, especially in the early campaign stages (usually before July of an election year). Incumbents who have proven to be surefire vote-getters over the long haul—with five or more terms—may establish such commanding positions that they rarely face serious challenges.

Sometimes established incumbents deliberately overspend for reasons beyond the race at hand. Decisive victories can establish claims for higher office: Many House members yearn for a Senate seat; some senators (including several 2008 presidential contenders) have presidential ambitions. Others strive to impress colleagues with their electoral prowess by distributing funds to needier candidates. Durbin, for example, used his extra campaign funds in 2008 to make himself one of the top contributors to the DSCC.[22]

Incumbents' overspending is motivated, finally, by a sense of uncertainty and risk. "Because of uncertainty," Gary C. Jacobson explains, "members tend to exaggerate electoral threats and overreact to them. They are inspired by worst-case scenarios—what would they have to do to win if everything went wrong?—rather than objective probabilities."[23] In other words, incumbents often enjoy the luxury of raising, and spending, more funds than necessary—which they do to ward off worst-case scenarios.

Challengers' Money. Challengers and open-seat candidates typically do not enjoy the same embarrassment of riches. They need to raise money to gain visibility, win credibility, and get a head start over other contenders. (For one open-seat candidate's fundraising efforts, see Table 4-1.) In this arena as in so many others, nothing succeeds like success. "Failure to raise enough money creates a vicious spiral," explains political analyst Thomas B. Edsall. "Some donors become reluctant to invest their cash, and then state and national parties are less likely to target...party building and get out the vote drives in those races."[24]

Challengers, for their part, spend all the money they can raise to make their names and faces known to voters. Because they normally start far behind the incumbent, challengers' campaign dollars tend to be more cost-effective than incumbents'. As Jacobson has demonstrated, the more a challenger spends, the more votes he is likely to attract.[25] The five challengers who bested Senate incumbents in 2008 were all adequately financed, though none of them actually matched their opponents' resources.

Spending Campaign Funds

As exercises in communication, campaigns are driven by the need to find a cost-effective way of reaching citizens and getting them to vote. Spending patterns vary widely between the House and the Senate, among congressional districts and states, and between incumbents and challengers.

As a rule, statewide Senate races are mass media contests with messages conveyed mainly through radio and television. Costs are especially high in densely populated states with large metropolitan media markets. Senate candidates spend far more on media advertising and fundraising than do their House counterparts, who spend correspondingly more on traditional means of voter contact. The most expensive House contests often occur in states where the population is small and spread out.[26] Consider central and western Nebraska's Third District, which spans 85 percent of the state's land area and is served by nine media markets in six states (only three of them within Nebraska). When the seat was open in 2006, the two major-party candidates spent between them about $2.5 million to reach voters in those wide-open spaces.

Despite its astronomic costs, television advertising is popular because candidates believe it works. They are probably right. In the 1980s, political scientist Thomas Patterson estimated that it cost only about one-half cent to get to a single television viewer, compared with one-and-a-half cents to reach a newspaper reader and twenty-five cents to reach a direct-mail recipient.[27]

The character of candidates and their party organizations also affects the media mix and budgeting. Confident incumbents can channel their money into telephone or door-to-door appeals that direct their messages to activists, partisans, and supporters. Lesser-known candidates must turn to broad-scale media, such as television or billboards, to promote name recognition.[28] Both House and Senate challengers spend more on media and less on traditional campaigning than do incumbents. And, although challengers presumably need more money to get their messages across, they spend less in fundraising than incumbents do.

Incumbents also spend more than challengers on constituent gifts, entertainment, and donations to local causes. Although the issue presents thorny problems of legal definition, the Federal Election Commission (FEC) allows gifts of nominal value to constituents. Spending reports from members' campaigns and their related political action committees (PACs) disclose a surprising array of activities, such as buying flowers and tickets to sports events, organizing athletic teams, sponsoring contests and prizes, and subsidizing travel and entertainment.[29]

Organizing the Campaign

Implementing the campaign strategy is the job of the candidates and their organizations. Waging a campaign is not for the fainthearted. Take the case of psychology professor Brian Baird, a Democrat who won Washington's Third District (comprising Olympia and southwest Washington state) seat in 1998. Having lost to the incumbent by a mere 887 votes two years earlier, Baird vowed to run full tilt the second time, when the incumbent bowed out to run for the Senate. His campaign schedule is summarized in Table 4-1. Baird spent almost all of his waking hours on the campaign during the peak months (July through October)—more than ten hours a day for 123 days. By far the largest block of time—more than one-third—was spent raising the $1.3 million he needed to win the open seat. Most of those hours he sat in a tiny room he called his bunker, wearing a headset and phoning potential contributors. Many of his meetings with individuals, groups, or other politicians also involved fundraising. And travel consumed many valuable hours in his average-sized district.

Few localities today boast tight party organizations. In some strong party areas, voter contact is the job of ward, precinct, and block captains. Candidates in some such areas still dispense "walking-around money" to encourage precinct captains to get out the vote and provide small financial rewards for voting. But in most places today traditional local parties have often been replaced by hybrid organizations that partner with state and national parties and their allied interest groups.

When they can pay the price, today's candidates can purchase campaign services from political consulting firms, most of them operating within partisan networks. According to an independent survey of the 2004 federal election cycle, political candidates, national parties, and advocacy (527) groups paid nearly $1.8 billion to some 600 professional consultants—half of their total campaign spending. Two-thirds of that money went to media consultants.[30] Some firms offer a wide array of services; others specialize in polling, direct

TABLE 4-1 **See How He Ran: Candidate Brian Baird's Time Budget, July–October 1998**		
Activity	Hours and minutes spent[a]	Percentage of time
Fundraising call time	397:30	32
Other fundraising	36:00	3
Meeting with individuals, groups, politicians	146:00	12
Public events	96:00	8
Meeting with media	31:00	2
Voter contact	89:15	7
Meeting with staff	58:45	5
Travel	203:15	16
Personal time	201:30	16
Total hours	1,259:15	101[b]
Average hours per day	10:12	

Sources: Baird for Congress Campaign, 1998; and James A. Thurber and Carolyn Long, "Brian Baird's 'Ring of Fire': The Quest for Funds and Votes in Washington's Third District," in *The Battle for Congress,* ed. James A. Thurber (Washington, D.C.: Brookings Institution, 2001), 188.

[a] Excludes the three days of campaigning in November: 33 hours, 15 minutes, mostly in voter contact.

[b] Does not add to 100 percent because of rounding.

mail, phone banks, advertising, purchasing media time, coordinating volunteer efforts, fundraising, or financial management and accounting. Despite the hype they often receive, consultants by themselves rarely turn a campaign around. At best they can make the most of a candidate's resources and help combat opponents' attacks. They cannot compensate for an unskilled or lazy candidate or for a candidate's staff that does not follow through on details.

CAMPAIGN TECHNIQUES

Campaigns are designed to convey candidates' messages to people who will lend support and vote in the election. Campaigns are not necessarily directed at all voters. Often narrower groups are targeted—most notably, the political parties' core supporters.

The Air War: Media and Other Mass Appeals

Candidates reach the largest numbers of voters by running broadcast ads and making televised appearances. Television is the broadest spectrum medium and often the most cost-effective. But its costs eat up the bulk of most campaign budgets.

Media efforts vary in the degree to which candidates control their preparation and distribution. Some of the most effective appeals—news coverage and endorsements, for example—are determined by persons other than the candidate. Because journalists can raise unwanted or hostile questions, many politicians seek out the friendlier environments of talk shows hosted by nonjournalists. Even more congenial are appeals the candidates themselves buy and pay for— newsletters, media ads, and direct mail. The drawback is that self-promotion is seen as less credible than information from independent sources.

Nearly three-fourths of all voters receive campaign news from television— network, cable, or local. A third turn to the Internet as their primary campaign news source, and 29 percent rely on newspapers.[31] Yet local news programming largely ignores congressional campaign coverage. In the weeks preceding the 2004 elections, for example, 92 percent of the scheduled half-hour local news programs in eleven select media markets offered no coverage at all of local candidate races, including U.S. House races. In the ten markets with statewide Senate races, the "blackout rate" was 94 percent.[32] Most candidates must thus pay to reach voters: Local television stations nationwide took in an estimated $3 billion from candidate advertising in 2008.[33]

Positive Themes. Most campaign themes call for promotions that evoke positive responses from citizens. Little-known candidates must initially boost name familiarity. Running in Virginia's Fifth District in 2008, challenger Tom Perriello constructed a television ad making light of the fact that most people did not know how to pronounce his name. After showing a series of voters endorsing Perriello, each one pronouncing his name differently, the candidate himself comes on the screen to say, "I'm Tom Perriello, and I approve this message because knowing how to pronounce my name isn't what's important. Recognizing it on the ballot is what is." In the course of this thirty-second ad, Perriello's name was used five times, shown on a mock ballot, and displayed continuously along the bottom of the screen. The lighthearted ad, in conjunction with an energetic campaign, helped Democrat Perriello to a long-shot victory over seven-term Republican incumbent Virgil Goode in a largely rural, Republican-leaning district.[34]

Positive ads present candidates in warm, human terms to which citizens can relate. Democrat Dennis Moore, a 1998 challenger in Kansas's Third District (located in the northeast and Kansas City suburbs) had a superb résumé, but it was his talent as an amateur singer and guitar player that enabled him to connect with voters on a personal level. Moore had to be coaxed into making a hokey TV spot entitled "Guitar Lessons." After mentioning a style of music (country, rock, blues), he would play a short tune and then apply it to an issue. Example: "Rock: We need to make Social Security solid as a rock."[35] Moore captured the seat, a feat he has repeated five times.

If skillfully done, TV ads can be artful as well as effective in bringing home the candidates' themes. A case in point was the series of brilliant, funny—and inexpensive—television ads that helped a little-known Wisconsin state legislator, Russell D. Feingold, win the Democratic primary over better-known and better-financed rivals and then to defeat a two-term incumbent senator.[36] As his opponents battered each other with negative ads, Feingold ran clever, personal spots describing himself as the "underdog candidate." One showed Elvis, alive and endorsing Feingold. Another showed Feingold walking through his modest home, opening up a closet and saying, "No skeletons." In another he posted his three key pledges on his garage door. Although outspent in both the primary and the general election, Feingold became one of five successful Senate challengers in 1992 (he has kept his seat through subsequent elections).

Some media appeals are coordinated with field operations. Trolling for the student vote in Madison, Wisconsin, Democratic candidate Tammy Baldwin ran what her staff called the "Bucky" ad (for "Bucky Badger," the University of Wisconsin mascot). It ran on MTV and youth-oriented shows. The ad said that "there is one candidate who understands our issues" and ended with a pitch to get out and vote, with a phone number and Baldwin's Web site. Every time the ad ran, all the headquarters' phone lines would light up.[37]

Negative Themes. Candidates can also use campaign resources against their opponents. Different from positive ads are those known as contrast ads, which distinguish the candidate from the opponent on grounds of policy and experience, and attack ads, which strike at the opponent's record or personal character. Rep. Leonard Lance's, R-N.J., 2008 winning bid for an open seat in New Jersey's Seventh District offers an example of an effective contrast ad. The ad featured a series of "man on the street"-style shots, showing male and female voters of different ages and races, each saying "Linda Stender is a Spender." The ad's tone is high-spirited, using bright colors and punctuated with a cash register sound. One voter is even shown cracking up laughing as he attempts the line. The repetition, combined with the rhyme on his opponent's name, memorably conveyed the central contrast Lance sought to draw in his campaign.

Negative campaign themes are often the result of opposition research (called "oppo" by campaigners). Its purpose is "to get the skinny on the client's opponents and, if all goes well, expose them as hypocrites, liars, thieves, or just plain unsavory characters."[38] Both national parties and many campaigns invest in opposition research. Because challengers are usually less known than incumbents, they are more vulnerable to attacks and unflattering personal revelations.

Although not technically a campaign ad, the "push poll" is another negative campaign technique. These are not actual polls designed to elicit public attitudes, but instead advocacy phone calls with questions aimed at changing the voter's opinions. The caller divulges negative information—often false or misleading—in the hope of pulling the voter away from the opponent and toward the candidate paying for the call.

Negative ads are common in modern campaigning because politicians believe they work. The strategy was forcefully described by Rep. Tom Cole, R-Okla., in a memo to his House colleagues:

> Define your opponent immediately and unrelentingly....Do not let up— keep the tough ads running right up to election day. Don't make the mistake of pulling your ads in favor of a positive rotation the last weekend.[39]

Referring candidly to his party's 2006 playing field, Cole added, "When people are looking at national issues that are not breaking our way, what you want to do is focus on your opponent."[40]

Recent experiments by two noted communications researchers tend to confirm the power of negative ads. Such ads, these scholars found, lift voters' information levels, even if the information conveyed is distorted or trivial. Ads tend to reinforce previously held views and only slightly raise (or lower) the likelihood of voting. While neither positive nor negative ads have much effect on strong partisans, negative ads can work powerfully on citizens who have little information to begin with and on those with little or no party allegiance.[41]

Some researchers take a benign view of negative ads. "We should not necessarily see negative ads as a harmful part of our electoral system," contends Kenneth Goldstein, head of the University of Wisconsin's political advertising project. "They are much more likely [than positive ads] to be about policy, to use supporting information, and to be reliable. Few negative ads are on personal issues."[42] One study of 189 different Senate campaigns found that "negative campaigning…generally *mobilizes*, rather than *de*mobilizes, the electorate."[43]

Distortions and Dirty Tricks. Like other forms of product promotion, political ads often stretch or distort the truth. Sometimes the disinformation is so blatant that the term "dirty tricks" applies. This includes not only spreading falsehoods but also using doctored photographs or faking news reports or news headlines. An especially sinister tactic is associating an opponent with bad events over which the person had no control. For example, several candidates have been slandered by ads that morphed their portraits into Osama bin Laden or Saddam Hussein.

One of the most controversial attack ads in the 2008 campaign was aired by Sen. Dole in her unsuccessful attempt to retain her seat against Hagan's challenge. Dole's ad began with the question, "If Godless Americans threw a party in your honor, would you go?"[44] The ad then described her opponent's attendance at a Boston fundraiser at the home of an advisor to the Godless Americans PAC (which seeks to remove references to God from U.S. currency, among other similar goals). The ad concluded by showing Hagan's photo, with an off-camera woman's voice saying, "There is no God." That quote seemed to suggest that Hagan herself made the statement, though the creator of the ad denied any intent to mislead people into thinking that the voice was Hagan's.[45] The subject matter of the ad is obviously inflammatory, particularly in North Carolina, one of the most religious states in the country.[46] Dole had held back on this charge until the last week before the election, but when polls continued to show her trailing at that point, she signed off on the "Godless ad."[47]

Victims of smear tactics have some means of defense, even when attacks are leveled close to election day. The campaign can promptly air response ads to set the record straight or at least accuse the offender of mudslinging. In the case of Dole's ad, Hagan, a Sunday school teacher and elder at her Greensboro Presbyterian church, initially responded with a lawsuit against Dole, claiming that the ad was false and defamatory.[48] She then aired a response ad in which she said, "My faith guides my life and Senator Dole knows it....My campaign is about creating jobs and fixing our economy, not bearing false witness against fellow Christians."[49] In the end, many Republicans felt that Dole's ad backfired on her campaign. The ad "alienated her from moderate independents and potentially from evangelicals," remarked one longtime GOP strategist. "In my mind it was political malpractice by Dole's advisors."[50] "When you're making ads that say, 'There is no God,' it usually means your campaign doesn't have a prayer," quipped GOP consultant Alex Castellanos.[51]

Formal complaints can sometimes persuade opponents to disavow attack ads or local broadcasters to pull them off the air. Media outlets find themselves in the unwanted role of arbitrating between contending candidates. The legal situation is murky. Courts have held that candidates have a right to buy ads even if their content is challenged, but broadcasters are not legally required to air ads from party organizations or advocacy groups.[52]

The Bipartisan Campaign Reform Act (BCRA) of 2002 requires that candidates personally appear and vouch for their advertisements. Some have proposed tighter controls on campaign advertising—for example, requiring candidates to appear in all ads that talk about their opponents. Others argue that formal or legal remedies against misrepresentations raise thorny constitutional questions, not to mention the specter of excessive regulation and protracted litigation. Citizens may be better off trusting that "the give-and-take of campaign thrust-and-parry and the activity of a free and skeptical press create a balance" between contenders.[53]

Evolving Mass Media. The old-fashioned media—newspapers, radio, and television networks—are on the decline. The newspaper business in the United States, in particular, appears to be in crisis. Even before the current recession, newspapers around the country had cut staff and closed bureaus in an effort to remain economically viable. This evolution is partly a result of generational replacement: recent surveys indicate that while two-thirds to three-quarters of the oldest age cohorts are daily newspaper readers, only about 20 percent of the youngest cohorts are.[54] A similar generational trend has been seen in network news viewership. The Internet is becoming an increasingly important news source. A study by the Pew Research Center reported a 130 percent increase in Internet usage for campaign news between 2004 and 2008, with the shift most pronounced among young people.[55]

Web outlets are thus far unregulated. In 2006, the FEC decided to treat the Internet "as a unique and evolving mode of mass communication and political speech that...warrants a restrained regulatory approach."[56] Critics of the hands-off approach point out that Web political messages can be costly to produce, and sometimes far edgier than would be permitted in traditional media outlets. The public at least has an interest in learning who instigates these messages, who prepares them, and who pays for them.

Still, the variety and seeming spontaneity of the Web intrigues many political observers. One observer of the Web scene calls it "word of mouth on steroids." Although campaign organizations use the medium, the knowledge and skills to make compelling videos—like those unleashed on YouTube and other outlets for and against the 2008 presidential contenders—have "moved out of campaign headquarters" and onto the computer screens of private citizens.

In this decentralized and diverse media environment, campaigns increasingly display what political scientist Darrell West describes as a law of diminishing returns. "It becomes difficult to break through the clutter," he observes, "and at this point there is a lot of clutter out there."[57]

The Ground War: Pressing the Flesh and Other Forms of Close Contact

Direct appeals to voters through personal appearances by candidates or their surrogates—at shopping centers, factory gates, or even door to door—are part of every campaign. In his successful 1948 Senate campaign, Lyndon B. Johnson swooped out of the sky in a helicopter to visit small Texas towns, grandly pitching his Stetson from the chopper for a bold entrance. (An aide was assigned to retrieve the hat for use at the next stop.)[58] Other candidates, preferring to stay closer to the ground, stage walking tours or other events to attract attention. Few elected officials get by without doing a great deal of what is inelegantly called "pressing the flesh."

Contemporary politicians have rediscovered the virtues of retail as opposed to wholesale campaigning. As political reporter David S. Broder put it: "More and more political strategists are coming to believe that the high-tech tools that have dominated campaigns for the past four decades—TV spots, mass mailings and professionally staffed phone banks—are far less effective [in motivating voters] than the old-fashioned way of turning out the vote."[59] Personalized techniques target those most apt to go to the polling booth: loyalists within the parties' core constituency groups. With computer databases and improved demographic data, campaigners in recent decades have engaged in "strategic mobilization": pinpointing people with demographic and political traits favorable to one's party.[60]

An obvious advantage of so-called shoe-leather campaigning is cost, at least when compared with mass media appeals. "Door-to-door canvassing is the tactic of choice among candidates and campaigns that are short on cash," explain Yale political scientists Donald P. Green and Alan S. Gerber. "Precinct walking is often described as the weapon of underdogs."[61] Former representative Dan Glickman, D-Kan. (1977–1995), then a thirty-one-year-old and now the film industry's chief lobbyist, describes his first House campaign:

> I walked door-to-door to 35,000 homes over an eight-month period. I walked from 10:30 a.m. to 2 p.m. and again from 5:30 to 8 p.m. I lost 35 pounds and learned to be very realistic about dogs. I met a woman my father had lent $100 or $150 to 30 years before. She embraced me and said, "You saved us." I won by three percentage points.[62]

Face-to-face campaigning is obligatory in smaller communities, where people expect politicians to show up at festivals, parades, or annual county fairs. "If you ain't seen at the county fair, you're preached about on Sunday," remarked a politician as he led his party's Senate candidate around the hog and sheep barns in Ada, Oklahoma.[63] In small states, first-name relationships are often valued. Of Vermont's voters, political scientist Garrison Nelson remarks, "They want to know you." The state's Independent senator Bernard Sanders's bumper stickers simply say, "Bernie."[64] In Bristol, on Rhode Island's coast, the Fourth of July parade—the oldest in the country—is "the first and perhaps biggest event of the campaign season."[65]

One-on-one campaigning is physically and emotionally challenging, and the payoff is often elusive. "The hardest doorbell for a candidate to ring is the first one," campaign specialist Ron Faucheux recalls of his canvassing days. "Canvassing takes an enormous amount of time and a serious commitment."[66] At best, he cautions, canvassers reach only about 30 percent of an area's voters. Only about 60 percent of the people will be home, and the person who comes to the door may represent only half the household's eligible voters. To reach more voters per visit, candidates seek out shopping malls, organized groups, fairs, or rallies.

Some campaigns make a point of mobilizing cadres of volunteers. Representative Baldwin's winning run in 1998 for an open seat in Wisconsin's Second District (comprising Madison) was boosted by some 3,000 volunteers, 1,700 of them University of Wisconsin (UW) students. Most of these helpers did a literature drop or two, or they worked the phones for an evening. Some—at least thirty-five during the general election race—worked full-time. Much of the volunteer effort targeted Madison's 40,000 UW students, traditionally indifferent voters who make up 10 percent of the district's potential electorate. The volunteer effort paid off. Baldwin topped 70 percent of the vote in the six wards with the highest concentration of UW students.[67]

Getting Out the Vote. Personal encounters by candidates or their surrogates are essential for GOTV drives: making sure constituents are registered and getting voters to the polls. All these tasks (staffing phone banks or canvassing) can be hired for a price, but they are most effective when carried out by someone who can connect with the potential voter. According to Green and Gerber, face-to-face canvassing raises turnout by seven to twelve percentage points and in the end is more cost effective than alternative media–based campaigns.[68]

Recognizing the importance of personalized voter contact, both parties have developed sophisticated GOTV operations. Each now relies on "microtargeting" to reach sympathetic voters. This employs computer models to exploit a wide array of data, such as the groups people belong to or the magazines they read, to identify potential voters and the issues that are important to them. "Microtargeting has become so widespread that it is now used by all House and Senate candidates, on both sides, in state legislative races, and in some cases, all the way down the ballot to local school board elections."[69]

The Republican party began using microtargeting with its famous "72-hour plan" (devised by White House strategist Karl Rove and Republican National Committee chair Ken Mehlman), first rolled out in 2002. Under the plan, the party recruited more volunteers, made more live phone calls, rang more doorbells, left more door hangers, and pulled out more votes from Republican households than ever before. "In the last election cycle [the money] would've been spent on TV," a Georgia campaign manager explained. "This cycle, it went into manpower."[70] The scheme's heart was the "Voter Vault," a $15-million national database labeling voters worth contacting as "socos," or social conservatives, "fiscos," fiscal conservatives, and "soft Dems," crossover voters.[71] The database helped candidates "track down likely supporters and avoid wasting time on those who couldn't be persuaded."[72] The 72-hour plan was widely credited for many Republican party successes between 2000 and 2008.

Democrats responded with their own stepped-up GOTV efforts in 2006 and 2008. The Democratic National Committee appropriated the microtargeting approach and invested millions of dollars in a national voter database that could be used by Democratic candidates throughout the country. For its part, the Obama campaign took ground operations to a new level. "In scale and ambition, the Obama organization goes beyond even what Rove built," wrote journalist Alec MacGillis. "The campaign has used its record-breaking fundraising to open more than 700 offices in more than a dozen battleground states, pay several thousand organizers, and manage tens of thousands more volunteers."[73] Obama's campaign created a neighborhood-based team structure: each team was led and staffed to the extent possible by local residents and linked to the campaign's field operations with text messages, email, and social networking Web sites. As part of its ground operation, the campaign also launched an ambitious voter registration drive in all fifty states, "Vote for Change," in which volunteers were recruited and then trained in the basics of voter registration. In light of the effort, DCCC Chairman Chris Van Hollen, D-Md., declared that turnout was "the big wild card for Republicans," who "can't plan on a conventional turnout scenario," given the Obama campaign's voter registration successes.[74]

According to many accounts, the 2008 presidential campaign of John McCain suffered from a lack of focus on GOTV operations. Outmatched financially by the Obama forces and unable to compete in paid media, McCain allocated fewer resources to mobilize voters than President Bush had in 2000 and 2004. "The desire for parity on television comes at the expense of investment in paid boots on the ground," said one top Republican strategist privy to McCain's plans. "The folks who will oversee the volunteer operation have been told to get out into the field on their own nickel."[75]

For both parties, many groups are prepared to "get out into the field on their own nickel." In this sense, the parties' GOTV efforts are just part of a broader campaign waged by their allied groups. For example, "in most states union members will be contacted between fourteen and twenty-four times by other union members in some fashion," AFL-CIO's political director reported in 2002.[76] Labor unions further escalated their ground efforts in 2008, spending more than $300 million in their efforts to organize and mobilize voters on behalf of Democratic candidates.[77] For their part, Republicans depend on a wide array of pro-life, evangelical, and socially conservative organizations to do GOTV for their candidates. In 2008, McCain's choice of Sarah Palin as his running mate was instrumental in motivating members of such groups to volunteer time and effort to turning out voters.[78]

Both parties are sure to expand their ground-war troops in future elections. Their computers are crammed with exhaustive precinct-by-precinct, even block-by-block, data defining targeted residents. Also in their computers are the names of millions of volunteers who will be called upon to wage campaigns for the 2010 election and beyond.

THE PARALLEL CAMPAIGNS

The scene is a hospital operating room, patient surrounded by surgeons and nurses. One surgeon in a voice of astonished concern exclaims, "Oh my." A nurse asks, "Colitis?" Another nurse asks, "Hepatitis?" A third, "Diverticulitis?" The surgeon replies, "No, I'm afraid it's Dina Titus. Taxes up the yingyang. Her tax policy is killing us." The target of this television ad was 2008 Democratic House challenger Dina Titus, a former political science professor at University of Nevada-Las Vegas and now representative for Nevada's Third District. The ad was paid for by Freedom's Watch, a lobbying group bankrolled by wealthy conservatives, notably billionaire developer Sheldon Adeson.

An important story in recent congressional campaigns is the role played by groups not formally affiliated with the candidates or the parties. Campaigns no longer resemble boxing matches between two combatants. They have become free-for-alls in which multiple combatants throw punches and land roundhouse kicks. Incumbents compete not only against their challengers, but also scores of groups that join the fray.

Groups interested in congressional election outcomes have every reason to mount their own campaigns. Individual donations to candidates by themselves have limited impact: Legal limits on contributions mean that they are tiny drops in the bucket. And since passage of BCRA in 2002, individuals and groups are barred from donating soft money to the parties for organizational and GOTV purposes.

Private groups, by contrast, can indulge in unlimited independent spending for or against candidates, as long as it is reported to the Federal Election Commission and not coordinated with the candidates' own fundraising. Better yet is issue advocacy—messages aimed at influencing voters' choices without explicitly advocating the election or defeat of specific candidates. Such efforts, largely indistinguishable from candidate advertising, are clearly designed to sway federal elections. Courts have on First Amendment grounds rebuffed the FEC's attempts to limit such ads, but in upholding BCRA's Title II, the U.S. Supreme Court endorsed certain restrictions upon "electioneering communications"— television advertising that refers to specific candidates for federal office sixty days before a general election and thirty days before a primary.[79]

There are several categories of groups, some known by sections of the Internal Revenue Code. PACs raise and spend limited hard-money contributions to elect or defeat candidates. Tax-exempt groups under Section 527 of the tax code raise money for political activities, including issue advocacy and GOTV efforts. Nonprofit, tax-exempt groups under several parts of Section 501(c) can engage in certain activities, mainly not directed at specific candidates.

Republicans can count on support from business and industry, whose PACs and other groups have the deepest pockets. One power center is the Business Industry Political Action Committee (BIPAC), a group that advises and coordinates election activities of businesses and industry associations. Another group, spearheaded by the U.S. Chamber of Commerce, embraces a wide spectrum of business groups such as the 600,000-member National Federation of Independent Business (NFIB). Besides mobilizing its members, the NFIB in 2002 rolled out a GOTV drive aimed at some twenty House races and eight Senate-race states.[80] In 2008, the NFIB and its Save America's Free Enterprise Trust disbursed more than $2.3 million, focusing its contributions on some of the hardest fought races involving conservative Republicans.[81]

Another GOP power cluster is made up of right-wing ideological groups—those opposed to taxes, gun control, abortion, and gay rights, and those favoring prayer in schools and homeschooling. These include such familiar names as the Partnership for American Families, the National Rifle Association, and the Club for Growth, along with conservative religious forums.

On the left side of the spectrum, the AFL-CIO—the umbrella organization for dozens of labor unions—began with media campaigning but increasingly pours its money and personnel into GOTV efforts. "Magically, we have learned that when we talk to union members on the phone or face to face in the workplace and get them information, they vote—and they vote for the candidates and positions we have endorsed," explained the AFL-CIO's political chief.[82]

Liberal ideological groups compose the Progressive Network, described as "a progressive political coffee klatch where…information, gossip, hearsay and innuendo" are exchanged.[83] It is an alliance of environmental, feminist, and gay and lesbian organizations. Key players include the Sierra Club, the League of Conservation Voters, the Natural Resources Defense Council, the National Abortion and Reproductive Rights Action League (NARAL), and the Human Rights Campaign (gay and lesbian rights). Left-wing bloggers, such as Duncan Black (*Eschaton*) and Markos Moulitsas Zúniga (*Daily Kos*), are relatively new players in campaigns.[84] In recent years, the so-called netroots have taken an increasingly active role in congressional elections, assisting with fundraising, communication, and grassroots organizing.

Interest group involvement in elections resembles an arms race. Hundreds of organizations engage in congressional campaigning, most of them in league with one or the other major political party. Advocacy groups (527s) alone poured more than $216 million into the 2008 elections, over and above what candidates and parties spent.[85]

WHO VOTES?

Although Congress is supposed to be the people's branch of government, only around half of voting-age citizens normally take part in House elections.

FIGURE 4-1   **Turnout in Presidential and Congressional Elections, 1946–2008**

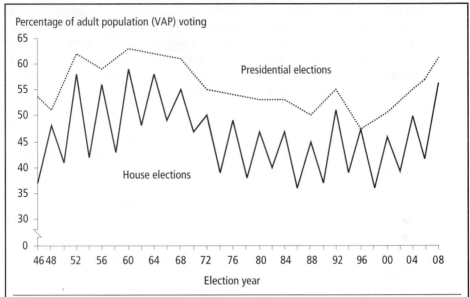

Percentage of adult population (VAP) voting

Sources: U.S. Bureau of the Census, Statistical Abstract of the United States: 2001 (Washington D.C.: U.S. Government Printing Office, 2001), Tables 401–404; Curtis Gans, "African-Americans, Anger, Fear and Youth Propel Turnout to Highest Level Since 1960," Center for the Study of the American Electorate, American University, http://www.american.edu/ia/cdem/csae/pdfs/2008pdfoffinaledited.pdf; Michael P. McDonald, "Voter Turnout," *United States Election Project,* George Mason University, http://elections .gmu.edu/voter_turnout.htm; Norman J. Ornstein, Thomas E. Mann, and Michael J. Malbin, *Vital Statistics on Congress, 2001–2002* (Washington D.C.: American Enterprise Institute, 2002), Table 2-1; and Martin P. Wattenberg, "Turnout in the 2004 Presidential Election," *Presidential Studies Quarterly* 35 (March 2005): 138–146.

In the 2008 House elections 58 percent of the voting-age population, or VAP (all eligible residents age eighteen and over), participated.[86] In the midterm elections two years earlier the turnout was 55 percent.

As Figure 4-1 indicates, turnout varies according to whether the election is held in a presidential or a midterm year. Midterm races lack the intense publicity and stimulus to vote provided by presidential contests. Since the 1930s, turnout in midterm congressional elections has averaged about 12 percent below that of the preceding presidential election. Midterm electorates include more people who are interested in politics, and—not unrelated—who are also more affluent and better educated.[87] Voter turnout in congressional races fails to match that of presidential elections—even in presidential election years.

Reasons for Not Voting

Political analysts disagree over the reasons for the anemic voting levels in the United States, near the bottom among established democratic countries. Several explanations—not all of them compatible—have been suggested.[88]

One explanation for nonvoting is simply demographic. Groups with low voting rates, such as young people, African Americans, and Latinos, have been growing as a share of the U.S. population. Young people (ages eighteen through twenty-nine) are traditional no-shows, perhaps because they have fewer life experiences (mortgages, taxes, school-age children, community ties) that propel older people toward activism. Four out of ten young people are unregistered to vote (three times greater than those aged fifty and older).[89] Turnout levels among young people have grown in recent years and were higher in the 2008 election than in 2004.[90] Youth turnout was especially improved in battleground states, such as Pennsylvania, Nevada, and Virginia, where the Obama campaign managed to reach an unusually high percentage of young voters.[91]

A second explanation stresses legal barriers to voting. Only about 70 percent of the VAP are registered to vote. Many democracies automatically register all adults; some even require that people vote. In contrast, U.S. citizens must take the initiative to register and vote. The National Voter Registration Act of 1993 (the so-called Motor Voter law) aimed to increase citizens' access to voter registration by, among other things, requiring states to offer voter registration as an option when citizens apply for a driver's license. Registration of eligible voters soon rose about 3.8 percent nationwide, but voting levels failed to rise, especially among the young and the poor, the targets of the measure.[92] "Motor Voter is a howling success as a registration tool," remarked Kentucky's chief election officer, "but turnout is still a dog."[93]

Other disincentives can be blamed on electoral arrangements. U.S. citizens are asked to vote far more often than voters in parliamentary regimes; and election days are held on weekdays, not on the weekend or national holidays. One study found that nearly 30 percent of those registered but not voting said they were too busy or could not take time off from work.[94] Biased or careless election administration can turn away voters or miscount their ballots—as uncovered in voting scandals in Florida (2000), Ohio (2004), and other states and localities. Local election practices often weigh most heavily on minority or socioeconomically disadvantaged (SES) citizens, who are more likely to encounter insufficient numbers of poll workers, antiquated or badly designed voting machines, longer waiting lines, and even official discouragement from going to the polls. Twenty-four states have sought to raise further barriers through voter ID requirements—such as photo IDs or proof-of-citizenship papers.[95] These laws were passed under the pretext of combating "voter fraud," but were really partisan measures intended "to depress voter turnout in minority and poor communities."[96] In 2008 the Supreme Court upheld the strictest such law, Indiana's 2005 statute that requires all voters to present a valid government ID.[97] Federal officials have likewise seemed more eager to pursue voter fraud cases (which are very rare) than those involving discrimination against voters.[98]

State laws govern most aspects of voting, which localities carry out with dizzying diversity. A number of states and localities have, however, modernized their election procedures, making it easier to register and vote. Absentee balloting is common. Some states permit ballots to be submitted over a period of time. Oregon citizens may vote by telephone. And, prompted by the 2000 fiasco, the BCRA raised federal election standards and promised (but did not assure) money to help states meet those standards.

A third explanation for low voter turnout is citizen disaffection. Noncompetitive elections, poor candidates, and contentious or negative campaigning are thought to keep people away from the polling booths. Apathy and cynicism are, to be sure, part of the picture. Surveys sponsored by Harvard University's *Vanishing Voters* project found that four out of ten nonvoters in 2000 claimed to care little about politics and public affairs. A quarter were dismayed or confused by the barrage of campaign messages. And another quarter were simply angry or cynical about politics.[99]

Finally, even conceding all these disincentives, the level of nonvoting may be seriously exaggerated. As Michael P. McDonald of George Mason University concludes, "The much-lamented decline in voter participation is an artifact of the way in which it is measured." In calculating turnout, many scholars fail to take into account the large number of voting-age residents who are not eligible to vote. Sizable and growing segments of the population are not entitled to vote and must be excluded when properly calculating turnout: jailed felons (two million), barred from voting in all but two states; ex-felons (1.4 million), barred from voting in fourteen states; and undocumented aliens (twelve million or more). According to McDonald and Samuel L. Popkin, failure to take account of these ineligible residents "artificially depresses the turnout rate." Recalculating the VAP for every national election since World War II, the two political scientists estimated turnout ranging from 52.7 to 60.6 percent—still nothing to be proud of, but "a lot less dismal than is generally believed."[100]

Biases of Voting. Although voting is the simplest and most accessible form of political involvement, it is still biased in favor of people at the higher rungs of the social and generational ladders—those who are older, more affluent, better educated, and more in touch with political events. Eight in ten people whose annual incomes exceed $50,000 vote in a typical election. This is twice the voting rate of the poor, defined as people with incomes of less than $15,000.

Alternative forms of political participation are even more sharply biased. For example, giving money is mainly an elite activity. In the sample Sidney Verba and his colleagues examined, 35 percent of all political money flowed from the 4 percent of people making more than $125,000 a year. Poor people, who were 19 percent of the sample, made only 2 percent of political donations.[101]

HOW VOTERS DECIDE

What induces voters to cast their ballots for one candidate and not another? As a general rule, voters reach their decisions on the basis of party loyalty. But candidate assessments and salient issues also figure into voters' decisions. The relative strength of these elements varies over time and among specific races.

Although American voters are often uninformed or indifferent about political issues and candidates, they employ what is called low-information rationality, or gut reasoning, to make voting-booth decisions. As Popkin explains, people "triangulate and validate their opinions in conversations with people they trust and according to the opinions of national figures whose judgments and positions they have come to know."[102] Thus voters work through imperfect information to make choices that will often roughly approximate the choices they would have made with more perfect information.

Party Loyalties

Party identification is the single most powerful factor in determining voters' choices. It remains the strongest single correlate of voting in congressional elections. In recent elections, at least nine in every ten Democrats and Republicans voted for their parties' nominees. Independents tend to split their votes more evenly between the parties, though in the most recent elections they have leaned Democratic. In 2006, they veered toward Democratic candidates by a three-to-two margin.[103] In 2008, they preferred Obama to McCain by six percentage points.[104]

According to surveys, most people who claim to be Independents are in fact closet partisans who lean toward one party or the other. These Independent leaners—about a quarter of the total electorate—hold attitudes similar to those of partisans. Not only do they favor one party over the other, but they also share many (though not necessarily all) of the party's values and say they will vote for the party's candidates—if they vote.

Only a small percentage of citizens (5 to 10 percent) are true Independents; they are unpredictable, however, and have dismal turnout rates. "I would encourage candidates not to play to them," advises David Magleby of Brigham Young University, "because they tend to jump on bandwagons, to follow tides. You're better off [working] on getting your weak partisans and your leaners."[105]

Party Decline and Surge. Today's voters are as loyal to their professed party identification as they have ever been.[106] Few voters who identify as either Republicans or Democrats defect from their party when they cast votes in particular congressional races. However, today's high level of party loyalty is a notable shift from the 1970s and 1980s.

Between 1950 and 1980, partisan loyalty declined among the American electorate, with voters identifying with one party and often supporting candidates from the other party. These weakened party ties led to an epidemic of split-ticket voting—with voters supporting one party's presidential candidate and the opposition party's congressional candidate. Between 1952 and 1988 the number of voters who reported in surveys that they split their ticket between presidential and House candidates increased from 12 percent to 25 percent. Those who split their ballots between different parties' House and Senate candidates grew from 9 percent to 27 percent.[107]

Most of these ticket splitters, it turned out, were in the throes of moving from one party to another. White southern conservatives made up a large share of ticket-splitters during this era. Targeted by the GOP's so-called southern strategy, these voters were attracted to such presidential candidates as Barry Goldwater, Richard Nixon, and Ronald Reagan. But southern conservatives kept backing Democrats in congressional and state races because strong Republican candidates often were unwilling to challenge entrenched incumbents, because the Democratic party put up conservative candidates, and because long-serving Democrats won the "personal vote" of constituents: they could deliver more benefits back home through their party's control of legislative chambers. The same phenomenon occurred to a lesser degree in the Northeast, where voters were drawn to the Democrats' national policies and candidates, but continued to support moderate to liberal Republican representatives or senators.[108]

Recent party realignment has brought party affiliation into sync with policy and ideological preferences. Although the process extended over many years, the long Republican courtship of southern conservatives was consummated in 1994. Merle Black of Emory University estimates that more than 80 percent of white conservatives in the South are Republicans; only 10 percent are Democrats.[109] A parallel trend, no less dramatic, has been the Democratic Party's absorption of GOP moderates and liberals. Finding acceptable candidates up and down the ballot, these voters have less need to pick and choose— hence, revived partisanship and dwindling split tickets.

In short, the bulge in split-ticket voting was a by-product of gradual partisan realignment. Over the past five presidential elections, ticket splitting has plummeted to less than 10 percent—exactly the level of fifty years ago. By the same token, the number of congressional districts voting for one party's presidential candidate and the other party's House candidate—which had spiked dramatically—fell back. In 2008 fewer than 19 percent of House members won in districts carried by the opposite party's presidential candidate.

Midterm and Presidential Election Years. Politicians have long talked about coattails: how House and Senate candidates could be pulled into office by the strength of a popular presidential candidate. The idea is that successful presidential candidates will pull in new voters not just for themselves, but for their whole party.

In presidential election years the party that wins the presidency typically does increase its numbers in Congress. As shown in Table 4-2, the winning presidential candidate's party gains on average 15.5 seats in the House and 4.3 seats in the Senate. Boosts for the president's congressional party were considerably more modest in recent election years than they were in the 1930s and 1940s, and George H.W. Bush, Bill Clinton, and George W. Bush all began their presidencies with some congressional seat losses for their party. Nevertheless, political scientists who have analyzed the influence of presidential candidates on the outcome of congressional elections have found that "nontrivial coattail effects have been discernible in recent elections."[110]

TABLE 4-2 **Seats in Congress Gained or Lost by the President's Party in Presidential Election Years, 1934–2008**

| Year | President | Seats gained or lost | |
		House	Senate
1932	Franklin D. Roosevelt (D)	+90	+9
1936	Roosevelt (D)	+12	+7
1940	Roosevelt (D)	+7	−3
1944	Roosevelt (D)	+24	−2
1948	Harry S. Truman (D)	+75	+9
1952	Dwight D. Eisenhower (R)	+22	+1
1956	Eisenhower (R)	−2	−1
1960	John F. Kennedy (D)	−22	+2
1964	Lyndon B. Johnson (D)	+37	+1
1968	Richard M. Nixon (R)	+5	+6
1972	Nixon (R)	+12	−2
1976	Jimmy Carter (D)	+1	0
1980	Ronald Reagan (R)	+34	+12
1984	Reagan (R)	+14	−2
1988	George H. W. Bush (R)	−2	0
1992	Bill Clinton (D)	−10	0
1996	Clinton (D)	−9	−2
2000	George W. Bush (R)	−3	−4
2004	Bush (R)	+3	+4
2008	Barack Obama (D)	+21	+8
Average seats gained (20 elections)		+15.5	+4.3

Source: Compiled by the authors.

Ronald Reagan, for example, boosted his party's congressional votes by 2 to 3 percent in 1980 and 5 percent in 1984.[111] In 1996 President Clinton's reelection added about 2.6 percentage points to Democrats' House and Senate totals. President Obama began his presidency with the largest increases in his party's numbers in Congress for any president since Reagan in 1980.

The president's party normally suffers significant reversals in the midterm congressional elections. As evident in Table 4-3, the effect was so consistent and

TABLE 4-3	**Midterm Fortunes of Presidential Parties, 1934–2006**		

		Seats gained or lost	
Year	President	House	Senate
1934	Franklin D. Roosevelt (D)	+9	+10
1938	Roosevelt (D)	−71	−6
1942	Roosevelt (D)	−55	−9
1946	Roosevelt and Harry S. Truman (D)	−45	−12
1950	Truman (D)	−29	−6
1954	Dwight D. Eisenhower (R)	−18	−1
1958	Eisenhower (R)	−48	−13
1962	John F. Kennedy (D)	−4	+3
1966	Lyndon B. Johnson (D)	−47	−4
1970	Richard M. Nixon (R)	−12	+2
1974	Nixon and Gerald R. Ford (R)	−48	−5
1978	Jimmy Carter (D)	−15	−3
1982	Ronald Reagan (R)	−26	+1
1986	Reagan (R)	−5	−8
1990	George H. W. Bush (R)	−8	−1
1994	Bill Clinton (D)	−52	−8
1998	Clinton (D)	+5	0
2002	George W. Bush (R)	+7	+2
2006	Bush (R)	−31	−6
Average seats lost (19 elections)		−25.9	−3.4

Source: Compiled by the authors.

dramatic that political scientists regarded it as nearly a natural law of American politics. In midterm elections since 1934 the presidential party has lost an average of 26 House seats and 3.4 Senate seats.

The 1998 and 2002 results were anomalies, however. Democrats gained five seats in the House and held their own in the Senate in 1998, in the midst of President Clinton's impeachment proceedings. While voters deplored Clinton's personal behavior, his job ratings remained robust; Republicans were rebuked for insisting on impeaching him. Four years later President Bush's GOP gained seven House and two Senate seats, no doubt because of the post-9/11 rally effect. The only other anomaly occurred in 1934, when President Franklin D. Roosevelt's popularity strengthened the Democrats' grip on both chambers.

One theory to explain this pattern is known as "surge and decline." This theory posited that the visibility and excitement of a winning presidential campaign attracts intermittent voters who tend to support the president's party in downticket races. When these presidential candidates are not on the ballot, the shrunken electorate of midterm years contains fewer supporters of the president's party. That is, a presidential surge, swollen by less motivated voters attracted by presidential campaigns, is followed two years later by a decline as intermittent voters drop out of the electorate. But other studies suggest that midterm voters are no more or less partisan than those in presidential years and share most of their demographic characteristics.[112]

Another theory argues that midterm elections serve in part as a referendum on the president's popularity and performance in office during the previous two years.[113] Voters may hold the president's party responsible for unpopular military ventures, economic reverses, or a declining political or moral climate. In some midterm years, the referendum aspect is hard to discern. But no other single factor better explains such outcomes as the Democrats' 1974 post-Watergate bonus of fifty-two representatives and four senators, their 1982 recession harvest of twenty-six House seats, Republicans' 1994 bonanza, and the Democrats' retaking of the majority in 2006. In that year, no less than 36 percent of citizens—the highest such figure in the last five midterm contests—regarded their midterm vote as one against President Bush (whose approval rating at the time was 40 percent).[114] The opposition Democrats picked up thirty seats in the House and six in the Senate.

The Appeal of Candidates

"My theory on politics is ultimately that people vote for the person they like most," declared the revered former senator David Pryor, D-Ark. (1979–1997).[115] Apart from partisan loyalties, the appeal of given candidates is the strongest force in congressional voting. Not surprisingly, candidate appeal normally tilts toward incumbents. When voters abandon their party to vote for House or Senate candidates, they usually vote for incumbents.

Incumbency, Yet Again. As discussed in Chapter 3, incumbents rarely lose their bids for reelection. Indeed, incumbents' success rates go well beyond what one should expect, given the partisan character of their constituencies. In other words, the sheer fact of incumbency offers advantages in that candidates fare better running as incumbents than they would running as nonincumbents.[116]

To measure this advantage, scholars often look to the "sophomore surge" and the "retirement slump." The sophomore surge refers to the average gain in vote share won by candidates running for reelection for the first time, compared to their performance in their first election. The retirement slump is the average drop in a party's vote share when an incumbent retires and the seat opens up. Scholars then average together these two calculations into a single index, known as the "slurge," that is often used to measure overall incumbency advantage. According to this measure, contemporary incumbents enjoy about a six-percentage point increase in their share of the vote simply by virtue of being incumbents.[117] Incumbency confers powerful benefits upon officeholders who shrewdly exploit their available resources.

Incumbents are better known than their opponents. Jacobson surely captures the normal state of affairs when he observes that "most incumbents face obscure, politically inexperienced opponents whose resources fall far short of what is necessary to mount a formidable campaign."[118] Even if voters cannot recall officeholders' names in an interview, they can recognize and express opinions about them when the names are presented to them—as in the voting booth. In National Election Study (NES) surveys spanning almost thirty years, nearly all respondents were able to recognize and rate Senate and House incumbents running for reelection (means of 97 percent and 92 percent, respectively). Senate challengers were recognized and rated by 77 percent of the respondents, House challengers by only 53 percent. Open-seat candidates fell somewhere between incumbents and challengers in visibility. The unequal visibility of candidates is a key context for voting decisions.[119]

In evaluating candidates, voters normally favor incumbents over challengers. Voters in the NES surveys tend to evaluate incumbents according to personal characteristics and noncontroversial activities such as casework and constituent outreach. Even on the issues, references to incumbents were overwhelmingly positive. More than two-thirds claimed to have agreed with their legislator's votes, although only one in ten could cite how the representative had voted on a piece of legislation during the preceding two years. On the eve of the 2008 balloting, in a year in which overall approval of Congress was at a historic low,[120] 57 percent of likely voters agreed that their member of Congress deserved reelection.[121]

Incumbents' popularity depends in large part upon their success in shaping information that constituents receive about them and their performance— through advertising, credit claiming, and position taking.[122] Not surprisingly, voters report having high levels of contact with House and Senate incumbents. The more contact voters have with their legislators, the more positive their evaluations are likely to be. According to NES surveys, at least nine out of ten voters said they had some form of contact with their representative. A fifth of them reported having met the lawmaker in person. Many constituents receive mail from their representatives or read about them in newspapers. Virtually all voters reported some contacts with their senators, mostly through mailings, TV appearances, or other media coverage.

Incumbents far outpace their challengers in visibility, though the visibility gap between incumbents and challengers is wider in House races than in Senate races. Half of voters, at best, report contact with House challengers, but as many as 85 percent of voters report contacts with Senate challengers (mostly through media coverage or candidate mailings).

Senate and House. These findings help explain why senators are more vulnerable at the polls than are their House counterparts. First, surveys indicate that representatives are more warmly regarded than senators—probably because they are judged more on positive actions, such as personal contacts or constituent service, whereas senators are more closely linked to divisive national issues.

Second, Senate challengers are far more conspicuous than House challengers. Senate contests are more widely reported by the media, and challengers can gain almost as much exposure as incumbents. Media coverage of House races is more fragmentary than that of Senate races, throwing more weight to incumbents' techniques of contacting voters.

Third, senators cannot manipulate voter contacts as much as representatives do. Voters get their information about Senate races largely through organized media, which senators do not control. Representatives gain exposure through focused means—personal appearances, mailings, and newsletters—which they fashion to their own advantage. "Somewhat ironically," observed Michael J. Robinson, "powerful senators are less able to control their images than 'invisible' House members."[123] Finally, Senate elections are simply more competitive than House elections. That is, one-party states are rarer, proportionately, than one-party congressional districts. Further, it is often easier to recruit well-known, well-financed Senate challengers. Among the several challengers who won Senate contests in 2008 was nationally-known political comedian Al Franken—who took on incumbent Minnesota GOP senator Norm Coleman in a razor-close contest whose results remained undecided for months.

Among senators, constituency size is a crucial variable in elections. Small-state senators in many respects resemble representatives. Compared with their large-state colleagues, they are more visible, more accessible, and more able to raise the campaign money they need. But they are not electorally safer—probably because their challengers, too, have an easier time mounting their campaigns and gaining visibility.[124]

Issue Voting

Issue preferences and even ideological beliefs figure prominently in congressional campaigns. A significant number of voters are attuned to issues and base their choices on a specific issue or cluster of issues. Not a few elections turn on those margins.

Congressional Party Platforms. Partisans care deeply about the issues with which their parties are linked. In studying the 1998 House elections, Owen Abbe and his colleagues found that "voters are more likely to support candidates whom they deem competent on their issues." They concluded that "party leaders and individual candidates must campaign on a well-defined agenda for party-owned issues to have an impact."[125]

At least since the mid-1970s, congressional parties have forged campaign platforms. The most notable example was the Contract with America, the brainchild of then-Rep. Newt Gingrich of Georgia, signed by more than three

FIGURE 4-2 Who Were the Voters in 2006?

Percentage of Voters		For Democrat		For Republican
	Total Vote	**53**		**45**
79	White	47		51
10	Black	89		10
8	Hispanic	69		30
2	Asian	62		37
49	Men	50		47
51	Women	55		43
12	18–29 years old	60		38
24	30–44 years old	53		45
34	45–59 years old	53		46
29	60 and older	50		48
3	Did not complete high school	64		35
21	High school graduate	55		44
31	Some college education	51		47
45	College graduate	53		46
44	White Protestants	37		61
24	White fundamentalist	28		70
26	Catholics	55		44
2	Jewish	87		12
7	Family income under $15,000	67		30
12	$15,000–$29,999	61		36
21	$30,000–$49,999	56		43
22	$50,000–$74,999	50		48
39	over $75,000	49		50
36	Republicans	8		91
26	Independents	57		39
38	Democrats	93		7
22	East	63		35
27	Midwest	52		47
30	South	45		53
21	West	54		43

Source: Adapted from Harold W. Stanley and Richard G. Niemi, *Vital Statistics on American Politics, 2007–2008* (Washington, D.C.: CQ Press, 2007), Table 3-10.

Notes: Percentages based on Democratic, Republican, and other (not shown) votes. Data based on questionnaires completed by voters leaving polling places around the nation on election day. 2006 data are shown because they reflect voters' party preferences in congressional elections without the complicating presence of a presidential contest.

hundred Republican candidates on the steps of the Capitol's West Front in September 1994.[126] It was a set of ten proposals that included a balanced-budget amendment, a presidential line-item veto, internal House reforms, term limits for lawmakers, and policy proposals on crime, welfare, business regulation, and tax cuts. If a GOP majority were elected, the candidates pledged that they would put the measures to a House floor vote within the first hundred days of the new Congress. Flush with victory that November, Speaker-elect Gingrich quickly claimed a popular mandate to enact the Contract with America. House Republicans staged votes on most of these items, but in the end few became law.

More than a year before the 2006 balloting, Senate Democrats announced they would campaign for a five-point agenda—embracing such universally-supported goals as national security, energy independence, and economic strength. Their House counterparts, led by then-Minority Leader Nancy Pelosi of California, came up with a similarly broad "Six for '06" platform. When Pelosi became Speaker, she pursued the so-called 100-legislative-hour plan to gain approval of six measures—involving the minimum wage, stem cell research, health care, national security, education, and energy. House action was completed after some forty-two legislative hours. As with Gingrich's GOP plan twelve years earlier, however, many of the new House majority's proposals were thwarted by Senate inaction or presidential opposition.

Issues and Partisanship. Voters' responses to political issues show up in the different patterns of choice displayed by demographic groups. (See Figure 4-2.) Americans sort themselves out politically according to their age, sex, income, education, race or ethnicity, region, and even by frequency of attendance at religious services.

A demographic snapshot of the two parties' voters would start at the much-discussed gender gap, the difference in voting between men and women. Women lean toward Democratic candidates, men toward Republicans. The gender gap appears in virtually all recent contests. As pollster Celinda Lake remarked, "You'll get [a gender gap] in a race for dogcatcher in Montana, if it's a Republican against a Democrat."[127] The gender gap was seven percentage points in 2008 and has been as much as ten percentage points in other recent elections. The explanation for the gender gap probably lies in differing responses to political and social issues. Men are generally more favorable toward military expenditures, tough anti-crime laws, and restrictions on welfare recipients and immigrants. Women respond more positively than men to social programs such as government-sponsored health benefits, job training, child care, and assistance to needy families.[128]

A host of similar patterns is found among congressional voters. "There's a family gap, a generation gap, a gender gap," said GOP pollster Neil Newhouse of the fissures among the voting population.[129] Many of the patterns are familiar. The Republicans attract upper-income and conservative voters; the Democrats engage lower-income and liberal voters. The Republicans draw upon married people, white Protestants, regular churchgoers, gun owners, and small business owners; the Democrats attract singles, African Americans, mainstream Catholics, Jews, seculars, and occasional churchgoers. Such loyalties are built on issues and themes adopted by parties and candidates over the years.

Issues and Campaigns. Legislators and their advisers are highly sensitive to voters' expected reactions to stands on issues. Much energy is devoted to framing positions, communicating them (sometimes in deliberately vague language), and assessing their effect. Moreover, every professional politician can relate cases in which issues tipped an election one way or another. Frequently cited is the electoral influence of single-interest groups. Some citizens vote according to a single issue they regard as paramount, such as gun control, abortion, or gay marriage. Even if few in numbers, such voters can decide close contests. That is why legislators often shrink from taking positions on hot-button issues such as these.

Public policy issues also have powerful indirect effects upon election outcomes. Issues motivate "opinion leaders," voters who can influence support far beyond their single vote. Issues are carefully monitored by organized interests and their PACs, which can channel or withhold funds, publicity, and volunteer workers for the candidate's cause. Legislators devote time and attention to promoting and explaining issues to attentive publics because it pays for them to do so.

ELECTION OUTCOMES

The two Congresses are manifested throughout congressional elections. House and Senate contests are waged one by one on local turf, but always against a backdrop of national events, issues, and partisan alignments. The involvement of national party entities and their allied interest groups has imposed a greater degree of national coordination upon congressional campaigns, especially those in marginal states and districts. The resulting fusion of local and national forces shapes the content and results of congressional elections.

Party Balance

Despite the oft-claimed independence of candidates and voters, virtually all races are run under either the Democratic or Republican party label, fought on playing fields tilted toward one party or the other, and aimed mainly at loyalists who are likely to turn out for their parties' candidates.

Shifting Majorities. As discussed in Chapter 3, the overall partisan outcomes of the 2008 contests were largely fixed months and even years before the actual balloting. First, the parties' successes or failures over the recruitment season determined whether quality candidates or long-shot contenders were on the ballots. Many of the Republican losses of 2008—twenty-one seats in the House and eight seats in the Senate—can be attributed to a larger number of retirements among Republican than Democratic incumbents.[130] In the House, Republicans had to defend twenty-seven seats opened up because of retiring incumbents, while Democrats only had to protect six open seats. In the Senate, five Republicans and no Democrats retired. At the same time, a political environment favorable to Democrats helped the party recruit strong challengers for the 2008 elections, while Republicans had difficulty inducing good candidates to risk a congressional bid.[131]

Second, many states and districts are generally safe for one party or the other. Although Democrats enjoyed a good recruitment season in the 2008 cycle, many safe Republican constituencies still remained. At most, 25 percent of all House races and no more than 20 percent of Senate elections were even remotely competitive.[132]

Either the Democrats or the Republicans have controlled Congress since 1855. (Appendix A lists the partisan majorities in the House and Senate since 1901.) Between 1896 and 1920 the two parties had approximately equal numbers of partisans in the electorate, but lower participation rates in Democratic areas favored the Republicans. The GOP's relative position improved further after 1920, when women received the vote.

The New Deal realignment of the 1930s shifted the balance to the Democrats. For many years after that, the Democrats were virtually a perennial majority and the Republicans a permanent minority on Capitol Hill. Between 1932 and 1994, the Republicans controlled both chambers simultaneously for only four years (1947–1949, 1953–1955) and the Senate alone for six years (1981–1987). Democratic sweeps in 1958, 1964, and 1974 padded their majorities. Republicans found the Democratic dominance in Congress hard to overcome, even in years when voters strongly backed Republican presidential candidates. Incumbents effectively exploited their reelection assets, thus maintaining Democratic control.

In 1994, for the first time in forty years, Republicans won control of both houses of Congress. Not one Republican incumbent was defeated that year, while thirty-one Democratic representatives and two senators lost their seats. In succeeding elections Republicans clung to their narrow majority in the House, with Democrats gaining ten seats (1996), then five (1998), and two (2000). Democrats pulled even with Republicans in the Senate in 2000, but in 2002 and 2004, the Republicans added to their majorities in both chambers.

In 2006, Democrats returned to majority status in both House and Senate. Democrats then expanded these margins of control in the 2008 elections. Indeed, a major question in the lead-up to the 2008 elections was whether Democrats would reach sixty seats in the Senate, a threshold that could allow the party to overcome the Senate minority party's ability to filibuster and obstruct majority party initiatives.[133]

Regional Patterns. Recent elections have cemented long-term shifts in the two parties' power bases. Historically, the Grand Old Party was dominant in the populous states of the Northeast and Midwest. "The Democracy," by contrast, owned the solid South from the Civil War era through the 1970s, as well as the large urban political machines. Today, many of the old patterns are precisely reversed, with the Republican Party dominant in the South and the Democratic Party ascendant in the Northeast.[134] The tectonic plates of political alliances move slowly, but they sometimes produce changes of earthquake proportions.

The 1994 earthquake signaled the Republicans' conquest of the South. For the first time in history, the GOP claimed a majority of the South's seats. The party's grip on the region continued to tighten in the ensuing decade. Republicans now claim 55 percent of House seats and 68 percent of Senate seats from the eleven states of the Confederacy. The modern-day GOP is the party of choice for conservative white southerners and unquestionably their true philosophical home.

Regionally, the South and the Mountain West form the backbone of the congressional GOP. Indeed, between 43 and 45 percent of the Republican conference in both chambers is now from the South, even though that region only accounts for a quarter of the Senate and a third of House districts. In the Mountain West the party claims 61 percent of senators and 39 percent of House districts. The Upper Midwest, from Ohio to Wisconsin, is generally a competitive region, with Republicans controlling 42 percent of the region's House seats, but only 21 percent of its Senate seats.

Democrats are strongest on the edges of the national map—the two coasts and parts of the Upper Midwest. The eleven states of New England and the mid-Atlantic are overwhelmingly Democratic (though some have lost population and thus House seats). In these states (all were in the Democratic party's presidential column in 2004 and 2008), the party claims 75 percent of House seats and seventeen of twenty-two Senate seats. The GOP lost its last remaining New England House seat when Rep. Chris Shays, R-Conn., was defeated for reelection in 2008. Similarly, Democrats dominate the country's westernmost coast. In the four Pacific-rim states (excluding Alaska), all were won by Democratic candidates in the last three presidential elections—Democrats control forty-five of sixty-nine House seats and all eight Senate seats.

Looking beyond such regional patterns, the two parties tend to represent different kinds of districts. Democratic strength lies in cities, inner suburbs, and majority-minority districts, including those in the South and Midwest. Republicans dominate rural, small town, and exurban areas. Relatedly, Democratic voters are more packed together in the districts held by Democrats than are Republican voters in the districts held by their party, meaning that Democratic candidates tend to win by larger majorities than Republican winners normally do. Put another way, more Democratic votes are wasted (that is, inefficiently distributed across congressional districts), giving the GOP a structural advantage.[135]

Polarized Parties, Polarized Voters? Underlying this geographic distribution is what might be called a cultural divide between the two parties. Democrats tend to represent urban areas, where most voters favor social welfare spending and environmental and other business regulations. Urban voters also tend to take a more tolerant view on the diversity of racial, ethnic, and sexual identities. Republicans tend to be traditionalists—economic and cultural conservatives who promote businesses large and small, advocate certain religious causes, and generously support military expenditures. Such long-standing issue commitments flatly contradict anyone who claims that there is scant difference between the two parties.

How pervasive are these partisan differences within the electorate? Political elites—candidates, officeholders, activists, and strong party identifiers—have long been found at the extremes of the ideological spectrum: Democrats to the left, Republicans to the right.[136] Such activists do not represent the majority of citizens, average voters, or even average party identifiers. Most voters identify as either "moderate" or refuse to use any ideological term to describe themselves.[137] If recent surveys are to be believed, however, rank-and-file party identifiers have become more ideologically polarized than in the past.[138] Many, after all, respond to the rising amount of ideological rhetoric in the contemporary political context, including that dispensed by congressional representatives and biased cable, Internet, and other news outlets. Moreover, these loyal voters are ardently wooed by parties and candidates—who seek reliable supporters (rather than waverers) to turn out at the polls.

Party Alignment and Realignment

Historically, political upheavals have shifted party control in the House or Senate with decisive results. Political scientists and journalists often talk of "critical elections" or "critical periods," in which one party yields preeminence to another, or major voting groups alter the shape of the parties' coalitions, or both. Such watershed eras include the Civil War, the turbulent 1890s, the New Deal of the 1930s, the Republican revolution of 1994. Each of these upheavals brought to Capitol Hill new lawmakers, new voting patterns, and new legislative priorities.[139]

Between the Civil Rights upheavals of the 1960s and the middle of the 1990s, the congressional party system went through a gradual transformation that realigned the parties on ideological lines and brought them into competitive balance. The Republican Party achieved ideological consistency by coopting southern and rural conservatives and by shedding most of its moderate wing—especially members from Northeastern, mid-Atlantic, and Pacific states. In losing most of the South to Republicans, the Democrats also became more ideologically coherent. Long split by divisions between conservative southerners and northern liberals, the Democratic party of the 1990s was smaller than in the past, but considerably more unified.

The intriguing question is whether the 2006 and 2008 elections represent a temporary roadblock for Republicans or an enduring shift in Americans' attitudes toward the parties and their approaches to governing. In some respects, the recent elections just continue trends set during the 1990s. The Republican Party now dominates the South and is a minority in almost every other region. Rep. Peter King, R-N.Y., for example, is now the last remaining

Republican east of the Hudson River. Along with their losses outside the South, Republicans lost many of their moderate voices. With the retirements of senators John Warner in Virginia and Wayne Allard in Colorado and the defeats of senators John Sununu in New Hampshire, Gordon Smith in Oregon, and Norm Coleman in Minnesota, the Senate Republican conference is notably more conservative. Accordingly, the party's congressional leaders uniformly hail from its conservative wing.

However, the 2008 elections made the Democratic caucus more diverse, with members representing a broader coalition in terms of geography and ideology. Democrats won some surprising victories in rural and exurban areas—conservative territory—in 2008. They won seats in rural areas of Colorado, Michigan, Nevada, New Mexico, and southwestern Alabama. They captured the military-oriented district in Norfolk and Virginia Beach of Rep. Thelma Drake, R-Va. They won Maryland's first district on its rural eastern shore. They even picked up a seat in rural Idaho. The ranks of the conservative Blue Dog Coalition grew. As a result of its recent victories, the Democratic party has become larger and more ideologically diverse.

Realignments of the party system are only apparent in hindsight. It is possible that the post-2006 Democrats will enjoy an enduring congressional majority, especially given the hurdles to defeating incumbents. It is likely, though, that Democrats will have difficulty retaining many of their new holdings. If so, today's party system will remain in the same tight competitive balance characteristic of the 1990s, even though Democrats enjoy margins of control wider than any held by Republicans during their recent period of majority status.

Turnover and Representation

Reelection rates should not be confused with turnover rates. Even in years when few members are turned out of office by the voters, many leave Capitol Hill voluntarily—to retire, to run for another office, or to follow other pursuits. In other words, a natural process of membership change is continuous. When the new Congress convened in January 2009, a majority of senators and representatives had served less than a decade. Fifteen senators and fifty-seven representatives are newcomers to the 111th Congress.[140]

For Congress to be a responsive institution, constant turnover of members is a given—whether by steady increments or by watershed elections. Even when few lawmakers are turned out of office, all of them are keenly aware of the threat of defeat. Most take steps to prevent that eventuality by continually monitoring constituents' needs and opinions through personal visits and polls. But are voters' views accurately reflected by the representatives they elect to Congress? This question is not easily answered. Popular control of policymakers is not the same thing as popular control of policies. Constituents' views are not precisely mirrored by legislators' voting behavior and the laws passed by the legislature.

CONCLUSION

What link exists between voters' attitudes and members' voting on issues? Miller and Stokes found that constituency attitudes correlated differently according to the kind of policy.[141] In foreign affairs a negative correlation existed between constituents' attitudes and legislators' votes (a gap that persists to this day); in social and economic welfare issues the correlation was moderate; in civil rights issues the correlation was very high. In other words, in at least one and possibly two major policy areas the linkage was weak enough to cast some doubt on constituency control.

Political scientists explain the absence of strong linkages by noting how difficult it is to meet all the conditions needed for popular control of policies. Voters would have to identify the candidates' positions on issues, and they would have to vote by referring to those positions. Differences among candidates would have to be transparent, and winners would have to vote in accord with their preelection attitudes. These conditions are not routinely met. Candidates' stands are not always clear, and candidates do not invariably differentiate themselves on issues.

Nonetheless, winning candidates learn from their campaign experiences, even from issues raised by their opponents. "Issue uptake" is the term coined by political scientist Tracy Sulkin to describe this effect. From her study of the issue agendas of 473 House and Senate campaigns and the winners' subsequent legislative activity, she demonstrates that the victors embrace many of their opponents' campaign themes when they return to Capitol Hill. "Congressional campaigns have a clear legacy in the content of legislators' agendas," she writes, "influencing the areas in which they choose to be active and the intensity with which they pursue these activities."[142] Legislative responsiveness is best thought of as a process:

> It begins in campaigns as candidates learn about the salience of issues and their strengths and weaknesses on them; continues throughout winning legislators' terms in office, influencing not just how they vote but also the content of legislation they introduce, cosponsor, and speak about on the floor; goes on to inform their career decisions and future electoral prospects; and leaves a tangible trace on public policy outputs.[143]

If ideological or attitudinal links between voters and their representatives are rough and variable, actual contacts between constituents and individual legislators are numerous and palpable. Much of lawmakers' time and effort while in office is devoted to responding to the folks back home. Constituency politics are ever present in the daily lives of senators and representatives. The two Congresses are distinct, but inextricably linked.

SUGGESTED READINGS

Cain, Bruce, John Ferejohn, and Morris Fiorina. *The Personal Vote: Constituency Service and Electoral Independence.* Cambridge: Harvard University Press, 1987.

Dolan, Kathy. *Voting for Women: How the Public Evaluates Women Candidates.* Boulder, Colo.: Westview Press, 2003.

Fiorina, Morris P., Samuel J. Abrams, and Jeremy C. Pope. *Culture War? The Myth of Polarized America,* 2nd ed. New York: Pearson Longman, 2005.

Herrnson, Paul S. *Congressional Elections: Campaigning at Home and in Washington.* 5th ed. Washington, D.C.: CQ Press, 2008.

Jacobson, Gary C. *The Politics of Congressional Elections.* 6th ed. New York: Pearson Longman, 2004.

Krasno, Jonathan S. *Challengers, Competition, and Reelection.* New Haven: Yale University Press, 1994.

Sulkin, Tracy. *Issue Politics in Congress.* Cambridge and New York: Cambridge University Press, 2005.

Thurber, James A., ed. *The Battle for Congress: Consultants, Candidates, and Voters.* Washington, D.C.: Brookings Institution, 2001.

Wattenburg, Martin. *Is Voting for Young People?* New York: Pearson Longman, 2007.

*L*awmakers on the Hill and at Home. Sen. Max Baucus (D-Mont.) shovels dirt as part of his "work days" program at a highway construction site north of Kalispell, Montana (top left). On Capitol Hill, as chair of the Senate Finance Committee (bottom left, with ranking Republican Charles Grassley of Iowa standing to the right), Baucus oversees Senate negotiation on health care reform—a prime goal of President Obama. Two House candidates meet with voters in 2008: Aaron Schock (R-Ill.) appears at the Illinois State Fair (top right), while Lynn Jenkins (R-Kan.) talks with voters in Valley Falls, Kansas (bottom right). Schock captured the Peoria, Illinois, seat vacated by Rep. Ray LaHood (chosen as the Obama administration's Transportation Secretary); Jenkins ousted a Democratic incumbent in her Wichita, Kansas, district.

chapter 5

Being There: Hill Styles and Home Styles

"We are Americans; we're different from Canada, we're different than the United Kingdom," explained Sen. Max Baucus (D-Mont.). "We have to come up with a uniquely American solution, probably a combination of private and public coverage."[1] Baucus was leading a discussion on health care issues at St. Peter's Hospital in Helena, the Montana state capital—in the sort of town hall meeting that members of Congress regularly hold around the country. But Baucus was no ordinary member of Congress seeking his constituents' views on health care. As chair of the Senate's powerful Finance Committee, Baucus is a central congressional player in the Obama administration's attempts to overhaul the nation's health insurance system.

It is safe to say that Max Baucus is no household name. A low-profile senator from one of the nation's least populated states, Baucus is nevertheless "arguably the most consequential legislator in America."[2] A considerable share of the most significant legislation of recent years bears Baucus's mark. While in the minority party in 2001, Baucus worked closely with Senate Finance Committee Chair Charles Grassley, R-Iowa, to shepherd President Bush's $1.35 trillion tax cut through a chamber divided 50–50 between Republicans and Democrats.[3] In 2003, Baucus was one of only two Democrats permitted in the room during conference committee negotiations over landmark legislation creating a new federal prescription drug benefit program for seniors.[4] He was a prominent leader on the 2009 reauthorization of the State Children's Health Insurance Program, the 2007 minimum wage increase, the 2004 major corporate tax cut, and the 2000 fight for normalizing trade relations with China.[5] With his broad-ranging influence, Baucus is a resource for other members seeking to accomplish their own goals. "He gets bombarded by members with pet issues," remarks a former committee staffer. "Every time he walks on the floor he comes back with 12 sticky notes. And he looks at that as a way of putting legislation together."[6]

Baucus's reputation as a lawmaker is matched only by his reputation for constituency service. On his desk stands a plaque that reads, "Montana comes first."[7] He grants open access to Montanans: "He still takes all phone calls from constituents, unscreened."[8] Baucus is renowned for his ability to bring federal dollars to Montana. Dubbed a "high plains grifter" by the *Washington Post*,[9] Baucus has coaxed federal help for his state, including its roads, farmers, ranchers, and doctors. The shape of national policy is indelibly influenced by the concerns of Baucus's local constituency. To get out of Baucus's Finance Committee, trade legislation must take account of Montana's beef producers.[10] Health legislation must make special provision for rural providers.[11]

Baucus's political success has not always come easy. Representing a state that has voted Republican in nine of the last ten presidential elections, Baucus has faced some tough electoral challenges, and so takes nothing for granted. To stay in close touch with constituents, he schedules regular "work days," working a full day alongside Montanans in various jobs and professions.[12] He consistently raises large sums for his reelection efforts, long before the identity of his challenger is known. In 2008, Baucus raised more than $11 million, opened nine offices around the state, employed more than fifty campaign workers, and spent thousands of dollars on television ads.[13] In the end, having failed to find a top-tier candidate, the GOP was stuck with self-recruited Bob Kelleher, an eighty-five-year old perennial aspirant who raised virtually no money and who took idiosyncratic political positions.[14] Baucus was reelected with 73 percent of the vote.

Local champion and national leader, Max Baucus personifies the two Congresses. All members live and work in these two worlds: one on Capitol Hill and the other back home in their states and districts.

HILL STYLES

Congress is a body of transplanted locals who naturally speak up for their constituents. A majority of representatives in one survey agreed with the statement: "I seldom have to sound out my constituents because I think so much like them that I know how to react to almost any proposal."[15] However, the ability of Congress to reflect the nation's large and varied population is affected by the diversity of its membership. There is no substitute for having a member of one's own group in a position of influence, and many groups do not receive representation commensurate with their presence in the population.

Who Are the Legislators?

The Constitution names only three criteria for individuals serving in Congress: age, citizenship, and residency. However, entrance requirements are far more restrictive. Elections, as Aristotle first observed, are essentially oligarchic affairs that involve few active participants.

By almost any measure, senators and representatives constitute an economic and social elite. They are well educated. They come from prestigious occupations. The pay of senators and representatives ($169,300 in fiscal year 2009) alone puts them in the top 1 percent of the nation's wage earners, but many members also have earned or inherited considerable wealth. In 2008 nearly two-thirds of senators and 39 percent of House members were millionaires.[16]

The elite character of the congressional membership raises questions of representation. One central purpose of a representative body is to bring together diverse individuals to deliberate on public policy. When the diversity of viewpoints is systematically limited, important interests and concerns within society are likely to be overlooked or undervalued. As John Stuart Mill argued nearly a century and a half ago, "In the absence of its natural defenders, the interest of the omitted is always in danger of being overlooked; and when looked at, is seen with very different eyes from those of the persons whom it directly concerns."[17]

To meet Mill's standards for representation, must Congress closely mirror the demographics of the populace? Hannah Finichel Pitkin distinguishes between two types of representation: *descriptive* and *substantive*.[18] "Descriptive representation" refers to whether a legislature's membership reflects the diversity of backgrounds and interests in society. "Substantive representation" occurs when legislators consciously act as agents for constituents and their interests, an activity legislators can perform regardless of their personal background or group memberships. Legislators from farming districts can voice farmers' concerns even though they have never plowed a field; whites can champion equal opportunities for minorities. Few Asian Americans serve in Congress, but their proportion in a district affects a member's support of issues advocated by that group.[19]

Although descriptive and substantive representation are distinct concepts, a wide range of empirical research has found that they are intertwined in the real world. The social identity of legislators affects representation in myriad ways. Representatives' racial, ethnic, and gender identities shape their priorities, positions, and legislative styles.[20] Whether constituents and representatives share a common identity has also been shown to affect trust and patterns of contact between them.[21]

Education and Occupation. By every measure, Congress is a highly educated body. Some 95 percent of the members have university degrees. Two-thirds have graduate degrees. Seventeen have medical degrees.

Historically, law and politics have been closely linked in the United States. A humorist once quipped that the U.S. government "of laws and not men" is really "of lawyers and not men." When the 111th Congress convened in January 2009, 167 representatives and 57 senators were law school graduates.[22]

That a large number of members have law degrees does not necessarily mean that they possess extensive experience in the practice of law. "They are not, by and large, successful lawyers who left thriving partnerships to run for public office," observes Alan Ehrenhalt, "Rather, they are political activists with law degrees."[23] Legal training develops skills that are useful in gaining and holding public office, such as verbalization, advocacy, and negotiation. A law degree also serves as a stepping-stone into public service at many levels. Congressional staffers are often expected to have law degrees, for example, and many members of Congress start out on Capitol Hill as staff aides. The 111th Congress contains 112 former congressional staffers. Lawyers also monopolize elected law enforcement and judicial posts, two other pathways to Congress.

The historical dominance of lawyers on Capitol Hill has nonetheless declined in recent decades. Lawyers are now outnumbered by members with other careers. Today's Congress is filled with professional public servants or, in common parlance, "career politicians." The 111th Congress included thirteen former governors, ten lieutenant governors, three former cabinet secretaries, a former secretary of the Navy, a federal judge, three state supreme court justices, and thirty-eight mayors. More than half of all members of the House previously served in their state or territorial legislatures. Nearly half of the Senate (forty-five senators) are former House members.[24]

Many members of Congress have served in the military, though the veterans' ranks have thinned over time. Following World War II, returning veterans surged into Congress. Among them were Reps. John F. Kennedy, D-Mass.; Richard M. Nixon, R-Calif.; Gerald R. Ford, R-Mich.; and Bob Dole, R-Kan. By the 1970s more than seven of ten members were veterans. As World War II faded from view and draftees were replaced by a volunteer force, fewer veterans have been elected. About a quarter of the 111th Congress's members have served in the military.[25]

Today's media-centered campaigns have spawned a few celebrity legislators. Several astronauts, including Sen. Bill Nelson, D-Fla., have served. Former athletes and coaches in the 111th Congress include a member of the Baseball Hall of Fame: Sen. Jim Bunning, R-Ky., who once pitched a perfect game for the Philadelphia Phillies.

Many occupations are, and always have been, drastically underrepresented in Congress. Low-status occupations—including farm labor, service trades, manual and skilled labor, and domestic service—are rare on Capitol Hill. Not a few members, however, held menial jobs at some point in their lives. At a hearing on Social Security taxes for household help, for example, Rep. Carrie P. Meek, D-Fla. (1993–2003), a granddaughter of slaves, brought her own vivid experiences to the proceedings. "I was once a domestic worker," she told her colleagues. "My mother was a domestic worker. All my sisters were domestic workers."[26] Such perspectives are valuable for congressional representation and deliberation.

Race. African Americans, who make up 13.5 percent of the nation's population, account for 8 percent of Congress's members. In 2009, forty-two African Americans (including two delegates) served in the House and one in the Senate; all were Democrats. Although their representation in Congress does not reflect the proportion of African Americans in the nation's population, black legislators are beginning to occupy positions of greater influence in Congress.[27]

Other minorities are underrepresented, as well. Latinos make up 15 percent of the U.S. population but only 5.7 percent of the members on Capitol Hill. Of the twenty-eight Latino representatives and three senators, most are Mexican Americans, four are Cuban Americans, and three are of Puerto Rican descent. Twenty-six are Democrats and five are Republicans. Asians and Pacific Islanders claim nine representatives and two senators—all but two of them Democrats. There is one Native American, a House Republican.

The growing presence of racial minorities in Congress has had beneficial effects on representational bonds with minority communities. African Americans represented by black lawmakers, for example, tend to be more knowledgeable about their representatives and to hold them in higher esteem.[28] "Even controlling for party membership," Katherine Tate's survey of black constituents found, "black legislators received significantly higher ratings on average than their white counterparts."[29] Another study showed that constituents of the same race as the incumbent were 27 percent more likely than constituents of other races to recognize the name of their representative.[30]

A growing scholarly literature also suggests that wider descriptive representation of minority populations on Capitol Hill yields greater substantive benefits for African American communities. Black legislators are more active on issues of importance to their constituents of color. They are more likely than their white colleagues to introduce bills on subjects of special concern to black Americans.[31] Based on a systematic study of legislative activity on three House committees (Judiciary, Financial Services, and Education and Labor), Katrina Gamble finds that, on policy issues of special interest to African Americans, black members were more active than white members in attending committee meetings, voting, offering amendments, and participating in deliberations.[32]

A serious question for minority representation in Congress focuses on the creation of majority-minority House districts. Most minority House members represent majority-minority districts. Only a handful of African Americans and Latinos are now elected from areas with less than 50 percent minority residents. The creation of such districts, however, tends to concentrate minority voters into a small number of districts and diminish their presence in neighboring districts. In this sense, majority-minority districts may create a trade-off between descriptive and substantive representation.[33] Minority constituents are enabled to elect minority representatives, but by being packed into relatively few districts they lack the influence they would otherwise exert as a plurality in other, more mixed districts. Meanwhile, white representatives from districts that lost black voters in post-1990 racial gerrymandering became more conservative and less supportive of policies preferred by African Americans.[34] Some scholars have suggested that the best way to enhance African American representation is to maximize the number of Democrats in Congress, regardless of race.[35] But the issue involves complex trade-offs—because maximizing the ranks of minority lawmakers enriches representational relationships and advances policies affecting African American communities.

Gender. Neither chamber accurately reflects the nation in terms of gender. Congress historically has been a male bastion. In international comparisons, it still is: The United States ranks sixty-ninth worldwide in the proportion of women serving in the national legislature.[36] Diversity has developed slowly.

Unable to vote nationally until 1920, women have always been underrepresented in Congress. Beginning in 1917 with Rep. Jeannette Rankin, R-Mont., women's presence in Congress has grown very slowly. A record number of women serve in the 111th Congress—seventy-seven representatives (nineteen of them in the California delegation) and seventeen senators (two each from California, Maine, and Washington).[37] For the first time in history, a woman—Nancy Pelosi, D-Calif.—presides as Speaker of the House.

The advent of a critical mass of women has changed Congress. Policy concerns once labeled "women's issues"—which in truth affect everyone—began to receive a respectful hearing. Gender discrimination, women's health, and issues involving the balance between family and workplace have begun to be seriously addressed. Rep. Nita M. Lowey, D-N.Y., whose mother died of breast cancer, asked for increased funding for research on the disease. During debate over family leave policy, Sen. Patty Murray, D-Wash., talked about having to quit a secretarial job sixteen years earlier when she was pregnant with her first child. "When a person in this body gets up and speaks from personal experience, it changes the whole nature of the debate," observed Sen. Chris Dodd, D-Conn.[38] Referring to the women serving in the Senate, Senator Murray declared, "We've made it okay for men to talk about these [women's] issues, too."[39] Political science research offers systematic confirmation that the presence of women has had notable effects on Congress. Women legislators are more likely than men to introduce, sponsor, and press for bills of special concern to women and children.[40]

Only a handful of women members are mothers of school-age children. They face special challenges, but their presence on the Hill undoubtedly enriches representation. "If we are supposed to be 'the people's House,' we need to look like America," contends Rep. Shelley Berkley, D-Nev. "Mothers with kids at home understand what other women deal with across the country."[41] "Having kids is very relevant for a member of Congress," says former representative Pat Schroeder, D-Colo. (1973–1997), whose children were young when she arrived on Capitol Hill. "I totally understood the need for child care."[42] "In the Senate Finance Committee, we were talking about higher education and I looked around the room and thought, 'I'm the only one saving for college,'" said Sen. Blanche Lincoln (D-Ark.), mother of preteen twin boys, "I'm not professing that my colleagues with grown children are any less compassionate. They're just not going through it."[43]

Women legislators today are active far beyond the so-called women's issues. For example, Sen. Susan Collins, R-Maine, steered a complex intelligence reform bill through fierce turf battles while chairing the Senate Homeland Security and Governmental Affairs Committee in 2004.[44] Indeed, in the post-9/11 environment, it has become especially important for women legislators to establish a profile on national defense. Voters tend to view female candidates as less competent on military and security issues.[45] To counter voters' stereotypes of female politicians, Michele Swers finds that women legislators expanded their activity and visibility on defense issues, particularly on homeland security matters.[46]

Sexual Orientation. Gays and lesbians passed a milestone in 1998 when Tammy Baldwin, D-Wis., became the first lesbian representative whose sexual orientation was known before her initial election. (Other congressional gays and lesbians revealed their sexuality or were outed after they had served for some time; some remain in the closet.) Baldwin, who served six years in the state legislature, did not shy away from the issue. Her campaign slogan was "A different kind of candidate." Baldwin is one of three openly gay members of the 111th Congress.[47]

As with other types of social identity, electing gay and lesbian representatives matters for the group's representation. Indeed, one recent study found that the presence of lesbian and gay elected officials was the single most important factor affecting local adoption of domestic partner benefits.[48] Still, as Rep. Barney Frank, D-Mass., observed, the hardest part of running as a gay is "convincing voters that you will not disproportionately focus on that minority's issues."[49] That lesson applies to all candidates contending in districts where they are in the minority—for example, blacks running in majority white areas.

Religion. Nearly all members of Congress cite a specific religious affiliation. By comparison, about 16 percent of Americans do not identify with any particular faith; indeed, the fastest growing category in recent surveys of American religion is "unaffiliated."[50] Protestants collectively make up a majority of the 111th Congress, but more than one-quarter of all House and Senate members are Roman Catholics, the largest single religious denomination. Jews, who make up 2.6 percent of the total U.S. population, accounted for 8 percent of the 111th Congress.[51] The House includes nine Mormons, two Buddhists, two Muslims, and one avowed atheist.

Age and Tenure. When the 111th Congress convened in 2009, the average age of members was the highest in history: fifty-seven for representatives, sixty-three for senators.[52] Tenure as well as age has risen since the early days. "Few die, and none retire," it was said as the twentieth century began. Today, the average member of Congress has served more than twelve years.[53]

Age and tenure levels fluctuate over time. Periods of relatively low turnover (the 1980s, for example) are punctuated by dramatic changing-of-the-guard periods, as in the 1970s and the 1990s, involving both senior and junior members of Congress.[54] Electoral defeats play some role, but the majority of members leave voluntarily. Of course, many departing members "voluntarily" retire, anticipating electoral difficulties and wishing to avoid waging a losing campaign.[55]

A certain balance between new blood and stable membership is undoubtedly optimal for legislative bodies. Rapid turnover—the early 1990s and 2006–2008, for example—can sharpen generational conflict. Many newly elected members indulge in Congress-bashing in their campaigns and want to shake up the institution; not a few of them shun the idea of making a career of public service. As the new members settle in, however, many have second thoughts; incumbency is no longer a dirty word.

Equal Representation of States. The equal voice that all states have in the Senate has huge effects on congressional representation. States vary widely in population, with the most populous state (California) nearly seventy times the size of the least populous state (Wyoming). As a consequence, the Senate's representation scheme gives some citizens far more per capita representation in Congress than others. Indeed, the forty senators from the twenty least populous states represent only about 10 percent of the U.S. population. By comparison, more than a quarter of the nation's population resides in only three states and thus has only six senators. By the standard of "one person, one vote" the Senate is one of the most malapportioned legislatures in the democratic world.[56]

The Senate's divergence from a population-based representation affects the welfare of many social and economic groups. It enlarges the voice of farmers, ranchers, mining interests, and users of federal lands—all groups that have more presence in the less populous states than in the nation as a whole. At the same time, racial and ethnic minorities—already underrepresented in Congress relative to their share of the nation's population—are further disadvantaged by the Senate's makeup.[57] The nation's populous states are more racially and ethnically diverse than its less populous ones, so one effect of Senate representation is to boost the voting power of the predominantly white residents of lightly populated states and to confer less voting power on the more racially diverse residents of populous states. Based on an analysis of Senate roll-call voting on issues of concern to racial minorities, John Griffin finds that senators from more populous states are more attuned to the interests of racial minorities than senators from less populous states. He concludes that "the Senate's apportionment method appears to skew decisions [that racial and ethnic minorities] groups care about most in a direction adverse to their interests."[58]

Equal state representation in the Senate has other meaningful effects. Bonds between senators and their constituents are closer and more personalized in less populous states than in more populous states.[59] And when Congress makes decisions about distributing federal dollars, less populous states receive more benefits than they pay in taxes, whereas populous states provide more revenue but receive fewer returns. "An extensive empirical literature has documented a strong, positive association between a geographical area's per capita seats in the [Senate] and the share of public expenditures it receives."[60] Small-population states are advantaged across most federal spending programs, with the effect most pronounced on the types of programs over which Congress maintains tightest control.[61]

Collective Representation. Representation does not always follow state or district boundaries. Representation occurs when citizens feel they are served by any member of Congress, not just their local member. Congressional representation is, as Robert Weissberg put it, "collective," not just "dyadic."[62] In other words, representation involves more than the interactions between individual members and the residents of their geographic constituencies. Citizens can feel a sense of connection to Congress when the body as a collective whole includes any members who speak for them. When someone from an ethnic or racial minority background goes to Congress, it is often a matter of pride for an entire identity group. Such legislators speak for people like them throughout the nation.[63]

Many constituencies are represented in the same way. One member who suffers from epilepsy defends job rights for other sufferers of the disease; another whose grandson was born prematurely champions funds for medical research into birth defects; members who are openly gay speak out for the rights of homosexuals everywhere. Such causes are close to members' hearts, even though they may pay scant political dividends. Legislators' backgrounds, religious beliefs, social identities, and experiences all shape their views and priorities. Political scientist Barry Burden refers to such influences as "the personal roots of representation," and he argues that analysts must take them into account to understand legislators' policy activism in Congress.[64]

Congressional Roles

Members of Congress, as Richard F. Fenno Jr. says, spend their lives "moving between two contexts, Washington and home, and between two activities, governing and campaigning."[65] The two contexts and the two activities are continuously interwoven. How members govern is deeply affected by their constituency roots and their campaign experiences. In turn, their Capitol Hill activities affect all their subsequent contacts with people back home. As members carry out their representational functions, it is possible to distinguish three roles undertaken to some degree by most members of Congress: legislator, constituency servant, and partisan.

Legislator. The rules, procedures, and traditions of the House and Senate impose many constraints on members' behavior. To be effective, new members must learn their way through the institutional maze. Legislators therefore stress the formal aspects of Capitol Hill duties and routines: legislative work, investigation, and committee specialization. Charles E. Schumer, D-N.Y., an elective official for more than half his life (he was elected to the state assembly at age twenty-three and served nine terms in the U.S. House), explained his commitment as a professional legislator during his successful 1998 Senate campaign:

> I love to legislate. Taking an idea—often not original with me—shaping it, molding it. Building a coalition of people who might not completely agree with it. Passing it and making the country a little bit of a better place. I love doing that.[66]

Legislators pursue information and expertise on issues, not only because of their personal interest in public policy but also because it sways others in the chamber. To influence other members, a legislator must be perceived as credible and knowledgeable—in other words, someone worth listening to.

The legislator's role often dovetails with that of representing constituents. Most members seek committee assignments that will serve the needs of their states or districts. One House member related how his interest in flood control and water resource development impelled him to ask for a seat on the committee handling those issues. "The interests of my district dictated my field of specialization," he explained, "but the decision to specialize in some legislative field is automatic for the member who wants to exercise any influence."[67]

Members soon learn the norms, or folkways, that expedite legislative bargaining and maximize productivity. Examining the post–World War II Senate, Donald R. Matthews identified six folkways governing behavior that were enforced informally. Senators should (1) serve an apprenticeship (exercising restraint and deference to elders in the early years); (2) concentrate on Senate work instead of on gaining publicity; (3) specialize in issues within their committees or affecting their home states; (4) act courteously to colleagues; (5) extend reciprocity to colleagues—that is, provide willing assistance with the expectation that it will be repaid in kind one day; and (6) loyally defend the Senate, "the greatest legislative and deliberative body in the world."[68]

These folkways have faded in importance in the contemporary Senate, though they have not entirely disappeared. Barbara Sinclair's major reassessment of senators' Hill styles concluded that the restrained activism of the 1950s Senate had given way to unrestrained activism in the contemporary era.[69] New senators now actively take part in most aspects of the chamber's work, ignoring the apprenticeship norm. Many senators, especially those with an eye on the White House, work tirelessly to attract national publicity and personal attention. Committee specialization, although still common, is less rigid than it once was. Senators now have many overlapping committee assignments and are expected to express views on a wide range of issues. The norms of courtesy and reciprocity are still invoked, but institutional loyalty wears thin in an era of harsh partisanship and public cynicism about government.

The House relies more on formal channels of power than on informal norms. From interviews, however, Herbert B. Asher uncovered seven norms: friendly relationships are desirable; the important work of the House should be done in committees, not on the floor; learning the procedural rules of the House is essential; members should not personally criticize a colleague on the House floor; members should be prepared to trade votes; members should be specialists; and freshmen should serve apprenticeships.[70]

As in the Senate, the norms of earlier eras have weakened. New members, impatient to make their mark, assert themselves more quickly—aided by party leaders who worry about getting the freshmen reelected. Leadership comes earlier to members than it used to. Specialization is more compelling in the House than in the Senate—but many members branch out into unrelated issues. No longer are committees the sole forums for influencing legislation. Today's members, more partisan and ideologically driven than their predecessors, shun norms such as reciprocity and compromise.

Legislatively minded members champion the decaying norms and decry the rancor that has marked recent Congresses. Efforts to preserve traditional institutional norms have not been entirely unsuccessful. Asked to compare the House with his earlier career (as an economics professor), former majority leader Dick Armey, R-Texas (1985–2003), remarked, "Here you're working with a more pleasant group of people. There isn't the petty meanness in Congress that you find in university politics."[71] Even in an era of high partisanship, reciprocity and compromise are necessary if members' disparate goals are to be reconciled into legislation that can be passed.

Constituency Servant. As constituency servants, members of Congress attempt to give voice to local citizens' concerns, solve problems they have with federal programs, and ensure that constituents receive their fair share of federal dollars. Often the task is performed by legislators and their staffs as casework—individual cases triggered by constituent letters or visits. Even though mostly delegated to staff aides, this is a chore that weighs heavily on members. A House member expressed the philosophy of most legislators like this:

> Constituent work: that's something I feel very strongly about. The American people, with the growth of the bureaucracy, feel nobody

cares. The only conduit a taxpayer has with the government is a congressional office. [72]

Sometimes members stress constituency service to gain breathing room for legislative stands that stray from district norms.

Constituency servants champion their states' or districts' needs when federal funds are distributed. One member's view of this role was expressed in frank terms in a famous undercover interview during the Abscam probe of influence peddling in the late 1970s. Rep. Michael "Ozzie" Myers was recorded as saying to Federal Bureau of Investigation (FBI) agents posing as aides of an Arab sheik:

> It's a big pie down in Washington. Each member's sent there to bring a piece of that pie back home. And if you go down there and you don't—you come back without milkin' it after a few terms…you don't go…back. [73]

Myers' words are inelegant and the context sleazy, but they characterize members' traditional view of constituency advocacy. Research has shown that obtaining local benefits does indeed help members "go back" to Congress. It improves their name recognition back home, [74] reduces their likelihood of facing a strong challenger, [75] and improves vulnerable members' reelection chances. [76] Even if they rail against pork-barrel spending in other people's areas, members recognize that their constituents expect them to bring home the bacon.

Members have especially strong incentives to perform the constituency servant role whenever Congress considers government programs with highly visible local benefits, such as highway or mass transit grants, water projects, and homeland security contracts. If members fail to win earmarked funds for their constituents, they can nonetheless seek other benefits—for example, favorable regulatory rules or trade concessions for local industries. [77] An Arkansas lobbyist tells the story of going to visit one of his state's Republican members known for his anti-pork speeches. "I know you're anti-pork," the lobbyist began, "but I have to tell you about our needs and how to position yourself." "What do you mean?" the representative retorted. "As far as I can tell, it's not pork if it's for Arkansas." [78]

Partisan. Members of Congress are elected not just as individual representatives, but as members of a political party. Nearly every member of Congress formally affiliates with one of the two major parties, and even the few members elected as independents organize with one or the other party to receive their committee assignments. Party affiliation is more than a mere label for most members. Members actively work with and for their parties, and members' partisan activities have a pervasive effect on congressional elections, representation, and legislation.

Members have a personal stake in the collective fate of their parties. Whether their party commands a majority of seats in the House or Senate affects members' power in the chamber and their ability to achieve their legislative goals. The majority party elects leaders with agenda-setting responsibilities and controls the chairmanships of all committees and subcommittees in the two chambers. In addition, members know that voters' feelings about the parties will affect their own electoral chances. Former senator Lincoln Chafee, R-R.I., lost his seat in

2006 despite high personal approval ratings in great part because of his party's unpopularity in Rhode Island. "I give the voters credit," he said. "They made the connection between electing even popular Republicans at the cost of leaving the Senate in the hands of a leadership they had learned to mistrust."[79]

Many members hold posts within their congressional parties. Legislative party organizations are extensive, with whips, deputy whips, regional whips, and a variety of task forces. Elections for party positions are often hotly contested. As will be discussed in more detail in Chapter 6, members who hold or seek party positions dedicate significant effort to party causes. They engage in internal party communications, party message development, and partisan public relations. They do favors for fellow partisans and exhort them to vote the party position. They seek to impress leaders and other party members with their prodigious fund-raising and campaigning on behalf of their party's candidates.[80]

Even those members who do not serve as party officers attend and participate in party caucus. In the contemporary Congress, the House and Senate caucuses of both parties meet at least weekly. Most members of Congress also personally contribute to help their party's candidates win or hold office.[81] In 2006, for example, House Democrats collectively gave their candidates $14 million; House Republicans contributed $24.6 million to their partisans.[82] On top of that, they also donate funds to their congressional campaign committees. During the 2006 elections, Republican members provided $37.3 million to their campaign organizations, and Democratic members $51.1 million to their counterpart entities.

Partisan activities today place significant demands upon legislators' time and energy. Not only do members seek to enact good policy as legislators and advance local concerns as constituency servants, but they are also partisans, heavily invested in the collective fortunes of their parties.

How Do Legislators Spend Their Time?

Time is the most precious commodity for senators and representatives. The lack of it is their most frequent complaint about their jobs.[83] Allocating time requires exceedingly tough personal and political choices.

For a breakdown of how members' time is spent, see Table 5-1. According to a 1993 congressional survey, members' daily priorities are roughly as follows: (1) meeting on legislative issues with constituents, either at home or in Washington; (2) attending committee hearings, markups, and other committee meetings; (3) meeting with government officials and lobbyists; (4) studying pending legislation or discussing legislation with other members or staff; (5) working with informal caucus groups of colleagues; (6) attending floor debates or watching them on television; (7) doing nonlegislative work (casework) for constituents in Washington; (8) managing personal office operations and staffs; (9) raising funds for the next campaign, for others' campaigns, or for the political party; (10) working with party leaders to build legislative coalitions; (11) overseeing how agencies are carrying out laws or policies; and (12) making appearances on legislation outside the state or district.[84] Staff members usually prepare daily schedules for members of Congress to consult

TABLE 5-1   **Activities of Members of Congress: Actual and Ideal (in percentages)**

Activity	Members actually spending time				Members preferring to spend more time
	Great deal	Moderate amount	A little	Almost none	
Representation					
Meet with citizens in state or district	68%	30%	1%	0%	17%
Meet in Washington, D.C., with constituents	45	50	5	0	17
Manage office	6	45	39	10	13
Raise funds for next campaign, for others, for party	6	33	45	16	7
Lawmaking					
Attend committee hearings, markups, other meetings	48	46	6	0	43
Meet in Washington on legislative issues	37	56	6	0	31
Study, read, discuss pending legislation	25	56	17	2	78
Work with informal caucuses	8	43	36	13	25
Attend floor debate, follow it on television	7	37	44	12	59
Work with party leaders to build coalitions	6	33	43	18	42
Oversee how agencies are carrying out policies and programs	5	22	43	29	53
Give speeches about legislation outside state or district	5	23	49	23	16

Source: U.S. Congress, Joint Committee on the Organization of Congress, *Organization of the Congress, Final Report,* H. Rep. 103–413, 103d Congress, 1st sess., December 1993, 2:231–232, 275–287.

Note: A total of 161 members of Congress (136 representatives, 25 senators) responded to this survey, conducted in early 1993 under the auspices of the Joint Committee on the Organization of Congress. This series of questions elicited responses from 152 to 155 members.

as they whirl through a busy day on Capitol Hill. A handful of lawmakers post their schedules on their Web sites. "I just wanted to give people an opportunity to see who I meet with," explained Sen. Jon Tester, D-Mont.[85]

Scheduling is complicated by the large number of formal work groups—mainly committees and subcommittees, but also joint, party, and ad hoc panels. The average senator sits on three full committees and seven subcommittees; representatives average two committees and four subcommittees.

With so many assignments, lawmakers are hard-pressed to control their crowded schedules. Committee quorums are difficult to achieve, and members' attention is often focused elsewhere. All too often working sessions are composed of the chairman, the ranking minority member, perhaps one or two interested colleagues, and staff aides. House rules tightening quorum requirements only made scheduling problems worse.

Repeated floor votes, which lawmakers fear to miss, are another time consuming duty. In a typical Congress more than one thousand recorded votes may be taken in the House chamber and perhaps six hundred in the Senate. "We're like automatons," one senator complained. "We spend our time walking in tunnels to go to the floor to vote."[86] "A member of Congress is like an island, surrounded by staff and perpetually in motion," says Rep. Debbie Wasserman-Schultz, D-Fla. "The pressure never stops." Wasserman-Schultz shuns the House gym and explains, "I get my exercise running around the Capitol."[87]

Lawmakers' daily schedules in Washington are "long, fragmented, and unpredictable," according to a study based on time logs kept by senators' appointment secretaries.[88] "In Congress you are a total juggler," recalls former representative Schroeder, D-Colo., now a trade association executive. "You have always got seventeen things pulling on your sleeve."[89] Members' schedules are splintered into so many tiny fragments that effective pursuit of lawmaking, oversight, and constituent service is hampered. According to a management study of several senators' offices, an event occurs every five minutes, on average, to which the senator or the chief aide must respond personally.[90] Often members have scant notice that their presence is required at a meeting or a hearing. Carefully developed schedules can be disrupted by changes in meeting hours, by unforeseen events, or by sessions that run longer than expected. (After the terrorist attacks in 2001, members were issued BlackBerries so they could keep track of schedules and developments.)

Political scientists may claim that Congress runs in harmony with members' needs, but the members know otherwise. In a survey of 114 House and Senate members, "inefficiency" was the thing that most surprised them about Congress (45 percent gave this response).[91] "[Congress] is a good job for someone with no family, no life of their own, no desire to do anything but get up, go to work, and live and die by their own press releases," quipped former representative Fred Grandy, an Iowa Republican who left Congress in 1995. "It is a great job for deviant human beings."[92]

Nearly half the respondents in a 1987 survey agreed that they had "no personal time after work"; a third said they had "no time for family."[93] In the last years of Republican control Congress largely adhered to a Tuesday-to-Thursday schedule that gave members more opportunity to spend time back home with families,[94] although constituency business consumes a great deal of members' time when Congress is not in session. When Democrats regained the majority in 2006 the leadership promised five-day workweeks, but members immediately began to complain about the loss of family time. "Keeping us up here eats away at families," said Rep. Jack Kingston, R-Ga. "Marriages suffer."[95]

The dilemma legislators face in allocating their time is far more than a matter of scheduling. It is a case of conflicting role expectations. Look again at Table 5-1, where lawmakers' activities are arrayed to illustrate the tensions inherent in the two Congresses, from the representative Congress (at the top of the list) to the legislative Congress (at the bottom). More members want to devote extra time to legislative duties than would choose to spend more time on constituency and political chores. According to the 1993 survey, an average of 43 percent of the members would like to spend more time on the eight legislative tasks, whereas on average only 14 percent of them would give more time to the four representation items. Eight of ten members would study more thoroughly the legislation they vote on; six of ten would follow floor debate more closely.[96] The two Congresses pull members in different directions. As a retiring House committee chairman remarked:

> One problem is that you're damned if you do and damned if you don't. If you do your work here, you're accused of neglecting your district. And if you spend too much time in your district, you're accused of neglecting your work here.[97]

The Shape of the Washington Career

Once a short-term activity, congressional service has become a career. Accompanying this careerism, or longevity, is a distinctive pattern of Washington activity: The longer members remain in office, the more they sponsor bills, deliver floor speeches, and offer amendments. Despite the democratizing trends of the reform era (1960s and 1970s), senior lawmakers continue to lead in all these categories. "The *apprenticeship norm* may or may not be dead, but *apprenticeship* is stronger than it has been in decades," John R. Hibbing concluded from his painstaking study of four cohorts of members who entered the House between 1957 and 1971.[98]

Long tenure also tends to pull members toward legislative specialization. Settling into their committee slots, members gain expertise in a distinct policy field, and spend their time managing legislation and conducting oversight in that field. Seniority tends to boost legislative achievement. Veterans usually enjoy more success than do freshmen in getting their bills passed.

The link between members' service and their effectiveness reflects the indispensable role careerists play in the legislative process. As Hibbing observed:

> Senior members are the heart and soul of the legislative side of congressional service....Relatively junior members can be given a subcommittee chairmanship, but it is not nearly so easy to give them an active, focused legislative agenda and the political savvy to enact it. Some things take time and experience, and successful participation in the legislative process appears to be one of those things.[99]

The wisdom of this statement is repeatedly borne out. One recent study drawing on the uniquely detailed data available for the North Carolina General Assembly reports that legislators' "effectiveness rises sharply with tenure," and "there is no evidence that effectiveness eventually declines with tenure, even out to nine terms."[100] Controlling for other factors affecting legislators' influence, the authors conclude that "the increased effectiveness [of senior legislators] is due to the acquisition of specific human capital, most likely through learning-by-doing."[101] A comprehensive study of U.S. House members' ability to get their bills past significant stages in the legislative process reports that "as members become more senior they become more efficient at arranging deals with key office-holders."[102] Newcomers bring with them zeal, energy, and fresh approaches. On the other hand, many of them lack patience, bargaining skills, institutional memory, and respect for the lawmaking process.

LOOKING HOMEWARD

Not all of a representative's or a senator's duties lie in Washington, D.C. Legislators not only fashion policy for the nation's welfare, but they also act as emissaries from their home states or districts.

Independent Judgment or Constituency Opinion?

Although found in virtually every political system, representation is the hallmark of democratic regimes dedicated to sharing power among citizens. In small communities decisions can be reached by face-to-face discussion, but in populous societies such personalized consultation is impossible. Thus, according to democratic theory, citizens can exert control by choosing "fiduciary agents" to act on their behalf, deliberating on legislation just as their principals, the voters, would do if they could be on hand themselves.[103] In attempting to serve as a faithful agent for constituents, legislators are faced with a central dilemma of representation: whether to take actions that are popular with constituents or to do what the legislator believes is in their best interest. As Pitkin explains:

> The representative must act in such a way that, although he is independent, and his constituents are capable of action and judgment, no conflict arises between them. He must act in their interest, and this means he must not normally come into conflict with their wishes.[104]

Recent opinion surveys seem to echo Pitkin's formulation. As one analyst puts it, "[T]he public seems to want elected officials to internalize the majority's values and then try to assess how those values come to bear on an issue." No less than 85 percent agreed with the statement: "The goal of Congress should be to make the decisions that a majority of Americans would make if they had the information and time to think things over that Congress has."[105]

For Burke, a legislator must do more than register prevailing constituency opinion. Legislators must instead use their superior information about policy, their broader perspective, and their personal judgment in making decisions. This conception of the legislator as Burkean trustee has always had its admirers. Speaking to a group of newly elected House members, Rep. Henry J. Hyde, R-Ill. (1974–2007), voiced the Burkean ideal:

> If you are here simply as a tote board registering the current state of opinion in your district, you are not going to serve either your constituents or the Congress well....You must take, at times, a national view, even if you risk the displeasure of your neighbors and friends back home....If you don't know the principle, or the policy, for which you are willing to lose your office, then you are going to do damage here.[106]

Nearly every member can point to conscience votes cast on deeply felt issues. A few, such as Rep. Mike Synar, D-Okla. (1979–1995), compile a contrarian record, challenging voters to admire their independence if not their policies. Synar was an unabashed liberal Democrat from a state that now elects mostly conservative Republicans. "I want to be a U.S. congressman from Oklahoma, not an Oklahoman congressman," Synar declared when he arrived in the capital.[107] If turned out of office by hostile sentiment (as Synar later was), the Burkean can at least hope for history's vindication.

Electoral realities imperil the Burkean ideal. Burke himself was ousted from office for his candor. Today's voters similarly prefer instructed delegates rather than lawmakers who exercise too much independent judgment. Nevertheless, citizens' expectations (and hence their "instructions") for representatives can vary widely. As a recent study revealed, "Some citizens desire assistance in dealing with government; others want their representative to focus on national policy concerns. Still others want their member[s] to devote most of their time to local policy concerns."[108]

In practice, legislators assume different representational styles according to the occasion. They ponder factors such as the nation's welfare, their personal convictions, and constituency opinions. "The weight assigned to each factor," writes Thomas E. Cavanagh, "varies according to the nature of the issue at hand, the availability of the information necessary for a decision, and the intensity of preference of the people concerned about the issue."[109]

Members of Congress are challenged to explain their choices to constituents—no matter how many or how few people truly care about the matter.[110] The anticipated need to explain oneself shapes a member's decisions and is part of the dilemma of choice. A cynical saying among lawmakers asserts that "a vote on anything [is] a wrong vote if you cannot explain it in a 30-second TV ad."[111]

What Are Constituencies?

Senators and representatives cannot respond equally to all the people within a given state or district. A subset of their constituents elected them, and so they interact more with supporters than with opponents. The constituencies that legislators see as they campaign or vote are quite different from the boundaries found on maps. Fenno describes a "nest" of constituencies, ranging from the widest (geographic constituency) to the narrowest (personal constituency), which is made up of supporters, loyalists, and intimates.[112]

Geographic and Demographic Constituencies. The average House district today numbers more than 700,000 people. As for senators, fourteen represent states with only one House district; the rest represent multi-district states with as many as 37 million people.[113] Such constituencies differ sharply from one another. More than half (57 percent) of the people in Manhattan's Upper East Side (New York's Fourteenth District) have college degrees, compared with only 6 percent in California's central valley (Twentieth District). Median family income ranges from $92,000 (New Jersey's Eleventh District, Morris County) to less than $21,000 in New York's Sixteenth District in the South Bronx, where 40 percent of the families live in poverty.[114] Such disparities among districts shape their representatives' outlooks.

There are also political "microclimates." Democrat Nydia M. Velázquez's Twelfth District in New York begins in a Hispanic area of Brooklyn, jumps across the East River to take in Manhattan's Chinatown, Little Italy, and its Lower East Side, and then doubles back again to encompass neighborhoods in north Brooklyn and Queens. Republican Mary Bono's sprawling southern California Forty-fifth District embraces smog-ridden suburbs east of Riverside, irrigated farmland of the Coachella Valley, and the wealthy desert oases of Palm Springs and Palm Desert. Even these geographical distinctions grossly simplify the complex and subtle ethnic, economic, and social mixture of these communities.

Demographically, constituencies may be homogeneous or heterogeneous.[115] Some constituencies, even a few whole states, remain uniform and one-dimensional—mostly wheat farmers or urban ghetto dwellers or small-town citizens. Because of rising population, economic complexity, and educational levels, however, virtually all constituencies, House as well as Senate, have become more heterogeneous than they used to be. The more diverse a constituency, the more challenging is the representative's task.

Another attribute of constituencies is electoral balance, especially as manifested in the incumbent's reelection chances. Heterogeneous districts tend to be more competitive than uniform ones. Incumbents predictably prefer safe districts—those with a high proportion of groups leaning toward their partisan or ideological stance. Not only do safe districts favor reelection, but they also imply that voters will be easier to please.[116]

Truly competitive districts are not the norm, especially in the House of Representatives. The 2008 contests produced a number of surprises; but seven out of ten House victors that year boasted margins of 60 percent or more; 54 of them faced no major party foe. Only 14 percent of the seats were truly competitive (won by 55 percent or less), and more than a third of those seats shifted from one party to the other. As Table 5-2 shows, competitiveness varies over time. Senate seats are more likely to be closely contested than House races, but many senators, including most of those up for reelection in 2008, still win in a walk.

Whatever the numbers might show, few incumbents regard themselves as truly safe. The threat of losing an election is very real. Most lawmakers have a close call at some time in their congressional careers, and many of them eventually suffer defeat.[117] In addition to the incumbents who went down to defeat in 2008, a number of others—including four senators and some thirty House members—survived while receiving what might be called warning messages from the home folks. Incumbents thus worry not only about winning or losing but also about their margins of safety. Downturns in normal electoral support narrow the member's breathing space in the job, may invite challengers in future years, and could block chances for further advancement.[118]

Political and Personal Constituencies. As candidates or incumbents analyze their electoral base, three narrower constituencies can be discerned: supporters (the reelection constituency), loyalists (the primary constituency), and intimates (the personal constituency).[119] Supporters are expected to vote for the candidate on election day, but some do not. Candidates and their advisers constantly monitor these voters, reassessing precinct-level political demography—registration

TABLE 5-2 **House and Senate Margins of Victory, 1974–2008**

Chamber and election year	Percentage of vote				Number of seats
	Under 55	55–59.9	60 plus	Unopposed	
House					
1974	24	16	46	14	435
1976	17	14	56	12	435
1978	17	14	53	16	435
1980	18	14	60	8	435
1982	16	16	63	6	435
1984	12	13	61	14	435
1986	9	10	64	17	435
1988	6	9	67	18	435
1990	11	16	58	15	435
1992	20	18	58	3	435
1994	22	17	52	9	435
1996	22	18	57	3	435
1998	10	17	63	10	435
2000	23	12	59	15	435
2002	10	10	80	18	435
2004	7	14	64	15	435
2006	15	14	62	9	435
2008	14	16	57	12	435
Senate					
1974	41	18	35	6	34
1976	30	33	30	6	33
1978	24	33	36	6	33
1980	58	18	21	3	34
1982	30	27	43	—	33
1984	18	21	58	3	33
1986	38	15	47	—	34
1988	33	15	52	—	33
1990	26	11	49	14	34
1992	34	34	32	—	35
1994	32	34	34	—	35
1996	59	18	24	—	34
1998	29	9	62	—	34
2000	29	15	55	—	34
2002	38	18	44	4	34
2004	32	15	50	3	34
2006	24	21	55	—	33
2008	26	20	51	3	35

Sources: CQ Weekly and authors' calculations.

Note: Percentages may not add to 100 because of rounding. "Unopposed" includes districts or states where only one major-party candidate was on the ballot.

figures, survey data, and recent electoral trends. The more elections incumbents have survived, the more precisely they can identify supporters. Areas and groups with the biggest payoffs are usually targeted.

Loyalists are the politician's staunchest supporters. They may be from preelectoral ventures—civil rights, environmental, or antiabortion activists, for example. They may be centered in religious or ethnic groups, or political or civic clubs. They may be friends and neighbors. They are willing volunteers who can be counted on to lend a hand in reelection campaigns.

Candidates dare not ignore these loyalists. A favorite story of House Speaker Thomas P. "Tip" O'Neill Jr., D-Mass. (1953–1987), came from his first, failed, campaign for city council. A neighbor told him, "Tom, I'm going to vote for you even though you didn't ask me." "Mrs. O'Brien," replied a surprised O'Neill, "I've lived across the street from you for 18 years. I shovel your walk in the winter. I cut your grass in the summer. I didn't think I had to ask you for your vote." To this the lady replied, "Tom, I want you to know something: people like to be asked."[120] Expressions of gratitude are equally important. The elder George Bush reportedly "always carried a box of note cards with him on the campaign trail and penned a personal note immediately following each event to the volunteers and hosts."[121]

Even entrenched officeholders worry about keeping their core supporters energized. Loyalists are a politician's defenders in times of adversity. "There's a big difference between the people who are for you and the people who are excitedly for you," an Iowa politician told Fenno, "between those who will vote if they feel like it and those for whom the only election is [your] election. You need as many of that group as you can get." An inadequate base of core support, the informant explained, brought down two of the state's one-term Democratic senators. "One had a base that was a mile wide and an inch deep; the other's support was an inch wide and a mile deep."[122]

Intimates are close friends who supply political advice and emotional support. They may be members of the candidate's family, trusted staff members, political mentors, or individuals who shared decisive experiences early in the candidate's career. The setting and the players differ from state to state and from district to district. Tip O'Neill's inner circle was made up of the "boys" of Barry's Corner, a local clubhouse in Cambridge, Mass., whose families O'Neill had known intimately over more than fifty years of political life. When Rep. David E. Price, D-N.C., first decided to run for Congress, he relied on what he called the "Wednesday night group," which he described as "an inner circle without whom the effort would never have gotten off the ground."[123] Such intimates play an indispensable role. Beyond their enthusiastic support, they provide unvarnished advice on political matters and serve as sounding boards for ideas and strategies.

Home Styles

Legislators evolve distinctive ways of presenting themselves and their records to their constituents—what Fenno calls their home styles. These styles are exhibited in members' personal appearances, mailings, newsletters, press releases, telephone conversations, radio and television spots, and Internet Web sites. Little is known about how home styles coalesce, but they are linked to members' personalities, backgrounds, constituency features, and resources. The ways members interact with constituents have a powerful effect on their electoral success. As Fenno states, "It is the style, not the issue content, that counts most in the reelection constituency."[124]

Presentation of Self. A successful home style will elicit trust—constituents' faith that legislators are what they claim to be and will do what they promise.[125] Winning voters' trust does not happen overnight; it takes time, persistence, and consistency. Members must establish their qualification for office—the belief that they are capable of handling the job. Members also strive to convey identification, the impression that legislators resemble their constituents; and empathy, the sense that legislators understand constituents' problems and care about them.

Given variations among legislators and constituencies, countless available home styles can effectively build the trust relationship. The legendary Speaker "Mr. Sam" Rayburn represented his East Texas district for nearly fifty years (1913–1961) as a plain dirt farmer. Once back in his hometown of Bonham, his drawl thickened; his tailored suits were exchanged for khakis, an old shirt, and a slouch hat; and he traveled not in the Speaker's limousine, but in a well-dented pickup truck. His biographer relates:

> If Rayburn ever chewed tobacco in Washington, a long-time aide could not recall it, but in Bonham he always seemed to have a plug in his cheek. He made certain always to spit in the fireplace at his home when constituents were visiting, so that if nothing else, they would take away the idea that Mr. Sam was just a plain fellow.[126]

Today's legislators are no less inventive in fashioning home styles. Representative A's direct style features face-to-face contacts with people in his primary constituency. He rarely mentions issues because most people in his district agree on them. Representative B, a popular local athlete, uses national defense issues to symbolize his oneness with a district supportive of the military. Representative C displays himself as a verbal, issue-oriented activist, an outsider ill at ease with conventional politicians. Senator D, articulate and personable, comes across as "a mom in tennis shoes." Senator E, who recently ousted an incumbent of the opposite party, presents herself as an independent-minded person for whom party labels are "irrelevant." The repertoire of home styles is virtually limitless.

Voters are likely to remember style long after they forget issue statements or voting records. Even so, legislators know full well that they must explain their decisions to others.[127]

Explaining Washington Activity. Explaining is an integral part of decision making. In home district forums, constituents expect members to be able to describe, interpret, and justify their actions. If they do not agree with the member's conclusions, they may at least respect the decision-making style.

> They don't know much about my votes. Most of what they know is what I tell them. They know more of what kind of a guy I am. It comes through in my letters: "You care about the little guy."[128]

Although few incumbents fear that a single vote can defeat them, all realize that voters' disenchantment with their total record can be fatal—more so in these days of Internet communications when lobby groups publicize voting records. Members stockpile reasons for virtually every position they take, often more than are needed. Facing especially thorny choices (for example, on aid to Wall Street firms, Social Security reform, or the war in Iraq), they might follow a middle-of-the-road route. More often, they huddle under the umbrella of their party's line. Whatever course they choose, they will find that inconsistency is mentally and politically costly. Contrary to the popular stereotype of politicians speaking out of both sides of their mouths, members give much the same account of themselves regardless of the group they are talking to.

Rep. John P. Murtha, D-Pa., a Vietnam veteran with close ties to the Pentagon, faced a dilemma in late 2005 when he decided to reveal his doubts about the Iraq war to his constituents. "I just came to the conclusion finally that I had to speak out," he said. "I'm hopeful I didn't go too far."[129] He received three standing ovations when he recounted the federal aid he had delivered to his district. But when he spoke briefly about Iraq, his audience was unsure how to react; no questions were raised. Murtha's credibility on military affairs changed the debate on Capitol Hill. It also appears to have affected his electoral prospects at home. Murtha had escaped any significant challenge since 1990 and had been unopposed in 2004; but in 2006 he received 61 percent of the vote and 58 percent in 2008.

Constituency Careers. Constituency bonds evolve over the course of a lawmaker's career. Constituency careers have at least two recognizable stages: expansionism and protectionism. In the first stage the member builds a reelection constituency by solidifying the help of hard-core supporters and reaching out to attract added blocs of support. Aggressive efforts to reach out to new voters—exploiting the perquisites of incumbency, such as fund-raising and an election-year avalanche of messages to constituents—accounts for the "sophomore surge," in which newcomers typically boost their margin in their first reelection bid.[130] In the second stage the member stops expanding the base, content with protecting support already won. Once established, a successful home style is rarely altered.

Certain developments, however, can lead to a change in a member's home style. One is demographic change in the constituency, as population movement or redistricting force a member to confront unfamiliar voters or territory. A second cause is strategic reaction, as a fresh challenger or a novel issue threatens established voting patterns. Because coalitions may shift over time, members and their advisers pore over the results of the most recent election (and available survey results).

Finally, home styles may change with new personal goals and ambitions. Achieving positions of power in Washington can divert a member's attention from home state business. Family responsibilities or a need to improve one's financial situation may also lead to a shift in priorities. Faced with new aspirations or shifting constituency demands, some members decide to retire. Others struggle ineffectively and are defeated. Still others survive by rejuvenating their constituency base.

OFFICE OF THE MEMBER INC.

Home style includes the way a member answers day-to-day questions: How much attention should I devote to state or district needs? How much time should I spend in the state or district? How should I keep in touch with my constituents? How should I deploy staff aides to handle constituents' concerns?

Road Tripping

During the nineteenth century legislators spent most of their time at home, traveling to Washington only when Congress was in session. After World War II (and the advent of both air travel from home and air conditioning on Capitol Hill), however, congressional sessions lengthened until they spanned most of the year.

By the 1970s both houses had adopted parallel schedules of sessions punctuated with district work periods (House) or nonlegislative periods (Senate). At the same time, members were permitted more paid trips to states or districts. Today senators and representatives are allowed as many trips home as they want, subject to the limits of their official expense allowances. Many members (even those from the West Coast) go home every weekend.

Currently fashionable home styles thus entail frequent commutes. Although travel has increased for all members, the more time-consuming the trips home, the less often they are made. When their families remain at home, members are more inclined to return regularly. Most members stay close to their districts as election day approaches.[131]

Seniority is also a factor. Senior members tend to make fewer trips to their districts than do junior members, perhaps reflecting junior members' greater attentiveness to their districts or senior members' greater Washington responsibilities. Finally, members' decisions to retire voluntarily are usually accompanied by large drops in trips home.

Constituency Casework

"All God's chillun got problems," exclaimed Rep. Billy Matthews, D-Fla. (1953–1967), as he pondered mail from his constituents.[132] In the early days lawmakers lacked staff aides and wrote personally to executive agencies for help in such matters as pension or land claims and appointments to military academies. The Legislative Reorganization Act of 1946 provided de facto authority for hiring caseworkers, first in Senate offices and later in the House.

What are these cases all about? As respondents in a nationwide survey reported, the most frequent reason for contacting a member's office (16 percent of all cases) is to express views or obtain information on legislative issues. Requests for help in finding government jobs form the next largest category, followed by cases dealing with government services such as Social Security, veterans' benefits, or unemployment compensation. Military cases (for example, transfers, discharges, personal hardships) are numerous, as are tax, legal, and immigration problems. Constituents often ask for government publications. And there are requests for flags that have flown over the U.S. Capitol.

Many citizen appeals, moreover, betray a hazy understanding of the office-holder's duties. Rep. Luis V. Gutierrez, D-Ill. (1993–2009), reported being barraged with all manner of complaints and requests when he shops in his North Side Chicago neighborhood. Examples of what he has heard are: "They haven't picked up my trash!" (the city's job); "Can you get my son a scholarship to the state university?" (a state matter); or "I can't pay my child support" (personal). Representative Gutierrez's personal favorite was: "I own property in Puerto Rico and someone is blocking my driveway."[133]

Cases come to legislators' offices by letter, phone, e-mail, fax, or in person at district or mobile offices. All representatives and senators now have e-mail addresses and Web sites with contact information. Occasionally, members themselves pick up cases from talking to constituents. Many hold office hours in their districts for this purpose. When a constituent's request is received, it is usually acknowledged promptly by a letter that either fills the request or promises that an answer will be forthcoming.

Keeping up with incoming communications is a priority for all congressional offices. If the constituent's request requires contacting a federal agency, caseworkers communicate by e-mail, phone, letter, or buckslip (a preprinted referral form).[134] Usually, the contact in the executive agency is a liaison officer, although some caseworkers prefer to deal directly with line officers or regional officials. Once the problem has been conveyed, it is a matter of time before a decision is reached and a reply forwarded to the congressional office. The reply is then sent along to the constituent, perhaps with a cover letter signed by the member. If the agency's reply is deemed faulty, the caseworker may challenge it and ask for reconsideration; in some cases the member may intervene in person to lend weight to the appeal.

Casework loads vary from state to state and from district to district. In both chambers senior legislators receive proportionately more casework requests than do junior members.[135] Perhaps senior members are considered more powerful and better equipped to resolve constituents' problems. Legislators themselves certainly cultivate this image in seeking reelection. Demographic variation can affect casework volume. Some types of citizens simply are more likely than others to have contact with government agencies.

Comparing senators and representatives, Frances E. Lee and Bruce I. Oppenheimer found that casework loads are affected by constituency size:

> Senators as a group are not different from House members in the amount of contact they have with constituents. Instead, senators who represent constituencies that are similar in size to House districts have contact levels that mirror or exceed those of House members.[136]

Senators representing populous states draw fewer per capita requests from constituents than senators representing small states. Large-state senators are perceived as more distant, so constituents in those states are more likely to turn to their House members for their casework requests. "As state population decreases," however, "House members and senators look increasingly similar in accessibility and responsiveness."[137] As for clout, senators win hands down (they are 1 out of 100 instead of 1 out of 435). So constituents in small states are more than twice as likely to contact their senator than people in larger states.

From all accounts, casework pays off in citizens' support for individual legislators. In one National Election Study (NES) survey, 17 percent of all adults reported that they or members of their families had requested help from their own representatives. Eighty-five percent of them said they were satisfied with the response they received; seven in ten felt the representative would be helpful if asked in the future.[138] "Casework is all profit," contends Morris P. Fiorina. Unlike the positions members take on issues, casework wins friends without alienating anyone. But casework benefits do not entirely supplant issue positions or party loyalties.

Some criticize constituency casework as unfair or biased in practice. Citizens may not enjoy equal access to senators' or representatives' offices. Political supporters or cronies may get favored treatment at others' expense. But in the great bulk of cases, help is universally dispensed.

Personal Staff

Legislators head sizable office enterprises that reflect their two-Congresses responsibilities within the institution and toward their constituents. Staff members assist with legislative and constituency duties. Constituent representation is deemed so essential that when a member dies, resigns, or is incapacitated, the staff normally remains on the job (supervised by the Secretary of the Senate or the Clerk of the House, as the case may be).

Each House member is entitled to an annual member representational account (MRA) of some $1.3 million annually—paying salaries of no more than eighteen full-time and four part-time employees. The average House member's full-time staff actually numbers about fifteen. Representatives also are entitled to an annual office allowance, used for travel, telecommunications, district office rental, office equipment, stationery, computer services, and mail.[139]

Senators' personal staffs range in size from thirteen to seventy-one; the average is from thirty to thirty-five full-time employees. Unlike the House, the Senate places no limits on the number of staff a senator may employ from their two personnel accounts: an administrative and clerical account (which varies according to a state's population) and an account for hiring legislative assistants. A senator's office expense account depends upon factors such as the state's population and its distance from Washington, D.C.

Members' offices always seem crowded and overburdened, but freezes on staff size have been partially offset by computerization, shifting work to state and district offices, and use of volunteers. Congressional offices depend heavily on unpaid help, mainly college-age interns. On average, each House and Senate office uses about nine interns every year (see Appendix B for information on internships).

Staff Organization. No two congressional offices are exactly alike. Each is shaped by the personality, interests, constituency, and politics of the individual legislator. State and district needs also influence staff composition. A senator from a farm state likely will employ at least one specialist in agricultural problems; an urban representative might hire a consumer affairs or housing expert. Traditions are important. If a legislator's predecessor had an enviable reputation for a certain kind of service, the new incumbent will dare not let it lapse.

The member's institutional position also affects staff organization. Committee and subcommittee chairmen have committee staff at their disposal. Members without such aides rely heavily on personal staff for their committee work.

Staff Functions. Most personal aides in the House and Senate are young, well educated, and transient. Senate and House aides have served on average less than four years in their posts. Their salaries, although somewhat above the average for full-time workers in the United States, fall well below those for comparably educated workers.[140]

The mix of personal staff functions is decided by each member. Most hire administrative assistants (AAs), legislative assistants (LAs), caseworkers, and press aides as well as a few people from the home state or district. AAs supervise the office and impart political and legislative advice. Often they function as the legislator's alter ego, negotiating with colleagues, constituents, and lobbyists. LAs work with members in committees, draft bills, write speeches, suggest policy initiatives, analyze legislation, and prepare position papers. They also monitor committee sessions that the member is unable to attend.

To emphasize personal contacts, many members have moved casework staff to their home districts or states. Virtually all House and Senate members have home district offices in post offices or federal buildings. Some members have as many as five or six offices. Members' district staffs fill the role once performed by local party workers, and simultaneously enhance members' reelection prospects. Senators have an average of four home state offices and deploy a third of their staff there. Representatives have an average of 2.3 offices and deploy almost half of their aides in their districts.[141]

Other reasons are cited for decentralizing constituent functions. Capitol Hill office buildings are crowded. Field offices have lower staff salaries, cheaper rents, and less overhead. They also are more accessible to constituents, local and state officials, and regional federal officers. Computers and fax machines make it easy for Washington offices and district offices to communicate. This decentralizing trend implies a heightened division between legislative functions based on Capitol Hill and constituency functions based in field offices. In other words, "Office of the Member Inc." is increasingly split into headquarters and branch divisions—with the Capitol Hill office dealing with legislative duties and the state or district office dealing with constituents.

Because members' resources—offices, staffs, and allowances—are funded by the taxpayers, they are restricted to the conduct of official business. "Any campaign work by staff members must be done outside the congressional office, and without using any congressional office resources," states a 2006 House ethics memorandum.[142] This may seem a cloudy distinction: members' offices are suffused with electoral concerns, and what constitutes "campaign activity" is unclear. During the campaign season, certain aides go on leave and transfer to the campaign organization's payroll. Members' families are also barred from the congressional payroll, although some of them work without pay or within the campaign apparatus. A recent study found that thirty-nine House members had family members on their campaign payrolls—totaling $3 million in salaries over the two election cycles (2002–2004).[143]

MEMBERS AND THE MEDIA

Office allowances in both chambers amply support lawmakers' unceasing struggle for media attention. A member's office bears some resemblance to the communications division of a medium-size business. Nearly every day, stacks of printed matter and electronic messages are released for wide distribution. In addition to turning out press releases, newsletters, and individual and mass mailings, members communicate through telephone calls, interviews, radio and TV programs, e-mail and text messages, personal Web sites, and even through Internet social networking services. Most of the time, these publicity barrages are aimed not at the national media but at individuals and media outlets back in the home state or district.

Direct Mail

The traditional cornerstone of congressional publicity is the franking privilege— the right of members to send out mail at no cost to them with their signature (the frank) instead of a stamp. The practice, which in the United States dates from the First Continental Congress in 1775, is intended to facilitate official communication between elected officials and the people they represent (a ratio- nale accepted by federal courts in upholding the practice). In recent times mem- bers found that aggressive use of the frank could aid reelection. Rep. Bill Frenzel, R-Minn. (1971–1991), noted that both parties teach newcomers three rules for getting reelected: "Use the frank. Use the frank. Use the frank."[144]

Critics point out that franked mail is largely unsolicited and politically moti- vated. Outgoing mail costs are much higher in election years than in nonelection years. Most items are mass mailings, not individual letters. Mass mailings are either general-purpose newsletters blanketing home states or districts or special messages targeted to certain categories of voters. Recipients are urged to share their views or contact local offices for help. Sometimes the newsletter may feature an opinion poll asking for citizens' views on selected issues. Whatever the results, the underlying message is that the legislator cares what folks back home think.

The current franking law forbids using franked mail "unrelated to the official business, activities, and duties of members." It also bars the frank for a "matter which specifically solicits political support for the sender or any other person or any political party, or a vote or financial assistance for any candidate for any political office." In addition, chamber rules forbid mass mailings (500 or more pieces) 60 days (Senate) or 90 days (House) before a primary, runoff, or general election. In the two months before the beginning of each cutoff period, streams of U.S. Postal Service trucks are seen pulling away from loading docks of the congressional office buildings.

Caps have been placed on newsletters and on total outgoing mail—one piece for each address in the state for senators, three pieces for each address in the district for representatives. Rules governing newsletters curb their advertising features, for example, personal references or pictures of the member. Recent reforms reversed the upward spiral of congressional mail costs.[145]

Although it can still be abused, the franking privilege is essential to sustain communications between lawmakers and their constituents. A former chairman of a House oversight commission posed the issue: "How do you write rules and regulations that distinguish between a thoughtful discussion of some important public issue and a self-promoting thing with the photograph of a member on every other page?"[146]

The advent of e-mail poses the problem of whether, or how, the much-debated franking restrictions should apply. The Senate has generally applied the franking rules to electronic mail. The House, however, has declined to adopt such strict rules. As Rep. Vernon J. Ehlers, R-Mich., says of the e-mail issue:

> It is not partisan, it is just simply an informational summary of these bills that were taken up, this is the result of the bills. My constituents are finding that useful, the e-mail list is growing. I think my constituents…will find it a bit strange to suddenly, three months before the election, they are not allowed to hear from me about what the Congress has done in a nonpartisan way.[147]

Americans increasingly rely on the Internet for news.[148] It's no wonder, then, that lawmakers have rapidly set up Web sites, and even blogs.[149] Most (but not all) sites feature the member's biography, committee assignments, and votes on major issues. Capitol Hill Web sites exhibit variety in their content, usability, and interactivity.[150] Some members' Web sites include streaming audio or video of members' speeches or appearances on news programs. Few of them include such potentially sensitive information as the member's financial disclosure reports, earmark requests, travel spending, and meetings with lobbyists.

Members are quick to embrace new technologies to communicate with constituents. Many members now make use of social networking Web sites such as Facebook and Twitter. Reporting on lawmakers using their BlackBerries throughout President Barack Obama's first address to a joint session of Congress, *Washington Post* journalist Dana Milbank joked, "It's bad enough that Americans are paralyzed by economic jitters. Now the president has to deal with lawmakers paralyzed by Twitter."[151] Milbank quotes some of the members' tweets that describe the president's speech: "'Sounds like nationalization—very bad news.'…'Not many applause lines. Some in the audience not sure to react.'…'First big divide: he thanks Congress for recovery act. D's cheer, R's silent.'"

Feeding the Local Press

News outlets in North America are decentralized and dispersed. These include daily and weekly newspapers, radio and TV stations, and cable systems.

Virtually all these media outlets are locally based because of the vitality of local issues and local advertising.

Most local media outlets have inadequate resources for covering what their congressional delegations are doing in the nation's capital. Few of them have their own Washington reporters. Most rely on syndicated or chain services that rarely follow individual members consistently. "If they report national news it is usually because it involves local personalities, affects local outcomes, or relates directly to local concerns," stated a Senate report.[152]

Relations with the press receive close attention from members. Most legislators have at least one staffer who serves as a press aide; some have two or three. Their job is to generate coverage highlighting the member's work. Executive agencies often help by letting incumbents announce federal grants or contracts awarded in the state or district. Even if the member had nothing to do with procuring the funds, the press statement proclaims, "Senator So-and-So announced today that a federal contract has been awarded to XYZ Company in Jonesville." Many offices also prepare weekly or biweekly columns that small-town newspapers can reprint under the lawmaker's byline.

The House, the Senate, and the four Capitol Hill parties (House and Senate Republicans and Democrats) have fully equipped studios and satellite links where audio or video programs or excerpted statements (called actualities) can be produced for a fraction of the commercial cost.[153] Some incumbents produce regular programs that are picked up by local radio or television outlets. More often, these outlets insert brief audio or TV clips on current issues into regular news broadcasts—to give the impression that their reporters have gone out and obtained the story. Members also create their own news reports and beam them directly to hometown stations, often without ever talking to a reporter. With direct satellite feeds to local stations, members regularly go "live at five" before local audiences.

Like printed communications, radio and TV broadcasts pose ethical questions. House and Senate recording studios are supposed to be used only for communicating about legislation and other policy issues, but the distinction between legitimate constituent outreach and political advertising remains blurred. (The studios run by the parties have no such limits.) Some radio and television news editors have qualms about using members' programs. "It's just this side of self-serving," said one television editor of the biweekly "Alaska Delegation Report."[154] Others claim to see little difference between these electronic communications and old-fashioned press releases. Local editors and producers still have to decide whether to use the material, edit it, or toss it.

Local Press Boosterism?

With a few notable exceptions, local media fail to convey even minimal information about their representatives. Most stories are uncritically positive: only 6 percent of the news stories compiled by Douglas Arnold cited anyone who criticized the incumbent's performance.[155] As a result of this pervasive positive tilt, when members successfully cultivate local coverage, they are more likely to win reelection.[156]

In the eyes of home district media outlets, incumbents simply fare splendidly. Michael J. Robinson cited the case of "Congressman Press," a midlevel House member, untouched by scandal, who had an average press operation. Drawing on 144 press releases from his office over the course of a year, his local paper ran 120 stories featuring or mentioning him. "On average, every other week, Congressman Press was featured in a story virtually written in his own office."[157]

Even when local stories are not drawn from press releases, they tend to be respectful if not downright laudatory. A detailed study of the local press corps in eighty-two contested races highlighted the journalists' tendency toward "safety and timidity." Incumbents were rendered respectful coverage based on their experience; in contested open seats, journalists tended to keep their distance.[158] However, one recent study finds that local media give closer scrutiny to House members who are perceived as out of step with constituents' views than to members who are perceived as in-step, suggesting that these media do a better job of promoting accountability in cases where members are thought to have strayed from constituency preferences.[159]

Electronic media are even more benign than print media. As one legislator said, "TV people need thirty seconds of sound and video at the airport when I arrive—that's all they want."[160] Most local reporters for radio and TV are on general assignment and do little preparation for interviews. Their primary goal is to get the newsmaker on tape. This is especially true of outlets in smaller markets, few of which have access to a Washington bureau.

Local radio and television's weakness for congressionally initiated communications magnifies the advantages incumbents enjoy. ABC-TV correspondent Cokie Roberts concludes, "The emergence of local TV has made some members media stars in the home towns and, I would argue, done more to protect incumbency than any franking privilege or newsletter ever could, simply because television is a more pervasive medium than print."[161] A recent study reports a strong link between the expansion of local television stations across the country and the rise of incumbency advantage in the post-1960s era.[162]

Reports on Congress from the national press corps are far more critical than those from local news organizations. Following the canons of investigative journalism, many national reporters are on the lookout for scandals or evidence of wrongdoing. The national press reports primarily on the institution of Congress, whereas the local press focuses mostly on local senators and representatives. Individual members tend to be reported on far more favorably than the institution. The content and quality of press coverage in local and national media underscore the differences between the two Congresses. Congress as collective policymaker, covered mainly by the national press, appears in a different light from the politicians who make up the Congress covered mainly by local news outlets.

CONCLUSION

How members of Congress manage the two Congresses dilemma is reflected in their daily tasks on Capitol Hill and in their home states or districts. Election is a prerequisite to congressional service. Legislators allocate much of their time and energy, and even more of their staff and office resources, to the care and cultivation of voters. Their Hill styles and home styles are adopted with this end in mind.

Yet senators and representatives do not live by reelection alone. Many bemoan the need for constant campaigning. "What drives me nuts about this place is that, when I came here, it used to be that you had at least a year after you were elected where you could get the people's business done before the next election intruded," complained veteran legislator David Obey, D-Wis. "Now the way politics has been nationalized, the election intrudes every day."[163] For those who remain in office, reelection is not usually viewed as an end in itself, but as a lever for pursuing other goals—policymaking or career advancement, for example. Fenno challenged one of the representatives whose constituency career he had followed, remarking that "sometimes it must be hard to connect what you do here with what you do in Washington." "Oh no," the lawmaker replied, "I do what I do here so I can do what I want to do there."[164]

SUGGESTED READINGS

Arnold, R. Douglas. *Congress, the Press, and Political Accountability.* Princeton: Princeton University Press, 2004.

Baker, Ross K. *House and Senate.* 3d ed. New York: Norton, 2001.

Burden, Barry C. *Personal Roots of Representation.* Princeton: Princeton University Press, 2007.

Cook, Timothy. *Making Laws and Making News: Media Strategies in the U.S. House of Representatives.* Washington, D.C.: Brookings Institution Press, 1989.

Davidson, Roger H. *The Role of the Congressman.* Indianapolis: Bobbs-Merrill, 1969.

Fenno, Richard F., Jr. *Home Style: House Members in Their Districts.* Boston: Little, Brown, 1978.

Fiorina, Morris P. *Congress: Keystone of the Washington Establishment.* 2d ed. New Haven: Yale University Press, 1989.

Hibbing, John R. *Congressional Careers: Contours of Life in the U.S. House of Representatives.* Chapel Hill: University of North Carolina Press, 1991.

Lipinski, Daniel. *Congressional Communication: Content and Consequences.* Ann Arbor: University of Michigan Press, 2004.

Price, David E. *The Congressional Experience: A View from the Hill.* 2d ed. Boulder, Colo.: Westview Press, 2004.

Rosenthal, Cindy Simon, ed. *Women Transforming Congress.* Norman: University of Oklahoma Press, 2002.

Swers, Michele L. *The Difference Women Make: The Policy Impact of Women in Congress.* Chicago: University of Chicago Press, 2002.

P *arty Leaders.* Surrounded by children—her own grand-children and other members' children, House Speaker Nancy Pelosi (D-Calif.) raises her hand to take her oath of office in January 2007 (top). She became the first woman to hold the office when her party took control for the first time in twelve years. The three Democratic leaders (center) meet the press after a White House meeting: From left to right, House Majority Leader Steny H. Hoyer (Md.), Speaker Pelosi, and Senate Majority Leader Harry Reid (Nev.). Republican leaders (bottom, from left to right): Senate Minority Leader Mitch McConnell (Ky.) and House Minority Leader John A. Boehner (Ohio) stand on stage at the 2008 Republican National Convention in St. Paul, Minnesota.

Leaders and
Parties in Congress

On January 6, 2009, Speaker of the House Nancy Pelosi, D-Calif., stood on the rostrum in the House chamber, surrounded by her grandchildren and those of other representatives, to administer the oath of office to all House members. The opening day ceremony for the 111th Congress was for the Speaker not only a new beginning, but also a culmination. Long before that day, Speaker Pelosi had been laying the foundation for this new legislative session.

For more than a year, Pelosi had worked tirelessly to expand the Democratic majority. The large class of thirty-two Democratic newcomers were taking the oath for the first time in part because of Pelosi's efforts, as well as the party campaign committee she had assembled. The House's top fundraiser, Pelosi had raised a reported $40 million for Democratic candidates in 2007–2008.[1] She campaigned all over the country: "In a single weekend, her itinerary had her campaigning in New York, Chicago, Dallas, Los Angeles, and Atlanta—and aides say that pace was not unusual."[2]

Ever since the November elections two months earlier, Pelosi had also been engaged in organizing Democrats for the upcoming Congress. The first order of business was to work with the Steering Committee to fill committee positions, a complex balancing of the two Congresses. Committee chairs need members with whom they can work. Members want assignments that take advantage of their talents and expertise. Vulnerable members require positions that will allow them to build reputations among constituents; more senior members seek seats on key committees to exert a wider influence. These complicated organizational matters needed to be resolved before the new Congress convened; otherwise, progress on the sizable Democratic agenda would be stalled in the session's critical early months.[3]

One of Pelosi's most delicate organizational responsibilities is managing intraparty conflicts. A leader's best course of action is often to discourage ambitious members from challenging party colleagues. After successfully managing the Democratic Congressional Campaign Committee (DCCC), for example, Rep. Chris Van Hollen, D-Md., wanted to step up in the leadership by bidding for caucus chair. Pelosi persuaded him to stay on at DCCC for another cycle, thus avoiding an "all out fight."[4] To make her request more attractive, Pelosi gave him the new title of special assistant to the Speaker.[5]

In another case, Pelosi faced an explosive conflict over the chairmanship of the Energy and Commerce committee—whose expansive jurisdiction encompassed President Barack Obama's expected initiatives in energy sustainability and health care. Two distinguished lawmakers sought that important post at the beginning of the 111th Congress. The House's longest-serving member, John Dingell, D-Mich., chaired the committee in the 110th Congress and from 1981 until 1995, when the GOP took over the House. Dingell faced a challenge from the more activist, and more liberal, Henry Waxman, D-Calif. The battle was ideologically charged and split the Democratic caucus down the middle.[6] With her well-known environmentalist record and close relationship with her fellow Californian, Pelosi was known to prefer Waxman. Nonetheless, Pelosi handled the issue with great care to avoid alienating Dingell and his supporters—nearly half the Democratic caucus. She remained aloof from the dispute.[7] She even instructed her close allies not to use her name in any efforts to help Waxman.[8] By not taking a clear position on the issue, her preferred outcome was achieved without heavy-handed interference. Soon afterwards, Pelosi held a ceremony in honor of Dingell's record-breaking congressional service to say, "We love and respect John Dingell."[9]

As a final step to prepare for the new Congress, Pelosi also worked behind the scenes to put together a package of rule changes to facilitate the passage of the Democratic agenda. The most controversial modification placed new limits on the motion to recommit, a procedural tactic that Republicans had repeatedly used in the previous Congress to block Democratic initiatives.[10] The package also removed term limits on committee chairs, a move that could impede junior members hoping to move up into leadership.[11] Despite the potential for conflict, the measures were adopted with little fanfare as one of the first acts of the new Congress.

Building electoral majorities, managing internal party organization, presiding over the House and its internal rules are among the Speaker's wide-ranging duties. These tasks must always be carried out with careful attention to the forces of the two Congresses. Leaders must facilitate lawmaking, while at the same time attending to party members' representational ties with their constituents. "[Pelosi] knows each and every [Democratic] member," explains Rep. Anna Eshoo, D-Calif. "So much of her work is one-on-one with members, in identifying what is troubling to them and what is important to their constituents."[12] Making national policy means finding ways of persuading individual members who represent different constituencies, regions, ideologies, values, and interests to support legislation that addresses national concerns. "The only thing that counts is 218 votes, and nothing else is real," a House Democratic leader declares. "You have to be able [to attract a majority of the House] to pass a bill."[13]

Implicit in this party leader's statement is recognition that mobilizing winning coalitions is not easy. Party leaders encounter what scholars call a "collective action" dilemma.[14] How can leaders mobilize a majority to pass legislation (for the collective or public good) when it is often in the self-interest of many lawmakers to do little or nothing to secure the measure's enactment, even if they favor it, because the bill's advocates will invest the necessary time and effort to secure its passage? Thus, many lawmakers may take a free ride on the efforts of their colleagues and then claim credit and receive benefits from the bill's enactment. If there are too many free riders though, little lawmaking gets done.

Congressional leaders resolve the collective action problem in two main ways: devising sufficient incentives (political, policy, or procedural, for example) to attract majority support, and coordinating the work of the bill's champions to win desired objectives. Leadership in legislatures, then, "can be seen as having been instituted to ameliorate the problems of collective action…. [P]arty leaders are seen as agents of the members who select them and charge them" with acting on their behalf to achieve a number of goals, including the production of collective goods.[15]

Taking account of the two Congresses also requires party leaders to assume leadership roles both inside and outside the institution. In their inside role, party leaders formulate national policy agendas and use their procedural and organizational authority to advance them. In their outside role, party leaders articulate and publicize issue agendas designed to galvanize partisan support and swing voters. They help recruit candidates for Congress and assist in their campaigns. Leaders also must serve as the party's link to the president, the press, the public, and the party faithful. In 2004 Speaker Dennis Hastert, R-Ill., was heavily involved in both House electoral races and President George W. Bush's reelection campaign. "I see us all in this together," Hastert told a reporter. "It is important for us to go and run a good campaign for our own survival and that's good for the president. If the president does well and he gets people excited positively, that helps us. There is a cumulative effect here."[16]

The leaders' inside and outside roles interrelate. In today's era of ideological polarization and intense electoral competition, the line between campaigning and governing has all but disappeared. Locked in a permanent campaign, leaders try to generate public support and momentum in order to force legislative action on party priorities. "The reality is, to get something done in this town you've got to deal with the policy and the politics," explained former representative Rob Portman, R-Ohio.[17]

Congress is a partisan body. That is, legislative organization is partisan organization. The majority party in the House or the Senate controls not only the top leadership posts and each chamber's agenda of activities, but also the chairmanships and majorities on committees and subcommittees.

LEADERS OF THE HOUSE

House rules permit a determined majority to achieve its policy objectives, but it was not always so. Before 1890, intense battles were fought over the majority party's right to govern and the minority party's right to have input. The minority party was able to use a variety of stalling tactics to prevent action in the pre- and post–Civil War House. In the 1890s, however, Republican Speaker Thomas "Czar" Reed of Maine finally broke the minority's capacity to frustrate House decision making. The House adopted new rules (the famous Reed Rules) to facilitate majority rule and action. An 1890 House rule, which remains in effect today, states: "No dilatory motion shall be entertained by the Speaker."

The Speaker of the House

No other member of the House possesses the visibility and authority of the Speaker. The Constitution states that the House "shall choose their Speaker." Although the Constitution does not require the Speaker to be a House member, all of them have been. Under the Presidential Succession Act of 1947, the Speaker is next in line behind the vice president to succeed to the presidency.

The office of Speaker combines procedural and political prerogatives with policy and partisan leadership. Speakers preside over the House, rule on points of order, announce the results of votes, refer legislation to the committees, name lawmakers to serve on conference committees and select committees, and maintain order and decorum in the House chamber. In addition to these procedural prerogatives, they exercise important political powers. They set the House's agenda of activities, control the Rules Committee, chair or influence the decisions of their party's committee assignment panel, bestow or withhold various rewards, coordinate policymaking with Senate counterparts, and, in this age of video and Internet politics, expound party and House positions to the public at large. In practice, Speakers today seldom actually preside over the House because they focus considerable attention on external activities, such as campaigning for party members, fund-raising, and message development.

Speakers are formally elected by the members of the House. Today this means that Speakers have served long careers in the House to build relationships with fellow members and to rise through the ranks of the party. Before 1899, however, it was not uncommon for Speakers to have only a few years of service as representatives. Henry Clay of Kentucky was elected to the speakership on November 4, 1811—his first day in the House. Speakers elected since 1899 have served, on average, more than twenty years before their election to the post. Pelosi served twenty years before becoming Speaker in 2007.

Once in office, Speakers traditionally have been reelected as long as their party controlled the House. Members typically vote for the speakership along straight party lines. Not since 1923 has there been a floor battle over the speakership, because one party has always enjoyed a clear majority. As chief parliamentary officer and leader of the majority party (see Figure 6-1), the Speaker enjoys unique powers in scheduling floor business and in recognizing members during sessions. Occasionally, Speakers will relinquish the gavel to join in floor debate. Recent Speakers, such as Hastert and Pelosi, often vote on issues before the House.[18]

The Speaker is also in charge of administrative matters. When Speaker Newt Gingrich took office after forty years of Democratic control, he revamped the administrative structure and management of the House. Gingrich's reforms abolished administrative units and positions, streamlined and modernized management, undertook an outside independent audit of the accounting systems, and assigned responsibility to a new chief administrative officer—elected by the House at the start of each Congress—for running the House's administrative operations in a professional manner.[19] Like Hastert, Speaker Pelosi retained this administrative structure.

Cannon and Rayburn. Speakers gradually accrued power during the Republic's first 120 years. By 1910 Speaker Joseph G. Cannon, R-Ill., dominated the House. He assigned members to committees, appointed and removed committee chairmen, referred bills to committee, regulated the flow of bills to the House floor as chairman of the Rules Committee, and controlled floor debate. Taken individually, Cannon's powers were little different from those of his immediate predecessors; but taken together and exercised to their limits, they bordered on the dictatorial. The result was a revolt against Cannon. Progressive Republicans combined with discontented minority Democrats to reduce the Speaker's authority.

The House forced Cannon to step down from the Rules Committee in 1910 and required the House to elect the committee's members. The next year, when Democrats took control of the House, the new Speaker (James B. "Champ" Clark of Missouri) was denied the authority to make committee assignments, and his power of recognition was curtailed. The speakership then went into long-term eclipse as power flowed briefly to party caucuses and then to the committee chairs.

Over time after the 1910 revolt, committees became more powerful relative to party leaders. Power in Congress was diffused among a relatively small number of committee chairmen who were often called the "dukes" or "barons" of Capitol Hill. These chairmen rose to power by means of a nearly inviolable seniority system, in which the committee's longest serving majority party member served as chair until death, resignation, or retirement. This system tended to elevate conservative southern Democrats from safe seats to top committee posts, a process that often installed committee chairs who were out of step with the preferences of party leaders.

Speakers after Cannon exhibited various leadership styles that reflected their personalities, the historical context in which they operated, and the extent of conflict both within their party and the chamber as a whole. The longest serving Speaker in history, Democrat Sam Rayburn of Texas (1940–1947, 1949–1953, 1955–1961), functioned largely as a broker or mediator, negotiating with and persuading the powerful chairs to report out legislation supported by the Democratic majority. Rayburn used his personal prestige as well as his long political experience and immense parliamentary skills to provide coherence for a decentralized chamber. As he explained, "The old day of pounding on the desk and giving people hell is gone....A man's got to lead by persuasion and kindness and the best reason—that's the only way he can lead people."[20]

FIGURE 6-1   Organization of the House of Representatives, 111th Congress (2009–2011)

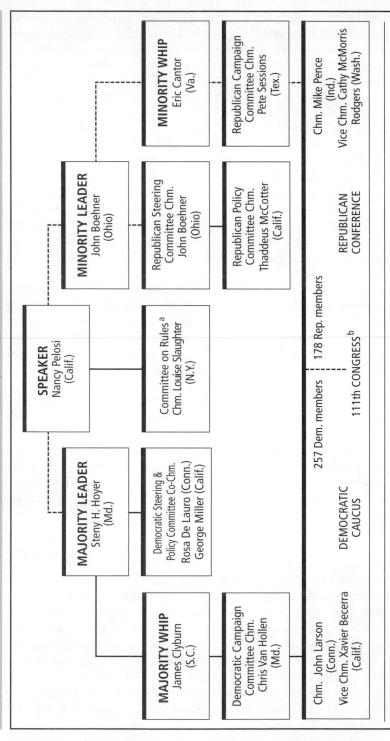

[a] Although not strictly a party panel, the Rules Committee in modern times functions largely as an arm of the majority leadership.

[b] As of May 2009.

The relationship between these two centers of institutional power— committee and party—provides a useful analytical framework for assessing the extent of centralized (party dominance) versus decentralized (committee autonomy) authority in the legislature. The Cannon era was plainly a time of party power. Over much of the twentieth century, the balance of power tilted toward committee leaders—with the seniority principle governing the selection of House and Senate committee chairmen. Today, although committees and their leaders remain powerful, party leaders are more pivotal in influencing action on the major issues of the day. Both power centers, meanwhile, can be fettered by majority vote of the chamber's membership.

Revival of the Speakership. The distribution of internal power changed fundamentally after Rayburn. Activist, liberal lawmakers elected during the Vietnam War and the Watergate era found themselves frustrated by the conservative tilt of the committee barons. This liberal bloc joined forces with other longtime members disgruntled with the status quo to curb the power of committee chairs. These reformist Democrats took a two-pronged approach to transform the distribution of power in the House.

First, they aimed to limit the ability of committee chairs to act independently. They made chairs more accountable to their party. Rather than allowing them to hold their chairmanships regardless of their adherence to their party's agenda, the new party rules required that committee chairs be elected by secret ballot of the Democratic Caucus. Committee chairs were also obligated to share power with subcommittee chairs.

Second, the reformers strengthened the hand of the party leadership. The Speaker, for example, gained the right to name all the majority party members of the Rules Committee, including the chair. The Speaker was also permitted to refer measures to more than one committee. By the late 1970s, majority Democrats recognized that dispersing power to more subcommittees had hampered their ability to accomplish policy and political goals. Accordingly, rank-and-file Democrats encouraged their party leaders to use their new powers to overcome institutional fragmentation and to curb minority Republicans' ability to obstruct action on the floor.

Three Democratic Speakers—Thomas P. "Tip" O'Neill Jr. of Massachusetts (1977–1987), Jim Wright of Texas (1987–1989), and Thomas S. Foley of Washington (1989–1995)—were the immediate beneficiaries of these changes. Just as intended, the reforms of the 1960s and 1970s had strengthened leaders' ability to assemble winning coalitions. O'Neill held the speakership for ten consecutive years, the longest uninterrupted service of any Speaker. Using a strategy of inclusion to draw Democratic rank-and-file members into the leadership orbit, he expanded the whip structure and encouraged junior Democrats to back partisan priorities by appointing them to leadership task forces.[21] During the first six years of the Reagan presidency—when the Senate was in Republican hands—O'Neill became the Democratic Party's national spokesman. In the process he transformed the speakership into an office of high national visibility.

O'Neill's successor was Jim Wright, who pushed the prerogatives of the office even further. In domestic and foreign policy, Wright took bold risks. Whereas O'Neill strived for consensus, Wright laid out an agenda and then worked diligently—by himself if necessary—to mobilize support. "The Congress," declared Wright, "should not simply react, passively, to recommendations from the president but should come forward with initiatives of its own."[22] His unyielding personal style and knack for making "minority status more painful," as one House GOP leader put it, embittered Republicans (and even some of his own party).[23]

"If Wright consolidates his power, he will be a very, very formidable man," warned the GOP's Representative Gingrich. "We have to take him on early to prevent that."[24] Gingrich brought ethics charges against the Speaker, and they were investigated by the Committee on Standards of Official Conduct. That panel eventually charged Wright with violating House rules by accepting gifts from a close business associate and circumventing limits on members' outside income through bulk sales of his 1984 book *Reflections of a Public Man* to lobbyists and interest groups. Wright did not survive these ethical and political challenges and left the House in June 1989.

End of an Era: Foley (1989–1995). Wright's successor was then–majority leader Foley. Elected to the House in 1964, Foley had risen through the ranks during an era of sharp partisan, political, and personal infighting. He had a reputation for being a judicious, low-key, and consensus-oriented leader. His initial objectives as Speaker were to restore civility, integrity, and bipartisan cooperation to the House and to provide policy direction. Although Republicans found Foley easier to deal with than Wright, they soon lamented the Speaker's willingness to use procedural rules to frustrate GOP objectives. Moreover, problems that afflicted the Wright speakership—intraparty divisions and bipartisan scandals (revelations of check bouncing at the House bank by nearly 300 members)—continued under Foley. Republicans targeted Foley for defeat in November 1994, hammering him for opposing term limits for lawmakers—a major issue at the time. After a thirty-year congressional career, Speaker Foley lost reelection as Democrats lost the House.

Gingrich: A New Style of Speaker (1995–1999). Speaker Newt Gingrich, R-Ga., took the office to new heights. As minority whip before the 1994 elections, Gingrich had spearheaded a ten-point party platform titled "The Contract with America." Almost all House Republican candidates pledged to act on every item in the platform within the first 100 days of the 104th Congress if their party won a majority in the House. Gingrich was widely credited for the GOP's sweeping victory in the 1994 elections. One of his House GOP colleagues articulated the conventional wisdom: "[Gingrich is] the one responsible for leading the Republican Party out of the wilderness of the minority [where it had wandered for forty years before the 1994 elections] to the promised land of the majority. He is singularly responsible for us being where we are now."[25] Gingrich was his party's unanimous choice for Speaker, taking the place of retiring GOP Leader Bob Michel.

Gingrich had an expansive idea of the Speaker's role. His Democratic predecessors, Gingrich once said, were "essentially legislative leaders speaking to the press about legislative matters." He went on to say, "I, on the other hand, was essentially a political leader of a grassroots movement seeking to do nothing less than reshape the federal government along with the political culture of the nation."[26] Gingrich, a commentator observed, was "first a leader of a national movement, then a Republican spokesman and, only third, Speaker of the House."[27]

Gingrich was a strikingly effective Speaker, although his power waned over time. During the initial 100-day period, the House observed a parliamentary model of governance as GOP lawmakers marched in lockstep to follow the lead of their "prime minister." Gingrich centralized power by reducing the independence of committees. He selected committee members and leaders who would strongly support his agenda. He personally chose the chairs of several standing committees, ignoring seniority in the process. In addition, he required the GOP members of the Appropriations Committee to sign a written pledge that they would heed the leadership's directives for spending reductions. During his speakership, he often bypassed committees entirely by establishing leadership task forces to process legislation. Most significantly, he changed House rules to impose six-year term limits for all committee and subcommittee chairs—so that no chairperson could accumulate enough influence to challenge the central party leaders. In short, party power dominated committee power.

Everything in the ten-point contract except term limits for lawmakers passed the House within 100 days. In an unprecedented event that tracked what presidents often do, Gingrich gave a prime-time, nationally televised address on April 17, 1995, highlighting the House's achievements during its first 100 days and outlining the country's future direction. Not since the early 1800s—when Speaker Henry Clay put forward an agenda ("The American System") for strengthening the nation's infrastructure—had a Speaker so exploited the position's bully pulpit. Under Gingrich, the speakership became a platform for focusing public debate on crucial issues of national governance.

Gingrich's Contract set the agenda for Congress and the nation long after the election that made it possible. Although the Contract's items encountered many legislative roadblocks thrown up by President Bill Clinton and the Senate, they eventually resulted in a substantial legislative record. Tracing out all the Contract measures through the end of Gingrich's speakership, Randall Strahan concludes that "sixteen bills originating in the Contract or containing major Contract provisions had been signed into law by 1998."[28]

Despite early successes, however, Gingrich's confrontational strategy with the White House eventually produced political disaster for Republicans. Two extended face-offs with President Clinton in late 1995 and early 1996 resulted in failures to pass appropriations bills needed to fund ongoing government operations. As a result, the government was forced to shut down. Opinion polls showed that the public blamed Republicans, not President Clinton, for these government shutdowns.[29] Further, Republicans' revolutionary plans for down-sizing government by eliminating cabinet departments and reducing spending for education, environment, and health programs were successfully character-ized by Democrats as extreme. Gingrich's public popularity plummeted, and the Speaker became a campaign issue in many 1996 congressional races.

After President Clinton won reelection to a second term, Gingrich had to contend with the difficulties of legislating with a smaller majority in the 105th Congress (1997–1999). In addition, he faced ethics charges of his own. Shortly after the 1996 elections, Gingrich admitted that he had provided inaccurate and incomplete information to the House Ethics Committee regarding his solicitation of tax-deductible contributions, which were used for partisan pur-poses contrary to federal law. Two weeks after Gingrich's reelection as Speaker, the House voted 395–28 to reprimand him for ethical misconduct and to fine him $300,000. He thus became the first Speaker formally disciplined by the House for ethical wrongdoing.

Weakened by the ethics charge, Gingrich no longer dominated the House as he once did. Rank-and-file Republicans and his top leadership lieutenants became frustrated with Gingrich's leadership. Rep. Peter T. King, R-N.Y., urged Gingrich to step aside as Speaker because his low popular standing—job approval ratings below 30 percent—reduced his ability to advance Republican priorities. "As roadkill on the highway of American politics," King wrote, "Newt Gingrich cannot sell the Republican agenda."[30] *Time Magazine*'s 1995 "Man of the Year" had fallen far in the next year. Other GOP leaders and a small band of ideologically hard-line junior conservatives complained that Gingrich com-promised too much with the Democrats. As a result, they hatched a plot to remove him from the speakership in the summer of 1997. Although the scheme was uncovered and averted, it exposed the deep frustration with the Speaker within Republican ranks.[31]

On the eve of the 1998 elections, the Speaker took a high-risk political gamble. Despite polls showing the public was sick of hearing about President Clinton's sexual relationship with White House intern Monica S. Lewinsky, Gingrich gave the order to GOP campaign officials to blanket selected House districts with multimillion-dollar TV ads highlighting the scandal. When the House adjourned two weeks before the election, Clinton-fixated Republicans had no coherent agenda to promote.

When the 1998 midterm results came in, Republicans were shell-shocked at their poor showing. Scores of Republicans blamed Gingrich for another elec-tion in which they lost seats despite early predictions (including those of the Speaker) that their party would gain seats and coast to victory. Gingrich became an early casualty of the election, abruptly departing the race for the speakership and resigning from the House. A skillful insurgency leader, Gingrich had diffi-culty adjusting to the formidable job of governing the House.

The Coach as Speaker: Dennis Hastert (1999–2007). After Gingrich's pre-sumptive successor, Appropriations chair Robert Livingston, La., announced that he, too, was resigning from the House (having admitted to adultery),

Republicans turned to Hastert, the GOP's chief deputy whip since 1995. A respected, well-liked conservative lawmaker, he quickly lined up the support of his party colleagues. As such, he became Speaker without having served in an elective leadership post—something that had not occurred since Frederick Gillett, R-Mass., was Speaker (1919–1925). But his GOP colleagues sensed that Hastert was the right person for the job. "We needed somebody who was not nuclear, that was not controversial, that members trusted," said Majority Leader Tom DeLay, R-Texas, a key supporter and vote-gatherer for Hastert.[32]

A former high school wrestling coach, Hastert employed coaching metaphors to explain his leadership role. "A good coach knows when to step back and let others shine in the spotlight," he said.[33] He added, "They call me speaker, but they probably ought to call me the listener because I just do a lot of it."[34] The longest-serving GOP Speaker, Hastert maintained a modest public profile, sharing his national spokesman's role with other Republicans. As Hastert said: "I don't think I have to be [at] the head of every news release or press conference...and...on every Sunday talk show."[35] Hastert, noted one account, was "not known for the pithy sound bites that modern politics demands."[36]

Despite his lower public profile, Hastert exercised "top down" command of the House and followed a partisan governing strategy on party-preferred measures. "The job of the Speaker," he said, "is not to expedite legislation that runs counter to the wishes of the majority of his majority."[37] Further, he consolidated power in a trio of leaders—himself, the majority leader (DeLay), and the majority whip (Roy Blunt, Mo.).

This leadership team was not reluctant to direct rank-and-file members or committee chairmen to toe the line on issues of importance to the party. For example, during a GOP Conference meeting, Veterans Affairs chairman Christopher H. Smith, N.J., criticized the Republicans' budget resolution and the White House's spending proposals for veterans. Speaker Hastert "got up and shut him down," said a witness to the tongue-lashing. "That was off the charts. I've never seen anything like that....It was scathing."[38] Smith nevertheless refused to curb his advocacy of more spending for veterans, setting himself against the wishes of Republican leaders and the Bush administration. In a precedent-setting action, GOP leaders removed Smith as Veterans chair at the start of the 109th Congress (2005–2007), even though he had served only four of the six years allowed. Smith was even removed as a member of the panel.

Hastert's leadership role changed when Republican George W. Bush became president. No longer was he required to develop agendas and strategies to counter the plans of a Democratic president. Instead, he worked with President Bush to coordinate communications strategies and to move the administration's priorities through Congress. "It's my job to make sure that we can pass bills the president can sign," he stated, "and if we [pass] bills the president can't support, then I'm derelict in my duty."[39]

The 2006 elections ended Hastert's tenure as Speaker; he left the GOP leadership and resigned his House seat in November 2007.

The "History Maker" as Speaker: Nancy Pelosi. On January 4, 2007, in her inaugural speech as Speaker, Nancy Pelosi acknowledged that this is "a historic moment for the Congress, and it is a historic moment for the women of America." Her path to power merits brief mention. As Pelosi noted in her address to the House, her experience in politics "began in Baltimore where my father was the mayor" (he was also an eight-year member of Congress). As the daughter of a political leader, Pelosi learned the art of politics, including keeping a "favor file," as her Dad called it, of the assistance she provides to congressmen along with their responses to her requests. As Rep. Jim McDermott, D-Wash., noted, "She won't say, 'Vote this way.' She'll say, 'You are free to do what you want.' But you can be sure she'll remember if you don't do the right thing."[40]

Upon graduation from college, Pelosi married, moved to San Francisco, and raised five children. Active in California politics, she became state party chair and a major fund-raiser for Democrats. She was also an avid supporter of the labor-liberal policies of Rep. Phil Burton, a dominant figure in San Francisco politics. When he died in 1983, his wife Sala succeeded him in the House. Four years later, on her deathbed, Sala Burton endorsed Nancy Pelosi to succeed her. Pelosi defeated a number of rivals in the Democratic primary, won the safe seat, and in June 1987, at the age of 47, began her service in the House.

Her twenty-year rise to the speakership began when her party colleagues elected her minority whip of the 107th House (2001–2003), defeating her long-time rival Steny Hoyer of Maryland. Two years later, following the disappointing loss of seats in the November 2002 elections, Richard Gephardt, Mo., stepped down as Democratic leader. Pelosi easily won the post and became the first woman to head a political party in Congress. For the next four years she set her sights on reclaiming the House for Democrats. Unsuccessful in the 2004 elections, she worked tenaciously for the next two years to reverse that result.

During the 2006 election cycle, she raised $50 million and campaigned indefatiguably to boost the electoral chances of Democratic incumbents and challengers.[41] She kept her fractious Democrats united, limiting Speaker Hastert's ability to persuade her Democratic colleagues to back GOP bills. House Democrats voted together 88 percent of the time, "the most unified voting record in 50 years."[42] Pelosi imposed message discipline on her colleagues as they showcased a "Six for '06" agenda during the 2006 campaign: raising the minimum wage, funding stem cell research, reducing student loan interest rates, eliminating tax subsidies for oil and gas companies, adopting the remaining recommendations of the 9/11 Commission, lowering drug prices, enacting ethics and lobbying reforms, and restoring fiscal discipline.

Three things at least are clear from her early period as Speaker. First, she knows how to achieve results. She won House adoption of the "Six for '06" agenda within the promised 100 legislative hours.[43] The swift passage of the agenda— which won the support, on average, of about a third of the Republicans—showed the electorate that Democrats had a program and could act in concert to advance it. Like the Contract with America, however, the Democrats' agenda quickly faced difficulties with the Senate and an opposition-party president. Nevertheless, a number of the agenda items won final passage in the 110th Congress—including a minimum wage hike, tougher gas mileage standards for autos, increased veterans' benefits, and congressional ethics legislation. With a Democratic president in the White House in the 111th Congress, additional items in the '06 agenda were likely to progress further in the legislative process. President Obama signaled support for a number of those priorities, including negotiating lower prices for prescription drugs, increasing federal assistance to college students, and ending tax benefits for companies that outsource jobs abroad.

Second, like Gingrich, Pelosi must closely attend to her national public image. It is unlikely that the first woman Speaker of the House will be able to maintain Hastert's low profile, even if she wants to. Indeed, one Republican strategy is to direct critical attention on Pelosi to undermine the Democratic Party's popularity—an approach similar to the way Democrats targeted Gingrich as the face of the Republican Party in the 1990s. As long as President Obama's early approval ratings remained positive, focusing on Pelosi allowed Republicans to resist Democratic priorities without confronting Obama directly.[44] "Republicans realize that taking on a president with more than 70 percent approval rating isn't very wise," said Ron Bonjean, a former aide to Republican congressional leaders, "Speaker Pelosi says she wrote the [stimulus] bill, so that gives you permission to try to triangulate her."[45] By consistently portraying Pelosi as an ideologically extreme "San Francisco Democrat," Republicans aim to shape Pelosi's public image over time. Rep. Patrick McHenry, R-N.C., explained the strategy: "Our goal is to bring down approval numbers for [Speaker Nancy] Pelosi and for House Democrats. That will take repetition. This is a marathon, not a sprint."[46] Of this strategy, Pelosi has remarked, "It doesn't bother me—I'm in the arena." Given the intense scrutiny she receives, the Democratic Party's success will nevertheless depend in part on Pelosi's image, as well as her ability to successfully shepherd legislation through the House.[47]

Third, Speaker Pelosi's leadership style largely tracks the "top down," centralized model of her two immediate predecessors, Gingrich and Hastert. Despite having criticized the Republican majority's restrictions on open debate and full committee consideration of bills, Pelosi has employed similar limitations on committees and inputs from the minority party. "After months of promising bipartisanship and a return to the regular order," complained Rep. Jack Kingson, R-Ga., "Pelosi's first act was to cut off...all amendments and bypass all of her own committees, in a rush to meet an arbitrary and meaningless [100-hour] deadline."[48] Under Pelosi's leadership, committee chairs have enjoyed a somewhat more prominent role. Reflecting on differences between Pelosi and her predecessors, journalists Richard E. Cohen and Brian Friel observe, "In the two years since Democrats regained House and Senate control, an elite group of committee chairmen who deal with key national issues has enjoyed a resurgence of influence."[49] The enhanced role for committee leaders, however, did not imply a decentralized process in which committees enjoyed free rein. Instead, legislation was often worked out in an "ad hoc" manner behind closed doors in leadership offices.[50] A wide-ranging Brookings Institution report on congressional operations and policy-making in the new Democratic Congress concluded that, "a pattern of tighter, more centralized control—which began more than two decades ago under Democratic rule and then intensified under Republican majorities, especially after the 2000 election—continues unabated."[51]

The Speaker's Influence: Style and Context. Congressional analysts disagree about the extent to which congressional leaders can influence policy outcomes. Compared to legislative party leaders in many other democracies, party leaders in Congress unquestionably have fewer tools to induce party loyalty among lawmakers. Nevertheless, congressional leaders enjoy greater institutional authority at some times than at others. (See Box 6-1 for a brief review of the principal scholarly theories of congressional leadership.) In general, political scientists stress context over personal style as the main factor affecting the Speaker's institutional clout.

Personal style refers to the skills, abilities, and qualities of the Speaker, such as intelligence, talent for coalition building, or political acumen. It also refers to a leader's willingness to utilize the full range of his or her parliamentary prerogatives, to pressure colleagues to vote a certain way, or to advance policy positions independent of consensus within their party.

Context refers to the House's external and internal environment. External elements include whether the Speaker's party controls the White House, the public's demand for legislation, the complexity of national problems, the popularity of the president, and the partisan leanings of the voting public. Internal elements that condition the Speaker's influence are the size and cohesiveness of the majority party, the diffusion of power among members, and the autonomy of committees.

The policy views of rank-and-file party members constitute one of the most important elements of a leader's context. A prominent scholarly theory, called conditional party government, suggests that if partisans share common policy views and confront an opposition party with sharply different policy preferences, then these dual conditions favor strong centralized leadership. Rank-and-file partisans will empower their party leaders to advance an agenda that nearly all of them support. As the two leading proponents of this theory state:

> These two considerations—preference homogeneity [or policy agreement within parties] and preference conflict [or policy disagreement between parties]—together form the "condition" in the theory of conditional party government. As they increase, the theory predicts that party members will be progressively more willing to create strong powers for leaders and to support the exercise of those powers in specific instances. But when diversity grows within parties, or the differences between parties are reduced, members will be reluctant to grant greater powers to leaders. This is the central prediction of [conditional party government].[52]

BOX 6-1   **Theories of Congressional Leadership**

Political scientists have developed different theories to explain why congressional leaders appear to be stronger during some eras than others. The most prominent is called conditional party government.[a] A competing theory—the pivotal voter theory—suggests that the influence of party leaders is marginal with respect to their ability to shift policy outcomes away from what a majority of the chamber prefers toward the policy preferences of the majority party.[b]

Proponents of each theory view party leaders as agents of their principals—their rank-and-file partisans. Members want their party leaders to help them accomplish their fundamental goals: getting reelected, making good policy, and gaining—or maintaining—power in the House or Senate. A correspondence in leader-member views means that party leaders will work to advance the majority preferences of the rank-and-file. After all, party leaders hold their positions at the sufferance of their partisan colleagues, and they usually want to be reelected to those leadership posts.

Conditional Party Government Theory

◄ The power of congressional leaders hinges on the degree of homogeneity within the majority party concerning policy and on the extent of interparty conflict between Democrats and Republicans.

◄ With both conditions in play, rank-and-file party members are supportive of changes that strengthen their party leaders, such as the Speaker. Thus, a cohesive majority party can pass legislation without any support from the minority party.

◄ Conversely, when parties' policy goals are fragmented, partisan lawmakers have little incentive to give their leaders more authority. They may use their power against the political and policy interests of many in the rank-and-file.

Pivotal Voter Theory

◄ Suggests that policy outcomes on the floor rarely diverge from what is acceptable to the pivotal voter—the member who casts the 218th vote in the House.

◄ Rarely does everyone in the majority party support a particular policy. Why, then, should majority members change their policy views to back a party position with which they disagree? Instead, they will join with members of the other party to form the winning coalition. According to this theory, these pivotal voters determine chamber outcomes.

◄ If each party is internally united in its policy preferences, as the conditional party government theory states, there will be no difference between what the majority party wants and what the chamber membership will agree to.

◄ Simply observing party leaders engaged in frenetic activity—often seeking pivotal votes—does not mean they can skew legislative outcomes beyond what is acceptable to a majority of the entire membership.

[a] See, for example, John H. Aldrich and David W. Rohde, "The Transition to Republican Rule in the House: Implications for Theories of Congressional Politics," *Political Science Quarterly* 112, no. 4, (winter 1997–1998): 541–567.
[b] See Keith Krehbiel, *Pivotal Politics: A Theory of U.S. Lawmaking* (Chicago: University of Chicago Press, 1998).

The theory of conditional party government illuminates the role of the Speakership at different times in House history. Speaker Sam Rayburn's role as cautious broker and negotiator, for example, makes sense in light of fractures within the Democratic Party during the 1950s. During Rayburn's era—and for many years afterwards—congressional Democrats were deeply divided between their northern and southern wings. For a century after the Civil War, the "Solid South" almost always elected Democrats to Congress. Southern Democrats tended to be more conservative than their northern colleagues on a number of significant political issues, particularly civil rights and labor regulations (such as minimum wage laws, union organizing, and business-labor relations). On such matters, southern Democrats often allied themselves with Republicans in a voting pattern known as the conservative coalition. Recognizing these divisions, Rayburn had to lead cautiously. Just bringing the Democratic caucus together could be politically explosive, so Rayburn rarely convened the caucus.[53] Instead, Rayburn dealt with members on a personalized, individual basis. According to the theory of conditional party government, Rayburn's style of leadership was not merely a personal stylistic choice; it was a way of coping with intractable conflict within the party. Under such conditions, rank-and-file Democrats simply would not trust their Speaker with expansive procedural and political powers.

By the same token, the conditional party government perspective views the forceful leadership of Gingrich, Wright, and Pelosi in light of changes in the political context. Since the 1960s, regional realignments have created far more ideological consensus *within* each of the two congressional parties, and considerably less ideological agreement *between* the two parties than existed during the 1950s and 1960s. After the enfranchisement of southern African Americans in the 1960s, the Democratic Party in the South began to elect Democrats (John Lewis of Georgia, for instance) who were more responsive to African American constituents and more ideologically compatible with their party colleagues from the rest of the country. Meanwhile, conservative southern voters—mainly whites—gradually moved into the Republican Party. Because the South is now largely in the GOP camp, today's Democratic party mostly lacks the deep regional divisions that characterized the earlier era. Constituency change in the North reinforced this ideological homogenization of the parties. Liberal "Rockefeller Republicans" have largely disappeared in the Northeast. The conservative coalition is no longer an important voting bloc in Congress. As a result of these constituency changes, the two parties are more internally coherent in their policy preferences and more different from one another.

This changed context helps explain the assertive styles of recent Speakers. Because the two parties are more cohesive internally, and more different from each other, rank-and-file members of both parties are more willing to trust their leaders with institutional authority. For example, contemporary Speakers of both parties were given more influence over committee assignments, allowing them to appoint like-minded members to coveted committees. By stacking important committees with loyal partisans, a Speaker raises the likelihood that they will report legislation that the Speaker favors. Individual members also recognize that they owe their committee assignments in part to the Speaker. Given the greater willingness of rank-and-file members to tolerate hierarchical leadership, Speakers like Wright, Gingrich, Hastert, and Pelosi could all dictate to committee chairmen, advance party agendas, and take procedural actions to hamstring the minority party. Their personal talents were augmented by formal and informal procedural changes that raised the likelihood that their objectives would be realized.

Leadership, however, is by no means entirely determined by the congressional context. "Leadership in Congress occurs within an institutional context that imposes limits on leaders," writes Randall Strahan, "but some leaders take advantage of those opportunities and others do not. Leadership involves not only the conditions that make leadership possible but also the choice of the leader to act."[54] Adroit and forceful Speakers can lead by molding circumstances and seizing opportunities favoring their own objectives.[55] Speakers' personal capacities, in short, allow them to exercise that elusive quality called leadership—persuading others to follow their lead even when they disagree with their leaders' views. A committee chairman during the Contract with America period, for example, explained why he voted for a Gingrich-advocated policy that he opposed: "At times like these," he said, "many of us subordinate our preferences to the greater good of the team."[56] Context and style interact in dynamic ways that are hard to untangle.

Floor Leaders

The Speaker's principal deputy—the majority leader—is the party's floor leader. As former majority leader Tom DeLay, R-Tex., said of his relationship with Speaker Hastert: "I see it that Hastert is the chairman of the board and I am the chief executive officer."[57] Elected every two years by secret ballot of the party caucus, the floor leader is not to be confused with a floor manager. Floor managers—usually two for each bill and frequently the chairman and ranking minority member of the committee that reported the bill—are appointed to steer particular bills to a final decision.

The House majority leader is usually an experienced legislator. Two recent examples—DeLay and Steny Hoyer, D-Md.—make the point. When Tom DeLay took the post at the start of the 108th Congress (2003–2005), he had served in the House for eighteen years. He was elected majority whip when Republicans took control of the House following the 1994 elections. As majority whip, DeLay established himself as perhaps the most effective party whip in the House's history and, aside from Gingrich, the chamber's most influential Republican. Nicknamed "The Hammer" by colleagues for his combative style, DeLay was an accomplished vote counter and enforcer, a shrewd campaign and legislative strategist, an aggressive fund-raiser, and a skillful coordinator of the party's connections to lobbyists.

DeLay pushed the powers of the majority leadership to their limits. His heavy-handed tactics, win-at-any-cost legislative style, and ties to unsavory lobbyists (such as the now-imprisoned Jack Abramoff) prompted the House Ethics Committee to rebuke him three times (including improperly pressuring a GOP colleague to support a Medicare drug bill during an extraordinary three-hour roll-call vote). As his standing in the party eroded and legal and political controversies threatened his 2006 reelection—giving credence to the Democrats' "culture of corruption" campaign theme—DeLay relinquished his majority leadership post and resigned from the House.

Democrat Steny Hoyer is the majority leader of the 111th House (2009–2011). First elected to the House in May 1981 (a special election), Hoyer was always ambitious to become a party leader. He was first successful in 1989 when he became chairman of the Democratic Caucus. Despite losses in contests for party whip in 1991 and 2002, Hoyer persisted in his efforts to woo his party colleagues and finally became minority whip when the position came open following the 2002 elections. When Pelosi ascended to the speakership, Hoyer became majority leader. He did not win the majority leadership without a contest, however. John Murtha, D-Pa., a close ally and friend of Pelosi's, challenged Hoyer for the post. To the surprise of many Democrats, Pelosi publicly endorsed her friend and vigorously lobbied Democrats to vote for Murtha. This action reflected her coolness toward Hoyer and her personal loyalty to Murtha (who had managed her successful race against Hoyer to become minority whip). But her involvement was widely regarded as miscalculated, as Hoyer easily defeated Murtha by a 149 to 86 caucus vote.[58]

Hoyer, a more centrist and less partisan leader than DeLay or Pelosi, is known for his ability to work well with majority and minority members. Comfortable in front of the cameras, he also excels at fund-raising and campaigning for his partisan colleagues. The Pelosi-Hoyer leadership team, despite their personal and policy differences, appears to be working well. "They're pros," remarked Anna Eshoo, a close friend of Pelosi's. As professional politicians who recognize the importance of working together to enact Democratic priorities and maintain majority control of the chamber, both "understand the responsibility and the burden given to them," said Eshoo. Another Democratic lawmaker, Ron Kind of Wisconsin, noted: "If there is any tension, it's not visible to the average member [of Congress]."[59]

House and party rules are largely silent about the majority leader's duties. By tradition, the primary duties are to serve as principal strategist and spokesperson for the party and to monitor the House floor. By modern custom, neither the Speaker nor the Democratic or Republican floor leader chairs committees.[60] The majority and minority leaders, as well as the Speaker, may serve on formal or informal task forces or panels. For example, the Speaker and minority leader are ex officio members of the Permanent Select Intelligence Committee.

The majority leader helps to plan the daily, weekly and annual legislative agendas. To do so, Hoyer must consult with a wide array of players. He meets weekly with the committee chairs to discuss their schedule of activities, review pertinent legislative issues, and coordinate chamber action with the party's floor managers. He confers with the president about administration proposals, particularly when the president is of the same party. He also gauges sentiment on legislation among rank-and-file members and urges them to support or defeat measures. As one majority leader said: "The Majority Leader has prime responsibility for the day-to-day working of the House, the schedule, working with the committees to keep an eye out for what bills are coming, getting them scheduled, getting the work of the House done, making the place function correctly." He added: "[Y]ou are also compelled to try to articulate to the outside world what [your party stands] for, what [your party is] fighting for, what [your party is] doing."[61]

The minority leader is the floor leader of the loyal opposition. Like the majority leader, the minority leader promotes unity among party colleagues, monitors the progress of bills through committees and subcommittees, and forges coalitions in support of proposals. However, the minority leader is more often in a reactive position, criticizing the majority party's initiatives and developing alternatives to them. Bertrand Snell, R-N.Y., minority leader from 1931 to 1939, described the duties:

> He is spokesman for his party and enunciates its policies. He is required to be alert and vigilant in defense of the minority's rights. It is his function and duty to criticize constructively the policies and program of the majority, and to this end employ parliamentary tactics and give close attention to all proposed legislation.[62]

John Boehner, R-Ohio, is minority leader in the 111th Congress. Boehner became the Republican leader in the 109th Congress when DeLay stepped down from his post. Nevertheless, he had to withstand challenges to his leadership from the right wing of his party at the start of both the 110th and the 111th Congresses. On both occasions, the GOP Conference decided to keep Boehner, a seasoned leader, rather than go with a newcomer. Boehner, who served previously as chairman of the GOP Conference and head of the Education Committee (he was a principal author of the No Child Left Behind Act), understands the intricacies of putting together successful legislative coalitions.

The minority leader must forge party unity by managing internal conflict and resolving intraparty disagreements. Perhaps the most important job of the minority leader is to craft a strategy to win back majority control of the House. In this respect, the minority leader must decide whether to cooperate with or to confront the majority party. By working with the majority, the minority party can often influence legislation more to its followers' liking. However, cooperation entails supporting the majority party's legislation on the floor— often an unpleasant task. A minority party can instead pursue a strategy of confrontation. By consistently offering an alternative vision on issues of the day, the minority party can build the case for its return to power. In the 111th Congress, Boehner signaled that House Republicans would focus more on confrontation than on cooperation. "I have been trying to get my Republican colleagues to understand that we are not in the legislative business," Boehner remarked at a lunch with reporters. "We will spend more time communicating [with the American people] because that is what we can do."[63] There is no set formula on how to win back majority control of the House, because many of the electoral and political forces and events that influence majority status are beyond party leaders' control.[64]

The Whips

Another top elective party post is the chief whip, who nowadays heads a team of deputies and regional whips. As the term implies, the duties of whips are to encourage party discipline, count votes, and, in general, mobilize winning coalitions on behalf of partisan priorities. To do so, the chief whip serves as a liaison between the party's rank-and-file membership and the leaders. The whip communicates political and policy intelligence between the leadership to the rank-and-file; assigns deputy whips to take the "temperature" of the various factional groups within the party; and polls members. A standard polling classification to identify lawmakers' voting predilections on important procedural and substantive issues is "yea," "leaning yea," "undecided," "leaning no," and "no." Majority Whip James Clyburn, D-S.C., used a fishing and hunting metaphor to explain his procedure for forging winning coalitions:

> When it comes to working with the Democratic Caucus I have to fish in a lot of ponds. I go fishing with the Blue Dogs [fiscally conservative Democrats]. I go fishing with the New Dems [moderate Democrats]. I go fishing with the Hispanics and I go fishing with the Asian Pacific Islanders, trying to cobble together the 218 votes I need. But a lot of time, I have to be a hunter, even though I never hunt, they tell me that a good hunter knows how to work both sides of the ditch. I fish among my Caucus, Democratic Members, and I go hunting sometimes, among my Republican Members.[65]

In recent years both parties have expanded their whip teams. House Democrats in the 111th House, for example, had a senior chief deputy whip, eight chief deputy whips, and a number of assistant, regional, and other whips. The whip team meets regularly to discuss issues and strategy. Naming more members as whips involves them in leadership decision making and gives them additional incentives to back their top leaders. As a former GOP majority whip stated, with a sixty-person GOP whip organization, it is feasible "to reach everybody in the [Republican] conference and deliver their votes when it counts."[66] Having more whips also ensures leadership representation for important party groups and broadens the party's appeal to outside constituencies.

Each party's whip prepares notices advising members of the daily and weekly floor schedule with updates as warranted. They identify, for instance, the time when the House will convene, the measures to be considered each legislative day, and when the last vote for the week is expected. Information about the House schedule is available on the Web sites of the majority and minority whips as well as the House majority leader.

The minority whip in the 111th House, Rep. Eric Cantor, R-Va., and his chief deputy whip Kevin McCarthy, R-Calif., meet weekly with their deputy and assistant whips to count votes, exchange information, and ensure that members have a handle on the Republican Conference's talking points on upcoming issues. Cantor works to bridge divisions within the Republican Conference and to build party consensus on a message. With Republicans in the minority, Cantor has been less focused on arm-twisting and marshalling votes. "When one is in a 257–178 minority, it is rare that you'll do a lot of vote corralling," explained Rep. Mike Conaway, R-Texas, a whip team member.[67] Instead, Cantor has focused more on outreach, disseminating the Republican message to activists within and beyond the Beltway.[68] "In the minority, without the presidency, we have to think and act as guerrilla advocates, using the Internet and other avenues to quickly and cheaply connect with middle-class families about their real concerns about the economy and their jobs," said Rob Collins, Cantor's chief of staff.[69] "Now that you've got a huge deficit in votes…finding a tight message that can be repeated in multiple forms and multiple voices…becomes a key thing for the whip operation to do," said Rep. Mark Kirk, R-Ill. "The whip team under Roy [Blunt, the previous Republican whip] was very much a creature of running a majority, and that is not the mission of this team."[70] Cantor's whip team nonetheless managed an impressive display of Republican unity in response to President Obama's stimulus package in February 2009, when not a single House Republican supported the measure.[71] "What transpired, and will give us a shot in the arm going forward," Cantor remarked about the vote, "is that we are standing up on principle and just saying no."[72]

LEADERS OF THE SENATE

Unlike the House, today's Senate is an institution that tolerates and even promotes individualism. Candidate-centered elections, the proliferation of policy- and ideologically-oriented interest groups, the large role of money in campaigns, the staff resources available to every senator, and senators' need to seek news media coverage are among the factors that have led to today's individualistic Senate. Senators cherish and assert their independence, which intensifies the challenges faced by those elected to lead them. Unlike their House counterparts, Senate leaders lack institutional prerogatives and rules designed to facilitate majority rule, and so must rely heavily on personal skills and negotiation with colleagues of both parties.

Presiding Officers

The House majority's highest elected leader, the Speaker, has the authority to preside over the House. By contrast, the Senate majority leader, the majority party's highest leader, almost never presides in the Senate chamber.

The Senate has three kinds of presiding officers. First, the constitutional president of the Senate is the vice president of the United States (see Figure 6-2). Except for ceremonial occasions, the vice president seldom presides over Senate sessions, and he can vote only to break—not make—a tie. When votes on major issues are expected to be close, party leaders make sure that the vice president is presiding so that he can break the tie.

Second, the Constitution provides for a president pro tempore to preside in the vice president's absence. In modern practice this constitutional officer is the majority party senator with the longest continuous service. Sen. Robert C. Byrd of West Virginia, for example, became president pro tempore of the Democratic controlled 111th Senate (2009–2011). By passing a simple resolution, the Senate sometimes appoints a deputy president pro tempore. This majority party official presides over the Senate in the absence of the vice president and president pro tempore.

Third, a dozen or so senators of the majority party, typically junior members, serve approximately one-hour stints each day as the presiding officer. The opportunity to preside helps newcomers become familiar with Senate rules and procedures.

Floor Leaders

The majority leader is the head of the majority party in the Senate, its leader on the floor, and the leader of the Senate. Similarly, the minority leader heads the Senate's minority party. (Nowadays, minority leaders prefer to be called "Republican leader" or "Democratic leader," as the case may be.) The majority and minority leaders are elected biennially by secret ballot of their party colleagues. Neither position is mentioned in the Constitution; they are relatively recent creations that date from the early 1900s.

The Emergence of the Floor Leader. Historically, the Senate has always had leaders, but no single senator exercised central management of the legislative process in the fashion of today's floor leader. During the Senate's first century or so—especially in the 1790s and early 1800s, when there was no system of permanent standing committees or organized senatorial parties—leadership flowed from the personal talents and abilities of individual legislators. The small size of the early Senate promoted an informal and personal style of leadership.

Throughout the nineteenth century scores of prominent senators were called "leaders" by scholars and other observers. Some were sectional or factional leaders; others headed important committees (by the mid- to late 1840s, committees and their chairmen were centers of power); and still others (such as Henry Clay, John C. Calhoun, and Daniel Webster) exercised wide influence because of their special political, oratorical, or intellectual gifts. Even as late as 1885, however, Woodrow Wilson could write, "No one is *the Senator*....No one exercises the special trust of acknowledged leadership."[73]

By the turn of the twentieth century the political landscape had changed. Party structures and leaders emerged as clearly identifiable forces

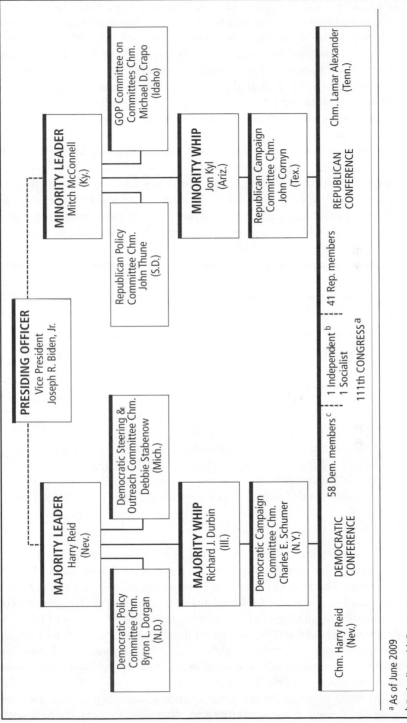

FIGURE 6-2 Organization of the Senate, 111th Congress (2009–2011)

PRESIDING OFFICER
Vice President
Joseph R. Biden, Jr.

MAJORITY LEADER
Harry Reid
(Nev.)

MINORITY LEADER
Mitch McConnell
(Ky.)

Democratic Policy
Committee Chm.
Byron L. Dorgan
(N.D.)

Democratic Steering &
Outreach Committee Chm.
Debbie Stabenow
(Mich.)

Republican Policy
Committee Chm.
John Thune
(S.D.)

GOP Committee on
Committees Chm.
Michael D. Crapo
(Idaho)

MAJORITY WHIP
Richard J. Durbin
(Ill.)

MINORITY WHIP
Jon Kyl
(Ariz.)

Democratic Campaign
Committee Chm.
Charles E. Schumer
(N.Y.)

Republican Campaign
Committee Chm.
John Cornyn
(Tex.)

DEMOCRATIC
CONFERENCE

REPUBLICAN
CONFERENCE

Chm. Harry Reid
(Nev.)

Chm. Lamar Alexander
(Tenn.)

58 Dem. members [c]   1 Independent [b]   41 Rep. members
                      1 Socialist
                      111th CONGRESS [a]

[a] As of June 2009

[b] Both align with Democrats.

[c] This total includes Arlen Specter of Pennsylvania, who shifted parties in April 2009, and Al Franken of Minnesota, who was declared winner by 312 votes but who had not been certified at press time. Although most observers believe he will be seated eventually, his opponent's legal appeal could alter the outcome.

for organizing and managing the Senate's proceedings. This important development occurred, according to a historian of the Senate, because of the influx of a "new breed" of senator who valued party unity and "the machinery of [party] organization," especially the party caucus.[74] Soon those senators who chaired their respective party caucuses acquired levers of authority over senatorial affairs. They chaired important party panels, shaped the Senate's agenda of business, and mobilized party majorities behind important issues. The position of majority leader had informally emerged out of the caucus chairmanship by 1913.[75]

Not until Lyndon B. Johnson (LBJ) became majority leader in 1955 was the post transformed into one of great authority and prestige.[76] Considered by many analysts to be the most influential majority leader ever, the Texas Democrat had an extensive network of trusted aides and colleagues who gave him better information about more issues than any other senator. Opposition party control of the White House (Eisenhower's presidency) gave the aggressive Johnson the luxury of choosing which policies to support and which strategies to employ to get them enacted. And his pragmatic outlook, domineering style, and arm-twisting abilities made him the premier vote gatherer in the Senate. The majority leader's awesome display of face-to-face persuasion was called "the Johnson Treatment."

> The Treatment could last ten minutes or four hours. It came, enveloping its target, at the LBJ Ranch swimming pool, in one of LBJ's offices, in the Senate cloakroom, on the floor of the Senate itself....Its tone could be supplication, accusation, cajolery, exuberance, scorn, tears, complaint, the hint of threat. It was all of these together. It ran the gamut of human emotions. Its velocity was breathtaking, and it was all in one direction. Interjections from the target were rare. Johnson anticipated them before they could be spoken. He moved in close, his face a scant millimeter from his target, his eyes widening and narrowing, and his eyebrows rising and falling. From his pockets poured clippings, memos, statistics. Mimicry, humor, and the genius of analogy made The Treatment an almost hypnotic experience and rendered the target stunned and helpless.[77]

Buttressing Johnson was an inner club, a bipartisan group of senior senators. A particularly important ally within this inner club was Richard B. Russell of Georgia. The leader of southern Democrats and a lawmaker of immense influence, Russell endorsed Johnson as Democratic leader. (The Russell Senate Office Building on Capitol Hill is named after the Georgia senator.) The club, observers said, wielded the real power in the Senate through its control of chairmanships and committee assignments.[78] Furthermore, unwritten rules of behavior (for example, junior members should be seen and not heard) encouraged new senators to defer to the establishment.

Majority leaders today encounter a much different Senate from the one led by Johnson. Gone is the seniority-ruled, club-like, relatively closed Senate of old—ended largely by three key developments: the influx of independent-minded and activist senators who wanted and expected to be major policy participants; internal senatorial changes that promoted egalitarianism, such as the provision of staff resources to all members; and external developments in the broader political environment (the twenty-four-hour news cycle, for instance).

Together, these developments led to an individualistic Senate where leaders are expected to serve members' personal needs and advance their individual agendas. As former majority leader Byrd (1977–1981; 1987–1989) once remarked about the egalitarian, individualistic, and C-SPAN-covered Senate: "Circumstances don't permit the Lyndon Johnson style. What I am saying is that times and things have changed. Younger Senators come into the Senate. They are more independent. The 'establishment' is a bad word. Each wants to do his 'own thing.'"[79] Unlike the demanding and aggressive Johnson, Byrd as majority leader referred to himself as "slave" to the needs of his senatorial colleagues.

Limits on Today's Leadership: Individualism and Partisanship. If individualism characterizes the post-Johnson Senate, another development has added to the leader's difficulties in managing and processing the Senate's business: escalating partisanship. Unlike the House, possessing a strong and cohesive majority party does not necessarily enable a Senate leader to govern. As discussed in more detail in Chapter 8, the Senate's rules do not permit the majority party leadership to set the agenda without input from the minority party. The majority leader must negotiate with the minority leader in scheduling legislation for floor consideration. Successfully leading the Senate thus requires Senate leaders to achieve considerably more cross-party consensus than is necessary in the House.

As in the House, the two Senate parties have become, in the words of journalist David S. Broder, "more cohesive internally and further apart from each other philosophically."[80] Or as Sen. Orrin G. Hatch, R-Utah, phrased it: "Today, most Democrats are far left; most Republicans are to the right; and there are very few in between."[81] Such differences between the parties are grounded not only in members' personal policy preferences; they are also fostered by groups allied with the parties. The two Congresses are very much in evidence as Democratic senators champion policies favored by their core national constituencies (environmentalists, single women, gays, minorities, and union members, for instance) and Republican lawmakers do the same for their constituency base (the religious right, business owners, white males, rural Americans, gun owners, and antiabortion advocates, for example).

By any measure, party conflict is at a historic high for the modern Senate. One indicator of this heightened partisanship is the large number of party-line votes (a majority of Democrats facing off against a majority of Republicans). In the 1970s, only 39 percent of roll-call votes divided a majority of Republicans from a majority of Democrats. In 2007, fully 60 percent were party votes. In 2008, 52 percent of roll-call votes divided the Senate along party lines. Even more striking is the growth in cohesion—call it discipline or philosophical agreement—within both party caucuses. In the 1970s, the average senator backed the party position 65 percent of the time on partisan roll calls. In the 1980s, the average degree of partisan loyalty rose to 73 percent; in the 1990s to 81 percent. In 2008, it was 86 percent.[82]

What all this means for the majority leader is extraordinary difficulty in achieving the necessary consensus to enact legislation and approve nominations. Any senator, regardless of party, has awesome parliamentary powers to stymie action, which puts a premium on the leader's skill in negotiating and deal-making. Lacking formidable leadership tools to exert tight control over chamber proceedings, Senate leaders rely heavily on patience, perseverance, personal ties, and, on occasion, procedural hardball to move legislation. Yet if one or more senators employ a filibuster (extended debate) on a matter, the leader needs sixty votes to invoke a procedure called cloture (closure of debate) if he is to provide the Senate with an opportunity to vote on the measure or matter. As a former majority leader stated:

> It's a tough job [being majority leader], and it has gotten tougher and tougher. Part of it is that now you don't need 50 votes—you've got to have 60 votes. The filibuster and cloture used to be used occasionally for big issues. [In more recent years], it has become an instrument used on almost every bill. You can have 51 votes, you can have 55 votes, but if you don't get 60 votes, [the bill] can die. And it is very hard to dredge up 60 votes.[83]

Dredging up 60 votes is especially taxing in the context of the chamber's heightened partisanship. When the minority leader organizes a partisan filibuster, a majority leader with fewer than 59 fellow partisans will have to persuade members of the opposing party to vote against their own party leader in order to end debate—a tall order. In the 111th Senate, the switch of Pennsylvania senator Arlen Specter from Republican to Democrat gave the Democratic party control of 60 seats, pending the seating of Al Franken once the disputed Minnesota Senate contest is settled. Control of 60 seats will enable Democrats to stop an organized minority-party filibuster, if they are able to maintain perfect party unity. But the diverse Democratic caucus will undoubtedly create challenges for Reid in controlling extended debate.

Recent Majority Leaders. Senate leadership has turned over rapidly in recent years. Part of this turnover has been the result of election returns. Narrow margins during most of this time meant that small shifts in senate seats could transfer party control of the chamber—which happened three times between 2000 and 2007. In 2001, a single senator, James Jeffords of Vermont, changed his party affiliation from Republican to Independent and announced he would caucus with the Democrats. His action transferred partisan control of the chamber. Democratic Leader Tom Daschle, S.D., said of the Jeffords switch: "We have just witnessed something that has never happened before in all of Senate history—the change of power during a session of Congress."[84] Republican Leader Trent Lott of Mississippi blamed Jeffords for staging a "coup of one" to give Democrats control of the Senate.[85]

Scandal is another cause of leadership turnover. Soon after Republicans returned to power following the November 2002 elections, Republican Leader Lott made racially charged comments at retiring GOP South Carolina senator Strom Thurmond's 100th birthday party. Lott praised Thurmond's 1948 run for the presidency on a segregationist Dixiecrat platform. A political firestorm developed, and Lott's remarks were denounced by many in his party. Even though he apologized five times for his comments, pressure built for Lott's resignation until he stepped down as majority leader.

After Lott's resignation, Senate Republicans elected, by acclamation, Tennessee senator Bill Frist as the new majority leader. Frist had received help from President Bush to succeed Lott and enjoyed close relations with the White House. Nevertheless, Majority Leader Frist's job in leading a narrowly divided Senate was not easy. He was an untested party leader with limited procedural and senatorial experience. Frist observed, "The frustration here of needing 60 votes" to get action on almost anything that becomes controversial "requires collaboration, reaching out, negotiation."[86] A low-key, inclusive leader who worked well with committee chairs and colleagues, Frist faced a feisty Democratic minority armed with ample parliamentary means to frustrate action.

Democrat Harry Reid of Nevada is the majority leader of the 111th Senate. A former Golden Gloves boxer and House member, Reid was elected to the Senate in 1986 and served as minority whip under Democratic Leader Daschle. After Daschle's electoral defeat in 2002, Reid became minority leader and then, by acclamation, the majority leader when Democrats regained the majority after the 2006 elections. By all accounts, he is a blunt, tough, and savvy leader. "He's very shrewd and effective," remarked Sen. John Ensign, R-Nev. "Behind the scenes he is tenacious."[87]

Despite his leadership skills and extensive legislative experience, Reid faced difficulties similar to Frist's. Reid frequently found it impossible to push legislation past the procedural hurdles that a Senate minority can erect. "The biggest challenge I have is results," he said. "If you have more than half [in the Senate], that doesn't mean you are going to win. You need to have multiple instances where you can create different coalitions to get to 60."[88] Part of Reid's game plan for achieving results is "a highly centralized leadership operation" with floor strategy and message operations managed from his office.[89] He promoted partisan cohesion by keeping note cards in a breast pocket of his jacket "on which he records favors asked and promises made."[90] In addition, Reid enjoyed a good working relationship with the Republican leader. Even so, the legislative record of the 110th Senate was lackluster. Senate Democrats prevailed on only around 54 percent of party votes in 2008, considerably below Senate Republicans' success rates on party votes between 1995 and 2006.[91] Many measures that cleared the Democratic majority House failed to pass the Senate.

Minority Leader. The Senate minority leader consults continually with the majority leader, because the Senate usually operates by consensus. "I'm very fond" of Majority Leader Reid, stated Republican Leader Mitch McConnell, Ky.

"I think he wants to get solutions to problems, and so do I."[92] To get things done typically requires cooperation across party lines. In addition, the minority leader represents his party to the president. When a member of the president's party, the minority leader has the traditional duties of pushing the administration's program and responding to partisan criticisms of the president. When a member of the opposite party, the minority leader has to calculate when to cooperate with and when to confront the president.

McConnell meets regularly with Senate Republicans to build party consensus, craft policy alternatives, and devise tactics to block or modify Democratic initiatives. He also works with his House counterpart to coordinate strategy and to develop and communicate a party agenda. As Sen. Lamar Alexander, Tenn., said of his leader: "Mitch McConnell's strength is he knows the Senate and understands it is almost entirely based on personal relationships. Most successful leaders' strategy is silent, but he has a very good understanding of where each of us is, and he works with us privately."[93] For his part, McConnell has made it clear that the only way the Senate can function is on a bipartisan basis with legislation containing provisions that appeal to Republicans. During the closely divided 110th Congress, he remarked that there is nothing Democrats "can do without some degree of cooperation from a very robust forty-nine-vote minority."[94] To be sure, the minority leader is also always striving to win back control of the Senate.

Party Whips. The Senate's whip system carries out functions similar to those of the House's, such as counting noses before crucial votes, monitoring floor activity, and fostering party consensus. Richard J. Durbin of Illinois is the majority whip of the 111th Senate, the Democrats' second-in-command. He heads a whip structure that includes a chief deputy whip and four deputy whips. Durbin and Reid complement each other. Reid excels at knowing the procedural "nuts and bolts" of the Senate. Durbin, also quite knowledgeable about procedures, is "very good at taking issues and making them resonate with the public, and he is good on the [Senate] floor and at message" development.[95] As Sen. Patty Murray, D-Wash., noted, "He puts issues we're dealing with in real American language. I think he's really a good face for our party."[96]

The Senate's minority whip is Jon Kyl, R-Ariz. Elected to the post in 2007 after Democrats won control of the Senate, Kyl does not face the majority leader's difficulties of moving a legislative agenda through the Senate. Nevertheless, his tasks are similar to the majority whip's. He serves as a public face for the GOP, articulating its positions on the Sunday morning political talk shows and in other public venues. He works to build consensus around party positions and initiatives. He identifies effective communicators within his party to take the lead on issues. Indeed, his skill at tapping effective advocates for partisan causes was among the reasons *Time Magazine* selected him as one of "America's 10 Best Senators."[97] He develops parliamentary strategies to force votes on Republican issues or to block the Democratic agenda. In general, Kyl works to help Republicans "see the advantages of sticking together."[98]

SELECTION OF LEADERS

Before the beginning of each new Congress, senators and representatives elect their top leaders by secret ballot in their party caucuses. Although the whole House votes for the Speaker, the election is pro forma. With straight party voting the modern unspoken rule on this and other organizational matters, the majority party has always elected the Speaker.

Candidates for party leadership positions usually wage elaborate campaigns to win support from their partisan colleagues, with some launching Web sites to support their candidacy. Jack Kingston, R-Ga., used the Internet to make his unsuccessful plea to be the House GOP Conference chair, "with a video blog outlining his credentials for the post."[99] Occasionally, last-minute entrants successfully bid for leadership positions. But whether brief or lengthy, campaigns for party leadership positions are intense. Members understand that a party leadership post can be a "career launching pad...either within the [Congress] or outside it."[100]

The two parties treat their hierarchies differently in the House: the Democrats view it as sort of a ladder and the Republicans as a slippery slope. Democrats have a history of elevating their next-in-line officer—from whip to majority (or minority) leader to Speaker—as vacancies occur. Republicans have a history of pushing people off the leadership track because of turmoil in their ranks. For example, in 1959 Charles A. Halleck of Illinois ousted Joseph W. Martin Jr. of Massachusetts as the GOP leader; in 1965 Gerald R. Ford of Michigan turned the tables on Halleck; in 1980 John J. Rhodes of Arizona was persuaded by his colleagues to step down as party leader; in 1994 Robert H. Michel of Illinois retired in the face of Gingrich's stated intention to challenge him. Four years later, Gingrich resigned the speakership, having lost the support of many House Republicans.

Seniority in Congress is only one of many criteria that influence the election of party leaders. Other considerations are ideological or geographical balance within the leadership; parliamentary expertise; competency in organizational matters; skill in forging winning coalitions; fund-raising prowess; communication skills; sensitivity to the mood of the membership; and personal attributes, such as intelligence, fairness, persuasiveness, political shrewdness, and media savvy.

Although serving as a party leader in the House is typically a full-time position, every party leader in the Senate sits on one or more committees. The smaller size of the Senate allows leaders to participate in committee work while discharging their leadership duties. In the 111th Senate, for example, Reid, McConnell, Durbin, and Kyl each serve on standing committees.

LEADERSHIP ACTIVITIES

House and Senate leaders have basically the same job: to bring coherence, direction, and efficiency to a legislative body. Leadership duties can be broadly described as institutional maintenance (ensuring that Congress and its members perform their lawmaking and oversight duties and preserving Congress's reputation and integrity) and party maintenance (crafting winning coalitions among partisan colleagues and providing assistance to their members).[101] The basic point is to influence policymaking in line with their party's objectives. Leaders are also expected to assist their partisan colleagues electorally by championing legislative initiatives that convey partisan messages to the electorate.

Institutional Tasks

From an institutional perspective, party leaders have a number of obligations. They are provided with extra staff resources beyond those accorded individual lawmakers to assist in carrying out these diverse responsibilities.

Organizing the Chamber. Party leaders select the top administrative officers. These officers are important for the day-to-day functioning of the chambers even if their holders are invisible to the public. Examples include the clerk of the House and the secretary of the Senate. Party leaders also oversee committee jurisdictional revisions and revise congressional rules. Speaker Gingrich backed the abolition of three standing committees in 1995; Speaker Hastert supported a major recodification of House rules in 1999, the first since 1880. In 2007, Speaker Pelosi endorsed House adoption of new ethics and lobbying rules.

Scheduling Floor Business. "The power of the Speaker of the House is the power of scheduling," Speaker O'Neill once declared.[102] Or, as Newt Gingrich put it, "When you are Speaker you get to set the agenda.... [Y]ou get to decide what legislation is up."[103] After consulting with committee leaders, interested members, the president, and others, House and Senate party leaders decide what, when, how, and in which order measures should come up for debate. Setting the chamber's agenda and schedule—determining what each chamber will debate—is perhaps the single most important prerogative of the Speaker and Senate majority leader.

Once a bill is scheduled for action, the job of the leaders is to see that members vote—a task more difficult than merely herding bodies into the chamber. Party leaders may seek out certain members to speak on an issue because their endorsement can persuade other legislators to support it. Or they may delay action until the bill's sponsors are present. "The leadership must have the right members at the right place at the right time," said Byrd when he was the Senate majority whip.[104] In short, the leaders' scheduling prerogatives mold policy; arranging the time that bills reach the floor can seal their fate. A week's delay in scheduling a controversial White House initiative, for instance, may give the president, lobbying groups, and others additional time to muster votes for the proposal. Delay may also afford the opposition an opportunity to mobilize their forces.

Legislative business is also scheduled with forthcoming elections in mind. Measures are postponed to avoid an electorally embarrassing defeat, or they may be brought to the floor to satisfy groups allied with the party. What better time to take up legislation revamping the Internal Revenue Service than on or around April 15, the filing deadline for federal income taxes? Reflecting the two Congresses, both parties use the floor as an election platform to raise issues that appeal to their outside partisans. After passing measures advocated by its electoral base, a party can say, "Look what we did for you." Conversely, a party that fails to pass a measure can say to its bedrock supporters, "Look what we tried to do."

Influencing Colleagues. Party leaders also have the task of persuading members to support their legislation. In the modern Congress arm-twisting means pleading and cajoling to coax votes. "If you have no sense of what other people's judgments, values or goals are," stated Speaker Foley about the negotiating process, "you're in a very poor position to evaluate how you might accommodate them."[105] Although leaders generally seek to influence members of their own party and chamber, they also try to win cooperation from the other chamber and from the opposition party.

Party leaders do not have to rely solely on their powers of persuasion. Informal political networks and access to strategic information give them an edge in influencing colleagues.

> Because members will respond more candidly to leadership polls than to lobbyist or White House polls, [leaders] have perhaps the most important information in a legislative struggle—information on where the votes are and (sometimes) what it will take to win certain people over.[106]

Top leaders also can bestow or withhold a variety of tangible and intangible rewards, such as naming legislators to special or select committees, influencing assignments to standing committees, aiding reelection campaigns, and smoothing access to the White House or executive agencies.

Consulting the President. A traditional duty of party leaders is to meet with the president to discuss the administration's goals and to convey legislative sentiment about what the executive branch is doing or not doing. Although presidents spend more time dealing with leaders of their own party in Congress, they also consult with opposition leaders.

Party Tasks

From a party perspective, congressional party leaders have a number of formal and informal responsibilities. Each party's rules formally specify certain functions and responsibilities for their leaders. Parliamentary precedents and chamber rules also assign certain duties to party leaders. Informally, party leaders have assumed a wide range of duties, such as devising and implementing strategic decisions.

Organizing the Party. Congressional leaders help to organize their party by selecting partisan colleagues for standing committees, revising party rules, choosing other party leaders, and appointing party committees. Just a few examples illustrate the point. Senate GOP rules authorize their leader, Senator

McConnell, to appoint party colleagues to certain committees. By party rule, Speaker Pelosi names the chairs and Democratic members of two "leadership" committees—House Administration and Rules. To reward Sen. Charles Schumer, D-N.Y., for his stellar work in helping Democrats win back majority control of the Senate, Senator Reid "installed him in a newly created leadership post—vice chairman of the Democratic Conference, which is now No. 3 in the [leadership] lineup…He also named Schumer as chairman of the Joint Economic Committee, a panel on which the New Yorker had never even served."[107]

Promoting Party Unity. Another leadership assignment is to encourage party unity in Congress on priority legislation. Sen. Everett Dirksen, R-Ill., (minority leader, 1959–1969) used social gatherings to accomplish this goal.

> Dirksen brought party members together in a series of social affairs. He held cocktail parties at a Washington country club, inviting all Republican senators and sometimes their wives too. These were calculated by Dirksen to improve party harmony and to build a friendly feeling for himself with the Republican senators.[108]

Party leaders' efforts to foster party cohesion go far beyond extending them social invitations. Leaders perform many services for their party rank-and-file that build goodwill and a sense of common purpose. They schedule members' bills, provide them with timely political information, advise them on electoral issues, visit with their constituents, help them obtain good committee assignments, and work with them to forge policy agendas. "You really have to make people feel part of the process, and I guess it is a little bit like a shepherd," remarked a Senate Democratic leader. "You really want to keep as much as you can the flock together, and that takes different approaches with different people."[109] Periodically, leaders organize partisan retreats where members discuss party and policy goals, consider specific legislative initiatives, air differences, and resolve disputes.

Publicizing Party Views. Leaders are expected to publicize their party's policies and achievements. They give speeches in various forums, appear on radio and television talk shows, write newspaper and journal articles, hold press conferences, organize town meetings around the country, and establish Web sites that highlight party issues and images. Leaders are also expected to develop public relations strategies to neutralize the opposition's arguments and proposals. The advocacy role has increased in importance in recent years in part because of the twenty-four-hour news cycle. "We've created a situation," noted a scholar, "where the real way you drive the legislative process is by influencing public opinion, rather than by trading for votes."[110]

Party leaders also provide members with talking points for meetings with journalists or constituents. Parties often create communications teams that meet regularly to discuss message development and delivery and to recommend their more telegenic members to present party positions. "We're focused on making sure we deliver the [party] message both here in Washington and out in the hinterlands," said a chairman of the Senate Republican Conference.[111]

Providing Campaign Assistance. Leaders must be energetic campaigners and fund-raisers on behalf of their partisan colleagues. They help party candidates raise campaign funds. They establish their own leadership political action committees (PACs) to solicit contributions and donate to candidates of their party. They direct campaign dollars to groups running issue ads in the months leading up to the November elections. They travel to numerous states or House districts to campaign for incumbents and challengers from their party. They encourage outside groups to contribute to the party's electoral efforts. They also help vulnerable colleagues gain a higher profile by giving them a lead role on a major issue or creating working groups to provide members running for reelection with greater public exposure.[112]

Members anticipating a run for a leadership post distribute campaign funds as standard operating practice. "It seems that the job of fundraiser is becoming more important to senators' expectations of what a majority leader should do. The candidates [for this leadership position] thus are not trying to buy votes so much as to demonstrate how well they can fulfill that role," according to one account.[113] In both House and Senate, the ability to raise funds for colleagues is an increasingly important criterion for judging prospective party leaders.[114] Leaders stand at the conjunction of the two Congresses— the representative assembly, where money is needed to join, and the lawmaking body, where power calls the shots.

PARTY CAUCUSES, COMMITTEES, AND INFORMAL GROUPS

House and Senate leaders operate in diverse institutional settings. In the larger, more impersonal House, majority party leaders sometimes ignore the wishes of the minority party. This seldom happens in the Senate, where leaders must cope with the extensive rights of individual senators and the minority party. Despite these differences between House and Senate, parties in the two chambers are organized into the same three components: caucuses, committees, and informal party groups.

Party Caucuses

The organization of all partisans in a chamber is called the conference or (in the case of House Democrats) the caucus. Party conferences or caucuses elect leaders, approve committee assignments, provide members with services, debate party and legislative rules and policies, appoint task forces or issue teams, develop themes to keep members on message, enable members to vent their frustrations, and discuss outreach programs that appeal to voters. To promote Republican initiatives, a House GOP Conference chair announced, "We're going to operate more like a Madison Avenue public relations firm— more emphasis on benchmark polling, more direct-to-constituent contact, editorial placement and town hall meetings."[115] In an explanation that applies equally well to both parties and chambers, a senior House Democrat said:

> The caucus is the place where a great deal of freewheeling debate over an issue takes place and where sometimes a consensus develops. …Most of the discussions, although they have taken place at leadership meetings and at chairmen's meetings and in whips' meetings, have ended up in the broader forum of the caucus where every member of the Democratic party participates. You don't take a vote, but you try to develop a consensus and make concessions where they're necessary and develop the strongest possible position that can be supported by the maximum number of Democrats.[116]

In brief, party caucuses are useful forums where party members and leaders can assess sentiment on substantive or procedural issues and forge party unity. Sometimes presidents attend their party's House or Senate caucus to rally the troops. On rare occasions, party caucuses vote to strip members of their committee seniority or to oust committee leaders. The Senate Democratic Caucus met in November 2008, for example, to consider whether to allow Sen. Joe Lieberman, I-Conn., to continue to chair the Homeland Security Committee after Lieberman had actively supported Republican John McCain for president. Perhaps fearing that Lieberman would leave the party if he were stripped of his gavel, the caucus voted to permit him to keep his chairmanship, though they removed him from an Environment and Public Works post. Committee and party leaders are removed from their posts when legal action is taken against them (for example, if they are indicted).

Party Committees

Each of the four congressional parties—Senate and House Democrats, Senate and House Republicans—establishes committees to serve partisan needs and objectives (see Table 6-1). Three of the four parties on Capitol Hill have policy committees, for example. House Democrats disbanded their policy committee at Pelosi's direction. In its place, she established a revamped Steering Committee, which has a policy component (headed by George Miller of California) and a committee assignment component (chaired by Rosa DeLauro of Connecticut).[117] Party committees do not make policy, but they provide advice on scheduling, study substantive and political issues, distribute policy papers, track votes on issues, and discuss and implement party policy. Their influence has varied over the years, assuming greater importance when the party does not control the White House and thus needs policy and oversight assistance. Byron Dorgan, N.D., chair of the Senate Democratic Policy Committee, directed the panel to conduct extensive oversight activities during President George W. Bush's tenure, including investigations of government contracting in Iraq and Afghanistan, the implementation of the Medicare prescription drug policy, and gas prices, among other topics.[118] The two Senate and House GOP policy committees maintain Web sites that party

TABLE 6-1 **Party Committees in the Senate and House**	
Committee	Function
Senate Democratic	
Policy	Considers party positions on specific measures and assists the party leader in scheduling bills
Steering and Outreach	Assigns Democrats to committees and works to coordinate policy, legislative, and message issues for the Democratic Conference
Campaign	Works to elect Democrats to the Senate
Senate Republican	
Policy	Provides summaries of GOP positions on specific issues; researches procedural and substantive issues; drafts policy alternatives
Committee on Committees	Assigns Republicans to committees
Campaign	Works to elect Republicans to the Senate
House Democratic	
Steering	Assists the leadership and Democratic Caucus in establishing, implementing, researching, and communicating party priorities; assigns Democrats to committees
Campaign	Aids in electing Democrats to the House
House Republican	
Policy	Considers majority party proposals and works for consensus among Republican members
Steering	Assigns Republicans to standing committees
Campaign	Seeks to elect Republicans to the House

Note: The official names of the parties' campaign committees are as follows: Democratic Senatorial Campaign Committee, National Republican Senatorial Committee, Democratic Congressional Campaign Committee, and National Republican Congressional Committee.

members and staff can access at any time for information. Other important party panels are the campaign committees (discussed in Chapter 3) and the committee assignment committees (discussed in Chapter 7).

Informal Party Groups

In addition to party committees, a variety of informal groups operate on Capitol Hill. House and Senate leaders also employ party task forces to devise policy alternatives, formulate strategy, and coordinate floor action. Informal groups on Capitol Hill number around 300 in the 111th Congress. They may be unicameral or bicameral in composition. Many have a policy focus, such as the boating, steel, mining, soybean, rural health, electricity, automotive, children's, bicycle, or Internet caucuses. They strive to promote specific policies and heighten congressional and public awareness of their importance. There are also partisan and bipartisan groups. The House, for instance, has such party groups as the conservative Republican Study Committee, the centrist New Democrat Coalition, and the fiscally conservative Blue Dog Democrats. Some of these informal House groups, such as the Republican Study Committee, the 30-Something Caucus (moderate to liberal Democrats), and the Countdown Crew (GOP conservatives) regularly reserve time at the end of the legislative day to spotlight their own party's priorities and successes and to criticize the other party.

PARTY CONTINUITY AND CHANGE

Several features of the contemporary party system on Capitol Hill stand out: the intensity of party conflict, the persistence of the two-party system, and the advent of new coalition-building practices.

Intense Party Conflict

By any test one can use, the four Capitol Hill parties are flourishing. The organizational elements are healthy and active, their leaders are increasingly prominent, and their party voting is at relatively high levels. The congressional parties are assisted by well-staffed, professional party units.

The strength of today's parties has definite virtues. For one, it enables voters to better comprehend the divergent views, values, and principles of the two parties, and it may even encourage voter turnout. "Confrontation fits our strategy," stated Dick Cheney when he was in the House (1979–1989). "Polarization often has very beneficial results. If everything is handled through compromise and conciliation, if there are no real issues dividing us from Democrats, why should the country change and make us the majority?"[119]

Nevertheless, compromise is a traditional hallmark of legislative decision making. The intensity and extent of partisan conflict in the contemporary Congress raises questions about the body's ability to engage in meaningful bipartisan deliberation and mutual accommodation. Partisan polarization is decried by observers and members alike. In today's House, the two parties are not "just opponents or rivals now. [They] are enemies, with every fight being zero-sum," exclaimed a senior GOP lawmaker. "Compromise is seen as weakness by many of your constituents, and by all your potential opponents in the next primary."[120]

The call for bipartisanship is a commonly heard refrain—but an elusive goal—on Capitol Hill. President Obama campaigned by promising to "turn the page" on the bitter party politics that had characterized the Bush presidency. But his first major initiative, an economic stimulus package, elicited an almost purely partisan response in Congress. No House Republican and only three Senate Republicans supported the president's package.[121] Just before the opening of the 110th Congress, Senate majority leader Reid convened a closed-door meeting of all senators.[122] Its purpose: to infuse a spirit of bipartisanship in the working relationships between the two parties. A few weeks later the Senate was gridlocked as the two parties bitterly clashed over how to debate a measure disapproving of President Bush's deployment of more troops to Iraq.[123] Similarly, Speaker Pelosi promised that Democrats would run the House in an open and fair manner and allow Republicans the opportunity to offer their alternative amendments. Six weeks later, a newspaper headline proclaimed: "In Majority, Democrats Run Hill Much as GOP Did."[124]

The partisan rancor got so bad in the House (in the mid-1990s Speaker Gingrich and Minority Leader Gephardt refused to speak to each other for a year) that a bipartisan group of lawmakers organized a weekend retreat in 1997 for all members and their families. The so-called civility retreat was designed to allow members of the two parties to get to know each other better and to facilitate greater bipartisanship in resolving the nation's problems. Only marginal improvements flowed from this event. Three other civility retreats were held—in March 1999, March 2001, and March 2003—with similar limited improvements in comity among the members and between the parties. As a result, no further civility retreats have been held.

Episodes of sharp partisanship occur even in the more sedate Senate, in part because so many House members have been elected to that body. In recent Congresses nearly half of senators had served in the House. Many bring to the Senate the hard-edged partisanship that they learned in the House.[125] As Sen. Olympia J. Snowe, R-Maine, observed, "The whole Congress has become far more polarized and partisan so it makes it difficult to reach bipartisan agreements. The more significant the issue, the more partisan it becomes."[126]

The Two-Party System

The Democratic and Republican parties have dominated American politics and Congress since the mid–nineteenth century. Scholars have advanced various theories for the dualistic national politics of a country as diverse as the United States. Plurality elections in single-member congressional districts encouraged the creation and maintenance of two major parties. Under the winner-takes-all principle, the person who wins the most votes in a state or district is elected to the Senate or House. This principle discourages the formation of third parties. Some also trace the origins of the national two-party system to early conflicts between Federalists (advocates of a strong national government) and Antifederalists (advocates of limited national government). This dualism continued in subsequent splits: North versus South, East versus West, agricultural versus financial interests, and rural versus urban areas.[127] In addition, many states have laws that make it difficult to create new parties. Constitutional, political, and legal arrangements all contribute to the existence and maintenance of the two-party system.

Whatever mix of causes produced the two-party system, one thing is clear: Few third-party or independent legislators have been elected to Congress during the last century. The high-water mark was the 63d Congress (1913–1915), which had one Progressive senator and nineteen representatives elected as Progressives, Progressive-Republicans, or independents. In the post–World War II period, only a handful of lawmakers have been elected from minor parties or as independents.[128] Most of these legislators have converted to one of the major parties or have voted with them on procedural and substantive matters. The 111th Congress has only two Independent lawmakers, each of whom affiliates with the Democratic party: socialist senator Bernie Sanders of Vermont and former Democratic senator Joseph Lieberman of Connecticut. Third-party or independent members participate in Democratic or Republican affairs by invitation only.

Advances in Coalition Building

In Capitol Hill's highly competitive environment, party leaders are constantly searching for new ways to get the legislative results they desire. Recent innovations include media strategies, omnibus bills, and strategic planning.

Media Strategies. Party leaders understand that media strategies (the use of the press, television, radio, polls, the Internet, speeches, and so on) are essential to advance or block legislation. They form issue teams, message groups, "war rooms," or theme teams to orchestrate, organize, and coordinate political events and communications strategies that promote the party's message to the general public. No longer is the inside game—working behind-the-scenes to line up votes—sufficient to pass major legislation.

Also necessary is the outside game—influencing public opinion, coordinating with advocacy groups, and creating grassroots support for policy initiatives. Today, both parties use media to complement their parliamentary strategies in order to raise issues, define and frame priorities, and respond to partisan criticisms. Both congressional parties understand the importance of words as political weapons. GOP consultants found, for example, that characterizing the tax on inheritances as the "death tax"—and having GOP officeholders repeat it again and again over several years—aroused public ire against the tax. This sentiment was instrumental in the temporary repeal of the estate tax as part of President Bush's successful 2001 tax cut plan. Republicans continue to advocate for the permanent demise of the "death tax."

As compared to President Obama's bully pulpit to advance Democratic initiatives, congressional Republicans understand that they lack a single messenger who can focus the nation's attention in the same manner. As a result, Republicans have embraced a wide array of communications techniques to shape national debate, and they have augmented the number of leadership staff handling new media, communications, and grassroots outreach. "Our effort will work to help build dynamic multilayered, outside-the-Beltway coalitions that will help the Republican Conference explain the value of our policies and the impact they will have on the American people," said Jeff

Burton, the new coalitions director for Minority Whip Cantor.[129] Republican leaders—especially Boehner and Cantor in the House, and McConnell and Kyl in the Senate—hold press conferences, appear on diverse media outlets, organize town meetings, prepare talking points for the press (and their own members), develop party themes, use Web forums and blogs, write newspaper editorials, circulate data and statistics, organize policy forums, and engage in a variety of other activities to promote their legislative agenda to the public and to challenge Democratic initiatives.

Omnibus Bills. A phenomenon of modern lawmaking is the rise of mega-bills—legislation that is hundreds or thousands of pages in length encompassing disparate policy topics. Many of Congress's most significant recent policy departures have been enacted through omnibus bills.

Joining several bills in a single package can help leaders garner support. In such megabills, sweeteners can be added to woo supporters, and provisions that couldn't win majority support in stand-alone bills can be tucked out of sight. Bundling popular programs with painful spending cuts limits the number of difficult votes lawmakers must cast and provides them with political cover. Members can explain to angry constituents or groups that they had to support the indivisible whole because its discrete parts were not open to separate votes. Leaders, however, must be wary of the reverse concern that a mega-bill can attract a coalition of minorities with the votes needed to reject the measure.

Megabills can also strengthen Congress's leverage with the executive branch. Measures that a president might veto if presented separately can be folded into megabills and signed in that fashion.

Party leaders command the resources and authority to influence the packaging process. "Omnibus bills place a huge amount of power in the hands of a few key leaders and their staffs," remarked one House member.[130] Rank-and-file members look to party leaders to formulate a package acceptable to at least a majority of members. Nevertheless, these megabills often arouse the lawmakers' suspicions and complaints. "These omnibus bills—often gauged more by weight than the number of pages—are abominations," one member complained. "No one member of Congress has a chance to read much of them, let alone understand them, before they are voted on."[131] Late in the 108th Congress, lawmakers were compelled to vote on an omnibus appropriations bill more than 3,000 pages long and with less than twenty-four hours to review it.

Strategic Planning and Coordination. On major policy and political issues, strategic planning and coordination are crucial to the leadership's ability to mobilize successful coalitions. House and Senate leaders meet regularly with their partisan allies to craft their plans, to anticipate the legislative moves of the opposition, to develop their countermoves, and to formulate effective public relations strategies. For example, party leaders employ defensive messages as a way to protect their members from political attack, known as the "inoculation strategy." The objective is to appropriate the other party's popular issues by blurring the distinctions between congressional Democrats and Republicans. For example, on an immigration reform issue, Democrats called their package the Latino and Immigrant Fairness Act; Republicans dubbed their initiative the Legal Immigration Family Equity Act.[132]

Both parties, too, focus attention on how to win the battle of ideas in Congress and the broader electorate. In the aftermath of their 2006 electoral defeat, Senate Republicans began working to "brand" the GOP nationally as the "reform party"—ironically stressing some of the themes that had won them the majority in 1994: limited government, fiscal restraint, and elimination of wasteful programs and expenditures. "In my view," stated Senate GOP leader McConnell, "minority status isn't our biggest cause for concern. In the long run, the public's perception of the Republican Party is more dangerous."[133]

CONCLUSION

Congressional parties have elaborate organizations, and their leaders fulfill a multiplicity of roles and duties. The Senate majority leader, explained Byrd when he held that post, performs the following duties: "[He] facilitates, he constructs, he programs, he schedules, he takes an active part in the development of legislation, he steps in at crucial moments on the floor, offers amendments, speaks on behalf of legislation and helps to shape the outcome of the legislation."[134] Party leaders can do many things, but they cannot typically command their colleagues. Their leadership rests chiefly on their skill in providing others with reasons to follow them.

The party principle organizes Congress.[135] The committee principle, however, shapes the measures Congress acts upon. These two principles are often in conflict. The first emphasizes aggregation, the second fragmentation. Party leaders struggle to manage an institution that disperses policymaking authority to so many work groups. In short, leaders provide the centripetal force to offset committees' centrifugal influence.

SUGGESTED READINGS

Aldrich, John H. *Why Parties? The Origins and Transformation of Party Politics in America.* Chicago: University of Chicago Press, 1995.

Baker, Richard A., and Roger H. Davidson, eds. *First among Equals: Outstanding Senate Leaders of the Twentieth Century.* Washington, D.C.: Congressional Quarterly, 1991.

Cox, Gary W., and Mathew D. McCubbins. *Legislative Leviathan: Party Government in the House.* Berkeley: University of California Press, 1993.

Cox, Gary W., and Mathew D. McCubbins. *Setting the Agenda: Responsible Party Government in the U.S. House of Representatives.* New York: Cambridge University Press, 2005.

Davidson, Roger H., Susan Webb Hammond, and Raymond W. Smock, eds. *Masters of the House: Congressional Leaders over Two Centuries.* Boulder, Colo.: Westview Press, 1998.

Peters, Ronald M., Jr. *The American Speakership: The Office in Historical Perspective.* 2d ed. Baltimore: Johns Hopkins University Press, 1997.

Rohde, David W. *Parties and Leaders in the Postreform House.* Chicago: University of Chicago Press, 1991.

Sinclair, Barbara. *Legislators, Leaders, and Lawmaking: The U.S. House of Representatives in the Postreform Era.* Baltimore: Johns Hopkins University Press, 1995.

_____. *The Transformation of the U.S. Senate.* Baltimore: Johns Hopkins University Press, 1989.

Strahan, Randall. *Leading Representatives: The Agency of Leaders in the Politics of the U.S. House.* Baltimore: Johns Hopkins University Press, 2007.

C *ommittee Politics.* Two activist House committee chairs in their element (top left): Barney Frank (D-Mass.) of the House Financial Services Committee addresses financial services reforms in a Capitol Hill news conference in early 2009. Henry Waxman (D-Calif.) (top right) of the House Energy and Commerce Committee during an oversight hearing about a *salmonella* outbreak traced to a peanut processing plant; he holds a photo of a dead rodent and a certificate of achievement from the firm. Center: Treasury Secretary Timothy F. Geithner, standing at left, and Federal Reserve Chairman Ben S. Bernanke, seated at Geithner's right, prepare to testify before Representative Frank's committee concerning the nation's financial crisis. Bottom: Committee aides sort through amendments during a break in the House Energy and Commerce Committee's markup of a 2009 bill designed to reduce greenhouse gasses.

Committees:
Workshops of Congress

Committees serve two broad purposes: individual and institutional. Individually, lawmakers look for ways from their committee perches to benefit their constituents. "As far as I can see, there is really only one basic reason to be on a public works committee," admitted a House member. "Intellectual stimulation" is not it. "Most of all, I want to be able to bring home projects to my district."[1] With scores of representatives seeking assignment to the Transportation and Infrastructure Committee, it has grown to be the largest (seventy-five members in the 111th Congress [2009–2011]) in congressional history. Members of Congress well understand the connection between their committee assignments and their reelection potential.

Committees also enable legislators to utilize and develop expertise in areas that interest them. A former teacher, for instance, may seek assignment to the committee overseeing education policy. And some panels, such as the tax and appropriations committees, enable members to wield personal influence among their colleagues. Members ask to be on the House Appropriations Committee, explained a GOP leader, because "instantaneously...they have a host of new friends, and we all know why"—that panel controls the distribution of discretionary federal money.[2]

Institutionally, committees are the centers of policymaking, oversight of federal agencies, and public information (largely through the hearings they hold). By dividing their membership into a number of "little legislatures," the House and Senate are able to consider dozens of proposed laws simultaneously.[3] Without committees, a legislative body of 100 senators and 441 House members could not handle roughly 10,000 bills and nearly 100,000 nominations biennially, a national budget over $3 trillion, and a limitless array of issues, many controversial. Although floor actions often refine legislation, committees are the means by which Congress sifts through an otherwise impossible jumble of bills, proposals, and issues.

Congressional committees serve another important institutional function in the political system. They act as safety valves, or outlets for national debates and controversies. Military and economic responsibilities, demographic shifts, trade agreements, global environmental concerns, the drug war, the social dislocations caused by technological advances, and the rising cost of health care place enormous strains on the political system. As forums for public debates, congressional committees help to vent, absorb, and resolve these strains. Moreover, the safety-valve function gives the citizenry a greater sense of participation in national decision making and helps educate members about public problems. For example, public outrage at the American International Group's (AIG) use of $165 million in tax dollars to pay bonuses to employees who helped to trigger the nation's economic meltdown prompted fast action by the House to impose large tax penalties on the recipients of the bonus money. As House Majority Whip James Clyburn, D-S.C., stated, "We are a political body; we are a body that's responding to people's dreams and aspirations, and sometimes we respond to their emotions."[4]

The individual and institutional purposes of the committee system can conflict. Because members tend to gravitate to committees for constituency or career reasons, they are not the most impartial judges of the policies they authorize. "It's one of the weaknesses of the system that those attracted to a committee like Agriculture are those whose constituents benefit from farm programs," acknowledged Sen. Charles E. Schumer, a Democrat from New York. "And so they're going to support those programs and they're not going to want to cut them, even the ones that are wasteful."[5]

THE PURPOSES OF COMMITTEES

Senator Schumer's comment highlights an ongoing debate about the development and fundamental purposes of the committee system. To explain the organization of legislatures and the behavior of their committees, scholars have advanced the distributional, informational, and party hypotheses.

The distributional hypothesis suggests that legislatures create committees to give lawmakers policy influence in areas critical to their reelection. Members seek committee assignments to "bring home the bacon" (public goods and services) to their constituents. Because lawmakers largely self-select their committees, committees can become filled with what scholars call preference outliers— members whose homogeneous preferences for benefits to their constituents put them out of step with the heterogeneous views of the membership as a whole. Chamber majorities, in brief, may need to restrain overreaching committees by rejecting or amending their recommended actions.[6]

The informational hypothesis proposes that legislative bodies establish committees to provide lawmakers with the specialized expertise required to make informed judgments in a complex world. Furthermore, the division of labor under the committee system augments Congress's role in relation to the executive branch. Instead of being composed primarily of preference outliers, committees under this model consist of a diverse membership with wide-ranging perspectives. The basic goal of committees, then, is to formulate policies that resolve national problems.[7]

The party hypothesis views committees as agents of their party caucuses. The basis of this theory is that all members owe their committee assignments to their parties, and members of the majority party chair all the committees in Congress. According to this perspective, committee chairs are "senior partners"— analogous to those in law and accountancy partnerships—who provide strategic and tactical direction for their parties.[8] By wielding power over the agenda, committee chairs block the consideration of legislation unacceptable to the majority of their party and facilitate the passage of party-sponsored legislation in the chamber.

Each of these hypotheses captures an aspect of the committee system. "All three of the theoretical perspectives...can explain some aspects of congressional behavior and organization, but none offers a complete account by itself," concludes one recent study of decision making on agricultural policy.[9] Lawmakers are concerned with local issues of immediate concern to constituents, but every district and state is also affected by broad national concerns— the condition of the economy and the environment, for example. Certain issues may lend themselves on occasion more to the distributional than to the informational or party theory of policymaking.

Because good public policy may be impeded by the parochial orientations of individual members, Congress has a small number of control, or centralizing, committees that promote institutional and policy integration over committee and programmatic particularism. For example, each house has a Budget Committee, which proposes limits on how much Congress can spend for designated functional areas.[10] However committees are characterized, they focus and concentrate the policy and oversight activities of individual lawmakers.

EVOLUTION OF THE COMMITTEE SYSTEM

Committees in the early Congresses generally were temporary panels created for specific tasks. Proposals were considered on the House or Senate floor and then were referred to specially created panels that worked out the details—the reverse order of today's system. The Senate, for example, would "debate a subject at length on the floor and, after the majority's desires had been crystallized, might appoint a committee to put those desires into bill form."[11] About 350 ad hoc committees were formed during the Third Congress (1793–1795) alone.[12] The parent chamber closely controlled these temporary committees. It assigned them clear-cut tasks, required them to report back favorably or unfavorably, and dissolved them when they had completed their work.

Both chambers had, by at least 1816, developed a system of permanent, or standing, committees, some of which are still in existence. Standing committees, as historian DeAlva Stanwood Alexander explained, were better suited than ad hoc groups to cope with the larger membership and wider scope of congressional business. Another scholar, George H. Haynes, pointed out that the "needless inconvenience of the frequent choice of select committees" taxed congressional patience. Lawmakers recognized that debating bills one at a time before the whole chamber was an inefficient way of processing Congress's legislative business. Perhaps, too, legislators came to value standing committees as counterweights to presidential influence in setting the legislative agenda.[13] Permanent committees changed the way Congress made policy and allocated authority. The House and Senate now reviewed and voted upon recommendations made by specialized, experienced committees. Standing committees also encouraged oversight of the executive branch. Members have called them "the eye, the ear, the hand, and very often the brain" of Congress.[14]

As committees acquired expertise and authority, they became increasingly self-reliant and resistant to chamber and party control. After the House revolt against domineering Speaker Joseph G. Cannon, R-Ill., in 1910, power flowed to the committee chairmen. Along with a few strong party leaders, they held sway over House and Senate policymaking during much of the twentieth century. In rare instances committee members rebelled and diminished the chairman's authority. But most members heeded the advice that Speaker John W. McCormack, D-Mass. (1962–1971), gave to freshmen: "Whenever you pass a committee chairman in the House, you bow from the waist. I do."[15]

The chairmen's authority was buttressed by the custom of seniority that flourished with the rise of congressional careerism. The majority party member with the most years of continuous service on a committee virtually always became its chairman. As a result, committee chairmen owed little or nothing to party leaders, much less to presidents. This automatic selection process produced experienced, independent chairmen but concentrated authority in a few hands. The have-nots wanted a piece of the action and objected that seniority promoted the competent and incompetent alike. They objected, too, that the system promoted members from safe one-party areas—especially conservative southern Democrats and midwestern Republicans—who could ignore party policies or national sentiments.

The late 1960s and 1970s saw a rapid influx of new members, many from the cities and suburbs, who opposed the conservative status quo. Allying themselves with more senior members seeking a stronger voice in Congress, they pushed through changes that diffused power and shattered seniority as an absolute criterion for leadership posts. Today, House and Senate committee chairmen (and ranking minority members) must be elected by their party colleagues. No longer free to wield arbitrary authority, they must abide by committee and party rules and be sensitive to majority sentiment within their party's caucus or conference.

TYPES OF COMMITTEES

Congress today has a shopper's bazaar of committees—standing, select, joint, and conference—and within each of these general types there are variations. Standing committees, for example, can be either authorizing or appropriating panels. Authorizing committees (such as Agriculture, Armed Services, and Judiciary) are the policymaking centers on Capitol Hill. As substantive committees, they propose solutions to public problems and advocate what they believe to be the necessary levels of spending for the programs under their

---

TABLE 7-1 **Standing Committees of the House and Senate, 111th Congress (2009–2011)**

House	Senate
Agriculture	Agriculture, Nutrition, and Forestry
Appropriations	Appropriations
Armed Services	Armed Services
Budget	Banking, Housing, and Urban Affairs
Education and Labor	Budget
Energy and Commerce	Commerce, Science, and Transportation
Financial Services	Energy and Natural Resources
Foreign Affairs	Environment and Public Works
Homeland Security	Finance
House Administration	Foreign Relations
Judiciary	Health, Education, Labor, and Pensions
Natural Resources	Homeland Security and Governmental Affairs
Oversight and Government Reform	Judiciary
Rules	Rules and Administration
Science and Technology	Small Business and Entrepreneurship
Small Business	Veterans' Affairs
Standards of Official Conduct	
Transportation and Infrastructure	
Veterans' Affairs	
Ways and Means	

Source: House and Senate committee Web pages, http://www.house.gov/house/CommitteeWWW.shtml and http://www.senate.gov/pagelayout/committees/d_three_sections_with_teasers/committees_home.htm.

---

jurisdictions. The House and Senate Appropriations Committees recommend how much money agencies and programs will receive. Continuing conflict, not surprisingly, exists between the two types of panels. Typically, authorizers press for full funding for their policies and programs while appropriators are in the habit of recommending lower spending levels.

Standing Committees

A standing committee is a permanent entity created by public law or House or Senate rules. Standing committees continue from Congress to Congress, except in those infrequent instances when they are eliminated. Table 7-1 identifies the standing committees in the 111th Congress.

Standing committees process the bulk of Congress's daily and annual agenda of business. Typically, measures are considered on the House or Senate floor after first being referred to, and approved by, the appropriate committees. Put negatively, committees are the burial ground for most legislation. More positively stated, committees sift through the thousands of measures introduced in each Congress, reporting those that merit floor debate. Of the hundreds of bills that clear committees, fewer still are enacted into law.

Sizes and Ratios. Biennial election results frame the party negotiations that establish committee sizes and ratios (the number of majority and minority members on a panel). At the beginning of each new Congress, each chamber adopts its own resolution that elects party members to the committees and thus sets their sizes and ratios. In practice, House committee sizes and ratios are established by the majority leadership. As rules of the House Democratic Caucus stipulate: "The Democratic Leadership shall work to ensure that committee ratios are at least as representative of the number of Democrats in the House and that each panel include the greatest number of Democrats possible." Because the majority party has the votes, it can be the final arbiter if the minority protests its allotment of seats. By contrast, the Senate minority has significant leverage in setting committee sizes and ratios; if minority senators believe they are being unfairly treated, they can filibuster the resolution assigning senators to committees.

In the 111th House, the ratio of Democrats to Republicans in the chamber was 59 percent (257 Democrats of 435 members) to 41 percent (178 Republicans). This ratio was roughly reflected within most House committees. Some key procedural committees, however, have traditionally had disproportionate ratios to ensure firm majority party control. This pattern continued in the 111th Congress, with Democrats advantaged on House Administration (67 percent to 33 percent) and Rules (69 percent to 31 percent), as well as tax-writing Ways and Means (64 percent to 36 percent). Standards of Official Conduct has an equal number of majority and minority members. The Speaker names the committee chair.

Several significant exceptions, however, aroused the ire of GOP leaders in the 111th Congress. Republican leader John Boehner of Ohio complained to Speaker Nancy Pelosi about GOP underrepresentation on several key committees, especially Appropriations, Energy and Commerce, and Financial Services, where significant legislation was likely to originate. He was especially annoyed that Democrats reduced the Appropriations Committee's size from 66 to 60, with the Republicans losing the six seats. The change netted the Democrats a bonus of two seats more than their entitlement, based on their 59 percent chamber majority.[16]

Rep. Tom Price of Georgia, who chaired the conservative Republican Study Committee, the largest informal partisan group in the House, underscored that it was only fair that most standing committees reflect the appropriate ratio. "[I]t appears," he said, "that on some of the most pivotal committees where issues like taxes and financial services and health care are going to be decided, [the ratio of 59 percent Democrat, 41 percent Republican] has not held. The ratio appears to be closer to 63 percent Democrat, 37 percent Republican."[17] Speaker Pelosi defended the committee ratios by saying that they were fair and "reflect the increased number of Democrats in the House."[18]

In the Senate, committee sizes and ratios are negotiated by the majority and minority leaders. (Senate rules, unlike the House's, establish the sizes of the standing committees, but these can be adjusted up or down with the agreement of both parties' leaders.) After weeks of negotiations following the November 2008 elections, the leaders agreed to committee ratios for the 111th Senate. The negotiating process, said Democratic leader Reid, was "tedious, and the giver always feels that they have given more, while the taker believes that they deserve more [seats]."[19] The negotiations took longer than in the previous Congress because of initial GOP opposition to treating Democrat Al Franken as the eventual winner of the Minnesota Senate seat. Leader Reid reserved seats on several committees for Franken, as McConnell did for the previous incumbent, Norm Coleman.

With Senate Republicans agreeing to a 59 to 41 percent ratio, Democrats gained a three-seat edge on most committees with two exceptions (Appropriations and Armed Services), where Democrats have a four-seat advantage. With more party members on the committees, Democrats will have an easier time advancing their priorities compared to the one-seat margin they had in the previous Congress. When GOP Sen. Arlen Specter, Pa., switched parties, it provided Democrats with an additional seat on the five committees on which he serves. The majority party gained a five-seat advantage on Appropriations and a four-seat edge on the Judiciary, Environment, Veterans, and Aging panels.[20]

Party leaders often enlarge panels to accommodate lawmakers competing for membership on the same committees. They recognize that intraparty harmony can be maintained by boosting the number of committee seats. Reductions in committee sizes are thus hard to achieve, but they do occur—as in the case of House Appropriations previously mentioned. Committee size is sometimes decreased to improve the chair's ability to manage the committee, as well as to provide greater opportunities for panel members to deliberate and raise questions at hearings. Typically, minority party members bear the brunt of the reductions.

Subcommittees. Subcommittees perform much of the day-to-day lawmaking and oversight work of Congress. Like standing committees, they vary widely in rules and procedures, staff arrangements, modes of operations, and their relationships with other subcommittees and the full committee. They are created for various reasons, such as lawmakers' need to subdivide a committee's wide-ranging policy domain into manageable pieces, their desire to chair these panels, thus gaining a platform to shape the legislative agenda, and their wish to respond to the policy claims of specialized constituencies.

Under House rules adopted in 2009, Democrats limited most standing committees to no more than five subcommittees, although there are several exceptions. Committees allowed to have more than five subcommittees are Appropriations (twelve), Armed Services (seven), Foreign Affairs (seven), Oversight and Government Reform (seven), and Transportation and Infrastructure (six). Various reasons account for these exceptions: for example, long-standing custom, workload demands, acquisition of additional jurisdiction, accommodation of an individual lawmaker, and bicameral considerations. Committees bound by the limit of five, moreover, are permitted to create a sixth subcommittee if it is devoted to oversight.

A committee authorized to establish additional subcommittees may choose not to do so. For example, when Henry Waxman, D-Calif., chaired the Oversight and Government Reform Committee in the 110th House, he decided to reduce the number of subcommittees from seven to five. His new subcommittee structure was created "so that the jurisdiction of each subcommittee will have broad appeal and will engage the attention of the subcommittee members."[21] As chair of the Energy and Commerce Committee, Waxman eliminated one subcommittee by merging the Subcommittees on Environment and Hazardous Materials and Energy and Air Quality into the new Subcommittee on Energy and Environment. This subcommittee merger enhances prospects for environmental legislation because Edward Markey, D-Mass., a staunch environmentalist and ally of Speaker Pelosi, claimed the chairmanship of the merged subcommittee. This post gives Markey a platform for advancing legislative proposals related to issues studied by a select committee he also chairs: the Select Committee on Energy Independence and Global Warming, which lacks legislative authority (the right to receive or report legislation).[22]

Another House rule limits members to service on no more than four subcommittees. Such assignment restrictions, along with the limits on the number of subcommittees within each standing committee, are designed to make Congress "more deliberative, participatory, and manageable by reducing scheduling conflicts and jurisdictional overlap."[23] When Republicans ran the House (1995–2007), their party conference rules stated that the "selection of Chairmen of the Committee's Subcommittees [and GOP subcommittee assignments] shall be at the discretion of the full Committee Chairman, unless a majority of the Republican Members of the full Committee disapprove the action of the Chairman." Now in the minority, Republicans allow their ranking members on the full committee to select the ranking subcommittee members.

The Democratic majority of the 111th House follows detailed procedures outlined in the party rules for determining subcommittee chairs and assignments. Simply put, once the subcommittee structure and jurisdictions are established, committee Democrats—in order of their seniority on the full committee (or seniority on the Appropriations subcommittee)—bid for a subcommittee chairmanship (or assignment), which is then subject to approval by secret ballot of the Democratic committee members.

Since March 2004, House Democrats have also had a rule in place to encourage party loyalty among subcommittee leaders. The rule came about after sixteen Democrats voted with the Republican majority in November 2003 to pass a controversial Medicare prescription drug bill. Under the change instigated by then minority leader Nancy Pelosi, Calif., once the exclusive committees select their subcommittee chairs, they are then subject to approval by the

Steering and Policy Committee as well as the Democratic Caucus. (Subcommittee chairs of the Rules Committee, which is known as "the Speaker's committee," are exempt from this procedure.) According to Democratic aides, the party rule is designed to discourage members from voting against the Democratic Caucus "out of fear they could get passed over for subcommittee leadership."[24]

Under Democratic rules, the exclusive committees are Appropriations, Energy and Commerce, Financial Services, Rules, and Ways and Means. Democrats who serve on these panels, largely because of their importance and workload, may serve on no other standing committees—unless they are granted an exemption, or waiver, from this requirement. Waivers of the rule are quite common, however. In the 111th House, most of the nine Democrats on the Rules Committee also serve on another standing committee. Party leaders also grant waivers to permit members to sit on an extra major committee that they deem important to their reelection prospects. This is another example of the two Congresses, where the institution bends to suit the preferences and needs of individual members.

In the Senate, chamber and party rules are silent on the number of subcommittees that standing committees may establish. However, rules set subcommittee assignment limits for senators and prohibit them from chairing more than one subcommittee on any given committee. The number of subcommittees not surprisingly often equals the number of majority party members on a committee eligible to chair a subcommittee. Subcommittee chairmen and assignments are determined in one of two ways: by the full chair in consultation with the ranking member or by senators' order of seniority on the full committee. It is traditional for committee members to defer to the chair on organizational matters, such as the number of subcommittees and their respective jurisdictions. These matters, to be sure, are subject to majority approval of the panel.

Senate subcommittee chairmanships came into play following the November 2008 elections. Many Senate Democrats, dismayed at Independent Connecticut senator Joe Lieberman's strong backing of Arizona Republican senator John McCain's presidential candidacy, wanted to punish Lieberman by ousting him from the chairmanship of the Homeland Security and Governmental Affairs Committee. (Lieberman, who was Al Gore's 2000 vice presidential running mate, has caucused with Senate Democrats as an Independent.) In the end, wanting to keep Lieberman in the Democratic fold, Majority Leader Reid used a milder form of rebuke: the two gavel rule. Under a long ignored Senate rule (Rule XXV) committee chairs may head only one subcommittee. In Lieberman's case, he was allowed to retain his full committee chairmanship and his Armed Services subcommittee chairmanship, but he relinquished his chairmanship of an Environment and Public Works subcommittee.[25] To give Senate Democratic newcomers a chance to head subcommittees, Reid considered enforcing the Senate two gavel rule against twelve other full committee chairs who also headed at least two subcommittees.[26]

Unlike the House, where every standing committee except Budget and Standards of Official Conduct has subcommittees, four Senate standing committees customarily function without subcommittees—Budget, Rules and Administration, Small Business, and Veterans' Affairs—as do four other permanent panels: Indian Affairs, Ethics, Intelligence, and Aging. These panels are able to process their legislative business without subcommittees, given their typically modest workloads.

Select, or Special, Committees

Select, or special, committees are temporary panels that typically go out of business after the two-year life of the Congress in which they are created. But some select committees take on the attributes of permanent committees. The House, for example, has a Permanent Select Intelligence Committee. Select committees usually do not have legislative authority unless it is granted by their authorizing measure; typically they can only study, investigate, and make recommendations.

Select panels serve both individual and institutional concerns. They accommodate the interests of individual members. The chairmen of these panels may attract publicity that enhances their political careers. For example, Democrat Harry S Truman of Missouri came to the public's (and President Franklin D. Roosevelt's) attention as head of a special Senate committee investigating World War II military procurement practices. Second, special panels can be a point of access for interest groups, such as the elderly. In addition, select committees supplement the standing committee system by overseeing and investigating issues that the permanent panels may lack adequate time for or prefer to ignore. As noted earlier, a recent example of an issue-based select committee is the 111th House's creation of a select panel to give full-time attention and public focus to a major planetary issue: global warming.

They can also be set up to coordinate consideration of issues that overlap the jurisdictions of several standing committees. At the start of the 108th Congress, for example, the House created a Select Committee on Homeland Security. Scores of House standing committees had jurisdiction over various issues pertaining to homeland security. To strengthen supervision of the new Department of Homeland Security, formed from the merger of twenty-two agencies with around 180,000 employees, Speaker J. Dennis Hastert and other lawmakers wanted "a single point of oversight for the massive new department."[27]

Joint Committees

Joint committees, which include members from both chambers, have been used since the First Congress for study, investigation, oversight, and routine activities. In the 111th Congress there were four joint committees: Economic, Library, Printing, and Taxation. The Joint Library Committee and the Joint Printing Committee oversee, respectively, the Library of Congress and the Government Printing Office. The Joint Taxation Committee is essentially a holding company for staff who work closely with the tax-writing committees of each house. The Joint Economic Committee conducts studies and hearings on a wide range of domestic and international economic issues. Unless their composition is prescribed by statute, House members of joint committees are appointed by the Speaker, and senators are formally appointed by that chamber's presiding officer. The chairmanship of joint committees rotates each Congress between House and Senate members.

Conference Committees

Before legislation can be sent to the president for his consideration, it must pass both the House and the Senate in identical form. Conference committees, sometimes called the third house of Congress, reconcile differences between similar measures passed by both chambers. They are composed of members from each house. A representative highlighted their importance:

> When I came to Congress I had no comprehension of the importance of the conference committees which actually write legislation. We all knew that important laws are drafted there, but I don't think one person in a million has any appreciation of their importance and the process by which they work. Part of the explanation, of course, is that there never is a printed record of what goes on in conference.[28]

Conference bargaining roughly can be classified in four ways: traditional, offer-counteroffer, subconference, and pro forma. Traditional conferences are those in which the participants meet face to face, haggle among themselves about the items in bicameral disagreement, and then reach an accord. The bulk of conferences are of this type. In offer-counteroffer conferences, often used by the tax-writing committees, one side suggests a compromise proposal; the other side recesses to discuss it in private and then returns to present a counteroffer. Conferences with numerous participants (on omnibus bills, for example) usually break into small units, or subconferences, to reconcile particular matters or to address special topics. Pro forma conferences are those in which issues are resolved informally—by preconference negotiations between conferee leaders or their staffs. The conference itself then ratifies the earlier decisions.[29]

Some scholars argue that congressional committees are influential because they possess unilateral authority at the conference stage to veto or negotiate alterations in legislation. Others dispute this contention and claim that the "ex post veto is not a significant institutional foundation of congressional committee power."[30] Another model suggests that conferees serve as agents of their respective chamber majorities and advocate their policy positions instead of committee viewpoints.[31] Increasingly, the top party leaders in each chamber are taking a more direct and active role in the conference process and in determining who should (or should not) be a conferee.

The Senate or House majority leaders sometimes serve as conferees on priority measures to increase their leverage in the bicameral bargaining process. On occasion, party leaders will simply bypass conference committees and employ another method (the exchange of amendments between the chambers, see Chapter 8) to resolve interchamber substantive disagreements.[32]

THE ASSIGNMENT PROCESS

Every congressional election sets off a scramble for committee seats. Legislators understand the linkage between winning desirable assignments and winning elections. Reelected incumbents often seek to move to more prestigious panels. Newly elected representatives and senators quickly make their preferences known to party leaders, to members of the panels that make committee assignments, and to others. For example, freshman Democratic representative Frank Kratovil quickly began lobbying for committees important to his constituents and to his reelection in 2010. (He narrowly won, by 2,852 votes, a hard-fought election in 2008.) As the first Democrat elected from Maryland's Eastern Shore (the First District) in eighteen years, Kratovil lobbied for seats on Agriculture (his district is rural), Armed Services (many of his constituents work at Fort Meade and the Aberdeen Proving Ground), and Transportation (the Chesapeake Bay Bridge is in his district).[33] He won two (Agriculture and Armed Services) of his top choices and even his third assignment (Natural Resources) allows him to work on an issue of paramount importance to his constituents: improving the health of the Chesapeake Bay.

The Pecking Order

The most powerful, and thus most desirable, standing committees deal with taxing and spending: the House Ways and Means and Senate Finance, which pass on tax, trade, Social Security, and Medicare measures, and the House and Senate Appropriations Committees, which hold the federal purse strings. The Budget Committees, established in 1974, have become sought-after assignments because of their important role in economic and fiscal matters and their guardianship of the congressional budgeting process. The House and Senate Commerce Committees, as well as each chamber's banking committees, are also influential panels for two main reasons: their significant jurisdictional mandate and the campaign cash that committee members can raise from the many interest groups affected by the panel's decisions.

Among those panels that seldom have waiting lists are the Senate Ethics and House Standards of Official Conduct committees. These committees in both chambers are unpopular because legislators are reluctant to sit in judgment of their colleagues. "Members have never competed for the privilege of serving on the ethics committee, and I am no exception," remarked Rep. Howard L. Berman, D-Calif., after the Democratic leader prevailed on him to join the ethics panel. Or as a GOP member said after serving as ethics chairman, "I've paid my debt to society. It's time for me to be paroled."[34] Still, lawmakers who are appointed to the panel recognize its institutional importance. After she was named by Speaker Pelosi to head the House ethics panel in the 111th Congress, Rep. Zoe Lofgren, D-Calif., said: "The Committee on Standards of Official Conduct exists to ensure that the House of Representatives maintains [the public] trust and confidence, and in turn its legitimacy."[35] GOP representative Jo Bonner of Alabama is the panel's ranking minority member.

A committee's attractiveness can change over time. The Senate Foreign Relations Committee, for example, was historically a panel that elicited great interest among members (especially during the Vietnam War era). After the cold war ended, however, the committee had trouble in filling vacancies. Throughout the 1990s senators viewed it as largely a debating society without much influence. But today, the committee plays a major role in influencing international decision making, given heightened public concern about the global war on terrorism, Iraq and Afghanistan, and a large array of other important international issues. A foreign policy expert conceded the panel's renewed importance: "Yeah, they've got clout. You control money, you control nominations, you control treaties, and you control the microphone" to discuss an array of global issues. "That's a lot of power in Washington."[36]

Preferences and Politicking

In an analysis of six House committees, Richard F. Fenno Jr. found that three basic goals of lawmakers—reelection, influence within the House, and good public policy—affect members' committee assignment preferences. Reelection-oriented members were attracted to committees such as Natural Resources (then called the Interior Committee). Appropriations and Ways and Means attracted influence-oriented members. Policy-oriented members sought membership on committees such as Education and Labor or Foreign Affairs. Members with similar goals find themselves on the same committees, Fenno concluded. This homogeneity of perspectives may result in harmonious, but biased, committees (see Table 7-2 for a House-Senate comparison).[37]

Since Fenno's study, scholars have elaborated on the relationship between members' goals and committee assignments. They have divided House committees into reelection (or constituency), policy, and power panels and concur that some mix of the three goals motivates most activity on the committees. They agree, too, that members' goals "are less easily characterized in the Senate than in the House."[38] Almost every senator has the opportunity to serve on one of the top committees, such as Appropriations, Armed Services, Commerce, and Finance. Hence, the power associated with a particular committee assignment is less important for senators than for representatives.

Members campaign vigorously for the committees they prefer. A freshman House member explained how he set out to win a coveted spot on the Appropriations Committee. He solicited the help of the majority leader and lobbied each member who sat on his party's committee assignment panel. "It was almost like this was another congressional campaign," the lawmaker explained. "While a lot of [new] members were driving around house hunting and interviewing staff members, I was working" to win appointment to Appropriations.[39] His electoral vulnerability (50 to 48 percent in a nationally targeted race) persuaded party leaders to put him on Appropriations where he "brought home more highway and sewer money" than most of his party colleagues.[40]

TABLE 7-2 **House and Senate Committee Comparison**

Category	House	Senate
Number of standing committees	20	16
Committee/subcommittee assignments per member	About 6	About 11
Power or prestige committees	Appropriations, Budget, Commerce, Financial Services, Rules, Ways and Means	Appropriations, Armed Services, Commerce, Finance, Foreign Relations[a]
Treaties and nominations submitted by the president	No authority	Committees review
Floor debate	Representatives' activity is somewhat confined to the bills reported from the panels on which they serve	Senators can choose to influence any policy area regardless of their committee assignments
Committee consideration of legislation	More difficult to bypass	Easier to bypass[b]
Committee chairs	Subject to party and speakership influence that limits their discretionary authority over committee operations	Freer rein to manage committees
Committee staff	Often assertive in advocating ideas and proposals	More aggressive in shaping the legislative agenda
Subcommittee chairmanships	Representatives of the majority party usually must wait at least one term	Majority senators, regardless of their seniority, usually chair subcommittees

[a] Almost every senator is assigned to one of these committees.

[b] For example, by allowing riders—unrelated policy proposals—to measures pending on the floor.

A senior Republican House member provided all incoming GOP freshmen with a how-to booklet on securing committee assignments. (Her ideas also apply to Democrats seeking committee assignments.) She devised a three-part strategy emphasizing personal, political, and geographical factors. For example, she suggested face-to-face meetings with members of the Steering Committee, letters and phone calls to committee chairmen, and personal contact with party leaders. "Do not be afraid to go to each Member of the Leadership to let them know of your political needs. Leadership has proven…open to placing freshmen Members on key committees," the lawmaker advised the newcomers. She also urged freshmen to seek help from key party members in their state or region.[41] Sometimes party leaders recruit stellar candidates by promising them favorable committee assignments should they win; they may also entice former House members to run again by pledging to restore their previous seniority on their old committees.

Although both parties try to accommodate assignment preferences, some members inevitably receive unwelcome assignments. A classic case involved Democratic representative Shirley Chisholm of Brooklyn (1969–1983), the first African American woman elected to Congress. She was assigned to the House Agriculture Committee her first year in the House. "I think it would be hard to imagine an assignment that is less relevant to my background or to the needs of the predominantly black and Puerto Rican people who elected me," she said. Chisholm's protests won her a seat on the Veterans' Affairs Committee. "There are a lot more veterans in my district than there are trees," she later observed.[42]

How Assignments Are Made

Each party in each house has its own panel to review members' committee requests and hand out assignments to standing committees (the Democratic and Republican Steering Committees, the Republican Committee on Committees for Senate Republicans, and the Steering and Outreach Committee for Senate Democrats.) These panel's decisions are the first and most important acts in a three-step procedure. The second step involves approval of the assignment lists by each party's caucus. Finally, there is pro forma election by the full House or Senate. In January 2009, for example, Senate Majority Leader Harry Reid asked and received the unanimous consent of the chamber to adopt resolutions assigning Democrats and Republicans alike to the Senate's standing, select, and special committees, as well as the Joint Economic Committee.[43]

Formal and Informal Criteria. Both formal and informal criteria guide the assignment panels in choosing committee members. Formal criteria are designed to try and ensure that each member is treated equitably in committee assignments. For example, House Democrats have a rule that states that in making committee assignments, "the Democratic Steering and Policy Committee shall consider all relevant factors, including merit, length of service on the committee and degree of commitment to the Democratic agenda, and the diversity of the Caucus."

Since 1953, when Senate Democratic leader Lyndon B. Johnson of Texas announced his "Johnson rule," all Senate Democrats have been assigned one major committee before any party member receives a second major assignment. In 1965 Senate Republicans followed suit. Senate rules also classify committees into different categories, which are popularly called "A," "B," and "C." There is also a separate category in the A group informally called "Super A." Senators may serve on only one of the four Super A panels (Appropriations, Armed Services, Finance, and Foreign Relations) unless the rule is specifically waived for them. Senate Rule XXV states that members must serve on no more than two committees in the A category, which includes the four Super A panels; one in the B grouping (Budget, Rules and Administration, and Small Business, for example); and any number of C committees (Ethics, Indian Affairs, Joint Library, Joint Printing, and Joint Taxation).

Many criteria affect committee assignments, such as party loyalty, geography, substantive expertise, gender, or electoral vulnerability. Members' own wishes and electoral needs are other important criteria. Lawmakers who represent districts or states with large military installations may seek assignment to the Armed Services Committee. Or lawmakers with a specific policy interest (education, health, and so on) may strive to win appointment to panels that deal with those topics. Moreover, the committee assignment panels of each congressional party typically respect what is referred to as a "property norm." Returning lawmakers are generally permitted to retain their committee seats before new members bid for vacant committee positions.

Worth underscoring is the reality of the two Congresses in assignment decisions. Each party seeks through the appointments process to give electoral advantage to lawmakers of their party. House Democratic and GOP leaders, for instance, sometimes grant their electorally vulnerable freshmen an extra committee assignment or two to broaden their appeal as they head into the November elections. "All of these committees have constituents," explained Democratic leader Steny H. Hoyer of Maryland. "And all of these [freshmen Democratic appointees] have people in their districts who are members of these constituencies."[44] More seasoned members who could face tough electoral competition may also seek plum assignments to boost their influence and capacity for fund-raising.

Seniority. Normally, the assignment panels observe seniority when preparing committee membership lists. The member of the majority party with the longest continuous committee service is usually listed first. Senate Republicans, unlike House Republicans and House and Senate Democrats, apply seniority rigidly when two or more GOP senators compete for either a committee vacancy or chairmanship. As a senator noted: "When I first came to the Senate, I was skeptical [of the seniority tradition]. But as I've become more senior, I've grown more fond of it."[45] (The Senate GOP leader fills half of all vacancies on the "A" committees; seniority determines the other half.) Senate Democrats typically follow the seniority principle in making committee assignments with the party leader having a significant say in who goes onto which committees. By contrast, the two House parties do not observe seniority as strictly as Senate Republicans. House Democratic Caucus rules even state that the party's committee on committees (the Steering and Policy Committee) "need not necessarily follow seniority" in nominating members for committee posts. (See Box 7-1 on party assignment committees.) A summary overview of how the three most recent Speakers—Gingrich, Hastert, and Pelosi—handled the selection of chairmen spotlights the changing character of the process.

Gingrich. Speaker Newt Gingrich (1995–1999) bypassed the seniority custom on several occasions to give chairmanships to Republicans who could move the party's agenda despite their having less committee longevity than some others on those panels. Importantly, Gingrich was instrumental in having the House adopt a rule imposing a six-year term limit on committee and subcommittee chairmen, which promoted party direction of committees,

BOX 7-1   **Party Assignment Committees**

House Republicans. Before the 104th Congress began in 1995, incoming Speaker Newt Gingrich, R-Ga., revamped his party's committee on committees, which he would chair. Gingrich renamed it the Steering Committee; transformed it into a leadership-dominated panel; eliminated a weighted voting system wherein a GOP member of the assignment panel cast as many votes as there were Republicans in his state delegation; and granted the GOP leader the right to cast the most votes (five). These reforms continued in the subsequent Congresses. The Republican leader also appoints all GOP members of the Rules, House Administration, and Standards of Official Conduct Committees.

House Democrats. Democrats on the House Ways and Means Committee functioned as their party's committee on committees from 1911 until 1974, when the Democratic Caucus voted to transfer this duty to the Steering and Policy Committee. The Steering Committee, chaired by Rosa DeLauro of Connecticut in the 111th Congress, recommends Democratic assignments to the caucus, one committee at a time.

Senate Republicans. The chairman of the Republican Conference appoints the assignment panel of about eight members. In addition, the floor leader is an ex officio member. Idaho senator Michael D. Crapo chaired the panel during the 111th Congress.

Senate Democrats. The Steering and Outreach Committee makes assignments for Democrats. Its size (about twenty-five members) is set by the party conference and may fluctuate from Congress to Congress. The party's floor leader appoints the members of this panel and its chair (Sen. Debbie Stabenow of Michigan, for the 111th Congress).

constrained the ability of chairs to accrue power, and triggered "musical" chairmanships at the expiration of the chairs' six-year limit. (The GOP Rules chair, who is appointed by the Speaker, or minority leader, as the case might be, is not subject to the six-year limit.)

Hastert. When Dennis Hastert became Speaker (1999–2007), he decided to use an interview procedure to determine replacements for full committee chairs who had completed their six-year terms. In a letter to GOP members, Speaker Hastert explained several basic features of the interview process. "The candidates [for each open chairmanship] will be given an opportunity to discuss their legislative agenda, oversight agenda, how they intend to organize the committees, and their communication strategy," he wrote.[46] Party loyalty and fund-raising prowess were also factors. "You can't tell me a Member who raises $1 million for the party and visits 50 districts is not going to have an advantage over someone who sits back and thinks he's entitled to a chairmanship. Those days are gone," said a top GOP leadership aide.[47] Even with the six-year term limit rule during this period, there was no guarantee that chairs would be permitted to serve their full six years if they aroused the ire of party leaders. In an unprecedented event, in 2004 GOP leaders ousted a colleague (Christopher Smith of New Jersey) as chair of the Veterans' Affairs Committee, removed him from the panel, and named another member as chair. Smith's offense: his outspoken advocacy for more spending on veterans' benefits, which angered

Speaker Hastert. The message of Smith's removal was plain to every Republican: toe the party line and be part of the team or you will be benched.

The GOP's return to minority status in the 110th Congress produced some controversy on interpreting the term-limit rule. Three term-limited former GOP chairs argued that they should be allowed to retain ranking minority member status on their respective committees. The GOP Conference decided otherwise. The six-year limit, said a majority of the Conference membership, applies to service as chair or ranking minority member. However, the conference stated that the three could seek the ranking minority post on another panel where they are senior on the committee. Although the 111th House repealed the term-limit rule (see below), GOP party rules still impose the six-year limit on Republican committee leaders.[48]

Pelosi. Speaker Nancy Pelosi of California (2007-), who as minority leader directed the leadership-dominated Steering Committee to emulate Hastert's interview process for several of her top committee leaders, asserted control over Democratic assignments. Tracking the centralized models of Gingrich and Hastert, "Pelosi has near-total say in committee assignments, although her picks are voted on" by the Steering Committee.[49]

Pelosi, unlike her GOP predecessors, chose to follow seniority in designating committee chairs. As a result, many of the Democratic chairs are liberal "old bulls" who either headed or were senior members of several of the most influential committees prior to the GOP takeover in 1995—lawmakers such as David Obey, Wis., of Appropriations; George Miller, Calif., of Education and Labor; Barney Frank, Mass., of Financial Services; John Conyers, Mich., of Judiciary; and Charles Rangel, N.Y., of Ways and Means. In addition, the chairs of Agriculture, Armed Services, Budget, Foreign Affairs, Homeland Security, and Transportation are the most senior Democrats on those panels. The Pelosi-led 111th House also repealed the six-year term limit on Democratic committee chairs. Majority Leader Hoyer explained that the six-year rule had fallen victim to the law of unintended consequences. "With chairmanships up for grabs" every six years, "fundraising ability became one of the most important for job qualification, and legislative skill was sacrificed to political considerations."[50] Nevertheless, Pelosi signaled her unwillingness to return to the days of independent committee chairs. At the outset of her speakership in the 110th Congress, she stated that she would keep her committee leaders on a tight leash. Further, she assured "conservative Democrats that she would personally temper the legislative impulses of her most liberal chairmen while keeping close tabs on the investigations that could dominate the final two years of the Bush presidency."[51]

In addition, Pelosi deliberately challenged one of the most powerful old bulls: John Dingell, Mich. Currently the longest-serving House member in history, Dingell is known for his vigilance and assertiveness in protecting his Energy Committee's jurisdiction, which he chaired in the 110th Congress. Pelosi initiated the successful creation of the Select Committee on Energy Independence and Global Warming despite the opposition of Dingell and several other chairs, who viewed it as an invasion of their "turf."[52] After extensive negotiations between Pelosi and Dingell, the Speaker prevailed, and the select committee was created.[53]

On the Senate side, Republicans adopted a party rule, effective in 1997, restricting committee chairmen (or ranking members) to six years of service. "The whole thrust behind this," said the Senate author of the term-limit change, "is to try to get greater participation, so new members of the Senate don't have to wait until they've been here 18 years to play a role."[54] This goal is not easy to achieve, because long-serving Republicans are often senior on more than one committee. Thus, when they hit the six-year limit, party rules permit them to seek the chairmanship (or ranking minority position) of another committee and leapfrog over a party member with less committee seniority.

Senate Democrats do not have a term-limit rule for their committee leaders. Their long-standing tradition is to allow seniority to determine who will be either the chair or ranking minority member of a standing committee. This criterion does not mean that the Democratic senator with the most seniority on a committee is always its chair, because Senate rules limit members to one chairmanship. In the 111th Senate, Sen. Barbara Boxer, D-Calif., is head of the Environment and Public Works Committee even though she is outranked by two of her colleagues: Democrat Max Baucus, Mont., who chose to remain as chair of the Finance Committee, and Lieberman, who was permitted to continue heading the Homeland Security and Governmental Affairs Committee.

Biases. The decisions made by the assignment panels inevitably determine the geographical and ideological composition of the standing committees. Committees can easily become biased toward one position or another. Farm areas are overrepresented on the Agriculture Committees and small business interests on the Small Business Committees. No wonder committees are policy advocates. They propose laws that reflect the interests of their members and the outside groups and agencies that gravitate toward them.

Who does or does not sit on a committee affects the committee's policy-making. Committees that are carefully balanced between liberal and conservative interests can be tilted one way or the other by new members. The number of women on a committee could change committee dynamics and outcomes. After the 1991 Clarence Thomas-Anita Hill Supreme Court confirmation hearings (during which law professor Anita Hill testified that she was sexually harassed by Thomas when they worked in the same federal agency), a full-page advertisement in the *New York Times* asked: "What if fourteen women, instead of fourteen men, had sat on the Senate Judiciary Committee during the Clarence Thomas confirmation hearings?"[55] New committee leaders can shift a panel's policy agenda and outlook. The environmental views of Senator Boxer on environmental policy are diametrically opposed to those of the previous chair, Sen. James Inhofe, R-Okla.: "Inhofe calls global warming a hoax; Boxer ranks curbing global warming as one of her two top priorities."[56] A committee's political philosophy influences its success on the House or Senate floor. Committees ideologically out of step with the House or Senate as a whole are more likely than others to have legislation defeated or significantly revised by floor amendments.

Approval by Party Caucuses and the Chamber

For most of the twentieth century party caucuses in both chambers exerted little influence over committee assignments. Indeed, this pattern largely continues in the twenty-first century Senate. Although Senate parties can exercise control over committees, they nearly always defer to the seniority rankings of lawmakers in determining who heads a committee or subcommittee.

In the House, however, party caucuses became major participants in the assignment process beginning in the 1970s. Chairmen and ranking minority members were subjected to election by secret ballot of their party colleagues. Clearly, committee leadership is no longer an automatic right. Seniority still encourages continuity on committees, but that criterion has now become more flexible and is under caucus control.

A dramatic example of caucus control occurred at the start of the 111th Congress when two titans of the House—Dingell, the longest-serving House member, and Henry Waxman, the most senior Democrat behind Dingell on the Energy panel and a close confidant of Speaker Pelosi—faced off against each other for the chairmanship of the Energy and Commerce Committee. Waxman took Dingell by surprise when he announced soon after the November 2008 elections that he would challenge Dingell for the Energy and Commerce chairmanship. The two lawmakers had clashed over the years on various issues, especially the environment. Californian Waxman stressed stricter automobile emission standards whereas Michigan's Dingell, with the Big Three car manufacturers headquartered in his state, took a more industry-friendly approach.

Both men quickly mobilized whip teams to win the support of Democratic colleagues. Waxman won the first victory when the Steering and Policy Committee, headed by Speaker Pelosi, voted 23 to 20 to recommend that Waxman replace Dingell as Energy and Commerce chair. The final contest then occurred in the Democratic Caucus. By secret ballot, the Caucus voted 137 to 122 for Waxman over Dingell. Following the vote, Waxman, as the new chair, stressed the theme of change in his remarks. "The argument that we made is for a committee to have leadership that will work with [the Obama] administration and members of both the House and the Senate in order to get important issues passed in health care, environmental policy and energy policy. We are at a unique moment in history; we have an opportunity that comes only once a generation."[57] Waxman's win, according to two congressional correspondents, weakened the seniority system and empowered Pelosi, "fueling the perception that chairmen should avoid defying her."[58] Dingell was given the ceremonial post of "chairman emeritus" of the panel but he did not head any subcommittees.

COMMITTEE LEADERSHIP

Committee chairs call meetings and establish agendas, hire and fire committee staff, arrange hearings, recommend conferees, act as floor managers, allocate committee funds and rooms, develop legislative strategies, chair hearings and markups, and regulate the internal affairs and organization of the committee.

A chairman's procedural advantages are hard for even the most forceful minority members to overcome. The chairman may be able to kill a bill simply by refusing to schedule it for a hearing. Or he or she may convene meetings when proponents or opponents of the legislation are unavoidably absent. The chairman's authority derives from the support of a committee majority and a variety of formal and informal resources, such as substantive and parliamentary experience and control over the agenda, communications, and financial resources of the committee. When told by a committee colleague that he lacked the votes on an issue, a House chairman reminded him, "Yeah, but I've got the gavel."[59] The chair banged his gavel, adjourned the meeting, and the majority had no chance to work its will before the legislative session ended.

This example highlights the formidable ability of chairs to stymie action on legislation they oppose. Moreover, committee chairs are also among the most substantively and strategically knowledgeable members on their panel and in the chamber. They are advantageously positioned to advance ideas into law. When Bill Thomas, R-Calif., headed the Ways and Means Committee (2001–2007), he was acknowledged to be an especially skilled lawmaker: hardworking, assertive, and procedurally sophisticated. On numerous controversial issues (tax, trade, and health), he mobilized winning coalitions in committee, in the chamber, and in conference with the Senate. Thomas even sought out senatorial advice on how to move legislation in the House so as to maximize its chances in the Senate. "[H]e will venture to the Senate floor to run options by key senators of both parties, or to stop in Senate leadership offices, before returning to the House to brief appropriate leaders on the latest state of play."[60] At times, however, Thomas was sometimes also a difficult and acerbic partisan, even calling the Capitol police to oust Democratic committee members from the panel's library where they were meeting during a markup.

The top minority party members on a committee are influential figures. Among their powers (which may vary by committee) are nominating minority conferees, hiring and firing minority staff, sitting ex officio on all subcommittees, assisting in setting the committee's agenda, managing legislation on the floor, and acting as the party's committee spokesperson. Ranking members, as appropriate, present minority alternatives to majority proposals, challenge the chairs on procedural and policy matters, develop tactics and strategies to foil the majority's plans, and highlight minority party goals and views to an attentive public.

Committee chairs often cultivate productive working relationships with ranking members. When Charles Rangel, D-N.Y., assumed the chairmanship of Ways and Means in the 110th Congress, mindful of the heightened partisanship on the panel, he reached out to the ranking minority member, James McCrery, R-La., to reduce the partisan divide and encourage opportunities for bipartisan policymaking.[61] Rangel used the same approach to Dave Camp, R-Mich., the new ranking member in the 111th Congress upon McCrery's retirement from the House. Over in the Senate, Max Baucus, D-Mont., the head of the Finance Committee, meets at least twice a month with the ranking minority member, Charles Grassley, R-Iowa, to review committee business. That is the way "to encourage understanding, minimize misunderstandings, work . . . things out, and so forth—because relationships really count," said Baucus.[62]

POLICYMAKING IN COMMITTEE

Committees foster deliberate, collegial, fragmented decisions. They encourage bargaining and accommodation among members. To move bills through Congress's numerous decision points from subcommittee to committee, authors of bills and resolutions typically make compromises in response to important committee members. These gatekeepers may exact alterations in a bill's substance. The multiplicity of committees also increases members' and outside interests' routes of influence over any given issue or measure.

Overlapping Jurisdictions

The formal responsibilities of a standing committee are defined by the rules of each house, various public laws, and precedents. Committees with overlapping jurisdictions sometimes formulate a written memorandum of understanding that informally outlines how policy topics are to be referred among them.[63] Committees do not have watertight jurisdictional compartments. Any broad subject overlaps numerous committees. The Senate has an Environment and Public Works Committee, but other panels also consider environmental legislation; the same is true in the House. These House bodies, along with a brief sketch of some of their environmental responsibilities, are as follows:

> *Agriculture:* pesticides; soil conservation; some water programs
> *Appropriations:* funding for environmental programs and agencies
> *Energy and Commerce:* health effects of the environment; environmental regulations; solid waste disposal; clean air; safe drinking water
> *Financial Services:* open space acquisition in urban areas
> *Foreign Affairs:* international environmental cooperation
> *Natural Resources:* water resources; power resources; land management; wildlife conservation; national parks; nuclear waste; fisheries; endangered species
> *Oversight and Government Reform:* federal executive branch agencies for the environment
> *Science and Technology:* environmental research and development
> *Small Business:* effects of environmental regulations on business
> *Transportation and Infrastructure:* water pollution; sludge management
> *Ways and Means:* environmental tax expenditures

Given such overlaps it is no surprise that committees sometimes clash over their respective jurisdictional prerogatives, in part because they are a "lawmaker's power base. It is no wonder that committee boundaries are hotly contested."[64] Hence the oft-repeated adage on Capitol Hill: "turf is power." As one House chairman stated, "Nobody in this institution gives up jurisdiction they believe is rightfully theirs."[65] Committee staff are alert both to repel "border poachers" and to search for opportunities to expand their own panel's jurisdictional reach. Jurisdictional conflicts sometimes break out between or among subcommittees of the same standing committee, requiring the full committee chair to mediate the internal turf war.[66]

Jurisdictional overlaps can have positive results. They enable numerous members to develop expertise in several related policy fields, prevent any one group from dominating an issue, and promote healthy competition among committees. If healthy competition turns to battles over turf, then chamber leaders can employ various conflict-resolving techniques. One such device would be a memorandum of understanding between committees that clarifies how certain overlapping issues are to be referred to two or more committees that have shared policy interests.[67] Other devices include creating select committees, encouraging joint committee hearings, promoting informal staff consultations between or among committees with shared policy mandates, or having lawmakers serving on two committees with shared policy interests mediate jurisdictional controversies that might arise between them. For example, Sen. Mike Enzi, R-Wy., won assignment to the Finance Committee in the 111th Congress while retaining his ranking position on the Health, Education, Labor, and Pensions (HELP) Committee. Both panels share jurisdiction over major health issues. As Senator Enzi said, "I always hoped I could be a liaison between the HELP Committee and the Finance Committee."[68]

Multiple Referrals

When a bill is introduced in the House, it usually is referred to a single committee. On occasions when a bill is referred to more than one committee, the Speaker must "designate a committee of primary jurisdiction upon the initial referral of a measure to a committee." The Speaker has flexibility in determining whether, when, and for how long other panels can receive the measure. But the primary committee has predominant responsibility for shepherding the legislation to final passage. The Speaker may also send the measure to secondary panels. The House parliamentarian calls this practice an "additional initial referral." In the following example of referral language, the Energy and Commerce Committee is the primary committee and Ways and Means is the additional initial panel.

> H.R. 515. A bill to prohibit the importation of certain low-level radioactive waste into the United States; to the Committee on Energy and Commerce, and in addition to the Committee on Ways and Means, for a period to be subsequently determined by the Speaker, in each case for consideration of such provisions as fall within the jurisdiction of the committee concerned.

Multiple referrals may promote integrated policymaking, broader public discussion of issues, wider access to the legislative process, and consideration of alternative approaches. They also enhance the Speaker's scheduling prerogatives. The Speaker can use the referral power to intervene more directly in committee activities and even to set deadlines for committees to report multiply referred legislation. The reverse is also possible: the Speaker can delay action on measures by referring them to other committees. Thus, multiple referrals can be employed to slow down legislative decision making.

The Senate usually sends measures to a single committee—the committee with jurisdiction over the predominant subject matter of the legislation. Although multiple referrals have long been permitted by unanimous consent, they are infrequently used, mainly because senators have many opportunities to influence policymaking on the floor. Senate procedures provide lawmakers with relatively easy ways either to bypass the referral of legislation to committees or to raise issues for chamber consideration.

Where Bills Go

Many bills referred to committee are sent by the chairman to a subcommittee. Others are retained for review by the full committee. In the end, committees and subcommittees select the measures they want to consider and ignore the rest. Committee consideration usually consists of three standard steps: public hearings, markups, and reports.

Hearings. When committees or subcommittees conduct hearings on a bill, they listen to a wide variety of witnesses. These include the bill's sponsors, federal officials, pressure group representatives, public officials, and private citizens— sometimes even celebrities. Celebrity witnesses can help give a bill national visibility. As Sen. Arlen Specter, D-Pa., put it, "Quite candidly, when Hollywood speaks, the world listens. Sometimes when Washington speaks, the world snoozes."[69]

Equally important are witnesses who add drama to hearings because of their first-hand experience with an issue or the actions they have taken. The chief executive officer of AIG was lambasted at a House hearing for awarding bonuses to employees from taxpayer bailout funds.

The Senate Finance Committee, as another example, attracted national headlines with its hearings on alleged wrongdoings by the Internal Revenue Service (IRS). Taxpayers recounted their horrendous experiences, and IRS agents donned black hoods to tell about the organization's mistreatment of taxpayers.[70] Testimony by employees who lost their retirement savings because of corporate scandals helped to galvanize congressional enactment of corporate accounting and accountability laws. Sometimes the drama of testimony cuts against the interests of the witnesses. Consider the corporate leaders of General Motors, Chrysler, and Ford in 2008. Each flew separately to Washington, D.C., in their corporate jet to present testimony urging Congress to provide billions of taxpayer dollars to bail out their companies. As one lawmaker asked at the hearing, "I mean, couldn't you all have downgraded to first class or jet-pooled or something to get here?"[71] When given a second chance to plead their cases after defeat of the first auto industry bailout bill, the automotive bigwigs drove from Detroit to D.C. in their most fuel-efficient models. Hearings, in brief, are often orchestrated as political theater where witnesses can put a human face on a public problem, tell a story that may generate public momentum for legislation, or serve as "heroes" or "zeroes" in a larger narrative.[72]

Hearings provide opportunities for committee members to be heard on issues. Frequently, lawmakers present their views on legislation in their opening statements and in their questioning of witnesses. A two Congresses theme is sometimes evident in these questions. In April 2009, Senator Specter, up for reelection in 2010, abandoned the GOP and became a Democrat. A moderate, Specter faced bleak prospects in the upcoming GOP primary. Before the party switch, however, Specter worked diligently to win the support of conservative primary voters. For example, he grilled Eric Holder, Obama's nominee for attorney general, when he appeared before the Judiciary Committee. Sharp questioning of Holder had the "benefit of helping Specter shore up support among conservatives" back home. [73] His efforts were in vain, however.

Most hearings follow a traditional format. Each witness reads a prepared statement. Then each committee member has a limited time (often five minutes) to ask questions before the next witness is called. To save time and promote give-and-take, committees occasionally use a panel format in which witnesses sit together and briefly summarize their statements.

Committees will sometimes convene joint hearings with other relevant House or Senate panels. They may also organize field hearings in selected cities around the country to generate and solicit public support for an issue, or, in a two Congresses theme, schedule hearings in the chair's state or district to win him or her favorable publicity and visibility prior to the November elections. Committees may even hold pre-hearings so committee members can be better informed about the issues likely to be raised during a scheduled hearing.

Gradually, committees are beginning to harness contemporary technology to conduct Capitol Hill hearings. Speaker Pelosi has urged all committees to utilize technology to provide live broadcasts of their hearings online ("Webcasts") to make the legislative process "fully accessible and transparent" to the public.[74] Several House and Senate panels have used interactive video, teleconferencing, e-hearings, and other technology to collect testimony from witnesses who may be located in other parts of the nation or world. The Internet has been used to transmit testimony, and cable television viewers have e-mailed or faxed questions to witnesses.[75] In a first, an astronaut became the first person ever to deliver testimony from space to a House Science committee hearing held on Capitol Hill.[76]

Among the overlapping purposes served by hearings are:

- to explore the need for legislation;
- to build a public record in support of legislation;
- to publicize the role of committee chairmen;
- to stake out committee jurisdictions;
- to review executive implementation of public laws;
- to provide a forum for citizens' grievances and frustrations;
- to educate lawmakers and the attentive public on complex issues;
- to raise the visibility of an issue; and
- to test whether a bill is worth taking to the floor, by airing substantive problems and weighing support and opposition.

BOX 7-2 **Committee Decision Making: A Formal Model**

Political scientists use a variety of sophisticated techniques to understand legislative decision making. Employing concepts from economics such as rational choice—the notion that individuals (or lawmakers) have preferences or desires and that they will act in their self-interest to achieve their goals—these scholars utilize a number of analytical tools to consider how lawmakers devise strategies to accomplish their policy objectives. One such analytical approach is called spatial theory. The term spatial refers to a mathematical idea that theorists rely on called a policy space. An easy-to-understand example is that certain policy preferences can all be arrayed along a straight line, or unidimensional continuum. So, for example, one end of the line might be labeled "more spending" and the other "less spending." Different spending preferences could be placed at different points, or spaces, along the line.

In employing spatial theory to model legislative decision making, scholars make a number of assumptions. Two are especially important: (1) lawmakers hold consistent preferences and (2) members have an ideal policy outcome that they prefer. Put differently, lawmakers will vote for policy alternatives that bring them closer to their policy ideal and oppose those that do the reverse. The work of these scholars highlights the importance of institutional rules and procedures in determining which of several policy alternatives will prevail. Analysts have also found that the median voter—the midpoint lawmaker with an equal number of other members to his left or right—is the ultimate determiner of outcomes in unidimensional cases. Another way to view the median voter is the 218th vote in the House, the Supreme Court justice who casts the fifth vote in a 5 to 4 decision, or the member who casts the sixth vote in a committee of eleven members.

To depict this graphically, assume that a House Appropriations subcommittee has sent to the floor a spending bill that reflects its committee median (CM). The subcommittee also must take into account a floor median (FM) if it wants its majority position to carry the day on the floor. The current policy status quo (Q) means that, if the bill does not pass, last year's funding level remains in force. If the subcommittee's bill is brought to the floor under a no-amendment rule, then the House membership can either accept or reject the panel's position. If the House rejects the subcommittee's policy recommendation, it has agreed to retain the status quo. Whether the subcommittee's position prevails on the floor can be depicted using these two examples.

If the subcommittee's position is to win on the House floor, it must devise a strategy that takes account of the majority preferences of the membership. Furthermore, the subcommittee

Hearings are shaped mainly by the chairman and staff, with varying degrees of input from party leaders, the ranking minority member, and others. Chairmen who favor bills can expedite the hearings process; conversely, they can kill with kindness legislation they oppose by holding endless hearings. When a bill is not sent to the full chamber, the printed hearings are the end product of the committee's work.

Markups. After hearings have been held, committee members decide the bill's actual language; that is, the bill is marked up or amended (see Box 7-2 on committee decision making). Chairs may circulate their "mark" (the measure open for amendment) to committee colleagues via e-mail and solicit their comments and suggestions. Some panels adhere closely to parliamentary rules must have some way to acquire information about the policy options likely to be accepted by at least a majority of the House. These types of considerations are commonplace in the real world of Capitol Hill policymaking.

Example 1

More Spending			Less Spending
FM	CM		Q

In Example 1, the preferences of a majority of the House clearly are closer to the committee's position than the status quo. Hence, the committee's position prevails.

Example 2

More Spending			Less Spending
FM		Q	CM

In Example 2, a majority of the House clearly favors the policy status quo instead of the committee's position, which loses in an up-or-down floor vote.

Most bills concern not a single dimension, such as more or less spending, but a multitude of dimensions. For example, a bill might be close to a member's ideal point on the spending dimension but be far away on another dimension, such as which governmental level (federal or state) should handle the issue. The introduction of additional dimensions (multidimensionality) produces greater difficulty in analyzing legislative decision making. By employing spatial theory and other analytical approaches, political scientists strive to better understand and explain congressional politics and decision making.[a]

---

[a] See, for example, Kenneth Shepsle and Mark Boncheck, *Analyzing Politics* (New York: W. W. Norton, 1977); Charles Stewart, *Analyzing Congress* (New York: W. W. Norton, 2001); and Gerald Strom, *The Logic of Lawmaking: A Spatial Theory Approach* (Baltimore: Johns Hopkins University Press, 1990).

during this committee amending phase, others operate by consensus with few or no votes taken on the issues, and still others have "conceptual markups." A senator explained that Finance Committee markups "are not about legislative language. There are concept documents that are then put into legislative language and brought to the floor."[77] Concepts may include, for instance, whether going to school counts as work for welfare recipients or what kind of tax plan best fosters economic growth.

Proponents try to craft a bill that will muster the backing of their colleagues, the other chamber, lobbyists, and the White House. On the controversial issue of immigration reform, Senate Judiciary chairman Patrick Leahy, D-Vt., refused to schedule a markup of a comprehensive immigration bill in the 110th Congress until President George W. Bush publicly backed the measure. "We're not going to waste time on something" congressional Republicans are "going to shoot down," he said.[78]

The markup process can be arduous because members often face the two Congresses dilemma: whether to support a bill that might be good for the nation or oppose it because of the opposition of their constituents. Not surprisingly, the bill that emerges from markup is usually the one that can attract the support of the most members. As a former chair of the House Ways and Means Committee stated, "We have not written perfect law; perhaps a faculty of scholars could do a better job. A group of ideologues could have produced greater consistency. But politics is an imperfect process."[79] Or as Senator Pat Roberts, R-Kan., said about a bill revamping the intelligence community: "While this is not the best possible bill, it is the best bill possible."[80]

Outside pressures often intensify during markup deliberations. Under House and Senate sunshine rules, markups must be conducted in public, except on national security or related issues. Compromises can be difficult to achieve in markup rooms filled with lobbyists watching how each member will vote. Hence, committees sometimes conduct pre-markups in private to work out their positions on various issues.

After conducting hearings and markups, a subcommittee sends its recommendations to the full committee. The full committee may conduct hearings and markups on its own, ratify the subcommittee's decision, take no action, or return the matter to the subcommittee for further study.

Reports. If the full committee votes to send the bill to the House or Senate, the staff prepares a report, subject to committee approval, describing the purposes and provisions of the legislation. Reports emphasize arguments favorable to the bill, summarizing selectively the results of staff research and hearings. Reports are noteworthy documents. The bill itself may be long, highly technical, and confusing to most readers. "A good report, therefore, does more than explain—it also persuades," commented a congressional staff aide.[81] Furthermore, reports may guide executive agencies and federal courts in interpreting ambiguous or complex legislative language.

The Policy Environment

Executive agencies, pressure groups, party leaders and caucuses, and the entire House or Senate form the backdrop against which a committee makes policy. These environments may be consensual or conflictual. Some policy questions are settled fairly easily, while others are bitterly contested. Environments also may be monolithic or pluralistic. Some committees have a single dominant source of outside influence, while others face numerous competing groups or agencies.

Environmental factors influence committees in at least four ways. First, they shape the content of public policies and thus the likelihood that these policies will be accepted by the full House or Senate. The Judiciary Committees are buffeted by diverse and competing pressure groups that feel passionately on volatile issues such as abortion, school prayer, and gun control. The committees' chances for achieving agreement among their members or on the floor depend to a large extent on their ability to deflect such issues altogether or to accommodate diverse groups through artful legislative drafting.

Second, some policy environments foster mutual alliances among committees, federal departments, and pressure groups—the "iron triangles." The House and Senate Veterans' Affairs Committees, for example, regularly advocate legislation to benefit veterans groups, the second point in the triangle. This effort is backed by the Department of Veterans Affairs, the third point in the triangle. At the very least, issue networks emerge. These are fluid and amorphous groups of policy experts who try to influence any committee that deals with their subject area.[82]

Third, policy environments establish decision-making objectives and guidelines for committees. Clientele-oriented committees, such as the House and Senate Small Business Committees, try to promote the policy views of their clientele groups, small business enterprises. Alliances between committees and federal departments also shape decisions, such as the traditional support given the military by the House and Senate Armed Services committees.

Finally, environmental factors influence the level of partisanship on committees. Some committees are relatively free of party infighting, but other committees consider contentious policy issues that often divide the two parties. The formation of unions without a secret ballot is an example of a contentious topic that divides Republicans and Democrats on the House Education and Labor and Senate HELP Committees.

COMMITTEE STAFF

Throughout the three principal stages of committee policymaking—hearings, markup, and report—staff aides play an active part. Representatives and senators (to a greater degree because there are fewer of them) cannot handle the large workload on their own and so must rely heavily on their unelected employees. Congress needs qualified professional staff to counter the expertise lodged in the executive branch and in the lobbying community. In the House and Senate, committee resources are roughly divided between the majority and minority parties on a two-thirds to one-third basis. Informally, both parties rely on a network of outside experts to help them evaluate proposals from the executive branch, forge policy proposals, or provide strategic advice.

The discretionary agenda of Congress and its committees is powerfully shaped by the professional staff. Their influence can be direct or indirect, substantive or procedural, visible or invisible. "Most of the work and most of the ideas come from the staffers," conceded a senator. "They are predominantly young men and women, fresh out of college and professional schools. They are ambitious, idealistic, and abounding with ideas."[83] However, staff tenure is short. According to a recent study by the Congressional Management Foundation, "Over 60 percent of House staff have two or less years of experience in their current position, including 39 percent of Chiefs of Staff, 64 percent of Legislative

Directors, and 66 percent of Press Secretaries."[84] The average tenure for Senate aides is about 5.3 years. Many committee, personal, and leadership aides use their experience as a stepping-stone to other jobs, such as lobbying.

Policy proposals emanate from many sources—the White House, administrative agencies, interest groups, state and local officials, scholars, and citizens—but staff aides are strategically positioned to advance or hinder these proposals. As one Senate committee staff director recounted, "Usually, you draw up proposals for the year's agenda, lay out the alternatives. You can put in some stuff you like and leave out some you don't. I recommend ideas that the [chairman's] interested in and also that I'm interested in."[85] Many staff aides actively communicate with relevant issue networks (health or environment, for example) that enhance the flow of informed advice to lawmakers.[86]

Staff aides negotiate with legislators, lobbyists, and executive officials on issues, legislative language, and political strategy. Staff members do the essential spadework that can lead to changes in policy or new laws. For example, a "team totaling 20 [Senate Governmental Affairs] aides, including detailees from the FBI and [Central Intelligence Agency]," drafted the 2004 bill that reorganized the nation's intelligence community and created the post of Director of National Intelligence (DNI).[87] Staff aides sometimes make policy decisions. Consider their crucial role on a defense appropriations bill.

> The dollar figures in the huge piece of legislation [were] so immense that House-Senate conferees, negotiating their differences…, relegated almost every item less than $100 million to staff aides on grounds that the members themselves did not have time to deal with such items, which [one lawmaker] called "small potatoes."[88]

During hearings, aides recruit witnesses, on their own or at the specific direction of the chairman, and plan when and in what order they appear. In addition, staff aides commonly accompany committee members to the floor to give advice, draft amendments, and negotiate compromises. The number of aides who can be present on the floor is limited, however, by House and Senate regulations.

For information, analyses, policy options, and research projects, committee staff can turn to the three legislative support agencies: the Congressional Research Service (CRS), established in 1914; the Government Accountability Office (GAO), established in 1921 (as the General Accounting Office and renamed in 2004); and the Congressional Budget Office (CBO), established in 1974. Unlike committee or personal aides, these agencies operate under strict rules of nonpartisanship and objectivity. Staffed with experts, they provide Congress with analytical talent matching that in executive agencies, universities, and specialized groups.

Staffing reflects members' dual roles in the two Congresses: individual policymaker and constituency representative. During the electoral season, staffers frequently take unpaid leave to work as campaign volunteers for their boss or "to boost their party's prospects in pivotal races."[89]

COMMITTEE REFORM AND CHANGE

Since passage of the Legislative Reorganization Act of 1946, Congress has tried twice to revamp the committee system in a comprehensive way, each with rather marginal success. One attempt occurred in the House in the early 1970s and the other in the Senate in the latter part of the 1970s.[90] Since then, the House and Senate have focused less on major committee system overhaul and more on advancing incremental changes. Two fairly recent examples make the point. When Republicans captured control of the House in November 1994 after forty unbroken years of Democratic control, they eliminated three standing committees with close ties to Democratic constituencies—District of Columbia, Merchant Marine and Fisheries, and Post Office and Civil Service. The functions of these panels were assigned to other standing committees. When Democrats recaptured control of the House in November 2006, the Pelosi-led Democrats implemented a recommendation of an outside commission to strengthen congressional oversight of intelligence agencies. On January 9, 2007, the House adopted a resolution establishing a Select Intelligence Oversight Panel as a component of the Committee on Appropriations. Recent committee changes have responded to shifting policy needs—for example, the creation of homeland security committees in both chambers in the aftermath of the September 11, 2001, al Qaeda attacks.

Homeland Security Committees

The National Commission on Terrorist Attacks upon the United States (the 9/11 Commission) urged the House and Senate to each create a single authorizing committee for homeland security. Its report stated that at least eighty-eight committees and subcommittees in Congress had some jurisdiction over the Department of Homeland Security (DHS). The formation of House and Senate homeland security panels would minimize turf conflicts, reduce the number of panels top DHS officials had to appear before as witnesses, and strengthen congressional oversight of the new department. Both chambers responded to the commission's suggestion, but in different ways.

Senate GOP and Democratic leaders created in August 2004 a twenty-two-person working group (headed by Senators Mitch McConnell and Harry Reid) to review the commission's recommendations for improving oversight of intelligence and homeland security. Two months later, the Senate debated the McConnell-Reid plan (S. Res. 445), which called for renaming the Governmental Affairs Committee the Homeland Security and Governmental Affairs Committee and assigning it broad authority for overseeing domestic security and DHS. That objective, however, required ten standing committees to relinquish some of their jurisdiction to the renamed Governmental Affairs panel.

During floor action on S. Res. 445, committee chairs and ranking members offered several amendments that reclaimed the jurisdiction that would have been lost to the new committee if the resolution were adopted unchanged. "We're creating a shell," lamented Senator Lieberman, the ranking Democrat on the Governmental Affairs Committee. "We're calling a committee a homeland security committee. But if you pick up the shell, there's not much homeland security under it."[91] The Governmental Affairs Committee's chair, Susan Collins, R-Maine, said the changes made to S. Res. 445 left her newly renamed panel with "less than 38 percent of the Department of Homeland Security's budget and 8 percent of its personnel."[92] Dismayed by these events, both Collins and Lieberman voted against S. Res. 445, which was agreed to on October 9 by a 79–6 vote

At the opening of the 109th Congress in 2005, the House replaced its temporary homeland security panel with a standing committee. The new permanent panel was granted, among other things, jurisdiction over overall homeland security policy and the organization and administration of the Department of Homeland Security. The new committee also was assigned broad oversight authority over all government "activities relating to homeland security, including the interaction of all departments and agencies with the Department of Homeland Security." Even with creation of the new panel, oversight of homeland security is still spread among nine other authorizing committees.[93]

Turf-conscious committee chairs negotiated with their party leaders to preserve their panels' jurisdiction. A detailed analysis of how homeland security legislation is to be referred among all the committees with homeland security jurisdiction was included in the *Congressional Record*.[94] To illustrate, the Homeland Security Committee is to receive bills dealing with "transportation security"; the Transportation and Infrastructure Committee retains its jurisdiction over measures dealing with "transportation safety." Plainly, this jurisdictional distinction is somewhat akin to being "two sides of the same coin."

Committees, in sum, are remarkably durable, resilient, and stable institutions despite the periodic forces for change (public criticism of Congress, reformist sentiment among institutionally minded lawmakers, and so on) that buffet them. Major committee restructuring plans, as the several committee reform efforts in the post–World War II period attest, almost always fail or produce only marginal adjustments in committees' jurisdictional mandates, policymaking influence, or method of operation. Scholars and lawmakers posit various theories to explain why it is difficult to accomplish major jurisdictional realignment. For example, given that the control of jurisdictional turf is viewed as power, Speaker Thomas P. "Tip" O'Neill Jr., D-Mass., explained the House's rejection of a major 1973–1974 committee realignment plan in this succinct manner: "The name of the game is power, and the boys don't want to give it up."[95] A political scientist offered an electoral explanation, which embodies the two Congresses concept, for the demise of committee reshuffling plans.

> [A] primary and constant force hindering committee restructuring movements has been the electoral objectives of members of Congress. Under pressure to bolster their reelection prospects in order to achieve long-term legislative and personal goals, rational politicians with the ability to shape legislative structures utilize the arrangement

of rules and procedures to secure targeted government benefits for needy constituents and voting blocs. Any widespread change in the established order of policy deliberation—particularly its center-piece—the committee system—would create far too much uncertainty in members' electoral strategies and therefore would be broadly opposed from the start.[96]

Whatever factors (interest group, party leadership, or committee member and staff opposition, for instance) impede major committee overhaul, these workshops of Congress evolve in response to new events and circumstances. Several recent developments highlight the dynamic quality of the committee system. These include ebbs and flows in the authority of committee chairs, the use of task forces, and the circumvention of the committee process.

Constricting the Authority of Committee Chairs

When Republicans took control of both houses of Congress in the mid-1990s, many GOP committee chairs had to take more direction from their party's leaders, especially in the House. Committee chairs "have been at the mercy of top House and Senate Republican leaders," wrote two congressional analysts, "who—given the high level of partisanship and the small size of their majorities—have resorted to dictating legislation from the top down in order to maintain some semblance of control."[97] Centralized control over committees was conspicuous during the speakership of Newt Gingrich (1995–1999), who sometimes circumvented committee consideration of legislation, dictated legislative changes to committees, used the Rules Committee to redraft committee-reported measures, and engaged in other actions that undermined the committee system, such as creating partisan task forces.

Speaker Hastert (1999–2007), too, was not reluctant to rein in committee chairs. The removal of the Veterans' chair and the leadership's tight control over the Appropriations Committee illustrate his large influence. After Hastert won adoption in 2003 of a party rules change requiring the Appropriations subcommittee chairs to be approved by the party's Steering Committee, one of the subcommittee leaders said, "Now the leadership gets to have the [subcommittee chairs] come in and grovel before them."[98] Two years later, the Steering Committee warned a subcommittee chair that he could lose the chairmanship of his Appropriations subcommittee if he "does not raise or donate more money to Republicans."[99]

Speaker Pelosi also keeps the committee chairs under some control. After all, Pelosi is focused on retaining and expanding Democratic control of the House. Permitting independent-minded committee chairs to go their own way would jeopardize these party goals. At the same time, Speaker Pelosi needs to have a good working relationship with her chairs, because much of the House's work is carried out by these "little legislatures." Balancing "top down" command and committee autonomy is no easy task. Henry Waxman, the chair of the Energy and Commerce Committee and a Pelosi ally, put it this way: "I think there has to be a lot more direction from the leadership to the committees of jurisdiction. We don't want to return to the days of committee chairs that felt they didn't have to be accountable. There has to be a balance."[100] Another ally of Speaker Pelosi, Appropriations Committee chair David Obey, expressed a similar view. "When you have the right balance between leadership defining what the goals are and the committee having the chance to impact how you get there, that's the best way to produce legislation," said Obey.[101] An unanswered question is whether the correct balance has been achieved between party primacy and committee authority.

Obey, Waxman, and a few other committee chairs—George Miller, Calif., of Education and Labor; John Spratt, S.C., of the Budget Committee, and Barney Frank, Mass., of Financial Services—have seen an expansion of their lawmaking influence. A number of factors explain this development: their panels deal with important national issues, the chairs themselves are talented and assertive leaders, and, perhaps most importantly, "they derive their power from alliances with the speaker."[102] Other senior committee and subcommittee chairs express dismay that they sometimes have to wait on the sidelines as major bills which normally would fall under their panel's jurisdiction are written in the Speaker's office. As one subcommittee chair stated, "We're allowed to make suggestions…[b]ut it's still a substantially top-down process." Another said: "The question is: Are we actually going to get a chance to legislate? There's an opportunity to turn this corner, but we have not done that yet."[103]

Occasions also arise when Senate committee chairs are subject to party leadership direction. For example, Senate majority leader Harry Reid, D-Nev., instructed the Senate Finance and Budget Committee chairs "to take a look at what we can do with entitlements [mandatory spending programs]."[104] When political momentum began to build for a patients' bill of rights bill, the majority leader took the issue away from the chairman of the Health, Education, Labor, and Pension Committee and "created a [party] task force to write the bill."[105] Another majority leader gave the Finance Committee a deadline to report a priority bill or else he would call up the proposal that he favored. "I told the Finance Committee they have a window, and I'd love to have them pass out a bill and give it to us and then we'll take it up," he declared. "If that fails, we'll have to go to the floor with another vehicle."[106] On measures of utmost party importance, congressional leaders will override the prerogatives of committee chairs to take control of crucial agenda items. But such leadership direction occurs less frequently in the Senate than the House—simply because the chairs (like all senators) retain the ability to stymie floor action on legislation they disagree with.

The ability of today's party leaders, particularly in the House, to exercise significant control over committee leaders represents a major change in how today's Congress works. The chairs are subject to leadership direction on the party's top priorities and may face sanctions if their performance does not meet party expectations. On the one hand, this development ensures that the chairs (and ranking minority members) are ultimately held accountable for their actions to the Democratic Caucus or Republican Conference. On the other hand, tight leadership control could gradually diminish the traditional role of committees as the legislature's policy experts. Why bother to devote years of effort to become substantive experts, committee members might say, if policy on major issues is decided at the top?

Party Task Forces

Speaker Gingrich was noted for creating numerous party task forces, in part because he could determine their mandate and timetable, appoint the chair and members, and assign a deadline for drafting a product. Many of these task forces did little, but some wrote legislation. Task forces can forge consensus, draft legislation, coordinate strategy, promote intraparty communication, and involve noncommittee members and junior members in issue areas.

Speaker Hastert deemphasized the use of party task forces, but he still occasionally employed them to address issues important to the party. For instance, he created task forces to deal with health and terrorism issues. House Republican leader John Boehner, Ohio, named an earmark reform panel to recommend changes in how Washington spends taxpayer dollars to the GOP Conference early in the 111th Congress. Speaker Pelosi established a bipartisan task force to consider whether the House should create an outside body to investigate ethical misconduct by lawmakers.[107] The result: the House adopted a resolution (H. Res. 895) in March 2008 that for the first time in its history established a new Office of Congressional Ethics composed of private citizens appointed jointly by the Speaker and the minority leader. The Office has the authority to receive ethical complaints against lawmakers, conduct investigations, and refer serious ethical and legal matters to the House Committee on Standards of Official Conduct for action.

Senate leaders also form party task forces to showcase senators up for reelection and to promote party priorities on crucial issues. For example, Republican leader Mitch McConnell, Ky., established a health reform team "to lead Senate Republicans' health care effort in the 111th Congress."[108]

Bypassing Committees

It is not unusual for House and Senate party leaders to bypass some or all of the stages of committee consideration of legislation.[109] In general, the circumvention of committees reflects the dominance of party power over committee power.

A variety of considerations impel party leaders to bypass committees. For instance, heightened partisanship in certain committees encourages party leaders to take charge of priority measures to avoid negative media coverage of committee markups. Factional disputes within committees may also prevent committees from reaching agreement on measures deemed important to party leaders. Party leaders, too, may believe insufficient time exists for committees to hold hearings and markups on major bills for which they want consideration. For example, at the start of the 111th Congress, House leaders wanted fast action on high-profile bills, such as the Lilly Ledbetter Fair Pay Act (making it easier for plaintiffs to sue employers for pay discrimination).

Bypassing committee action, however, often provides opponents of the legislation with added grounds for criticism. As one lawmaker complained, "this bill did not make its way through the committee process during this Congress, thereby abandoning the critical committee vetting and amendment process."[110] When the House considered a bill reforming the troubled asset relief program (TARP), a member lamented that there were no "hearings, testimony, markup" of the legislation.[111] Senate committees are also bypassed. Sen. Barbara Mikulski, D-Md., stated that "legislative malpractice" occurred during Senate debate on a medical liability bill. "First of all, the procedure for considering this bill is seriously flawed. The bill was brought to the full Senate without hearings, without consideration by the Judiciary Committee."[112] Whether these procedural complaints are well-grounded is an open question. Some analysts contend that "there are few consequences if [committees are bypassed] because nobody outside Congress cares whether a bill went through committee or not."[113]

CONCLUSION

Several generalizations can be made about congressional committees today. First, they shape the House and Senate agendas. Not only do they have negative power—pigeonholing legislation referred to them—but they have positive power as well. The bills they report largely determine what each chamber will debate and in what form. As one House chairman stated in his testimony before the Joint Committee on the Organization of Congress,

> [Committees] provide Congress with the expertise, skill, and organizational structure necessary to cope with the increasingly complex and technical questions in both the domestic and international arenas. They also ensure a forum for the broadest possible participation of diverse interests and constituencies in the formative stages of the legislative process. They are, in short, the window through which much of the democratic participation in lawmaking is made possible.[114]

Second, committees differ in their policymaking environments, mix of members, decision-making objectives, and ability to fulfill individual members' goals. Recruitment methods reinforce the committees' autonomy. Committees frequently are imbalanced ideologically or geographically. They are likely to advocate policies espoused by agencies and outside groups interested in their work.

Third, committees often develop an esprit de corps that flows across party lines. Committee members usually will defend their panels against criticisms, jurisdictional trespassing, or any attempt to bypass them.

Fourth, committees typically operate independently of one another. This longtime custom fosters an attitude of mutual noninterference in the work of other committees. However, multiple referrals of bills spawn broader interrelationships among committees.

Fifth, the committee system contributes fundamentally to policy fragmentation, although a few committees—Rules and Budget, for example—act as policy coordinators for Congress. "This is one of the anomalies here," remarked a House member. "In order to attain legislative efficiency, we say that we have to break down into committees with specialized jurisdictions. When you do that, you lose your ability to grapple with the big problems."[115] Party leaders, as a result, are more involved than ever in coordinating policymaking and forging winning coalitions in committees and on the floor.

Finally, committee autonomy is increasingly under pressure from assertive party leaders who strive to move the party's agenda forward with or without the committee leaders' cooperation. In theoretical terms, the pressure on autonomy may be seen as a shift in committee roles from distributional purposes to partisan-programmatic goals.

SUGGESTED READINGS

Deering, Christopher J., and Steven S. Smith. *Committees in Congress.* 3d ed. Washington, D.C.: CQ Press, 1997.

Evans, C. Lawrence. *Leadership in Committee: A Comparative Analysis of Leadership Behavior in the U.S. Senate.* Ann Arbor: University of Michigan Press, 1991.

Fenno, Richard F., Jr. *Congressmen in Committees.* Boston: Little, Brown, 1973.

Hall, Richard L. *Participation in Congress.* New Haven: Yale University Press, 1996.

Frisch, Scott A. and Sean Q. Kelly, *Committee Assignment Politics in the U.S. House of Representatives* (Norman: University of Oklahoma Press, 2006).

King, David C. *Turf Wars: How Congressional Committees Claim Jurisdiction.* Chicago: University of Chicago Press, 1997.

Krehbiel, Keith. *Information and Legislative Organization.* Ann Arbor: University of Michigan Press, 1991.

Maltzman, Forrest. *Competing Principals: Committees, Parties, and the Organization of Congress.* Ann Arbor: University of Michigan Press, 1997.

Wilson, Woodrow. *Congressional Government.* Reprint of 1885 ed. Baltimore: Johns Hopkins University Press, 1981.

View from the "Back Benches." The House chamber, seen from the rear, spotlights the Speaker's rostrum, the clerks' seats in front, the gallery, and lawmakers' seats. Unlike senators, House members do not have assigned seats, but note the committee leaders' tables at the right.

Congressional
Rules and Procedures

Congress needs written rules to do its work. Compiling the Senate's first parliamentary manual, Thomas Jefferson stressed the importance of a known system of rules.

> It is much more material that there should be a rule to go by, than what the rule is; that there may be uniformity of proceeding in business not subject to the caprice of the Speaker or captiousness of the members. It is very material that order, decency, and regularity be preserved in a dignified public body.[1]

Jefferson understood that how Congress operates affects what it does. Thus Congress's rules protect majority and minority rights, divide the workload, help contain conflict, ensure fair play, and distribute power among members. Because formal rules cannot cover every contingency, precedents—accumulated decisions of House Speakers and Senate presiding officers—fill in the gaps. These precedents are codified by House and Senate parliamentarians, printed, and distributed. There are also informal, unwritten codes of conduct such as courtesy to other members. These folkways are commonly transmitted from incumbent members to newcomers.[2]

Before bills become laws, they typically pass successfully through several stages in each house (see Figure 8-1 for a simplified view of lawmaking). Bills that fail to attract majority support at any critical juncture may never be passed. Congress, in short, is a procedural obstacle course that favors opponents of legislation and hinders proponents. This defensive advantage promotes bargaining and compromise at each decision point.

Congressional rules are not independent of the policy and power struggles that lie behind them. There is very little that the House and Senate cannot do under the rules as long as the action is backed by votes and inclination. Yet votes and inclination are not easily obtained, and the rules persistently challenge the proponents of legislation to demonstrate that they have both resources at their command. Little prevents obstruction at every turn except the tacit understanding that the business of the House and Senate must go on. Members recognize that the rules can be redefined and prerogatives taken away or modified. Rules can also be employed against those who use them abusively. In brief, rules can be employed to block or advance actions in either chamber, and proponents or opponents of measures or matters do not regard them as neutral devices.

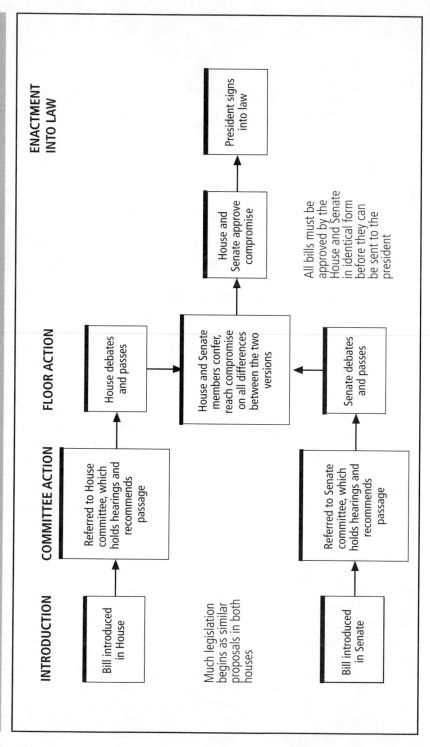

FIGURE 8-1 How a Bill Becomes Law

INTRODUCTION

COMMITTEE ACTION

FLOOR ACTION

ENACTMENT INTO LAW

Bill introduced in House

Referred to House committee, which holds hearings and recommends passage

House debates and passes

House and Senate members confer, reach compromise on all differences between the two versions

House and Senate approve compromise

President signs into law

Much legislation begins as similar proposals in both houses

Bill introduced in Senate

Referred to Senate committee, which holds hearings and recommends passage

Senate debates and passes

All bills must be approved by the House and Senate in identical form before they can be sent to the president

INTRODUCTION OF BILLS

Only members of Congress can introduce legislation. As a long-standing custom, however, lawmakers introduce "by request" measures proposed by the executive branch. Introducing one such bill, Sen. Carl Levin, D-Mich., explained: "As is the case with any bill that is introduced by request, [I] introduce this bill for the purpose of placing the administration's proposals before Congress and the public without expressing [my own view] on the substance of these proposals."[3]

Measures that members of Congress introduce have varied sources and sometimes complex origins. Often embedded in these measures are a number of assumptions—for example, that a problem exists; that it can best be resolved through enactment of a federal law instead of allowing administrative agencies or state and local governments to handle it; and that the proposed solution contained in the bill ameliorates rather than exacerbates the problem. There is also a two Congresses element to the introduction of legislation. Party leaders often allow their vulnerable members, such as narrowly elected freshmen, to sponsor popular legislation that will appeal to voters back home.

> Lawmakers are led to their choice of legislation by many factors: parochial interests, party preferences, and crass calculations linked to campaign fund raising. But one motivator—that is rarely discussed—can be just as potent: a member's personal brush with adversity. Congress is an intensely human place where personal experience sometimes has powerful repercussions.[4]

As former senator Gordon H. Smith, R-Ore., stated, "Each of us, as United States senators, comes to…this public place with the sum of our beliefs, our personal experience and our values, and none of us checks them at the door."[5] Lawmakers whose family members suffer from mental illness or who themselves have addiction problems often become advocates for legislation to address those personal issues. For example, Rep. Patrick Kennedy, D-Mass., was addicted to alcohol. He worked closely over several years with his Alcoholics Anonymous sponsor, Rep. Jim Ramstad, R-Minn., and two senators (his father, Edward Kennedy, D-Mass., and Pete Domenici, R-N.M.) to pass legislation requiring health insurers to provide mental health and addiction benefits equal to the benefits for other medical conditions. The legislation was signed into law on October 3, 2008, as a small section of the $700 billion Wall Street bailout bill (the Emergency Economic Stabilization Act).[6] Often members get ideas for bills from the executive branch, interest groups, scholars, state and local officials, constituents, the media, and their own staff.

A member who introduces a bill becomes its sponsor. He or she may seek cosponsors to demonstrate wide support for the legislation. Outside groups also may urge members to cosponsor measures. "We were not assured of a hearing," said a lobbyist of a bill that his group was pushing. "There was more hostility to the idea, so it was very important to line up a lot of cosponsors to show the overall concern."[7] As important as the number of cosponsors are their leadership status and ideological stance. Members often seek out cosponsors from the opposing party to signal that the bill transcends partisan politics. When President Barack Obama was a senator, he regularly cosponsored bills with one of the most conservative Senate Republicans, Tom Coburn of Oklahoma. Although they had polar opposite views on many issues, Obama and Coburn regularly cosponsored bills to ensure that taxpayer dollars were well spent. Massachusetts senator Edward Kennedy, a liberal Democrat, once said of the late senator Strom Thurmond, a conservative South Carolina Republican (1954–2003), "Whenever Strom and I introduce a bill together, it is either an idea whose time has come, or one of us has not read the bill."[8]

Although identifying a bill's sponsors is easy, pinpointing its real initiators may be difficult. Legislation is "an aggregate, not a simple production," wrote Woodrow Wilson. "It is impossible to tell how many persons, opinions, and influences have entered into its composition."[9] Although President John F. Kennedy, for example, is usually credited with initiating the Peace Corps, his special counsel, Theodore Sorensen, recalled that the idea was

> [b]ased on the Mormon and other voluntary religious service efforts, on an editorial Kennedy had read years earlier, on a speech by General [James] Gavin, on a luncheon I had with Philadelphia businessmen, on the suggestions of [Kennedy's] academic advisers, on legislation previously introduced and on the written response to a spontaneous late-night challenge he issued to Michigan students.[10]

In short, many bills have complex origins.

Required legislation, particularly funding measures, makes up much of Congress's annual agenda. Bills that authorize programs and specify how much money can be spent on them (authorization bills) and bills that provide the money (appropriation bills) appear on Congress's schedule at about the same time each year. Other matters recur at less frequent intervals—perhaps every four or five years. Emergency issues require Congress's immediate attention. Activist legislators also push proposals onto Congress's program. Bills not acted upon die automatically at the end of each two-year Congress. "Anybody can drop a bill into the hopper [a mahogany box near the Speaker's podium where members place their proposed bills]," said a House GOP leader. "The question is, Can you make something happen with it?"[11]

Drafting

"As a sculptor works in stone or clay, the legislator works in words," observed one member.[12] Words are the building blocks of policy, and legislators frequently battle over adding, deleting, or modifying terms and phrases. How measures are framed often influences how they are viewed by the public. "Whoever controls the language controls the debate," asserted one commentator.[13] Thus, imaginative labels for bills can sometimes attract publicity for or against legislation.

Members often give their bills eye-catching titles, such as the USA-PATRIOT Act ("Uniting and Strengthening America by Providing Appropriate Tools Required to Intercept and Obstruct Terrorism"). Lawmakers sometimes use the names of notable people to gain publicity and support for their ideas, such as the Muhammad Ali Boxing Reform Act, or they affix popular phrases to legislation, such as the "patients' bill of rights." Instead of proposing to reduce estate and inheritance taxes, conservatives call for an end to "the death tax."

Conversely, opponents of measures try to attach unattractive labels to them. Defenders of the estate tax refer to its abolition as the "Paris Hilton Benefit Act." Critics of an energy bill dubbed it the "Hooters and Polluters Bill" because the legislation contained a provision benefiting a Hooters restaurant in Louisiana. Upset that bank and financial executives who received bailout funds had such large salaries and bonuses, Sen. Bernie Sanders, I-Vt., introduced a bill titled "Stop the Greed on Wall Street Act." [14]

Although bills are introduced only by members, anyone may draft them. [15] Expert drafters in the House and Senate offices of legislative counsel assist members and committees in writing legislation. Executive agencies and lobby groups often prepare measures for introduction by friendly legislators. Many home-state industries, for instance, draft narrowly tailored tariff or regulatory measures that enhance their business prospects. These proposals are then introduced by local lawmakers—another instance of the two Congresses linkage. As a senatorial aide explained, the senator "just introduces it as a courtesy to his constituents." [16] (See Box 8-1 outlining the four basic types of legislation: bills, joint resolutions, concurrent resolutions, and simple resolutions.)

Nowadays, Congress frequently acts on comprehensive (omnibus) bills or resolutions (called packages or megabills by the press). Packages contain an array of issues that once were handled as separate pieces of legislation. Their increasing use stems in part from members' reluctance to make hard political decisions without a package arrangement. A House Budget Committee chairman once explained their attractiveness.

> Large bills can be used to hide legislation that otherwise might be more controversial. By packaging difficult issues in measures that command broad support, they enable members to avoid hard votes that they would have to account for at election time and allow members to avoid angering special-interest groups that use votes [to decide] contributions to campaigns. Leaders can also use them to slam-dunk issues that otherwise might be torn apart or to pressure the President to accept provisions that he objects to. [17]

Sometimes Congress has little choice but to use the omnibus approach. Months overdue in passing nine regular appropriations bills, Congress in early 2009 packaged the unfinished bills into a huge omnibus measure. In this way, procedural action on the outstanding measures was expedited by majority party leaders, who minimized opportunities for further delay if each bill had been taken up separately.

Timing

"Everything in politics is timing," Speaker Thomas P. "Tip" O'Neill Jr., D-Mass., used to say. A bill's success or failure often hinges on when it is introduced or brought to the floor. A bill that might succeed early in a session could fail as adjournment nears. But controversial legislation can sometimes be rushed through during the last hectic days of a Congress.

Elections greatly influence the timing of legislation. Policy issues can be taken off or kept on Congress's agenda because of electoral circumstances—a

BOX 8-1 Types of Legislation

Bill

◄ Most legislative proposals before Congress are in a bill form.

◄ Bills are designated H.R. (House of Representatives) or S. (Senate) according to where they originate, followed by a number assigned in the order in which they were introduced, from the beginning of each two-year congressional term.

◄ *Public bills* deal with general questions and become public laws if approved by Congress and signed by the president.

◄ *Private bills* deal with individual matters, such as claims against the government, immigration and naturalization cases, and land titles. They become private laws if approved and signed by the president.

Joint Resolution

◄ A joint resolution, designated H. J. Res. or S. J. Res., requires the approval of both houses and the president's signature, just as a bill does, and has the force of law.

◄ No significant difference exists between a bill and a joint resolution. The latter generally deals with limited matters, such as a single appropriation for a specific purpose.

◄ Joint resolutions are used to propose constitutional amendments, which do not require presidential signatures but become a part of the Constitution when three-fourths of the states have ratified them.

Concurrent Resolution

◄ A concurrent resolution, designated H. Con. Res. or S. Con. Res., must be passed by both houses but does not require the president's signature and does not have the force of law.

◄ Concurrent resolutions generally are used to make or amend rules applicable to both houses or to express their joint sentiment. A concurrent resolution, for example, is used to fix the time for adjournment of a Congress and to express Congress's annual budgeting plan. It might also be used to convey the congratulations of Congress to another country on the anniversary of its independence.

Resolution

◄ A simple resolution, designated H. Res. or S. Res., deals with matters entirely within the prerogatives of one house.

◄ It requires neither passage by the other chamber nor approval by the president and does not have the force of law.

◄ Most resolutions deal with the rules of one house. They also are used to express the sentiments of a single house, to extend condolences to the family of a deceased member, or to give advice on foreign policy or other executive business.

good illustration of how the two Congresses are inextricably connected. Following their major success in the 2006 elections, for example, House Democrats moved to capitalize on their momentum with quick action early in the 110th Congress to adopt their "Six for '06"—or 100-hour—legislative agenda, that included such popular measures as lobbying reform, interest rate reductions for student loans, and an increase in the minimum wage. Two years later the deep recession triggered rapid action on a nearly $800 billion economic stimulus package. The 1,100-page bill was introduced on January 26, 2009, and signed into law a mere three weeks later.

REFERRAL OF BILLS

After bills are introduced, they are referred formally to appropriate standing committees by the Senate presiding officer or the House Speaker. (In practice, these referrals are done by the Senate or House parliamentarians, who are the official procedural advisers to each chamber's presiding officer.) A bill's phraseology can affect its referral and hence its chances of passage. This political fact of life means that members use words artfully when drafting legislation. The objective is to encourage the referral of their measures to sympathetic rather than hostile committees. If a bill mentions taxes, for example, it invariably is referred to the tax panels. In a classic example, Senator Domenici sidestepped the tax-writing Finance Committee by avoiding the word *tax* in a bill proposing a charge on water-borne freight.

> If the waterway fee were considered a tax—which it was, basically, because it would raise revenues for the federal treasury—the rules would place it under the dominion of the Senate's tax-writing arm, the Finance Committee. But Finance was chaired by Russell B. Long, of Louisiana, whose state included two of the world's biggest barge ports and who was, accordingly, an implacable foe of waterway charges in any form. Domenici knew that Long could find several years' worth of bills to consider before he would voluntarily schedule a hearing on S. 790 [the Domenici bill]. For this reason, [Domenici staff aides] had been careful to avoid the word *tax* in writing the bill, employing such terms as *charge* and *fee* instead.[18]

Domenici's drafting strategy worked. His bill was jointly referred to the Commerce Committee and the Environment Committee, on which he served. Because committees' jurisdictional mandates are ambiguous and overlap, it is not unusual for legislation to be referred to two or more committees—the concept of "one bill, many committees." (See Box 8-2 illustrating how that parliamentary convention affects the reference of legislation.)

Of the thousands of bills introduced annually, Congress takes up relatively few. During the 110th Congress (2007–2009), nearly 10,000 public bills and joint resolutions were introduced; of these only 416 (4 percent) became public laws, about a third of them simply naming post offices or federal buildings. Part of the general decline in the number of laws enacted can be explained by the use of omnibus or megabills, or the widespread sentiment in both chambers that more laws may not be the answer to the nation's problems. But the decline may also reflect a political stalemate resulting from the complexity of issues, the intensity of partisanship, legislative-executive conflicts, and the narrow party divisions in Congress. Lawmakers understand that most of the bills they introduce are unlikely, as stand-alone measures, to become law. However,

BOX 8-2 **Rules and Referral Strategy**

Sometimes, the Senate's rules can be so arcane that it takes major strategy sessions to get even the most routine bills through the legislature.

That was the case when Sen. Bob Graham, D-Fla. (1987–2005), drafted a bill (targeted only at Florida) to permit the Forest Service to sell eighteen tracts of land and use the proceeds to buy up patches of private lands within the Apalachicola National Forest. To ensure that such a low-profile bill moved, Graham wanted it to go through the Energy and Natural Resources Committee, on which he sat.

Instead, Parliamentarian Alan S. Frumin told Graham's aides that the bill, which was soon to be introduced, would be referred to the Agriculture, Nutrition, and Forestry Committee. Because Graham was not a member, such a move could have guaranteed the bill a quiet death.

Why the Agriculture Committee? For at least three decades, the jurisdiction over land bills was split between the two committees. Bills affecting land east of the 100th Meridian—which runs through North Dakota and South Dakota and the middle of Texas—are assigned to Agriculture, while bills that affect lands west of it go to Energy.

Graham's bill dealt with the wrong side of the country. To change Frumin's mind, Graham's aides needed to turn the rules to their advantage.

They found their opportunity by uncovering the roots behind the 100th Meridian rule. The idea was to divide jurisdiction between public lands and privately owned lands. Because most land on the East Coast is privately owned, that side of the country went to Agriculture, which had jurisdiction over private lands. Everything in the West fell to Energy, which had jurisdiction over public lands.

Graham's aides, however, found out that a majority of tracts in Florida were always public lands. That persuaded Frumin that the bill belonged to the Energy panel.

Source: Adapted from David Nather, "Graham Turns Rules to His Advantage," *CQ Weekly,* June 8, 2002, 1494.

the ideas embedded in their legislation can be "added as amendments to a larger bill or negotiated into a markup or conference report."[19] The mere act of introducing legislation can attract public attention to a neglected topic, stimulate debate, or lay the groundwork for action in the next Congress.

Lawmaking is an arduous and intricate process. As a Senate GOP leader noted, "That's the way Congress works. You work for two years and finally you get to the end and either it all collapses in a puddle or you get a breakthrough."[20] Or as Rep. John D. Dingell, D-Mich., the longest-serving House member in history, phrased it: "Legislation is hard, pick-and-shovel work," and it often "takes a long time to do it."[21] Some ideas, such as universal health care, can take years or even decades of legislative incubation before they might make it into law.

Once committees complete action on the bills referred to them, House and Senate rules require a majority of the full committee to be physically present to report (vote out) any measure. If this rule is violated and neither waived nor ignored, the proposal that reaches the floor may be subject to a point of order—a parliamentary objection that halts the proceedings until the chamber's presiding officer decides whether the contention is valid.

Bills reported from committee have passed a critical stage in the lawmaking process. The next major step is to reach the House or Senate floor for debate and amendment. We begin our discussion with the House because tax and appropriation bills originate there—the former under the Constitution, the latter by custom.

SCHEDULING IN THE HOUSE

All bills reported from committee are listed in chronological order on one of several calendars—lists that enable the House to put measures into convenient categories. Bills that authorize, raise, or spend money are assigned to the Union Calendar (see Box 8-2) The House Calendar contains all other public measures. Private bills, such as immigration requests or claims against the government, are assigned to the Private Calendar. There is no guarantee that the House will debate legislation placed on any of these calendars. The Speaker, in consultation with other party and committee leaders, largely determines if, when, how, and in what order bills come up. The power to set the House's agenda constitutes the essence of the Speaker's institutional authority. The Speaker's agenda-setting prerogative is bolstered by rules and precedents upholding the principle of majority rule. This means that the rules and precedents of the House allow a determined voting majority—whether partisan or bipartisan—to prevail over a determined opposition.

Shortcuts for Minor Bills

Whether a bill is major or minor, controversial or noncontroversial, influences the procedure employed to bring it before the House. Most bills are relatively minor and are taken up and passed through various shortcut procedures.

One shortcut is the designation of special days for considering minor or relatively noncontroversial measures. An especially important time-saving procedure is *suspension of the rules*. It is in order Monday, Tuesday, and Wednesday of each week. The procedure is controlled by the Speaker through the power of recognizing who may speak. Most public laws enacted by the House are accomplished through this procedure. A study by Donald Wolfensberger, former staff director of the House Rules Committee, determined that in the 107th Congress (2001–2003) nearly three-quarters of bills enacted into public law came to the floor via this procedure, compared with around 33 percent two decades ago.

Legislation considered under suspension of the rules does not have to be reported from committee before the full House takes it up. The procedure permits only forty minutes of debate, allows no amendments, and requires a two-thirds vote for passage. The procedure is often favored by bill managers who want to avoid unfriendly amendments and points of order against their legislation. Bills that fail under suspension can return again to the floor by a rule issued by the Rules Committee (see the discussion below).

Why is the suspension procedure—which requires bipartisanship to attract the two-thirds vote—employed so frequently in such a polarized, closely-divided institution? The answer seems to involve a trade-off. "As members are increasingly being denied opportunities in special rules to offer amendments to more substantive bills on the floor," explains Wolfensberger, "the leadership is providing alternative mechanisms to satisfy members' policy influence and reelection needs through the relatively non-controversial and bipartisan suspension process."[22] Thus, greater use of suspensions serves two prime purposes: providing an outlet for members to achieve their policy and political goals, and keeping the lid on members' frustration with limited or closed amendment procedures.

The current rules of the House Democratic Caucus establish specific guidelines for using suspension procedure. The guidelines can only be enforced by the caucus and not by any point of order raised on the House floor. Under Caucus Rule 38, the suspension procedure is not to be used for major legislation, bills opposed by more than one-third of the committee members of jurisdiction, and measures estimated to exceed $100 million in cost for any fiscal year. Despite the Caucus Rule, major legislation is sometimes brought up via suspension procedure. For example, when prices at the gas pump in 2008 were approaching four dollars a gallon, the Speaker used the suspension procedure to prevent Republicans from offering amendments that would allow drilling in the Arctic National Wildlife Refugee or off the nation's coasts. With public opinion in favor of offshore drilling, the Speaker was uncertain whether she had the votes to defeat these unwanted amendments. Further, with the two Congresses in mind, she wanted to protect many of her Democratic colleagues from casting tough votes that would arouse the ire of various environmental groups, a core Democratic Party constituency. Ordinarily, the majority leadership does not "schedule bills for suspension unless confident of a two-thirds vote."[23]

At times, the majority leadership is chastised by the minority party for not scheduling enough of their bills via suspension procedure. To protest, minority party members may vote against suspension bills until more of their preferred measures are taken up on the floor. They may also castigate the majority leadership for using the suspension device for bills that they believe ought to receive more than forty minutes of debate, or ought to be subject to floor amendments.

Sometimes the minority will contend that noncontroversial bills that could easily pass by suspension are instead brought up with an open rule—granted by the Rules Committee—that permits more than forty minutes of debate and allows amendments. As David Dreier, R-Calif., the ranking member on Rules and its former chair (1999–2007), complained, he "would very much like to see these good, well-crafted utterly noncontroversial bills where they belong, and that is on the [informal] suspension calendar" where they can be passed quickly without wasting the House's time by using open rules to bring noncontroversial measures to the floor. The minority contends that majority leaders inflate the number of open rules for routine bills so they can claim credit for respecting minority rights. In response, Rep. Barney Frank, D-Mass., responded: "Equating a suspension of the rules procedure which allows only 40 minutes of debate and no amendments with an open rule simply because the final bill will get a large vote misunderstands, indeed, denigrates the democratic process....Very often the questions are not whether the bill will pass ultimately or not, but in what form."[24]

Another expedited procedure is *unanimous consent*. However, the Speaker will recognize a lawmaker to call up bills or resolutions by unanimous consent "only when assured that the majority and minority floor leadership and committee chairmen and ranking minority members have no objection."[25] Lacking these clearances, unanimous consent is not a viable avenue to the floor.

Major measures reach the floor by different procedures. Budget, appropriation, and a limited number of other measures are considered privileged—the House rulebook grants them a "ticket," or privileged access, to the floor. They may be called up from the appropriate calendar for debate at almost any time. Most major bills, however, do not have an automatic green light to the floor. Before they reach the floor they are assigned a rule (a procedural resolution, designated H. Res. and numbered) by the Rules Committee.

The Strategic Role of the Rules Committee

The House Rules Committee has existed since the very First Congress (1789–1791). During its early years the committee prepared or ratified a biennial set of House rules and then dissolved. As House procedures became more complex—with increases in membership and workload—the committee became more important. In 1858 the Speaker became a member of the committee and the next year its chairman. By 1880 Rules was a permanent standing committee. Three years later the committee launched a procedural revolution. It began to issue rules (sometimes called special rules): privileged resolutions that grant priority for floor consideration to virtually all major bills.

Arm of the Majority Leadership. In 1910 the House rebelled against the arbitrary decisions of Speaker Joseph G. Cannon, R-Ill., and removed him from the Rules Committee. During the subsequent decades, as the committee became an independent power, advancing those measures it favored, blocking measures it opposed, and extracting substantive concessions in bills in exchange for rules—often reflecting the wishes of the House's dominant coalition of conservative Republicans and southern Democrats.

The Rules Committee chairman from 1955 to 1967, Howard W. "Judge" Smith, D-Va., was a diehard conservative and a master at devising delaying tactics. He might abruptly adjourn meetings for lack of a quorum, allow requests for rules to languish, or refuse to schedule meetings. House consideration of the 1957 civil rights bill was temporarily delayed because Smith absented himself from the Capitol. His committee could not meet without him. Smith claimed he was inspecting a barn that had burned on his Virginia farm. Retorted Speaker Sam Rayburn, D-Texas, "I knew Howard Smith would do most anything to block a civil rights bill, but I never knew he would resort to arson."[26]

Liberals' frustration with the bipartisan coalition of conservatives who dominated the committee boiled over. After John F. Kennedy was elected president in 1960, Speaker Rayburn recognized that he needed greater control over the Rules Committee if the House was to advance the president's activist New Frontier program. Rayburn proposed enlarging the committee from twelve members to fifteen. This proposal led to a titanic struggle between Rayburn and the archconservative Rules chairman.

> Superficially, the Representatives seemed to be quarreling about next to nothing: the membership of the committee. In reality, however, the question raised had grave import for the House and for the United States. The

House's solution affected the tenuous balance of power between the great conservative and liberal blocs within the House. And in doing so, the House's answer seriously affected the Congress's response to the sweeping legislative proposals of the newly elected President, John Kennedy.[27]

In a dramatic vote the House agreed to expand the Rules Committee. Two new Democrats and one Republican were added, loosening the conservative coalition's grip on the panel.

During the 1970s the Rules Committee came under even greater majority party control. In 1975 the Democratic Caucus authorized the Speaker to appoint, subject to party ratification, all Democratic members of the committee. (Thirteen years later Republicans authorized their leader to name their members of the committee.) The majority party maintains a disproportionate ratio on the panel (nine Democrats and four Republicans in the 111th Congress). The Rules Committee, in short, once again serves as the Speaker's committee. As a GOP Rules member said about the panel's relationship with the Speaker, "How much is the Rules Committee the handmaiden of the Speaker? The answer is, totally."[28] Rep. Louise Slaughter, D-N.Y., the first female to chair Rules, heads the panel in the 111th Congress.

The Speaker's influence over the Rules Committee ensures that the Speaker can both bring measures to the floor and shape their procedural consideration. Because House rules require bills to be taken up in the chronological order listed on the calendars, many substantial bills would never reach the floor before Congress adjourned. The Rules Committee can put major bills first in line. Equally important, a rule from the committee sets the conditions for debate and amendment.

A request for a rule usually is made by the chairman of the committee reporting the bill. The Rules Committee conducts hearings on the request in the same way that other committees consider legislation, except that only members testify. The House parliamentarian usually drafts the rule after consulting with majority committee leaders and staff. The rule is considered on the House floor and is voted on in the same manner as regular bills (see Box 8-3 for an example of a structured, or restrictive, rule from the Rules Committee).

Types of Rules. Traditionally, the Rules Committee has granted open, closed, or modified rules as well as waivers. An open rule means that any germane amendments can be proposed. A closed rule prohibits the offering of amendments. A modified rule comes in two forms: modified open and modified closed (often called a "structured" rule). The distinction hinges on the number of amendments made in order by the Rules Committee—few under modified closed, more under modified open. Waivers of points of order set aside technical violations of House rules to allow bills or other matters to reach the floor. Waivers are commonly included in the different types of rules.

Whether Democrats or Republicans control the House, their majority on the Rules Committee displays procedural creativity and imagination.

Instead of choosing from among a few traditional patterns, the Rules Committee has demonstrated their willingness to create unique

BOX 8-3   **Example of a Rule from the Rules Committee**

This is a structured, or restrictive, rule (H. Res. 190) that sets the terms for debating and amending the Helping Families Save Their Homes Act of 2009 (H.R. 1106). It was adopted by the House on February 26, 2009, by a vote of 224 to 198.

Resolved, That at any time after the adoption of this resolution the Speaker may, pursuant to clause 2(b) of rule XVIII, declare the House resolved into the Committee of the Whole House on the state of the Union for consideration of the bill (H.R. 1106) to prevent mortgage foreclosures and enhance mortgage credit availability. The first reading of the bill shall be dispensed with. All points of order against consideration of the bill are waived except those arising under clause 9 of rule XXI. General debate shall be confined to the bill and shall not exceed one hour equally divided among and controlled by the chair and ranking minority member of the Committee on Financial Services and the chair and ranking minority member of the Committee on the Judiciary. After general debate the bill shall be considered for amendment under the five-minute rule. The bill shall be considered as read. All points of order against provisions in the bill are waived. Notwithstanding clause 11 of rule XVIII, no amendment to the bill shall be in order except those printed in the report of the Committee on Rules accompanying this resolution. Each such amendment may be offered only in the order printed in the report, may be offered only by a Member designated in the report, shall be considered as read, shall be debatable for the time specified in the report equally divided and controlled by the proponent and an opponent, shall not be subject to amendment, and shall not be subject to a demand for division of the question in the House or in the Committee of the Whole. All points of order against such amendments are waived except those arising under clause 9 or 10 of rule XXI. At the conclusion of consideration of the bill for amendment the Committee shall rise and report the bill to the House with such amendments as may have been adopted. The previous question shall be considered as ordered on the bill and amendments thereto to final passage without intervening motion except one motion to recommit with or without instructions.

Source: Congressional Record, February 26, 2009, H2839.

designs by recombining an increasingly wide array of elements, or by creating new ones as the need arises, to help leaders, committees, and members manage the heightened uncertainties of decision making on the House floor.[29]

The trend toward creative use of complex rules reflects several trends. Among these are: wider use of multiple referrals, which requires Rules to play a larger coordinative role in arranging floor action on legislation; the rise of megabills—hundreds of pages in length, containing priorities the Speaker does not want picked apart on the floor; the desire of majority party leaders to exert greater control over floor proceedings; members' restlessness with dilatory floor challenges to committee-reported bills; members' demand for greater certainty and predictability in floor decision making; and efforts by committee leaders either to limit the number of amendments or to keep unfriendly amendments off the floor. The sharp rise in partisanship has also provoked an increase in creative, typically structured, rules (see Box 8-4 on examples of creative rules).

BOX 8-4   **Examples of Creative Rules**

Queen-of-the-Hill Rule

◄ Under this special rule, a number of major alternative amendments—each the functional equivalent of a bill—are made to the underlying legislation, with the proviso that the substitute that receives the most votes is the winner.

◄ If two or more alternatives receive an identical number of votes, the last one voted upon is considered as finally adopted by the membership.

Self-Executing Rule

◄ This special rule provides that when the House adopts a rule it has also agreed simultaneously to pass another measure or matter.

◄ Adoption of a self-executing rule means that the House has passed one or more other proposals at the same time it agrees to the rule.

◄ Whether this rule is controversial or not usually depends on the nature of the policy being agreed to in the two-for-one vote.

Restrictive Rule

◄ The essential feature of the restrictive rule is that it limits the freedom of members to offer germane amendments to the bills made in order by those rules.

◄ The number of restrictive rules has increased since the 1980s.

◄ Rank-and-file members often rail against these rules because they restrict their opportunities to amend committee-reported measures or majority party initiatives.

Multiple-Step Rule

◄ This type of rule facilitates an orderly amendment process.

◄ One variation is for the Rules Committee to report a rule that regulates the debating and amending process for specific portions of a bill and then report another follow-on rule to govern the remainder of the measure and amendments to it.

◄ Another variation is for the Rules Committee to state publicly that, if a measure encounters difficulties on the floor, the panel will report a subsequent rule that limits time for further debate or further amendments.

Anticipatory Rule

◄ To expedite decision making on the floor, the Rules Committee may grant a rule even before the measure or matter to which it would apply has been reported by a House committee or conference committee.

When Republicans took control of the House in 1995 after decades in the minority, they promised more openness and greater chances for all lawmakers to offer floor amendments to pending legislation. Initially they worked toward this goal; but as their majorities declined in subsequent Congresses, the number of open rules dropped markedly (see Table 8-1)—the result of sharpened partisan conflict and the GOP's preference for enacting its agenda priorities

TABLE 8-1 **Open and Restrictive Rules, 95th–110th Congresses**

Congress and years	Total rules granted	Open rules Number	Open rules Percent	Restrictive rules Number	Restrictive rules Percent
95th (1977–1979)	211	179	85	32	15
96th (1979–1981)	214	161	75	53	25
97th (1981–1983)	120	90	75	30	25
98th (1983–1985)	155	105	68	50	32
99th (1985–1987)	115	65	57	50	43
100th (1987–1989)	123	66	54	57	46
101st (1989–1991)	104	47	45	57	55
102d (1991–1993)	109	37	34	72	66
103d (1993–1995)	104	31	30	73	70
104th (1995–1997)	151	86	57	65	43
105th (1997–1999)	142	72	51	70	49
106th (1999–2001)	184	93	51	91	49
107th (2001–2003)	112	71	37	71	63
108th (2003–2005)	128	33	26	95	74
109th (2005–2007)	138	22	16	116	84
110th (2007–2009)	159	23	15	136	85

Sources: U.S. Congress, Congressional Record, daily ed., 103d Cong., 2d sess., October 7, 1994, H11278. For the 104th Congress, see House Rules Committee, press release, December 10, 1996. For the 105th Congress, the Rules Committee issued a total of 207 rules, but many did not directly involve bills and resolutions. As a result, the authors selected 142 as the number of rules granted for bills and resolutions. Minority Democrats have made their own calculation of the kinds of rules granted by the committee. They identify a total of 163 rules of which 38 are open (23 percent) and 115 (77 percent) are restrictive. See *Survey of Activities of the House Committee on Rules* (Washington, D.C.: U.S. Government Printing Office, 1999). For the 106th Congress, the Rules Committee issued 267 rules with 184 directly affecting the amending process on the floor. Hence, the authors employ the 184 figure instead of 267, which included rules, for example, that permitted the House to go to conference with the Senate. See *Survey of Activities of the House Committee on Rules* (Washington, D.C.: U.S. Government Printing Office, 2001). For the 107th Congress, the panel issued 191 rules with 112 directly related to the amendment process for the consideration of bills and resolutions. See *Survey of Activities of the House Committee on Rules* (Washington, D.C.: U.S. Government Printing Office, 2003). During the 108th Congress, the panel issued 192 rules with 128 either open (28), modified open (5), structured or modified closed (59), or closed (36). See *Survey of Activities of the House Committee on Rules* (Washington, D.C.: U.S. Government Printing Office, 2005). During the 109th Congress, the panel issued 193 rules with 138 directly related to the amending process. Of these, 22 were open, 2 modified open, 65 modified closed, and 49 closed. See *Survey of Activities of the House Committee on Rules* (Washington, D.C.: U.S. Government Printing Office, 2007) amd *Survey of Activities of the House Committee on Rules* (Washington, D.C.: U.S. Government Printing Office, 2009).

with few or no changes. "Whenever an issue is the least bit contentious, whenever there is even the hint of disagreement about a bill," a Rules Democrat complained, "the majority clamps down on [the] Members, chokes debate, and forces a closed rule through the House."[30] Open rules clash with a fundamental objective of any majority party: passage of priority legislation even at the cost of restricting members' amending opportunities.

Like the Republicans in 1995, the Democratic majority in the 110th House (2007–2009) pledged to manage the House in an open, fair, and deliberative manner. Nonetheless, Democrats brought their legislative priorities to the floor under closed or structured rules. Closed rules prevented Republicans from offering "gotcha" amendments designed for campaign attack ads or from undermining the majority's priorities.

Republicans repeatedly took the floor to castigate the Democrats for reneging on their promises. "When it comes time to shutting down debate, silencing ideas, restricting minority rights, ignoring rules they themselves wrote, and running the House in a top-down, shut-up, sit-down manner," exclaimed a Rules Republican, "this Democrat[ic] majority has no peer.... They have passed more closed rules that block all amendments and debate than any House in history."[31] Responding to the GOP complaints, Democrats like Rules chair Slaughter charged that Republicans "have a lot of nerve complaining about how the House has been run," given the procedural abuses Democrats suffered when the GOP ran the House.[32] As Majority Leader Steny Hoyer put it: "I said we were going to be fair, not stupid."[33]

Again in control of the 111th House, Democrats continued to use closed or structured rules. Only this time many rank-and-file Democrats became upset with leadership circumvention of the "regular order": that is, committee vetting and amending on the floor. No less than 66 Democrats wrote to Speaker Pelosi urging a return to the regular order. At the Democrats' annual retreat, she promised her colleagues that "we will go forward now under regular order."[34]

In summary, rules establish the conditions under which most major bills are debated and amended. They determine the length of general debate, they permit or prohibit amendments, and they often waive points of order. Writing the rules is the majority party's way of ensuring that measures reach the floor under terms favorable to its preferred outcomes. Put differently, the majority party limits and structures the votes to get the results it intends, which can include the two Congresses. In this era of message politics and partisan polarization, innovative rules can both protect majority party members from casting electorally perilous votes, or from offering amendments that might appeal to narrow party factions.

For their part, minority lawmakers object strongly to the wider use of restrictive rules that block them from offering and getting votes on a number of their policy alternatives. "We don't expect to win," said a minority member, "but we do expect to be able to at least offer amendments so the two parties can define their differences."[35] However, the political reality today is that in a highly polarized House, the members' ability to offer amendments is not a right but a privilege accorded them by the Rules Committee. Special rules, in short, are often as important to a bill's fate as a favorable committee vote.

Dislodging a Bill from Committee

Committees do not necessarily reflect the point of view of the full chamber. What happens when a standing committee refuses to report a bill, or when the Rules Committee does not grant a rule? To circumvent committees, members have three options: the discharge petition, the Calendar Wednesday rule, and the Rules Committee's power to extract a bill from committee. These are rarely employed and seldom successful.

The discharge petition allows the House to relieve a committee of jurisdiction over a stalled measure. This procedure also provides a way for rank-and-file members to force a bill to the floor even if the majority leadership, the committee chairman, and the Rules Committee oppose it. If a committee does not report a bill within thirty legislative days after the bill was referred to it, any member may file a discharge motion (petition)—requiring the signature of 218 members, a majority of the House. Once the signatures are obtained, the discharge motion is placed on the Discharge Calendar for seven days. It can then be called up on the second and fourth Mondays of the month by any member who signed the petition. If the discharge motion is agreed to, the bill is taken up right away. Since 1910, when the discharge rule was adopted, only three discharged measures have ever become law. Its threatened or actual use, particularly as the number of signatures approach 218, may prompt a committee to act on a bill and the majority leadership to schedule it for floor action. The discharge procedure is rarely successful as a lawmaking device. For one thing, 218 signatures are hard to obtain. Moreover, members are reluctant to second-guess committees, to write legislation on the floor without the guidance of committee hearings and reports, and to use a procedure that might one day be used against their own committees.

The minority party often employs discharge petitions to spotlight the two Congresses. For example, minority members may promote and publicize their high-priority issues and then circulate discharge petitions "in an attempt to force House votes—and provide a contrast with [the majority party] in an election year."[36] A month before the November 2008 elections, the House Republican campaign committee issued statements blasting fourteen vulnerable House Democrats for failing to sign a discharge petition to force an up-or-down vote on lifting the offshore oil drilling ban.[37]

The discharge rule also applies to the Rules Committee. A motion to discharge a rule is in order after seven legislative days, instead of thirty days, as long as the bill made in order by the rule has been in committee for thirty days. Any member may enter a discharge motion, but majority members rarely break ranks with their party leaders to sign the petition. When Rep. Christopher Shays, R-Conn., signed a successful discharge petition to force House action on a major campaign finance reform bill (the Bipartisan Campaign Reform Act of 2002) opposed by the GOP leadership, his party colleagues accused Shays of disloyalty and warned that he might face a challenger in the Republican primary. Signing discharge petitions, "along with other kinds of procedural betrayals, are being considered and discussed by members" of the GOP's committee on committees, remarked the GOP Conference chair.[38] Shays was subsequently passed over as chair of the Government Reform Committee, even though he had more seniority than the two other Republicans in contention. (Shays was defeated in the November 2008 elections.)

Adopted in 1909, the Calendar Wednesday rule provides that on Wednesdays committees may bring up from the House Calendar or Union Calendar their measures that have not received a rule from the Rules Committee. Calendar Wednesday is cumbersome to employ and seldom used. It was sometimes employed by the minority to tie up the floor and thus signal their displeasure with majority party actions.[39] As a result, the Democratically-controlled House changed the Calendar Wednesday rule on the opening day of the 111th Congress. Under the revision only committee chairs, upon one legislative day's notice, are authorized to call up bills on Calendar Wednesday. It would be very unlikely that a chair will use the new procedure. Since 1943 fewer than fifteen measures have been enacted into law under this procedure.[40]

Finally, the Rules Committee has the power of extraction. The committee can propose rules that make bills in order for House debate even if the bills have neither been introduced nor reported by standing committees. Based on an 1895 precedent, this procedure is akin to discharging committees without the required 218 signatures. It stirs bitter controversy among members who think it usurps the rights of the other committees; therefore it is seldom used.

HOUSE FLOOR PROCEDURES

The House meets Monday through Friday, often convening at noon. Its usual practice is to conduct the bulk of its committee and floor business during the middle of the week (called the "Tuesday to Thursday Club"). This scheduling pattern helps representatives juggle legislative business with weekend trips to their districts—weekly testimony to the tug and pull of the two Congresses.

Speaker Pelosi and Majority Leader Hoyer nonetheless promised a full five-day workweek for the 110th House (2007–2009). They chided Republicans for having kept the House in session fewer days (103) than the "do-nothing" 80th Congress (110 days) targeted by Harry Truman during his 1948 presidential campaign. Hoyer explained that most weeks the House would come in "Monday at 6:30 p.m. and be working on Fridays, as we used to do, until about [2:00 p.m.] to give people time so they can get home" to their districts.[41] Two years later he announced that the 111th House would be in Monday through Friday for eleven weeks in 2009. "This is in keeping," he said, "with a pledge by Democratic leaders who, after taking control of Congress in 2006, vowed to extend the typical workweek of three days to five days."[42] The Democratic leaders' goal was not merely to contrast their management of the House with the Republicans', but to provide more time for committees and members to consider and debate legislation. (Needless to say, the five-day schedule is likely to slip as the 2010 midterm elections loom and lawmakers push to return home to campaign.)

At the beginning of each day's session, bells ring throughout the Capitol and the House office buildings, summoning lawmakers to the floor. The bells also notify members of votes, quorum calls, recesses, and adjournments. Typically, the opening activities include a daily prayer; approval of the *Journal* (a constitutionally required record of the previous day's proceedings); recitation of the Pledge of Allegiance; receipt of messages from the president (such as a veto message) or the Senate; announcements (if any) by the Speaker; and one-minute speeches by members on any topic. A period of morning hour debate takes place after the opening preliminaries on Mondays and Tuesdays before the start of formal legislative business.

After these preliminaries, the House generally begins considering legislation. For a major bill, a set pattern is observed: adopting the rule, convening in

Committee of the Whole, allotting time for general debate, amending, voting, and moving the bill to final passage.

Adoption of the Rule

The Speaker, having consulted other majority party leaders and affected committee chairmen, generally decides when the House will debate a bill and under what kind of rule. When the scheduled day arrives, the Speaker recognizes a majority member of the Rules Committee for one hour to explain the rule's contents. By custom, the majority member yields half the time for purposes of debate only to a minority Rules Committee member. (Yielding time for debate purposes only prevents the minority member from offering an amendment to the special rule.) At the end of the debate, which may take less than the allotted hour, the House votes on the previous question motion. Its approval brings the House to an immediate vote on the rule; its rejection (a rare occurrence) allows the minority party to offer a germane amendment to the rule. The final step is the vote on House passage of the rule.

Opponents of a bill can try to defeat the rule and avert House action on the bill itself. But rules are rarely defeated because the Rules Committee usually anticipates the chamber's wishes, and because such procedural votes are normally supported by majority party members. Speaker Pelosi has yet to see the House reject a special rule. Only two such rules were rejected during the speakership of her predecessor, J. Dennis Hastert, R-Ill. (1999–2007). Once the rule is adopted, the House is governed by its provisions. Most rules state that "at any time after the adoption of [the rule] the Speaker may declare the House resolved into the Committee of the Whole."

Committee of the Whole

The Committee of the Whole House on the state of the Union is a parliamentary artifice designed to expedite consideration of legislation. It is simply the House in another form with different rules. For example, a quorum in the Committee of the Whole is only 100 members, compared with 218 for the full House. The Speaker appoints a majority party colleague to preside over the committee, which then begins general debate of a bill.

General Debate

A rule from the Rules Committee specifies the amount of time, usually one to two hours, for general discussion of the bill under consideration. Controversial bills require more time, perhaps four to ten hours. Control of the time is divided equally between the majority and minority floor managers—usually the chairman and ranking minority member of the committee that reported the legislation. (When bills are referred to more than one committee, a more complex division of debate time is allotted among the committees having jurisdiction over the legislation.) The majority floor manager's job is to guide the bill to final passage; the minority floor manager may seek to amend or defeat the bill.

After the floor managers have made their opening statements, they parcel out several minutes each to colleagues on their side of the aisle who wish to speak. General debate rarely lives up to its name, because most legislators simply read prepared speeches. "There's no real debate in Congress," noted a House GOP leader. "I mean, there are a series of speeches for and against a given issue."[43] Give-and-take exchange occurs infrequently at this stage of the proceedings.

The Amending Phase

The amending process is the heart of decision making on the floor of the House. Amendments determine the final shape of bills and often dominate public discussion. Former Illinois Republican Henry J. Hyde (1975–2007), for example, repeatedly and successfully proposed "Hyde amendments" barring the use of federal funds for abortions.

An amendment offered in the Committee of the Whole is considered under the five-minute rule, which gives the sponsor five minutes to defend it and an opponent five minutes to speak against it. The amendment then may be brought to a vote. Amendments are routinely debated for more than ten minutes, however. Legislators gain the floor by saying, "I move to strike the last word" or "I move to strike the requisite number of words." These *pro forma* amendments, which make no alteration in the pending matter, simply serve to give members five more minutes of debate time.

If there is an open rule, opponents may try to load the bill with so many objectionable amendments that it will sink of its own weight. The reverse strategy is to propose sweetener amendments that attract support from other members. Offering many amendments is an effective dilatory tactic because each amendment must be read in full, debated for at least five to ten minutes, and then voted on.

In this amending phase the linkage of the two Congresses is evident: Floor amendments can have electoral as well as legislative effects. Amendments allow lawmakers to take positions that enhance their reputations with the folks back home, put opponents on record, and shape national policy. For example, "put-them-on-the-spot amendments," as one representative dubbed them, are artfully fashioned by minority lawmakers to force the majority to vote on issues such as gun control or stem cell research that can be used against them in the next campaign.[44] The majority party's control of the Rules Committee minimizes their use of this tactic, because the panel commonly "scripts" the amendment process—by specifying, for example, that only certain amendments can be offered, often in a set order, and only by a particular member.

The minority guards the floor to demand explanations or votes on amendments brought up by the majority. "So long as a floor watchdog exists," one floor guardian wrote, "all members of the House are afforded some additional protection from precipitous actions."[45] Reps. Lynn Westmoreland, R-Ga., Tom Price, R-Ga., and others have assumed this role for the GOP in the 111th House.

Voting

Before the 1970 Legislative Reorganization Act was passed, the Committee of the Whole adopted or rejected amendments by voice votes or other votes with no public record of who voted and how. Today, any legislator supported by twenty-five colleagues can obtain a recorded vote. (The member who requested a recorded vote is counted as one of those who rise to be counted by the chair.)

Since the installation of an electronic voting system in 1973, members can insert their personalized cards (about the size of a credit card) into one of more than forty voting stations on the floor and press the "Yea," "Nay," or "Present" button. A large electronic display board behind the press gallery provides a running tally of the total votes for or against a motion. The voting tally is watched carefully by many members:

> I find that a lot of times, people walk in, and the first thing they do is look at the board, and they have key people they check out, and if those people have voted "aye," they go to the machine and vote "aye" and walk off the floor.
>
> But I will look at the board and see how [members of the state delegation] vote, because they are in districts right next to me, and they have constituencies just like mine. I will vote the way I am going to vote except that if they are both different, I will go up and say, "Why did you vote that way? Let me know if there is something I am missing."[46]

Both parties use difficult and controversial votes against vulnerable lawmakers. In the lead-up to the November 2008 elections, for example, House Democratic Caucus Chairman Rahm Emanuel (now President Obama's chief of staff) told vulnerable Republicans that if they did not back expansion of the State Children's Health Insurance Program (SCHIP), their vote would be used against them in the election. Ten Republicans did vote against SCHIP and that, among other factors, contributed to their defeat.[47] (An early priority of the 111th Congress was to pass the SCHIP expansion, which President Obama signed into law.)

After all pending amendments have been voted on, the Committee of the Whole rises. The chairman hands the gavel back to the Speaker, and a quorum once again becomes 218 members.

Final Passage

As specified in the rule, the full House must review the actions of its agent, the Committee of the Whole. The Speaker announces that under the rule the previous question has been ordered, which means in this context that no further debate is permitted on the bill or its amendments. The Speaker then asks whether any representative wants a separate vote on any first-degree amendment. (A first-degree amendment is offered to the text of the bill, a second-degree amendment is offered to the first-degree one.) If not, all the amendments agreed to in the committee are approved.

The next important step is the recommittal motion, which provides a way for the House to return, or recommit, the bill to the committee that reported it. There are two forms of this motion: the rarely used "straight" motion to return the measure to committee (which effectively kills it), and a motion to recommit with instructions—these contain the minority's policy alternative and must be germane to the bill—that the committee report "forthwith" (which means the bill never really leaves the House). If this form of the motion is adopted, the bill—as modified by the instructions—is automatically before the House again.

By precedent, either form of the motion to recommit is always made by a minority party member who opposes the legislation. These motions are seldom successful because they are considered an opposition party device; but they do serve to protect the rights of minority members by granting them a final opportunity to reshape the measure. When Republicans won majority control in 1995, they amended House rules to guarantee the minority leader or his/her designee the right to offer a recommittal motion with instructions. Although Democrats retained this guarantee following their election victories in 2006 and 2008, they did change two specific features of the rule on the opening day of the 111th Congress.

These changes eliminated the controversial word "promptly" for the traditional "forthwith" in the instructions. In the 110th House, Republicans increasingly used the word "promptly" rather than "forthwith" in their instructions. If the "promptly" motions are agreed to, they have the practical effect of killing the bill. The motion reads: "Mr. X moves to recommit the bill, H. R. 1234, to the Committee on Natural Resources with instructions to report back to the House promptly with the following amendment" [the minority's policy alternative]. When Democrats were in the minority for a dozen years (1995–2007), they used the word "promptly" thirty-three times and all were unsuccessful. But during the 110th Congress, Republicans used "promptly" motions on forty-six occasions, all also unsuccessful.[48]

The majority party complained that Republicans cleverly designed their "promptly" motions to try and compel vulnerable or other Democrats to vote for the GOP motions, undermining the majority party's priority legislation. A few examples make the point. Such motions were offered that either enforced the Second Amendment's right to bear arms or repealed gun control laws in various areas. However phrased, these motions led to votes that split the Democratic membership. Other such motions would have prohibited federal tax subsidies for localities that refused to enforce immigration laws (so-called "sanctuary" cities for illegal immigrants). In short, Republicans "launched a coordinated effort [in the 110th House] to use recommital motions to force Democrats to cast uncomfortable votes or make unwelcome changes to bills."[49] The Democratic response was often to yank the bill off the floor in order to rethink their next moves.

To end these procedural headaches, the Democratic majority on January 7, 2009, amended the House rulebook to forbid the minority party from offering "promptly" motions. Now, only "forthwith" motions to instruct are in order: "Mr. X moves to recommit the bill H.R. 5678 to the Committee on Ways and Means with instructions to report the same back to the House forthwith with the following amendment." Moreover, House rules were further amended to permit ten minutes of debate, equally divided, on the straight motion to recommit. Previously, this was not subject to debate. The straight motion is now procedurally equivalent to the promptly motion. Its adoption kills the underlying legislation. If the motion to recommit with forthwith instructions is adopted, the amendment (or instructions) is then voted on by the House. Once the amendment is either adopted or rejected, the Speaker then declares, "The question is on final passage."

Passage of the bill by the House marks about the halfway point in the lawmaking process. The Senate must also approve the bill, and its procedures are strikingly different from those of the House.

SCHEDULING IN THE SENATE

Compared with the larger and more clamorous House, which needs and follows well-defined rules and precedents, the Senate operates more informally. And unlike the House, where the rules permit a determined majority to make decisions, the Senate's rules emphasize individual prerogatives (unlimited freedom to debate and to offer amendments), including nongermane amendments and minority rights (those of the minority party, a faction, or even a single senator). "The Senate," said one member, "is run for the convenience of one senator to the inconvenience of 99."[50] No wonder some commentators say the Senate has only two rules (unanimous consent and exhaustion) and three speeds (slow, slower, and slowest). As Sen. Byron L. Dorgan, D-N.D., said, "The only thing it's easy to do in the Senate is slow things down. The Senate is 100 human brake pads."[51] Sen. Judd Gregg, R-N.H., underscored Dorgan's observation when he stated: "The Founding Fathers intended us to be inert, and we've expanded that ability to a point where a single senator can block action."[52]

The scheduling system for the Senate appears relatively simple. The Calendar of Business is used for all public and private bills and the Executive Calendar for treaties and nominations. The Senate has nothing comparable to the House Rules Committee's scheduling duties, and the majority and minority leadership actively consult about scheduling. The Senate majority leader is responsible for setting the agenda and is aided in controlling the scheduling by the priority given him when he seeks recognition on the floor. To be sure, the two Congresses phenomenon suffuses scheduling. The majority leader, for instance, may bring bills to the floor that energize the party's core supporters just prior to the November election. Conversely, the leader may call up controversial issues early in a Congress "rather than risk fighting them out in the weeks immediately before the November election."[53]

Despite the Senate's smaller size, establishing a firm agenda of business is harder in the Senate than in the House. As a former majority leader once said:

> The ability of any Senator to speak without limitations makes it impossible to establish total certainty with respect to scheduling. When there is added to that the difficult and very demanding schedules of 100 Senators, it is very hard to organize business in a way that meets the convenience of everybody.[54]

Legislation typically reaches the Senate floor in two ways: by unanimous consent ("I ask unanimous consent to call up the bill S. 1234") or by motion ("I move to take up the bill S. 1234"). Unanimous consent agreements are crucial to the smooth functioning of the Senate. Without these orders of the Senate, the institution would have a hard time processing its large workload. Remember, these agreements can be blocked by a single objection ("I object!"). And individual senators can force the Senate to consider their proposals by offering them as nonrelevant amendments to pending business.

Unanimous Consent Agreements

The Senate frequently dispenses with its formal rules and instead follows negotiated agreements submitted to the Senate for its unanimous approval (see Box 8-5

BOX 8-5   **Example of a Unanimous Consent Agreement**

*O**rdered,* that at 10:00 a.m. on Tuesday, March 10, 2009, the Senate resume consideration of H.R. 1105, an act making omnibus appropriations for the fiscal year ending September 30, 2009, and for other purposes; provided, that the following be the only first degree amendments remaining in order to the bill; further, that no amendment be in order to the listed amendments prior to a vote in relation thereto; further, that the amendments must be offered and debated Friday, March 6, 2009, Monday, March 9, 2009, or Tuesday, March 10, 2009:

◄ Amdt. No. 615, offered by the Senator from Nevada (Mr. Ensign),
◄ Amdt. No. 621, offered by the Senator from Louisiana (Mr. Vitter),
◄ Amdt. No. 604, offered by the Senator from Alabama (Mr. Sessions),
◄ Amdt. No. 593, offered by the Senator from Arizona (Mr. McCain),
◄ Amdt. No. 662, offered by the Senator from South Dakota (Mr. Thune),
◄ Amdt. No. 637, offered by the Senator from Wyoming (Mr. Barrasso),
◄ Amdt. No. 668, offered by the Senator from Wyoming (Mr. Enzi),
◄ Amdt. Nos. 629, 630, 631, offered by the Senator from Arizona (Mr. Kyl),
◄ An amendment on dues notification offered by the Senator from Arizona (Mr. Kyl) or his designee, with a copy of the proposal at desk,
◄ Amdt. No. 673, offered by the Senator from Texas (Mr. Cornyn), and
◄ Amdt. No. 665, offered by the Senator from Kentucky (Mr. Bunning).

Ordered further, That on Tuesday, the remaining amendments be considered and debated and that after all debate has been concluded on the remaining amendments, the Senate proceed to vote in relation to the amendments in a sequence established under a subsequent order, with two minutes of debate, equally divided and controlled in the usual form prior to a vote in relation to each; provided, that after the first vote in the sequence, the remaining votes be limited to 10 minutes each.

Ordered further, That upon disposition of all remaining amendments, there then be 30 minutes of debate, equally divided and controlled between the Leaders or their designees, prior to a vote on the motion to invoke cloture on H.R. 1105.

Ordered further, That upon disposition of the amendments and the Senate having voted on the motion to invoke cloture on H.R. 1105 and cloture having been invoked, all post-cloture time be considered yielded back, the bill be read a third time, and the Senate proceed to vote on passage of the bill.

Ordered further, That with respect to the motion to invoke cloture on H.R. 1105, the mandatory quorum required under Rule XXII be waived.

Source: U.S. Senate, *Calendar of Business,* 111th Cong., 1st sess., March 10, 2009, 2.

---

on unanimous consent agreements). The objectives are to expedite work in an institution known for extended debate, to impose a measure of predictability on floor action, and to minimize dilatory activities. As a party floor leader observed:

> We aren't bringing [measures] to the floor unless we have [a unani-
> mous consent] agreement. We could bring child-care legislation
> to the floor right now, but that would mean two months of fighting.
> We want to maximize productive time by trying to work out as much
> as we can in advance [of floor action].[55]

It is not uncommon for party leaders to negotiate piecemeal unanimous consent agreements (UCAs)—limiting debate on a specific amendment, for example—and to discuss and hammer them out in public on the Senate floor. Comprehensive unanimous consent agreements—which might address the exact date and time when the Senate is to consider a bill, under what debating and amending conditions, and when precisely it will be voted upon—are hard to reach in today's polarized Senate. Drafts of UCAs are privately circulated among senators to solicit their ideas and support. Sometimes it can take days, weeks, or months before a UCA is acceptable to all senators. And they can be quite complicated, as this classic example illustrates:

> It took more than two weeks to negotiate, sometimes in closed-door meetings among senators and staff, other times on the floor of the Senate, with tempers flaring and the traditional senatorial courtesy frayed almost to the breaking point. When completed, it took nearly an hour for the majority leader to read aloud to his colleagues, and when printed in the *Congressional Record* it consumed three pages. It was so complicated that many senators admitted they could not understand the [UCA] even after two or three readings.[56]

Unanimous consent agreements (also called time-limitation agreements) limit debate on the bill, any amendments, and various motions. Typically, they impose constraints on the amendment process: how many may be offered and under what restrictions. To facilitate enactment of an omnibus crime package that contained provisions with widespread Senate support, for example, senators agreed to a unanimous consent request barring floor amendments on such controversial issues as gun control or the death penalty.[57]

The Senate's unanimous consent agreements are functional equivalents of special rules from the House Rules Committee. Both waive the rules of their respective chambers and must be approved by the members—in one case by majority vote and in the other by unanimous consent. These accords are binding contracts that can be terminated or modified only by another unanimous consent agreement. Senators and aides often negotiate and draft unanimous consent agreements privately, whereas the Rules Committee hears requests for special orders in public sessions.

Ways to Extract Bills from Committee

If a bill is blocked in committee, the Senate has several ways to obtain floor action. It can add the bill as an unrelated floor amendment to another bill, bypass the committee stage by placing the bill directly on the calendar, suspend the rules, or discharge the bill from committee. Only the first two procedures are effective; the other two are somewhat difficult to employ and seldom succeed.[58]

Because the Senate has no general germaneness (relevancy) rule, senators can take an agriculture bill that is stuck in committee and add it as a nonrelevant floor amendment to a pending health bill. "Amendments may be made," Thomas Jefferson noted long ago, "so as to totally alter the nature of the proposition." However, unanimous consent agreements can limit or prohibit nonrelevant amendments.

Bypassing committees also occurs when senators invoke one of its formal rules: Rule XIV. Typically, when senators introduce bills or joint resolutions (or when bills or joint resolutions are passed by the House and sent to the Senate), they are referred to the appropriate committee of jurisdiction. Senate Rule XIV specifies that those measures are to be read twice by title on different legislative days—when the Senate is in session—before they are referred. If no senator raises an objection after the first reading and again the next legislative day after the second reading, the bill or joint resolution is automatically placed on the Senate's calendar of business. Although not used for the vast majority of measures, the rule is often invoked on party issues of high priority. The majority leader, for example, may employ it to circumvent committees because no time is available for a lengthy committee review, or because he wants a measure ready to be called up at his discretion.

SENATE FLOOR PROCEDURES

The Senate, like the House, often convenes at noon, sometimes earlier, to keep pace with the workload. Typically, it opens with a prayer. This is followed by the Pledge of Allegiance and then leaders' time (for example, ten minutes each to the majority leader and the minority leader to discuss various issues). If neither leader wants any time, the Senate typically either permits members who have requested time to make their statements, or it resumes consideration of old or new business under terms of a unanimous consent agreement. The Senate, too, must keep and approve the *Journal* of the previous day's activities. Commonly, the *Journal* is "deemed approved to date" by unanimous consent when the Senate adjourns or recesses at the end of each day.

Normal Routine

For most bills the Senate follows four steps:

1. The majority leader secures the unanimous consent of the Senate to an arrangement that specifies when a bill will be brought to the floor and the conditions for debating it.
2. The presiding officer recognizes the majority and minority floor managers for opening statements.
3. Amendments are then in order, with debate regulated by the terms of the unanimous consent agreement. Amendments are approved or rejected by voice or roll-call vote.
4. A roll-call vote commonly takes place on final passage.

As in the House, amendments in the Senate serve various purposes. For example, floor managers might accept "as many amendments as they can without undermining the purposes of the bill, in order to build the broadest possible consensus behind it."[59] Some amendments highlight the two Congresses pressures—bestow benefits to the electorate or embarrass members who must vote against them. "My amendment can be characterized as a 'November amendment,'" remarked a Republican senator, "because the vote…will provide an opportunity for senators to go home and say, 'I voted to reduce federal taxes' and

'I voted to cut federal spending.'"[60] As another example, Senate Democrats make "vigorous use of amendments to strike a contrast with Republican policies."[61] Unless constrained by some previous unanimous consent agreement, senators generally have the right to offer an unlimited number of floor amendments.

A bill is brought to a final vote whenever senators stop talking. This can be a long process, particularly in the absence of a UCA. (A number of laws restrict a senator's right to prolong debate, such as trade or reconciliation measures. As a former Senate parliamentarian noted: "We have on the books probably a couple hundred laws that set up specific legislative vehicles that cannot be filibustered or only amended in a very restricted way.")[62] On some bills UCAs are foreclosed because of deliberate obstructive tactics, particularly the threat or use of the filibuster. In these instances, bills cannot be voted upon until the filibuster has ended. Every measure might face at least two primary filibusters: the first on the motion to take up the legislation and the second on the bill itself.

Holds, Filibusters, and Cloture

The old-style filibuster has long been associated with the 1939 movie *Mr. Smith Goes to Washington,* which featured a haggard Jimmy Stewart staging a dramatic solo talkathon on the floor of the Senate to inform the public about political wrongdoing. In its current form, however, filibusters are rarely invoked but often threatened—to gain bargaining power and negotiating leverage.

Filibusters involve many blocking tactics besides extended debate in which senators hold the floor for hours of endless speeches. Many contemporary filibusters are waged by those who skillfully use Senate rules. For example, senators might offer scores of amendments, raise points of order, or demand numerous and consecutive roll-call votes. Holds are another form of silent filibuster.

Holds. A hold permits one or more senators to block floor action on measures or matters by asking their party leaders not to schedule them. A hold, explained Sen. Charles E. Grassley, R-Iowa, is "a notice by a Senator to his or her party leader of an intention to object to bringing a bill or nomination to the floor for consideration."[63] Neither Senate rules nor precedents provide for holds; they are an informal custom. The majority leader decides whether, or for how long, he will honor a colleague's hold. The power of holds is grounded in the implicit threat of senators to conduct filibusters or to object to unanimous consent agreements.

Holds are attacked because they often lead to delays or even the death (choke holds) of measures or nominations. Originally intended as a way for senators to get information about when the majority leader planned action on a measure, they have become devices to kill measures by delaying them indefinitely, or to gain bargaining leverage (holds as hostage) by, for instance, stalling action on presidential nominees. On one occasion, so many holds on nominations were pending before the Senate that a Democratic leader felt left out. As he explained: "I'm going to have to pick out a nominee to get to know him or her a lot better because it works that way. I mean, it's 'Hello, I'm your holder…come dance with me.'"[64]

Proposals are repeatedly made to reform the practice but not end it. Senators long complained about the use of secret holds, because they had no idea who to contact to determine if some compromise or adjustment might be made that would permit the anonymous member to lift the hold. The Senate did address secret holds in 2007 when Congress passed and the president signed the Honest Leadership and Open Government Act, a major lobbying reform bill. Although the Act established a procedure for ending anonymous holds, it is not effective in practice. A senator, for example, has six session days to decide whether formally to place a hold. If so, the member so informs the majority or minority leader, as the case may be. Then that member's name will be publicized in the *Congressional Record* and elsewhere. However, if a senator forgoes using a hold, then for at least six session days there is a secret hold in effect. Furthermore, a senator could arrange to have a number of like-minded colleagues, at the expiration of each six-day period, place a hold (so-called "rolling holds"). Thus, secrecy continues today to surround the holds process. There are, of course, senators who publicly inform their colleagues that they have holds on measures or nominees.

Filibusters and Cloture. The right of extended debate is unique to the Senate. Any senator or group of senators can talk continuously in the hope of delaying, modifying, or defeating legislation. In 1957 South Carolina senator Strom Thurmond, then a Democrat, set the record for the Senate's longest solo performance—twenty-four hours and eighteen minutes—trying to kill a civil rights bill.

The success of a filibuster depends not only on how long it takes but also on when it is waged. A filibuster can be most effective late in a session because there is insufficient time to break it.[65] Even the threat of a filibuster can encourage accommodations or compromises between proponents and opponents of legislation.

Defenders of the filibuster say it protects minority rights, permits thorough consideration of bills, and dramatizes issues. "In many ways," noted Sen. Robert C. Byrd, D-W.Va., "the filibuster is the single most important device ever employed to ensure that the Senate remains truly the unique protector of the rights of our people."[66] Critics contend that talkathons enable minorities to extort unwanted concessions. During most of its history, the Senate had no way to terminate debate except by unanimous consent, exhaustion, or compromise. In 1917 the Senate adopted Rule XXII, its first cloture (debate-ending) rule. After several revisions, Rule XXII now permits three-fifths of the Senate (60 members) to shut off debate on substantive issues or procedural motions. (A two-thirds vote is required to invoke cloture on a proposal to change the rules of the Senate.) Once cloture is invoked, thirty hours of debate time remain before the final vote.

Senators complain about the frequent use of filibusters and cloture attempts. In the past, filibusters generally occurred on issues of great national importance; today they occur on a wide range of less momentous topics. As one majority leader pointed out:

> Not long ago the filibuster or threat of a filibuster was rarely under-taken in the Senate, being reserved for matters of grave national importance. That is no longer the case....The threat of a filibuster is now a regular event in the Senate, weekly at least, sometimes daily. It is invoked by minorities of as few as one or two Senators and for reasons as trivial as a Senator's travel schedule.[67]

Unsurprisingly, many commentators scorn the "60-vote Senate." Or as a senator observed: "It isn't good enough to have the majority. You've got to have 60 votes."[68] Coupled with the chamber's underlying malrepresentation—favoring lightly populated states over populous ones—the forty-one senators who can theoretically halt floor action may often comprise a minority who in turn represent an even smaller minority of citizens.

Attempts to invoke cloture also have increased. For example, in the decade from 1961 to 1971, there were 5.2 cloture votes per Congress; during the narrowly divided 51 to 49 110th Senate (2005–2007), a record-number 139 cloture petitions were filed. The cascade of cloture petitions responded to Minority Leader Mitch McConnell of Kentucky, whose threats to filibuster legislation were aimed at impeding action on the majority's agenda and persuading the majority leader to negotiate with the Republicans. With 59 Democratic senators following the November 2008 elections, Majority Leader Harry Reid, Nev., was in the 111th Congress capable of invoking cloture by keeping his party united and winning the support of one or more moderate GOP senators. (In February 2009, three GOP moderates—Sens. Susan Collins and Olympia Snowe of Maine and Arlen Specter, Pa. [now a "D"]—provided the winning margin to enact President Obama's nearly $800 billion economic stimulus package.)

The norm of one cloture vote per measure has also changed. The modern Senate reached a record of eight cloture votes (all unsuccessful) on a controversial campaign financing measure during the 100th Congress (1987–1989).

These upward trends reflect contemporary senators' willingness to employ their procedural prerogatives to gain concessions, delay legislation and nominations, or accomplish other objectives through greater use of filibusters and threatened filibusters (as well as holds and nonrelevant amendments). Political scientist Barbara Sinclair's research underscores the extent of the contemporary Senate's difficulties with extended debate. In the 1960s, only about 10 percent of major measures considered in the Senate experienced problems with extended debate. By the 1970s and 1980s, around 30 percent of major measures suffered delay, and since the 1990s around half of all major measures have encountered difficulties related to extended debate.[69]

Cloture is also sometimes employed for purposes unrelated to ending a filibuster. The purposes are usually twofold: to expedite the Senate's business by limiting debate and to impose a germaneness, or relevancy, requirement on all amendments. (If invoked, Rule XXII requires all amendments to be germane to the clotured measure.) Majority party leaders sometimes file cloture as soon as the Senate takes up a measure—to prevent the minority party from offering their agenda priorities as nonrelevant amendments to the pending legislation, thus protecting electorally vulnerable majority senators from casting votes on difficult issues. Cloture votes can also be useful to a majority leader as a way to test senatorial sentiment or as evidence for labeling opposition party members as obstructionists.

The procedural and political "hardball" actions of recent years reflect an erosion of the Senate's customary norms of collegiality, civility, and accommodation. The various explanations for this development include the arrival in the Senate of former House members imbued with the aggressive partisanship common to that chamber, heightened demands placed on senators by constituents and lobbyists, intense electoral competition, and the rising costs of campaigns. "Daily priorities [are] shaped more by personal agendas—campaign needs, interest-group demands, personal staff, obligations to meet constituents, and off-the-Hill speeches—and less by the expectations of colleagues and the needs of Senate colleagues," wrote Steven S. Smith. "Pressed by constituencies and lobbyists and more strongly motivated to grab a headline, senators now more routinely and more fully exploit their procedural prerogatives than at any other time in the Senate's history."[70] These developments result in a more individualistic and partisan Senate, which means that compromises and agreements are harder to achieve on weighty substantive and/or procedural issues.

RESOLVING HOUSE-SENATE DIFFERENCES

Before bills can be sent to the president, they must be passed in identical form by both the House and the Senate. Most public laws are approved without direct negotiation between the chambers. They may pass each chamber without any changes (roughly 70 percent), or the House and Senate amend a bill in turn until both chambers agree on the wording (about 20 percent of laws follow this "ping-ponging" route). Only about 10 percent of the measures passed by Congress—usually the most important and controversial—are subject to bicameral reconciliation by conference committees.

Before focusing on conference committees, called "the third house" of Congress, it is useful to review briefly the exchange of amendment procedure (the "ping-pong" approach) as a way to reconcile bicameral disagreements. The amendment exchange procedure will probably occur less frequently in the 111th Congress than in its predecessor because of the larger number of Democratic senators likely to vote for cloture.

The Bicameral Exchange of Amendments

The House and Senate can message—or "ping-pong"—amendments back-and-forth between them until substantive disagreements on a measure are worked out. Under this approach, one chamber may adopt the other house's amendments or further modify those amendments until both houses eventually agree to the same version of the legislation. The ping-pong method is often used on relatively noncontroversial bills and frequently in the closing days of a Congress to save time. "Bills may be sent back and forth on an hourly basis until there is a meeting of the minds, or one side backs down, or the two chambers give up in failure."[71]

Ping-ponging took on heightened importance during the 110th Congress because of the Senate's inability to convene a conference with the House because of threatened filibusters. So the exchange of amendments between the two chambers became the only practical way to resolve interchamber differences on legislation. To convene a conference in the Senate, the majority leader or majority floor manager will usually ask and receive unanimous consent when this request is made: "Mr. or Madam President, I ask unanimous consent that the Senate insist on its amendments [or disagree to the House's amendments to the

Senate's bill], request a conference with the House on the disagreeing votes thereon, and that the Chair be authorized to appoint conferees."

Notice that there are three distinguishable parts to this request: insistence (or disagreement); request for a conference; and authorization for appointing of conferees. If a lawmaker objects to the unanimous consent request, then the majority leader or floor manager must move each step separately, with each motion subject to a filibuster. As former Senate parliamentarian Bob Dove explained: "The three steps are usually bundled into a unanimous consent agreement and done within seconds. But if some senators do not want a conference to occur and if they are determined, they can force three separate cloture votes to close debate and that takes time. It basically stops the whole process of going to conference."[72] If conferences cannot be convened because of delaying tactics—or if time constraints prevent their use—then an important result of ping-ponging is that the principal negotiators on major legislation will be the House and Senate majority leaders. They meet in secret, along with a limited number of other invited lawmakers, to fashion the major bicameral compromises.[73] (The House has little difficulty in convening conferences because of the "majority rule" principle that undergirds its procedural operations.)

Conference Committees

Under each chamber's rules and precedents, conference committees meet to resolve the matters in bicameral dispute. They are not supposed to reconsider provisions already agreed to, and they should not write new law by inserting matter that neither house may have considered. However, parliamentary rules are not self-enforcing, and either chamber can waive or ignore them. It is not unusual for conference reports to contain new matter that neither chamber debated nor amended in committee or on the floor. No wonder conference committees are called the third house of Congress. As Senator Specter stated,

> [Conference committees] are when the work is concluded. Everything else which is done is really of much less significance than the conferences, where the final touches are put on legislation which constitutes the laws of the country.[74]

Selection of Conferees

Conferees usually are named from the committee or committees that reported the legislation. Congressional rules state that the Speaker and the Senate presiding officer select conferees. In fact, that decision typically is made by the relevant committee chairmen and the ranking minority members. House and Senate party leaders are usually involved in naming conferees on major legislation to ensure that they will uphold leadership positions on the legislation.

House and Senate party leaders are sometimes named as conferees—a sign that they want to direct conference negotiations on high-stakes issues important to their party. The House majority leader, for example, often serves on important tax conferences. When the top majority party leaders of either chamber are named as conferees, this signals, as one senator declared, a "majority-party driven" conference.[75]

Each chamber may name as many conferees as it wants, and some conference delegations have become very large. The 1981 omnibus reconciliation conference set the record, with more than 250 House and Senate conferees working in fifty-eight subconferences to resolve more than 300 matters at issue. The ratio of Republicans to Democrats on a conference committee generally reflects the proportion of the two parties in the two chambers.

Today's conference committees represent a sharp departure in size and composition from the pre-1980 era, when conference delegations generally ranged from five to twelve conferees from each house. And before the mid-1970s conferees nearly always were the most senior lawmakers from the committees that reported the legislation. Although seniority still often dictates who the conferees will be, it is not unusual for junior and even first-term members to be conferees. Further, conferees today commonly are chosen from several standing committees and reflect intricate selection arrangements. For example, House conferees may be named to negotiate only certain items in disagreement instead of the entire bill. Multiple referrals and megabills are the driving forces behind these two developments.

Openness and Bargaining

Secret conference meetings were the norm for most of Congress's history. In 1975 both houses adopted rules requiring open meetings unless the conferees from each chamber voted in public to close the sessions. Two years later the House went further, requiring open conference meetings unless the full House agreed to secret sessions. Sometimes the Cable-Satellite Public Affairs Network (C-SPAN) televises conference proceedings.

The open conference is yet another instance of individual–institutional cleavage. Under the watchful eye of lobbyists, conferees fight fiercely for provisions they might have dropped quietly in the interest of bicameral agreement. To be sure, private bargaining sessions still permeate conference negotiations.

Senators and representatives expect certain bills to go to conference and plan their bargaining strategy accordingly. Whether to have a recorded vote on amendments, for example, can influence conference bargaining. In the absence of a recorded vote, amendments are easier to drop in conference. Bargaining techniques in conference cover a range of techniques: from logrolling ("you accept my chamber's position on this provision and I'll accept yours on another provision") to threats to walk out of the negotiations unless the other side compromises. One side may struggle on behalf of a position on which it plans to yield, so the conferees can assure their parent chamber that they put up a good fight but the other side would not relent. Conference committees are where the final version of the law is often written, sometimes making changes or additions to legislation that neither chamber ever reviewed or considered in committee or on the floor.

The Conference Report

A conference ends when its report (the compromise bill) is signed by a majority of the conferees from each chamber. House and Senate staffs then prepare the conference report and the accompanying joint explanatory statement, which summarizes the conferees' recommendations. The House and Senate then vote on the conference report without further amendment. (Senators can filibuster a conference report.) If either chamber rejects the conference report—an infrequent occurrence—a new conference may be called or another bill introduced. Once passed, the compromise bill is sent to the president for approval or disapproval.

CONCLUSION

The philosophical bias of House and Senate rules reflects the character of each institution. The majority rules in the House, whereas individual (often minority) rights are stressed in the Senate. In both chambers, however, members who know the rules and precedents have an advantage over procedural novices in affecting policy outcomes. Senator Byrd, an acknowledged procedural expert in the Senate, understands that passing measures often involves unorthodox processes and procedures (for example, forgoing committee hearings or markups or even floor debate).[76]

In addition to congressional rules, other elements in the lawmaking process include persistence, strategy, timing, compromise, and pure chance. To make public policy requires building majority coalitions at successive stages where pressure groups and other parties can advance their claims. Political, procedural, personal, and policy considerations shape the final outcome. Passing laws, as one former representative said, is like the "weaving of a web, bringing a lot of strands together in a pattern of support which won't have the kind of weak spots which could cause the whole fabric to fall apart."[77]

SUGGESTED READINGS

Binder, Sarah A. *Stalemate: Causes and Consequences of Legislative Gridlock.* Washington, D.C.: Brookings Institution, 2003.

Binder, Sarah A., and Steven S. Smith. *Politics or Principle? Filibustering in the United States Senate.* Washington, D.C.: Brookings Institution, 1997.

Cox, Gary W., and Mathew D. McCubbins. *Setting the Agenda: Responsible Party Government in the U.S. House of Representatives.* New York: Cambridge University Press, 2005.

Evans, Diana. *Greasing the Wheels: Using Pork Barrel Projects to Build Majority Coalitions in Congress.* New York: Cambridge University Press, 2004.

Krehbiel, Keith. *Pivotal Politics: A Theory of U.S. Lawmaking.* Chicago: University of Chicago Press, 1998.

Krutz, Glen. *Omnibus Legislating in the U.S. Congress.* Columbus: Ohio State University Press, 2001.

Longley, Lawrence D., and Walter J. Oleszek. *Bicameral Politics: Conference Committees in Congress.* New Haven: Yale University Press, 1989.

Loomis, Burdett, ed. *Esteemed Colleagues: Civility and Deliberation in the U.S. Senate.* Washington, D.C.: Brookings Institution, 2000.

Oleszek, Walter J. *Congressional Procedures and the Policy Process.* 7th ed. Washington, D.C.: CQ Press, 2007.

Sinclair, Barbara. *Unorthodox Lawmaking: New Legislative Processes in the U.S. Congress.* 3d ed. Washington, D.C.: CQ Press, 2007.

Smith, Steven S. *Call to Order: Floor Politics in the House and Senate.* Washington, D.C.: Brookings Institution, 1989.

*C*ongressional Decision Makir
(Top, from the left): Hou
Appropriations chair David R. Ob
(D-Wis.) consults with the committe
staff director and deputy during mark
of the fiscal 2007 supplemental appr
priations bill. Center right: The Hou
uses an electronic system to record me
bers' floor votes. Members insert plas
cards into voting boxes throughout t
chamber and vote "yea," "nay," or "pr
ent." Members' votes are scrutinized a
rated by hundreds of interest groups
including the League of Conservati
Voters (bottom right). Bottom left a
center left: Senate and House vote tot
are displayed on C-SPAN.

ON AGREEING TO THE
RESOLUTION

H RES   495

	YEA	NAY	PRES	NV
REPUBLICAN	211		8	3
DEMOCRATIC	207	1	1	2
INDEPENDENT	2			
TOTALS	420	1	9	5

TIME REMAINING   0:00

YEA NAY PRES

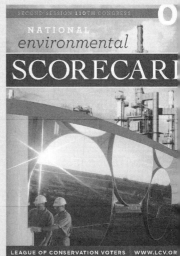

SECOND SESSION 110TH CONGRESS
NATIONAL
environmental
SCORECARI

LEAGUE OF CONSERVATION VOTERS   WWW.LCV.OR

Alito
Confirmation

Y = 58   N = 42

Clinton (D)	N
Coburn (R)	Y
Cochran (R)	Y
Coleman (R)	Y
Collins (R)	Y
Conrad (D)	Y
Cornyn (R)	Y
Craig (R)	Y
Crapo (R)	Y
Dayton (D)	N

YEA 58   NAY 42

Nomination of Samuel A. Alito, Jr.,
of New Jersey, to be an Associate
Justice of the Supreme Court
of the United States

chapter 9

Deliberation in Congress

"I know that everyone is anxiously awaiting the 8:15 time," joked Senate majority leader Harry Reid to a group of unhappy senators waiting on the Senate floor at 8:40 p.m. on a Thursday evening. Only a few could even muster a smile in response.[1] Earlier that day, Reid had announced that senators could tentatively expect a roll-call vote to take place at 8:15 p.m. Nearly half an hour after the vote was expected, it had become clear that Democrats lacked the support needed to advance a critical $410 billion omnibus spending measure. "It appears at this time that we are going to have to continue work on this bill," said Reid, "We would probably be a vote short."[2]

Democratic leaders were thrown off guard by dissent in their party's ranks. With newly enlarged majorities in both House and Senate, Democrats had expected to pass the measure easily.[3] But passing the bill turned out to be a "tough slog."[4] Republicans denounced as wasteful the bill's increased spending—an average boost of 8 percent for domestic programs.[5] In the wake of the controversy, a few centrist Democrats signaled their concern, with Sen. Evan Bayh, D-Ind., publishing an opinion piece in the *Wall Street Journal* that criticized the bill as "bloated" and "business as usual."[6] Sen. Russ Feingold, D-Wis., objected to the bill's $8 billion for legislators' pet projects.[7] Even with these defections, Reid thought that he had won the needed support. Instead, he was blindsided by the opposition of Sen. Robert Menendez, D-N.J., who was "deeply offended" by a few provisions in the 1,132-page measure that would relax some travel and trade restrictions on Cuba.[8] Menendez's opposition was especially unexpected because senators serving in the party leadership—Menendez is chair of the Democratic Senate Campaign Committee—rarely oppose their party on priority issues. "It's been surprising," Reid said of the failure to move the bill.[9]

Reid postponed the vote to buy time for building support. In the interim, he was forced to allow Republicans to offer a series of amendments intended to force Democrats to cast politically painful votes. Sen. David Vitter, R-La., for example, successfully demanded a vote on an amendment to eliminate automatic cost-of-living increases in congressional salaries.[10] Senators of both parties knew these votes would figure in future ads against Democratic candidates. "This is all about developing campaign commercials," said Sen. Mark Begich, D-Alaska.[11] "Democrats effectively used the pay raise issue against several

Republican candidates in past cycles," noted a National Republican Senatorial Committee spokesman, "so I don't think they should be at all surprised if this emerges as an issue in some of their own campaigns."[12]

While debate on amendments went forward, leaders began to round up new support for the bill. "We're working on it," said Majority Whip Richard J. Durbin, "I hope at the end of the day we don't lose [as many as four or five Democrats]."[13] Of the whip team's efforts, Sen. Claire McCaskill, D-Mo., commented, "I think it's fair to say that there's an extraordinary amount of pressure on this particular bill."[14] Treasury Department officials were dispatched to discuss the Cuba trade provisions with Menendez. Having received assurances about the way the administration would interpret the legislative language, Menendez finally announced his support of the bill at a Democratic caucus meeting, to a round of applause.[15]

In the end, the Senate passed the legislation after an additional week of work, and President Obama signed the measure on March 11, 2009. The leadership's difficulties with the measure nevertheless raised questions about the Democratic Congress's ability to pass the Obama administration's ambitious energy and health care proposals. "What does this mean for the Obama agenda?"[16] asked Rep. Louise M. Slaughter, D-N.Y., chair of the House Rules Committee. "We have a lot to accomplish, and people have high expectations," said Rep. Jim McGovern, D-Mass., "We need to get our act together."[17]

This large-scale spending measure (and hundreds more that have a lower profile) required lawmakers to make tough policy choices collectively—after discussion, debate, bargaining, and problem solving. "The Senate requires consensus," remarked Senate leadership staffer Jim Manley, "Senator Reid is not a king. If he had the ability to snap his fingers and make things fall into place, he would."[18] The end product is almost always an imperfect compromise. Indeed, "imperfect" was precisely how President Obama described the omnibus spending bill when he signed it.[19] Legislative assemblies are deliberative bodies, and in the United States this deliberation always takes place in the context of the two Congresses. Individual members confront thousands of choices: how and when to participate, how to decide, how to find allies, and how to explain their actions to constituents back home.

THE POWER TO CHOOSE

All members of Congress have the ability to shape public policy, although some members are far more influential than others. At minimum, every legislator has the right, indeed the obligation, to vote. Legislators must cast their own votes; no colleague or staff aide may do it for them. To exchange their votes or other official acts for money or for any other thing of value is a federal crime. But aside from bribery or corruption there are no legal grounds for challenging legislators' deliberations or decisions. As discussed in Chapter 2, the U.S. Constitution specifies that "for any speech or debate in either House, [members of Congress] shall not be questioned in any other place."

Policymaking in Congress involves far more than casting roll-call votes. Matters that come before Congress for a vote have already been shaped by the participation of members at many prior stages. Some of this work, like members' votes, is a matter of public record: formal meetings, markups, debates, and amending activities. Of equal importance are the less visible informal negotiations that surround nearly every enactment—away from the eyes of reporters and lobbyists. Separating formal and informal modes of participation in his study of members' committee activity, Richard L. Hall found that members' formal and informal activities do not always coincide.[20] Sometimes members use formal actions to signal concern to constituents and other groups, but then do not follow through with the hard informal work necessary to shape the legislation.

A full accounting of lawmakers' performance, then, would embrace not only how members participate in floor and committee deliberations but also how much effort they expend overall. How much attention do they pay to issues? How do they gain expertise? Whom do they look to for information on legislative decisions? How influential are party leaders? How do they hire, deploy, and supervise their staff? Countless such decisions define what it means to be a member of Congress.

TYPES OF DECISIONS

One basic decision facing legislators is how to spend their time and energy while in the nation's capital. Some try to digest the mountains of studies and reports that cross their desks. They "do their homework," in Capitol Hill parlance. Others seem to know or care little about legislative matters. They pursue other duties—communication, outreach, visits with constituents or lobby groups, partisan politics, and fund-raising. Such members may rarely contribute to committee or floor deliberations. Their votes usually follow cues from party colleagues, staff aides, the White House, or interest groups. Some are found in the ranks of the "Obscure Caucus," a list of unnoticed members compiled periodically by *Roll Call*, a Capitol Hill newspaper. "These Members pay strict attention to parochial issues and would much rather attend a hog-calling contest back home than appear on a cable news show. They deliver for their districts and shun any entreaties to become part of the Washington, D.C., culture."[21]

Successful legislators can focus solely on local matters, while avoiding contentious national disputes. Indeed, many voters cannot tell the difference between a prominent national legislator and an effective constituency servant. Still, most legislators claim to prefer legislative tasks. They strive to make time for their legislative duties, regardless of distractions.

Specializing

Within the legislative realm, members may dig deeply in a particular area or range widely across issues and policies. Senators are more apt to be generalists, while representatives tend to cultivate a few specialties. Sen. Jim DeMint,

R-S.C., then head of the House GOP's class of 1998 caucus, explained why members should specialize:

> If you've got twenty things you want to do, see where everything is. You'll find that maybe ten of those are already being worked on by people, and that while you may be supportive in that role, you don't need to carry the ball. But you can find those two or three things that are important to you that no one seems to be taking the lead on. But if you try to play the lead on everything, you'll be wasting your time.[22]

In both houses key policymaking roles are played by those whom Rep. David E. Price, D-N.C., a political scientist, calls *policy entrepreneurs*—those recognized for "stimulating more than . . . responding" to outside political forces on a given issue.[23] Often nearly invisible to the mass of citizens, these legislators are known to specialized publics for their contributions to specific policies—for example, Rep. Ike Skelton, D-Mo., on military readiness; Rep. Earl Blumenauer, D-Ore., on bike trails; Rep. C. W. Bill Young, R-Fla., on bone-marrow transplant programs; and Sen. Tom Harkin, D-Iowa, on policies for the disabled.

Members' policy reach can go beyond their committee assignments—through speeches, floor amendments, caucuses, and task forces, to name a few. When only in his second term, and although not a member of the Armed Services Committee, Rep. Dick Armey, R-Texas (1985–2003), devised an ingenious scheme to employ an outside commission to decide which unneeded military bases should be closed. His proposal smoothed political sensitivities and won bipartisan support for passage in 1988. Such feats are not everyday occurrences, but the fluidity of today's procedures makes even the most junior member a potential policy entrepreneur.

A member's knowledge and perceived expertise on issues is a vital source of legislative influence. As Sen. Edmund S. Muskie, D-Maine (1959–1980), once explained:

> People have all sorts of conspiratorial theories on what constitutes power in the Senate. It has little to do with the size of the state you come from. Or the source of your money. Or committee chairmanships, although that certainly gives you a kind of power. But real power up there comes from doing your work and knowing what you're talking about. Power is the ability to change someone's mind. . . . The most important thing in the Senate is credibility. Credibility! That is power.[24]

Timing of Decisions

Lawmakers do more than specialize in a particular policy field. They are constantly forced to make decisions on issues, many far from their areas of specialization. Timing is key. *When* members make decisions has important consequences for the deliberative process, a point that Richard F. Fenno Jr. elaborates in his work on the "politics of timing."[25]

From a study of a 1981 vote on selling AWACS (airborne warning and control system) reconnaissance planes to Saudi Arabia, Fenno identified three types of decision makers: early deciders, active players, and late deciders.

Early deciders are fervent supporters who want to get out front in the debate. "I'd rather come out early and be part of the fight," said Rep. Peter T. King, R-N.Y., of his ready support for fast-track trade authority.[26] These members are buoyed by friendly lobbyists but ignored by others—because their commitments are known at the outset from declarations, bill sponsorship, or prior voting records.

Active players, in contrast, delay their commitments, inviting bids from various sides of the issue at hand and often gaining leverage over the final language of legislation.

Late deciders delay their decision (or reconsider an earlier commitment) until the very last moment. They forfeit influence over the basic framework of the measure. Chiding colleagues who resisted supporting President George W. Bush's 2001 tax cuts, then GOP whip Don Nickles of Oklahoma (1981–2005) warned, "People that don't support [the budget] won't have very much impact on how it's put together."[27]

But late deciders are eagerly courted by all sides and may gain specific concessions. At the end of 2005, then Senate majority leader Bill Frist, R-Tenn., lacked only one vote to rescue his party's $39.7 billion budget-saving package (S.1932). His targets were two GOP senators who had opposed an earlier version of the bill: Gordon H. Smith of Oregon, incensed that the measure cut Medicaid patients' benefits, and Norm Coleman of Minnesota, worried about cuts of $30 million in subsidies to sugar beet growers, many residing in his home state. House leaders insisted on gaining Medicaid savings through benefits cuts, instead of imposing higher costs for drug companies and other providers. So the deal went to Coleman. "Karl Rove called me and asked me what I wanted," he related. "A few hours later it was out of the bill."[28] Coleman's flip gave Frist the needed 50–50 tie which, with Vice President Dick Cheney as the tie-breaker, sent the measure to the White House. It was a victory for crop subsidies and Medicaid providers, but a loss for poor people needing medical care.

Taking the Lead

Senators and representatives differ widely in the rate at which they introduce and sponsor bills. Some lawmakers are inveterate initiators of bills and resolutions; others shy away from sponsoring measures. A study by Wendy Schiller found that bills in the Senate are most likely to be introduced by senior senators, those who are chairs or ranking members of high-volume committees (such as Commerce), and those who represent large, diverse states.[29]

Senate and House rules do not limit the number of members who can cosponsor bills or resolutions. Thus cosponsorship has become common. Most bills are cosponsored; according to one study, the average Senate bill had 7.2 cosponsors, and the average House bill had 22.2 cosponsors.[30] Authors of measures often circulate a "Dear Colleague" letter detailing the virtues of the bill and soliciting cosponsors to demonstrate broad support and urge committee action. A recent study found that more than 12,000 such letters were sent electronically by House members in 2007—an increase of 238 percent since 2003, and an average of more than 25 letters per member.[31]

Cosponsorship, no less than sponsorship, is politically motivated, as freshman senator Dan Quayle, R-Ind. (1981–1989), understood when he asked the Senate's preeminent liberal, Edward M. Kennedy, D-Mass., to cosponsor his first major bill, the 1982 Job Training Partnership Act. Soliciting Kennedy's cooperation was a daring move for a young conservative embarking on his first subcommittee chairmanship. "The decision to travel the bipartisan route…was his earliest strategic decision," wrote Fenno of Quayle's eventual legislative success. "It caused him a lot of trouble, but he never looked back."[32] Despite right-wing opposition and stonewalling from the Reagan administration, Quayle's decision helped win passage of the job training act. It was his greatest Senate achievement—and a notable entry in his résumé when he was later tapped for the vice presidency by George H.W. Bush.

Occasionally, however, cosponsors are shunned. Introducing his waterway users' fee bill, Sen. Pete V. Domenici, R-N.M., decided against seeking cosponsors for several reasons.[33] First, as ranking Republican on the subcommittee, he could arrange for hearings without the support of cosponsors. In addition, single sponsorship is easier. ("If you've got cosponsors you have to clear every little change with them.") And, finally, if the bill became law, he would get more credit on his own.

Do legislators favor the bills and resolutions they introduce? Normally they do, but as Sportin' Life, the *Porgy and Bess* character, said, "It ain't necessarily so." Members may introduce a measure to stake out jurisdiction for their committee or to pave the way for hearings and deliberations that will air a public problem. Or they may introduce measures they do not personally favor to oblige an executive agency or to placate an important interest group.

Taking Part

As members in any organization, some lawmakers take a passionate interest in what goes on; others pay selective attention to issues; a few seem just to be going through the motions. In his detailed study of three House committees, Richard L. Hall uncovered great variation in members' levels of participation.

Although members' attendance at committee and subcommittee sessions was respectable (about three-quarters of the members showed up for at least part of each session), active participation—taking part in markup debate, offering amendments, and the like—was far less common. Perhaps half a subcommittee's members could be considered players, by a generous counting. The rest were nonplayers. As a subcommittee staffer remarked, "On a good day half of [the members] know what's going on. Most of the time it's only five or six who actually mark a bill up."[34]

Constituency interests, as might be predicted, strongly propel members to participate in committee business. This is true even when the negotiations are informal and out of the public's sight. In formal subcommittee markup sessions, "the public forum has the benefit of allowing members to at once promote—through their votes, arguments, amendments, obstructionism—constituency interests and be seen doing so."[35]

Constituency-driven activity is especially common in the House Agriculture Committee, a panel historically driven by regional and commodity pressures. Given the committee's composition, its membership is more favorable to agriculture programs than the House of Representatives as a whole. Furthermore, only a subset of the committee's members participates on most matters, and those who choose to take part tend to be more biased in favor of the programs under consideration than even the rest of the Agriculture Committee. Members representing constituencies with large numbers of dairy farmers and peanut growers, for example, were most active in influencing policy affecting dairy and peanut interests. Neither the full committee nor floor deliberations counterbalanced the enthusiastic advocacy of the dozen or so lawmakers from districts that produced those commodities. Although participation on Agriculture was the most biased toward members with a constituency stake in the legislation being considered, Hall also found that in debates over job training legislation in another committee, participating members tended to represent areas with higher unemployment rates than those of nonparticipants. In cases where concentrated district benefits were not at stake, Hall found no participatory biases.

Members in formal leadership positions are also more likely to take an active part in committee deliberations. Members often forgo participation because there are so many demands on their time that they must prioritize issues that are important to their constituents. Committee and subcommittee leaders, however, face fewer obstacles to participation because their seniority and authority "places them at the epicenter of the communications network in which most important legislative interactions take place."[36] In other words, holding leadership posts puts members "in the know" and enables them to be major players on legislation even when they do not personally have a significant constituency stake in the outcome.

Participation in House or Senate floor debates is equally varied: members who do not serve on the relevant committees, or who have only peripheral interests in the matter, are tempted to speak simply "for the record." "Congressional debate is typically no better than moderately informed," Gary Mucchiaroni and Paul J. Quirk concluded from their detailed analysis of three major congressional debates. "Legislators frequently assert claims that are inaccurate or misleading, and reassert them after they have been effectively refuted."[37]

The good news about floor debates is that opposing members often—though not always—counter erroneous or distorted arguments. Senate debates, moreover, appear to Mucchiaroni and Quirk to be superior to House debates:

> Senate debates had more frequent and in-depth discussion of the issues, and provided far more information. Senators displayed more knowledge of the issues and policies than their House counterparts, and approached them with greater sophistication.[38]

Senators' participation surely benefits from the chamber's more leisurely debate schedules and their more generous staff assistance. However, certain gadflies might counter that senators are, if anything, less informed than House members about the subjects of their speeches—which are invariably recited from scripts and often concern subjects beyond their committee assignments.

Offering Amendments

Another important way of participating is to offer amendments to bills or resolutions. Amendments propose specific changes in legislative language: they delete or add words or substitute one provision for another. They are a chief means of shaping legislation during committee and floor deliberation. However, amendments are not always intended to enact policy changes. They can instead be used as a tool of obstruction. They can also serve political purposes by putting members on the record on specific issues.

House leaders, who control the floor agenda, regularly employ special rules to limit the amendments that members can offer to particular bills. By so doing, the leaders often can engineer favored policy outcomes. In 2003, for example, Republican leaders wanted to fulfill the Bush administration's $87 billion request for the Iraq war effort, which included $20 billion for Iraqi reconstruction projects. At a time of large federal budget deficits, however, many Republicans and most Democrats worried about the high price tag.[39] The reconstruction expenditures were also unpopular with voters.[40] A Republican member of the Appropriations Committee, Rep. Zach Wamp, R-Tenn, sought to offer an amendment strongly opposed by the administration that would have treated reconstruction projects as a loan that Iraq would have to repay out of its future oil revenues.[41] Such an amendment would undoubtedly have drawn the support of nearly all Democrats and a significant number of Republicans. To prevent this outcome, leaders merged the Iraq reconstruction money and the military funds into a single bill and prohibited any amendment that would separate the two expenditures. Packaging the bill in this way allowed supporters to claim that their vote was merely "support for the troops." The emergency appropriations passed the House 303–125 with near universal support from Republicans and substantial support from Democrats. Had Wamp's amendment been in order, however, the House would very likely have reduced or restricted the reconstruction funds.

In the Senate, given individual senators' prerogatives, amendments are more freely offered and form a central part of floor debate. In a GOP-controlled Senate, with elections looming in 1996, Senator Kennedy won passage of two popular measures by vowing to introduce them as amendments to a variety of floor bills. These were a hike in the minimum wage and a provision that insurance companies could neither drop coverage when people switch jobs nor deny coverage for preexisting medical conditions. Although GOP leaders strongly opposed both measures, they allowed the floor votes to avoid facing repeated embarrassments in an election year.

Amendments can also derail legislation. A 2009 effort to give the District of Columbia a voting seat in the House of Representatives, for example, ran into a serious legislative roadblock when the Senate adopted an amendment by Sen. John Ensign, R-Nev., that would have invalidated the District's restrictive gun control laws.[42] President Bill Clinton's 1993 economic stimulus package similarly came unglued in the Senate under a barrage of hostile amendments. The bill's Democratic managers labored to keep the measure intact in the face of Republican amendments to drop what they claimed were pork projects. When Democrats shut off amendments by a parliamentary maneuver, the Republicans' opposition hardened, and cloture could not be invoked.

Sometimes amendments are offered simply to test the strength of support for a proposal, rather than to immediately alter policy outcomes. During a debate on reauthorizing the National Aeronautics and Space Administration, Rep. Tim Roemer, D-Ind. (1991–2003)—then a junior committee member— introduced an amendment to cancel the costly space station program. Instead of losing by a wide margin (as in previous years), the amendment failed by only a single vote. That narrow margin signaled plunging support for the space station and other "big science" projects.[43]

Some amendments are designed to force members to declare themselves on issues that command public attention. Amendments on abortion funding or balanced budgets are prime examples. Sen. David Vitter's amendment to the 2009 omnibus appropriations bill to end automatic cost-of-living increases in congressional salaries is another example.

Other amendments are poison pills. So-called "killer amendments" are intended to make a bill so unpalatable that if adopted will kill the underlying measure. Senate and House sponsors of campaign finance reform faced opponents who offered what are called non-severability amendments, meaning that the entire act would fall if courts ruled against any portion of the measure. Advocates and opponents alike knew that one or more of the bill's provisions— the soft-money ban, issue ad restrictions, or hard-money limits—might well be struck down by the courts. The authors of the Senate bill, John McCain, R-Ariz., and Russ Feingold, D-Wis., beat back those amendments in close votes. Although killer amendments upset the sponsors and managers of bills, they rarely alter a measure's ultimate fate. Examining seventy-six killer amendments considered in the mid-1990s, John D. Wilkerson concluded that they "rarely, if ever, cause bills to fail.…Most were easily defeated."[44]

Casting Votes

Lawmakers' most visible choices are embodied in the votes they cast. Voting is a central ritual in any legislative body. Members know that their voting records communicate a great deal of information about their policy commitments to their constituents. Reflecting on his vote on the Bush Administration's financial institutions bailout package, then-Rep. Chris Shays, R-Conn., said "This is a legacy vote; these are the votes you have to live with for the rest of your life."[45] Members anticipate that constituents will review their votes at reelection time. Outside groups closely follow members' votes on specific measures and publicize them during election campaigns. Nevertheless, members' own personal judgment will sometimes outweigh political expedience. "I'm willing to give up my seat over this," said Rep. Jim Marshall, D-Ga., a conservative in a Republican-leaning seat, explaining his vote on the 2008 bailout package.[46]

Senators and representatives strive to be recorded on as many floor and committee votes as they can. The average member participates in more than 95 percent of recorded votes on the floor. Members seek to compile a record of diligence to forestall charges of absenteeism by potential opponents. House and Senate leaders make it easier for members to fulfill high expectations by avoiding votes on Mondays and Fridays, stacking votes back to back in midweek, and promising no votes several evenings each week.[47]

If members cannot vote in person, they can still be recorded on an issue. They may announce their views in floor statements or in press releases. A member who wishes to be recorded on an issue but cannot be present for the roll-call vote may also ask another member who plans to vote on the other side for a "pair" arrangement in which both announce their positions in the *Congressional Record* but neither casts a vote. Members often grant such requests as a courtesy to their colleagues. Pairing is a voluntary arrangement that allows members to go on record without voting or affecting the final tabulation.

What Do Votes Mean?

Like other elements in the legislative process, votes are open to multiple interpretations. A vote may not mean what it appears to, at first glance. Therefore, one must be cautious in analyzing legislative votes.

House and Senate floor votes do not perfectly register members' views. Members sometimes vote against a bill that they prefer to the status quo because they hope that a better bill on the matter might emerge later. Members know that weak reform can sap political will for more comprehensive action. Politicians will also refuse to accept a compromise when they can force a confrontation that will sharpen the differences between the parties. On some occasions, members prefer to keep the issue alive rather than to pass a bill. As John B. Gilmour writes, "advocates often anticipate that having the party differences clearly displayed will help them win in the next election, after which they will be able to enact an unadulterated form of the bill."[48] Killing a modest measure may lead to action on a more wide-ranging proposal later.

Members may also vote for a bill that they do not approve of because they fear that if they fail to support it, the end result will be something even worse. In 2003, a number of conservative Republicans voted for a new federal program providing prescription drug coverage for elderly Americans because they believed it was the best bill they could get. "I don't think we'll write a better bill if we defeat this," said conservative senator Jon Kyl, R-Ariz., explaining why he did not push for a less expensive, more targeted program. "I don't think the no-action alternative is realistic. I don't think that the alternative of helping only those who need the help is likely to occur. There's too much momentum for a universal benefit for that to be the situation. Given the close nature of the House and Senate we may have the best that we can do under the circumstances with this bill."[49] Members will often go along with legislation because on the whole they deem the bill a step forward, even though they dislike specific portions.

In some cases recorded votes are wholly misleading. Given the multiplicity of votes—procedural as well as substantive—on many measures, lawmakers can come out on more than one side of an issue, or at least appear to do so. For instance, members may vote to authorize a program and then against funding it. Or they may vote against final passage of a bill but for a substitute version. This tactic assures the bill's backers that the lawmaker favors the concept, while pleasing voters who oppose the bill. Such voting patterns may reflect either a deliberate attempt to obscure one's position or a thoughtful response to complex questions. As in so many aspects of human behavior, lawmakers' motivations can be judged fully only in light of specific cases.

Members can also take advantage of "free votes" when their own individual vote will not affect the final outcome. Some members delay voting until the outcome of the vote is already assured. During the 1990 debate on a constitutional amendment to prohibit flag burning, David King and Richard Zeckhauser observed "strategic waiting" on the part of members.[50] Democratic members were cross-pressured on the issue—Democratic leaders opposed the anti-flag-burning amendment, but it was very popular with constituents. Before it was clear that the amendment was going to fail, only 28 percent of the voting Democrats supported the amendment. Once enough votes had been cast to defeat the amendment, 73 percent of the remaining Democrats voted in favor of it. After the amendment had failed, members could take the popular position without any legislative consequences. Opportunities for insincere votes proliferate in the U.S. system of the separation of powers. Members can deliberately vote for measures that they believe will fail in the other chamber of Congress or be vetoed by the president. They can support popular measures that they expect the courts to strike down as unconstitutional.

Lawmakers' voting rationales are sometimes hard to explain to outsiders. In some cases members face a dilemma: Either vote their convictions and deal with the consequences, or swallow their misgivings and vote for appearance's sake. Rep. Mark Sanford, R-S.C. (1995–2001), chose the former course in 1998, when he joined fourteen other Republicans in voting against a popular bill authorizing U.S. sanctions against nations that persecute religious minorities—an appealing idea but fraught with problems. "This was an awfully awkward vote, and I know I'll hear from the folks back home," he explained. "But the devil was in the details."[51]

More often lawmakers decide to go with the crowd. Regarding a highly appealing constitutional amendment requiring a balanced budget, Sen. Ernest F. Hollings, D-S.C. (1967–2005), admitted that he planned to vote for it because he got "tired of explaining" its deficiencies. It was easier "just to say put it in."[52] Such was the case in the Homeland Security Act of 2002—a massive, deeply flawed bill that threw some 180,000 federal workers into a new executive department. Members went along, despite misgivings, because they feared being labeled as opposing homeland security.

Scholars and journalists often mistakenly treat votes as if they were unambiguous indicators of legislators' views. Lobbyists, too, are prone to assess lawmakers on the basis of floor votes. Many groups construct voting indexes that label legislators as "friendly" or "unfriendly." Citizens should be cautioned to examine such indexes closely. How many votes does the index comprise? Are they a fair sample of the group's concerns? Does the index embody a partisan or ideological agenda, hidden or otherwise? The bottom line is: Beware of an interest group's voting scorecards, even if you agree with its policy leanings.

DETERMINANTS OF VOTING

Votes, particularly on single issues, should be examined, interpreted, and categorized with care. Several factors shape congressional voting: party affiliation, ideological leanings, constituents' views, and presidential leadership.

Party and Voting

Party affiliation is the strongest single correlate of members' voting decisions. In a typical year from half to two-thirds of all floor votes could be called party unity votes, defined as votes in which a majority of voting Republicans oppose a majority of voting Democrats. In the 110th Congress (2007–2008), 58 percent of all House votes and 57 percent of Senate votes fell into this category. Figure 9-1 depicts House and Senate party unity votes from 1970 through 2008. Party voting is far more prevalent today than in the 1970s and early 1980s.[53] Indeed, contemporary levels of party voting recall the militant parties of the late nineteenth century.

Party unity scores can be calculated for individual members—the percentage of party unity votes in which individual members voted in agreement with the majority of their party colleagues. According to these scores, the average legislator now toes the party line on nearly nine out of ten party unity votes.[54] Aggregate party unity scores for Democrats and Republicans from 1970 through 2008 are displayed in Figure 9-2. Party voting levels in both houses have risen by about 20 percent since the 1970s.[55]

Party cohesion stems from a number of roots. Members of a political party vote similarly because they are elected by many of the same sorts of constituencies and organized interests throughout the country. Party members also vote together because of their shared ideological commitments. Changes in the ideological composition and the constituency base of the two congressional parties have contributed to the increased levels of partisanship in the contemporary Congress. Each of these sources of party unity—constituency and ideology—will be discussed below. However, it is important to note that congressional party unity also has a source in explicitly *partisan* motives, meaning party members' shared political interests in helping their party win elections and control Congress.[56] These interests bring fellow partisans together despite the diversity of their policy preferences. Indeed, even when party conflict in Congress was at a low ebb in the late 1960s and early 1970s, the parties still successfully organized

FIGURE 9-1   Party Unity Votes in Congress, 1970–2008

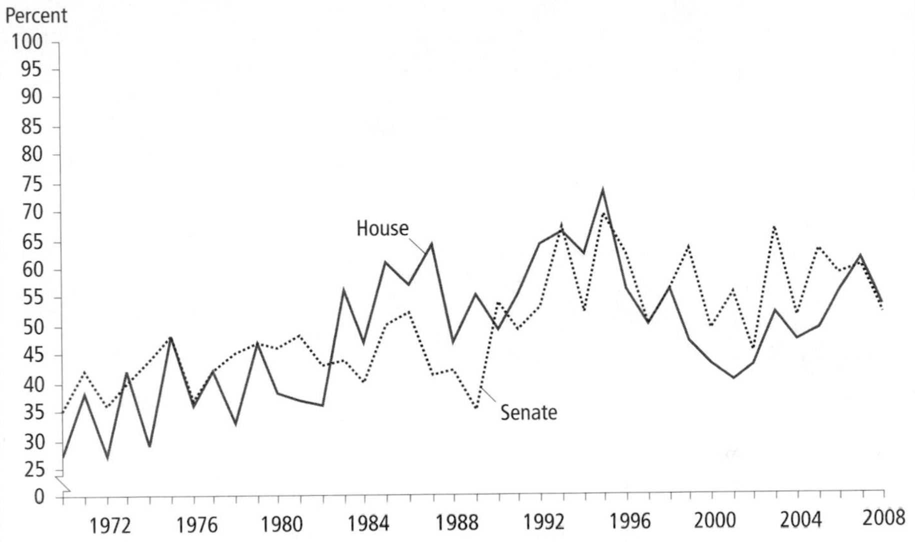

Percent

```
100
 95
 90
 85
 80
 75
 70
 65                                    House
 60
 55
 50
 45
 40
 35                                                  Senate
 30
 25
  0
     1972    1976    1980    1984    1988    1992    1996    2000    2004    2008
```

Source: "Party Unity History," CQ Weekly, January 1, 2007, 39; "Frequency of Party Unity Votes Drops," CQ Weekly, December 15, 2008, 3334.

Note: Party unity votes are defined as the percentage of all House and Senate votes in which a majority of Democrats opposed a majority of Republicans

the committees and leadership of Congress, and party affiliation remained the strongest single predictor of members' voting behavior.

Members of Congress cooperate with their fellow partisans in part because their personal fate as politicians is bound up with their party's public image. Members know that they do not win or lose elections solely as individual legislators. Voters' attitudes about the national parties affect their choices in particular congressional elections.[57] As a result, members take into account how their individual actions will affect public perceptions of their party as a whole. As one congressman explained to political scientist Randall Ripley, "We need a party record—and principles—as well as an individual record. The decline of the party image between 1962 and 1964 cost me 6 percent at the polls."[58]

Members also care about the collective image of their party because they want their party to command a congressional majority. Members gain power personally when their party is in the majority. Members of the majority party chair all committees and subcommittees, and majority leaders set the floor agenda. It is easier for members to advance their personal policy initiatives when they are in the majority.

Members concerned with winning elections and wielding influence will therefore pay attention to their party's collective image. To foster positive public impressions of their party, fellow partisans work to find common ground. They collaborate

FIGURE 9-2   **Levels of Party Voting in Congress, 1970–2008**

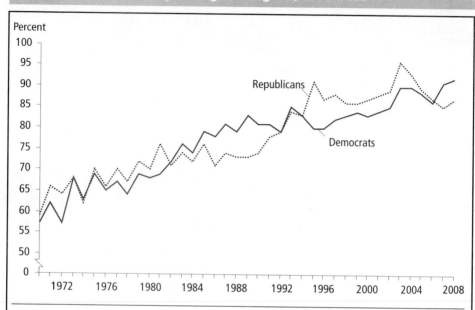

Sources: Derived from annual CQ voting studies reported in *CQ Weekly,* December 15, 2008, 3337.

Note: The graph shows the percentage of times the average Republican or Democrat in Congress voted with his party majority in partisan votes for the years listed. These composite party unity scores are based on votes that split the parties in the House and Senate—a majority of voting Republicans opposing a majority of voting Democrats. The scores have been recomputed to correct for absences.

in efforts to construct an appealing policy agenda and then cooperate in promoting it. They also exploit opportunities to call into question the other party's competence and integrity. Although the parties unquestionably face some collective action problems and are not always successful in their efforts to develop a consensus agenda, these electoral and power motives remain a potent source of party unity.

Common political interests nurture bonds of trust and communication among fellow partisans. To deepen these bonds, the congressional parties also sponsor organizations and activities designed to reinforce party loyalty and shared purpose. The parties hold regular lunches, conferences, and retreats for members. In addition, the socialization of new members largely takes place in partisan settings. Fewer friendships cross party lines than they used to. Former senator John Breaux, a habitual cross-party bargainer, blames social patterns for some of today's partisan cleavages.

> If the only knowledge you have of "the other side of the aisle" is what you have read in an attack press release written by the party operatives, you wouldn't want to talk to them, and you certainly wouldn't want to be friends.[59]

Party leaders regularly appeal to their members' common partisan interests in order to rally their troops behind the party agenda. In the lead-up to the 2008 congressional elections, for example, Minority Leader John Boehner, R-Ohio, told his caucus behind closed doors that "Americans won't vote for Republicans until they fix their 'brand' and convince voters they will fix Washington."[60] Democrats suffered similar anxieties during their years in the congressional minority. In 2005, for example, Democratic leaders invited in a variety of consultants to help them figure out how to reposition their party image.[61] One of the leaders of this effort, Sen. Byron Dorgan, D-N.D., expressed concern that the Democratic Party had failed to communicate effectively its legislative goals to the public. Contrasting his party's image with the clearer Republican brand, Dorgan said, "I can tell you what the Republicans stand for in eight words: family values, strong defense, lower taxes and less government."[62] Reflecting on these partisan motives, political scientists Gary W. Cox and Mathew D. McCubbins write, "Modern political parties facing mass electorates, similar to corporations facing mass markets, have a strong incentive to fashion and maintain a brand name."[63]

Because of the common political interests they share with fellow partisans, members are predisposed to support their party. Political scientists who have studied members' voting decisions have found that members decide mainly by consulting the views of their political party colleagues.[64] The typical member of Congress "feel[s] duty bound to ascertain the views of the party leaders and [to] go along in the absence of contrary inclinations."[65] In other words, members cooperate with their parties as a default position. They go along unless they have a reason to defect. Wavering members who have reservations about the party's position may be subject to considerable pressure from party leaders. Rep. Mark Souder, R-Ind., described the exhortations of House Speaker Newt Gingrich, R-Ga. (1995–1999), and his lieutenants during the GOP's first year in power:

> They pull us into a room before almost every vote and yell at us.... They say, "This is a test of our ability to govern," or "This is a gut check," or "I got you here and you hired me as your coach to get you through, but if you want to change coaches, go ahead."[66]

Party leaders can rely on a high level of reflexive support from fellow partisans, especially on procedural matters. Political scientists have repeatedly shown that members are more likely to vote with their parties on procedural motions than directly on the substance of legislation.[67] Indeed, members often support their party leaders on procedural matters related to a bill, even when they don't intend to support the bill on final passage. One recent study comparing how House members voted on closed rules (which force the House to take an up-or-down vote on a bill with no opportunity for amendment) with their votes on final passage of the bills governed by those closed rules found dramatic partisanship on procedural matters, regardless of the members' votes on final passage.[68] Majority party members opposing the legislation nevertheless supported their leaders on the relevant procedural rule fully 88.4 percent of the time; meanwhile, minority party members who supported the bill on final passage were almost never willing to support the rule. Procedural votes are similarly partisan in the Senate.[69] Sen. Bob Packwood (1969–1995) (R-Ore.) once observed, "[T]his is a procedural vote, and in the Senate we traditionally stick with the leadership on such votes."[70]

Because leaders find it easier to muster support if a vote is defined in procedural terms, they use procedural tactics to engineer substantive policy outcomes. David W. Rohde calls this "process partisanship," which means "the degree to which each institution is structured or operates in a partisan fashion."[71] House leaders have considerable ability to exploit procedures to strengthen party unity. Through their control of key committees, scheduling powers, and the use of special rules, majority party leaders arrange for votes they are likely to win and avoid those they are apt to lose. Senate leaders have fewer procedural tools than House leaders, but they can use their right to be recognized first on the floor to regulate the timing, order, and content of debates to partisan advantage.

Ideology and Voting

Just as lawmakers are committed partisans, most of them also harbor broad ideological views on the proper role and purpose of government.[72] Indeed, many members of Congress entered politics through various ideological causes. The civil rights, environmental, and antiwar movements spurred political activism for many members on the left of the ideological spectrum. Many members on the right entered politics because of their "small-government" views or traditionalist social values. Long before they take their first oath of office, members bring ideological loyalties that inspire voting decisions throughout their political careers.

Both political parties encompass ideological diversity. The Republican Party, for example, embraces both economically conservative voters—educated, higher-income cohorts who are often associated with business—along with less-educated, lower- or middle-income people—called "Sam's Club" Republicans by one commentator—who are drawn to the party's traditional social values and its hard line on crime. These two viewpoints are not always in perfect harmony. Indeed, the Republican losses of Congress in 2006 and the White House in 2008 sparked earnest internal party debate about how to balance the party's ideological wings. Conservative strategist David Frum, for example, recommended that the party reach out more aggressively to highly educated voters by adopting an approach that is "less overtly religious and less polarizing on social issues."[73] Others urged the party to renew its ties to its core conservative voters. Regardless of their views on such debates, Republican Party leaders in Congress must accommodate both the party's social-conservative and economically conservative business wings. Republican Conference Chair Mike Pence, R-Ind., says that he seeks compromise positions that will be broadly acceptable to Republicans: "The journey to the middle starts from both ends of the spectrum."[74]

The Democratic Party also embraces ideological variety. It includes across-the-board liberals who are committed to a vigorous government redressing of economic grievances, to tolerant stances on social and lifestyle issues, and to international treaties and institutions guiding foreign policy. The party also includes moderates who hold conservative views on contentious social or foreign policy issues. Recent elections have somewhat enlarged the ranks of these moderate members, as centrist Democrats have captured a number of seats formerly held by GOP moderates in swing states and districts. The party's diversity reflects its voters, who range from union members—who are concerned with economic issues but unsupportive of liberalism on social causes—to the "creative-class" professionals in university towns and urban enclaves who are far more libertarian on social issues.[75] Free-trade pacts also tend to split these groups: Union members fear losing jobs to low-wage foreign labor, while educated professionals tend to be more open toward globalization. Democratic leaders have to navigate these ideological divisions, often by avoiding issues that fracture the party. Reflecting on the few votes that took place on social issues in the 110th Congress, moderate Rep. Jason Altmire, D-Pa., said, "The reason, in my opinion, they didn't have those votes is because they wouldn't have won them."[76]

When political scientists began seriously to analyze congressional roll-call voting in the 1950s, ideological diversity within each of the two parties was far greater than it is today. Conservatives and liberals had a meaningful presence in both legislative parties. Although members often voted along party lines, at other times they would unite across parties in recognizable ideological coalitions. Frequently, Republicans and southern Democrats would cooperate in a voting pattern known as the conservative coalition.[77] Historically, this coalition was stronger in the Senate than in the House, but its success rate was impressive in both chambers during the 1939–1965 period—no matter which party controlled the White House or Capitol Hill.

Since the 1960s, the two parties have sorted themselves out along ideological lines, with conservatives largely in the Republican Party and liberals almost exclusively in the Democratic Party. As a consequence, the cross-party conservative coalition surfaces so rarely these days that the respected *CQ Weekly* has stopped scoring it.[78] Bipartisan conservatism fell victim to the increasing ideological consistency of both political parties. "Democrats are perched on the left, Republicans on the right, in both the House and the Senate as the ideological centers of the two parties have moved markedly apart," writes Sarah A. Binder.[79]

The party polarization of the contemporary Congress—in which partisanship and ideology are closely intertwined—can be shown spatially on a left-right (liberal to conservative) continuum. Using the congressional roll-call voting record, political scientists Keith T. Poole and Howard Rosenthal have devised a scaling methodology to generate ideological scores for all members of Congress.[80] Their data show marked divergence between the parties in recent years.

FIGURE 9-3 Ideological Divisions in Congress and the Public

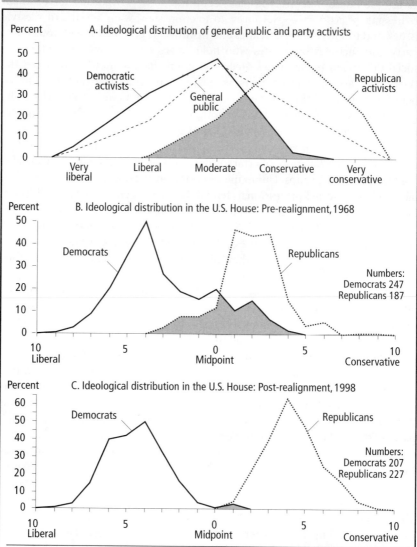

A. Ideological distribution of general public and party activists

B. Ideological distribution in the U.S. House: Pre-realignment, 1968

Numbers:
Democrats 247
Republicans 187

C. Ideological distribution in the U.S. House: Post-realignment, 1998

Numbers:
Democrats 207
Republicans 227

Sources: Panel A: Washington Post/ABC News survey, Washington Post, August 11, 1996, M8 and August 25, 1996, M4. Panels B and C: Adapted from Sean M. Theriault, "The Case of the Vanishing Moderates: Party Polarization in the Modern Congress" (paper presented at the Western Political Science Association, Denver, Colorado), March 2003, Fig. 1. These data are derived from Keith T. Poole and Howard Rosenthal's DW-NOMINATE ideology scores. See Keith T. Poole and Howard Rosenthal, Congress: A Political-Economic History of Roll-Call Voting (New York: Oxford University Press, 1997). Scores for adjacent years (1969–1970 and 1999–2000) yield virtually identical results. See Morris P. Fiorina et al., Culture War? The Myth of a Polarized America, 2d ed. (New York: Pearson Longman, 2006), Fig. 2.2.

Figure 9-3 displays the distribution of ideological preferences for Republicans and Democrats among activists, the general public, and in Congress. When voters are asked to locate themselves on the ideological spectrum, the result roughly follows a normal bell-shaped curve. As shown in Panel A, citizens are bunched together around the middle of the ideological spectrum, with relatively few respondents identifying themselves as very liberal or very conservative.[81] The same centrist pattern appears when voters are asked to position themselves on specific policy issues, even on hot-button topics like taxes and abortion. In contrast, political activists are more likely to identify as either liberal or conservative. The surveys of delegates to the national presidential nominating conventions displayed in Panel A of Figure 9-3 reveal Republican and Democratic activists clustering to the left or right of the median, with far less overlap between the two parties at the elite level than exists in the mass public.

In 1968 the ideological divisions in the House of Representatives (displayed also in Panel B in Figure 9-3) looked similar to those of the party elites. Democrats appeared in almost every ideological niche, from far left to far right; Republicans were more tightly clustered on the right, but a number spilled over to the liberal side of the scale.[82] Political moderates—members at or near the midpoint between the parties—constituted a substantial bloc.

The contemporary Congress (represented by Panel C), however, is almost completely polarized along party lines. Only a handful of members fall at the midpoint; not a single Republican falls on the liberal side of the scale, and only a few Democrats stray into the conservative category. (Panels B and C were compiled from the Poole-Rosenthal data by scholar Sean M. Theriault.)

In today's Congress, members' party affiliation and ideological views overlap almost perfectly. (These figures are for the House; patterns in the Senate are similar though somewhat less dramatic.) This polarization, and the resulting collapse of the middle, has produced clear ideological battle lines between the parties. Although partisan rigidity gets a bad rap from commentators, one must consider how closely political convictions are linked to partisanship in the minds of lawmakers and their activist supporters. "If you can't find common ground, that doesn't mean you're partisan," Speaker Pelosi explained. "It just means you believe different things." Of her Republican foes—often blamed for obstructing her party's proposals—the Speaker noted that, "They vote the way they believe.... I think that they vote with more integrity than they get credit for."[83]

The proportion of political moderates—conservative Democrats or liberal Republicans—hovered at about 30 percent in the 1960s and 1970s. Fewer than one in ten of today's lawmakers fall into this centrist category.[84] Conservative Democrats, the larger of the two centrist groupings, once represented a third of their party's members; today they could caucus in a small cloakroom. In the 110th Congress (2007–2008), they represented at most 8 to 10 percent of either the Senate or the House's members. Even rarer were moderate to liberal Republicans, who accounted for no more than 2 percent of all House GOP members and no more than 6 percent of senators.[85]

This "incredible shrinking middle" (former Sen. Breaux's term) on Capitol Hill, as political scientist Binder explains, "seems to substantially hamper the ability of Congress and the president to reach agreement on issues before them."[86]

Constituency and Voting

Constituency context is another powerful influence on members' vote choices. Constituencies control lawmakers' choices in two ways. First, people usually elect representatives whose views mirror their own. In this sense, representatives vote their constituency because they are simply transplanted locals. Second, members listen to constituents because it is in their electoral interest to do so. Representatives feel great electoral pressure to respond to the dominant political interests and opinions in their constituencies.

Constituency context can either reinforce or undermine party unity in Congress. For much of the twentieth century, it was not unusual for conservative-leaning states to elect Democrats and for liberal-leaning states to elect Republicans. During that period, constituency influence often led members to buck their party. But since the 1960s constituencies have gradually sorted themselves out according to ideological and policy preferences. In the current era, constituency pressure tends to bolster party unity.

Relatively few Democrats in the 111th Congress represent conservative districts or states. In 1960, all senators from the South were Democrats, and they constituted a large conservative bloc who often resisted Democratic Party leaders and cooperated across party lines with Republicans. But in the current Congress, there are only seven southern Democrats in the Senate. Republicans hold 68 percent of all southern Senate seats and 59 percent of all southern House seats. By the same token, many areas once represented by GOP liberals have been captured by Democrats. New England, an area of the country that was once a moderate Republican stronghold, now elects Democrats almost exclusively. The decline of conservative Democrats and moderate Republicans underlies much of the ideological cohesion within, and the chasm between, today's Capitol Hill parties.[87]

Partisans in the contemporary Congress vote together in great part because they reflect the same kinds of states and districts. Republicans tend to represent rural areas and outer suburbs. Democrats tend to represent urban areas, inner-ring suburbs, and majority-minority districts.[88]

The few remaining party mavericks in today's Congress tend to come from parts of the country where their party generally does not do well electorally. Democratic mavericks tend to be from nonminority southern or midwestern areas. The Senate Democrat most likely to defect from the Democratic Party's position in 2008 was Louisiana's Sen. Mary Landrieu, who opposed her party on 31 percent of party unity votes.[89] Similarly, the most independent Republicans are those representing northeastern and mid-Atlantic states. In 2008, for example, Maine's two Republican senators, Susan Collins and Olympia Snowe, opposed their party on 51 and 54 percent of party unity votes, respectively. In his last year in the Republican Party, Sen. Arlen Specter also opposed his party on 38 percent of such votes. Party leaders acknowledge their members' need to reflect constituency opinion. Indeed, then-House Democratic Caucus chair Rahm Emanuel of Illinois (now President Obama's chief of staff) advised his vulnerable freshman class of 2006 to "vote more for their districts and less for their party."[90]

Constituency affects congressional decision making as politicians take both attentive and inattentive publics into account. Political scientist R. Douglas Arnold tracks how both groups can influence members' electoral calculations.[91] Attentive publics are those citizens who are aware of issues facing Congress and hold decided opinions about what Congress should do. It is thus relatively easy for politicians to consider their views. A politician's natural instinct is to yield to the strongly voiced preferences of an attentive public, unless the issue in question mobilizes two equally vociferous but opposing interests. Especially feared are single-interest groups that threaten to withhold electoral support if their preferences—for example, on abortion or gun control—are ignored.

Inattentive publics are those who lack extensive knowledge or firm preferences about a specific issue. Frankly, this describes most people most of the time. People pay attention to only a small fraction of the issues before Congress. Yet a reelection-minded legislator dare not ignore those who seem indifferent to an issue. "Latent or unfocused opinions," Arnold cautions, "can quickly be transformed into intense and very real opinions with enormous political repercussions. Inattentiveness and lack of information today should not be confused with indifference tomorrow."[92] Legislators are well advised to approach even the most minor choices with this question in mind: Will my decision be defensible if it were to appear on the front pages of major newspapers in my state or district?

Calculating the electoral consequences of a lawmaker's multitude of daily decisions is no easy task. Arnold summarizes the components of such calculations:

> To reach a decision, then, a legislator needs to (1) identify all the attentive and inattentive publics who might care about a policy issue, (2) estimate the direction and intensity of their preferences and potential preferences, (3) estimate the probability that the potential preferences will be transformed into real preferences, (4) weight all these preferences according to the size of the various attentive and inattentive publics, and (5) give special weight to the preferences of the legislator's consistent supporters.[93]

Fortunately, lawmakers need not repeat these calculations every time they face a choice. Most issues have been around for some time. The preferences of attentive and even inattentive publics are fairly well known. Moreover, Congress is well structured to amass and assess information about individual and group preferences. And prominent officials—party leaders and acknowledged policy experts, for example—can often legitimize members' choices and give them cover in explaining those choices to voters.

FIGURE 9-4   **Presidential Success History, 1953–2008**

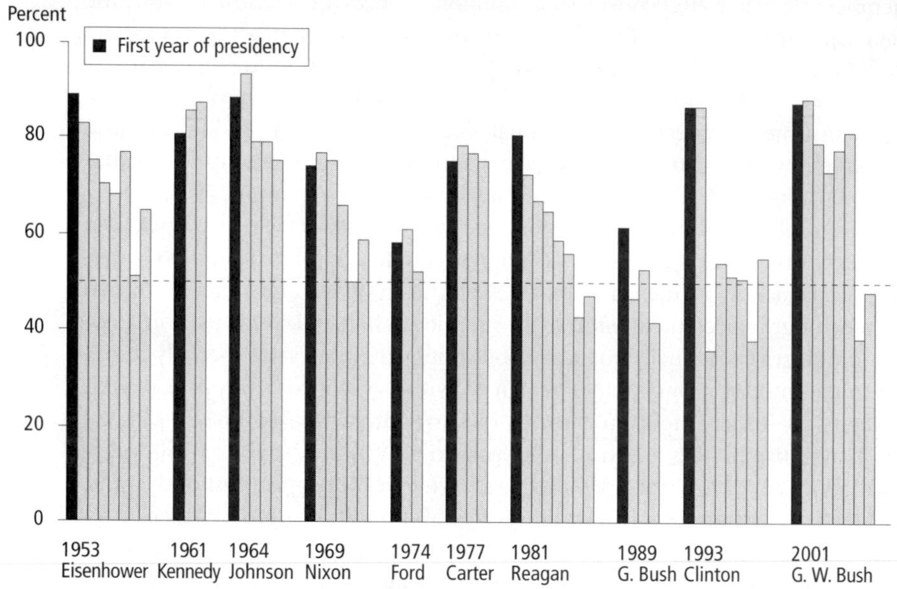

Source: CQ Weekly, December 15, 2008, 3323.

Note: Presidential success is defined as the percentage of the times the president won his way on roll-call votes on which he had taken a clear position.

The Presidency and Voting

Although Congress often pursues an independent course and members differ in their feelings toward the occupant of the White House, presidents can persuade members to support their agendas. Figure 9-4 depicts the percentage of the time presidents—from Dwight D. Eisenhower to George W. Bush—have prevailed in congressional roll-call votes on which they announced a position. Presidents take positions on a wide range of issues, from the momentous (tax cuts and the Iraq war, in Bush's case) to large numbers of routine and noncontroversial matters (most Senate confirmations of executive nominations, for example).[94]

President George W. Bush won 81 percent of the roll-call votes on which he took a position over his first six years in office. This was the best success record since President Lyndon B. Johnson's remarkable victories during 1964–1965.[95] Indeed, Bush's success rates remained high through his sixth year in office (2006), even though the public's assessment of his performance tumbled.[96] However, congressional support for Bush's agenda collapsed when Democrats took control of Congress. In 2007, Bush prevailed on only 38 percent of roll-call votes on which he took a position, the second worst record for a president in the modern era. His success rate improved in 2008—but only to 48 percent, still an exceedingly low level of support by historical standards.

The congressional reaction to Bush's presidential leadership reflected a basic political reality: Presidents do far better with their own partisans than with those of the opposition party. Members of the president's party feel obliged to lend their support whenever they can. The party ratio that presidents confront in Congress is the single most important determinant of success or failure. "We don't live in a parliamentary system," observed Vermont's Sen. James M. Jeffords (1989–2007), when in 2001 he left the Republican Party, "but it is only natural to expect that people such as myself, who have been honored with positions of leadership, will largely support the president's agenda."[97] In 2008 House Republicans supported President Bush 64 percent of the time, and Senate Republicans 70 percent of the time. For Democrats, the figures were 15 percent for House members and 34 percent for senators.[98] (The disparity between the two chambers might seem odd, but is explained by the Senate's many votes on the president's relatively noncontroversial executive branch nominees.)

By the same token, party control of Congress dramatically affects presidential success rates. As long as their party controls Congress, presidents win at least three of every four votes on which they take a position; when the government is divided, presidents fall well below that level. In his first two years in office, with Democrats controlling both chambers, President Bill Clinton prevailed on 86.4 percent of all roll-call votes. After the GOP took over Congress in 1995, Clinton's success rates on Capitol Hill plummeted to its modern-day low of 36 percent.[99]

A second important pattern emerges out of Figure 9-4: Presidents tend to lose congressional support as their administrations age. Presidents' best years in dealing with Congress are usually their first. A downward trend is evident for almost all modern presidents, though it was less pronounced for Clinton, whose congressional support settled at a relatively steady low level after the Republican takeover of Congress. The pattern of declining support over time was also evident over George W. Bush's first six years in office, even though Republicans maintained control of Congress throughout that period.

LEGISLATIVE BARGAINING

Whatever their sources of influence, individual legislators in the end have only a single vote on any given bill or, more typically, on an amendment. At that moment, the vote is reduced to a "yea" or "nay" question, with no hedging or nuance allowed. Legislators have to decide how to cast these binary votes on a bewildering array of issues. They rarely have adequate—or even much—information on any particular bill or amendment. Legislators must weigh their goals—which often may conflict—and process their limited information in a relatively short period of time to arrive at a decision.[100]

Such a state of affairs—disparate goals and widely scattered influence—is hazardous. Stalemate is a constant threat. The "collective action problem" is how political scientists refer to the challenge of merging individual goals into group achievements. To overcome this predicament, members have to resort to politicking; that is, they must trade off goals and resources to get results. No wonder, then, that Congress is "an influence system in which bargain and exchange predominate."[101]

Implicit and Explicit Bargaining

Bargaining is a general term that refers to several related types of behavior. It describes, generally, the process by which two or more parties define the terms of a mutually beneficial exchange. Such processes may be implicit or explicit.

Implicit Bargaining. Implicit bargaining occurs when legislators take actions designed to elicit certain reactions from others, even though no negotiation has taken place. For example, legislators often introduce bills or sponsor hearings not because they expect the measure to pass but to prod someone else—an executive branch official, or a committee chairman with broader jurisdiction on the question—to take action on the problem. Or a bill's managers may accept a controversial amendment knowing full well that the objectionable provision will be dropped in the other chamber or in conference. These are examples of the so-called law of anticipated reactions.[102]

Another type of implicit bargaining occurs when legislators seek out or accept the judgments of colleagues with expertise on a given matter, expecting that the situation will be reversed in the future. Exchanges of voting cues are endemic in both chambers. What is being traded is information. The exchange not only saves the recipient the time and trouble of mastering the subject matter, but it can also provide credible cover in defending the vote. A number of moderate House Republicans took cues from Sherwood Boehlert of New York (1983–2007) on environmental issues. "I pay attention to how Sherry votes, and think other people do as well," said Connecticut's then-Rep. Christopher Shays (1987–2009). "He would not be in the mainstream of the Republican Party, but I think he's in the mainstream of American politics when it comes to the environment."[103] Similarly, Sen. John H. Chafee, R-R.I. (1977–1999)—the Senate's most liberal Republican—served as cue-giver for his younger friend, Vermont senator Jeffords, who said:

> I remember that if I ever had a question on how to vote or if I came in at the last minute and did not know what the issue was—I hate to admit that—I would first look to see how John voted. I knew, if nothing else, that if I voted as he did, I would probably not get in trouble.[104]

Exchanging cues is a key element in John W. Kingdon's model of representatives' decisions, derived from interviews with members immediately after their votes on specific issues.[105]

Legislators have little difficulty making up their minds when they receive no conflicting cues from party leaders, respected fellow members, constituents, or key interest groups. If all the actors in their field of vision concur, members operate in a consensus mode of decision making. Fellow members emerge in Kingdon's study as the most influential cue-givers, with constituencies ranking second. As one lawmaker observed:

I think that the other members are very influential, and we recognize it. And why are they influential? I think because they have exercised good judgment, have expertise in the area, and know what they are talking about.[106]

When members deviate from a consensus stance among their cue-givers, it is usually to follow their own conscience or their constituencies. Adding up these short-term forces, Kingdon's model successfully predicted about 90 percent of the decisions.

Explicit Bargaining. Explicit bargains also take several forms. In making compromises legislators may agree to split their differences. Compromises are straightforward on issues dealing with quantitative elements that can easily be adjusted upward or downward—for example, funding levels or eligibility criteria. Compromise on substance is also possible. For example, members who favor a major new program and members who oppose any program at all may agree to a two-year pilot project to test the idea.

"You cannot legislate without the ability to compromise," declared Sen. Alan K. Simpson, R-Wyo. (1979–1997), who often found fault with militant junior members of his own party. He recounted the following tale:

> On a recent bill, I went to [conservative House members] and said: "Here's what I'm doing. I've got six senators who will vote this far, and then the next time if you go any further, they will not be there." So [Sen.] Larry [E.] Craig [R-Idaho] and I delivered on this singular bill, and they said, "We want you to get more." And we said, "There is no more to get." Next vote on this bill, we lost six votes. Then they came in and said, "We are going to probably kill the whole thing...." [A]nd they got nothing.[107]

The lesson is that compromise is inevitable in crafting laws; those who are unwilling to give ground are bound to be disappointed.

Logrolling

Logrolling is bargaining in which members exchange support so that all parties to the deal can attain their individual goals. The term originated in the nineteenth century when neighbors helped each other roll logs into a pile for burning. Its most visible form is a something-for-everyone enactment, sometimes called a "Christmas tree" bill. Such bills are prevalent in legislative areas such as public works, omnibus taxation, or tariffs and trade. Describing the classic logroll, former representative Edward J. Derwinski, R-Ill. (1959–1983), explained how the country's two million farmers put together a majority coalition every five years to pass the omnibus farm bill's basket of price supports, acreage allowances, and marketing agreements:

> What [the farmers] do is very interesting. The agriculture people from North Carolina, where agriculture means tobacco, discuss their problems with the man representing the rice growers in Arkansas or

California. The sugar beet growers in Minnesota and sugar cane interests in Louisiana and Hawaii and the wheat and corn and soybean and
other producers just gather together in one great big happy family to
be sure there is a subsidy for every commodity. They put those numbers together again so that they have at least 218 supporters in the
House and 51 in the Senate. A supporter of the tobacco subsidy automatically becomes a supporter of the wheat subsidy, or the sugar
quota, or the soybean subsidy, or whatever else follows.[108]

One of the most successful logrolling achievements in farm policy is the
food stamp program. It brought together farm lobbies that wanted to boost
the agricultural market and urban welfare interests that wanted to feed low-
income people. In 1998, for example, a House-Senate agriculture conference
report included a crop insurance provision for farmers and a provision restor-
ing food stamps to a quarter-million immigrants who had lost them in the
1996 welfare overhaul. House Republican leaders decided to strip the food-
stamp provision from the agreement—a move calculated to please conservatives. The rule for debate was soundly defeated by an urban-rural coalition of
98 Republicans and 190 Democrats. "After today's vote, there is no doubt about
food stamps," said Rep. Lincoln Diaz-Balart, R-Fla.[109]

Logrolling draws lawmakers into the finished legislative product by
embracing their special interests, proposals, or amendments. Henry M. "Scoop"
Jackson, D-Wash. (House, 1941–1953; Senate, 1953–1983), when asked how he
had assembled a majority for a new proposal, responded something like this:
"Maggie said he talked to Russell, and Tom promised this if I would back him
on Ed's amendment, and Mike owes me one for last year's help on Pete's
bill."[110] (Note: Anyone who can identify all these senators deserves a special
award from the authors of this book! All entries accepted.) Such reciprocity
especially pervades the Senate, dominated as it is by individuals. Sponsors of a
Senate bill often must placate most or all interested legislators to gain clearance
to bring a bill to the floor.

Lawmakers who enter into, and stand to profit from, a logroll are expected
to support the final package, regardless of what that package looks like. A
broad-based logroll is thus hard to stop. "It's not a system of punishment. It's
a system of rewards," explained Rep. Bill Frenzel, R-Minn. (1971–1991).[111]

In a hostile fiscal environment, logrolling is often aimed at equalizing
sacrifices instead of distributing rewards. Broad-spectrum bills—authorizations, omnibus tax measures, continuing resolutions, and budget resolutions—
may include numerous less than optimal provisions, many of which would fail
if voted on separately. Such a negative logroll enables lawmakers to support the
measure as "the best deal we can get."

Logrolling often turns narrowly targeted programs into broad-scale ones.
In negotiating for passage of two high-priority measures—crime reduction
and a national service corps—the Clinton administration had to scatter benefits so broadly that their effectiveness was severely impaired. The 1994 crime

bill provided for 100,000 more police officers on the nation's streets, but the bill's impact was diluted by spreading the funds throughout the entire country, not just in high-crime urban areas. Similarly, funds for the volunteer Americorps program were spread too thinly among too many sites for it to make a noticeable difference in any single area.[112]

In a time logroll, members agree to support one measure in exchange for later support for another measure. A time logroll was crucial to the initial House passage of the new prescription drug benefit for seniors in 2003. Rep. Jo-Ann Emerson, R-Mo., had been fighting for years to allow U.S. consumers to purchase generic drugs from Canada and other countries where prices were lower, but she could not convince her Republican leadership to permit a vote. "I felt like a darned broken record," Emerson said.[113] When Emerson realized that Republican leaders would need her vote to pass the new prescription drug benefit, she took advantage of the opportunity. She demanded that they promise to bring her reimportation bill up for a vote. She was able to get a good-faith pledge from the leadership to greenlight her bill. "I'm extremely pleased with the outcome," she said.[114] Republican leaders fulfilled their promise to Emerson the following month by permitting the House to take a vote on the matter.[115]

Sometimes logrolls can be constructed on the basis of side payments, in which support is exchanged for benefits on an unrelated issue—for example, a federal project for the state or district, a better committee assignment, inclusion in an important conference, help with fund-raising, or access to the White House. With liberal use of campaign contributions, for example, sugar interests have expanded their influence far beyond the fifteen states where fewer than 6,000 farmers grow sugar. Sugar farm industries make wide-ranging political contributions to members, parties, and labor unions. In 2007, sugar farmers mustered an overwhelming coalition of 282 House members to vote against a challenge to a $1 billion, ten-year growers' subsidy plan. "When you take on Big Sugar, you take on a huge political money operation," said Rep. Mark Steven Kirk, R-Ill.[116] Although such side payoffs may seem trivial or parochial, they can enable members to achieve valued goals.

Bargaining Strategy

For bargaining to take place, participants must be able to rely upon one another's future actions. Rep. John P. Murtha, D-Pa., a master dealmaker, cites two elements of power on Capitol Hill: "Develop expertise on an issue that makes you vital to colleagues, and keep your word."[117] Relying on his expertise and contacts within the defense community, he often deals quietly in the back corner of the Democratic side of the House. His orbit has embraced liberal House Speaker Pelosi and ultra-conservative former Republican floor leader Tom DeLay of Texas, whom he regarded as an honest broker. When DeLay needed something, Murtha told a reporter, "He comes over to the corner and we work it out." On the Senate side of the Capitol, former GOP majority leader Frist did not hesitate to do business with liberal icon Edward Kennedy. "He has always dealt straight with me," Frist said. "You know exactly where he's coming from."[118]

For bargaining to succeed, the participants must agree on the need for a legislative product. That is, the benefits of reaching a decision must exceed the costs of failing to do so. In many cases politicians may prefer a course of strategic disagreement, which John B. Gilmour describes as "efforts of politicians to avoid reaching an agreement when compromise might alienate supporters, damage their prospects in an upcoming election, or preclude getting a better deal in the future." [119]

According to bargaining theory, a measure's sponsors will yield only what they absolutely must to gain a majority of supporters. "[P]arties wish to use their votes efficiently, winning victories at the cheapest possible price." [120] According to this logic, if bargainers act rationally and have perfect information about one another, minimum winning coalitions should predominate. [121] Recounting Senate majority leader Lyndon B. Johnson's meticulous vote counting before a floor fight, political scientist John G. Stewart concluded, "And once a sufficient majority had been counted, Johnson would seldom attempt to enlarge it: Why expend limited bargaining resources which might be needed to win future battles?" [122]

Most legislative strategists, however, lack Johnson's extraordinary skills. Uncertainty about outcomes leads them to line up more than a simple majority of supporters. Moreover, at many points in the legislative process supermajorities are required—for example, in voting under suspension of the rules, in overriding vetoes, or in ending Senate filibusters. Not surprisingly, therefore, minimum winning coalitions are not typical of Congress, even in the majoritarian House of Representatives. [123]

Yet coalition size is the crux of legislative strategy. Bargainers repeatedly face the dilemma of how broadly or how narrowly to frame their issues and how many concessions to yield in an effort to secure passage.

CONCLUSION

Congressional deliberation is at risk today. With both parties unified and seemingly uninterested in debate or compromise, life on Capitol Hill has become, in Hobbes's words, "nasty" and "brutish" (though hardly "short"). Take-no-prisoners strategies are encouraged by today's highly competitive, polarized party system. As former Sen. Breaux observed,

> The pressure on congressional leaders both from interests in the party and from outside groups is severe. Many would rather fight and lose, rather than reach out and find common ground. Congress should not be like the Super Bowl, in which one team always has to win and the other team inevitably loses. There's nothing wrong with reaching legitimate compromise and getting something done for the American people. [124]

Sarah Binder's findings echo this sentiment. "The decline of the political center," she writes, "has produced a political environment that more often than not gives legislators every incentive not to reach agreement."[125] The result is often legislative inaction—which can be interpreted as stalemate or gridlock.

Yet the enterprise of lawmaking rests on the premise that, at least where urgent matters are concerned, bargainers will normally prefer some sort of new outcome to none at all. As the legendary Senate Republican leader (1959–1969) Everett M. Dirksen, R-Ill., once remarked: "I am a man of fixed and unbending principle, and one of my principles is flexibility."[126] Flexibility is especially crucial with "must-pass" legislation that, if not approved, can imperil government functions. When dealing with some reauthorizations, appropriations, and debt ceiling adjustments, the alternative to action can be shutdown of the federal government. Indeed, budget impasses have resulted in government shutdowns seventeen times in the last twenty-five years.[127]

Bargaining is a necessary part of legislative life. It shapes the character of bills, resolutions, and other forms of congressional policymaking. It also underlies many attributes of the legislative process—delay, obfuscation, compromise, and norms such as specialization and reciprocity.

Deliberation is the hallmark of legislative decision making. Coalitions are constructed as diverse views are voiced, and a variety of members and interest groups participate. It is yet another point of contact and conflict between the two Congresses—the Congress of individual wills and the Congress of collective decisions.

SUGGESTED READINGS

Arnold, R. Douglas. *The Logic of Congressional Action.* New Haven: Yale University Press, 1990.

Binder, Sarah A. *Stalemate: Causes and Consequences of Legislative Gridlock.* Washington, D.C.: Brookings Institution Press, 2003.

Brownstein, Ronald. *The Second Civil War: How Extreme Partisanship Has Paralyzed Washington and Polarized America.* New York: The Penguin Press, 2007.

Edwards, George C. *At the Margins: Presidential Leadership of Congress.* New Haven: Yale University Press, 1989.

Kingdon, John W. *Congressmen's Voting Decisions.* 3d ed. Ann Arbor: University of Michigan Press, 1989.

Mucchiaroni, Gary, and Paul J. Quirk. *Deliberative Choices: Debating Public Policy in Congress.* Chicago: University of Chicago Press, 2006.

Sulkin, Tracy. *Issue Politics in Congress.* New York: Cambridge University Press, 2005.

Theriault, Sean M. *Party Polarization in Congress.* New York: Cambridge University Press, 2008.

M *ultiple Presidential Roles.* President Barack Obama meets with bipartisan Senate leaders to discuss his Supreme Court nomination of Judge Sonia Sotomayor (top). From left to right, Sen. Jeff Sessions (R-Ala.), ranking minority member of the Judiciary Committee; Minority Leader Mitch McConnell (R-Ky.); Vice President Joseph R. Biden Jr.; President Obama; Majority Leader Harry Reid (D-Nev.); and Judiciary Committee chair Patrick Leahy (D-Vt.). Members of Congress (bottom left) applaud the president's signing of an act to prevent home foreclosures and ease access to credit. Members mob the president (bottom right) after he addressed a joint session of Congress in February 2009. Although not formally billed as a State of the Union address, it was the president's first formal report to Congress, and included his views on the nation's health and his proposals for the future.

Congress and the President

T he 44th president, Barack Obama assumed his office at a moment of huge domestic and international challenges. The United States was in the midst of a deep economic recession that scholars compare to the Great Depression of the 1930s. The country was bogged down in ongoing military conflicts in Iraq and Afghanistan. The federal deficit and debt zoomed upward at a disturbing rate. Yet the country had high expectations that the Congress—under expanded Democratic control—and the president could deliver the plans and policies to put the country back on the right track. One of Obama's promises was to change the way Washington does business. The president pledged to employ a "post-partisan" style of governance, working to end the often acrimonious battles between congressional Democrats and Republicans and the partisan gridlock that stymied many of his recent predecessors.

Winning the support of the minority party is no easy assignment for President Obama, despite his efforts to reach out to numerous GOP lawmakers. He has met personally with Republicans on Capitol Hill, invited them to the White House, traveled with GOP lawmakers to their states or districts, and solicited their advice on legislation. Yet on the most significant bill of his early administration, the nearly $800 billion economic stimulus package, not a single House Republican voted for it and only three GOP senators supported the measure, Susan Collins and Olympia Snowe of Maine and Arlen Specter of Pennsylvania. Specter's support for the stimulus package so eroded his support among grassroots Republicans that he chose to switch to the Democratic Party rather than attempt to win a contested Republican primary in 2010. Meanwhile, House and Senate Republicans launched a coordinated public relations campaign against the president's stimulus package and other budget plans, castigating them as "spends too much, taxes too much, and borrows too much." Congressional Republicans, with the two Congresses in mind, are gambling that their opposition to the stimulus package will pay electoral dividends in 2010.

> The stimulus package has emerged as the first major campaign issue of the 2010 election cycle, and a Republican Party eyeing a return to the majority is going all-in. The near-universal GOP opposition to the stimulus means that, for 2010 at least, Democrats own the result. Republicans, meanwhile, are banking on it, at least electorally, to fail.[1]

For his part, the president has derided the GOP's criticisms. Republican proposals, he said, are "rooted in the idea that tax cuts alone can solve all our problems, that government doesn't have a role to play, that half measures and tinkering are somehow enough, that we can afford to ignore our most fundamental economic challenges. Those ideas have been tested and they have failed."[2]

From a purely institutional perspective, reaction against the "Bush-Cheney" regime has shaped the relationship between the Democratically controlled 111th Congress (2009–2011) and the Obama White House. The previous administration—of President George W. Bush and his powerful vice president, Dick Cheney (2001–2009)—asserted, often successfully, vast executive powers at the expense of the legislative branch, a position that largely met with congressional acquiescence. Speaker Nancy Pelosi and Senate Majority Leader Harry Reid have both insisted that they are leaders of an independent and coequal branch of government—even with a president of their own party. "I don't work for Obama," asserted Senator Reid.[3] For her part, Speaker Pelosi promised that Democrats would not function as congressional Republicans often did during the George W. Bush years, marching in lockstep to support the president and his administration. Speaker Pelosi, for example, backed a resolution requiring House committees to conduct at least three oversight and investigative hearings a year on waste, fraud, and abuse in the Obama-led executive branch.[4]

Tensions between the executive and legislative branches are inevitable. The two policymaking branches have divergent responsibilities; they have different constituencies and terms of office; and they are typically jealous of their prerogatives. Executive officials see the decentralized Congress as inefficient and meddlesome. Legislators perceive the hierarchical and highly centralized executive branch as arrogant and arbitrary. At times these differences lead to conflicts that the news media dramatize as "battles on the Potomac."

Yet day in and day out, Congress and the president work together. Even when their relationship is guarded or hostile, bills are passed and signed into law. Presidential appointments win Senate approval. Budgets are eventually enacted and the government is kept afloat. This cooperation continues even when control of the White House and the Capitol is divided between the two major parties. Conversely, as Presidents Carter and Clinton (in his first two years in office) learned, unified partisan control of both branches is no guarantee of harmony. Political scientist Ross Baker summarized President Clinton's rocky start with Congress.

> Clinton's problems started with his proposal to enable gays to serve openly in the armed forces. His principal antagonist in this fight was not a Republican, but the Democratic chairman of the Senate Armed Services Committee, Sam Nunn of Georgia. After backing down on that issue, Clinton proposed an emergency stimulus package that quickly passed the House but was scuttled by the outnumbered Republicans in the Senate through a filibuster—Democrats didn't have the 60 votes to end it. Clinton's early missteps, combined with

collapse of the national health insurance initiative, captained by Hillary Clinton, contributed to the Republican capture of both houses of Congress in the 1994 elections.[5]

Early in his administration, President Obama experienced "push back" by various congressional Democrats to his major initiatives. Some state the president was overloading the legislative circuits by proposing so many major initiatives all at once—a massive stimulus package, a $3.6 trillion budget plan, and major proposals to reform health care, energy, and education. "There's only so much that we can absorb and do at one time," explained Sen. Daniel Inouye, D-Hawaii, chair of the Senate Appropriations Committee.[6] The president responded that Congress is capable of dealing with more than one major problem at a time.

The president's budget priorities have also been challenged by several influential Democratic committee chairs. "This is a very stupid idea," the House Agriculture Committee chair remarked about an administration proposal to eliminate subsidies to farmers earning more than $500,000 annually.[7] The chair's comment underscored the two-Congresses theme: protect core constituent interests, or the twoyear electoral contract might be terminated sooner than a lawmaker wants.

THE PRESIDENT AS LEGISLATOR

Presidents are sometimes called the chief legislators because they are closely involved in the decisions Congress makes. Article II, Section 3, of the Constitution directs the president from time to time to "give to the Congress Information of the State of the Union and recommend to their Consideration such Measures as he shall judge necessary and expedient." (Today, this means annually and during television's prime time.) Soon after delivering the annual State of the Union address, the president sends to Congress draft administration bills for introduction on his behalf. By enlarging the list of messages required from the president—the annual budget and economic reports, for example—Congress has further involved the chief executive in designing legislation. Congress often delegates authority to the president because it appreciates the strengths of the White House—such as its capacity for coordination—and recognizes its own shortcomings, such as its decentralized committee structure, which inhibits swift and comprehensive policymaking. Crises, partisan considerations, and public expectations all make the president an important participant in congressional decision making. And the president's constitutional veto power ensures that White House views will be listened to, if not always heeded, on Capitol Hill.

The concept of the legislative presidency became widespread only after World War II. By then it could be conceded that the role was institutionalized, performed not because of some unique combination of personality and circumstance but because everyone expected it—including Congress, the press, and the public.[8] This deeply entrenched expectation will not change any time soon.

Understanding the chief executive's relations with Congress is no easy task. The Founders did not clearly define the legislative-executive relationship, so it has always been a work in progress. Presidents bring their own style to the relationship, which Charles O. Jones characterizes as either the "partnership model" or the "independent model." The partnership model means that presidents consult regularly with lawmakers and involve them directly in the policy and political affairs of the White House. The independent model holds that presidents should minimize their involvement with Congress and strive on their own to accomplish their top priorities.[9]

Scholars and others have long analyzed America's complex system of separate institutions sharing, and competing for, power. Different theories or models, such as Jones's, have been formulated to define effective presidential leadership. In recent decades scholars have produced an array of studies, "a bewildering succession of new models of the presidency, each the product of an admixture of empirical and normative assessments."[10] Some studies focus on the person in the White House; others on the bureaucracy and the institutional functions and structures of the presidency; and still others analyze discrete aspects of the relationship between Congress and the president, such as presidential spending power versus the legislative branch's power of the purse.[11] Here we discuss five prominent presidential theories—persuasion, rhetoric, administrative, political time, and the "two presidencies"—as a way to illuminate important aspects of the chief executive's relations with Congress. To varying degrees, these analytical perspectives overlap and capture the activities of all presidents.

The Power to Persuade

"Presidential *power* is the power to persuade," wrote Richard E. Neustadt (a former staff aide in the Truman White House and adviser to president-elect John F. Kennedy).[12] Power, Neustadt asserted, meant more than the executive's ability to persuade Congress to enact a bill. "Strategically, the question is not how he masters Congress in a peculiar instance, but what he does to boost his chances for mastery in any instance."[13] To be successful, presidents are urged to employ all their varied powers (constitutional, political, bureaucratic, personal, and more) to persuade Congress and others to follow their lead. Setting Congress's agenda—determining the policies that the legislature pays attention to by taking them up in committee and on the floor—epitomizes the president's power to persuade.

Presidents have shaped Congress's agenda from the very beginning. The First Congress of "its own volition immediately turned to the executive branch for guidance and discovered in [Treasury secretary Alexander] Hamilton a personality to whom such leadership was congenial."[14] Two decades later (by 1825) the "initiative in public affairs remained with [Speaker Henry] Clay and his associates in the House of Representatives" and not with the president.[15] Thus, dominance in national policymaking may pass from one branch to the other. Strong presidents sometimes provoked efforts by Congress to reassert its own authority and to restrict that of the executive. Periods of presidential ascendancy often are followed by eras of congressional assertiveness. Still, Congress usually has expected the White House to outline its legislative program in the annual State of the Union message and in other formal and informal presidential messages.

Presidents follow different patterns in setting agendas. Two presidents— Ronald Reagan (1981–1989) and Jimmy Carter (1977–1981)—were opposites in their ability to persuade Congress to enact their policy priorities. Agenda control was the hallmark of Reagan's leadership during his first year in office. By limiting his legislative priorities, Reagan focused Congress's and the public's attention on one priority issue at a time. Most were encapsulated as "Reaganomics"—tax and spending cuts. He exploited the usual honeymoon period for new presidents by moving his agenda quickly, during a moment of widespread anticipation of a new era of GOP national political dominance.

Reagan also dealt skillfully with Congress: meeting, negotiating, and socializing with lawmakers, including a private dinner with Democratic Speaker Thomas P. "Tip" O'Neill Jr. of Massachusetts and his wife. Enjoying a Republican majority in the Senate, the Reagan White House focused primarily on lobbying the Democratic-controlled House to pass the president's economic program— the "greatest selling job I've ever seen," said Speaker O'Neill. Reagan himself personally called or telegraphed all of the "Boll Weevils," the forty-seven southern Democrats in the Conservative Democratic Forum.[16] He persuaded several governors to meet with members from their states who were opposing the program. Top executive officials were dispatched to targeted Democratic districts to drum up public support. On the key House vote, all 191 GOP members and sixty-three Democrats backed the president's budget plan. After only eight months in office, Reagan scored some of the biggest victories of his entire eight years in office. Later, when his control over the agenda slackened, Congress was still confined to a playing field he had largely set out. Lawmakers were forced to respond to, although not always accept, the positions the president had staked out on taxes, spending, defense, and social issues.

By contrast, Reagan's predecessor in the White House, Jimmy Carter, quickly overloaded Congress's agenda and never made clear what his priorities were. Three major consequences resulted:

> First...there was little clarity in the communication of priorities to the American public. Instead of galvanizing support for two or three major national needs, the Carter administration proceeded on a number of fronts.... Second, and perhaps more important, the lack of priorities meant unnecessary waste of the President's own time and energy.... Third, the lack of priorities needlessly compounded Carter's congressional problems.... Carter's limited political capital was squandered on a variety of agenda requests when it might have been concentrated on the top of the list.[17]

Carter lacked the temperament for doing personal lobbying. Although he met in formal sessions with a large number of members, he shunned informal, personal contacts. He did not view informal discussions or negotiating meetings with members as a productive use of his time.

It is too early to evaluate how President Obama—the first sitting senator since John F. Kennedy (1960) to move directly to the White House—and Congress will legislate together. His agenda-setting approach, it would appear, borrows a little from both Carter and Reagan. From Carter, President Obama has tried to capitalize on his early popular support to accomplish an activist agenda in a relatively short period of time. Obama promised the voters "change" if elected, and he has advanced a presidential agenda as ambitious as Franklin Roosevelt's "New Deal" or Lyndon Johnson's "Great Society." On top of the worst economic calamity in decades, Obama has urged Congress to accept major and costly policy initiatives at a time that the government was spending trillions of dollars to get the economy back on track.

President Obama also sent Congress a budgetary blueprint for fiscal 2010 with an annual deficit projected to be about $1.2 trillion and a national debt estimated to soar to over $13 trillion. Little surprise that Obama and his top aides, like the Reagan administration, have expended considerable time and effort trying to win the backing of lawmakers for his economic, domestic, and fiscal plans. "We remain confident," said Peter Orszag, director of the Office of Management and Budget (OMB), "that the four key principles that the president put forward for the budget—in particular, that it must invest in health care, that it must invest in education, that it must invest in clean energy and that it must cut the deficit in half by the end of his first term—will all be accomplished."[18] Others were not so certain. "The early word is that the latest [budget] numbers will make an already difficult [lawmaking] task even more difficult," said Sen. Thomas Carper, D-Del.[19] The fundamental issue is whether Congress can produce all the changes that Obama wants. Former Democratic representative Lee Hamilton, a highly respected legislator who began his House career in 1965, compared today's demands on Congress with those of President Lyndon Johnson's era.

> There is a big difference. In the Great Society, Johnson presented very specific legislation—Medicare, Medicaid, the elementary and secondary education act—that had really been debated. The legislation was sent to the Hill in quite specific form. [But that is not what Obama has done.]
>
> He has these major issues—energy, health care, education—and set out principles and, in effect, asked the Congress to do the drafting of the legislation. That is a huge difference. Today the Congress is a very different institution and I think the initiatives that Obama has put forward represent an extraordinary, even historic, challenge to the Congress. [The question] is whether they can do it. And I think the game is in doubt. It represents as great a challenge to the leadership in Congress as any I can recall.[20]

Needless to say, most presidents recognize the importance of maintaining informal contacts with Congress because they understand that it is not easy to persuade Congress to act in a certain way. As Lyndon Johnson—who had served as Senate minority leader (1953–1955) and majority leader (1955–1960)—once declared, "Merely placing a program before Congress is not enough. Without constant attention from the administration, most legislation moves through the congressional process at the speed of a glacier."[21] Johnson regularly (and sometimes crudely) admonished his aides and departmental officers to work closely with Congress. "[Get off] your ass and see how fast you can respond to a congressional request," he told his staff. "Challenge yourself to see how quickly you can get back to him or her with an answer, any kind of an answer, but goddamn it, an answer."[22]

At least since Harry S. Truman, presidents have maintained a formal White House legislative liaison office to promote the administration's program in Congress; to lobby outside groups, state officials, and others to do the same; to target members who could be coaxed for votes on certain issues; and, more generally, to foster a cooperative legislative-executive atmosphere.

To persuade members to support their programs, presidents often grant or withhold their patronage resources. Broadly conceived, patronage involves not only federal and judicial positions but also federal construction projects, location of government installations, campaign support, access to strategic information, plane rides on *Air Force One,* White House entree for important constituents, and countless other favors, large and small. Some presidents even keep records of the political favors they grant to lawmakers, IOUs that they can cash in later for needed support in Congress. Limits, however, do exist to the persuasive power of patronage. As one White House congressional relations chief said, "The problem with congressional relations is that with every good intention, at the end of the day you can't accommodate all the requests that you get."[23] More importantly, many factors influence how members vote on issues important to the White House. Although a president's persuasive skills can sometimes tip the balance, other considerations—lawmakers' constituency interests, policy preferences, and ideological dispositions, as well as public opinion and the number of partisan seats in each chamber—usually are more important in shaping congressional outcomes.

Going Public: The Rhetorical President

"With public sentiment, nothing can fail; without it nothing can succeed," Abraham Lincoln once observed.[24] Lincoln's idea is the essence of the rhetorical presidency: how and when a chief executive strategically employs contemporary campaign techniques and the technology of the mass media to promote "himself and his policies in Washington by appealing to the American public."[25] The rhetorical president's ultimate objective is to produce an outpouring of public support that encourages lawmakers to push his ideas through the congressional obstacle course.

Going public on an issue, however, is not without its risks. The strategy often alienates legislators who feel that the president is going over their heads, cutting them out of the process, and disregarding their constitutional role. The president can also raise expectations that cannot be met, make inept appeals, or stiffen the opposition. Furthermore, many legislators are more popular than the president in their districts or states. The president goes public to gather support because "if he had the votes he would pass the measure first and go to the public only for the bill-signing ceremonies."[26]

President Reagan was an acknowledged master at using the electronic media to orchestrate public support. The Hollywood actor-turned-president was at home in front of cameras and microphones, and he had a keen sense of public ritual and symbolism as means of rallying support. After the March 30, 1981, assassination attempt, Reagan returned a month later and made a dramatic appeal for his economic program. "The White House shrewdly tied Reagan's return to action to the budget and tax debate, scheduling an April 28 comeback speech before a joint meeting of Congress. It was a triumph, and people began to call him the 'Great Communicator.'"[27] Reagan's adroitness with the media, primarily during his first year in office, is a legacy that looms large for subsequent presidents and Congresses. He showed that "one man using the White House's immense powers of communication can lift the mood of the nation and alter the way it does business."[28]

President George H. W. Bush's public relations techniques "abandoned the elaborate, tightly controlled machinery developed in recent years to project, manipulate and polish a presidential image" in the television age.[29] Instead, the senior Bush used traditional methods—meeting with small groups of reporters, inviting journalists to lunch, or traveling outside Washington, D.C.—to build public support through communication.

President Clinton, by contrast, used media technologies to reach voters and employed campaign-style practices to generate public support for his programs. His empathetic response to the April 1995 bombing of a federal office building in Oklahoma City reminded people of the human face of the federal government, the very entity Republican "revolutionaries" were warring against. When Republicans added qualifying provisions that Clinton opposed to a flood relief bill, the president used the bully pulpit to paint the GOP position as "extreme" and generated a flurry of favorable publicity for his position. As one reporter noted,

> News accounts portrayed Republicans as, well, crazy extremists bent on playing games with flood victims. Rank-and-file Republicans writhed in political agony. Michigan Republican Fred Upton's mother watched the news accounts with alarm and warned her son, "You're getting killed." "When your mom tells you that, you know you're in trouble," said Upton.[30]

The White House also used "nightly tracking polls and weekly focus groups to help determine its daily message and the approach President Clinton should take to important national issues."[31]

George W. Bush was initially dubbed "the reticent president" by some analysts on several grounds: his preference for not seizing the public spotlight and addressing every major event or issue that might arise; his determination to stay "on message" by sticking to prepared talking points; his predilection for carefully staged and scripted appearances; and his propensity for committing verbal gaffes. Nonetheless, Bush worked diligently to win public and political support for his policy and political objectives.[32] Bush also became the first president to deliver his weekly radio address in Spanish—political recognition of the electoral potential of the growing Hispanic population.

Bush came into his own as both communicator in chief and commander in chief in the aftermath of the terrorist attacks on the World Trade Center in New York City and the Pentagon. He gave powerful and eloquent speeches in a variety of forums, such as before Congress and at the United Nations (UN), on the need to go after terrorists who threatened the United States and to disarm Saddam Hussein's regime in Iraq. His direct and confident manner resonated with most Americans and boosted domestic and congressional support for his antiterrorism and war plans.

In addition, the Bush White House went to great lengths to use television to promote the president, employing former network television aides with expertise in lighting, camera angles, and backdrops. The most elaborately staged event was Bush's flight to, and speech on, the aircraft carrier *Abraham Lincoln,* prematurely announcing the end of major military combat in Iraq. White House aides "choreographed every aspect of the event, even down to the members of the *Lincoln* crew arrayed in coordinated shirt colors over Mr. Bush's right shoulder and the 'Mission Accomplished' banner placed to perfectly capture the president and the celebratory two words in a single shot."[33] As the war lengthened for years without producing stability and security in Iraq, those same images were used to ironic effect by war critics, Democratic candidates, and late-night comedians.

After the Democrats won control of Congress in 2006, President Bush continued to go public against Congress in pursuit of his war policies. The strategy became increasingly untenable as the violence in Iraq escalated, antiwar sentiment increased in the United States, and Bush's job approval ratings plummeted to less than 30 percent.[34] Challenged by the Democratic-controlled Congress, Bush appeared before supportive audiences using strong rhetoric demanding that the Democrats continue to finance the war. Senate Majority Leader Harry Reid, D-Nev., responded: "The days of a blank check and a green light for escalation are over."[35] In the end, Bush left office in January 2009 "with some of the lowest [popular approval] marks of any president in recent history."[36]

President Obama, like Reagan, is an exceptionally skilled and eloquent speaker who enjoys addressing citizens in a variety of locales and settings. Winston Churchill once said that of "all the gifts bestowed upon [modern leaders], none is so precious as the gift of oratory."[37] Obama has that gift.[38] In a modern version of Franklin Roosevelt's "fireside" chats, Obama became the first president to appear with Jay Leno on "The Tonight Show," a late-night television program that draws about five million viewers. The president's purpose was "to broaden his audience beyond cable news junkies and political elites, appealing to those who don't already know the intricacies of his budget blueprint and health care overhaul plan."[39] President Obama recognizes that "in a fragmented media universe, presidents must communicate nearly constantly across an array of platforms, both traditional and new."[40] One of those new platforms was a live Internet "town hall" meeting in which Obama fielded questions in the White House from citizens across the nation as well as from a live audience in the East Room. That video chat was the first of its kind for any modern presidency.[41]

President Obama pledged to leave Washington every week to stay connected with the country, listening to peoples' concerns and explaining his policies. His many trips to cities around the nation underscored that campaigning and governing are inextricably linked activities (the so-called "permanent campaign"). Many of the states he visited (Florida and Indiana, for example) are electorally important should Obama run for reelection in 2012. Significantly, Obama has enlisted the nationwide army of supporters that he mobilized, many through the Internet during the 2008 presidential campaign, to build public support for his legislative agenda.

The president's grassroots operation, run by a group ("Organizing for America") overseen by the Democratic National Committee, includes an estimated "13 million e-mail addresses, 4 million cellphone contacts and 2 million active supporters."[42] These Obama supporters have received numerous e-mails urging them to contact their members of Congress, encouraging them to back the president's agenda. One e-mail told supporters to use their campaign experience to promote the president's agenda in their communities. "In the next few weeks, we'll be asking you to do some of the same things we asked of you during the [2008] campaign—talking directly to people in your community about the president's ideas for long-term prosperity," wrote David Plouffe, the president's campaign manager.[43] A "post-partisan" presidency may be Obama's goal; but he and his followers are not reluctant to exert political pressure on wavering lawmakers to vote for his programs.

The Administrative President

Presidents understand that getting Congress to pass legislation is an arduous process; and that even when laws are enacted, bureaucratic indifference may hamper implementation of presidential initiatives. Thus, presidents' core administrative strategy is to win policy goals by statute whenever feasible, but when such effort falls short, to accomplish those aims through organizational or managerial techniques. Administrative presidents employ a variety of methods, such as naming loyal political appointees to supervise and monitor agency activities, reorganizing executive departments to advance presidential goals, using the budget process to reduce unwanted programs or increase favorite activities, and employing executive orders and rule-making authority to achieve outcomes blocked by Congress.[44]

Using executive orders and reorganization plans, presidents can act on their own to create entirely new administrative agencies. In doing so, presidents are able to institutionalize policies that Congress would never have created. Based on a study of all the administrative agencies established between the end of World War II and 1995, William G. Howell and David E. Lewis report that "presidents have unilaterally created over half of all administrative agencies in the United States."[45] Among them are such important agencies as the Peace Corps. Facing significant opposition in Congress to the Peace Corps idea, President Kennedy opted to create the agency by executive order. By the time Congress got around to reviewing the president's actions, the Peace Corps already had 362 employees and 600 volunteers at work in eight countries.[46] By establishing this "fact on the ground," the president pressured Congress into accepting the new organization. In the immediate aftermath of the September 11, 2001, terrorist attacks, President Bush unilaterally created an Office for Homeland Security in the White House and established a new court system for handling suspected terrorist noncitizens, calling them "unlawful enemy combatants."[47]

Presidents have long employed executive orders—a form of administrative lawmaking using (or expanding) authority that the legislative branch has delegated—to achieve objectives not explicitly authorized by Congress.[48] President Truman, for example, issued an executive order racially integrating the armed services. Stymied by the GOP-controlled Congress on issues such as antismoking legislation, a patients' bill of rights, and subsidies for school construction, President Clinton made extensive use of executive orders. "His formula include[d] pressing the limits of his regulatory authority, signing executive orders and using other unilateral means to obtain his policy priorities when Congress fail[ed] to embrace them."[49] Congressional Republicans railed against Clinton's "go-it-alone" governing.

George W. Bush similarly exploited administrative tools to advance his policy goals. First, he used the appointment power to staff the White House and executive branch with people who shared his goals and to place conservatives in prominent posts. Many of his allies claimed that Bush surpassed even Ronald Reagan in the ideological commitment of his appointments.[50] Bush also placed high value on loyalty in naming people to important governmental positions. For example, Condoleezza Rice, the president's national security adviser, confidante, and a frequent visitor to Camp David, replaced Colin Powell as secretary of state in Bush's second term.

Second, Bush quickly exercised executive authority to roll back, suspend, or challenge many Clinton-era regulations. He also was not reluctant to implement by executive fiat administration programs stalled in Congress. For example, when the Senate blocked action on Bush's faith-based initiative (assisting religious groups in winning government grants for charitable and social service work), the president ordered his administration to implement the program through executive orders and changes in agency regulations.[51]

Third, like presidents before him, Bush encouraged his departments and agencies to move rapidly to enact a wide array of so-called "midnight regulations." Rushing them through in the administration's waning months, executive officials could burnish the president's legacy and—as a senior think tank analyst observed—"extend its influence into the future, especially when they know the administration succeeding them does not share its philosophies."[52] Speaker Nancy Pelosi, familiar with the last-minute issuance of regulations by an outgoing administration, issued on Halloween a list of eleven Bush administration rules that she dubbed "Ghoulish Midnight Regulations."[53]

Needless to say, the Obama administration moved quickly to block or reverse many of Bush's rules and regulations. Even before he was sworn into office, Obama's transition team "compiled a list of about 200 Bush administration actions and executive orders that could be swiftly undone to reverse White House policies on climate change, stem cell research, reproductive rights and other issues."[54] True to form, in his first seven days in office, President Obama blocked action on Bush's last-minute rules; banned the use of torture; ordered the closing of the Guantánamo Bay prison and a review of detention policies for suspected terrorists; overturned the ban on funding international health groups that provide counseling on terminating pregnancies; directed the Transportation Department to develop new fuel-efficiency standards; and ordered the Environmental Protection Agency (EPA) to consider granting California and other states the ability to impose tougher tailpipe emission standards than the federal standards.

In addition, President Obama imposed new ethics standards on administration officials and issued a Freedom of Information Act memorandum instructing "all members of his administration to operate under principles of openness, transparency and of engaging citizens."[55]

The President and Political Time

Political scientist Stephen Skowronek spotlights the importance of what he terms "political time."[56] A president's place in political time refers to his relationship to the nation's dominant political regime and to the resources available to the presidency at that point in American history. Presidents can be compared by whether or not they are affiliated with the dominant national coalition of the period (if there is one) as well as by how they perform within that historical context. Given these two variables, presidents face divergent leadership tasks, as well as varying levels of resources for success.

Presidents Franklin D. Roosevelt, John F. Kennedy, and Jimmy Carter—all Democrats who enjoyed Democratic majorities in Congress—faced different problems in leading the nation because they occupied the White House at different points in a sequence of political change that saw the birth, expansion, and decay of the New Deal order. "In the modern Democratic period," starting with FDR's election, "regime outsiders like Republicans Dwight D. Eisenhower and Richard Nixon faced different problems from those confronted by regime insiders like John F. Kennedy and Lyndon Johnson."[57]

Painting in broad historical strokes, Skowronek observes that presidents elected in an election repudiating the ruling regime have much wider political authority than presidents who are elected merely to carry out a ruling regime's program. Presidents elected as repudiators have greater political latitude to define their own policies and priorities because the public expects them to do things differently from their predecessor. The presidents generally regarded as "great" are those elected immediately following presidents who were widely judged to be incompetent.

> John Adams and Thomas Jefferson, John Quincy Adams and Andrew Jackson, James Buchanan and Abraham Lincoln, Herbert Hoover and Franklin Roosevelt, Jimmy Carter and Ronald Reagan—this repeated pairing of dismal failure with stunning success is one of the more striking patterns in presidential history.[58]

By contrast, presidents elected to deliver on a dominant regime's existing program are more constrained. They face great political difficulties when they disappoint members of their coalition. Because the public expects them to "stay the course," they are not given the political freedom to disappoint any element of the party coalition. Presidents in this situation often find that they cannot prioritize. They must deliver on all items in the party's platform. President Lyndon Johnson, for example, a Democratic president in the post–New Deal era, was expected both to win the war in Vietnam and to fund the Great Society fully. For presidents in this situation, any choice among party priorities brings howls of outrage, charges of disloyalty and heresy, from within their own party.

Only tentative judgments can be made about where George W. Bush, much less Barack Obama, fit in Skowronek's theory. Bush ran for office in 2000 as an affiliate of the ascendant Reagan regime. Although the electoral outcome was hotly contested, he interpreted his election as authorizing a broad articulation of the Reagan agenda. This role was borne out by his statements and core policies, especially his broad tax cuts. Yet in the end he deviated from the Reagan legacy by what Skowronek would call "orthodox innovation" that enlarged the federal government's size and reach, and left a sea of red ink (two wars and costly domestic programs in education and drug benefits for seniors). Although Bush continued to command the loyalty of his core supporters, conservatives grew uneasy over his seeming abandonment of Reaganism.

Surely it is premature to judge President Obama's place in Skowronek's matrix. Given the multiplicity of challenges he confronts and the scope of his policy plans, Obama could be a transformative (that is, reconstructive) president, ushering in a new political regime akin to the New Deal presidency of

Franklin D. Roosevelt. White House Chief of Staff Rahm Emanuel's remark—"You never want a serious crisis to go to waste"—might well be the motto of such presidents.[59] And like all such presidents, Obama entered the office on the heels of what most regarded as a failed presidency. "Presidents elected upon the outright rejection of their predecessors will have at hand an expansive warrant for disruption," Skowronek wrote in 1997. "The exercise of presidential power will be relatively unencumbered in these circumstances because the incumbent is implicitly authorized by his election to constitute an alternative to the discredited past."[60]

The fate of Obama's presidency depends on whether he can successfully ride out the crises he faces: to revive the ailing economy, stimulate confidence in the marketplace, and engender public confidence in the government. It depends also on whether he is seen to address the deficiencies of his predecessors—the very circumstances that made his presidency possible. Fortunately, although earlier regime-changing presidents—Jackson, Lincoln, and Franklin Roosevelt, for example—made numerous mistakes during their time in office, they often proved resilient, even when their policies failed disastrously. So if Obama can produce the "change we can believe in"—a very tall order—then a new political order might emerge that might transform American society and the political order. If not, Obama could end up a one-term president.

The "Two Presidencies"

"The United States has one president, but it has two presidencies; one presidency is for domestic affairs, and the other is concerned with defense and foreign policy."[61] This formulation by political scientist Aaron Wildavsky stated that presidential proposals are likely to achieve more success in the international than in the domestic arena, in part because Congress asserts itself more in domestic policymaking than in foreign policy. Wildavsky's thesis has sparked considerable controversy: for example, how to measure success rates in the two arenas, and whether the concept is relevant today, when the international and domestic overlap constantly.[62] Whatever the strengths or weaknesses of the two-presidencies idea as Wildavsky laid it out, the concept can be applied to the presidency of George W. Bush before and after the September 11, 2001, terrorist attacks. If the pre-9/11 period comprised George W. Bush's first presidency with its focus on domestic issues, the post-9/11 era for Bush began on September 11, 2001.

The Pre-9/11 Phase. Despite Vice President Al Gore's plurality in the 2000 popular vote tally, the absence of any mandate from the voters, and the lack of any presidential coattails (the GOP lost seats in both chambers, though it held onto the majority in each), President Bush quickly advanced an ambitious agenda as though he had won a huge victory. This surprised many pundits who predicted that Bush would move slowly to implement his "compassionate conservative" campaign promises. "This is the farthest thing from a caretaker administration you could get," declared a Brookings Institution analyst. "It's the farthest thing from a president saying I lost the popular vote, I'm here because of a 5 to 4 vote on the Supreme Court [*Bush v. Gore*]. I'd better [advance] some centrist positions."[63]

Bush scored major policy successes early in his first term largely by staking out an assertive policymaking approach that combined bipartisan and partisan governing strategies. Three days after being sworn into office, for example, Bush proposed the No Child Left Behind Act—later signed into law. The measure established standards of learning and accountability for elementary and junior high schools across the nation. A bipartisan and bicameral group of lawmakers—Reps. John Boehner, R-Ohio, and George Miller, D-Calif., and Sens. Edward Kennedy, D-Mass., and Judd Gregg, R-N.H., worked cooperatively with the administration to win passage of the legislation. Bush took a more partisan approach in pushing Congress to enact the largest across-the-board tax cut ($1.35 trillion) since Ronald Reagan's presidency. Although there were partisan complaints that the tax cut was too large, lawmakers on both sides of the aisle were reluctant to vote against tax reductions for their constituents.

A different legislative dynamic emerged after May 2001, when Senate Democrats suddenly became the majority party following Vermont GOP senator Jim Jeffords's party switch. (Jeffords became an Independent but caucused with the Democrats.) Democratic control of the Senate produced significant problems for the Bush administration. Now the Democrats could initiate and force votes on their priorities, hold hearings to spotlight their agenda and critique Bush's, modify or block administration bills coming from the GOP House, reject the president's nominations, and require the White House to develop "a defensive strategy for responding to Democratic ideas."[64] Bush responded by renouncing bipartisanship and adopting a partisan model of governance. Given the choice "between making concessions that create a broader bipartisan majority and narrowly passing a bill that more closely tracks his preferences, Bush will choose the latter," said top White House aides.[65]

The president soon encountered vocal opposition to many of his ideas in Congress and the country. Polls indicated public concern about the country's direction and showed that the public preferred Democratic positions over the GOP's. In June 2001, Bush's public standing had fallen "to a tepid 50 percent approval rating, the lowest presidential approval rating in more than five years."[66] Congressional Democrats were increasingly optimistic that they would reclaim control of Congress in the midterm elections of November 2002. It was not to be, however.

The Post-9/11 Phase. The second George W. Bush presidency was transformed by the terrorist attacks. After an uncertain response during the first days, Bush became a confident, resolute, decisive, and strong commander in chief. Images of the president consoling firemen and others at the site of the World Trade Center, his calm and confident demeanor, and his eloquent statements to the public—including the September 20, 2001, national address before a joint meeting of Congress—rallied the nation to fight a global war against terrorists and the states that provided them safe haven. He called this global struggle "the first war of the twenty-first century," a war that could go on for years or even decades.

Bush's public approval ratings soared to a record-level 91 percent, breaking his father's previous record of 89 percent established during the 1991 Persian Gulf War.[67] The levels of bipartisanship on Capitol Hill were also remarkable in the initial weeks after the terrorist attacks. Congress moved quickly to enact a number of significant measures, including passage of legislation authorizing the president to employ "all necessary and appropriate force" against those groups or nations involved in the terrorist attacks. Subsequently, as directed by the president, the military ousted the Taliban regime in Afghanistan, which had provided safe haven for Osama bin Laden, the Al Qaeda leader behind the September 11 attacks.

President Bush's focus then turned to Iraq, a nation he declared to be part of the "axis of evil" that threatened the world. The administration persuaded Congress in October 2002 to enact a joint resolution granting him unilateral authority to launch a preemptive military strike against Iraq. On March 19, 2003, President Bush went on national television and informed the nation of the start of the war in Iraq. Three weeks later, on April 9, U.S. forces entered Baghdad, ending the Saddam Hussein regime.

President Bush justified the invasion of Iraq on several grounds: Al Qaeda operated in Iraq, and Saddam Hussein was somehow involved in the 9/11 attacks; Hussein had weapons of mass destruction (chemical and biological) and posed a threat to American and world safety; and as the president stated in his 2003 State of the Union address, Hussein was obtaining uranium from Niger for his nuclear weapons program. The rationales for invading Iraq proved to be false. A number of analysts, retired generals, government officials, and others opposed the invasion, but "their concerns carried no weight against a swelling of patriotism, a backdrop of fear and an administration determined to oust Saddam Hussein."[68] A few weeks before he left office, in a valedictory interview with ABC News anchor Charles Gibson, President Bush came close to suggesting that the invasion of Iraq had been a mistake. "The biggest regret of all the presidency has to have been the intelligence failure in Iraq," the president stated.[69] (Ironically, as some semblance of stability emerged in Iraq, the military situation in Afghanistan deteriorated because of a resurgent Taliban and a weak Afghan government.)

The Iraq war came to dominate national politics and policymaking. It consumed the time and energy of the administration and Congress and divided the country. Upset with the Iraq war, President Bush, and political scandals on Capitol Hill, voters put Democrats in charge of the House and Senate in the November 2006 elections. The return of divided government was a major power shift in national governance in at least two respects: First, the Democratic-controlled Congress launched hard-hitting investigations of executive branch actions—contracting abuses in Iraq and in the aftermath of

Hurricane Katrina, for example—that received little attention from Republican Congresses fearful of embarrassing the White House.

Second, Democratic leaders of the 110th Congress worked to restore Congress's role as a "check and balance" by confronting and challenging the president on a range of issues, such as trying to impose a timetable for the withdrawal of U.S. troops from Iraq. During his presidency, Bush and Vice President Richard Cheney expanded executive power through a combination of unilateral decision making; minimizing, even ignoring, the role of Congress; and interpreting broadly the commander in chief's wartime role. The Democratic Congress devised their legislative strategies and battled the White House in the court of public opinion, but lawmaking on many significant issues proved difficult given the combined potency of the president's veto and the difficulty in obtaining the sixty votes needed to overcome GOP filibusters in the Senate.

Divided government (a common occurrence since World War II) does not necessarily mean legislative stalemate, even with an assertive Democratic Congress and a lame duck but resolute president. A number of major policy achievements have occurred during periods of divided government, largely because it prompts the search for bipartisan solutions to difficult problems. Even with heightened partisan tensions between Bush and congressional Democrats, the 110th Congress won enactment of several major laws, such as a $700-billion bailout of banks and financial institutions; a major tightening of ethics rules for lawmakers and lobbyists; higher fuel efficiency standards for automobiles; a new GI Bill of Rights for veterans; and a $300-billion reauthorization of a farm bill (overriding Bush's veto).

President Obama confronts an array of overlapping issues that involve the two presidencies, because so many of today's problems are transnational in character. They range from global warming to international criminal organizations to the global economic crisis. No single nation is capable of effectively addressing these global issues alone, nor is any nation insulated from the effects of these issues. The global economic decline, triggered by America's sub-prime mortgage crisis, directly affects the United States because thousands of workers have been laid off and because foreign purchasers are not able to buy our exports in the quantities they once did. The president understands that America's prosperity and security are inextricably linked to the well-being of the global economy. His director of national intelligence, Dennis C. Blair, warned Congress that "the global economic crisis is the most serious security peril facing the United States," bolstering lawmakers' support for passage of the president's nearly $800 billion economic stimulus package.[70]

THE VETO POWER

Article I, Section 7, of the Constitution requires the president to approve or disapprove bills passed by Congress. In the case of disapproval, the measure dies unless it "shall be repassed by two thirds of the Senate and House of Representatives." Because vetoes are so difficult to override, the veto power makes the president, in Woodrow Wilson's words, a "third branch of the legislature."[71] Presidents usually can attract enough of their supporters in Congress to sustain a veto, who may also publicly pledge to sustain vetoes of certain bills to show solidarity with the chief executive. From 1789 through the end of the George W. Bush administration, "36 of 44 Presidents have exercised their veto authority a total of 2,562 times. Congress has overridden these vetoes on 110 occasions (4.3%)."[72]

The decision to veto is a collective administration judgment. Presidents seek advice from numerous sources, such as agency officials, the Office of Management and Budget, and White House aides. Various reasons are commonly given for vetoing a bill: the bill is unconstitutional, it encroaches on the president's independence, it is unwise public policy, it cannot be administered, or it costs too much. Political calculations may permeate any or all of these reasons. The veto is more than a negative power, however. Presidents use the threat of a veto to advance their policy objectives by, for example, inducing legislators to accommodate executive preferences and objections. "We try to use the veto threat wisely, to change votes or to change the language of the underlying document," explained a top White House legislative aide. "And we succeed."[73]

Presidents also practice the politics of differentiation through the veto: A veto fight with Congress may suit presidents who want to underscore how their views differ from the other party's. For its part, Congress can discourage vetoes by adding items to must-pass legislation or to measures the president strongly favors. Congress may also deliberately send the president of the opposite party a measure that lawmakers want him to veto, so that they can use the issue on the campaign trail—a "winning by losing" strategy. Bills may also be signed in a public ceremony closer to the November elections as a way to energize the electoral base of the president's party, another example of the two Congresses.

Veto Options

Once the president receives a bill from Congress, he has ten days (excluding Sundays) in which to exercise one of four options:

1. He can sign the bill. Most public and private bills presented to the president are signed into law. Presidents sometimes issue signing statements that express their interpretation of a new law's provisions.

2. He can return the bill with his veto message to the originating house of Congress.

3. He can take no action, and the bill will become law without his signature. This option, seldom employed, is reserved for bills the president dislikes but not enough to veto.

4. He can pocket veto the bill. Under the Constitution, if a congressional adjournment prevents the return of a bill, the bill cannot become law without the president's signature.

Veto Strategies

George H.W. Bush was among the most successful chief executives in employing the veto against an opposition Congress. He used it to block unwanted legislation and as a potent bargaining weapon to get concessions from the Democratic-controlled Congress. Not until his term was nearly over, and after thirty-five consecutive veto victories, did Congress manage to override a Bush veto—on a 1992 measure to reregulate the cable television industry. Part of the explanation for Bush's veto successes was that he announced his intentions early and stuck by them unless the compromises he wanted were agreed to. Furthermore, he convinced congressional Republicans that their strength depended on sustaining his vetoes. (Of his forty-six vetoes, only the cable bill veto was overridden by Congress.)

By contrast, President Clinton did not veto a single measure during his first two years in office—something that had not happened since the days of Millard Fillmore in the 1850s. Part of the explanation is that Clinton was dealing with a Democratic Congress. Not until 1995 did Clinton use his veto pen, rejecting an appropriations bill sent to him by the Republican Congress. Subsequently, the president either exercised or threatened to exercise the veto against numerous GOP-sponsored bills.

President George W. Bush claimed that he would not hesitate to use his veto power to enforce his budgetary goals if Congress passed legislation he considered excessive or objectionable. But he did not veto a single bill, spending or otherwise, during his entire first term, although he did issue 145 veto threats during that time. One has to reach back all the way to James Garfield (1881) to find a vetoless president, and Garfield did not even serve a full year before being assassinated. Partial-term presidents William Henry Harrison, Zachary Taylor, and Millard Fillmore never issued a veto, nor did one-termers John Adams and John Quincy Adams. Only Jefferson survived two terms without one.[74]

Several factors account for Bush's no-veto first term: unified Republican control of the House and Senate during much of the period and the resulting consensus on many issues; the refusal of top party leaders, such as Speaker Hastert, to send to the White House bills that Bush might veto; the desire of Republicans to demonstrate their capacity to govern with narrow majorities; the ability of the White House and GOP congressional leaders to work out their disagreements; and the president's pragmatism in redefining his positions "to accommodate the direction in which lawmakers were leaning."[75] In addition, Bush also developed a practice of signing measures into law but ignoring the provisions he did not like and issuing signing statements.

Bush's first veto came in July 2006 on a stem-cell research bill that violated his anti-abortion beliefs.[76] With the Democratic takeover of the 110th Congress (2007–2009), the number of vetoes and veto threats increased. Bush vetoed seven measures in 2007 and four more the next year. In 2003, with the GOP in charge of Congress, Bush issued ninety-one statements of administration policy (which often included veto threats); 141 were sent to the Democratic Congress in 2007.[77] Congress overturned four of Bush's twelve vetoes.

Bush sometimes choreographed bill-signing ceremonies to reward supporters and send messages. For example, "Bush signed [a bill dealing with corporate corruption] on a table adorned with a sign saying 'Corporate Responsibility,' a technique used by the White House image-makers to associate the president's picture with the gist of his message."[78] In a first, President Bush invited bloggers as a group to a signing ceremony for a measure creating a database of federal spending—"a recognition of their role in forcing the bill through Congress over the objections of senior senators."[79] For their part, the Democratic leaders of the 110th Congress, Speaker Pelosi and Senate Majority Leader Reid, sometimes held their own media-covered signing ceremonies, affixing their signatures to bills before they were sent to the White House.[80] Once they have signed a bill, along with the signatures of the clerk of the House and secretary of the Senate, it is printed on special paper called "parchment" and delivered by hand to the White House. A copy is also sent to the Government Printing Office for online public distribution.

Post-Veto Action

Just as the president may feel strong pressure to veto or to sign a bill, Congress may feel intense political heat after it receives a veto message. A week after President Nixon's televised veto of a 1970 bill funding welfare programs, House members received more than 55,000 telegrams, most of them urging support for the veto. Congress upheld the veto, in part because of Nixon's televised appeal. However, despite a massive telephone campaign to congressional offices (as many as 80,000 calls an hour) urging members to sustain President Reagan's veto of a 1988 civil rights bill, the House and Senate easily overrode the veto.[81] Congress need not act at all on a vetoed bill. If party leaders lack the votes to override, the chamber that receives a vetoed measure may refer it to committee or table it. Even if one house musters the votes to override, the other body may do nothing. A vetoed bill cannot be amended—it is all or nothing at this stage—and the Constitution requires that votes on vetoed bills be recorded.

Presidents may issue proclamations called "signing statements" to accompany bills they have signed into law. Signing statements, although not mentioned in the Constitution, have been used since James Monroe's presidency (1817–1825). George W. Bush, however, employed them more often than any other president, to reassert and strengthen what was called the "unitary theory" of executive power.[82] As interpreted by Bush, this theory allowed the president

---

BOX 10-1 **Examples of Signing Statements**

	Congressional Directive	Signing Statement
Intelligence Reform and Terrorism Prevention Act of 2004 (PL 108-458) Signed December 17, 2004	Created a position for a national intelligence director in response to past intelligence failures, and required the president to consult with Congress on ther person's responsibilities.	"To the extent that provisions of the Act… purport to require consultation with the Congress as a condition to execution of the law, the executive branch shall construe such provisions as calling for, but not mandating, such consultation."
Fiscal 2006 Defense Appropriations (PL 109-148) Signed December 30, 2005	Outlawed "cruel, inhumane or degrading treatment" of suspected terrorists in U.S. custody.	"The executive branch shall construe Title X in Division A of the Act, relating to detainees, in a manner consistent with the constitutional authority of the President to supervise the unitary executive branch and as Commander in Chief."
Department of Defense Appropriations Act, 2007 (PL 109-289) Signed September 29, 2006	Blocked money from being spent to process foreign intelligence if it was gathered unlawfully. Stipulated that information gathered on U.S. citizens must comply with constitutional limits on searches and seizures.	"The executive branch shall construe [the provision] in a manner consistent with the President's constitutional authority as Commander in Chief, including for the conduct of intelligence operations, and to supervise the unitary executive branch."

Source: Adapted from Chris Wilson, "Memo to Congress: Bush Asserts Final Say," *CQ Weekly,* October 30, 2006, 2863.

---

to override laws that he claimed would impinge upon his constitutional prerogatives as commander in chief. When Congress banned torture of war prisoners, for example, the president held that the law trespassed on his powers as commander in chief. President Reagan was the first to use signing statements as a way to challenge congressional enactments on constitutional grounds. Of his 276 signing statements, 71 (or 26 percent) raised constitutional objections. By comparison, 127 (or 85 percent) of President Bush's 149 signing statements contained "multiple constitutional and statutory objections…to over 700 distinct provisions of law."[83] (See Box 10-1 for three examples of Bush's signing statements.)

Even though the Constitution requires the president to "take care that the laws be faithfully executed," Bush's signing statements asserted that "he has the power to set aside the laws when they conflict with his legal interpretation."[84] Signing statements have aroused the concern of Congress because they seem to provide the president an unofficial line-item veto, allowing him to decide which parts of bills to implement or ignore. On the other hand, other observers believe that signing statements have little effect on the administration of laws. Studies have shown that "federal agencies seem to have generally complied with thousands of legislative provisions that [Bush] had questioned."[85]

When campaigning for president, Obama criticized President Bush's use of signing statements. As president, Obama vowed that he would use such statements with restraint and "only when it is appropriate to do so as a means of discharging my constitutional responsibilities."[86] On March 11, 2009, President Obama issued his first signing statement, "reserving a right to bypass dozens of provisions in a $410 billion government spending bill even as he signed it into law."[87] GOP senator Charles E. Grassley of Iowa blasted the signing statement for setting back "whistleblower protections and [violating] two promises with one stroke of the pen."[88] The two promises, according to Grassley, were protecting whistleblowers and avoiding Bush's sentiment that some parts of laws are optional. In a White House memorandum to all departments and agencies, President Obama made clear that signing statements are appropriate in limited circumstances, and "they promote a healthy dialogue between the executive branch and Congress."[89]

Pocket Vetoes

The pocket veto has been a source of some controversy and confusion over the years. Article I, Section 7, of the Constitution states: "If any bill shall not be returned by the President within ten days (Sundays excepted) after it shall have been presented to him, the same shall be a law, in like manner as if he had signed it, unless Congress by the adjournment prevents its return, in which case it shall not be a law." The Framers wanted to ensure that presidents would not be forced into signing last-minute legislation, and that Congress would have time to consider, and perhaps override, the president's objections. The issue, however, is exactly when a congressional adjournment prevents the return of the president's veto. Several court decisions (see, for example, the 1974 case *Kennedy v. Sampson*) established the principle that pocket vetoes are not to be used during congressional sessions but only after Congress's final adjournment at the end of its second session.

This understanding was followed by the Ford and Carter administrations but not by other presidents. For example, President Reagan twice used intersession (between the first and second sessions) pocket vetoes, and President Clinton employed intrasession (in the middle of a session) pocket vetoes. Clinton even returned the pocket vetoes to Congress, which tried unsuccessfully to override them. In December 2007, President Bush invoked the pocket veto and returned it to the House (which originated the measure) "to leave no doubt the bill is being vetoed." The House majority voiced strong objection, with Speaker Pelosi declaring, "Your successful return of H.R. 1585 establishes that you were not prevented from returning it.[90] Thus it appears that neither an intra- nor an intersession pocket veto prevents its return to Congress. Until the Supreme Court makes a definitive ruling involving the use of the pocket veto both during and between legislative sessions, it is likely that legislative-executive conflicts over the pocket veto will occur periodically. In sum, the scope of the pocket veto power, as public law scholar Louis Fisher has written, "has been left largely to practice and to political understandings developed by the executive and legislative branches."[91]

The Line-Item Veto

Congress's habit of combining numerous items into a single measure obliges the president to accept or reject the entire package. Presidents and supporters of executive power have long advocated allowing the president to veto items selectively. They argue that it would give the president an effective way to eliminate wasteful spending and reduce the federal deficit. Opponents counter that the item veto is about interbranch power and not fiscal restraint. Granting the item veto to the president, they argue, would undermine Congress's power of the purse and give chief executives added bargaining leverage over lawmakers. "The president could say, 'I'm going to zap your dam, but I've got another piece of legislation coming around, and I won't be so inclined to do that [if you support me],'" said Rep. Jack Kingston, R-Ga. [92] Critics also say that presidents already have the only tool they need to control spending: the veto.

After much debate, Congress in 1996 expanded the president's rescission (cancellation of spending) authority. It eventually passed the line-item veto, as part of the "Contract with America," despite concern among congressional Republicans that President Clinton would use it against GOP-passed riders (extraneous policy provisos) in appropriations bills. The Line-Item Veto Act gave the president a fifth veto option. After a president signed a bill into law, he could exercise the line-item veto prerogative to cancel dollar amounts specified in any appropriations law, or even in the accompanying House or Senate committee reports; strike new entitlement programs or expansions of existing programs; and delete tax breaks limited to one hundred or fewer beneficiaries. The measure required the president, after using the line-item veto, to send a special message to Congress identifying what he had rescinded. To overturn his decisions, Congress would have to pass another bill that the president could then veto, requiring Congress to override it by a two-thirds vote of each chamber. Under the law the president could block something if he had the support of only one-third plus one of the members of each chamber. The act became effective January 1, 1997, and was to expire at the end of 2004.

Contrary to the expectations of pundits, President Clinton exercised caution in his use of the line-item veto. The president apparently chose not to anger lawmakers whose support he might need later to enact administration priorities. As one account noted, the president "has deferred to Congress on the overwhelming majority of projects that members added to budget bills, even when the Administration could find no compelling public interest to justify them."[93]

On June 25, 1998, in the case *Clinton v. New York City*, the Supreme Court by a 6–3 vote declared the Line-Item Veto Act unconstitutional because it gave the president "unilateral authority to change the text of duly enacted statutes," as Justice John Paul Stevens wrote for the majority.[94] The Clinton administration soon announced that it would release funds for the projects that had been subjects of line-item vetoes. Since the Court's decision, and in view of today's record expenditures during the economic crisis and heightened concern about wasteful spending, there has been renewed interest in enacting a constitutionally valid line-item veto.

For example, Sens. Russell Feingold, D-Wis., and John McCain, R-Ariz., along with Rep. Paul Ryan, R-Wis., introduced in the 111th Congress the Congressional Accountability and Line-Item Veto Act. If enacted, it would grant the president the ability to cancel, or rescind, congressionally earmarked spending, tax breaks, or tariff benefits. The president would return his recommendations for cancellation to Congress for expedited consideration in the House and Senate. The bill would be constitutional, declared Senator McCain, because it protects Congress's prerogatives by requiring "both the House and Senate to pass a rescission request before it can become law."[95]

SOURCES OF LEGISLATIVE-EXECUTIVE COOPERATION

Unlike the legislative assemblies of many nations, where executive authority is lodged in the leader of parliament—called the prime minister or premier—Congress truly is separate from the executive branch. Yet the executive and legislative branches are mutually dependent in policymaking. The 120 volumes of the *United States Statutes at Large* underscore the cooperative impulses of the two branches. Each volume contains the joint product of Congresses and presidents over the years, from the 108 public laws enacted by the First Congress (1789–1791) to the 460 enacted by the 110th Congress (2007–2009). These accomplishments are the result of party loyalties and public expectations, bargaining and compromise, and informal links between the president and lawmakers.

Party Loyalties and Public Expectations

Presidents and congressional leaders have met informally to discuss issues ever since the First Congress, when George Washington frequently sought the advice of Virginia representative James Madison. But meetings between the chief executive and House and Senate leaders were not common until Theodore Roosevelt's administration (1901–1909). Today, congressional party leaders are two-way conduits who communicate legislative views to the president and inform other members of executive preferences and intentions.

Presidents and members of their party are linked psychologically and ideologically. This means that "bargaining 'within the family' has a rather different quality than bargaining with members of the rival clan."[96] Congressional Democrats want President Obama to succeed in moving his agenda, even though they do not always share his priorities. As Rep. Chris Van Hollen, Md., chair of the Democratic Congressional Campaign Committee, said: "Our political fortunes are tied to Barack Obama's." The 2010 midterm elections "will be a report card not only on Congress but the White House, too."[97]

Bargaining and Compromise

The interdependence of the two branches provides each with the incentive to bargain. Legislators and presidents have in common at least three interests: shaping public policy, winning elections, and attaining influence within the legislature. In achieving these goals, members of Congress may be helped or hindered by executive officials. Agency personnel, for example, can heed legislators' advice in formulating policies, help them gain favorable publicity back home, and give them advance notice of executive actions. Executive officials, meanwhile, rely on legislators for help in pushing administrative proposals through the legislative process.

President Obama has courted the legislative branch extensively, as have his Cabinet heads and top aides, to gain favorable action on his agenda priorities. To win allies on his budget plans, Obama went to Capitol Hill to meet with key factions of the House Democratic Caucus: the moderate New Democrats, the Congressional Black Caucus, and the moderate-to-conservative Blue Dog Democrats, strong advocates of fiscal restraint. He had key Senate Democrats to the White House and visited with all Senate Democrats at their weekly luncheon session. Sen. Ron Wyden, D-Ore., stated that during a White House meeting with Senate Democrats, the president was open to a range of budgetary compromises. "If you don't care for ideas that I have," remarked Obama, "I'm going to be open to alternatives."[98] Similarly, the president met with key congressional Republicans to test their sentiments.

Informal Links

Some presidents deal with Congress more adeptly than others. Lyndon Johnson assiduously courted members. He summoned legislators to the White House for private meetings, danced with their wives at parties, telephoned greetings on their birthdays, and hosted them at his Texas ranch. He also knew how to twist arms to win support for his programs. Johnson's understanding of what moved members and energized Congress was awe-inspiring. "There is only one way for a President to deal with the Congress," he said, "and that is continuously, incessantly, and without interruption."[99]

President Obama meets periodically with the bicameral leadership—the Speaker, House minority leader, Senate majority leader, and Senate minority leader—to discuss issues of common concern. His top legislative aides are present at every key stage of a bill's development, working in "real time" to resolve contentious issues. As a former senator, the president also has informal and friendly relationships with many lawmakers, such as Sen. Tom Coburn, R-Okla., as do Vice President Joe Biden and White House chief of staff Rahm Emanuel. Presidential scholars suggest, however, that the chief executive's style and skills affect legislative success only "at the margins."[100] Far more important are contextual factors: the mood of the country, the state of the economy, the popularity of the president, the president's partisan strength in Congress, and so on.

SOURCES OF LEGISLATIVE-EXECUTIVE CONFLICT

Legislative-executive conflicts were evident in 1789; they are present today; and they can be expected in the future for at least three reasons. First, the Constitution specifies neither the precise policymaking roles of Congress and the president nor the manner in which they are to deal with one another. Second, presidents and Congresses serve different constituencies. Third, important variations exist in the timetables under which the two branches operate.

Constitutional Ambiguities

Article I invests Congress with "all legislative powers," but it also authorizes the president to recommend and to veto legislation. In several specific areas the Constitution splits authority between the president and Congress. The Senate, for example, is the president's partner in treaty making and nominations under "advice and consent" clauses. And before treaties can take effect, they require the concurrence of two-thirds of the Senate. The Constitution is silent, however, on how or when the Senate is to render its advice to the president.[101]

In 1919 and 1920 a historic confrontation occurred when the Senate vehemently opposed the Treaty of Versailles negotiated by President Wilson. The treaty contained an agreement binding the United States to the proposed League of Nations. Many senators had warned the president against including the League provision in the treaty, and during floor deliberations the Senate added several reservations that the president strongly opposed. Spurning compromise, Wilson launched a nationwide speaking tour to mobilize popular support for the treaty. Not to be outdone, senators opposed to the pact organized a "truth squad" that trailed the president and rebutted his arguments. During his tour Wilson suffered a stroke from which he never fully recovered. In the end the treaty was rejected. This historical example illustrates that, under the Constitution's separation of powers, presidents' ability to achieve even their most urgent foreign policy goals is limited by Congress's institutional prerogatives.

Different Constituencies

Presidents and their vice presidents are the only public officials elected nationally. To win, they must create vastly broader electoral coalitions than are necessary for legislators, who represent either states or districts. Only presidents, then, can claim to speak for the nation at large. It is important to note, however, that

> there is no structural or institutional or theoretical reason why the representation of a "single" broader constituency by the President is necessarily better or worse than the representation of many "separate" constituencies by several hundred legislators. Some distortion is inevitable in either arrangement, and the question of the good or evil of either form of distortion simply leads one back to varying value judgments.[102]

Presidents and legislators tend to view policies and problems from different perspectives. Members of Congress often subscribe to the view that "what's good for Portland is good for the nation." Presidents are apt to say that "what's good for the nation is good for Portland." In other words, public officials may view common issues differently when they represent diverging interests.

For example, a president might wish to reduce international trade barriers. A representative from a district where a manufacturer is threatened by imported products is likely to oppose the president's policy, while retailers of imported products are likely to support the president. The challenge to national policymaking is to forge consensus within an electorate that simultaneously holds membership in two or more competing constituencies.

Disparities in constituencies are underscored by differences in the ways voters judge presidents and members of Congress. Studies of presidential popularity ratings suggest that presidents are judged on the basis of general factors—economic boom or bust, the presence or absence of wars or other crises, the impact of policies on given groups.[103] The news media, too, can affect the assessment of presidents. Legislators, by contrast, tend to be assessed on the basis of their personalities, their communication with constituents, and their service in material ways to the state or district. Not only do presidents and legislators serve different constituencies, but they also labor under divergent incentives.

Different Time Perspectives

Finally, Congress and the president operate on different timetables. Presidents have four years, at most eight, to win adoption of their programs. They are usually in a hurry to achieve all they can before they leave office. In practice, they have even less time—in view of the typical decrease in presidential support after any so-called initial "honeymoon." In reality, presidents and their advisers often have a year, perhaps less, to sell their basic program to Congress and the public. "A president's most effective year is his first," explained Sen.

Richard Durbin, D-Ill., President Obama's close friend and confidant. "He is brand new to the office, has a national mandate of varying degrees, and Congress is usually more open to working with him. After the first year, an election year [2010] is under way and people look at him differently."[104] Presidents think in four-year terms, most lawmakers think in two.

On major, long-standing issues, however, Congress typically moves slowly. Seldom does it pass presidential initiatives quickly, unless an emergency or crisis of some sort is looming. Moreover, many legislators are careerists. Once elected, House members are likely to be reelected, and senators serve six-year terms. Most members hold office a good deal longer than the presidents they deal with. Skeptical legislators, reluctant to follow the president, realize that if they resist long enough someone else will occupy the White House.

THE BALANCE OF POWER

"The relationship between the Congress and the presidency," wrote Arthur M. Schlesinger Jr., "has been one of the abiding mysteries of the American system of government."[105] Part of the mystery inheres in the Constitution, which enumerates many powers for Congress as well as those "necessary and proper" to carry them out, while leaving the president's powers largely unstated. Where does the balance of power lie? There is no easy answer, but at certain times the scale has tipped toward Congress and at other times toward the president. Scholars have even identified periods of "congressional government" or "presidential government."[106]

Four points need to be remembered about the ups and downs of Congress and the presidency. First, even during periods when one branch appears to dominate, the actual balance of power in specific policy areas is complex. The stature of either branch is influenced by issues, events, partisan circumstances, personalities, or public opinion.

The mid-1960s and early 1970s, for example, are cited as a time of "imperial presidents" and compliant Congresses.[107] This refrain was heard again when Republicans were in charge of Congress (2001–2007) and George W. Bush was in the White House. But Congress was by no means passive during that period. While it enacted much of President Johnson's Great Society program, it also initiated scores of laws, including consumer, environmental, health, and civil rights legislation. Nor did executive actions go unchallenged. Nationally televised hearings conducted in 1966 by the Senate Foreign Relations Committee helped to mobilize congressional and public opposition to the Vietnam War.

Second, power also shifts within each branch. In Congress aggressive leaders may be followed by less-assertive leaders. In the executive branch the forces for White House leadership regularly battle the forces for agency decentralization. These internal power fluctuations clearly affect policymaking. As recently as the Eisenhower presidency in the 1950s, powerful committee and party leaders could normally deliver blocs of votes to pass legislation. Today, even with the resurgence of partisanship on Capitol Hill, the president can never be sure which of the 535 members will form a winning coalition.

Third, legislative-executive relationships are not zero-sum games. If one branch gains power, the other does not necessarily lose it. If one branch is up, the other need not be down. The expansion of the federal government since World War II has augmented the authority of both branches. Their growth rates were different, but each expanded its ability to address complex issues, initiate legislation, and frustrate proposals of the other. Conventional wisdom states that wars, crises, nuclear weapons, military expansion, and public demands fostered the imperial presidency. Such factors certainly enlarge the likelihood of executive dominance, but in the wars of 1812 and 1898, for example, military action was encouraged in part by aggressive Congresses. Economic panics and depressions under Presidents James Monroe, James Buchanan, and Ulysses S. Grant did not lead to losses of congressional power.

Political scientist David Mayhew has asserted that, with respect to productivity of laws and investigations, it "does not seem to make all that much difference whether party control of the American government happens to be unified or divided."[108] Mayhew examined the period from 1946 to 1990, when the mobilization of cross-party majorities on Capitol Hill was commonplace. President Ronald Reagan, for instance, enjoyed large successes on his policy priorities (tax cuts, defense hikes, and program reductions) in 1981, when he won the support of conservative "Reagan Democrats" in the Democratic-controlled House. Today, in an era of strong, closely divided, and ideologically distinct congressional parties—reflecting the conditional party government model—presidents confront heightened potential for partisan impasses, especially in the Senate, regardless of whether the government is unified or divided.

Conflict between Congress and the president is embedded in the system of separation of powers and checks and balances. But the Founders also expected their governmental arrangement to promote accommodation between the branches. Historical patterns have veered between these two extremes. The two branches worked together in the early days of Woodrow Wilson's progressive New Freedom (1913–1916), during the New Deal (1933–1937) and World War II (1941–1945), in the brief Great Society years (1964–1966) following John F. Kennedy's assassination in 1963, for the even briefer "Reaganomics" juggernaut during Ronald Reagan's first year in office (1981), and for most of George W. Bush's first six years in office (2001–2007). At other times they fought fiercely—during Wilson's second term (1919–1921); after 1937 during the Franklin Roosevelt administration; after 1966 during the Lyndon Johnson administration; and for much of the Nixon, Reagan, George H.W. Bush, and Clinton administrations, and the final two years of George W. Bush's presidency.

Finally, a wide gap often separates what presidents want from what they can achieve. Congress can influence what, when, how, or even whether executive recommendations are sent to Capitol Hill. Expectations of what will pass Congress frequently shape White House agendas. This indirect priority-setting power of the House and Senate can affect whether the president even transmits certain proposals to Congress. It also works in the other direction. Recommendations may be forwarded or endorsed because the White House knows they have broad legislative support. "The president proposes, Congress disposes" is an oversimplified adage.

Congress and the president are institutions shaped by diverging imperatives. Executive officials want flexibility, discretion, and long-range commitments from Congress. They prefer few controls and consultations with a limited number of legislators. The executive tends to be hierarchical, or vertical, in decision making, whereas Congress tends to be collegial and horizontal—with power spread among 535 independent-minded lawmakers. One of the legislative branch's strengths is to give voice and visibility to diverse viewpoints that the executive branch may have overlooked or ignored. The dispersion of power can slow down decision making, but it can also promote public acceptance of the nation's policies. Hence, what are often viewed as Congress's vices are also genuine virtues.

CONCLUSION

Conflict would seem to be the inevitable result of a system that intentionally divides lawmaking and other powers between the executive and legislative branches. Much of the relationship between Congress and the executive, however, is better characterized as accommodation than as conflict. Neither branch is monolithic. Presidents find supporters in both chambers even when they are opposed by congressional majorities. Both branches seek support for their policy preferences from each other and from outside allies. Congress and the president must find ways to work together to achieve common goals.

Nevertheless, confrontation is a recurring element in dealings between Capitol Hill and the White House. The Framers of the Constitution consciously distributed and mixed power among the three branches. They left it unclear how Congress or the president would assert control over the bureaucracy and over policymaking. Even when both houses of Congress are controlled by the same party as the White House, the two branches have different constituencies and often become adversaries.

Lastly, legislative-executive relations are constantly evolving. Either branch may be active on an issue at one time and passive at another time. So many circumstances affect how, when, what, or why shifts occur in the relationship that it is impossible to predict the outlook.

Over the past generation Congress clearly has equipped itself with a formidable arsenal of resources. As a result, it can play a more active role, initiating policies of its own and overseeing executive branch actions. This development need not be a formula for stalemate. "Our proper objective," counseled Sen. J. William Fulbright, D-Ark. (1945–1974), "is neither a dominant presidency nor an aggressive Congress but, within the strict limits of what the Constitution mandates, a shifting of the emphasis according to the needs of the time and the requirements of public policy."[109]

SUGGESTED READINGS

Binkley, Wilfred. *President and Congress*. New York: Knopf, 1947.

Bond, Jon R., and Richard Fleisher, eds. *Polarized Politics: Congress and the President in a Partisan Era*. Washington, D.C.: CQ Press, 2000.

Edwards, George C., III. *On Deaf Ears: The Limits of the Bully Pulpit*. New Haven: Yale University Press, 2006.

Fisher, Louis. *Constitutional Conflicts between Congress and the President*. 4th ed. Lawrence: University Press of Kansas, 1997.

Gilmour, John B. *Strategic Disagreement: Stalemate in American Politics*. Pittsburgh: University of Pittsburgh Press, 1995.

Gregg, Gary L., II. *Considering the Bush Presidency*. New York: Oxford University Press, 2004.

Howell, William G. *Power without Persuasion: The Politics of Direct Presidential Action*. Princeton, N.J.: Princeton University Press, 2003.

Jones, Charles O. *Clinton and Congress 1993–1996*. Norman, Okla.: University of Oklahoma Press, 1999.

Mayhew, David R. *Divided We Govern: Party Control, Lawmaking, and Investigating, 1946–1990*. New Haven: Yale University Press, 1991.

Rudalevige, Andrew. *The New Imperial Presidency*. Ann Arbor: University of Michigan Press, 2005.

A *Far-Flung Bureaucracy.* During his confirmation hearings before the Senate Energy and Natural Resources Committee (top), Interior Secretary-designate Sen. Ken Salazar (D-Colo.) walks to the dais to speak with Sens. Blanche Lincoln (D-Ark.) and Lisa Murkowski (R-Alaska) and staff member Sam Fowler. (Salazar is the committee's first member to serve as Interior Secretary.) Federal agencies are charged with diverse tasks: a TSA (Transportation Safety Administration) officer screens a passenger at a security checkpoint at Baltimore-Washington International Airport (center). And a FEMA (Federal Emergency Management Agency) agent (bottom) hands a card to a resident of Parkersburg, Iowa, which had just been declared a federal disaster area after tornadoes struck in May 2008.

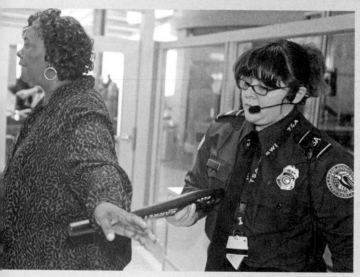

Congress and the Bureaucracy

I n his 1981 inaugural address, President Ronald Reagan declared that "government is not the solution to our problem, government is the problem." Fifteen years later, in a State of the Union address, President Bill Clinton exclaimed, "The era of big government is over."

Today, the era of big government is back, if it ever went away. Under presidents of both parties, the national government continues to grow. The administration of Republican president George W. Bush witnessed substantial governmental growth, only in part triggered by new domestic security, law enforcement, and military requirements after the September 11, 2001, terrorist attacks. As journalist David S. Broder wrote, President Bush presided over one of the largest expansions of government in history. "He has created a mammoth Cabinet department [the Department of Homeland Security], increased federal spending, imposed new federal rules on local and state governments, and injected federal requirements into every public school in America."[1]

Democratic president Barack Obama took office in the midst of the most serious national economic crisis since the Great Depression. Daily, the news media highlight the seriousness of the economic downturn: growing joblessness, plant closings, the collapse of major banks and financial institutions, and the spread of home foreclosures. As a result, the government has intervened dramatically in the marketplace, including the forced ouster of the General Motors chief executive as a condition for the company to receive additional federal bailout funds.[2] Trillions of taxpayer dollars are being spent to try and revive the ailing economy and prevent the deep economic recession from spiraling downward into another depression. "Not since Lyndon B. Johnson and Franklin D. Roosevelt," wrote a congressional journalist, has a president like Obama "moved to expand the role of government so much on so many fronts—and with such a demanding sense of urgency."[3] As one scholar said about this government-directed model of capitalism:

> We've gone from debates over privatizing the public sector to big steps toward governmentalizing the private sector. We're writing this new social contract with three guides: more public money in the private economy, more rules to shape how the private sector behaves, and more citizen expectations that government will manage the risks we face.[4]

Why is it so difficult for presidents or Congress to shrink the size, role, or reach of the federal government? Setting aside war and other national crises, one basic reason is the ambivalence of the public. Although professing to want to get government off their backs, Americans of virtually all ideological persuasions often turn to government to fulfill their goals and to provide assistance during times of need. As William S. Cohen, former GOP senator from Maine (1979–1997) and defense secretary during the Clinton administration, put it: "The government is the enemy until one needs a friend."[5]

The paradox, then, is that citizens oppose the general idea of big government (after all, few people like to pay taxes), but they support the government's specific roles—and may even welcome their selective expansion—in ensuring clean air and water, a strong national defense, access to quality health care, the safety of food and prescription drugs, crime prevention, and protection from terrorist attacks. Understandably, lawmakers typically defend government programs supported by their constituents. And to implement each government program, an organized bureaucracy is required.

The two Congresses contribute to an expanding bureaucracy. In today's complex and interdependent world, constituents look to the national government for security, services, justice, and protection. Members of Congress respond to their constituents' demands. Regardless of which party is in control, the national government is not reluctant to supersede state authority to regulate electricity, define what constitutes drunk driving, or combat child abductions. Similarly, nationwide corporations often lobby for federal regulation so they do not have to contend with the different rules of the fifty states. Indeed, businesses often prefer federal regulations because these are sometimes "considerably weaker than those being imposed these days by many of the tougher states."[6] As former senator Ernest F. Hollings, D-S.C. (1966–2005), said: "We have armies who protect us from enemies from without and the [Federal Bureau of Investigation] protects us from enemies within. We have Social Security to protect us from the ravages of old age. We have Medicare to protect us from ill health. We have clean air and clean water [laws] to protect our environment. We have [laws that mandate] safe working places and safe machinery. Our fundamental duties here are to protect."[7]

CONGRESS ORGANIZES THE EXECUTIVE BRANCH

Just as the president and Congress share influence over lawmaking, they share responsibility for the executive branch of government—the bureaucracy. The Constitution requires the president to implement the laws, and by implication it empowers him to manage the executive branch. But Congress "has at least as much to do with executive administration as does an incumbent of the White House."[8] Congress is constitutionally authorized to organize and fund the executive branch. The Framers, of course, did not foresee the huge federal bureaucracy that has arisen from their sparse references to "executive departments." George Washington supervised only three departments (State,

War, and Treasury); Barack Obama heads fifteen. Beyond the cabinet departments, the federal bureaucracy also includes independent agencies (the Central Intelligence Agency, e.g.), independent regulatory commissions, and government corporations (see Figure 11-1).

Congress has extensive influence over the structure and composition of the federal bureaucracy.[9] Congress can enact statutes that establish or abolish executive agencies and departments. (see Table 11-1). The newest cabinet creation, for example, is the Department of Homeland Security (DHS). Congress can also instruct departments and agencies to reorganize themselves or establish an outside commission to recommend how departments or agencies might be merged or abolished. Congress can authorize the president to reorganize on his own initiative or to propose reorganization plans subject to some form of congressional review. Besides establishing federal entities such as DHS, Congress has an array of other ways to affect bureaucratic behavior. The Senate confirms (or not, as the case might be) high-level administrative officials. Congress authorizes the basic personnel systems of federal entities. It also grants rule-making authority to administrative agencies.

Senate Confirmation of Presidential Appointees

High-level federal appointments—executive, diplomatic, and judicial—are subject to the Senate's "advice and consent" under Article II, Section 2, of the Constitution. After the president has decided whom to nominate, the Senate decides whether to confirm (see Figure 11-2).

Senators use their confirmation power to wield influence over executive branch priorities. Senate committees usually elicit the following promise from departmental and agency nominees they have confirmed: "The above nomination [a Cabinet secretary, for example] was approved subject to the nominee's commitment to respond to requests to appear and testify before any duly constituted committee of the Senate."[10] Or as Sen. Charles Grassley, R-Iowa, declared, "I'm going to hit every [Obama] nominee with the question, 'Are you open to congressional oversight?'"[11] The confirmation process also reflects the two Congresses principle. As a top Senate official once remarked, "It looks very, very good in California or some place to put out a press release that says, 'Today, I questioned the new Secretary of Transportation about the problems of our area.'"[12]

Presidents have three broad ways to bypass the Senate's advice and consent role for positions subject to advice and consent. Constitutionally, presidents can make recess appointments during Senate breaks, either within or between sessions.[13] The Constitution (Article II, Section 2) provides that "[t]he President shall have Power to fill up all Vacancies that may happen during a Recess of the Senate, by granting Commissions which shall expire at the End of their next Session." Recess appointees then serve until the end of the next Senate session; for example, a person named in 2009 could serve until late 2010. Senators often resent presidential use of this option; their opposition to some potential recess appointees may prompt the Senate technically to stay in session as a way to

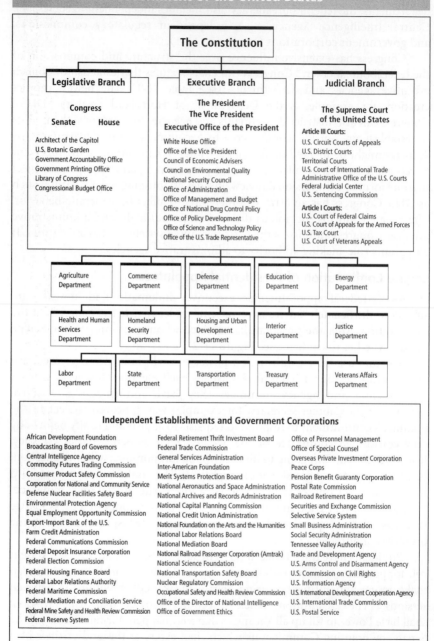

FIGURE 11-1 The Government of the United States

The Constitution

Legislative Branch

Congress

Senate **House**

Architect of the Capitol
U.S. Botanic Garden
Government Accountability Office
Government Printing Office
Library of Congress
Congressional Budget Office

Executive Branch

**The President
The Vice President
Executive Office of the President**

White House Office
Office of the Vice President
Council of Economic Advisers
Council on Environmental Quality
National Security Council
Office of Administration
Office of Management and Budget
Office of National Drug Control Policy
Office of Policy Development
Office of Science and Technology Policy
Office of the U.S. Trade Representative

Judicial Branch

**The Supreme Court
of the United States**

Article III Courts:
U.S. Circuit Courts of Appeals
U.S. District Courts
Territorial Courts
U.S. Court of International Trade
Administrative Office of the U.S. Courts
Federal Judicial Center
U.S. Sentencing Commission

Article I Courts:
U.S. Court of Federal Claims
U.S. Court of Appeals for the Armed Forces
U.S. Tax Court
U.S. Court of Veterans Appeals

Agriculture Department	Commerce Department	Defense Department	Education Department	Energy Department
Health and Human Services Department	Homeland Security Department	Housing and Urban Development Department	Interior Department	Justice Department
Labor Department	State Department	Transportation Department	Treasury Department	Veterans Affairs Department

Independent Establishments and Government Corporations

African Development Foundation
Broadcasting Board of Governors
Central Intelligence Agency
Commodity Futures Trading Commission
Consumer Product Safety Commission
Corporation for National and Community Service
Defense Nuclear Facilities Safety Board
Environmental Protection Agency
Equal Employment Opportunity Commission
Export-Import Bank of the U.S.
Farm Credit Administration
Federal Communications Commission
Federal Deposit Insurance Corporation
Federal Election Commission
Federal Housing Finance Board
Federal Labor Relations Authority
Federal Maritime Commission
Federal Mediation and Conciliation Service
Federal Mine Safety and Health Review Commission
Federal Reserve System

Federal Retirement Thrift Investment Board
Federal Trade Commission
General Services Administration
Inter-American Foundation
Merit Systems Protection Board
National Aeronautics and Space Administration
National Archives and Records Administration
National Capital Planning Commission
National Credit Union Administration
National Foundation on the Arts and the Humanities
National Labor Relations Board
National Mediation Board
National Railroad Passenger Corporation (Amtrak)
National Science Foundation
National Transportation Safety Board
Nuclear Regulatory Commission
Occupational Safety and Health Review Commission
Office of the Director of National Intelligence
Office of Government Ethics

Office of Personnel Management
Office of Special Counsel
Overseas Private Investment Corporation
Peace Corps
Pension Benefit Guaranty Corporation
Postal Rate Commission
Railroad Retirement Board
Securities and Exchange Commission
Selective Service System
Small Business Administration
Social Security Administration
Tennessee Valley Authority
Trade and Development Agency
U.S. Arms Control and Disarmament Agency
U.S. Commission on Civil Rights
U.S. Information Agency
U.S. International Development Cooperation Agency
U.S. International Trade Commission
U.S. Postal Service

Source: The United States Government Manual, 2007–2008 (Washington, D.C.: Office of the Federal Registrar, GPO), 21.

TABLE 11-1 **Growth of the Cabinet**	
Department	Year created
State	1789
Treasury	1789
War (reorganized and renamed Defense in 1947)	1789
Interior	1849
Justice (position of attorney general created in 1789)	1870
Agriculture	1889
Commerce (created as Commerce and Labor)	1903
Labor (split from Commerce and Labor)	1913
Health, Education, and Welfare (reorganized and renamed Health and Human Services in 1979)	1953
Housing and Urban Development	1965
Transportation	1966
Energy	1977
Education	1980
Veterans Affairs	1989
Homeland Security	2002

Source: *CQ Daily Monitor,* Jan uary 10, 2003, 3.

block these appointments. The Senate convenes pro forma sessions that last only seconds to prevent the chief executive's use of the recess authority. For example, the Democratic Senate held pro forma sessions to prevent Steven G. Bradbury from getting a recess appointment. President Bush had nominated Bradbury five times to be head of the Justice Department's Office of Legal Counsel, but many Senate Democrats had "concerns about Bradbury's views on interrogation techniques that critics say amount to torture."[14]

Second, the president can name individuals, on a temporary acting basis, to fill vacant positions that require confirmation by the Senate. Senate dissatisfaction with this procedure led to enactment of the Federal Vacancies Reform Act (P.L. 105-277), which imposed time restrictions on how long officials can serve in an acting capacity, typically 210 days.

Third, Congress has enacted laws that permit the president, an agency head, or an automatic mechanism to fill temporary vacancies. For example, if the director of the Office and Management and Budget (OMB) is absent or unable to serve, the deputy director then acts as the OMB director.[15]

Moreover, many prominent officials, such as White House advisors, are not subject to the advice and consent of the Senate. President Obama may be a

FIGURE 11-2 The Appointments Process

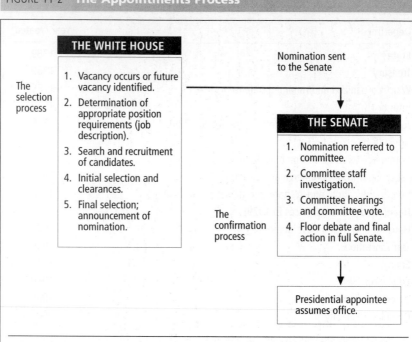

record-breaker in naming so many individuals, informally called "czars," to head up important policy initiatives—the "environmental czar," the "economic czar," or the "information czar."[16] A fundamental job of czars is to oversee and coordinate the forming of coherent policies that cross-cut the jurisdictions of several departments and agencies. The appointment of numerous czars also reflects the amassing of further power in the White House. Sen. Robert C. Byrd, D-W.Va., has objected to Obama's naming of multiple czars because they are not answerable to Congress, and they confuse the lines of administrative authority and "obscure the decisionmaking process."[17] Added Yale law professor Bruce Ackerman, "[W]e need to seriously consider requiring Senate approval of senior White House staff positions."[18] Others, however, question the value of confirmation hearings that are often dominated by fringe or unrelated matters, such as whether a nominee hired undocumented household help.

Indeed, nominations to high-level executive posts today are subject to standards of judgment and evaluation that go far beyond reasonable questions of competence or conflict of interest. Nominees' personal lives and backgrounds are scrutinized as well. As one commentator explained:

These days, if you want to run for office or accept a position of public trust, everything is relevant. Your moral, medical, legal and financial background, even your college records, become the subject of public scrutiny. In the old days, the scrutiny was done in private, and certain transgressions could be considered irrelevant.[19]

This shift in standards stems in part from a change in attitudes by the press, the public, the White House, and the Senate. The press, for example, now more aggressively reports on the private activities of public officials.[20] In the 1980s, use of marijuana could derail nominees; in the 1990s, it was hiring illegal immigrants as a nanny or domestic helper. In 2009, it has been tax issues that have caused problems for several of Obama's top nominees, such as Thomas Daschle's (the former Senate Democratic leader) withdrawal as the president's choice to head the Department of Health and Human Services because of failure to pay $146,000 in taxes.[21] This development is also driven, in large measure, by a hyperpartisan environment in which the president's opponents seek to embarrass or obstruct the administration at every turn.

The combination of these developments has produced a rigorous vetting process for nominees. Each nominee must fill out several lengthy questionnaires. The Senate Finance Committee has "borrowed" IRS staff to examine the tax returns of Obama's nominees. Several lengthy questionnaires must be filled out by each nominee. Investigators from the White House, the FBI, the IRS, and the Senate ask nominees difficult and uncomfortable questions about their personal and professional lives. "I have never been subjected to such personally insulting and expensive scrutiny in my life," said one Obama nominee, who was asked for receipts for furniture he donated to charity more than a decade ago. Another nominee was asked about "his wife's sexual activity when she was at university."[22] The importance of a thorough vetting process was emphasized by an Obama adviser. "The real purpose of vetting," he said, "is to understand the person's ability to perform the job and be confirmed for the position. We also want to avoid surprises."[23] ("Avoiding surprises," as well as ability, was a fundamental concern.) There were nonetheless surprises for President Obama, not only with Daschle but also with New Mexico governor Bill Richardson's sudden withdrawal for Commerce Secretary because of an ongoing investigation in his state and Treasury secretary Timothy Geithner's unexpected tax problems that delayed his eventual confirmation.

One result of the rigorous vetting process, according to a study done by the Brookings Institution (a Washington, D.C.–based think tank), is a drop-off in "the number of talented Americans willing to accept the call to presidential [service]. Presidential recruiters report that it takes more calls to find candidates willing to subject themselves to the process and more work to keep the candidates from bolting once the process begins."[24]

Today, there is substantial frustration with the confirmation process. "The nomination system is a national disgrace," wrote a scholar of the presidential appointment process.[25] The problems are many, afflicting the administrations of both parties—even when the same party controls the White House and the Senate. Although the Senate eventually confirms most nominees, three concerns with the process merit mention.

First, it takes ever longer to fill the full-time cabinet and agency positions requiring Senate confirmation. Whereas President John F. Kennedy had his administrative appointees in place by April 1961, only 2.4 months after his inauguration, "the first Bush administration was not fully confirmed until early October [1989], and the Clinton administration not until mid-October [1993], more than eight months after the start of their respective presidencies."[26] Four months into George W. Bush's first-term administration, "only 11 percent of its most senior government positions" had been filled.[27] For Bush's second term, however, all of his new cabinet secretaries were in place by mid-February 2005, with most confirmed during January.

Although senators have complained about the slowness of President Obama's nominating process, he is "still sending the Senate more names and winning confirmation faster than his predecessor" at the same point in time.[28] The senatorial complaints typically involve delays in filling key Health and Human Services and Treasury positions. For example, Paul Volcker, a former Federal Reserve chair and economic adviser to President Obama, lamented: "The secretary of the Treasury is sitting there without a deputy, without any undersecretaries, without any, as far as I know, assistant secretaries responsible in substantive areas at a time of very severe crisis. He shouldn't be sitting there alone."

Second, bureaucratic developments contribute to the slowness of the confirmation process. Congress and the president have created more executive positions requiring Senate confirmation. President Kennedy nominated fifteen undersecretaries and eighty-seven assistant secretaries in 1961; President George W. Bush appointed almost fifty undersecretaries and more than 220 assistant secretaries.[29] For his fifteen cabinet departments, President Obama has more than 700 Senate-confirmable positions to fill. Overall, there are 1,141 Senate-confirmable positions when other agencies are included in the count.[30]

In the 1970s, writes Professor Paul C. Light, "Congress discovered executive structure...and began to mine it."[31] Since then Congress and the president have made numerous changes in the top four layers of officials in cabinet departments (secretary, deputy secretary, undersecretary, and assistant secretary). More new job titles in the top echelons of government have been created than ever before. Additional bureaucratic layers result—in some federal agencies there are as many as fifty layers between the president and frontline executive employees—"a bureaucratic fog in which Congress and the president are hopelessly isolated from the people they most need to guide."[32] Among the numerous new titles are: deputy associate deputy secretary, principal assistant deputy undersecretary, principal senior deputy assistant secretary, deputy associate assistant secretary, and deputy executive associate administrator.[33]

As a result of "title creep," Professor Light explains that it is difficult to know whom to hold accountable for what goes wrong in the executive branch, and "impossible for the bottom to hear the top when messages go through dozens of interpretations on their journey down."[34] Light brands title creep as the "thickening of government" and attributes much of it to "an indelible belief that more leaders equals more leadership."[35] Several other reasons account for the invention of new titles, including the "use of promotions rather than pay raises to reward senior employees, the creation of new positions by Congress and attempts by presidents to tighten their hold on the bureaucracy with a greater number of political appointees."[36] New political posts are created by redefining civil service jobs as political or simply by creating new positions. Whatever the reason for their creation, the addition of nominees subject to advice and consent slows the confirmation process.

Third, the Senate's confirmation process can be mean and nasty, especially in this period of polarized politics. "With law so hard to make and so hard to change, influencing the choice of the implementers and adjudicators of the law becomes an essential strategic option."[37] Many nominees, therefore, are subjected to rough treatment. Ideological groups, for instance, may organize attack campaigns to defeat nominees who appear unsupportive of their agenda. Sometimes the purpose of Senate confirmation hearings "seems less to ensure that nominees are fit than to cripple the chief executive's political leadership. A defeated nomination can embarrass a president, demoralize his supporters, and reduce public confidence in his judgment."[38] Others argue that although the confirmation process may be tough, so are the positions for which nominees seek assignment. "If you can't fight your way through the process," stated a former head of the Central Intelligence Agency (CIA), "you might not just do a hot job as director."[39]

Individual senators, too, are not reluctant to threaten filibusters or to place holds on nominations. (Recall that holds are notices by senators to party leaders that they oppose floor consideration of certain nominees. See Box 11-1 for holds placed on nominations.) The filibuster of a nominee may also reflect the two Congresses. Sen. Arlen Specter, then R-Pa., expected a stiff primary challenge in 2010. As one GOP senator remarked, a Specter-led filibuster of a controversial nominee to head the Office of Legal Counsel in the Department of Justice "could be very good for him." It could potentially unite conservative primary voters behind him.[40] (To avoid the primary, Specter switched parties in 2009.) The Senate may also refuse to consider a nominee if members invoke senatorial courtesy. This tradition, dating from the nation's earliest years, means that the Senate will usually delay or not act upon nominees for offices in a state if opposed by a senator of the president's party from that state.

Fourth, some observers doubt the ability of political appointees to manage the federal government and regard the confirmation process as a limited tool for testing basic competence. "We entrust the administration of the largest 'company' in the country…to a cast of well-meaning political loyalists with little or no management experience," wrote a career civil servant with thirty-four years of federal service. "We accept the rather mindless notion that any bright and public-spirited dilettante can run a government agency, bureau, or office."[41]

BOX 11-1 **Senate Panel Approves Science Adviser Nominees Delayed by Anonymous Holds**

The Senate Commerce, Science, and Transportation Committee approved the nominations of two top science advisers that have been delayed by multiple anonymous holds.

The panel approved by voice vote the nominations of John P. Holdren, picked to head the White House Office of Science and Technology Policy, and Jane Lubchenco, who would direct the National Oceanic and Atmospheric Administration.

Majority Leader Harry Reid, D-Nev., was expected to later move to limit debate on the nominations in an effort to overcome the holds.

The source of the holds was still unclear. However, Jean Longo, a committee spokeswoman, said they were not placed by a Democrat.

Sen. Robert Menendez, D-N.J., had reportedly placed a hold on the two nominees over an unrelated matter dealing with Cuba policy in the recently enacted fiscal 2009 omnibus (PL 111-8), but it was apparently lifted.

Senate aides speculated that the holds were placed by Republicans opposed to the nominees' stance on global climate change, particularly as it regards the government's role.

Although a Feb. 12 nomination hearing was mostly amicable, Sen. David Vitter, R-La., gave Holdren a particularly lengthy grilling on his past stances on climate change.

"One of the lines from the president's inaugural address which I most appreciated was his comment about science and honoring that and not having it overtaken by ideology," Vitter said when he opened his questioning. "My concern is that, as one of his top science advisers, many statements you've made in the past don't meet that task, and so I wanted to explore that."

Science advocates have said they are frustrated by the blocking of administration officials they argue are needed now more than ever.

The holdup could slow timely science and environment policy work between Congress and the administration, particularly the spending of roughly $21.5 billion dedicated to science in the economic recovery package. (PL 111-5.)

Source: Kathryn A. Wolfe, "Senate Panel Approves Science Adviser Nominees Delayed by Anonymous Holds," *CQ Today,* March 13, 2009, 11.

The Personnel System

Congress wields constitutional, legal, and informal authority over the federal personnel system, as the creation of DHS shows. In establishing the newest cabinet department, Congress authorized both it and the Defense Department to revamp their personnel systems with an eye toward loosening civil service restrictions—that is, rewarding employees for the quality of their work instead of their longevity of service. The civil service itself was created after a disgruntled job seeker assassinated President James A. Garfield in 1881. That event prompted Congress to curb the abuses of the spoils system, the practice of handing out federal jobs to supporters of the party that had won the presidency. In 1883 Congress passed the first civil service law that substituted merit for patronage. But those patronage practices have a modern equivalent:

TABLE 11-2 **Political Appointees by Department and Appointment Type as of September 1, 2008**

Department	Pres. Appt. Requiring Senate Approval	Pres. Appt. Not Requiring Senate Approval	Non-Career Senior Executive Service	Schedule C	Total
Agriculture	16	0	43	168	227
Commerce	23	2	33	103	161
Defense	53	0	94	134	281
Education	17	1	14	112	144
Energy	22	0	30	66	118
Health and Human Services	20	1	48	66	135
Homeland Security	20	1	61	102	184
Housing and Urban Development	15	0	18	49	82
Interior	17	0	30	36	83
Justice	223	0	45	68	336
Labor	19	0	29	105	153
State	222	3	36	125	386
Transportation	23	0	31	41	95
Treasury	33	0	23	45	101
Veterans Affairs	15	0	8	9	32
Total	738	8	543	1229	2518

Source: Henry B. Hogue, Maureen Bearden, and Betsy Palmer, *Filling Advice and Consent Position at the Outset of a New Administration,* CRS Report RLWP19, December 18, 2008, 3.

the political appointee system. Currently, in the fifteen cabinet departments, there are more than 2,500 political appointees (see Table 11-2).[42] The number of political appointees, however, is small compared with the number of federal employees (2.7 million civil servants and 1.4 million uniformed personnel).

When Hurricane Katrina devastated the Gulf Coast in late August 2005, for example, the chief of the Federal Emergency Management Agency (FEMA) was Michael Brown. A former commissioner of the International Arabian Horse Association, Brown had little experience in emergency management. Despite President Bush's praise—"Brownie, you're doing a heck of a job"— FEMA's response in quickly ameliorating the misery of the people in this region was inept and inadequate. One response by Congress was to pass the Post-Katrina Emergency Management Reform Act of 2006 (P.L. 109-295), which requires that any nominee named to head FEMA must meet certain qualifications. The law provides that the administrator of FEMA "shall be appointed from among individuals who have—(A) a demonstrated ability in and knowledge of emergency management and homeland security; and (B) not less than 5 years of executive leadership and management experience in the public or private sector."[43]

Sens. Russell D. Feingold, D-Wis., and John McCain, R-Ariz., proposed that the number of political appointees be capped at two thousand.[44] They judged there were simply far more such officials than the president could manage effectively. Far from enhancing responsiveness, said another senator, the large number of political appointees undermines "presidential control of the executive branch."[45] Not everyone agrees. Amid rising partisanship one scholar argued, "presidents need to stock departments with people who understand politics and the importance of interaction with Congress, lobbyists and the media."[46]

Pay and Other Legal Standards. By law, Congress has wide control over federal employees. It can establish retirement programs; special requirements for holding office; personnel ceilings; employee performance standards; wages, benefits, and cost-of-living adjustments (COLAs); and protections from reprisals for whistleblowers (employees who expose waste and corruption). The 1939 Hatch Act, named for Sen. Carl Hatch, D-N.M. (1933–1949), restricts federal employees' partisan activity. The act was passed during the New Deal after reports that civil servants were being coerced to back President Franklin D. Roosevelt in his reelection efforts. Today, civil servants can engage in political activity in accord with regulations prescribed by the U.S. Office of Special Counsel. For example, most career civil servants can run for nonpartisan office, contribute to political organizations, or distribute campaign literature. They may not run for partisan office, use their authority to exert influence over an election, or wear political buttons while on duty.[47]

There are other limits on bureaucrats. After leaving public office, many executive offices, top legislative staffers, and legislators themselves pass through the "revolving door" to jobs with private firms that deal with the government. However, various laws impose a so-called "cooling-off" period before these officials and employees may lobby their former agency, department, or branch of government. For example, under the Honest Leadership and Open Government Act, which President Bush signed into law on September 14, 2007, high government officials and senators are subject to a two-year cooling-off period after leaving office; House members have a one-year cooling-off period.[48]

Size of Government. Americans have debated the size and reach of the federal government since the nation's founding. At least since the twentieth century—from the Progressive Era to World War I, from the New Deal to the Great Society to today's governmental interventions in the private sector—the national government has dramatically expanded. Growth has been driven by a number of overlapping factors. Wars and crises, of course, expand federal obligations. The intelligence community mushroomed during the Cold War as the United States faced a major threat from the other nuclear-armed superpower: the Soviet Union. Complexity is another factor triggering governmental growth. New problems and issues repeatedly demand national action.

Today, the federal government must address issues with global dimensions, from trade to currency exchange rates to climate change. As the nation's population increased to over 300 million and government expanded its responsibilities and capacities, it was only natural that individuals and groups would look to their national officeholders for the resolution of problems in health care, transportation, law enforcement, energy, and so on.

People often complain about the over-large federal establishment, but what does "too big" really mean? Much of the disagreement centers on how government size is measured: the share of the gross domestic product (GDP) devoted to federal expenditures, the magnitude of the federal budget, or the number of federal employees. As to the first standard, federal spending relative to the size of the American economy exhibits a mixed picture, from 21.8 percent of GDP in 1990 to 18.4 percent in 2000, 19.8 percent in 2004, and 20.2 percent in 2008. Another measure is the federal budget, which keeps growing (reaching $3.6 trillion in 2010), but so, too, have the nation's population and obligations.

Contrary to what many people believe, the federal workforce has remained relatively constant in size. How can the government continue to perform services while generally keeping its size down? One answer is that much of what the federal government does is to transfer money to eligible recipients, such as the elderly who receive Social Security. This function does not require large numbers of federal workers. Another answer is that federal work has been outsourced to contract firms, or privatized. The Pentagon, for instance, reached a milestone of sorts at the start of the twenty-first century when the number of its private sector employees (734,000) exceeded its civilian workforce (700,000). These contract employees "perform service jobs from mowing lawns to testing weapons systems."[49] As one analyst explained: "Everybody wants the federal government to look smaller than it really is. By contracting out jobs rather than having civilian workers in those jobs, you can say, 'Look, the government's smaller.'"[50]

One scholar has put the true personnel size of the government at about 15 million employees: the 4.1 million civilian, military, and postal workers plus the 10.5 million "shadow" employees who work "under federal contracts and grants or mandates imposed on state and local governments."[51] The number of private contractors seems certain to soar as "more and more companies" enter the government contracting world following enactment of President Obama's nearly $800 billion stimulus package.[52]

However this debate about government size is reconciled, privatizing (or outsourcing) the federal government's work has certain benefits and costs. Outsourcing has distinct advantages in many instances: contractors can be faster, more flexible, and cheaper than the career bureaucracy. However, many analysts believe that certain functions are inherently governmental and ought not to be turned over to outside organizations. Thus, there is concern that the government loses vital expertise as it outsources critical functions to the private sector.[53] Moreover, because contractors are not directly responsible to Congress, the so-called third-party (or shadow) government raises serious questions of accountability, resulting in fraud, waste, and cost overruns, as shown by the contracting abuses associated with post–Hurricane Katrina and Iraq reconstruction.[54]

The Rulemaking Process

Although Congress creates executive agencies and defines their legal mandate, rarely can it specify the details needed to implement policies. The landmark Telecommunications Act of 1996, for example, made it illegal to make "indecent" material available to minors. What material is indecent? That question rests with government regulators (the Federal Communications Commission already bars "seven dirty words" from broadcasts) and ultimately the federal courts. In such cases, specifications must be written, details filled in, and procedures set forth.

Thus agencies are empowered to make rules for carrying out the mandates contained in laws.[55] For example, in 2003 a new 1,100-page prescription Medicare drug benefit for the elderly became law; the drug benefit was the largest expansion of an entitlement program since the presidency of Lyndon Johnson. The following year the Department of Health and Human Services issued 1,956 pages of draft regulations for public comment on implementation of the new prescription drug benefit.[56] In 2008, nearly 81,000 pages of rules and regulations—compared to 3,450 in 1937—were published in the *Federal Register* as part of the rulemaking process.[57]

In the Administrative Procedures Act of 1946 and later amendments to it, Congress established standards for rulemaking by government agencies. Interested parties can take part in the process in such ways as testifying in public about the merits or demerits of proposed regulations. When regulators at the Food and Drug Administration (FDA) planned to redefine the ingredients that go into chocolate, many chocolate lovers and candy manufacturers across the nation began a grassroots campaign to oppose the change.[58]

When final, regulations have all the force and effect of law. All regulations, explained Sen. Charles E. Grassley, R-Iowa,

> are based ultimately on authority granted by this Congress. When an agency promulgates a rule, it is engaging in a legislative task—in effect, filling in the gaps on the implementation of policies that we in Congress have established through statute. Accordingly, all regulations must be accountable to this Congress.[59]

In other words, executive branch officials who write the rules are lawmakers operating in a bureaucratic context. Federal regulations may be declared unconstitutional or overturned. For example, federal judges can declare that rules issued by agencies violate public law. Courts can also compel agencies to issue regulations. The Supreme Court declared that the Environmental Protection Agency (EPA) violated the Clean Air Act by "improperly declining to regulate new-vehicle emissions standards to control the pollutants that scientists say contribute to global warming."[60] Recently, the Supreme Court upheld EPA's use of cost-benefit analysis under the Clean Water Act permitting utilities to decide "what technology is needed to protect fish from being killed by large industrial cooling water intake structures."[61]

Federal courts also ensure that executive officials do not repeal unwanted rules by fiat. Once a rule is published in the *Federal Register,* a federal appeals court held that "it cannot be reversed without a lengthy administrative process, even if [the rule] has not yet taken effect."[62] Although presidents can overturn executive orders with the stroke of a pen, they cannot treat regulations the same way. "It is not easy for a president to stop a final rule that has been published in the *Federal Register* short of putting the whole process [as prescribed in the Administrative Procedures Act of 1946] in reverse and beginning the process of rule making anew—with public notices, comment periods and agency reviews that could take years."[63]

Congress and the White House frequently skirmish over rulemaking. GOP administrations tend to have a pro-business regulatory bias, giving key regulatory jobs to corporate and industry officials who are keen on easing or reducing regulation. Democratic presidents appoint individuals to head agencies who support worker safety, consumer, and environmental protections. Unsurprisingly, just hours after being sworn into office, President Obama ordered "work halted on all federal regulations left unfinished at the end of the Bush era until they can be reviewed by the new president's team."[64] The president also directed the Office of Management and Budget (OMB) to solicit public comment on how to improve the regulatory process for "a new executive order on federal regulatory review."[65]

About 600 major rules and regulations are issued each year by executive agencies that require review by the White House regulatory "czar": the chief of the Office of Information and Regulatory Affairs (OIRA) within the Office of Management and Budget (OMB). OIRA analyzes regulations that would impose more than $100 million in costs upon affected industries. It then can reject them, require their revision, or approve them in line with the president's priorities.[66] In 2007 President Bush issued an executive order expanding OIRA's authority in two important ways: (a) requiring agencies to specify why market forces cannot fix a problem targeted by proposed rules, and (b) authorizing the regulatory czar to review informal agency "guidance documents," which are often viewed as official rules. Bush's executive order further enhanced presidential oversight of rulemaking by requiring each federal rulemaking agency to accept "a White House–picked regulatory policy officer, who has the authority to review and approve all major rulemaking activity by the agency."[67] Ten days into his administration, President Obama issued an executive order rescinding the Bush order. Obama also directed the heads of all agencies and departments to "promptly rescind any orders, rules, guidelines, or policies implementing or enforcing" Bush's directive.[68]

Proposed rules and regulations are typically subject to cost-benefit review. Measuring costs and benefits is at best a tricky undertaking. Risk analysis experts hold that this traditional tool should be used "to sort through a complex world of threats to human and environmental health so we can identify the choices that will do the most people the most good at the least cost?"[69] Critics of this approach, however, point out that measuring costs is usually easier than estimating benefits; costs are more easily quantified, while benefits are intangible and long-term.

President Obama is also able to undo regulations he opposes by encouraging Congress to pass legislation repealing them or to use laws on the books to overturn unwanted regulations. The Congressional Review Act (CRA) of 1996, for example, requires regulators to submit all proposed major rules and regulations to the House and Senate. Lawmakers then have sixty legislative days from the time a regulation is published in the *Federal Register* to reject it under expedited procedures by enacting a joint resolution of disapproval. (See Box 11-2 for a review of the CRA procedure.) The CRA prohibits filibusters in the Senate and requires presidential approval. The law has only been used once, in 2001 to repeal an ergonomic (repetitive motion injury) rule promulgated by the Clinton administration. Congressional Democrats in 2009 planned to use the CRA to undo "midnight rulemaking" by the Bush administration.[70]

The CRA also illustrates the two Congresses. Sen. Kent Conrad, D-N.D., led in invoking the act to block a regulation issued by the Agriculture Department that would lift restrictions on the importation of Canadian beef because of "mad cow" disease. Up for reelection in November 2006 and representing a "red" state carried by Bush, Conrad acted on behalf of North Dakota ranchers who were "worried that the imports will undermine the safety of the state's cattle industry."[71] The joint resolution of disapproval passed the Senate but not the House. Election years are also a time when administrations delay issuing regulations that could be politically controversial or costly—dubbed "slow rolling" by lobbyists and policymakers. "Slow rolling takes place before a presidential election because it is an axiom of political life that agencies take no action that could give an issue to the opponents of the incumbent administration."[72]

How valuable are regulations? Lawmakers, like their constituents, are of two minds. Some, such as Sen. Barbara Boxer, D-Calif., emphasize their positive achievements.

> The purpose of the Federal regulatory process is to improve and protect the high quality of life that we enjoy in our country. Every day, the people of our Nation enjoy the benefits of almost a century of progress in Federal laws and regulations that reduce the threat of illness, injury, and death from consumer products, workplace hazards, and environmental toxins.[73]

Others call for "more rational regulations," with "better analysis of costs, benefits, and risks, so that regulators will issue smarter, more cost-effective regulations."[74] A difficult challenge is to distinguish between inflexible, pointless, or overly burdensome and costly regulations and beneficial regulations that are necessary to promote and protect the public's health and safety.

BOX 11-2   **Resolution of Disapproval**

A resolution of disapproval is a privileged measure established by the Congressional Review Act of 1996 (PL 104-121). It allows Congress to nullify a rule issued by a federal agency.

These resolutions are intended to grant fast-track floor procedures in the Senate to head off some of the delaying tactics that can hang up floor consideration for days on end. Though the law grants fast-track procedures only in the Senate, the resolution must be endorsed by both chambers.

In the Senate, once a resolution of disapproval is brought to the floor, it cannot be amended and action cannot be interrupted for other business. A simple majority is needed for passage.

In order to take advantage of the fast-track procedures in the Senate, the resolution must be introduced in both chambers within 60 calendar days after the agency reports the rule to Congress. The Senate then has 60 legislative days from the date the rule is published in the *Federal Register* in which to act before the resolution's fast-track privileges expire.

To overturn the agency rule, the resolution must pass both chambers and be signed by the president. If the resolution is enacted, the rule cannot take effect, and the agency cannot issue a substantially similar rule without congressional authorization. The rule the resolution would nullify is deemed not to have had any effect at any time.

Source: Adrianne Kroepsch, "Senate Moves to Overturn FCC Decision to Relax Media Ownership Rule," *CQ Today,* May 16, 2008, 10.

The Electoral Connection

Some scholars argue that Congress enlarged the executive establishment by passing vague laws that bureaucrats had to embellish with rules and regulations. Regulatory laws, for example, may call for a "reasonable rate," without defining "reasonable." Frustrated by government rules, people turn to their senators and representatives for help. Lawmakers thus "take credit coming and going"—they claim credit for creating programs to help constituents and then for untangling the bureaucratic snarls they create.[75]

Electoral explanations, however, cannot account for overall bureaucratic growth. Although intuitively appealing, there is little support for the assertion that members' "incessant quest for local benefits has somehow contributed to growth in government spending." Lawmakers eagerly seek money for projects in their states or districts, but this practice usually just reallocates money that would have been appropriated anyway. In fact, the most costly non-defense federal programs, such as Medicare and Social Security, "deliver benefits as a matter of right, not privilege, and congressmen have fewer opportunities to claim responsibility for them."[76]

Many other considerations affect how federal benefits are distributed. An agency may process the requests of the president's congressional backers quickly, while other members' proposals are encased in red tape. Influential members of the committees with jurisdiction over certain agencies may receive the lion's share of federal benefits. Presidential pork is also commonplace as chief executives promise jobs and projects in states crucial to reelection.

Not all federal projects are worth attracting. Members weigh the political risks of backing missile bases, hazardous waste dumps, nuclear power plants, or other controversial projects strongly resisted by their constituents. Some lawmakers oppose spending for projects even if they are in their own district. Sens. Tom Coburn, R-Okla., and John McCain are especially vigilant in targeting what they consider to be wasteful spending. The Internet Web sites of both senators contain floor statements against legislation containing what they see as pork. Still other members want to challenge unnecessary tax and spending subsidies for businesses and industries ("corporate welfare").[77]

Whatever their view of federal projects, legislators must act as intermediaries between constituents and federal agencies. Constituents' problems are handled within members' offices by personal staff aides called caseworkers. In addition to courting the electoral payoff of effective casework—evidence of the two Congresses once again—some members appreciate its value as oversight. "The very knowledge by executive officials that some Congressman is sure to look into a matter affecting his constituents acts as a healthy check against bureaucratic indifference or arrogance," wrote a former senator.[78]

CONGRESSIONAL CONTROL OF THE BUREAUCRACY

"Congressional power, like chastity," explained a scholar, "is never lost, rarely taken by force, and almost always given away."[79] No law can be sufficiently detailed to cover every conceivable circumstance. So Congress allows executive officials wide discretion in implementing the laws it passes. This delegation of authority occurs because legislators lack the time, knowledge, or expertise to address the complexities of contemporary administration.

Congress is often sharply criticized for drafting vague or sloppy legislation that gives executive officials and judges too much leeway in interpretation and administration. "Administration of a statute is, properly speaking, an extension of the legislative process," and therefore Congress must watch over its programs lest they undergo unintended change.[80] Given the size and reach of the executive establishment, Congress's oversight role is even more important today than when Woodrow Wilson wrote in 1885 that "[q]uite as important as lawmaking is vigilant oversight of administration."[81]

The Constitution does not refer explicitly to the oversight role; but it implicitly flows from Congress's right, among other things, to make laws, raise and appropriate money, give advice and consent to executive nominations, and impeach federal officials. Congress, however, has formalized its oversight duties. The Legislative Reorganization Act of 1946 directed all House and Senate committees to exercise "continuous watchfulness" over the programs and agencies under their jurisdiction. Subsequent statutes and House and Senate rules extend Congress's authority and resources for oversight. The Government Accountability Office, the chief investigative arm of Congress, provides the House and Senate with "high risk" reports on the management and accounting practices of federal agencies and departments.

Members understand their review responsibilities. "Congress's duty didn't end in passing this law," remarked a senator. "We have to make sure the law works." Another senator said: "I have always felt that one-third of the role of Congress should be in oversight."[82] The purposes of oversight are many, but three are especially important: To check the power of the executive branch; to determine how laws are being implemented and whether they need adjustments and refinements; and to shine the spotlight of public attention on significant executive actions and activities. As Woodrow Wilson wrote in 1885, "The informing function of Congress should be preferred even to its legislative [lawmaking] function." He went on to say:

> Unless Congress [has] and use[s] every means of acquainting itself with the acts and dispositions of the administrative agencies of government, the country must be helpless to learn how it is being served; and unless Congress both scrutinize[s] these things and sift[s] them by every form of discussion, the country must remain in embarrassing, crippling ignorance of the very affairs which it is most important it should understand and direct.[83]

A number of political purposes are, of course, served by oversight, such as generating favorable publicity for programs; urging the elimination or reduction of agencies; responding to requests from special interests to influence agency decisions; or winning electoral support from constituents or groups. Oversight thus occurs in a political context, within which Congress's relationship with administrative agencies can range from cooperation to conflict.

To ensure that laws are working, Congress utilizes a varied array of formal and informal processes and techniques. Each has its strengths and weaknesses, and it is often necessary to employ several in combination if the House and Senate are to challenge or assess executive branch performance. Many oversight activities are indirect, ad hoc, and not subject to easy measurement or even recognition. "Oversight isn't necessarily a hearing," said John D. Dingell, D-Mich., a noted House overseer when he chaired the Energy and Commerce Committee. "Sometimes it's a letter. We find our letters have a special effect on a lot of people."[84]

Hearings and Investigations

Many of Congress's most dramatic historical moments have occurred in legislative probes into administrative or business misconduct or man-made or natural disasters. Examples include the Teapot Dome inquiry (1923), the Senate

Watergate hearings (1973–1974), the Iran-contra investigation (1987), the 2003 joint hearings into the disintegration of the space shuttle *Columbia* as it was returning to Earth, the 2007 hearings on the Iraq war, or the 2009 hearings into taxpayer-funded bonuses for Wall Street executives. The mere threat of a congressional hearing is often enough to keep agencies in line. But Congress's investigative authority is not without limits. Earl Warren, when he was chief justice of the U.S. Supreme Court, wrote in *Watkins v. United States* (1957):

> There is no general authority to expose private affairs of individuals without justification in terms of the functions of Congress....Nor is the Congress a law enforcement or trial agency. These are functions of the executive and judicial departments of government. No inquiry is an end in itself; it must be related to, and in furtherance of, a legitimate task of the Congress. [85]

By collecting and analyzing information, House and Senate inquiries can clarify whether new laws are needed to address public problems. They also sharpen Congress's ability to scrutinize executive branch activities, such as the expenditure of funds, the implementation of laws, and the discharge of duties by administrative officials. Investigations also inform the public by disseminating and revealing information. "Congress provides a forum for disclosing the hidden aspects of governmental conduct," wrote two Senate members of the Iran-contra investigating committee. It allows a "free people to drag realities out into the sunlight and demand a full accounting from those who are permitted to hold and exercise power." [86] Hearings and investigations, in short, are valuable devices for making government accountable to the people. They can spawn new laws or their functional equivalent: change in bureaucratic operations.

Congressional Vetoes

Congress has little choice but to delegate sweeping authority to administrative agencies. The question is then how Congress can control those agencies. One answer historically has been the legislative veto (or congressional veto), a statutory enactment that permits presidents or agencies to take certain actions subject to later approval or disapproval by one or both houses of Congress (or in some cases by committees of one or both houses). Legislative vetoes are arrangements of convenience for both branches. Executives gain decision-making authority they might not have otherwise, and Congress retains a second chance to examine decisions.

In 1983, many forms of the legislative veto were declared unconstitutional by the Supreme Court (*Immigration and Naturalization Service v. Chadha.*) The Court's majority held that the device violated the separation of powers, the principle of bicameralism, and the Presentation Clause of the Constitution (legislation passed by both chambers must be presented to the president for his signature or veto). The decision, wrote Justice Byron R. White in a vigorous dissent, "strikes down in one fell swoop provisions in more laws enacted by Congress than the court has cumulatively invalidated in its entire history."[87]

Congress has repealed some veto provisions since *Chadha* and amended others, while continuing to employ a wide range of oversight techniques to monitor executive actions. Yet, despite the *Chadha* ruling, legislative vetoes continue to be enacted into law. Public law scholar Louis Fisher sums up the status of legislative vetoes:

> Are they constitutional? Not by the Court's definition. Will that fact change the behavior between committees and agencies? Probably not. An agency might advise the committee: "As you know, the require- ment in this statute for committee prior-approval is unconstitutional under the Court's test." Perhaps agency and committee staff will nod their heads in agreement. After which the agency will seek prior approval of the committee.[88]

Self-interest impels agencies to pay close attention to the wishes of members of Congress, especially those who sit on their authorizing or appropriating panels.

Mandatory Reports

Congress can require the president, federal agencies, or departments to assess programs and report their findings.[89] Reports can act "as a mechanism to check that laws are having the intended effect." They can "drive a reluctant bureaucracy to comply with laws it would otherwise ignore."[90] The House Permanent Select Intelligence Committee, for instance, threatened to reduce funds for the Central Intelligence Agency director's office if the intelligence agency did not "file dozens of overdue reports required by law" within a reasonable period of time.[91] Periodically, Congress passes legislation to discard obsolete or unnecessary reports. (Occasions also do arise, though, when lawmakers object to the discontinuation of reports that they believe provide useful information to policymakers and the public.) However, the overall trend is toward more, not fewer, reports. As Senator McCain has noted, "Congress assigns about 300 new reports to the agencies each year."[92] By one estimate, executive agencies annually prepare more than 5,000 reports for submission to Congress.

Nonstatutory Controls

Congressional committees also use informal means to review and influence administrative decisions. These range from telephone calls, letters, personal contacts, and informal understandings to statements in conference reports, hearings, and floor debates.[93] Committee reports frequently contain phrases such as "the committee clearly intends that the matter be reconsidered" or "the committee clearly intends for the Secretary to promote" or "the committee clearly expects."

On occasion, OMB directors tell federal agencies to ignore report language because it is not legally binding. Lawmakers of both parties and chambers (and even executive officials), however, may seek to thwart such directives. Sometimes members threaten to make all report language legally binding on agencies, thus limiting the agencies' flexibility and discretion in resolving issues.[94] Although there is no measure of their usage, nonstatutory controls may be the most common form of congressional oversight.

Inspectors General

In 1978 Congress created a dozen independent offices for inspectors general (IGs). Since then Congress has established inspector general offices in nearly every federal department and agency. Given the trillions of dollars being spent to restore the economic health of the nation, Congress has created a special inspector general to oversee the $700 billion bailout of the financial system. To monitor the $787 billion economic stimulus package, twenty-three IGs from different agencies are "working on accountability, doing the oversight, the audits, and any necessary investigations," explained Earl Devaney, a former IG, who now heads the Recovery Act Transparency and Accountability Board. Delaney is in overall charge of coordinating and tracking how the stimulus money is being spent, uncovering fraud trends, and identifying the "best practices for detecting fraud."[95]

Inspectors general testify frequently before congressional committees and submit directly to Congress reports on their efforts to root out waste, fraud, and abuse. For instance, the Labor Department IG determined that a departmental initiative to improve worker safety in hazardous industries "rarely fulfilled its promise" because of uneven inspections and enforcement. The result: fifty-eight fatalities that might have been prevented.[96] The Pentagon's IG detailed billions of dollars in waste and fraud by military contractors.[97]

The Appropriations Process

Congress probably exercises its most potent oversight of agencies and programs through the appropriations process. By cutting off or reducing funds (or threatening to do so), Congress can abolish agencies, curtail programs, or obtain requested information. One agricultural funding bill, for example, stripped an Agriculture Department undersecretary of his supervisory authority over the U.S. Forest Service and the Natural Resources Conservation Service because of sharp and continuing clashes between appropriators and the appointee.[98] In another case, a House Appropriations subcommittee chairman, angry because the Homeland Security Department had not provided reports on its spending priorities, declared: "They've just been ignoring us. They'll pay for that."[99] By the same token, Congress can build up program areas by increasing their appropriations—sometimes beyond the levels that the administration has requested.

The appropriations power is exercised mainly through the Appropriations Committees in the House and Senate, especially through each panel's standing subcommittees. These panels annually recommend funding levels for federal agencies and departments so that they have the money to carry out their program responsibilities. The budgetary recommendations of the Appropriations subcommittees are generally accepted by their parent committee and by the House or Senate.

The Appropriations Committees and their subcommittees, or members from the House or Senate floor, may offer amendments that limit the purposes for which money may be spent ("limitation amendments") or that impose other spending limits on federal agencies. Funding bills also may contain various policy directives to federal agencies—for example, prohibiting agencies from using funds to promulgate or issue certain regulations. Such directives are often in the form of floor amendments called riders. "These amendments," wrote two GOP senators, "are an important way for Congress to save taxpayers from wasteful agency spending, and they enjoy a long-standing precedent because of their use by Republican and Democratic Congresses alike to rein in the excesses of Republican and Democratic administrations."[100]

Impeachment

Article II, Section 4, of the Constitution states: "The President, Vice President, and all Civil Officers of the United States, shall be removed from office on Impeachment for, and Conviction of, Treason, Bribery, or other high Crimes and misdemeanors." This removal power is the ultimate governmental check vested in Congress.[101] The House has the authority to impeach an official by majority vote. It then tries the case before the Senate, where a two-thirds vote is required for conviction.

Only impeached federal judges have been convicted by the Senate. As for presidents, the House impeached President Andrew Johnson in 1868, after Radical Republicans in the House charged that he had violated the Tenure of Office Act by dismissing the secretary of war. The Senate acquitted Johnson by a single vote. Facing probable impeachment and conviction, President Richard M. Nixon resigned in 1974, after the House Judiciary Committee voted articles of impeachment. In December 1998 President Clinton became the first elected president to be impeached by the House. (Johnson was not elected; he became president when Abraham Lincoln was assassinated.) The charges against Clinton were perjury and obstruction of justice. Two months later the Senate voted acquittal on both articles of impeachment.[102]

The controversy over the firings of U.S. attorneys during President George W. Bush's second administration led to calls for impeaching his attorney general, Alberto Gonzales, largely because of bipartisan concern that he was not truthful in his testimony before congressional committees. "If Alberto Gonzales will not resign, Congress should impeach him," exclaimed a law professor.[103] Censure had also been raised as another option. Bruce Fein, a former assistant attorney general in the Reagan administration, stated that: "Congressional oversight includes the authority to censure executive branch officials for maladministration or...to sharpen political accountability."[104] Two Democratic senators even suggested (emulating a practice of parliamentary regimes) that the Senate vote on a "non-binding resolution expressing 'no confidence' in Gonzales."[105] (Gonzales voluntarily resigned in August 2007.)

Oversight: An Evaluation

Congress's willingness to conduct regular and meaningful oversight stems from several factors: public dissatisfaction with government; revelations of executive agency abuses; the influx of new legislators skeptical of government's ability to perform effectively; concern that some regulatory agencies are tied too closely to the industries they regulate; the availability of congressional staff; and recognition by Congress that it must make every dollar count.[106]

The perspective of the two Congresses highlights the electoral, political, and policy incentives that encourage members to oversee the bureaucracy. One of these incentives is the opportunity to claim credit for assisting constituents and to receive favorable publicity back home. Another is prodding by interest groups and the media. Committee and subcommittee chairmen "seek a high pay off—in attention from both the press and other agencies—when selecting federal programs to be their oversight targets."[107] Members on the relevant committees of jurisdiction are also motivated to induce favorable agency and departmental action on pet policies or programs.

Divided government—the president of one party, Congress controlled by the other—encourages vigorous congressional oversight. Oversight simultaneously enables opposition lawmakers to supervise agency activities and look for ways to undermine the administration's policy goals or public reputation. By comparison, under unified government, the majority party in Congress tends to engage in less oversight. As one senior GOP lawmaker said of the unified period (2003–2007) when Republicans were in charge, "Our party controls the levers of government. We're not about to go out and look beneath a bunch of rocks to cause heartburn."[108] The reason for the lack of serious oversight during this unified period, former Representative Christopher Shays, R-Conn. admitted, was that we "ended up functioning like a parliament, not a Congress. We confused wanting a joint agenda with not doing oversight."[109] Party loyalty, in short, overcame institutional responsibility. With Democrats now in charge of the elective branches, it remains to be seen whether and to what extent congressional Democrats will conduct vigorous and rigorous oversight of the Obama administration.

Whether in unified or divided government, congressional oversight may not probe as deeply as some might wish. Friendly alliances can develop among the committees that authorize programs, the agencies that administer them, and the interest groups that benefit from governmental services. Many committees are biased toward the programs or agencies they oversee. They want to protect and nurture their progeny and make program administration look good. Without concrete allegations of fraud or mismanagement, committees may lack the incentive to scrutinize and reevaluate their programs. This kind of cooperative oversight can dissuade committees from conducting meaningful inquiries.

A standard rationale for oversight is that it ensures that laws are carried out according to congressional intent. Because many laws are vague and imprecise, however, they are difficult to assess. Proof that programs are working as intended, moreover, can take years to emerge. Congressional patience may wane as critics conclude that there are no demonstrable payoffs for the taxpayer. Alternatively, oversight may identify program flaws but not reveal what would work or even whether there is any ready solution.

Each oversight technique has limitations. Hearings may provide dramatic episodes, for example, but they often result in minimal follow-up. The appropriations process is usually hemmed in by programmatic needs for financial stability. And statutes are often blunt instruments of control. Other obstacles to effective oversight include inadequate coordination among committees sharing jurisdiction over a program; unsystematic review by committees of departmental activities; and frequent turnover among committee staff aides, a situation that limits their understanding of programs passed by Congress.

Critics who fault Congress's oversight may be erecting unattainable standards. Many analysts are looking for what scholars have come to call "police-patrol" oversight—active, direct, systematic, regular, and planned surveillance of executive activities. Instead, Congress often waits until "fire alarms" go off—from interest groups, the press, staff aides, and others concerned about administrative violations—before it begins to review in detail agencies' activities. [110]

Congress may be obtaining some extra police patrol assistance through the combination of civic-minded individuals and technology. A new trend involves the "public as watchdog." A good example is enactment of the Federal Funding Accountability and Transparency Act of 2006, informally called the "Google your government" law, because it requires OMB "to provide a user-friendly, searchable database" of nearly $1 trillion in federal grants and contracts. [111] There are new Web sites—recovery.gov or stimuluswatch.org, for example—that allow citizens to monitor the projects that receive money from the stimulus package. The GAO has launched a Web site and hotline (FraudNet) to enable citizens to report allegations of waste, fraud, or mismanagement of stimulus funds. The promise of these actions is that they enable any interested person or watchdog group to monitor federal spending and make evaluations known to congressional lawmakers. The blogosphere, in short, adds millions of extra eyes to congressional oversight of government spending and activities.

Micromanagement

Because oversight often means legislative intrusion into administrative details, executive branch officials sometimes complain about congressional micro-management. Even though it can cause dismay in the executive bureaucracy, Congress's focus on administrative details is as old as the institution itself. The structural fragmentation of the House and Senate encourages examination of manageable chunks of executive actions. Members realize that power inheres in details, such as prescribing personnel ceilings for agencies. Presidents who oppose certain programs can starve them to death by shifting employees to favored activities. Thus Congress may specify personnel ceilings for some agencies. "It is one of the anomalies of constitutional law and separated powers," writes Louis Fisher, "that executive involvement in legislative affairs is considered acceptable (indeed highly desirable) while legislative involvement in executive affairs screams of encroachment and usurpation."[112]

CONCLUSION

Because of continual shifts in the balance of legislative and executive prerogatives, the age-old issue of executive independence versus congressional scrutiny will not be settled. Yet the recent interest in oversight has had scant discernible effect on the size and scale of the executive branch or on the main roles and responsibilities of the legislative branch. After all, committees are not disinterested overseers, but rather guardians of the agencies and programs under their purview. Together with their satellite interest groups, committees and agencies form subgovernments or issue networks that dominate many policymaking areas.

SUGGESTED READINGS

Aberbach, Joel D. *Keeping a Watchful Eye: The Politics of Congressional Oversight.* Washington, D.C.: Brookings Institution, 1990.

Arnold, R. Douglas. *Congress and the Bureaucracy: A Theory of Influence.* New Haven: Yale University Press, 1979.

Foreman, Christopher J., Jr. *Signals from the Hill: Congressional Oversight and the Challenge of Social Regulation.* New Haven: Yale University Press, 1988.

Light, Paul C. *The New Public Service.* Washington, D.C.: Brookings Institution Press, 1999.

_____. *The True Size of Government.* Washington, D.C.: Brookings Institution Press, 1999.

_____. *A Government Ill Executed: The Decline of the Federal Service and How to Reverse It.* Cambridge, Mass.: Harvard University Press, 2008.

Mackenzie, G. Calvin, with Michael Hafken, *Scandal Proof: Do Ethics Laws Make Government Ethical?* Washington, D.C.: Brookings Institution Press, 2002.

Rosenbloom, David. *Building a Legislative-Centered Public Administration: Congress and the Administrative State, 1946–1999.* Tuscaloosa: University of Alabama Press, 2000.

Court Politics. Prior to their formal confirmation hearings, Supreme Court nominees are obliged to make courtesy visits with key senators. Nominees are often accompanied by "sherpas"—experienced insiders who advise nominees as to which senators must be seen and how to approach them. Top: Judge Sonia Sotomayor—the first Latina nominated for the high court—meets with Judiciary Chair Patrick Leahy (D-Vt.) in June 2009. Associate Supreme Court Justice Ruth Bader Ginsburg (center) arrives for President Obama's address to a joint session of Congress in February 2009. A variety of Court decisions mobilize interest groups: anti-war protesters (bottom) demonstrate in front of the Supreme Court building.

12

Congress and the Courts

"Scarcely any political question arises in the United States that is not resolved, sooner or later, into a judicial one," wrote the famous French chronicler Alexis de Tocqueville in *Democracy in America,* his classic 1835 study of early American life.[1] From the beginnings of the Republic, when federal courts handed down decisions that strengthened the national government, to many of today's most hotly debated issues—executive war powers, racial redistricting, and abortion—federal judges have been at the storm center of numerous controversies. Since the U.S. Supreme Court asserted the prerogative of judicial review in the landmark case of *Marbury v. Madison* (1803), the American public has come to view the highest court as the primary, but not exclusive, interpreter of the Constitution.[2] Bolstered by both public legitimacy and legal precedent, federal jurists regularly pass judgment on the compelling issues that confront the nation.[3] At the same time, Congress and the White House also interpret the Constitution. As the Supreme Court stated in *United States v. Nixon* (1974): "In the performance of assigned constitutional duties each branch of the Government must initially interpret the Constitution, and the interpretation of its powers by any branch is due great respect from the others."

The American constitutional system of separate institutions sharing power inevitably produces tension between Congress and the courts. Although the Framers outlined the structure and authority of Congress in some detail in Article I of the Constitution, Article III, which deals with the courts, is much less detailed. Indeed, Article III leaves the creation of the federal courts other than the Supreme Court wholly to the discretion of Congress. Thus, the judicial branch owes less to constitutional mandates and more to legislation establishing its structure and to the rulings of the early justices, such as Chief Justice John Marshall (1801–1835). As a noted legal scholar explained:

> Congress was created nearly full blown by the Constitution itself. The vast possibilities of the presidency were relatively easy to perceive and soon, inevitably materialized. But the institution of the judiciary needed to be summoned up out of the constitutional vapors, shaped and maintained. And the Great Chief Justice, John Marshall—not single-handed, but first and foremost—was there to do it and did.[4]

These early jurists rebuffed challenges to judicial power and established the courts' right to determine the constitutionality of state laws as well as acts of Congress.

Conflicts between Congress and federal courts are inevitable when the elective branches are called to account by decisions of the nonelective judicial branch, composed of judges with lifetime tenure. A famous instance occurred during the New Deal when the Supreme Court invalidated thirteen acts of Congress in one term (1935–1936). So frustrated was President Franklin D. Roosevelt that he tried to have Congress pass legislation expanding the size of the Court so he could nominate judges more sympathetic to his program. Widespread legislative and public opposition defeated Roosevelt's Court-packing scheme. Nonetheless, sensitive to the changes under way in the country, the Court soon began to shift its attitude in constitutional interpretation. In 1937 the Court handed down a decision that upheld a state minimum wage law similar to one that it had previously ruled unconstitutional.[5] In that same year, the Court upheld a federal law regulating management-labor relations, recognizing a far greater congressional power to regulate commerce than the Court's precedents had permitted. This abrupt turnabout by the Court, ending its penchant for limiting congressional power, was, as a wit of the period put it, "the switch in time that saved nine."

CONSTITUTIONAL REVIEW

Whether it is enacting minimum wage, health, or other laws, Congress derives its policymaking authority from two key parts of the Constitution: Article I and the Fourteenth Amendment. Article I, Section 8, grants Congress the right to legislate in many specific areas, such as laying and collecting taxes, coining money, and raising and supporting armies. In addition, an elastic clause gives Congress the authority to "make all laws which shall be necessary and proper" to carry out its enumerated powers.

The post–Civil War Fourteenth Amendment guarantees that no state shall deny any person life, liberty, or property without due process of law or deny any person the equal protection of the laws. The amendment provides that Congress "shall have the power to enforce [these provisions], by appropriate legislation." Finally, as the courts have noted, Congress also has "implied" and "inherent" powers not specifically mentioned in the Constitution, such as its right to conduct investigations as an adjunct to its lawmaking function. Federal courts, however, can impose constraints on the exercise of these constitutional pillars of legislative authority.

As for the courts, Article III of the Constitution states: "[T]he judicial power of the United States shall be vested in one Supreme Court, and in such inferior courts as the Congress may from time to time ordain and establish." Left to Congress was the formation of the elaborate judicial structure that exists today, including not only the Supreme Court, but also the district courts and courts of appeals (whose judges enjoy life tenure), as well as specialized courts, such as bankruptcy courts whose judges serve fixed terms. The federal court system now consists of district courts, which are trial courts of general jurisdiction, and regional courts of appeals, organized into units known as "circuits." The district courts are organized by states, with every state having at least one and larger states (for example, California and Texas) having as many as four. The Supreme Court has appellate jurisdiction, or the power to review cases not just from lower federal courts but also from the states' courts of last resort on matters that raise important issues of federal or constitutional law. Unlike the lower federal courts, the Supreme Court has the discretion, under statute, to determine whether or not it will review a case within its jurisdiction.

The Constitution specifies the "cases and controversies" over which the Supreme Court has original jurisdiction, such as issues involving the Constitution, federal law, and treaties. But the Supreme Court's appellate jurisdiction is subject to such exceptions as Congress may determine. In addition, Congress establishes the lower courts' jurisdiction through statute. It was only in 1875, for example, that Congress granted the lower federal courts "general" jurisdiction over cases arising under federal law or the Constitution, even though that jurisdiction has its basis in Article III.

Congress can alter the jurisdiction of the federal courts to achieve policy goals. Business and corporate interests, alarmed at state courts' handling of large-scale class action lawsuits, pressured Congress for many years to change the law to force such lawsuits into federal courts. After a number of failed attempts in previous Congresses, the 109th Congress enacted the Class Action Fairness Act (CAFA),[6] which expanded the jurisdiction of the federal courts over state-law-based class actions. According to one study, CAFA's intent—to shift class actions from plaintiff-friendly state courts toward the more defendant-friendly federal courts was quickly achieved.[7]

The federal courts' policymaking role is carried out in three main ways. First, their interpretive decisions can uphold or broaden the legislative powers of Congress. "Congress acted within its authority," said Supreme Court justice Ruth Bader Ginsburg, when the Court upheld a law further extending copyright privileges for authors, artists, and inventors, such as commercial artist Walt Disney, who created the world-famous animated cartoon character Mickey Mouse.[8] Second, it can check overreaching by Congress through its implied power of judicial review. Third, and equally significant, the Supreme Court can act as a policymaking catalyst, especially when the House or Senate is stymied in making decisions. The landmark civil rights case of *Brown v. Board of Education* (1954) is a classic example. The decision struck down the separate-but-equal doctrine that had upheld state laws mandating racially segregated public schools. Until this decision, filibusters by Southern senators thwarted enactment of meaningful civil rights bills. The *Brown* ruling galvanized Congress to enact the Civil Rights Act of 1957, the first civil rights law enacted by Congress since 1875. "The genius of a system of divided powers," wrote a law professor, "is that when one branch is closed to the desires of the populace or the demands of justice, another may open up."[9] The *Brown* decision in fact had little impact on the actual desegregation of public schools until Congress began to pass such landmark legislation as the Civil Rights Act of 1964 and the Elementary and Secondary Education Act of 1965.

Each national branch of government has the constitutional means of influencing the others. The Supreme Court affects Congress "whenever justices interpret the meaning of the Constitution, treaties, federal statutes, administrative [rules and regulations], and the decisions of [lower] federal and state courts."[10] In turn, Congress has the authority to affect the size, funding, and jurisdiction of federal courts, and the Senate is directed under the Constitution to approve or reject court nominees chosen by the chief executive. Federal courts issue rulings but they depend on the political branches to enforce those decisions. Alexander Hamilton distinguished judicial power from legislative or executive power in *The Federalist Papers* No. 78: The judiciary "has no influence over either the sword [the president] or the purse [Congress]…and can take no active resolution whatever. It may truly be said to have neither Force nor Will, but merely judgment." Nevertheless, federal courts have issued many rulings that require large costly expenditures in areas such as improvements in prison conditions and mental health institutions. In the area of war, contemporary presidents have taken military action either with or without authority from Congress. At least in theory, if rarely in practice, the federal courts may check executive overreach and adjudicate the proper allocation of war-making authority between Congress and the White House.

THE COURT AS REFEREE AND UMPIRE

The Supreme Court serves as both referee between the two nationally elective branches and as the umpire of federal-state relations. Ever since the Court claimed the power of judicial review in 1803 and voided part of an act of Congress, it has considered a large number of separation-of-power and federalism issues, most notably during the New Deal and in the past few decades. Whether acting as referee or umpire, the Supreme Court (and other courts) is often subject to criticism for usurping the prerogatives of the other national branches, or of state and local governments. Members of Congress "often reserve their most vituperative criticism of federal courts for decisions that, in their view, unduly limit the prerogatives of state and local governments to regulate such matters as abortion, school prayer, prison overcrowding, school busing, local elections, and so on."[11]

A common refrain in criticisms of the courts is that the judges are acting as a "super-legislature" in their rulings—that is, they are "legislating from the bench." The charge of "judicial activism" is premised on the view that, at least in some cases, judges make decisions based on their personal values and not the dictates of law, or that they are making decisions that their critics believe should be settled by the elective branches of government. One's view of activism, however, often depends on whether one supports the direction the court is taking. Decisions that expand Congress's authority to legislate may be opposed by those who prefer matters to be handled by the executive branch or the states. Conversely, decisions that restrict the reach of the legislative branch are likely to be opposed by those who favor a national approach to problems.

The Referee

Like federal courts, Congress also interprets the Constitution when it makes national policy through its lawmaking processes. As a result, it is not uncommon for the two branches to view issues differently. To be sure, the Supreme Court often exercises restraint when it addresses the powers of Congress or the president for two key reasons: to avoid charges of judicial overreaching and in recognition that only the elective institutions can implement judicial judgments. The following case reveals how a decision restricting Congress's authority under the Commerce Clause (Article I, section 8) of the Constitution can trigger a fast reassertion of legislative power.

In *United States v. Lopez* (1995), the Supreme Court overturned a federal law banning guns near school grounds. For the "first time since the New Deal...the Court found Congress to have exceeded the bounds of its constitutional authority to regulate interstate commerce"—in this case the presence of guns that had probably moved across state lines that ended up on school playgrounds.[12] Congress quickly moved to pass legislation reasserting its authority under the Commerce Clause to restrict guns from school zones. The measure, which the president signed, said that, "It shall be unlawful for any individual knowingly to possess a firearm that has moved in or that otherwise affects interstate or foreign commerce at a place that the individual knows, or has reasonable cause to believe, is a school zone."[13] When the revised statute was challenged in the lower federal courts, it was upheld as a constitutional exercise of Congress's power to regulate interstate commerce. The Supreme Court has not yet reviewed these lower court decisions.

Mindful of the courts' referee role, lawmakers seek to employ it for their own goals. Increasingly, members turn to the courts to accomplish ends they are unable to achieve in Congress. Often, they ask the courts to defend congressional prerogatives against usurpation by the president. War making is the principal example. Not since World War II has Congress declared war, although it has enacted legislation that is functionally equivalent. Recent presidents of both parties have committed American troops to combat on their own initiative. As for war power suits brought by lawmakers, scholar Louis Fisher takes a cautionary view:

> From the Vietnam War to the present day, members of Congress have gone to court to contest presidential wars and defend legislative prerogatives. In most of these cases, the courts held that the lawmakers lacked standing to bring the case. Even when legislators were granted standing, the courts refused relief on numerous grounds. Judges pointed out that the legislators represented only a fraction of the congressional membership and that often another group of legislators

had filed a brief defending the president's action. Courts regularly note that Congress as a whole has failed to invoke its institutional powers to confront the president.[14]

Usually, courts dismiss these suits and offer two rationales: first, the lawsuits raise political questions best left to the elective branches to resolve, and second, they represent conflicts between groups of lawmakers pitted against each other, not constitutional clashes between Congress and the president. A key issue in these suits is whether lawmakers meet the constitutional test of "standing": have they suffered an institutional injury "fairly traceable to the [president's] allegedly unlawful conduct and likely to be redressed by the requested [judicial] relief?" Assuming that the test of standing cannot be met, federal courts are unlikely to render a decision because suits against "coordinate branches of government by congressional [lawmakers] pose separation-of-powers concerns which may affect [members'] standing to invoke the jurisdiction of the federal courts."[15]

The Umpire

As the federalism umpire, the Supreme Court is the arbiter of federal and state powers. The claims of the federal government are anchored in the Supremacy Clause (Article VI) of the Constitution, which posits that the federal Constitution, as well as federal laws and treaties, prevail over conflicting state constitutions or laws. The states' claims are grounded in the Tenth Amendment, which reserves certain powers to the states or to the people, and the Eleventh Amendment, which protects states from being sued in federal court. The Eleventh Amendment comes into play when Congress seeks to make state governments subject to federal regulation. In *Alabama v. Garrett* (2001), for example, the Supreme Court held that states are immune from suits brought by handicapped state employees under the 1990 Americans with Disabilities Act (ADA). The Court held that states were not required "to make special accommodations for the disabled, so long as their actions toward such individuals had a rational basis." The reason lay in an expanded notion of states' "sovereign immunity" from suits by private citizens—a theory disputed by many legal scholars.[16]

Alabama v. Garrett also involved opposing views of legislative and judicial powers. Chief Justice Rehnquist asserted "that it is the responsibility of the Supreme Court, not Congress, to define the substance of constitutional guarantees." This claim was far broader than Chief Justice John Marshall's famous 1803 pronouncement in *Marbury v. Madison* that the duty of the courts is "to say what the law is."[17]

Rehnquist dismissed as anecdotal the extensive evidence of discrimination against disabled state employees that had been amassed by congressional panels. Justice Stephen G. Breyer, in a dissenting opinion, countered: "In fact, Congress compiled a vast legislative record documenting 'massive, society-wide discrimination' against persons with disabilities." He appended a thirty-nine-page list of findings from the ADA's legislative history. Breyer (a one-time Capitol Hill staff member) went on to remind his colleagues of the constitutional primacy of legislative judgments.

> Unlike courts, Congress can readily gather facts from across the Nation, assess the magnitude of a problem, and more easily find an appropriate remedy. Unlike courts, Congress directly reflects public attitudes and beliefs, enabling Congress to better understand where, and to what extent, refusals to accommodate disability amount to behavior that is callous or unreasonable to the point of lacking constitutional justification. Unlike judges, Members of Congress can directly obtain information from constituents who have first-hand experience with discrimination and related issues.

Three years later, in *Tennessee v. Lane,* the Court took a different view from *Garrett* regarding state sovereignty under the ADA. The case demonstrates the different dimensions or complexities associated with federalism decisions. Briefly, George Lane, a paraplegic who had been charged with a crime, had to crawl up two floors to reach a county courtroom in Tennessee because there was no elevator. At a subsequent hearing, he refused to crawl up the stairs and was arrested for failure to appear at the hearing on his case. He sued Tennessee under the ADA and won a financial settlement, which the court upheld. Why the different outcome in *Lane* compared with *Garrett?* Part of the explanation is that the Court considered a wider range of evidence. In *Garrett,* the Court considered only state employers such as the University of Alabama; in *Lane,* it also examined Tennessee's treatment of the disabled by county and city employers. Significantly, *Lane* involved access to the courts, one of the country's key political institutions. Although the Court is concerned about access to employment by disabled persons, it has traditionally shown greater sympathy for access to political institutions by disadvantaged groups.

The Rehnquist court (1986–2006) was noted for its advocacy of state authority over federal powers. Whether the court under Chief Justice John Roberts will be as active in the federal-state arena is unclear, especially given the terrorist attacks of September 11, 2001. In the judgment of one law professor, whenever "you see a national emergency, federalism disappears. In a national emergency, you give the national government the power to get done what needs to get done."[18] It is the president who gains power during wartime, when the balance between liberty and security tilts toward the latter and not the former.

Constitutional Values under Stress

The global struggle against terrorists raises a number of important issues: whether and to what extent federal courts will sanction infringements of individual privacy, allow terrorist suspects (citizens or aliens) to be imprisoned indefinitely as "enemy combatants" without legal protections, permit greater governmental secrecy, authorize warrantless eavesdropping, and permit enhanced interrogation (torture).[19] After September 11, 2001, federal district judge Gladys Kessler said, "[T]he court fully understands and appreciates that the first priority of the executive branch in time of crisis is to ensure the physical security of its citizens." By the same token, she added, "the first priority of the judicial branch must be to ensure that our government always operates within the statutory and constitutional constraints which distinguish a democracy from a dictatorship."[20] (Congress, as noted in Chapter 11, is also expected to check excessive assertions of executive power.)

The Supreme Court has shown that it is capable of reining in executive power even during a time when the nation is threatened by international terrorism. In June 2004 the Supreme Court handed down three rulings that denied the president's right to hold citizens or captured foreigners as prisoners without allowing them their day in court.[21] In *Hamdi v. Rumsfeld,* Yaser Hamdi, an American citizen who denied that he fought with the Taliban, was held incommunicado at Guantánamo Bay, Cuba without the right to see a lawyer or challenge his detention. The Court held that Hamdi had the right of due process before a judge. In *Rumsfeld v. Padilla,* José Padilla, an American citizen, was arrested in Chicago and jailed in a Navy brig without any right to challenge his incarceration for, among other things, allegedly seeking to detonate a "dirty bomb" in the United States. In *Rasul v. Bush,* the Court determined that the then 600 detainees held at Guantánamo Bay could have their cases heard in federal courts. This decision overturned President Bush's declaration that detainees at Guantánamo Bay had no right of access to federal courts, because they were jailed outside the sovereign territory of the United States.

Two years later in *Hamdan v. Rumsfeld,* the Supreme Court held that the military tribunals—established in 2001 without congressional authorization by President Bush to try the prisoners held at Guantánamo Bay, Cuba— violated federal law. The court stated that the type of military commission established by the Bush administration concentrated "in military hands a degree of adjudicative and punitive power in excess of that contemplated either by statute or by the Constitution." In response, Congress passed the Military Commissions Act of 2006 to authorize the tribunals at issue in the *Hamdan* decision. The act also stripped the federal courts of jurisdiction to consider petitions for writs of habeas corpus filed by the Guantánamo detainees. Habeas corpus (its literal meaning is that "you should have the body for submitting") is a procedure that enables a person in custody to challenge their detention by forcing the executive branch to appear in court and requiring it to justify the continued detention of that person (the "petitioner").

The Military Commissions Act was subsequently challenged on constitutional grounds in district court and the U.S. Court of Appeals for the District of Columbia Circuit. Article I, Section 9, of the Constitution states that Congress may not suspend the privilege of habeas corpus, except under certain circumstances. The detainees' counsel argued that the Military Commissions Act violated this provision, the Suspension Clause. In a legal victory for

President Bush, the D.C. Circuit Court in 2007 upheld the military tribunals law and ruled (*Boumediene v. Bush*) that detainees at Guantánamo Bay "do not have the right to challenge their imprisonment in federal courts"[22] because constitutional rights do not apply to foreign nationals incarcerated outside the territory of the United States. (Boumediene, a Bosnian citizen, was held at Guantánamo Bay. He was released in May 2009 and resides in France.)

Boumediene's case reached the Supreme Court in 2008, which reaffirmed the right of those prisoners to have their cases reviewed by the federal judiciary.[23] As Justice Anthony Kennedy wrote for the majority, "Liberty and security can be reconciled; and in our system they are reconciled within the framework of the law. The Framers decided that habeas corpus, a right of first importance, must be a part of that framework, a part of that law." President Obama, who vowed to close the prison at Guantánamo Bay, created a task force "to decide how to handle current and future detainees."[24] A federal district judge subsequently ruled that some detainees at Bagram Air Force base in Afghanistan also have a right to habeas corpus (the ability to challenge their detention in federal court).[25]

A fundamental issue raised by certain judicial rulings is how assertive the courts should be in overturning decisions of the popularly elected Congress. Lawmakers are accountable to their constituents every time they face reelection. Although judges are not immune to the tides of public opinion, they do not face accountability through elections. The tension between policymaking by lawmakers versus judge-made decisions is perennial. Thus, it is useful to explore two traditional features of the Congress-court connection: statutory interpretation and legislative checks on the judiciary.

The distinction between statutory and constitutional interpretation is very important. Statutory interpretation involves federal judges employing various methods—reviewing legislative history, for example—to find the meaning, or intent, of the often vague language embedded in laws. For example, in May 2007 the Supreme Court decided in *Ledbetter v. Goodyear Tire & Rubber Co.* that Lilly Ledbetter, despite doing the same job as men at Goodyear, received less pay than her male counterparts for many years. When she learned of Goodyear's discriminatory treatment after twenty years on the job, she sued on the grounds of gender-based pay and employment discrimination. The Supreme Court ruled, in a five-to-four decision, that Ledbetter's lawsuit was not timely because she did not file the suit within 180 days of the date on which the lower pay had been agreed upon by the parties. The Court majority rejected the argument that the statute of limitations (i.e., the time in which the lawsuit could be filed) restarted with every discriminatory paycheck. A vigorous dissent by Justice Ruth Bader Ginsburg chided the Court's majority for their ignorance of workplace realities and noted that Congress could clarify the law. Many lawmakers strongly disagreed with the *Ledbetter* decision and its interpretation of legislative intent. In one of its first actions, the 111th Congress passed legislation, which President Obama signed into law, overturning *Ledbetter*, making it easier for workers to challenge gender-based employment discrimination by resetting the statute of limitations with every discriminatory paycheck.[26]

Constitutional interpretation occurs when federal or state laws are challenged as violating our founding document or its various amendments. For example, in 2008 the U.S. Supreme Court overturned a decision of the Louisiana Supreme Court (*Kennedy v. Louisiana*), which upheld a state law allowing the death penalty for a child rapist who did not kill his victim. The Louisiana court said the death penalty was justified under the Eighth Amendment to the U.S. Constitution (prohibiting "cruel and unusual punishments") because execution was not an excessive or cruel punishment for a child rapist. The U.S. Supreme Court determined that executing a defendant convicted of a non-homicide child rape is unconstitutional.[27] In determining whether national or state actions violate the Constitution, federal judges typically examine the text of the Constitution, the intentions of the drafters, and judicial precedents relevant to the controversy—although in the death penalty area, the Court also considers society's evolving standards regarding such punishment.

The major difference between statutory and constitutional interpretation, of course, is that Congress could override the Court's (mis)interpretation of Title VII of the 1964 Civil Rights Act in the *Ledbetter* case; but neither it nor the Louisiana state legislature could override the Court's pronouncement in the *Kennedy* case. A constitutional decision of the Court can only be undone by a subsequent constitutional amendment—which is very rare—or by the Court itself, when it overrules one of its precedents.

Statutory Interpretation

Communications between Congress and the federal courts are less than perfect. Neither branch understands the workings of the other very well.[28] Judges generally sense that ambiguity, imprecision, or inconsistency may be the price for winning enactment of legislative measures. The more members try to define the language of a bill, the more they may divide or dissipate congressional support for it. Abner J. Mikva, a four-term House Democrat from Chicago who went on to become a federal judge and later counsel to President Bill Clinton, recounted an example from his Capitol Hill days. The issue involved a controversial strip-mining bill being managed by Arizona Democrat Morris K. Udall, then chairman of the House Interior (now called Natural Resources) Committee:

> They'd put together a very delicate coalition of support. One problem was whether the states or the feds would run the program. One member got up and asked, "Isn't it a fact that under this bill the states would continue to exercise sovereignty over strip mining?" And Mo replied, "You're absolutely right." A little later someone else got up and asked, "Now is it clear that the Federal Government will have the final say on strip mining?" And Mo replied, "You're absolutely right." Later, in the cloakroom, I said, "Mo, they can't both be right." And Mo said, "You're absolutely right."[29]

Called upon to interpret statutes, judges may not appreciate the efforts required to get legislation passed on Capitol Hill or understand how to examine legislative history, as manifested in hearings, reports, and floor debate. For example, prior to House passage in the 109th Congress (2005–2007) of CAFA, Judiciary chairman F. James Sensenbrenner Jr., R-Wis., and fellow proponents "read into the House record a lengthy colloquy meant to guide federal judges" in deciding class action lawsuits.[30]

Within the courts and among legal scholars, there is a lively debate over the proper way to approach statutory interpretation. Should judges focus only on the plain meaning of the statutory language, or should they delve into legislative history to ascertain what Congress intended when it employed certain statutory phrases? A group of federal judges, led by Supreme Court justice Antonin Scalia, argues that legislative history is unreliable as an indicator of legislative intent because it is open to manipulation by lawmakers, executive officials, and congressional staffers.

One remarkable example of the manipulation of legislative history occurred in the context of the Senate passage of the Detainee Treatment Act (DTA) in late 2005. An important issue before the federal courts at the time was whether the DTA would retroactively nullify all the Guantánamo detainees' pending legal challenges. Two sponsors of the legislation, Sens. Lindsey O. Graham, R-S.C., and Jon Kyl, R-Ariz., sought to quash all such cases, while another sponsor, Sen. Carl Levin, D-Mich., wanted to allow cases filed before the passage of the DTA to go forward.[31] But just before the passage of the legislation, Graham and Kyl inserted into the *Congressional Record* a colloquy designed to show that in passing the DTA the Senate intended to invalidate all pending legal challenges brought by Guantánamo detainees. Written in informal style, the colloquy contained controversial banter suggesting that the exchange occurred live on the Senate floor. Such a colloquy would have alerted all senators that Graham and Kyl believed the legislation would foreclose all pending cases, and the absence of subsequent objections would imply that senators agreed with this interpretation. However, a C-SPAN recording showed that the discussion never actually occurred on the Senate floor. Justice Department lawyers nevertheless cited the colloquy in their legal brief arguing that Congress intended to remove all the pending cases from federal jurisdiction.[32] In response, a lawyer for one of the detainees objected. "This colloquy is critical to the government's legislative history argument, and it's entirely manufactured and misrepresented to the court as having occurred live on the Senate floor before a crucial vote."[33]

Rather than relying on legislative history, Scalia contends that justices should follow a textualist approach, examining the wording of laws or constitutional clauses and interpreting them according to what they meant at the time of enactment.[34] Other federal judges, including Supreme Court justice Stephen G. Breyer, defend the value of legislative history, finding it useful in statutory interpretation. "It is dangerous," Breyer asserted, "to rely exclusively upon the literal meaning of a statute's words."[35]

The dispute over legislative history is well illustrated by Congress's passage of the Civil Rights Act of 1991. The law overturned, in whole or in part, seven civil rights cases decided by a conservative-leaning Supreme Court.[36] Yet because the 1991 legislation was filled with ambiguities, interested lawmakers created their own legislative history during floor debate. A memorandum was even put in the *Congressional Record* stating that the written statement was the exclusive legislative history for certain contested provisions. During debate on the legislation, a Republican senator pointed out the pitfalls of relying on legislative history. His position essentially endorsed Scalia's view that Congress should state clearly what it means or wants in the law itself, rather than in floor debates or other explanatory statements.[37]

Supreme Court justice John Paul Stevens expressed a contrary opinion, saying that a "stubborn insistence on 'clear statements' [in the law] burdens the Congress with unnecessary reenactment of provisions that were already plain enough." Rep. Barney Frank, D-Mass., once remarked that if Scalia's view on legislative history became dominant, Congress would be required to develop a new category of legislation: "the 'No, we really meant it' statute."[38] Disagreement between Congress and federal judges over the utility of legislative history were summed up by the Senate Judiciary Committee's chief counsel: "The textual interpretation encourages us to write clearer legislation. But unclear bills are still written. If they were not, we would not have this fight over [the confirmation of] judges."[39]

Legislative Checks on the Judiciary

Supreme Court rulings can have profound effects on Congress and its members. Cases involving the redistricting of House seats, the line-item veto, and term limits for lawmakers are recent examples. If the Court arouses the ire of Congress when it rules on statutory questions, the legislative branch can enact new legislation. Scores of interest groups also monitor court decisions, and, if they disagree with them, these groups are not reluctant to lobby Congress to seek their statutory reversal. Congress has other ways by which it can influence the Supreme Court and lower federal courts. In addition to the Senate's constitutional advice and consent role regarding judicial nominations, four legislative powers merit some mention.

Withdrawal of Jurisdiction. Under its constitutional authority to determine the Supreme Court's appellate jurisdiction, Congress may threaten to withdraw the Supreme Court's authority to review certain categories of cases. The cases that promote such threats by Congress share certain features: they are controversial (abortion and school prayer); they are triggered by state or federal court decisions; and they arouse partisan and ideological passions among lawmakers and the electoral groups affiliated with each party. Despite numerous legislative threats to constrict or withdraw jurisdiction, on only one occasion in U.S. history did Congress prevent the Supreme Court from deciding a case by removing its appellate jurisdiction.

> This extraordinary action was taken by a Congress dominated by Radical Republicans who wanted to prohibit the Supreme Court from reviewing the constitutionality of the Reconstruction Acts of 1867. The acts substituted military rule for civilian government in the ten

southern states that initially refused to rejoin the Union and established procedures for those states to follow to gain readmittance and representation in the federal government.[40]

Congress simply passed legislation repealing the Supreme Court's right to hear appeals involving these matters and prevented "a possibly hostile Court from using the power of judicial review to invalidate a piece of legislation that was of vital concern to those who controlled the legislative body."[41]

Recently, a number of conservative lawmakers who were offended by certain federal court decisions strove to remove those issues from judicial review. One issue concerned a Ninth Circuit Court of Appeals decision that a 1954 federal law adding the phrase "one Nation under God" to the Pledge of Allegiance was unconstitutional on First Amendment grounds. The then House majority leader Tom DeLay, R-Texas, remarked, "I think that [legislation limiting the court's jurisdiction] would be a very good idea to send a message to the judiciary [that] they ought to keep their hands off the Pledge of Allegiance."[42] Other topics—such as same-sex marriage and the public display of the Ten Commandments—evoked similar responses. Various lawmakers also used sharp and even threatening rhetoric against the judiciary. Retired justice Sandra Day O'Connor commented that "the breadth and intensity of rage currently being leveled at the judiciary may be unmatched in American history. The ubiquitous 'activist judges' who 'legislate from the bench' have become central villains on today's domestic political landscape."[43]

Still, legislative initiatives to strip federal courts of jurisdiction occur infrequently. Various scholars identify a variety of reasons: "the historically broad consensus in Congress to protect, or at least tolerate, an independent judiciary; judicial opponents' reluctance to emasculate an institution that they may someday need as an ally; the sheer difficulty of impeaching officials, ratifying constitutional amendments, and even enacting statutes that lack consensus support; and resistance by the organized bar."[44]

Impeachment of Judges. Federal judges, like other national civil officers, are subject to impeachment under Article II of the Constitution. They are appointed for life "during good behavior." Only one Supreme Court justice, Samuel Chase, has ever been impeached by the House. This occurred in 1804, during bitter partisan battles between Federalists and Jeffersonian Republicans. The judiciary was the last bastion of Federalist influence after Thomas Jefferson won the presidency in the 1800 election. Chase's intemperate and arrogant behavior—he even campaigned for John Adams's reelection in 1800—aroused the ire of Jefferson and his allies in Congress. On March 12, 1804, the House voted 73–32 along party lines to impeach Chase. The Senate, however, failed to convict him. The importance of Chase's acquittal by the Senate was underscored in a book written by Chief Justice Rehnquist.

The acquittal of Samuel Chase by the Senate had a profound effect on the American judiciary. First, it assured the independence of federal judges from congressional oversight of the decisions they made in the cases that come before them. Second, by assuring that impeachment would not be used in the future as a method to remove members of the Supreme Court for their judicial opinions, it helped to safeguard the independence of that body.[45]

Other Supreme Court justices have either been threatened with impeachment or been the subject of impeachment investigations (for example, William O. Douglas in 1953 and in 1970).

A dozen federal judges have been impeached and even a smaller number have been convicted and removed from office. (Three federal district judges resigned prior to impeachment consideration.)[46] Most recently were the impeachment and removal of three judges: Judges Harry E. Claiborne (1986), Walter Nixon (1989), and Alcee L. Hastings (1989).[47] Claiborne was removed for tax evasion, Nixon for perjury, and Hastings for bribery. None of the three, however, was barred from holding further federal office by a separate Senate vote following their conviction. In 1992 Hastings was elected to the House of Representatives as a Democrat from Florida, where he has served continuously ever since. The 111th House (2009–2011) adopted a bipartisan resolution directing the Judiciary Committee to inquire whether a federal district judge in Louisiana should be impeached.[48] The Judicial Conference of the United States—the administrative body of the federal court system, headed by Chief Justice John Roberts—gathered evidence that the judge committed perjury and solicited cash from lawyers who appeared before him.

Size, Procedure, and Pay. Historically, the size of the Supreme Court has varied anywhere from six to ten members. "Generally, laws decreasing the number of justices have been motivated by a desire to punish the president; increases have been aimed at influencing the philosophical balance of the Court itself" (such as Roosevelt's court-packing plan).[49] But since 1869 Congress has not changed the Court's size from its current nine justices, so this power is unlikely to be invoked in the foreseeable future.

Procedurally, lawmakers have occasionally proposed that court decisions overturning federal laws must be accomplished by a supermajority vote of the justices. Some of the "more extreme proposals have urged that such decisions be unanimous."[50] None of these proposals has been adopted. Rather, they serve as signals sent to the judiciary to highlight lawmakers' disapproval of certain court decisions. Lawmakers have communicated their complaints to the unelected members of the judicial branch by calling for stronger ethical guidelines for judges to ensure their impartiality.[51] Legislative proposals for the creation of an "inspector general" to oversee judicial branch ethics have met with judicial branch claims that such oversight would violate the separation of powers and undermine judicial independence.

Another legislative proposal that has generated interbranch controversy is opening federal courtrooms to television. At present, the district courts and the Supreme Court do not permit their proceedings to be televised; the courts of appeals have discretion, on a circuit by circuit basis, to allow their proceedings to be televised. A majority of Supreme Court justices oppose the televising of their proceedings, in part because the cameras might alter decision making, intrude on the privacy of the justices by making them public celebrities, and threaten their personal security. During an appearance before the Senate Judiciary Committee, Justice Anthony Kennedy implored the senators not to pass legislation mandating the televising of their open proceedings.[52] His concern was that televised Court sessions would eventually undermine the collegial character of the Court and encourage the justices to speak in "sound bites." Nevertheless, some justices (Scalia, Breyer, John Paul Stevens, Ginsburg, and Chief Justice John Roberts) have appeared on various television programs. "So there has been very extensive [televising of individual justices]," said Sen. Arlen Specter, D-Pa., a member of the Judiciary Committee, "which totally undercuts one of the arguments [against the televising of Court proceedings]: that the notoriety would imperil the security of Supreme Court justices." He added: "It is, I think, fundamental that the court's work, the court's operation, ought to be more broadly understood" by the general public.[53]

A current concern is that fewer aspirants are seeking federal judgeships. Part of the reason for this is pay. "Salaries are far lower [for federal judges] than what fresh-faced law-school grads can make at big corporate firms."[54] Chief Justice Roberts devoted much of his 2008 annual year-end report on the federal judiciary to the inadequacy of judicial salaries. The judicial branch as a whole made a major push in the 110th Congress for a judicial pay increase. The effort at what the judges term "salary restoration"—because judicial salaries had not kept pace with inflation—won the support of House and Senate leaders and President Bush. But opposition from a few powerful members of Congress nixed the bill. The key sticking point was what is called "linkage"—under current law, the salaries of federal judges and members of Congress are linked.[55] The congressional reluctance to raise their own salaries—for obvious political reasons—is a large part of the reason federal judges' salaries have not kept pace with inflation. To substantially raise judicial salaries, realistically, members of Congress would have to agree to "de-link" their salaries from those of judges—thus depriving members of Congress of some political cover when they decide to raise their own salaries in the future. The chief justice currently receives a salary of $223,500 per year; associate justices of the high court receive $213,900; appeals court judges get $184,500; and federal district judges earn $174,000.[56] By comparison, law school deans could earn over $400,000 and top law firm partners $1 million or more.[57] Some analysts, however, question whether there are benefits to paying judges more.[58] The present state of the federal budget—and the salary linkage question—would seem to make any substantial increase in judges' salaries unlikely in the near future.

Constitutional Amendments. On four occasions, Congress successfully used the arduous process of amending the Constitution to overturn decisions of the Supreme Court. In *Chisholm v. Georgia* (1793), the Court held that citizens of one state could sue another state in federal court. To prevent a rash of citizen suits against the states, the Eleventh Amendment reversed this decision. It protects the states' sovereign immunity from lawsuits brought by citizens of other states and foreign countries. The *Dred Scott v. Sandford* (1857) decision that denied African Americans citizenship under the Constitution was nullified by the Thirteenth (abolishing slavery) and Fourteenth (granting African Americans citizenship) Amendments. The Sixteenth Amendment overturned *Pollock v. Farmer's Loan and Trust Co.* (1895), which struck down a federal income tax. The Twenty-sixth Amendment invalidated *Oregon v. Mitchell* (1970), which said that Congress had exceeded its authority by lowering the minimum voting age to eighteen for state elections.[59]

Generally, lawmakers are reluctant to amend the Constitution. Rep. Melvin Watt, D-N.C., reflects the view of many members: "I just think the Constitution has served us very well over a long, long period of time, and one needs to make a compelling case before we start amending the Constitution to do anything."[60] However, certain constitutional amendments have sometimes appeared regularly on the legislative agenda. One is a constitutional amendment that would ban desecration of the American flag. The proposal is a response to a 1989 Supreme Court ruling (*Texas v. Johnson*) that state laws banning flag burning violate the First Amendment right of free speech. Justice William Brennan, who wrote the majority opinion in *Johnson*, held that: "We do not consecrate the flag by punishing its desecration, for in doing so we dilute the freedom that this cherished emblem represents." The House has passed the legislation several times, but the Senate has never approved the measure.

Eliminating life tenure for federal judges is another proposal that sometimes surfaces on Capitol Hill. Bitter judicial nomination battles have prompted some to suggest term limits (fifteen years, for example) for federal judges. "If the Senate can't figure out how to reach a [partisan] truce in its battles over these all-important jobs," wrote one analyst, "maybe the best solution is to make the jobs not quite so important."[61] Others simply contend that Supreme Court justices serve too long (18.7 years was the average length of service on the Rehnquist Court). Aging justices, it is contended, may become overly arrogant, out of touch with contemporary values, or too impaired to serve. To avoid the difficulties of winning approval of a constitutional amendment, they propose a complex legislative approach that would move "justices into senior status after roughly eighteen years on the high court."[62]

ADVICE AND CONSENT FOR JUDICIAL NOMINEES

Article II, Section 2, of the Constitution states that the president "shall nominate, and by and with the Advice and Consent of the Senate, shall appoint...Judges of the Supreme Court." The Founders opposed giving the power to appoint solely to the executive, or solely to Congress as a whole or to the Senate in particular. The Framers compromised and provided that judicial selections required joint action by the president and the Senate. The president has the sole prerogative to nominate, but the power to confirm (or not) belongs to the Senate. Alexander Hamilton, in *The Federalist Papers* No. 66, viewed this division of responsibility in stark terms. "There will, of course, be no exertion of CHOICE on the part of the Senate. They may defeat one choice of the Executive and oblige him to make another; but they cannot themselves CHOOSE—they can only ratify or reject the choice he may have made."

Hamilton's perspective, however, requires some refinement. Giving two elective institutions a voice in the appointments process necessarily meant that nominees would be subject to a political process. Individual senators, House members, interest groups, the American Bar Association (which, since 1952, has rated judicial candidates), the press and media, and even sitting judges all may play a role in influencing both the choice of judicial nominees and Senate action, if any, on those nominees.[63] The fact that federal district and appellate court jurisdictions are geographically based means that senators from those states (especially if they are of the president's party) commonly have a large say in recommending judicial candidates to the White House. (See Table 12-1 for judgeship appointments by president.)

Before discussing various norms, practices, and controversies associated with the confirmation process for all federal judges, it is worth highlighting the general steps in filling a vacancy on the Supreme Court. In summary form, these are the half-dozen principal stages.

First, given a vacancy on the high court, the president selects a nominee. Considerable thought goes into his choice with two considerations having special prominence. Presidents want to nominate individuals who reflect their political and policy views and who are generally perceived as highly competent and knowledgeable. Of course, other considerations also enter the selection process: age, gender, race, religion, party affiliation, the prospect of an easy or hard confirmation battle, and so on.

In a first for the Supreme Court, every justice today is a former federal appeals court judge, which gives rise to the question of whether membership on the highest court should reflect a broader diversity of backgrounds. From Chief Justice John Marshall's day through Earl Warren's, for example, the Court typically included members steeped in legislative or executive experience. In the recent history Court, only recently retired Supreme Court justice Sandra Day O'Connor ever held an elective office—as an Arizona state senator. Some legal scholars suggest that a wider range of occupational experiences on the Court would serve an important representational function and enhance decision making "with a variety of issues in the electoral and legislative spheres."[64]

Presidents also may make recess appointments to the Supreme Court when the Senate is not in session. Recess appointments are temporary, expiring at the end of the next session of Congress. "Despite the temporary nature of these appointments, every [one of the twelve] appointed to the Court during a recess of the Senate, except one [John Rutledge in 1795], ultimately received a lifetime appointment after being nominated by the President and confirmed by the Senate."[65]

Second, candidates under serious consideration for the Court are subject to an extensive investigation by the administration into their personal and professional background. (The American Bar Association also evaluates prospective

TABLE 12-1 **Judgeship Appointments by President**

President	Supreme Court	Regional Court of Appeals	USCAFC[a]	District Courts	Total
Roosevelt (1933–1945)	9	52	—	136	197
Truman (1945–1952)	4	27	—	102	133
Eisenhower (1953–1960)	5	45	—	127	177
Kennedy (1961–1963)	2	20	—	102	124
Johnson (1963–1968)	2	41	—	125	168
Nixon (1969–1974)	4	48	—	182	231
Ford (1974–1976)	1	12	—	52	65
Carter (1977–1980)	0	56	—	206	262
Reagan (1981–1988)	3	78	5	292	378
Bush (1989–1992)	2	37	5	149	193
Clinton (1993–1900)	2	62	4	306	374
Bush (2001–1908)	2	61	2	261	326

Source: Adapted from "Judgeship Appointments by President," *The Third Branch,* Newsletter of the Federal Courts, February 2009.

[a] The U.S. Court of Appeals for the Federal Circuit (USCAFC) was established in 1982.

judges.) Once the president has made his choice, he sends a written nomination to the Senate, which is then referred to the Judiciary Committee. The nominee is escorted to various Hill offices to meet and talk with key senators. Meanwhile, the nominee begins extensive preparation for the hearings before the Judiciary Committee. Part of the preparation commonly involves participation in mock confirmation hearings called "murder boards."

Third, the Judiciary Committee launches its own investigation of the nominee's background and qualifications. After that stage is completed, the

Judiciary chair schedules public hearings on the nomination. The members of the committee have the opportunity to ask the nominee questions and also to receive testimony from other witnesses. Although it is unthinkable today that the committee would not proceed in this way, it is notable that for most of the nation's history confirmation hearings were unheard of. The very first such hearing arose not in the context of a conflict between Congress and the Court, but between Congress and the executive branch. In 1925, then attorney general Harlan Fiske Stone became the first Supreme Court nominee to testify in public before the Judiciary Committee. In the midst of the Teapot Dome Scandal, Stone had made enemies cleaning up the Justice Department—and in vigorously enforcing the nation's antitrust laws. But the first confirmation hearing of a Supreme Court nominee was precipitated by the Justice Department's handling of an indictment against Montana senator Burton K. Wheeler. When certain senators appeared willing to block his nomination, Stone himself apparently offered to appear before the committee, in a public hearing, to answer its questions with respect to his handling of the Wheeler case.[66] Still, confirmation hearings did not become customary until the mid-1950s. The Judiciary panel also receives testimony about the nomination from outside witnesses.

Fourth, after the hearings are concluded, the Judiciary Committee meets in open session to report the nomination to the Senate either with a favorable or negative recommendation, or with no recommendation at all. Dating back to at least the 1880s, the "Judiciary Committee's traditional practice has been to report even those Supreme Court nominations that were opposed by a committee majority, thus allowing the full Senate to make the final decision on whether the nominee should be confirmed."[67] (This practice does not apply to nominees for district or appellate court judgeships.) Once reported by the committee, the nomination is assigned to the Senate's executive calendar.

Fifth, the Senate majority leader decides when to call up the nomination for chamber consideration after consultation with various lawmakers, including the minority leader, and other pertinent individuals. Once the nomination reaches the floor, all senators have an opportunity to discuss the nominee's credentials, philosophy, or anything else they believe is relevant for the public record. Extended debate, or filibusters, are unusual on Supreme Court nominations. Cloture is available to curb talkathons but has been moved only three times: in 1968, on Abe Fortas's nomination to chief justice; in 1971, on William Rehnquist's nomination to be an associate justice; and in 1986, on Rehnquist's nomination to be chief justice.[68] After debate ends, in a practice begun in 1967, the Senate decides whether to confirm a Supreme Court nominee by a roll-call vote.[69]

Sixth, if the Senate votes to confirm, the secretary of the Senate transmits the resolution of confirmation to the president. The president then signs a document, called a commission, that officially appoints the nominee to the Supreme Court. The attorney general signs the engraved commission and delivers it to the nominee, who then takes the constitutional oath of office making him or her a justice of the U.S. Supreme Court.

Norms and Practices

Extraconstitutional norms and practices shape the confirmation process. President George Washington quickly learned the importance of the newly emerging norm of senatorial courtesy—an informal practice in which presidents consult home-state senators before submitting nominees for federal positions in their state. When Washington "failed to seek the advice from the Georgia senate delegation regarding a nomination for a federal position in Savannah, Washington was forced to withdraw the nomination in favor of the person recommended by the senators."[70]

Related to senatorial courtesy is the blue-slip policy of the Judiciary Committee, which applies only to district and court of appeals nominees. It refers to "blue approval papers that senators are asked to submit on nominees for federal judgeships in their states. For the past few years, both home-state senators had to submit a positive blue slip for a nominee to be considered by the Judiciary Committee."[71] Although exceptions have been made to this policy, Judiciary chair Patrick J. Leahy, D-Vt., announced that for the 111th Congress he would follow the traditional practice of not advancing judicial nominees unless both home-state senators agree, but senators "won't be able to withhold blue slips anonymously."[72] Blue slips encourage the president to seek the advice of senators before he submits judicial nominees to the Senate. Senate Republicans underscored that expectation when they sent a letter to Senator Leahy and President Obama stating, "[I]f we are not consulted on, and approve of, a nominee from our states, the Republican Conference will be unable to support moving forward on the nominee," implicitly threatening to employ dilatory tactics such as the filibuster.[73] An array of other Senate practices influences whether any action occurs on judicial nominations, such as the hold, the committee chair's prerogative of determining whether hearings will be held, and the majority leader's willingness to schedule floor consideration of the nominations.

An unresolved issue is the balance between advice and consent. Presidents usually favor consent over advice. The Senate tilts in the other direction. "It's advice and consent, not nominate and rubber stamp," declared Senator Leahy.[74] The qualifications appropriate for service as a federal jurist are not self-evident. The Constitution makes no reference to what presidents or senators should consider when exercising their respective roles (being a lawyer is not even a prerequisite). Setting aside the standard qualifications that everyone expects in prospective judges—legal experience, ethical behavior, recognized competence, and so on—an age-old question is whether people should be subject to litmus tests to be either nominated or confirmed for a judicial position. What place should a person's legal philosophy or ideology have in the appointments process? Here, for example, is the approach taken during the George W. Bush administration.

> The people counseling Bush on judicial appointments are convinced that his father erred in appointing some judges, notably David Souter, who has become a reliable vote for the Supreme Court's moderate wing and cast a pivotal vote for reaffirming *Roe v. Wade* [upholding a

woman's right of abortion pre-viability]. Consequently, Bush's counselors conduct extensive interviews with prospective nominees about their judicial philosophies. Many of the nominees have been active members of the Federalist Society, established in the early 1980s to organize, cultivate and sharpen conservative thinking about the Constitution. Activity within the Federalist Society constitutes an important—and sometimes the only—evidence of a young conservative's ideological commitment.[75]

President Obama, a former law professor, has indicated he wants to move away from ideological tests and confirmation wars involving judicial nominees. The president has suggested that he wants to name people to the federal bench with varied experiences, good judgment, and "broader perspectives on how the world works, and the depth and breadth of one's empathy."[76] When Justice David Souter announced his departure from the Supreme Court at the end of the June 2009 term, Obama nominated Circuit Court Judge Sonia Sotomayor, a Hispanic woman who had grown up in the Bronx projects, attended Ivy League schools, and had an extensive career.

Nomination Battles

Over the past two centuries, the Senate has "rejected about 20 percent of all Supreme Court nominees."[77] Most of the rejections occurred in the nineteenth century, with President John Tyler holding the record: Five of his six nominees were rejected by the Senate (see Table 12-2). After the Senate turned down John Parker in 1930, no Supreme Court nominee was rejected until the presidency of Lyndon B. Johnson. In June 1968 Chief Justice Earl Warren informed Johnson of his intention to retire. "Concern that Richard Nixon might win the presidency later that year and get to choose his successor dictated Warren's timing."[78] Johnson nominated his close friend on the Court, associate justice Abe Fortas, to be the next chief justice. However, when Fortas's ethical violations (accepting private money) came to light, it prompted the first filibuster in the Senate's history on a Supreme Court nomination, which doomed Fortas.[79] Cloture could not be invoked to end the filibuster and Johnson withdrew Fortas's nomination. Enmeshed in further ethical controversies and threatened by impeachment, Fortas the next year resigned from the Court altogether.

In 1969 the Senate rejected President Nixon's nominee to fill the Fortas vacancy, Clement Haynsworth, on the grounds of insensitivity to civil rights issues and conflicts of interest while on the lower court. Six months later another Nixon nominee, G. Harrold Carswell, was rejected because of his mediocre record as a lower court judge. President Ronald Reagan's nomination of conservative Robert Bork to the Supreme Court in 1987 sparked the bitter confirmation battles that still continue today. During nationally televised hearings, members of the Democratically controlled Judiciary Committee probed Bork's extensive written record to evaluate his constitutional and philosophical beliefs. Because Bork's nomination came at a time of large public concern

TABLE 12-2 **Supreme Court Nominations Not Confirmed by the Senate**

Nominee	President	Date of nomination	Senate action	Date of Senate action
William Paterson	George Washington	February 27, 1793	Withdrawn[a]	
John Rutledge[b]	Washington	July 1, 1795	Rejected (10–14)	December 15, 1795
Alexander Wolcott	James Madison	February 4, 1811	Rejected (9–24)	February 13, 1811
John J. Crittenden	John Quincy Adams	December 17, 1828	Postponed	February 12, 1829
Roger Brooke Taney	Andrew Jackson	January 15, 1835	Postponed (24–21)[c]	March 3, 1835
John C. Spencer	John Tyler	January 9, 1844	Rejected (21–26)	January 31, 1844
Reuben H. Walworth	Tyler	March 13, 1844	Withdrawn	
Edward King	Tyler	June 5, 1844	Postponed	June 15, 1844
Edward King	Tyler	December 4, 1844	Withdrawn	
John M. Read	Tyler	February 7, 1845	Not acted upon	
George W. Woodward	James K. Polk	December 23, 1845	Rejected (20–29)	January 22, 1846
Edward A. Bradford	Millard Fillmore	August 16, 1852	Not acted upon	
George E. Badger	Fillmore	January 10, 1853	Postponed	February 11, 1853
William C. Micou	Fillmore	February 24, 1853	Not acted upon	
Jeremiah S. Black	James Buchanan	February 5, 1861	Rejected (25–26)	February 21, 1861
Henry Stanbery	Andrew Johnson	April 16, 1866	Not acted upon	
Ebenezer R. Hoar	Ulysses S. Grant	December 15, 1869	Rejected (24–33)	February 3, 1870
George H. Williams[b]	Grant	December 1, 1873	Withdrawn	

Name	President	Date nominated	Action	Date of action
Caleb Cushing[b]	Grant	January 9, 1874	Withdrawn	
Stanley Matthews	Rutherford B. Hayes	January 26, 1881	Not acted upon[a]	
William B. Hornblower	Grover Cleveland	September 19, 1893	Rejected (24–30)	January 15, 1894
Wheeler H. Peckham	Cleveland	January 22, 1894	Rejected (32–41)	February 16, 1894
John J. Parker	Herbert Hoover	March 21, 1930	Rejected (39–41)	May 7, 1930
Abe Fortas[b]	Lyndon B. Johnson	June 26, 1968	Withdrawn	
Homer Thornberry	Johnson	June 26, 1968	Not acted upon	
Clement F. Haynsworth Jr.	Richard M. Nixon	August 18, 1969	Rejected (45–55)	November 21, 1969
G. Harrold Carswell	Nixon	January 19, 1970	Rejected (45–51)	April 8, 1970
Robert H. Bork	Ronald Reagan	July 1, 1987	Rejected (42–58)	October 23, 1987
Douglas H. Ginsburg	Ronald Reagan	October 29, 1987	Withdrawn	
Harriet Miers	George W. Bush	October 3, 2005	Withdrawn	

Source: Joan Biskupic and Elder *Witt, Guide to the U.S. Supreme Court,* 3d ed., vol. 2 (Washington, D.C.: Congressional Quarterly, 1997), 707: authors' notes.

[a] Later nominated and confirmed.

[b] Nominated for chief justice.

[c] Later nominated for chief justice and confirmed.

about the Supreme Court's ideological balance, and because Bork's views were perceived as too conservative and controversial by many senators and interest groups, the Senate rejected the nominee by a 58 to 42 margin. (Bork's nomination fight even gave rise to a new verb—"to bork"—which means to attack nominees by launching a politically based campaign against them.)

Even more controversial was President George H. W. Bush's 1991 nomination of Clarence Thomas, who was narrowly approved by the Senate on a 52–48 vote. Law professor Anita Hill, who previously worked for Thomas, charged that he had sexually harassed her on the job. The charges and countercharges played out on national television during the Judiciary Committee's hearings. Many in the public were glued to their screens to witness the dramatic testimony of Hill and Thomas. Conservative groups were outraged at the way Bork and Thomas were treated by the Democratic controlled Senate. They bided their time until it was their turn to wreak havoc on Democratic nominees for the federal bench.

In 1995 Republicans took control of the Senate, while Democrat Bill Clinton was in the White House. Many of Clinton's nominees to the lower federal courts never received hearings or waited years before any action took place on their nomination. For example, Richard Paez waited four years from his original nomination before he was confirmed to sit on the Ninth Circuit Court of Appeals. The principal GOP methods for frustrating Clinton's nominees were denying them hearings or floor votes.

During the brief period from June 2001 to November 2002, when Democrats held the Senate because of Vermont GOP senator James M. Jeffords's party switch, they blocked many of President George W. Bush's judicial nominees through holds, blue slips, and other dilatory actions. In the 108th and 109th Congresses, with Democrats again in the minority and unable to control committees or the floor schedule, they were "compelled to use the more incendiary weapon of the filibuster to stop the Bush nominees they oppose[d]. But the result [was] the same: frustration in the White House and rising bitterness in Congress."[80]

In spring 2005, the anger over judicial filibusters was so intense that Senate majority leader Bill Frist, R-Tenn., planned to use a parliamentary maneuver called the "nuclear option" to end the talkathons. According to the maneuver—never executed because fourteen senators opposed Frist's plan—the majority leader would make a point of order that further debate on a controversial nominee was dilatory. The Republican presiding officer would rule in his favor, and if the Democrats appealed the ruling, Frist would move to table (or kill) the appeal. The result: judicial nominations would be subject to an up-or-down majority vote rather than the Senate's first invoking cloture (a sixty-vote requirement) to end debate and then confirming or rejecting judicial nominees by majority vote.

In the 111th (2009–2011) Congress, Senate Republicans have an array of dilatory tactics to stymie and frustrate governance by the Democratic majority. They remember that when Obama was a sitting senator he supported delaying actions against President Bush's judicial nominees. It will be interesting to see how confirmation battles evolve during Obama's presidency. But it is certain that they will continue "to resemble political blood feuds, in which each side seeks to avenge the earlier assaults by the other side."[81]

Consent and Dissent

Until recently, little controversy was associated with scrutinizing judges named to serve on the twelve regional courts of appeals, the Federal Circuit, and the ninety district (or trial) courts. Today, fierce political, strategic, and tactical conflicts between the parties and branches overlay the confirmation process for many judicial nominees, especially for the appellate courts. "The politicization of the judiciary has recently been the most focused, and most virulent, at the appellate, or circuit level," stated federal judge James Robertson.[82] Four main factors explain this development.

First, informed observers are aware that federal judges make critical decisions across a broad spectrum of policy issues. Both parties understand that although the Supreme Court is viewed as the "court of last resort," it decides only about seventy to eighty cases each year (a decade ago the number was 107).[83] Today, the twelve "regional appeals courts and the Federal Circuit Court decide more than 63,000 cases each year."[84] The courts of appeals are "playing a more important role in setting law for vast areas of the country. A decision by the 9th Circuit, for example, is binding on nine states, where 19 percent of the nation's population lives."[85] The courts of appeals, remarked a law professor, are "the Supreme Courts for their region."[86]

Second, the nomination battles over controversial court of appeals nominees—even Department of Justice appointments—are perceived by many as "warm-ups" for the looming battles over Supreme Court vacancies. In office only a little more than 100 days, President Obama, as noted earlier, already has nominated Sonia Sotomayor to fill a Supreme Court vacancy. Several current justices, moreover, are in their seventies and eighties with some having significant health issues. President Obama's nominee to head the Office of Legal Counsel in the Department of Justice, Dawn Johnsen, as well as her brother-in-law David Hamilton—a district judge nominated by Obama to the U.S. Court of Appeals for the Seventh Circuit—have both encountered critical commentary from Senate Republicans. "The combat over the [two] nominations is widely viewed as spring training for the [Supreme Court] confirmation battles to come," wrote a seasoned journalist.[87]

Third, the contemporary Senate is a highly partisan institution for reasons recounted in Chapter 6. The ideological chasm between the two parties—also evident on the Judiciary Committee—is wider than it has been in decades. It is simply far more difficult for the Senate to provide advice and consent for life-time judicial appointments in a polarized environment. Unlike legislation, once the Senate confirms a judicial nominee there is no opportunity for subsequent Senates to reverse the decision except through the arduous impeachment process. In addition, as a scholar explained:

Because presidents overwhelmingly seek to appoint judges who hail from the president's party, Senate scrutiny of judicial nominees should be particularly intense when two different parties control the White House and Senate. Not a surprise then that nominees considered during a period of divided control take significantly longer to be confirmed than those nominated during a period of unified control. Judicial nominees are also less likely to be confirmed during divided government: Over the past six decades, the Senate has confirmed on average 87 percent of appellate court nominees considered during a period of unified control, while confirming 70 percent of nominees during divided government.[88]

A two Congresses component also hampers easy resolution of judicial fights. Neither side "sees political gain in compromise. Each energizes its electoral base by standing firm."[89]

Moreover, in presidential election years there is often a dropoff in the number of justices that will be confirmed by the Senate. Majority Leader Harry Reid, D-Nev., even called this slowing down the informal "Thurmond rule," after Sen. Strom Thurmond, R-S.C. "After June," noted Senator Reid, "we will have to take a real close look at judges in a presidential election year."[90] (Other senators dispute that there is a so-called Thurmond rule.) The political reality, however, is a marked decline in the number of appellate judges confirmed during presidential election years. One study concluded that for "all judicial nominations submitted between 1947 and 2008, appointees for the Courts of Appeal pending in the Senate in a presidential election year were nearly 40 percent less likely to be confirmed than nominees pending in other years."[91] A law professor explained why this pattern occurs. "The priority for the party not in control of the White House," he said, "is not so much in stopping candidates based on their ideology, but keeping as many vacancies open as possible on the theory that the next president may be someone of your party and will be able to fill those slots."[92]

Fourth, the confirmation battles represent a clash between the president and the opposition party in the Senate over who will control the ideological balance of power on the courts. President George W. Bush, for example, was "more consistent and insistent than, say, [Gerald R.] Ford or Reagan" in nominating conservatives to the bench, said a law professor.[93] "If Democrats just rolled over on Bush's nominations," said an analyst, "they would be guilty of oppositional malpractice."[94] There is no doubt that President Bush was successful in recasting federal courts in a more conservative direction. GOP court appointees "now constitute a majority of judges on 10 of the nation's 13 federal appeals courts."[95] Republican-appointed judges "hold 54 percent of the 674 full-time federal District Court judgeships and 56 percent of the 179 full-time seats on the 13 federal Circuit Courts of Appeals."[96] Unsurprisingly, many Democrats and outside activists are urging President Obama to nominate judges who will reflect a different legal perspective. "We hope for a [Supreme

Court] justice who can replace the lost voice of an Earl Warren or Thurgood Marshall or William Brennan," exclaimed Nan Aron, president of the Alliance for Justice.[97]

Of course the party label of judicial nominees does not mean, for example, that GOP appointees will decide cases in a way that satisfies Republicans. After all, most Supreme Court justices and appeals court judges are GOP appointees, yet conservative activists and lawmakers rail against an "out-of-control" judiciary.

CONCLUSION

Federal courts, like Congress and the president, are central forums for resolving the political, social, and economic conflicts that characterize American society. All three branches of government interact constantly to shape and influence the laws Americans live under. Sometimes, as presidents say, "the buck stops here." In Congress the buck may stop nowhere, and either elective branch may pass the buck to the courts when it is unable to resolve certain issues. "Through this process of interaction among the branches," wrote scholar Louis Fisher, "all three institutions are able to expose weaknesses, hold excesses in check, and gradually forge a consensus on constitutional values."[98]

SUGGESTED READINGS

Berger, Raoul. *Congress v. The Supreme Court.* Cambridge: Harvard University Press, 1969.

Fisher, Louis. *Constitutional Dialogues.* Princeton: Princeton University Press, 1988.

Geyh, Charles Gardner. *When Congress and Courts Collide.* Ann Arbor: University of Michigan Press, 2006.

Katzmann, Robert A. *Courts and Congress.* Washington, D.C.: Brookings Institution Press, 1997.

Morgan, Donald. *Congress and the Constitution.* Cambridge: Harvard University Press, 1966.

Noonan, John T., Jr. *Narrowing the Nation's Power: The Supreme Court Sides with the States.* Berkeley: University of California Press, 2002.

Interest Group Influence. A staff member for AARP (American Association of Retired Persons)—the nation's largest membership lobby—weighs members' responses to the controversial Medicare prescription drug bill, which the organization backed (top). A poster from the physicians' trade group, the American Medical Association (AMA), urges citizens to oppose cuts for Medicare providers (bottom left). Mass demonstrations seek to impress lawmakers through sheer numbers: The Million More Movement (bottom right) brought thousands of African Americans to the Mall in 2005 to protest lingering racial inequalities.

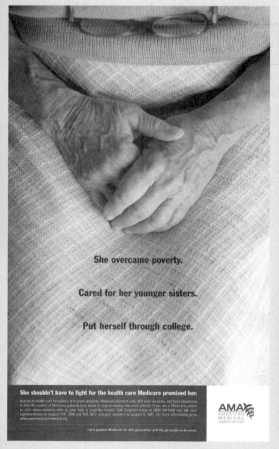

She overcame poverty.

Cared for her younger sisters.

Put herself through college.

She shouldn't have to fight for the health care Medicare promised her.

Access to health care for seniors is in great jeopardy. Medicare payment cuts, 26% over six years, will force physicians to limit the number of Medicare patients they serve or stop accepting new ones entirely. If you are a Medicare patient or care about someone who is, your help is urgently needed. Call Congress today at (888) 434-6200 and ask your representatives to support H.R. 2356 and H.R. 3617 and your senators to support S. 1081. For more information go to www.patientsactionnetwork.org

Let's protect Medicare for this generation and the generations to come.

AMA
AMERICAN
MEDICAL
ASSOCIATION

Congress and
Organized Interests

"Congress is playing chicken with your health care," the Military Officers Association told its members in a May 2008 bulletin.[1] That newsletter was just one small part of a major lobbying campaign in the summer of 2008 to persuade Congress to rescind a planned 11 percent cut in reimbursements to physicians serving patients on Medicare and other government health insurance programs.

In the Balanced Budget Act of 1997, Congress set long-term targets for federal health care spending. Since the passage of the act, however, health care costs have grown considerably faster than inflation, leading to regular cost over-runs.[2] In an effort to bring expenditures under control, the act included a formula to reduce reimbursements for medical services and equipment whenever Medicare spending targets were exceeded. Naturally, such cuts are highly unpopular with health care providers, who have launched all-out lobbying efforts to stop them each time they have been triggered. Indeed, the "doc fix" bill has become a "nearly annual ritual" in Congress.[3]

In the 2008 version of this recurring battle, the American Medical Association (AMA), pharmaceutical companies, and hospital associations from around the country, backed by scores of lobbyists, descended on Congress to fight the cuts. The AMA ran advertisements to sway wavering members of Congress, focusing on the states of vulnerable Senate Republicans up for reelection that fall.[4] The American Association of Retired Persons (AARP) enlisted 1.2 million of its members to contact Congress.[5] Doctors further increased the pressure on Congress by warning that they would no longer be able to take Medicare patients if reimbursements were reduced. "I lose money whenever I operate on a Medicare patient," said the president of Mississippi's State Medical Association, "In the last week, a number of doctors have told me they will quit seeing new Medicare patients or will cut back on the amount of Medicare work they do."[6] In addition, "Members received an outpouring of calls from doctors in their districts prior to the vote."[7]

The legislative result was what the medical lobbyists had sought. Despite strong opposition from President George W. Bush and Republican congressional leaders, a large bipartisan majority in Congress rescinded the Medicare cuts and provided for a 1.1 percent pay hike for doctors. During a House

Republican Conference meeting, Rep. Phil Gingrey, R-Ga., an ob-gyn physician himself, "questioned whether party leaders understood the significance of asking members to oppose a measure overwhelmingly supported by doctors and medical providers."[8] Confident of victory, the Democratic majority leadership put the legislation on the suspension calendar, which required a two-thirds majority to pass, even though they knew that Republican leaders were whipping members against the bill.[9] The tactic succeeded when the House voted 355–59 in favor of the bill, with 129 Republicans joining all Democrats in support. Although there was at first some question whether Senate Democrats would be able to clear the sixty-vote threshold to cut off debate, Sen. Edward M. Kennedy made a dramatic appearance returning from brain surgery to provide the sixtieth vote.[10] Once the outcome was assured, a number of other Senate Republicans switched sides, pushing the margin of support to sixty-nine votes.[11] President Bush vetoed the bill, calling it "fiscally irresponsible." But both chambers quickly and easily overrode the president's veto.[12]

AMERICAN PLURALISM

The 2008 "doc bill" battle illustrates the dual nature of American pluralism. On the one hand, a vast array of organized interests, most of them headquartered in the nation's capital, seek to influence government policy. This is the "Washington system" of lobbyists and insider access that inspires so much populist rhetoric and public distaste.[13] Narrow profit motives were hardly absent from the Medicare reimbursement debate, as manifold lobbyists sought legislative concessions to line their clients' pockets.[14]

Also weighing in on the issue, however, were membership organizations—some of them huge in size—through which American citizens assemble "to petition the government for redress of grievances," in the words of the Constitution's First Amendment. Groups of Americans legitimately concerned about how Medicare reimbursements might affect their access to health care made their concerns known. This case therefore displayed the ambivalence that characterizes both scholarly and journalistic considerations of American pluralism. The world of interest groups prompts fears of a government corrupted by narrow, special interests. Yet organized interests are not only constitutionally protected, but also a foundation of civil society and a natural by-product of democratic freedom.

A Capital of Interests

Capitol Hill lobbyists regularly fill committee hearings and markups, jam into conference committee rooms, and pack House and Senate galleries. These emissaries of organized interests do more than observe congressional events. They wield their vast resources—money, connections, personnel, information, and organization—to win passage of legislation they favor and reward the politicians who help them. Practically every major corporation, trade association, and professional group has Washington lobbyists. Lobbyists even have their own associations: the American Society of Association Executives and the American League of Lobbyists.

Looking in the Washington telephone directory under "associations" reveals as much about what moves Congress as does the Constitution. With more than 260,000 employees working in this sector, Washington is home to more national associations than any other city.[15] Numerous law firms have moved to the District of Columbia, and growing cadres of consultants and lawyers represent diverse clients, including foreign governments. The lobbying community probably constitutes the third largest industry employer in the nation's capital, behind government and tourism. The drug industry alone, for example, employed "1,274 lobbyists in 2005—more than two for every member of Congress."[16] As another example, the private equity industry spent $10 million in 2007 lobbying against efforts to tax the industry more heavily.[17] The Democratic takeover of Congress itself sparked a boost in lobbying hiring and expenditures, as organized interests sought out better access to new congressional leaders.[18]

Spending on lobbying has continued to grow, despite broader economic downturns. Lobbying expenditures by companies, associations, and their clients totaled $2.8 billion in 2007, a 9.8 percent increase over 2006 levels.[19] Both client registrations and spending on lobbying nearly doubled between 1999 and 2007.[20] "Washington is a kind of counter-cyclical town," explained H. Stewart Van Scoyoc, a high-profile lobbyist, "When companies have problems, they turn to people in town to help solve them."[21] Lobbyists of all sorts converged on Congress as it considered the 2009 economic stimulus package, for example.[22] High tech and pharmaceutical companies were seeking tax breaks for offshore income. Labor unions pressed for guarantees that green technology spending would produce jobs with good pay and benefits. Florida citrus growers and California wine growers, along with other agricultural interests, wanted more generous tax treatment for cultivating new fields. The industries in the sectors hardest hit in the recession, real estate and financial services, hired lobbyists all across Washington to seek various kinds of assistance.[23]

A Nation of Joiners

Americans' zest for joining groups was noted long ago by the French observer Alexis de Tocqueville. Americans of all "conditions, minds, and ages daily acquire a general taste for association and grow accustomed to the use of it," he wrote in 1835.[24] In 2000, 92 percent of the adult population in the United States belonged to at least one organization.[25]

Throughout American history, groups speaking for different subsets of "the people" have swayed public policies and politics. The nineteenth-century abolitionists fought to end slavery. The Anti-Saloon League crusaded for prohibition of alcohol in the 1900s. Liberal movements in the 1960s and 1970s protested the Vietnam War, racial discrimination, and abuse of the environment. In the 1970s and 1980s, interest groups galvanized support for or against equal rights for women. In the 1990s, conservative groups pushed term limits for lawmakers, a balanced budget amendment, and tax cuts. More recently, anti-abortion groups, anti-war groups, and both liberal and conservative membership organizations, from Moveon.org to the National Organization for Marriage, have played a prominent role in political debate.

A free society nurtures politically active groups. "Liberty is to faction what air is to fire," wrote James Madison in *The Federalist* No. 10. In recent years interest groups have grown in number and diversity. The American Medical Association dominated health lobbying for decades, for example, but today hundreds of health advocacy groups woo lawmakers and orchestrate grassroots activity. In 1975 there were about ninety health groups; today there are at least 750. "You name a disease, there's probably a Washington lobby for it," said an official of the American Heart Association.[26] In particular, there are more narrowly based groups that focus on single issues such as abortion or gun control. Many factors account for the proliferation of interest groups: social and economic complexity; scientific and technological developments; the government's regulatory role; the competition for federal dollars; and the diffusion of power in Congress and throughout the government, which enhances access for outside interests (see Box 13-1 on theories of interest group formation).

Some scholars contend that Americans' civic engagement has declined. Harvard University professor Robert Putnam has argued that citizen participation in associations is on the wane, drawing his most famous example from the nation's bowling alleys. Putnam's data show that more people are bowling, but do so outside of traditional bowling leagues, resulting in a drop in the number of bowling leagues.[27] They are, in short, "bowling alone." "People would rather be alone in front of a television set than out with a group," he wrote.[28] Several years later Putnam presented a more optimistic assessment of America's civic life, spotlighting citizens' engagement in a dozen community-building activities around the country.[29] Other scholars note that although membership in older groups such as Lion's Clubs, Elks, or Moose is down, membership is rising in newer organizations, such as environmental groups or youth soccer leagues.[30] The Internet also enables the formation of new social and political communities. Other important indicators of civic engagement—especially volunteering and charitable giving—have registered increases in participation.[31]

Biases of Interest Representation

Not all societal interests are organized and represented in the pressure group system. Organizations do not necessarily emerge just because people share a common policy goal or political interest. Economist Mancur Olson famously analyzed the difficulties of organizing to bring about policy change.[32] Organizing requires time and money, and individuals know that the small contributions they can make will usually not be decisive or even important. If a group exists and successfully presses for policy changes, the benefits will spread beyond those who worked to bring about the results. If, for example, an environmental group successfully presses for clean air regulations, urban

BOX 13-1   Some Theories on Interest Group Formation

Scholars have suggested a number of theories to explain the development of interest groups. Special interests have long been a source of fascination, in part because of their ability to influence policy making even though they may not reflect majority sentiment within the country. The case of intense minorities prevailing over apathetic or disengaged majorities often rivets scholarly attention. Among the various theories of group formation are the following.

▶ *The proliferation hypothesis* suggests that as society becomes more complex and interdependent, groups naturally form to reflect the country's intricate array of issues and entities. As new conditions, issues, or forces emerge, new groups are formed to reflect or respond to these developments. "The reasoning behind the proliferation hypothesis is straightforward: groups need a clientele from which to draw members."[a]

▶ *The disturbance hypothesis* posits the notion of an unstable equilibrium among groups. If something disturbs the equilibrium, such as war, technological innovations, the emergence of new concerns (acquired immune deficiency syndrome [AIDS], homeland security, and so on), and the like, then new groups emerge. As two scholars wrote, "Groups organize politically when the existing order is disturbed and certain interests are, in turn, helped or hurt." As an example, they noted: "Mobilization of business interests since the 1960s often has resulted from threats posed by consumer advocates and environmentalists, as well as requirements imposed by the steadily growing role of the federal government."[b]

▶ *The exchange hypothesis* states that groups form because of the efforts of "entrepreneurs." The argument asserts that "group organizers invest in a set of benefits which they offer to potential members at a price—joining the group. Benefits may be material [private gains], solidarity [camaraderie], or expressive [the reward of belonging to a group with shared values and causes]."[c] The implication is that organized interests are "deemed more powerful than unorganized interests."[d]

[a] Scott H. Ainsworth, *Analyzing Interest Groups* (New York: W. W. Norton and Co., 2002), 40.
[b] Alan J. Cigler and Burdett A. Loomis, eds., *Interest Group Politics,* 6th ed. (Washington, D.C.: CQ Press, 2002), 8. See also David B. Truman, *The Governmental Process,* 2d ed. (New York: Knopf, 1971).
[c] Robert Salisbury, "An Exchange Theory of Interest Groups," *Midwest Journal of Political Science* (February 1969): 1. Mancur Olson, in *The Logic of Collective Action* (Cambridge: Harvard University Press, 1965), suggests that many individuals are unlikely to join organizations that may benefit them personally because they will still receive the gains without the costs (fees, attending meetings, and so on) of participating in the group. This is called the free-rider problem. "For Olson, a key to group formation—and especially group survival—was 'selective' benefits. These rewards—for example, travel discounts, informative publications, and cheap insurance—go only to members." See Cigler and Loomis, *Interest Group Politics,* 9.
[d] Ainsworth, *Analyzing Interest Groups,* 39.

residents will benefit from smog reductions, regardless of whether they personally made any contribution to the group's efforts. As a consequence, individuals will prefer to free ride on the work of others.

The problem of free-riding is especially problematic for large groups, where failure to help with the collective effort is totally anonymous. According to Olson's analysis, organizing is easier for small groups with a strong material stake in policy outcomes. In small groups, social pressure can be effectively applied to discourage free-riding. In some cases, a single individual or firm will bankroll the cost of organizing, because it can benefit even after bearing the costs alone. Under this logic, the pressure group system should be tilted toward narrow economic interests that are easier to organize, and it should underrepresent broad public interests.

According to Olson's theory of collective action, Congress will receive more input from narrow groups with a financial stake in policy issues than from groups representing broader societal interests. Consistent with this theory, there are indeed biases in the composition of the interest group universe. One survey found that business interests make up 72 percent of all interests having Washington representation.[33]

The composition of the interest group world also reflects economic inequality. Put simply, it takes money to create and sustain organized interests, and so groups representing the well-off are more likely to emerge and survive. As political scientist E. E. Schattschneider famously put it, "the flaw in the pluralist heaven is that the heavenly chorus sings with a strong upper-class accent."[34]

The well-off and the well-educated in U.S. society participate more in politics compared with the less-fortunate, and lawmakers hear disproportionately from them. In her analysis of legislator-constituent interactions in health care policy, Kristina C. Miler discovers that legislators' perceptions of their constituencies were systematically distorted by the fact that they and their offices interact so much more frequently with resource-rich groups.[35] The rich and poor are interested in different things. The advantaged talk about taxes, government spending, and social issues, whereas the disadvantaged are primarily concerned about "basic human needs…[food], jobs, housing, and health."[36] Elected officials are inundated with messages from groups that represent the politically active (the elderly, veterans, and small-business owners, for example). Lawmakers receive comparatively little information about the policy preferences of the needy, who are often only marginally engaged in civic life.

PRESSURE GROUP METHODS

Groups have influenced congressional decisions from the country's beginning. During the nation's early technological and industrial expansion, railroad interests lobbied for federal funds and land grants to build their routes. Some of these early lobbyists' methods—offering bribes, for example—fueled public suspicion of pressure tactics. In 1874 Sen. Simon Cameron, R-Pa., described an honest politician as one who "when he is bought, stays bought."[37] Samuel Ward, the "king of the lobby" for fifteen years after the Civil War, once wrote to his friend Henry Wadsworth Longfellow:

When I see you again I will tell you how a client, eager to prevent the arrival at a committee of a certain member before it should adjourn, offered me $5,000 to accomplish this purpose, which I did, by having [the member's] boots mislaid while I smoked a cigar and condoled with him until they could be found at 11:45. I had the satisfaction of a good laugh [and] a good fee in my pocket.[38]

Lobbying methods have evolved in variety, sophistication, and subtlety. As government has expanded in size and scope, the mutual dependence of legislators and lobbyists has deepened. The legislator-lobbyist connection is a two-way street:

Groups turn to Congress as an institution where they can be heard, establish their positions, and achieve their policy goals. Members of Congress in turn rely on groups to provide valuable constituency, technical, or political information, to give reelection support, and to assist strategically in passing or blocking legislation that the members support or oppose. Groups need Congress, and Congress needs groups.[39]

Modern-day methods vary according to the nature and visibility of the issue and the groups' resources. Among the most important practices are direct and social lobbying, group alliances, grassroots support, and electronic advocacy.

These diverse techniques are typically employed in tandem. For example, House and Senate Democratic leaders and aides meet regularly with their lobbying allies, such as labor unions.[40] Sen. Debbie Stabenow, D-Mich., who heads the Democratic Steering and Outreach Committee, works "hand in hand with outside advocacy groups to raise public support for bills on the Democratic agenda."[41] Similarly, business lobbyists regularly consult with congressional GOP leaders to formulate strategy on the party's issues and goals. The lobbyists then mobilize grassroots support for these initiatives through petition drives, rallies, radio and television advertising blitzes, national door-to-door campaigns, and other techniques.[42] Sen. John Thune, R-S.D., the vice-chair of the Republican Conference, meets regularly with business groups and key GOP-leaning grassroots organizations to discuss ways to move the party's policy initiatives.[43]

Direct Lobbying

In the traditional method of direct lobbying, lobbyists present their clients' cases directly to members and congressional staff. When a group hires a prominent lawyer or lobbyist, such as Ken Duberstein, Chuck Brain, or Gerald Cassidy, the direct approach involves personal contact with senators or representatives. An aide to Speaker Thomas P. "Tip" O'Neill Jr., D-Mass. (1977–1987), explained the importance of the personal touch:

[Lobbyists] know members of Congress are here three nights a week, alone, without their families. So they…[s]chmooze with them. Make friends. And they don't lean on it all the time. Every once in a while, they call up—maybe once or twice a year [to] ask a few questions....Anne Wexler [a former official in the Carter White House, now a lobbyist] will call up and spend half an hour talking about...politics, and suddenly she'll pop a question, pick up something. They want that little bit of access. That's what does it. You can hear it. It clicks home. They'll call their chief executive officer, and they've delivered. That's how it works. It's not illegal. They work on a personal basis.[44]

Former members of Congress are particularly effective at direct lobbying. Recognizing their value, lobbying firms and clients eagerly enlist the services of former lawmakers. "Each member is part of a network of reciprocity," observed scholar James A. Thurber, "You help me, and I'll help you. That's what a lobbying client is buying."[45] A retired twenty-year House member wrote to prospective clients that he could "unravel red tape, open doors, make appointments, work with the Administration or government agencies, influence legislation, and assist in any other service required."[46] Drawing on recent disclosure filings, *CQ Weekly* reported that 195 former members of Congress are currently registered lobbyists.[47] Nearly a quarter of the members who retired or were defeated in the 2008 elections have registered as lobbyists.[48] (A Web site—www.opensecrets.org—allows citizens to track public officials who move between the government and the private sector: the so-called revolving door.) Former top Capitol Hill staff aides are similarly sought after because of their personal knowledge and understanding of key members and congressional processes.[49] Also advantaged in direct lobbying are the children and spouses of powerful members, Hollywood movie stars, famous sports figures, and prominent business executives (such as Microsoft's Bill Gates).[50]

Member-to-member lobbying can be uniquely effective. No outsider has the same access to lawmakers (and to certain precincts of Capitol Hill) that former colleagues have. For example, ex-GOP senators who may be lobbyists can attend the regularly scheduled Tuesday Republican Policy Committee lunch, "where legislative tactics are plotted on issues ranging from tax cuts to foreign policy," information "that gives them a decided edge over other lobbyists."[51] Some are offended by the access that lobbyists who are former legislators have to the floor and to other Capitol Hill locations that are not generally open to the public. Ethics reforms in 2007 imposed new limits on this access, although former members still retain privileges denied to others. Since 1991, former lawmakers have been prohibited from lobbying members of Congress directly for one year after they leave office, although they may plan strategy and advise others who do so. Efforts to lengthen this "revolving door" restriction in 2007 failed. As former House Speaker J. Dennis Hastert, R-Ill., explained, "It's hard to take away benefits for former members. We're all going to be former members one day."[52] Turnover in Congress hampers former members' direct lobbying. The longer former members have been out of Congress, the fewer personal contacts they have with current members.

The Jack Abramoff lobbying scandal of 2005–2006 made lobbying reform a top priority of the 110th Congress (2007–2009), especially because the "culture of corruption" was a key issue in the 2006 elections that returned control of Congress to the Democrats.[53] Abramoff had developed ties to influential lawmakers and staff aides, in part by providing them lavish travel, meals, and gifts. As one legislative aide said: "I was given tickets to sporting events, concerts, free food, free meals. In return, I gave preferential treatment to my lobbying buddies."[54] Abramoff, along with several lawmakers and legislative aides, is now serving a prison term for corruption. Another result of the Abramoff scandal was the new restrictions in the 2007 ethics reforms on members' receipt of gifts, meals, and travel subsidies from lobbyists.

Direct lobbying takes many forms. Lobbyists may organize focus groups of Hill staff aides to determine which arguments will most appeal to lawmakers.[55] The president of a telephone trade association underscored the importance of keeping congressional staffers informed. He even organized a retreat for congressional aides, in part to glean political intelligence about how best to frame his association's issues on Capitol Hill.[56] Lobbyists monitor committees; testify (or have their clients appear as witnesses) at hearings; interpret Hill decisions for clients; articulate clients' interests to legislators; draft legislation, speeches and "Dear Colleague" letters for members; and give campaign assistance. The House offers more occasions for contacting members directly than does the Senate, where lobbyists are more likely to target staff aides.

Taken together, lobbyists are major players in congressional policymaking. "Lobbyists contribute a lot to democracy," stated Rep. James P. Moran, D-Va. "They provide continuity and institutional memory. Most of them have been around longer than members."[57] Or as a GOP senator put it, "I would have to say the best information I get in the legislative process comes from people directly involved in the industry that is going to be affected—and from people who represent them: the 'nefarious' lobbyists."[58]

Social Lobbying

Lobbying also occurs in social settings outside the legislative context, such as at dinner parties, receptions, sporting and entertainment events, or on the golf course or tennis court. Successful direct lobbying is grounded in trust.[59] Legislators must believe that lobbyists are credible and knowledgeable before they will accept advice from or even devote time listening to them. Social interactions are extremely useful for fostering and developing the personal relationships that lobbyists need to be effective. Lobbyists thus seek out opportunities to interact casually with lawmakers, even when no client business will be discussed. On some occasions, of course, a conversation in a social setting can produce results for a lobbyist's client. As one experienced power dealer explained, "When you want to make an end run, meet someone at a party."[60]

Travel with members of Congress has long afforded many opportunities for lobbyists to engage in social lobbying, but recent ethics laws have placed new restrictions on the practice. Until the 2007 ethics rules were in place, for example, it was not unusual for legislators to accept flights on corporate jets, reimbursing their sponsors only for the cost of commercial airfare. Such settings afforded many possibilities for relationship-building and casual interaction between lobbyists, legislators, and lobbyists' clients. The 2007 ethics reforms, however, "effectively ban travel with registered lobbyists."[61] Lobbyists "may not accompany lawmakers or aides 'on any segment' of a trip."[62] And lawmakers must receive prior approval for all such travel from the Committee on Standards of Official Conduct.

Lobbyists are not permitted to pay for meals for legislators, banning the lobbyist-funded lavish dinners that were the source of so much public distaste. There is, however, the so-called "reception exception" or the "toothpick rule," which permits "members and aides to [eat] food [on toothpicks] at receptions, but bans them from attending sit-down meals with lobbyists."[63] As one lobbyist hosting a reception for legislators ruefully put it, "I'm sitting here as vice president of corporate affairs for the National Association of Manufacturers, and I'm making sure that there's nothing you need a fork for."[64] Members and aides may also attend lobbyist-paid events when carrying out "official duties" and when more than twenty-five people not connected with Congress are in attendance.

A large loophole in all these ethics rules involves political fund-raising. Social and direct lobbying can take place unrestricted at campaign events. Many fund-raising events offer wide-open opportunities for casual interactions with lawmakers: golf outings, fishing trips, and sit-down dinners. Lawmakers can continue to invite lobbyists to attend "lavish birthday parties in a lawmaker's honor ($1,000 a lobbyist), weekend golf tournaments ($2,500 and up), a Presidents Day weekend at Disney World ($5,000), or parties in South Beach in Miami ($5,000)."[65] Lobbyists end up paying for such events because "they pay a political fund-raising committee set up by the lawmaker. In turn, the committee pays the legislator's way."[66] In short, what is illegal if done directly—like paying for legislators' meals, travel, or gifts—is legal if done indirectly through campaign contributions. "I can get a $2 million earmark" setting aside money for a particular interest, remarked Sen. Tom Coburn, R-Okla., "and then they can give money through their friends to my campaign, but they can't buy me a $20 dinner."[67]

A variation on social lobbying is offering legislators speaking fees, or honoraria. Although members are banned by law from receiving honoraria, they may do so if they donate them to charities or other tax-exempt groups. Critics suggest that this arrangement enables members to "obtain political benefits by directing contributions to favored organizations, and some tax-exempt groups are affiliated with politicians."[68] Tax-exempt organizations are under increasing scrutiny by the Internal Revenue Service and other entities to determine if lawmakers and lobbyists "are using charities as a political-money subterfuge."[69]

Coalition Lobbying

To enhance their chances of success, lobbyists often construct coalitions in support of their legislative initiatives. Coalitions bring more resources, contacts, and money to lobbying efforts. With the diffusion of power on Capitol Hill, coalitions are better able than single groups to touch all the legislative bases. When individuals and organizations "band together and support one another," noted former senator John Breaux, D-La. (1987–2005), now a partner in a major Washington lobbying firm, it makes for "a smoother and more effective [legislative] operation than if fifty or more voices were all arguing for the same principle without any coordination."[70]

In 2004, for example, a group of companies and trade associations came together in the Homeland Investment Coalition to push for more favorable tax treatment of corporate income earned overseas. The Pharmaceutical Research and Manufacturers of America (PhRMA) worked with a variety of technology and financial interests to push for this tax provision, which was inserted in the American Jobs Creation Act of 2004. A study by researchers at the University of Kansas determined that this single tax break earned companies $220 for every dollar they spent lobbying on the issue, "a 22,000 percent rate of return on their investment."[71]

"We have no permanent friends or permanent enemies—only permanent interests." That oft-repeated line helps to explain why "coalitions, like politics, make strange bed fellows."[72] Rival lobbying interests sometimes forge temporary coalitions to promote or defend shared goals. For instance, a group of trade unions and liberal-leaning consumer groups joined with PhRMA and the health insurers' main trade association (America's Health Insurance Plans) in a coalition, known as the "Healthcare Reform Dialogue," to seek points of agreement as the Obama administration undertook an effort for national healthcare reform.[73] During the 110th Congress, an unusual coalition formed on a major farm bill to reduce subsidies for the traditional commodity crops—corn, wheat, cotton, rice, and soybeans—and provide more assistance to specialty crops, land conservation, environmental issues (biofuels research, for example), and nutritional programs. Upset that customary farm bills mainly subsidize rich farmers, while hurting poor farmers in developing countries and in rural areas of the United States, sixteen faith-based groups formed the "Religious Working Group on the Farm Bill." They were joined in the effort by the liberal Environmental Defense Fund and Oxfam and the conservative Club for Growth and Citizens against Government Waste.[74] In opposition were the large commodity trade associations, such as the American Farm Bureau Federation, the American Soybean Association, and the National Corn Growers Association.

A drawback of coalitions is that they are marriages of convenience. Multiple organizations are unlikely to cooperate on more than one issue, or for extended time periods. Lawmakers may also be wary of a coalition whose organizers, membership, or funding sources are murky. An attractive name (Coalition for Asbestos Reform, or the Climate Policy Group, for example) may simply be a way for a single interest to bankroll an initiative while masking its identity. To combat such efforts, Congress adopted reforms in 2007 to require more disclosure of the groups that fund and lead coalition efforts.

Grassroots Lobbying

Instead of contacting members directly, many organizations mobilize citizens in districts and states across the country to pressure their senators and representatives. Grassroots lobbying is perhaps the most effective pressure technique. For example, when eBay, the online auction Web site, wanted to influence federal telecommunications policy so that phone and cable companies could not favor certain types of Web traffic at the expense of others, it sent an e-mail to more than a million eBay users urging them to contact their members of Congress in support of "network neutrality."[75] Similarly, the Service Employees International Union (SEIU) announced in 2008 a plan to enlist its members to make ten million telephone calls to pressure members of Congress in support of universal health insurance coverage.[76]

Interest groups often send mass mailings to targeted congressional districts with letters or postcards enclosed for constituents to sign and mail to their legislators. Although lawmakers recognize that lobby groups orchestrate such mail campaigns, they realize also they may serve as a rough measure of sentiment and organizational strength behind an issue.

> Members have to care about this mail, even if it's mail that is almost identically worded. Labor unions do this sort of thing a lot. The congressman has to care that somebody out there in his district has enough power to get hundreds of people to sit down and write a postcard or a letter—because if the guy can get them to do that, he might be able to influence them in other ways. So, a member has no choice but to pay attention. It's suicide if he doesn't.[77]

Washington lobbying and public relations firms market grassroots lobbying services to clients. Masters of grassroots lobbying know how to guide citizens in their communications with members of Congress. Here is what one lobbyist said when he called a sportsman about a proposal to make hunting not tax deductible as a business expense: "Hello, Johnny Bob? This is J. D. in Washington. Got a pencil handy? Now, this is who your congressman is. This is how you write him."[78] Although the lack of disclosure requirements makes it difficult to track expenditures on grassroots lobbying, it has become a vital part of the Washington influence industry. "We are talking about lobbying firms that are providing paid advertising to influence specific legislation," observed campaign finance expert Thomas E. Mann, "These are massively funded lobbying campaigns using paid media."[79]

Lawmakers seek to distinguish between genuine grassroots and fake grassroots (often called "Astroturf"). Many so-called grassroots groups function as front organizations for their financial backers. A 2005 group with an environmentally friendly name, "Save Our Species Alliance," was actually pushing "a rewrite of the Endangered Species Act to ease paper and logging business's access to federal lands where those species live."[80] And when the House debated a major telecommunications bill, lawmakers were flooded with bogus mail from children, dead people, and constituents who said they had not sent any mailgrams. The uproar from members led to an investigation of the affair by the Capitol Police.[81]

Proponents contend that groups or individuals who can hire lobbying firms to concoct sham grassroots activity should be required to disclose publicly who they are and how much they are spending. "The point is to identify the messengers behind these communications," said a public interest advocate, "because that helps [people] evaluate the information."[82] Opponents argue that disclosure requirements run counter to the Constitution's guarantee of free speech and the right to petition the government. As noted in one federal court decision, "In a representative government such as this, these branches of government act on behalf of the people and, to a very large extent, the whole concept of representation depends upon the ability of the people to make their wishes known to their representatives."[83]

Mass mobilizations have become so common that some firms now specialize in "grass tops" lobbying. Whereas the goal of grassroots lobbying is to mobilize the masses, the goal of grass tops lobbying "is to figure out to whom a member of Congress cannot say no: his chief donor, his campaign manager, a political mentor. The lobbyist then tries to persuade that person to take his client's side" during talks with the lawmaker.[84] Big corporations may also hire "stealth" lobbyists—public relations specialists who work quietly to "influence the news media, sponsor grassroots activities and generate favorable scientific reports."[85]

Electronic Lobbying

As in most other areas of life, advances in communication technology have transformed the lobbyists' work. The mobile telephone and the Blackberry, for example, allow lobbyists sitting in a congressional markup to send out alerts on legislative developments to clients, coalition partners, and their home offices. The developments of the text message, e-mail, and the fax have all greatly increased the speed with which lobbyists can respond to the legislative process.

Messages can now be conveyed immediately to sympathizers anywhere in the country to bring pressure to bear when and where it is most needed. The potent combination of technology and politics makes "it easier to organize and send a political message across the country at warp speed."[86] To pressure the 110th Congress to act quickly on lobbying reform, Public Citizen (a consumer advocacy group) "faxed to congressional offices fake $1,000 bills called 'Lobbyist Cash'—complete with a picture of jailed lobbyist Jack Abramoff in his fedora."[87]

Groups use computer databases to identify supporters, target specific constituencies, recruit people, and generate personalized mass mailings.[88] With the emergence of interactive Web sites, lobbyists can communicate directly with prospective supporters, assign tasks, and get immediate feedback on any issue. Through increasingly sophisticated communications, "[lobbying] groups get to more of my voters, more often, and with more information than any elected official can do," complained one House member. "I'm competing to represent my district against the lobbyists and the special interests."[89]

Bloggers can activate an electronic network of political activists and organizations to lobby Congress on behalf of policies or issues they support or oppose. Talk-radio hosts, such as Rush Limbaugh (who is heard weekly on more than 600 stations by perhaps fourteen million listeners per week), can trigger from his (self-described) "Ditto-heads" an outpouring of letters, telegrams, e-mails, and faxes to lawmakers.

A subtle form of electronic lobbying occurs when advocacy groups purchase or establish Web sites or newspapers and buy radio and television stations to disseminate their views, blurring the "distinction between legitimate media and propaganda to promote their causes."[90] The National Rifle Association (NRA), for example, believes that more advocacy groups will emulate traditional media formats or buy radio stations to present their views to the general public without identifying them as NRA-owned. "We have as much right to be at the table delivering news and information to the American public as anyone else does," NRA's executive director explained.[91]

GROUPS AND THE ELECTORAL CONNECTION

Today it is often hard to differentiate the roles of interest groups and political parties in electoral politics. "The standard distinction between interest groups and parties used to be that parties were committed to winning elections and that pressure groups let elections happen and then tried to influence the people who got elected," remarked a political scientist. "Now interest groups through their PACs and a variety of other methods are very much involved in the pre-policy arena."[92] For an interesting example of a group blending issue advocacy and electoral politics, see Box 13-2 on union workers being trained as lobbyists in order to make them more effective advocates, organizers, and potential candidates for elective office.

Some groups are so extensively involved in partisan electoral politics that they are effectively "party allies," a vital part of their party's "enduring multi-layered coalition," in the words of Paul S. Herrnson.[93] For Democrats, group allies include labor unions, environmental and women's rights organizations, and liberal membership groups, such as People for the American Way and Moveon.org. For Republicans, allied groups include the U.S. Chamber of Commerce, pro-life organizations, and conservative ideological groups, like the Club for Growth.

In between elections, congressional party leaders and their allied interest groups cooperate to promote the party's message and enhance its public image. For instance, the National Association of Manufacturers coordinated with House GOP leaders to generate public support for President George W. Bush's tax-cut proposals. To communicate the point that the tax cuts would benefit all taxpayers and not just the well-to-do, the organization assembled a group of average Americans who would profit from the policies.[94] Similarly, Moveon.org organized petition drives and other mobilization efforts to pressure Congress to support President Obama's 2010 budget.

BOX 13-2   **Union Workers Trained as Lobbyists**

The United Steel Workers brings a group of legislative interns to the capital several times a year. It pays them what they make in their normal jobs plus expense allowances, lodges them in hotels, and gives them desks in the Steel Workers' offices near Dupont Circle. The visitors are technically on sabbaticals authorized by the union's collective bargaining agreements.

The program combines schooling and work. Interns often are sent to Capitol Hill to track down lawmakers or congressional aides to make the union's case on legislative issues. During a typical week, they also study congressional procedures and history, attend hearings, and observe union policy meetings. The purpose is to give rank-and-file workers a deeper knowledge of Congress and to inspire activism at the local level. The union hopes its interns will go home more politically savvy and better prepared to rally coworkers on union issues and at election time.

The steel union's program is unusual in intensity, length, and agenda. The union wants to bolster its grassroots efforts and deepen its pool of potential candidates for elected offices. A spokesman for the Steel Workers said the union hopes the six-year-old program will "get more plumbers and steamfitters and electricians into public office."

Source: Adapted from Matthew Tully, "Union Program Fields Blue-Collar Washington Lobbyists," *CQ Daily Monitor,* March 29, 1999, 7.

Interest groups help elect members to Congress in three principal ways: They raise funds and make financial contributions through political action committees, they conduct their own independent campaigns for or against issues and candidates, and they rate the voting records of legislators.

Groups and Campaign Fund-Raising

Legislators who dislike raising money—seemingly a majority of them—turn to lobbyists or professional fund-raisers to sponsor parties, luncheons, dinners, or other social events to which admission is charged. Lobbyists buy tickets or supply lists of people who should be invited. Lobbyists even serve as treasurers of members' reelection campaigns or political action committees.[95]

Fund-raising events consume more and more of legislators' limited time and create new scheduling conflicts—further evidence of the imperatives of the two Congresses, the representative assembly versus the lawmaking institution. Members cannot chase money and do legislative work at the same time. To minimize these conflicts, "windows" are opened in the Senate schedule:

> A window is a period of time in which it is understood that there will be no roll-call votes. Senators are assured that they won't be embarrassed by being absent for a recorded vote. Windows usually occur between six and eight in the evening, which is the normal time for holding fund-raising cocktail parties.[96]

Veteran senator Robert C. Byrd, D-W.Va., has complained that members must spend more time raising money than legislating.[97] A former senator said that he "had to become an expert [at fund-raising] to survive in California politics." He described three principles of raising money based on his experiences: First, "people who give once are likely to give again." If you stop asking, they will stop giving or give to someone else. Second, "it's a compliment…to ask someone for a large sum." Third, "people who have given to other causes may give to yours." For this reason, "keep track of all who give what to whom."[98] Congressional critics, and even legislators and lobbyists themselves, question the propriety of fund-raising practices. Members are concerned about implied obligations when they accept help or money from groups. For their part, lobbyists resent pressure from members to give repeatedly.

"Bundling" is a widely used fund-raising technique that allows lobbyists to raise more money for candidates than they can contribute personally under campaign finance laws. To bundle, a lobbyist or other fund-raiser will solicit checks from various sources and then give them all at once to a candidate's campaign committee. The candidate knows the bundler's identity because the checks are submitted to the campaign together or, in some cases, because the checks contain identifying information. Until the 2007 ethics reforms, the public was entirely in the dark about the identities of bundlers and the amounts they raised. Under current rules, limited disclosure requirements are imposed. Campaign committees must identify persons "reasonably known" to be registered lobbyists if they have provided two or more "bundled" contributions totaling more than $15,000 during any semi-annual reporting period.[99]

Groups and Advocacy Campaigns

Elections are contested today on interest group turf, with incumbents fighting opposing interests as well as other candidates. Interest group allies develop and fund advertising campaigns that are designed to influence electoral outcomes. Because such ads are not produced by the candidates or their political parties, they can be harder-hitting and more controversial. Sometimes, however, groups intervene in party primaries in ways not appreciated by party leaders. In 2006, for example, the right-wing Club for Growth's political action committee (PAC) aggressively funded ads in support of a Republican primary challenger to moderate Sen. Lincoln Chafee, R-R.I.[100] When Chafee won the primary, the Club for Growth took no further interest in the Rhode Island contest. But the primary challenge weakened Chafee, who lost his seat to a Democrat in the November 2006 elections.

When Republicans ran the House (1995–2007), GOP leaders such as Majority Leader Tom DeLay, Texas, instituted the "K Street Project" (named for the street in the nation's capital where many large lobbying firms have their offices).[101] House GOP leaders made it clear to lobbying firms that they would be wise to hire only Republicans for plum positions. The party's goals were to limit the influence of Democrats within the lobbying community and to gain leverage for GOP priorities in the form of campaign contributions and lobbying support. When Democrats won control of the 110th Congress, the House and Senate adopted rules prohibiting members from dictating "to any private entity the hiring or firing of anyone based on their political affiliation."[102]

Reverse lobbying also occurs. To achieve their policy objectives, lawmakers themselves encourage outside groups to support their legislative priorities. For example, the Republican leadership of Congress in 2003 recognized that obtaining the endorsement of AARP—the multi-million-member seniors' lobby—would greatly facilitate passage of one of President Bush's top priorities, a prescription drug benefit for Medicare enrollees. Shortly after President Bush's election, Speaker Hastert began talking with the AARP's chief executive, William D. Novelli. "He'd go to dinner with Novelli on occasion, have phone calls," said Hastert's spokesman John Feehry. "It was important to keep them in the loop."[103] It became much more difficult for Congress members to oppose the program after AARP backed the measure. "It's going to be hard for people to vote against this now," said Rep. Mike Bilirakis, R-Fla.[104] In short, lawmakers lobby the lobbyists. They aggressively solicit legislative input, as well as campaign funds, from their interest group allies.

Rating Legislators

About a hundred groups keep pressure on legislators by issuing "report cards" on their voting records. Groups select a number of major issues and then publicize Congress members' scores (on a scale of zero to one hundred) based on their "right" or "wrong" votes on them. Members are often warned by colleagues that certain votes will be scored. "You'll hear this as you walk into the chamber: 'This is going to be a scored vote. The environmentalists are going to score this vote, or the AFL-CIO is going to score this vote,'" stated a House member.[105] Congressional aides sometimes check with lobbying groups to determine if certain votes will be scored.

Interest groups use scorecards to influence members' decisions on selected issues. The liberal Americans for Democratic Action and the conservative American Conservative Union issue score-based ratings that are well known and widely used. One must beware of the ratings game, however. It is always simplistic. The selected votes are often inadequate to judge a member's full record, as they are selected with an agenda in mind. Group strategists defend ratings as "a shorthand way for voters to tell something about their congressman."[106] In targeting members in upcoming elections, many interest groups assign attention-getting names based on their scorecards, such as "heroes and zeroes" (from consumer advocates) or the "dirty dozen" (environmental polluters).

Groups use legislative scorecards to determine which candidates will win endorsement and receive campaign contributions. Incumbents who hold closely contested seats are usually careful when casting their votes. As a lawmaker who represents a marginal district once said, "If I cast a vote, I might have to answer for it. It may be an issue in the next campaign. Over and over I have to have a response to the question: Why did you do that?"[107] Some of the groups that rate lawmakers maintain Web sites that allow visitors to compare how they personally would vote on issues with the actual voting record of their senators or representatives.[108] Interest groups may also canvass door to door in certain areas, "to talk to voters about the results" of their scorecards.[109]

GROUPS, LOBBYING, AND LEGISLATIVE POLITICS

How much influence do organized interests wield over congressional legislation? The American public is convinced that their sway is excessive. Overwhelming majorities of survey respondents agree with the statement, "Congress is too heavily influenced by interest groups."[110] Political science research, by contrast, offers no such clarity on this question. According to a thorough review of the literature, the subject of interest group influence has "generated more smoke than fire, more debate than progress, more confusion than advance."[111] Despite the lack of scholarly consensus, the results of empirical research do not support sweeping populist characterizations of Congress as bought and paid for by moneyed interests.

The Role of Money

Journalists and campaign reform groups often posit a direct linear correlation between members' votes and the amounts they have received from various groups. The Center for Responsive Politics, a nonprofit research organization, analyzed fourteen heavily lobbied votes and found that "corporations that poured money into Congress typically got the votes they wanted."[112] The nonpartisan Center for Public Integrity also reported that "lawmakers devote themselves to protecting the industries that do them favors and pay for their campaigns."[113]

Scholarly researchers reject such simple cause-and-effect inferences. Simply correlating the campaign contributions legislators receive with their voting behavior ignores the possibility that members might just as well have voted as they did without any group influence or campaign contributions. Instead, it is necessary to determine whether lawmakers *change* their behavior after having received campaign assistance. The more careful research designs used by scholars frequently fail to find any causal connection between PAC contributions and members' votes.[114]

Rather than altering members' behavior, the principal finding of empirical research on interest group behavior is that lobbyists tend to donate to members who are already friendly to their objectives. Labor unions, for example, donate the bulk of their funds to Democrats.[115] Similarly, oil and gas interests contribute primarily to Republicans.[116] Generally speaking, groups do not regard it as a good investment of their campaign money to donate to legislative opponents. "If, as Schattschneider said, moneyed interests sing with an upper-class accent," write political scientists Richard L. Hall and Frank W. Wayman, "they also spend a good deal of effort singing to the choir."[117] In short, the patterns in campaign contributing simply do not conform to crude vote-buying theories.

Furthermore, as discussed in Chapter 3, the amount that interest groups can contribute to legislators' campaigns is limited. Under current campaign finance law, a PAC can donate no more than $5,000 per candidate per election. Given the current cost of election campaigns, a single group's contribution can make little difference—even when it contributes the maximum amount allowed under the law. In 2006, incumbent House members raised just under $1.4 million and incumbent senators about $4.4 million toward their reelection efforts.[118] With the proliferation of interest groups and PACs, candidates have many different groups to which they can turn for fundraising help. No single group exerts overwhelming financial leverage over any given member of Congress.

The relationship between lobbyists and legislators rarely resembles a simple economic exchange of money for support. Contributions signal and reinforce a relationship more often than they create one. The influence of money must be weighed along with other considerations influencing members' votes, including constituency pressures, party ties, friendships with fellow legislators or lobbyists, and personal conscience, idiosyncrasies, and prejudices. As Rep. Barney Frank, D-Mass., put it,

> Votes will beat money any day. Any politician forced to choose between his campaign contributions and strong public sentiment is going to vote public sentiment. Campaign contributions are fungible, you can get new ones. You can't get new voters.[119]

This is hardly to claim that the enormous sums that interest groups spend on political campaigns have no effect on legislative politics and policymaking. Contributions almost certainly buy access to legislators. "There is no question—if you give a lot of money, you will get a lot of access. All you have to do is send in the check," explained one corporate executive.[120] Nevertheless, the linkages between money and policymaking are not simple or easy to trace. Under the right circumstances, organized interests can reframe issues, sway members, mobilize support, or demobilize opposition, but there is very little evidence that organized interests are able to convert outright opponents.[121]

Lobbying and Legislation

An open, decentralized institution, Congress affords lobbyists multiple opportunities to shape the fate of legislation. Groups play a direct or indirect part throughout the congressional environment: in individual members' work, committee activities, legislative agenda setting, and floor decision making. Nevertheless, tracing the nature and extent of lobbyists' influence on legislation is no less difficult than untangling the relationship between campaign contributions and lawmaking.

Just as organized interests contribute primarily to their legislative allies, lobbyists also spend most of their time with friendly legislators. Lobbyists rarely target their opponents in Congress, nor do they generally devote significant effort trying to influence fencesitters.[122] Instead, they work with lawmakers who share their policy views—providing them with appropriate information, data, and political intelligence that they can perhaps use to persuade wavering colleagues.

Along these lines, many organized interests have ties to sympathetic informal congressional groups. For example, the Steel Caucus maintains links with the steel industry and the Textile Caucus with textile manufacturers. Interest groups can be instrumental in forming these informal legislative entities. The idea for the Mushroom Caucus (to protect mushroom producers from foreign imports) originated at a May 1977 luncheon for House members sponsored by the American Mushroom Institute.[123] The Institute of Scrap Recycling Industries lobbied for two years (successfully) to encourage formation of the Senate Recycling Caucus and the House Recycling Caucus. The focus of the two recycling groups is "on ways Congress can help improve recycling and develop new markets for recycled products."[124]

The relationship between lobbyists and legislators is better understood as a "legislative subsidy" than as a simple exchange in which legislators trade policy for political support.[125] Legislators benefit from the help of lobbyists because successful legislating requires so much work and expertise. Lobbyists' primary role is to assist and underwrite the efforts of their legislative allies. Lobbyists provide their congressional supporters with information, legislative language, policy analysis, useful arguments, and political advice. Working with friendly legislators, lobbyists steer policy toward their clients' goals, exerting influence that in practice is hard to distinguish from legislators' own policy preferences.

The value of lobbyists to legislators thus extends far beyond campaign contributions. "Essentially, we operate as an extension of congressmen's staff," explained one lobbyist. "Occasionally we come up with the legislation, or speeches—and questions [for lawmakers to ask at hearings] all the time. We look at it as providing staff work for allies."[126] Or, as one of Washington's premier lobbyists, Thomas Hale Boggs Jr. (son of former House majority leader Thomas Hale Boggs Sr., D-La. [1941–1943, 1947–1973], and former representative Lindy Boggs, D-La. [1973–1991]), explained, "Congressional staffs are overworked and underpaid. Lobbyists help fill the information vacuum."[127]

Lobbyists' information and expertise are thus one of their most valuable assets. An annual survey conducted by the American League of Lobbyists revealed that lobbyists rated "good information/analysis" given directly to the member as the most effective way to influence a lawmaker.[128] Reflecting on the changing styles of modern lobbying, a lawyer-lobbyist said, "Because of the increasing sophistication of staff, you have to be armed with facts, precedents and legal points. Sure it's a political environment, but it's much more substantive. The old-style, pat-'em-on-the-back lobbyist is gone, or at least going."[129]

Subgovernments

Many congressional committees deal with policies of concern to specific groups, such as farmers, teachers, or veterans. Lawmakers whose constituencies contain many members of these groups tend to seek seats on the relevant committees. Members from farming areas seek assignment to the Agriculture committees; members from states with many users of federal lands (e.g., ranchers, miners) seek assignment to the Natural Resources committees. Such committees often form alliances with the bureaucrats and lobbyists who regularly testify before them and with whom members and staff aides frequently meet. A few committees even have a staffer, such as a "director of coalitions," who works with "various coalitions that back legislation" that the committee advocates.[130] Scholars and journalists use the term *subgovernment* for the three-way policymaking alliances of committees, executive agencies, and interest groups.

These triangular relationships dominate policymaking less today than in the past. Other contending forces (citizens' groups, aggressive journalists, assertive presidents) have ended their policy monopoly. Fluid issue networks, in which diverse participants and groups influence decision making, better characterize current relationships within and among policy domains.

REGULATION OF LOBBYING

For more than 100 years Congress intermittently considered ways to regulate lobbying—a right protected by the First Amendment's free speech principle and "the right of the people...to petition the Government for a redress of grievances." Not until 1946 did Congress enact its first comprehensive lobbying law, the Federal Regulation of Lobbying Act (Title III of the Legislative Reorganization Act). This law's ineffectiveness finally led to passage of the Lobby Disclosure Act of 1995. (A "Guide to the Lobbying Disclosure Act" can be found on the Web site of the clerk of the U.S. House of Representatives: http://clerk.house.gov.) Congress recently enacted another major lobbying reform measure, the Honest Leadership and Open Government Act of 2007. In general, there have been three main statutory approaches to the regulation of lobbying: defining and prohibiting abusive lobbying practices; requiring registration for lobbyists; and providing for disclosure of lobbyists' activities.[131]

The 1946 Lobbying Law

The main objective of the 1946 act was public disclosure of lobbying activities. Persons trying to influence Congress were required to register with the clerk of the House or the secretary of the Senate and to report quarterly the amounts of money they received and spent for lobbying. The law's authors, although reluctant to propose direct control of lobbying, believed that "professionally inspired efforts to put pressure upon Congress cannot be conducive to well-considered legislation." Hence the law stressed registration and reporting:

> The availability of information regarding organized groups and full knowledge of their expenditures for influencing legislation, their membership and the source of contributions to them of large amounts of money, would prove helpful to Congress in evaluating their representations without impairing the rights of any individual or group freely to express its opinion to the Congress.[132]

The lobby law soon proved ineffective. In 1954 the Supreme Court upheld its constitutionality, but the decision *(United States v. Harriss)* significantly weakened the law. First, the Court said that only lobbyists paid to represent someone else must register—exempting lobbyists who spent their own money. Second, the Court held that registration applied only to persons whose "principal purpose" was to influence legislation. As a result, many trade associations, labor unions, professional organizations, consumer groups, and law firms avoided registering because lobbying was not their principal activity. Some lobbyists claimed immunity from the law on the pretext that their job was to inform, not influence, legislators. Finally, the Court held that the act applied only to lobbyists who contacted members directly. This interpretation excluded indirect lobbying activities that, for example, generated grassroots pressure on Congress.

Lawmakers tried repeatedly to plug the 1946 law's loopholes. The attempts foundered largely because it was difficult to regulate lobbying without trespassing on citizens' rights to contact their elected representatives. After repeated efforts to "change the way Washington does business"—a campaign theme that many members advocated—the two parties finally came together to enact the first major overhaul of the 1946 act.

The Lobby Disclosure Act of 1995

The Lobby Disclosure Act of 1995 applied new rules to individuals and firms that lobby Congress and senior executive branch officials. The law broadened the definition of those who must register as lobbyists to include all those who spend at least one-fifth of their time trying to influence lawmakers, congressional aides, or high-level executive officials, and who are paid $5,000 or more over a six-month period. Registrations of lobbyists quickly soared. A study by the Government Accountability Office determined that when the law took effect "only 6,078 individuals and organizations had registered" under the outdated 1946 act. "After the new law took effect, a total of 14,912 lobbyists registered," 10,612 of them first-time registrants.[133] In 2005, there were 34,785 registered lobbyists.[134] The law is administered by the public records offices of the House and Senate.

Lobbyists are required to "provide semi-annual disclosures showing who their clients are, what policies they are trying to influence, and roughly how much money they are spending for lobbying."[135] Civil fines of up to $50,000 can be imposed on those who fail to comply. Grassroots lobbying is exempt from the law, as are lobbyists paid $5,000 or less semi-annually and organizations that use their own employees to lobby.

Although the 1995 lobby law was an improvement over the old one, it was minimally enforced. A 2005 report by the Center for Public Integrity said that the disclosure system is in disarray.[136] Lee H. Hamilton, former Indiana representative, vice chair of the 9/11 Commission, and cochair of the 2006 Iraq Study Group, observed,

> Roughly one in five of the companies registered to lobby failed to file the required forms, and overall, 14,000 documents that should have been filed are missing, while another fifth of the required lobbying forms were filed late. The Center [for Public Integrity] found that "countless forms are filed with portions that are blank or improperly

filled out. An unknown number of lobbyists neglect or refuse to file any disclosure forms whatsoever." In essence, we have a lobby disclosure system in name only.[137]

Some firms and organizations also underreport their lobbying expenditures. "Companies, trade associations, and lobby firms often misreport—intentionally or inadvertently—how much money they shell out or take in."[138]

The Honest Leadership and Open Government Act of 2007

A confluence of events beyond the perception that the 1995 law was weakly enforced compelled the 110th Congress to take up another major lobbying reform bill. They included the Abramoff bribery scandal; the ethical violations and indictment in Texas of House GOP leader Tom DeLay; the imprisonment of several lawmakers and top congressional aides; and ongoing FBI investigations into alleged misconduct by a few sitting lawmakers. Seizing on that, the Democrats committed themselves on the campaign trail in 2006 to address what they called the "culture of corruption" on Capitol Hill. Highlighting the two Congresses, "We know we have to do [lobbying] reform in the 110th Congress or face the electoral consequences in November 2008 for reneging on our campaign promise to clean up Congress," declared House Democratic Caucus chairman Rahm Emanuel, Ill.[139]

Some of the most notable provisions of the 2007 ethics reforms are highlighted in Box 13-3. Allegations of ethical violations are handled by each chamber's ethics committee; lobbying violations are within the purview of the Department of Justice. Whether statutory or rule-based, enforcement of the requirements is essential to gain public trust.

During the consideration of the 2007 reforms, a number of more far-reaching proposals were rejected, including provisions to require disclosure of grassroots lobbying and further extensions to former members' "cooling off periods" to slow the revolving door. Several senators and House members have advocated creation in each chamber of an independent ethics commission, (which the House alone did in 2007) to investigate ethics and lobbying violations and report findings to the respective ethics committees. Clearly, many ideas for reform remain to be taken up during the next round of lobbying reform.

Foreign Lobbying

The 1995 Lobby Disclosure Act also amended the Foreign Agents Registration Act of 1938, which required those who lobby on behalf of foreign governments or political parties to register with the Justice Department. The 1995 law broadened the definition of foreign lobbyists to include individuals who lobby on behalf of foreign-owned commercial enterprises. About 500 lobbyists have registered with the Justice Department as agents representing foreign governments or parties (see www.usdoj.gov/criminal/fara).

Given the role of the United States in the global economy and in military security, many foreign governments and lobbyists who work for foreign clients

BOX 13-3 **The Honest Leadership and Open Government Act of 2007**

LOBBYING DISCLOSURE

Lobbyists must file quarterly reports for an electronic database, with a maximum fine of $200,000 for not complying.

GIFTS, MEALS, AND TRAVEL

Lobbyists may not give lawmakers or staff gifts, even those less than $50 in value, and they cannot pay for lawmakers' or staffers' meals or travel expenses.

Members and staff must receive advance approval from the appropriate ethics committee before accepting any travel with any private organization.

REVOLVING DOOR

Senators and very senior executive officials are prohibited from lobbying for two years after they leave government; House members, for one.

Senior staff members who left Capitol Hill would be prohibited from lobbying for one year.

All Senate staff members are prohibited from lobbying the member or committee for whom they worked for one year after leaving.

CAMPAIGN CONTRIBUTIONS

Registered lobbyists would have to reveal all their political contributions, including bundling of contributions from friends and colleagues.

Source: Adapted from Jack Maskell, Legislative Attorney, "Lobbying Law and Ethics Rules Changes in the 110th Congress," *Congressional Research Service Report,* September 17, 2007.

spend considerable time and money promoting their interests on Capitol Hill and with the broader citizenry. For example, after September 11, 2001, Saudi Arabia spent more than $20 million to improve its image among lawmakers, the press, and the public. (Fifteen of the nineteen airplane hijackers were Saudi-born.) Many other nations also hire lobbyists to forge closer ties with Congress, the executive branch, and various U.S. industries, such as oil.[140]

Local lobbyists also operate globally. Many U.S.-based corporations hire lobbyists who can protect their interests in Europe or other parts of the world when disputes arise about trade, agriculture, antitrust laws, the environment, and other issues.[141] The National Rifle Association formed a transnational organization of gun groups and firearm manufacturers from eleven other countries (the World Forum) to fight international restrictions and regulations that might adversely affect the gun trade.[142]

Globalization of the world's economy also influences congressional lobbying. Toyota is the world's largest auto manufacturer, with plants located in eleven states. By locating plants around the country, the company enhances its political clout on Capitol Hill, gaining supporters in the House, Senate, and state houses. Toyota can now "call on 151 House members, 22 senators, and 11 governors from the states where it operates."[143]

CONCLUSION

From the nation's beginning, lobbying and lawmaking have been closely intertwined. Lobbying "has been so deeply woven into the American political fabric that one could, with considerable justice, assert that the history of lobbying comes close to being the history of American legislation."[144]

Recent years have witnessed an explosion in the number and types of groups organized to pursue their ends on Capitol Hill. Compared with decades past, many more industry associations, public affairs lobbies (such as Common Cause), single-issue groups, political action committees, and foreign agents engage in the influence trade. Some of these groups employ new grassroots and technological lobbying techniques. Many victories today are won in Washington because of sophisticated lobbying campaigns waged in home states or districts.

No one questions that groups and lobbyists have a rightful public role, but some aspects of lobbying warrant concern. Groups often push Congress to pass laws that benefit the few and not the many. They inflate disagreements and hinder compromise. They often misrepresent the voting records of legislators in their rating schemes and pour money into the campaigns of their allies (mainly incumbents). Lawmakers who defy single-issue groups find at election time that those organizations are bent upon defeating them.

Built-in checks constrain group pressures, however. The immense number of organized interests enables legislators to play one competing group off against another. Knowledgeable staff aides also provide members with information to counter the lobbyists' arguments. Lawmakers' own expertise is another informal check on lobbyists. Finally, there are self-imposed constraints. Lobbyists who misrepresent issues or mislead members soon find their access permanently closed off.

SUGGESTED READINGS

Birnbaum, Jeffrey H., and Alan S. Murray. *Showdown at Gucci Gulch: Lawmakers, Lobbyists, and the Unlikely Triumph of Tax Reform.* New York: Random House, 1987.

Cigler, Allan J., and Burdett A. Loomis, eds. *Interest Group Politics.* 7th ed. Washington, D.C.: CQ Press, 2007.

Hall, Richard L., and Alan V. Deardorff. "Lobbying as Legislative Subsidy." *American Political Science Review* 100 (February 2006): 69–84.

Hojnacki, Marie and David Kimball. "Organized Interests and the Decision of Whom to Lobby in Congress." *American Political Science Review* 92(December 1998): 775–790.

Rozell, Mark, Clyde Wilcox, and David Madland. *Interest Groups in American Campaigns: The New Face of Electioneering.* 2d ed. Washington, D.C.: CQ Press, 2005.

Truman, David B. *The Governmental Process, Political Interests, and Public Opinion.* 2d ed. New York: Knopf, 1971.

Budgets, Taxes, and Policies in Hard Times. Two citizens fill out last-minute tax returns at a post office in northwest Washington, D.C. (top). House and Senate conferees (center) meet to consider the 2010 budget bills. Policymakers face the worst economic downturn since the Great Depression of the 1930s. Expecting a bear market in their search for jobs and careers, students and others (bottom) line up to attend a job fair at Miami Dade College.

Congress, Budgets, and Domestic Policymaking

"There is a tide in the affairs of men, which, taken at the flood, leads on to fortune."[1] So spoke Brutus, reflecting on his fate in Shakespeare's *Julius Caesar*. The sentiment could apply to President Barack Obama, whose career was hoisted by the winds of social and economic change. In office for only a short while, President Obama called upon a robust tide of popular support to advance a bold and ambitious agenda. The president moved swiftly to seize the moment—before the tides could reverse his fortunes.

The president moved at a brisk pace. In his first few weeks in the White House, he won enactment of a $787 billion economic stimulus package; signed a $410 billion omnibus appropriations bill into law; won congressional adoption of the major features of his $3.6 trillion budget proposal; achieved a $33 billion expansion of the State Children's Health Insurance Program (SCHIP); proposed major changes in health care, energy, and education; forced the head of General Motors (GM) into retirement; attended the G-20 summit of heads of state in London; met with American troops in Iraq, as well as the country's prime minister; reversed several policies of the Bush administration; urged an overhaul of the banking, housing, and financial sectors; requested supplemental spending for the conflicts in Iraq and Afghanistan; and opened discussion of major immigration reform.

Having campaigned on the theme of change, Obama set to work to deliver on his promises. Many lawmakers, however, balked at the high price tag of many of his major initiatives. Congressional Republicans criticized the trillion dollar deficits embedded in Obama's budget proposals. "It's a lot of money," noted Sen. John Thune, R-S.D. "That's going to cause a lot of heartburn for Republicans."[2] Moderate and conservative House and Senate Democrats also fretted about the size of the deficit and the amount of money being borrowed from countries like China. Fiscal commitments for bailing out the financial sector approached $3 trillion, according to the Special Inspector General for the Department of Treasury's Troubled Asset Relief Program (TARP). "It's like having a second US budget dedicated solely to saving the US financial system, and that truly is surreal," exclaimed Sen. Max Baucus, D-Mont., the chair of the Finance Committee.[3]

The Obama administration recognized the need to reduce the long-term deficit, even convening a "fiscal responsibility" summit a month after the president took office. The president and his allies, however, emphasized at least two fundamental points. First, the trillions of dollars being spent today are arguably required to revive the ailing economy. The cost is high, but the cost of doing little or nothing may turn a severe recession into a depression. As Alice Rivlin, a former director of the Congressional Budget Office (CBO) and a governor of the Federal Reserve, pointed out: "We have borrowed a lot. But...if we let our economy fall into depression we would be in even worse trouble, so we have to take the chance that we can borrow some more and get out of this recession."[4] Indeed, there were leading economists who faulted the administration for being too timid in requesting and allocating funds.

Second, the administration's bold plans and mammoth budget aim to recast domestic policies and introduce a new era of progressive federal activism. "We have fundamentally shifted the center of gravity in this budget, in the same way Reagan did [in 1981, reducing taxes, increasing defense expenditures, and cutting social programs]," declared Rahm Emanuel, Obama's chief of staff. "We are going to use this time and this moment to do what needs to be done."[5] As Sen. Ron Wyden, D-Ore., underscored, "The urgency of healthcare is now. After 60 years of yakking about health care, he's saying, 'I don't want to wait for year 61.'"[6] But House Minority Leader John Boehner's view was different. "The era of big government is back, and Democrats are asking you to pay for it."[7] Plainly, conflicts about policies and the money to pay for them lie at the vortex of today's lawmaking process.

DEFINITIONS OF POLICY

Defining "public policy" with any precision is difficult because the concept is inextricably entwined with the purposes of government. Nonetheless, several definitions exist. David Easton famously defined public policy as society's "authoritative allocation" of values or resources. To put it another way, policies can be regarded as determining "who gets what, when, and how" in a society. Randall B. Ripley and Grace A. Franklin offer a more serviceable definition of policy: Policy is what the government says and does about perceived problems.[8]

How can one recognize policies? The answer is not as simple as it may seem. Many policies are explicitly labeled and recognized as authoritative statements of what the government is doing, or intends to do, about a particular matter. The measures may be far-reaching (financing the Social Security system, for example); they may be trivial (naming federal buildings after deceased public officials). Nonetheless, these are obvious statements of policy. They are usually written down, often in precise legal language. They boast documented legislative histories in committee hearings, reports, and floor deliberations that indicate what lawmakers had in mind as they hammered out the policy's final provisions.

Not all policies, however, are so formal. Some are articulated by officials but, for one reason or another, are never set down in laws or rules. The Monroe Doctrine, which declared U.S. resistance to European intervention in the

Western Hemisphere, was inserted into the President James Monroe's 1823 State of the Union report, written by Secretary of State John Quincy Adams. Successive generations of policymakers have adhered to it ever since. Other policies, especially of a symbolic or hortatory nature, gain currency in the eyes of elites or the public without formal or legal elaboration.

Some policies stress substance—programs designed to build the nation's defense, for example. Others stress procedure, such as those imposing personnel ceilings on federal agencies, mandating program management standards, or requiring contractors' insurance for military weapons. Still others are amalgams of substance and procedure, such as fast-track provisions (renamed "trade promotion authority") written into trade laws and other laws that expedite committee and floor action in each house. Fast-track statutory provisions include time limits on committee consideration of a bill and on floor debate of a measure, prohibitions against floor amendments, and a requirement that each chamber pass identical legislation, thus dispensing with conference committees to iron out bicameral differences.

Finally, sometimes public policy is defined by governmental inaction. The United States had no general immigration law before 1924 and no overall national medical care program before 1965, but its policy of unregulated private activity and self-help on these issues was unmistakable.

The process of arriving at these policies is policymaking. The process may be simple or complex, highly publicized or nearly invisible, concentrated or diffuse. The policy may happen suddenly, such as military air strikes ordered by the president. Or it may require years or even decades to formulate, as in the case of civil rights or Medicare for the elderly.[9]

STAGES OF POLICYMAKING

Whatever the time frame, policymaking normally has four distinct stages: setting the agenda, formulating policy, adopting policy, and implementing policy.

Setting the Agenda

At the initial stage, public problems are spotted and moved onto the national agenda, which can be defined as "the list of subjects to which government officials and those around them are paying serious attention."[10] In a large, pluralistic country such as the United States, the national agenda at any given moment is extensive and vigorously debated.

How do problems arrive on the agenda? Some emerge as a result of a crisis or an attention-grabbing event—an economic depression, a terrorist attack, a school shooting, a devastating hurricane or earthquake, or a high-visibility corruption scandal. Others are occasioned by the gradual accumulation of knowledge, for example, rising awareness of an environmental hazard such as global warming. Still other agenda items represent the accumulation of past problems that no longer can be avoided or ignored, such as the safety of the nation's food supply and the crumbling infrastructure.

Agendas are also set in motion by political processes—election results (1964, 1980, 1994, 2006, and 2008 are good examples), turnover in Congress, or shifts in public opinion.[11] The 1994 election results gave the GOP control of the House for the first time in forty years and a chance to pursue its "revolution" in downsizing government. The next five elections produced a different outcome, reflecting the two Congresses theme, as many Republicans lost their zeal for shrinking the size and reach of government. "Too many people started to believe that the surest path to reelection is to spend money rather than cut government," remarked Rep. Jeff Flake, R-Ariz.[12] The election of 2006 produced a Democratic Congress and with it came a new set of priorities, including opposition to the president's handling of the Iraq war and aggressive congressional oversight of the executive branch. The 2008 elections ended with Democrats in charge of Congress and the White House and an agenda driven in large measure by a major economic crisis.

Agenda items are pushed by policy entrepreneurs, people willing to invest time and energy to promote a particular issue. Numerous Washington, D.C., think tanks and interest groups issue reports that seek to influence the economic, social, or foreign policy agenda of the nation, especially at the beginning of a new president's term. Health care and Social Security reforms, for instance, have long been advocated by various think tanks. Elected officials and their staffs or appointees are more likely to shape agendas than are career bureaucrats.[13] Notable policy entrepreneurs on Capitol Hill are party and committee leaders.

Lawmakers frequently are policy entrepreneurs because they are expected to voice the concerns of constituents and organized groups and to seek legislative solutions. Politicians generally gravitate toward issues that are visible, salient, and solvable. Tough, arcane, or controversial problems may be shunned or postponed because they arouse significant public controversy.

The nation's recent experience with record gasoline prices placed pressure on lawmakers to address difficult questions of energy policy. Energy independence has been a decades-long goal of the United States, particularly since the deliberate slowing-down of oil production in the 1970s by the OPEC cartel (Organization of Petroleum Exporting Countries). The result was long gasoline lines in cities across America as citizens waited for hours to fill their tanks before the stations ran out of gasoline. Some energy-saving and conservation innovations were introduced but these largely lapsed with the return of a global oil glut. Forecasters continue to predict more short- and long-term energy woes unless steps are taken to develop clean-energy alternative fuels, change consumption habits, encourage conservation, and reduce the spiraling demand for oil, especially oil from the volatile Middle East. The reality is that there are no quick fixes to the demand for energy. As one analyst suggested:

> We need an energy policy that understands that the world is going to require much more energy in the future. The math is pretty simple. Today, there are about 6.7 billion people on earth. By 2050 there will be 9 billion. To sustain these extra 2.3 billion people while still raising standards of living everywhere, we will need to consume about twice as much energy

as we do today. So the debate about oil vs. natural gas vs. biofuels vs. alternative energy is wholly unrealistic. If we are going to sustain and support this kind of population and economic growth, we'll need everything.[14]

This kind of creeping crisis is often difficult for members of Congress to grapple with, in part because of the two-Congresses dilemma. As conscientious lawmakers, members might want to forge long-term solutions. But as representatives of their constituents, they must respond to more immediate constituent concerns about, as Obama's energy secretary phrased it, being "at the mercy of [energy] price spikes" because of our oil dependency.[15]

Formulating Policy

In the second stage of policymaking, items on the political agenda are discussed and potential solutions are explored. Members of Congress and their staffs play crucial roles by conducting hearings and writing committee reports. They are aided by policy experts in executive agencies, interest groups, legislative support agencies, think tanks, universities, and private-sector organizations.

Another term for this stage is *policy incubation,* which entails "keeping a proposal alive while it picks up support, or waits for a better climate, or while a consensus begins to form that the problem to which it is addressed exists."[16] Sometimes this process takes only a few months; more often it requires years. During Dwight D. Eisenhower's administration (1953-1961), for example, congressional Democrats explored and refined domestic policy options that, while not immediately accepted, were ripe for adoption by the time their party's nominee, John F. Kennedy, was elected president in 1960.[17]

The incubation process not only brings policies to maturity but also refines the solutions to problems. The process may break down if workable solutions are not available. The seeming intractability of many modern issues complicates problem solving. Thomas S. Foley, D-Wash. (Speaker, 1989–1995), held that issues had become far more perplexing since he came to Congress in 1965. At that time "the civil rights issue facing the legislators was whether the right to vote should be federally guaranteed for blacks and Hispanics. Now members are called on to deal with more ambiguous policies like affirmative action and racial quotas."[18] Complex topics such as stem cell research, genetic discrimination, unconventional warfare, and global climate change are contemporary examples of difficult issues facing lawmakers. Solutions to problems normally involve "some fairly simple routines emphasizing the tried and true (or at least not discredited)."[19] A repertoire of proposals—for example, blue-ribbon commissions, trust funds, or pilot projects—can be applied to a variety of unsolved problems. Problem solvers also must guard against recommending solutions that will be viewed as worse than the problem.

Adopting Policy

Laws often embody ideas whose time has come. The right time for a policy is what scholar John W. Kingdon calls the "policy window": the opportunity presented by circumstances and attitudes to enact a policy into law. Policy entrepreneurs must seize the opportunity before the policy window closes and the idea's time has passed.

Once policies are ripe for adoption, they must gain popular acceptance. This is the function of legitimation, the process through which policies come to be viewed by the public as right or proper. Inasmuch as citizens are expected to comply with laws or regulations—pay taxes, observe rules, and make sacrifices of one sort or another—the policies themselves must appear to have been properly considered and enacted. A nation whose policies lack legitimacy is in deep trouble.

Symbolic acts, such as members' voting on the House or Senate floor or the president's signing a bill, signal to everyone that policies have been duly adopted according to traditional forms. Hearings and debates, moreover, serve to fine-tune policies as well as to cultivate support from affected interests. Responding to critics of Congress's slowness in adopting energy legislation, a senator posed these questions:

> Would you want an energy bill to flow through the Senate and not have anyone consider the impacts on housing or on the automotive industry or on the energy industries that provide our light and power? Should we ignore the problems of the miner or the producer or the distributor? Our legislative process must reflect all of the problems if the public is to have confidence in the government.[20]

Legitimating policies, in other words, often requires a measured pace and attention to procedural details. But a measured pace and painstaking attention to procedural niceties sometimes provide opponents of change with the opportunity to mobilize. In many circumstances, policymakers may be forced to enact bold changes quickly in response to public outcry or demand, knowing that the details will have to be refined and adjusted later. Legislative passage in three weeks of President Obama's economic stimulus package is an example.

Implementing Policy

In the final stage, policies shaped by the legislature and at the highest executive levels are put into effect, often by a federal agency. Most policies are not self-executing; they must be promulgated and enforced. A law or executive order rarely spells out exactly how a particular policy should be implemented. Congress and the president usually delegate most decisions about implementation to the responsible agencies under broadly worded guidelines. Implementation determines the ultimate effect of policies. Officials of the executive branch can thwart a policy by foot-dragging or sheer inefficiency. By the same token, over-zealous administrators can push a policy far beyond its creators' intent.

Congress, therefore, must exercise its oversight role. It may require executive agencies to report to or consult with congressional committees or to follow other formal procedures. Members of Congress receive feedback on the operation of federal programs through a variety of channels: media coverage, interest group protests, and even casework for constituents. With such information Congress can adjust funding, introduce amendments, or recast the legislation on which the policy is based.

TYPES OF DOMESTIC POLICIES

One way to understand public policies is to analyze the nature of the policies themselves. Scholars have classified policies in many different ways.[21] Our typology identifies three types of domestic policies: distributive, regulatory, and redistributive.

Distributive Policies

Distributive policies or programs are government actions that convey tangible benefits—subsidies, tax breaks, or advantageous regulatory provisions—to private individuals, groups, or firms. These benefits are often called "pork," a derogatory term for program benefits or spending specifically designated for members' states or districts. Pork is often difficult to define objectively, however. After all, "one person's pork is another person's steak." The projects come in several varieties:

> Dams, roads and bridges, known as "green pork," are old hat. These days, there is also "academic pork" in the form of research grants to colleges, "defense pork" in the form of geographically specific military expenditures and lately "high-tech pork," for example the intense fight to authorize research into super computers and high-definition television (HDTV).[22]

Distributive policymaking, which makes many interests better off and few, if any, visibly worse off—comes easy to Congress, a collegial and nonhierarchical institution that must build coalitions to function. A textbook example was the $1 billion-plus National Parks and Recreation Act of 1978. Dubbed the "Park Barrel Bill," it created so many parks, historic sites, seashores, wilderness areas, wild and scenic rivers, and national trails that it sailed through the Interior (now Resources) Committee and passed the House 341–61. "Notice how quiet we are. We all got something in there," said one House member, after the Rules Committee cleared the bill in five minutes flat. Another member quipped, "If it had a blade of grass and a squirrel, it got in the bill."[23] Distributive politics of this kind throws the two Congresses into sharp relief: national policy as a mosaic of local interests.

The politics of distribution works best when tax revenues are expanding, fueled by high productivity and economic growth. When productivity declines or tax cuts squeeze revenues, it can become difficult to add new benefits or expand old ones. Yet distributive impulses remain strong even in these circumstances as lawmakers in both parties work to ensure that money is spent for particular purposes in their districts or states. This type of particularistic spending is referred to by a variety of different names—"pork," "spending with a Zip code," "member projects," "congressional initiatives," "congressional directed spending," or, more common today, "earmarks." By whatever name, the fundamental purpose of this spending is to "bring home the bacon."

During the 1990s and 2000s, the number of earmarks increased in number and dollar value. According to Sen. John McCain, R-Ariz., a sharp critic of earmarks, in 1994 there were 4,126 earmarks included in appropriations bills; in 2005 there were 15, 877. "The level of funding associated with these earmarks has more than doubled from $23.2 billion in fiscal year 1994 to $47.4 billion in fiscal year 2005."[24] Various factors accounted for this trend. With narrow partisan divisions in the House and Senate, party and committee leaders used earmarks to attract the votes they needed to pass priority legislation and, in a two-Congresses tactic, helped electorally vulnerable lawmakers facing tough challenges at home. The proliferation of costly earmarks began to decline, however. In 2008, there were 11,610 earmarks at a cost of $17. 2 billion. Why the change?

There has been significant criticism of wasteful and unnecessary earmarks, as well as the unseemly and sometimes corrupt connection between earmarks to favorite clients who then contribute to lawmakers' campaigns. Aggressive watchdog groups and various lawmakers, such as representative Flake or Sen. Russell Feingold, D-Wis., publicized what they viewed as bad earmarks. Critics also pointed out that earmarks are often awarded to lawmakers based on their seniority and not on the merit or public value of the earmark. As a result, the 110th and 111th Congresses, as well as President Obama, enacted a series of reforms to bring transparency and accountability to the earmark process (see Box 14-1). For example, the procedures now require public disclosure of the lawmaker requesting an earmark; the name and location of the intended recipient; the purpose of the earmark; and certification that neither the requesting lawmaker nor his or her spouse has a financial interest in the earmark. Lawmakers continue to telephone and send letters to executive branch officials urging them to continue funding projects and activities earmarked in past years. This informal practice has been dubbed "phonemarking."[25]

Many lawmakers and analysts emphasize that eliminating every earmark would save a trivial amount of money (around $20 billion) compared to a $3.6 trillion budget, and the lengthy debates that occur over earmarks detract members' attention from the big budget items that dominate spending: entitlements, health care, or defense. Moreover, there are numerous earmarks that are not wasteful and serve worthwhile public purposes, such as repairing decrepit bridges. In the judgment of Rep. Ron Paul, R-Texas:

> To fight earmarks is to fight for an even more powerful executive branch. It is popular these days to condemn earmarks in the name of fiscal conservatism. The truth is that they account for less than 2 percent of the [$410 billion] spending bill just passed [in early 2009]. And even if all the earmarks were removed from the budget, overall, no money would be saved. That money would instead go to the executive branch to spend as it sees fit. Congress has the power of the purse. It is the constitutional responsibility of members to earmark, or designate, where funds should go, rather than to simply deliver a lump sum to the president.[26]

BOX 14-1   Earmarks: Here to Stay or Facing Extinction?

Attempting to quell the continuing uproar over earmarks, President Obama and House Democrats last week announced new procedures for publicizing and reviewing proposed projects. But Republicans denounced the plans as too little, too late, and Senate Democrats said they believed they already had taken steps to make the earmarking process more public.

On March 11, the same day he signed a fiscal 2009 spending bill containing $410 billion in discretionary funding, Obama announced several principles for an overhaul of the earmarking process. He said that members' earmark requests should be posted on their Web sites and that there should be public hearings on those requests. He also said any earmark for a for-profit company would have to be competitively bid. The House and Senate Appropriations panels already announced this year that members would have to post requests on their Web sites. They also announced a plan to limit the growth of earmarks by keeping the amount of funding devoted to the projects to less than 1 percent of overall discretionary spending.

The fiscal 2009 omnibus includes more than 8,500 earmarks totaling $7.7 billion, according to Taxpayers for Common Sense. House Democrats echoed Obama's call to require competitive bidding for for-profit companies. However, they took the additional step of saying executive agencies would be given twenty days to review an earmark request after it was made "to ensure that the earmark is eligible to receive funds and meets goals established in law."

Later in the day, Senate Appropriations Chairman Daniel K. Inouye, D-Hawaii, took a slightly different approach, saying his committee also would "work to ensure that congressional earmarks for private companies are subject to the same rules and regulations for competition as apply to items submitted as part of the president's budget." He also made clear, however, that his panel was not going to cede any of its authority. "Others have suggested that our hardworking and well-meaning federal employees should be the ones to make all these decisions," he said in a statement. "I could not disagree more. It is in the nature of a bureaucracy to be both risk-averse and to support the status quo."

Republican critics of earmarks, led by Obama's presidential campaign rival, Sen. John McCain of Arizona, dismissed the new Democratic moves as hollow. "The president's rhetoric is impressive, but his statement affirms we will continue to do business as usual in Washington regarding earmarks in appropriations legislation," McCain said in a statement. "The president could have resolved this issue in one statement—no more unauthorized pork barrel projects—and pledged to use his veto pen to stop them. This is an opportunity missed."

REPUBLICAN REQUESTS

The anti-earmark rhetoric of Republicans such as McCain did not mask the fact that Republicans requested 40 percent of the funding set-asides in the omnibus bill for these mostly parochial projects. The GOP also presided over a major proliferation of earmarks when it controlled Congress.

Republicans in both chambers, but especially the House, are divided over the issue. One camp would like to do away with earmarks entirely, arguing that the increase in earmarks during the twelve years that Republicans controlled Congress was a leading reason why the GOP is now in the minority. Other GOP members say they have an obligation to look out for their own districts and states and that it would be foolish to abandon the process if Democrats continue to seek earmarks.

House GOP leaders have railed against earmarks, but their Senate counterparts have been reluctant to do so, since some of them have served on the Appropriations Committee and request funding for projects in their states.

Source: David Clarke, "Earmarks: Here to Stay or Facing Extinction?," *CQ Weekly,* March 16, 2009, 613.

The two Congresses are a central factor in the ongoing debate on earmarks. For example, some lawmakers who want to emphasize their conservative and fiscal responsibility credentials have pledged not to take earmarks. Others have enlisted citizen groups back home to identify meritorious earmark requests. For example, Rep. Jackie Speier, D-Calif., has "formed a Citizens Oversight Panel made up of people from across the 12th District representing different views to review appropriations requests in public forums and pass their recommendations" to the congresswoman.[27]

Regulatory Policies

Regulatory policies are designed to protect the public against harm or abuse that might result from unbridled private activity. For example, the Food and Drug Administration monitors standards for foodstuffs and tests drugs for purity, safety, and effectiveness, and the Federal Trade Commission guards against illegal business practices, such as deceptive advertising.

Federal regulation against certain abuses dates from the late nineteenth century, when the Interstate Commerce Act and the Sherman Antitrust Act were enacted to protect against abuses in transportation and monopolistic practices. As the twentieth century dawned, scandalous conditions in slaughterhouses and food-processing plants led to meatpacking, food, and drug regulations. The stock market collapse in 1929 and the Great Depression of the 1930s paved the way for the New Deal's regulation of the banking and securities industries and of labor-management relations. Consumer rights and environmental protection policies came of age in the 1960s and 1970s, and the economic crisis of the 2000s triggered calls for greater regulation of financial firms to minimize excessive risk taking, maximize transparency, and mandate liquidity (cash-on-hand) standards.

Regulation inevitably arouses controversy. Much of the clean air debate, for instance, involves the basic issue of costs versus benefits: Do the public health benefits of cleaner air outweigh the financial costs of obtaining it?[28] Environmentalists and health advocates argue that tougher standards for regulating air pollution would prevent suffering and save the lives of thousands who are afflicted with asthma and other lung diseases. Industries and conservative groups attack these claims, contending that the "regulations are unnecessary, would be too costly and would yield only marginal health benefits."[29]

Redistributive Policies

The most difficult of all political feats is redistributive policy, which involves government's purposefully shifting resources from one group to another. Typically controversial, redistributive policies engage a broad spectrum of political actors—not only in the House and Senate but also in the executive branch and among interest groups and the public at large. Redistributive issues tend to be ideological, dividing liberals and conservatives on fundamental questions of equality, opportunity, and property rights. Tax cuts for the wealthy at a time of rising income inequality is an example of a redistributive controversy.

(Despite the controversy, when the tax cuts are brought up for a vote, they are usually approved by a solid margin.) Redistribution can even be future-oriented: excessive amounts of deficit spending today mean larger financial burdens for the next generation.

Most of the divisive socioeconomic issues of the past generation—civil rights, affirmative action, school busing, welfare, immigration, tax reform—were redistributive problems. A redistributive issue for the twenty-first century concerns the increasing share of the federal budget that goes to the elderly, compared with everyone else in society. Spending on entitlement programs, such as Social Security and Medicare, absorbs an ever-increasing proportion of federal dollars, which then are unavailable for other important social, domestic, or security needs. Universal health care is another redistributive issue because of concern over how to finance it and who would pay the program's cost, estimated to be $1.5 trillion over the next decade.[30]

When redistributive issues are at stake, federal budgeting is almost always marked by conflict. In recent years, the conflicts have tended to be over how to cut entitlements. Various techniques have been employed to disguise cuts and to make them more palatable. Omnibus budget packages permit legislators to approve cuts en bloc instead of one by one, and across-the-board formulas (such as freezes) give the appearance of spreading the misery equally to affected groups. In all such vehicles, provisions of this sort are added to placate the more vocal opponents of change.

CHARACTERISTICS OF CONGRESSIONAL POLICYMAKING

As a policymaking body, Congress displays the traits and biases of its membership and structure, as well as those of the larger political system. The two houses of Congress have divergent electoral and procedural traditions. Congress is representative, especially where geographic interests are concerned. It is decentralized, having few mechanisms for integrating or coordinating its policy decisions. It is often inclined toward enacting symbolic measures instead of substantive ones. And Congress is rarely ahead of the curve, or the public—tending to reflect conventional perceptions of problems.

Bicameralism

Differences between the House and Senate—their relative sizes, the members' terms of office, the character of their constituencies—shape the policies they make. Six-year terms, it is argued, allow senators to play the statesman for at least part of each term before approaching elections force them to concentrate on fence-mending. Although this distinction may be more apparent than real, empirical studies of senators' voting habits lend some support to the claim.

Various constituencies unquestionably pull in divergent directions. The more homogeneous House districts often promote clear, unambiguous positions on a narrower range of questions than those embraced by an entire state, represented by senators who must weigh the claims of many competing interests on a broad range of matters. The sizes of the two chambers, moreover, dictate procedural biases. House rules are designed to allow majorities to have their way. In contrast, Senate rules give individual senators great latitude to influence action. As a GOP senator once said: "The Senate has the strongest minority of any minority on Earth, and the weakest majority of any on Earth."[31]

The two chambers, in short, differ in outlook, constituency, and strategy. Bicameralism is less important in promoting or discouraging particular kinds of policies, writes Benjamin I. Page, than in "the furtherance of deliberation, the production of evidence, and the revealing of error."[32]

Localism

Congressional policies respond to constituents' needs, particularly those that can be mapped geographically. Sometimes these needs are pinpointed with startling directness. For example, an aviation noise control bill required construction of a control tower "at latitude 40 degrees, 43 minutes, 45 seconds north and at longitude 73 degrees, 24 minutes, 50 seconds west"—the very location of a Farmingdale, New York, airport in the district of the Democratic representative who requested the provision.[33]

Usually, however, programs are directed toward states, municipalities, counties, or geographic regions. Funds are often transferred directly to local government agencies, which in turn deliver the aid or services to citizens. But sometimes Congress will require states and localities to fund some national priorities without federal assistance. These "unfunded mandates" strain state budgets and arouse the ire of state and local officials. In 1995 President Bill Clinton signed into law the Unfunded Mandates Reform Act, which requires Congress either to make provision to pay for any mandate that the CBO estimates will cost state and local governments $50 million or more, or to "take a separate recorded vote to waive the requirement, thus holding members of Congress accountable for their decision."[34] Lawmakers are now supposed to consider the costs of any federal requirements they impose on state and local governments. However, the promise or intent of the law is not always met. The No Child Left Behind education law (P.L. 107-110), for instance, prescribes mandatory testing in all public schools for today's cash-strapped states. School systems in many states complain that the federal government has failed to provide enough money to cover the expense of meeting the law's requirements.

National and local policies are necessarily intertwined. National policies can be advanced by state and local governments; in turn, states or localities can develop innovations that spur national action. The threat of terrorist attacks in the United States demands that any such calamity be confronted by first responders—police officers, firefighters, public health officials, and others—at the state and local levels. On other issues as well, the states are the testing grounds, or laboratories, for social, economic, and political experiments.

Many policy debates revolve around not only which government level can most effectively carry out a responsibility, but also which level best promotes particular values. Liberals tend to prefer that the national government lead in enforcing civil rights and environmental protection. Conservatives support an activist national government on defense and security matters. When it suits their purposes, both liberals and conservatives are capable of advocating either national mandates or local autonomy, depending on which level of government would best serve their objectives.

Piecemeal Policymaking

Policies all too often mirror Congress's scattered and decentralized structure. Typically, they are considered piecemeal, reflecting the patchwork of committee and subcommittee jurisdictions. Congress's segmented decision making is typified by authorizing and appropriating processes in which separate committees consider the same programs, often without consulting each other.

The structure of a policy frequently depends on which committees have reported it. Working from varying jurisdictions, committees can take different approaches to the same problem. The taxing committees gravitate toward tax provisions to address problems, the appropriations committees will prefer a fiscal approach to issues, the commerce panels typically adopt a regulatory perspective, and so forth. Each approach may be well or ill suited to the policy objective. The approach adopted will depend on which committee was best positioned to promote the bill.

Symbolic Policymaking

Congressional policymaking can be more about appearance than substance. Bills are often passed to give the impression that action is being taken, even when the measure adopted is unlikely to have any real impact on the problem. The general public and interest groups continually demand, "Don't just stand there, do something." Doing something is often the only politically feasible choice, even when no one knows exactly what to do or whether inaction might be just as effective.[35]

Still, symbolic actions are important to all politicians. This is not the same thing as saying that politicians are merely cynical manipulators of symbols. Words and concepts—*equal opportunity, income inequality, cost of living, parity, affirmative action*—are contested earnestly in committee rooms and on the House and Senate floor. The result, however, is that federal goals are often stated in vague, optimistic language, not spelled out in terms of specific measures of success or failure.

Reactive Policymaking

It would be naive to expect a deliberative body routinely to adopt bold or radical solutions to problems. Elected officials are seldom far ahead of or far behind the collective views of their constituencies. Members know that out-of-the-mainstream views are unlikely to attract widespread public support. Congress is essentially a reactive institution. As one House member explained,

> When decision rests on the consent of the governed, it comes slowly, only after consensus has built or crisis has focused public opinion in some unusual way, the representatives in the meantime hanging back until the signs are unmistakable. Government decision, then, is not generally the cutting edge of change but a belated reaction to change.[36]

The reactive character of Congress's policymaking is evident in its budget process. Under pressures to reform, Congress reacted in 1974, 1985, and again in the 1990s with changes in the way it makes budget decisions. The current budget process, dating from the mid-1970s, was intended to bring coherence to the way standing committees handle the president's budget. It has decisively shaped both Congress's internal decision making and its relations with the executive.

CONGRESSIONAL BUDGETING

Congressional budgeting is a complex process that involves virtually all House and Senate members and committees, the president and executive branch officials, and scores of other participants. That congressional budgeting is usually contentious should come as no surprise considering the high political and policy stakes associated with fiscal decision making (see Box 14-2 for some of the terminology used in budgeting).

Authorizations and Appropriations

Congress's budget procedures are shaped by two customary and longtime processes: authorizations and appropriations. Generally, legislative rules stipulate that before agencies or programs receive any money, Congress should first pass authorization laws that do three fundamental things: (1) establish or continue (reauthorize) federal agencies and programs, (2) define the purposes, functions, and operations of programs or agencies, and (3) recommend (i.e., authorize) the appropriation of funds for programs and agencies. As Senate Democratic leader Harry Reid, Nev., explained:

> Authorizations allow programs to be created and funded. When we pass an authorizing bill, we hope the authorized level will be looked at in [the] appropriations committee—as I did as a longtime member. But we realize there are competing priorities, and full funding doesn't come very often.[37]

BOX 14-2   **A Budget Glossary**

Appropriations. The process by which Congress provides budget authority, usually through the enactment of twelve separate appropriations bills.

Budget authority. The authority for federal agencies to spend or otherwise obligate money, accomplished through enactment into law of appropriations bills.

Budget outlays. Money that is spent in a given fiscal year, as opposed to money that is appropriated for that year. One year's budget authority can result in outlays over several years, and the outlays in any given year result from a mix of budget authority from that year and prior years. Budget authority is similar to putting money into a checking account. Outlays occur when checks are written and cashed.

Discretionary spending. Programs that Congress can finance as it chooses through appropriations. With the exception of paying entitlement benefits to individuals (see mandatory spending below), almost everything the government does is financed by discretionary spending. Examples include all federal agencies, Congress, the White House, the courts, the military, and such programs as space exploration and child nutrition. About a third of all federal spending falls into this category.

Fiscal year. The federal government's budget year. For example, fiscal year 2010 runs from October 1, 2009, through September 30, 2010.

Mandatory spending. Made up mostly of entitlements, which are programs whose eligibility requirements are written into law. Anyone who meets those requirements is entitled to the money until Congress changes the law. Examples are Social Security, Medicare, Medicaid, unemployment benefits, food stamps, and federal pensions. Another major category of mandatory spending is the interest paid to holders of federal government bonds. Social Security and interest payments are permanently appropriated. And although budget authority for some entitlements is provided through the appropriations process, appropriators have little or no control over the money. Mandatory spending accounts for about two-thirds of all federal spending.

Pay-as-you-go (PAYGO) rule. This rule requires that all tax cuts, new entitlement programs, and expansions of existing entitlement programs be budget-neutral—offset either by additional taxes or by cuts in existing entitlement programs.

Reconciliation. The process by which tax laws and spending programs are changed, or reconciled, to reach outlay and revenue targets set in the congressional budget resolution. Established by the 1974 Congressional Budget Act (P.L. 93-344), it was first used in 1980.

Rescission. The cancellation of previously appropriated budget authority. This is a common way to save money that already has been appropriated. A rescissions bill must be passed by Congress and signed by the president (or enacted over his veto), just as an appropriations bill is.

Revenues. Taxes, customs duties, some user fees, and most other receipts paid to the federal government.

Sequester. The cancellation of spending authority as a disciplinary measure to cut off spending above preset limits. Appropriations that exceed annual spending caps can trigger a sequester that will cut all appropriations by the amount of the excess. Similarly, tax cuts and new or expanded entitlement spending programs that are not offset under pay-as-you-go rules will trigger a sequester of nonexempt entitlement programs.

Source: Adapted from Andrew Taylor, "Clinton's Strength Portends a Tough Season for GOP," *CQ Weekly,* February 6, 1999, 293.

As an example, the defense authorization bill might authorize the construction of three new submarines and recommend $15 billion for this purpose. Does that mean the Pentagon has the money to build the submarines? No. What needs to happen next is for Congress to enact the defense appropriations bill which would grant the Pentagon legal authority to spend a specific amount of money for the submarines. An authorization, in brief, can be viewed as a "hunting license" for an appropriation.

By custom, the House initiates appropriations bills. The House Appropriations Committee (usually one of its twelve subcommittees) would recommend how much money the Pentagon should receive for the submarines. The amount is called "budget authority" (BA). It is equivalent to depositing money in a checking account. The budget outlay (BO) is the check written by the Pentagon to the contractors hired to construct the submarines. The House Appropriations Committee can provide up to the $15 billion (but not more), propose less funding, or refuse to fund the submarine purchases at all. Assume that the House votes to approve $10 billion. The Senate Appropriations Committee, acting somewhat like a court of appeals, then hears Navy officials asking the Senate to approve the full $15 billion. If the Senate accedes, a House-Senate compromise is worked out, usually in a conference committee.

The authorization-appropriation sequence, which is often observed in the breach, is not required by the U.S. Constitution. The dual procedure dates from the nineteenth century and stems from inordinate delays caused by adding riders—extraneous policy amendments—to appropriation bills. "By 1835," wrote a legislator, "delays caused by injecting legislation [policy] into these [appropriations] bills had become serious and [Massachusetts representative] John Quincy Adams suggested that they be stripped of everything save appropriations."[38] Two years later the House required authorizations to precede appropriations. The Senate followed suit. (As discussed below, riders still exist, despite the dual procedure.)

The Constitution does provide, however, that "No Money shall be drawn from the Treasury, but in Consequence of Appropriations made by Law" (Article I, Section 9). As a result, appropriations have priority over authorizations. An appropriations measure may be approved even if the authorization bill has not been enacted. Some programs have not been authorized for years, but they still continue to operate. Why? If money is sprinkled on programs or agencies, they continue to exist and function even if their authorization has lapsed. As one House Appropriations subcommittee chairman said about the "must-pass" appropriations bills, "It's not the end of the world if we postpone the Clean Air Act or a tax measure. But the entire government will shut down if…appropriations" are not enacted annually.[39]

Authorizations can be annual, multiyear, or permanent. Through the end of World War II most federal agencies and programs were permanently authorized. They were reviewed annually by the House and Senate Appropriations Committees but not by the authorizing committees (such as Agriculture or Commerce). Since the 1970s the trend has been toward short-term authorizations, giving the authorizing committees more chances to control agency operations.[40] Generally, authorizing committees are eager to enact their bills on a timely basis, because otherwise they cede their lawmaking power to the appropriating panels. But authorizers also try from time to time to hitch a ride on an appropriations bill heading to the White House. "Ideally, it's not great to use [appropriations] bills," remarked House Financial Services Committee chair Barney Frank. "But they may be the only vehicles we can use [for] some [authorization measures] where we're facing a veto or we have problems in the Senate."[41]

In practice, it is hard to keep the two stages distinct. Authorization bills sometimes carry appropriations, and appropriation bills sometimes contain legislation (or policy provisions). Chamber rules that forbid these maneuvers can be waived. In the House, limitation riders make policy under the guise of restricting agency use of funds. Phrased negatively ("None of the funds…"), limitations bolster congressional control of bureaucracy. The Senate, too, is not reluctant to add extraneous policy proposals to appropriations bills. Angered that a major immigration proposal was added to a supplemental appropriations bill, Democratic leader Harry Reid of Nevada exclaimed, "This is the mother of all authorizing legislation on an appropriations bill."[42] Policy riders can provoke, as noted by Chairman Frank, bicameral and legislative-executive disputes.

Committee Roles and Continuing Resolutions. Among the authorizing committees, House Ways and Means and Senate Finance have especially powerful roles in the budget process. These tax panels have access to the staff experts of the Joint Taxation Committee. Because the House under the Constitution initiates revenue measures, it usually determines whether Congress will act on legislation to raise, lower, or redistribute the tax burden. Occasionally, however, the Senate takes the lead. The Senate technically complies with the Constitution by appending a major tax measure to a minor House-passed revenue bill. In 1981 the Republican-controlled Senate used this tactic to act on President Ronald Reagan's sweeping tax-cut plan. It used the same ploy the next year on the president's tax increase package. The House jealously guards its constitutional authority to originate tax measures and typically will return to the Senate any bill that violates the Origination Clause.[43]

Whenever Congress cannot complete action on one or more of the twelve regular appropriations bills (generally one for each subcommittee) by the beginning of the fiscal year (October 1), it provides temporary, stopgap funding for the affected federal agencies through a joint resolution known as a continuing resolution. In the past, continuing resolutions were usually employed to keep a few government agencies in operation for short periods (usually one to three months). Some years Congress has packaged all the regular appropriations bills into one massive continuing resolution. (A record twenty-one continuing resolutions were needed in 2000 before the GOP Congress and President Clinton compromised their differences on several appropriations bills that had not been enacted by the start of the fiscal year.)[44]

Each year Congress also passes one or more supplemental appropriations bills to meet unforeseen contingencies. To sum up, there are three basic types of appropriations: *regular* (made annually), *supplemental* (furnishing funds for unexpected contingencies), or *continuing* (providing funds when one or more annual appropriations bills have not been enacted by the start of the fiscal year).

Backdoor Spending Techniques

To sidestep the appropriators' ability to slash their recommended funding levels, authorizing committees evolved backdoor funding provisions to bypass the front door of the two-step authorization-appropriation sequence. Backdoors are authorization laws that mandate, rather than simply recommend, the expenditure of federal funds. This type of spending legislation, which is reported solely by the authorizing committees, is called direct (or mandatory) spending, as contrasted with the discretionary spending under the House and Senate Appropriations Committees. There are three types of backdoor or direct spending provisions: Contract authority permits agencies to enter into contracts that subsequently must be covered by appropriations. Borrowing authority allows agencies to spend money they have borrowed from the public or the Treasury. And entitlement programs grant eligible individuals and governments the right to receive payments from the national government.

The fastest growing of the three types is entitlements, which establish legally enforceable rights for eligible beneficiaries. Spending for entitlement programs (Medicare and Social Security, for example) is determined by the number of citizens who qualify and the benefit levels established by law. No fixed dollar amount is established for these programs.

The Challenge of Entitlements

Entitlements are the real force behind the escalation of federal spending (see Figure 14-1). More than half of all federal spending consists of entitlements that avoid the annual appropriations process review. This ratio of discretionary (determined through yearly appropriations) to mandatory spending represents a dramatic reversal from that of 45 years ago. (Interest on the federal debt is another uncontrollable expenditure.) Unlike defense or domestic discretionary programs—for which the Appropriations Committees recommend annual amounts and on which all lawmakers may vote—entitlement spending occurs automatically, under the terms outlined in the statute. Moreover, around four-fifths of these programs "are not 'means tested,' or linked to the incomes of recipients."[45]

Congress has done a reasonable job of containing discretionary spending. But reining in costly entitlements has proved a much more difficult task. In 1996 Congress passed legislation ending a decades-old national welfare entitlement program—Aid to Families with Dependent Children.[46] However, the recipients of the largest share of entitlement spending—senior citizens—are highly protective of these programs and also very likely to vote. In his second term President George W. Bush launched an intense lobbying drive to win

FIGURE 14-1 Federal Spending by Major Category, Fiscal Years 1965 and 2010 (outlays in billions of dollars)

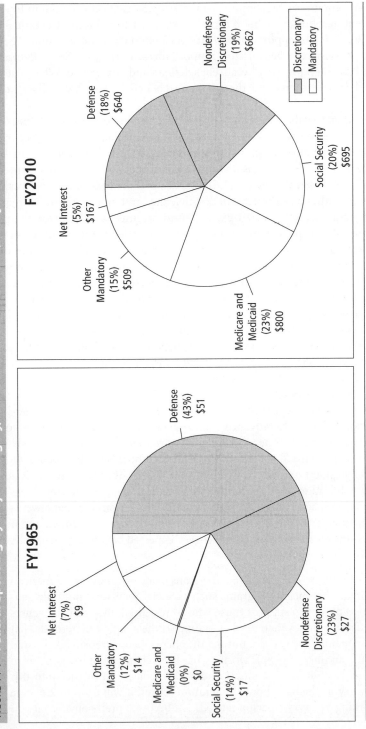

FY1965

Defense
(43%)
$51

Nondefense
Discretionary
(23%)
$27

Social Security
(14%)
$17

Medicare and
Medicaid
(0%)
$0

Other
Mandatory
(12%)
$14

Net Interest
(7%)
$9

FY2010

Defense
(18%)
$640

Nondefense
Discretionary
(19%)
$662

Social Security
(20%)
$695

Medicare and
Medicaid
(23%)
$800

Other
Mandatory
(15%)
$509

Net Interest
(5%)
$167

Discretionary
Mandatory

Source: Office of Management and Budget, *Budget of the United States Government: Fiscal Year 2008, Historical Tables* (Washington, D.C.: Government Printing Office, 2007), 133, 142. Charts prepared by Robert Keith, Government Division, Congressional Research Service.

public and congressional support for replacing Social Security with individual retirement accounts; but his reform effort failed to gain any traction. Even many Republicans opposed the plan's reliance on private accounts. "Social Security became the bedrock of support for seniors," said Sen. Olympia J. Snowe, R-Maine, "precisely because it's defined and guaranteed. What cost and what risk is it worth to erode the guaranteed benefit [through variable stock or bond investments]?"[47]

President Obama also has faced the challenge posed by the escalating costs of the major entitlement programs (Medicare, Medicaid, and Social Security). "We have to signal seriousness in [entitlement reform]," he said, "by making sure some of the hard decisions are made under my watch, not someone else's."[48] This is hardly news: Public officials and analysts have been warning for years—without too much effect—that the entitlement programs require reform, because the projected expenditures are unsustainable (for example, Medicare faces a prospective funding gap of at least $36 trillion; further, because of the current recession, the Medicare fund is expected to run out of money in 2017.[49]) Many lawmakers in both chambers agree upon the urgency of addressing entitlements. For example, the Senate Budget Committee Chair, Kent Conrad, D-N.D., and ranking member Judd Gregg, R-N.H., have called for a bipartisan commission to propose fundamental changes to the large entitlement programs with the recommendations subject only to limited debate and an up-or-down vote by each chamber. This drastic proposal recognizes that our political system is typically crisis-activated and prone to move slowly in dealing with problems looming over the horizon.

The long-term demographic challenge confronting Social Security (and Medicare) is that the United States is an aging society with a longer-lived population (thanks to advances in often-expensive medical technology). Already the nation is witnessing the gradual retirement of the seventy-six million members of the "baby boom" generation (those born between 1946 and 1964)—the largest number of retirees in the history of the country. This development will lead to huge retirement and medical expenditures for those who are eligible to receive Social Security benefits. Projections are that fewer workers (a "birth dearth") will be paying taxes to support the retirement and medical expenditures that will make up retirees' expected benefits. As Senate budget expert Gregg pointed out,

> In 1950 there were about 16 Americans working for every 1 American retired. That meant programs such as Social Security…not only generated money to support those who were retired, they actually generated more money than needed to support the people who retired. That is happening today even. But the number of people retiring compared to the number of people working has been changing. It has gone from 16 in 1950 down to about 3 and a half today. And further into this century, as the baby boom generation retires, it will drop to 2 people working for every 1 person retired.…It becomes pretty obvious, if you

have only two people working to pay for one person retired, those two people are going to have to pay a lot more in taxes to support that one person....So this creates a huge...unfunded liability [in future years as more money is taken out of Social Security than is paid in]. We do not know how we are going to pay for [Social Security and Medicare] in the outyears.[50]

With fewer workers supporting more retirees (without a further influx of immigrants, higher birthrates, or technological breakthroughs that enhance each worker's productivity), changes will be required to address the projected shortage of funds to pay for retirees' full benefits under current law.[51] Enough money is now coming into Social Security to cover the promised benefits to retirees.[52] In fact, Social Security has long taken in more from payroll taxes than it pays out in benefits. The current economic recession, however, is depleting the Social Security surplus faster than predicted. According to a report issued by the trustees of Social Security:

[T]he annual surpluses in the Social Security trust fund are expected to drop sharply [in 2009] and be nearly flat in 2010 because of the recession. The program will begin paying out more in benefits than it takes in from payroll taxes in 2016, a year earlier than estimated last year. Social Security will be insolvent by 2037, at which point enrollees would receive about three-fourths of their promised benefits through 2083.[53]

Many proposals have been put forth to deal with the long-term funding challenge, but each is controversial. Among the proposed changes are raising the retirement age, reducing benefits for future retirees, increasing the payroll tax rate, requiring affluent retirees to pay taxes on their benefits, and raising the amount of income subject to Social Security payroll taxes.[54] Resolving the long-term solvency problem requires putting more money into the system, cutting benefits, or some combination of the two.

Some analysts contend that the real entitlement budget buster of the future is not Social Security but Medicare. Peter Orszag, President Obama's budget director, has stated: "The long-term fiscal problem truly is fundamentally one involving the rate at which healthcare costs grow. Social Security and aging are important, but it is not where the money is."[55] With health-care costs rising faster than inflation, the graying of society, and costly new medical technologies, Medicare is already paying out more in benefits than it is receiving in taxes. Compounding the fiscal problem, Congress in 2003 added a prescription drug benefit to Medicare that is projected to cost $1.2 trillion over the next decade.[56] Elected officials often focus first on Social Security because there is a rough consensus on the solutions to constrain its soaring cost. Not so with Medicare. The "steps Congress could take now to restrain Medicare's growth are politically perilous. Deny end-of-life care? Restrict eligibility? Reduce treatments? Raise costs?"[57] Even more frightening from a budget perspective is the prospect of providing long-term nursing home or other care for the elderly. Long-term care, said Rep. Earl Pomeroy, D-N.D., is "the elephant in the living room that no one's talking about."[58] And Medicaid, a federal entitlement program for indigent and low-income persons that is jointly funded by the national and state governments, has "now surged past Medicare to become the nation's largest health care program."[59]

In short, an entitlement revolution is under way as the government today transfers more than half of federal monies to eligible families and individuals. "Call it government by ATM," remarked an analyst. "You walk up, hit the buttons, and the cash to which you're entitled pops out."[60] This transformation in the federal budget, away from discretionary to direct (or mandatory) spending, raises the question of the appropriateness of this funding ratio. Congress and the president face at least a dual fiscal challenge: the battle for scarce resources between entitlements and discretionary spending, and the struggle within the discretionary category between domestic versus defense and homeland security spending. Added to this mix is more than $900 billion in indirect spending—called tax expenditures or tax preferences—revenue that is forgone through various tax credits, subsidies, or deductions, such as the home mortgage interest deduction. Tax expenditures receive relatively little public attention, compared with direct or discretionary spending, yet in many years, said David Walker, a former U.S. comptroller general, "the total value of tax preferences exceeds the total value of discretionary spending. These items are off the radar screen, and they should [receive the same budgetary attention as discretionary and direct spending]."[61]

THE 1974 BUDGET ACT

Congress refocused its budgetary attention in the 1970s after its loose control of the purse strings gave rise to charges of financial irresponsibility. President Richard M. Nixon blamed Congress for annual deficits, consumer price hikes, high joblessness, and inflation. He also refused to spend monies duly appropriated by Congress, a practice called impoundment. Even though his administration lost every court challenge to the impoundments, Nixon held the political high ground. These diverse pressures prompted Congress to tighten its budget procedures.

The Budget and Impoundment Control Act of 1974 was landmark legislation. Among its principal features was the creation of House and Senate Budget Committees, as well as the Congressional Budget Office (CBO). The nonpartisan CBO prepares economic forecasts for Congress, estimates the costs of proposed legislation, and issues fiscal, monetary, and policy reports. The 1974 act also limited presidential use of impoundments and established a timetable for action on authorization, appropriation, and tax measures. The timetable has been changed periodically, and Congress commonly misses some of the target dates (see Box 14-3 for the timetable).

Of the many complex features of the 1974 act, two are central components of Congress's current budget process: the concurrent budget resolution and

BOX 14-3 **The Congressional Budget Timetable**	
Deadline	**Action to be completed**
First Monday in February	President submits budget to Congress
February 15	Congressional Budget Office submits economic and budget outlook report to Budget Committees
Six weeks after president submits budget	Committees submit views and estimates to Budget Committees
April 1	Senate Budget Committee reports budget resolution
April 15	Congress completes action on budget resolution
May 15	Annual appropriations bills may be considered in the House, even if action on budget resolution has not been completed
June 10	House Appropriations Committee reports last annual appropriations bill
June 15	House completes action on reconciliation legislation (if required by budget resolution)
June 30	House completes action on annual appropriations bills
July 15	President submits mid-session review of his budget to Congress
October 1	Fiscal year begins

Source: Bill Heniff Jr., *The Congressional Budget Process Timetable,* Congressional Research Service Report No. 98–472 GOV, March 20, 2008.

reconciliation. These two elements compel much of the time-consuming work of each annual legislative session, attract the attention of many interests and participants clamoring for fiscal resources, and influence policy decisions and outcomes.

Concurrent Budget Resolution

The core of Congress's annual budget process is adoption of a concurrent budget resolution. This measure is formulated by the House and Senate Budget Committees, which consider the views and estimates of numerous committees and witnesses.

The resolution consists of five basic parts: (1) The budget resolution estimates what the federal government will spend in a fiscal year and for at least the four following fiscal years. For each fiscal year, the spending is expressed in terms of both budget authority and budget outlays for each of the fiscal years. (2) The total aggregate spending is then subdivided among twenty functional categories, such as defense, agriculture, or energy. For each category, the spending indicates what Congress expects to expend in those substantive areas. (3) Next, the budget resolution stipulates the recommended levels of federal revenues needed to pay for the projected spending during each of the fiscal years. (4) Because the federal government consistently runs deficits, the budget resolution identifies the estimated deficits (or surpluses should they occur, which is infrequent). (5) The total outstanding public debt (savings bonds, Treasury securities, and other government obligations) permitted by law is also specified for at least the five-year period. The debt represents the accumulation of deficits (more spending than the revenue available) over time. From 1789 to 2000, for example, the national debt rose to $5.6 trillion. In 2009, the statutory debt ceiling was raised to over $13 trillion. In effect, the budget resolution sets the overall level of discretionary spending for each fiscal year. For 2010, the concurrent budget resolution set a spending ceiling of $1.086 trillion for appropriations bills in an overall budget of $3.6 trillion.[62]

The budget resolution is Congress's fiscal blueprint. It establishes the context of congressional budgeting; guides the budgetary actions of the authorizing, appropriating, and taxing committees; and reflects Congress's spending priorities. A senator described the purposes of the budget resolution:

> [The budget] resolution would be analogous to an architect's set of plans for constructing a building. It gives the general direction, framework, and prioritization of Federal fiscal policy each year. Those priorities then drive the individual appropriations and tax measures which will support that architectural plan.[63]

In a period of polarized politics, partisan issues dominate debate on these resolutions, as Democrats and Republicans battle over spending levels for their competing priorities. In 2009, for instance, not a single House or Senate Republican voted for the Democratic budget resolution.

The House and Senate each consider a budget resolution. In the House, budget resolutions are typically considered under special rules from the Rules Committee, which limit debate and impose restrictions on the number and types of amendments. In the Senate, the 1974 budget act sets a fifty-hour limitation for consideration of the budget resolution, unless members accept a unanimous consent agreement imposing other time restrictions. Amendments can be taken up and voted on after the fifty hours, but without debate. This circumstance often leads to so-called vote-a-ramas over several days, when senators may "cast back-to-back votes on a dizzying array of dozens of amendments," often with the two Congresses in mind. As national policymakers, members of Congress may have to cast tough, but responsible, votes, which will "serve as valuable campaign fodder" for opponents in the next election.[64]

When the chambers pass budget resolutions with different aggregate and functional spending levels, as is normal practice, House and Senate members usually meet in conference to resolve their disagreements. The conference report is then submitted to both chambers for final action. Recall that Congress's budget resolution is not submitted to the president and thus has no binding legal effect. Instead, it outlines a fiscal framework that enables Congress, through its budget committees, CBO, and other entities, to monitor all budget-related actions taken during the course of a year. When the House and Senate are late or unable to adopt a concurrent budget resolution—as has occurred several times because of bicameral disagreements over priorities and expenditures—each chamber usually adopts a resolution (H. Res. or S. Res.) reflecting the budget levels and enforcement procedures contained in the resolution adopted by one chamber but not the other.

Reconciliation

The 1974 budget act established a special procedure called reconciliation, which is an optional process authorized when Congress adopts the budget resolution. Its basic purpose is to bring revenue and direct spending (entitlement) legislation into conformity (or reconciliation) with the fiscal targets established in the concurrent budget resolution. As Sen. Robert C. Byrd, D-W. Va., explained, "A budget reconciliation process was established as an optional procedure to enhance Congress's ability to change current law in order to bring revenue and [direct] spending levels into conformity with the targets of the budget resolution."[65] Its basic objective is to make changes in federal policies that result in budgetary savings. First used in 1980, reconciliation has been employed twenty-one times (through 2008). It is a controversial process that "forces committees that might not want to reduce spending for entitlements under their jurisdiction to act and report legislation."[66]

Reconciliation is a two-step process. In the first step, Congress adopts a budget resolution containing a provision that usually instructs two or more House and Senate committees to report legislation that changes existing law. The instructions name the committees required to report legislation; they give each committee a dollar figure for mandated savings; and they establish a deadline for reporting legislation to achieve the savings. In the second step, the House and Senate Budget Committees compile into an omnibus reconciliation bill the legislative changes in revenue or direct (entitlement) spending programs recommended by the named committees. If the instructions involve only one committee in each chamber, then those panels would bypass the Budget Committee and report their recommendations to the full House or Senate. On several occasions reconciliation directives provided for more than one reconciliation bill. In 2005, for example, reconciliation instructions governed three measures: a spending bill involving cuts in mandatory programs; a $70 billion tax-cut bill; and a bill to raise the debt limit.[67]

Reconciliation in the House is considered under the terms of a rule from the Rules Committee. Procedurally, however, reconciliation is focused on the Senate, because measures governed by that optional process are treated differently from other bills or amendments. Reconciliation bills cannot be filibustered (a statutory time limit of twenty hours is placed on debate); passage requires a simple majority instead of the supermajority (sixty votes) needed to stop a talkathon; and amendments must be germane (the Senate has no general germaneness rule) and deficit neutral (tax cuts or spending increases must be offset by equivalent revenue increases or spending reductions). Little surprise that measures likely to arouse controversy in the Senate, such as tax bills, are attached to filibuster-proof reconciliation measures that could pass by majority votes.

At the outset of the Obama administration there was talk about using reconciliation to push the president's health and "cap and trade" energy priorities through the Senate. But Republicans announced their strong opposition, and moderate Democratic senators expressed unease about the procedure. "If you're going to talk about reconciliation, you're talking about something that has nothing to do with bipartisanship," declared GOP Senator Gregg, N.H. "You're talking about the exact opposite of bipartisan. You're talking about running over the minority, putting them in cement, and throwing them in the Chicago River."[68] Democratic Sen. Robert C. Byrd lamented that reconciliation "can be used by a determined majority to circumvent the regular rules of the Senate in order to advance partisan legislation. We have seen one party, and then the other, use this process to limit debate and amendments on nonbudgetary provisions that otherwise may not have passed under the regular rules."[69]

Senate Republicans threatened to shut down the Senate through dilatory actions if Democrats employ reconciliation on President Obama's health-care priority. They argued that reconciliation is for deficit reduction, not the enactment of major policy changes. The White House press secretary responded: "It's interesting to see the views on reconciliation and how they've changed since, say, the Bush tax cuts in 2001" when Republicans controlled the Senate and they used the technique on a number of major bills.[70] In 2009, the House budget resolution included reconciliation to protect health-care legislation from GOP filibusters; the Senate's version did not include that technique. When the two chambers met to settle their bicameral differences, reconciliation was included in the conference report. It was unclear whether this procedural technique would be employed; but, as Speaker Nancy Pelosi said, if "bipartisanship does not yield health care reform, then we'll to move to reconciliation," putting pressure on Senate Republicans to negotiate rather than block health-care reform through filibustering tactics.[71] Democratic Sen. Charles E. Schumer, N.Y., reinforced the view that reconciliation instructions for health-care reform, and perhaps an education bill, was a fallback procedure. "I know that we're certainly going to give Sen. [Max] Baucus, [the chair of the Finance Committee,] a chance to pass health care legislation with 60 votes," he said. "But it would be my view that if they can't do it by a certain time...we then move to reconciliation, where we need 51. And it's going to be hard enough to pass national health care with 51 votes."[72]

To prevent just such a usage of reconciliation bills, senators adopted the so-called Byrd Rule (named after Senator Byrd) in the mid-1980s. Under this complex rule, "measures cannot be included in the Senate reconciliation package [including conference reports] if they" are viewed as extraneous provisions that do not reduce the deficit. "It takes 60 votes in the Senate to waive the Byrd Rule."[73] Many senators, as a result, could challenge numerous health-care provisions as "Byrd droppings." As the former staff director of the Senate Budget Committee explained: "On something as massive as health care reform, there will be a number of provisions that don't have direct budgetary consequences.... [T]hose Byrd violations would be made and you'd end up making Swiss cheese out of the legislation."[74]

Reconciliation, in sum, is a powerful procedure for fiscal retrenchment. President Reagan and GOP congressional leaders used it for the first time on a grand scale in 1981. A reconciliation bill dictated deep, multi-year reductions (about $130 billion over three years) in domestic spending. Not long afterward, Congress also agreed to Reagan's tax legislation, the Economic Recovery Tax Act of 1981, which sharply cut tax rates for individuals and businesses. The revenue losses caused by the tax cut, combined with increased defense and entitlement expenditures and insufficient spending reductions in other areas, soon pushed annual budget deficits to levels unprecedented in peacetime, from double- to triple-digit shortfalls. Since the 1980s, Congress has been grappling with large deficits, with only a brief interlude of surpluses during the Clinton presidency.

Congress Changes Its Budget Process

The growth of budgetary deficits after 1981 became the prime congressional issue, as lawmakers and presidents adapted to a new world: the politics of deficit reduction. Numerous proposals were put forth to deal with the problem. A notable example in the mid-1980s was the *Gramm-Rudman-Hollings* plan (named after Sens. Phil Gramm, R-Texas; Warren B. Rudman, R-N.H.; and Ernest F. Hollings, D-S.C.).

The plan's core feature was the establishment in law of annual deficit reduction targets. If Congress did not meet the targets, the president would have to confiscate funds, that is, impose automatic, across-the-board spending cuts (called "sequestration") evenly divided between defense and domestic programs. This dire prospect was supposed to create an incentive for Congress and the president to decide how best to achieve deficit reduction. The plan did not work, and deficits continued to climb because the yearly targets were met through budget gimmicks.

As a result of dissatisfaction with this law, Congress enacted another major budgetary reform, the *Budget Enforcement Act (BEA)* of 1990. The BEA once again changed Congress's fiscal procedures. Three basic features undergirded the new legislation. First, it shifted Congress's attention from deficit reduction to spending control. Thus, the law removed the threat of sequestration if conditions beyond Congress's control (inflation, a worsening economy, or emergency funding for crises or disasters) pushed the deficit upward.

Second, the BEA established caps, or limits, for discretionary spending. The spending caps could be changed, but Congress and the president would have to agree to the modification. A loophole in the law enabled Congress and the president to escape tight spending caps if they designated expenditures above the cap as emergency spending.

Third, the BEA subjected tax and entitlement programs to a new pay-as-you-go (PAYGO) procedure, which required that any tax reductions or any increases in direct spending (that is, entitlement) programs be offset by tax hikes or reductions in other direct spending programs. As the chief counsel of the Senate Budget Committee explained, "The 'pay-as-you-go' label implies that Congress and the President may cut taxes or create [new direct spending] programs—that is 'go'—if they also agree to provide offsetting increased revenues or spending reductions—that is 'pay.'"[75]

Throughout much of the 1990s, the GOP-controlled Congress and President Clinton waged fierce battles over deficit reduction. As part of their political game plan, Republicans sent Clinton appropriations and reconciliation bills making deep cuts in federal programs. The president vetoed the measures, forcing two partial shutdowns of the government—the longest in congressional history. A fiscal breakthrough soon emerged, however.

SURPLUSES ARRIVE UNEXPECTEDLY

To the surprise of many lawmakers and pundits, who constantly lamented the pain and sacrifice (tax hikes and spending cuts) that balancing the budget would require, balanced budgets appeared sooner than anyone expected. By the end of September 1998, the national budget was $70 billion in the black, something that had last occurred in 1969. David A. Stockman, President Reagan's director of the Office of Management and Budget (OMB), once predicted deficits as far as the eye could see. Now economic forecasters were predicting surpluses as far as the eye could see.

Why the surge of black ink? Several factors contributed to the fiscal turnaround. First, the end of the Cold War led to reductions in defense expenditures. Second, despite some soft spots, the American economy was strong and healthy. The robust economy, combined with a booming stock market, flooded the federal Treasury with revenue from the capital gains taxes paid mainly by the richest one percent of the populace. Third, the Federal Reserve kept inflation and interest rates under control through an effective monetary policy that promoted economic expansion. Fourth, presidential and congressional budgetary decisions during the first George Bush administration, such as passage of the BEA of 1990, and President Clinton's 1993 economic package, encouraged fiscal restraint and led to budgetary savings. Finally, luck and timing contributed to the fiscal mix. "Just about everything broke right that could have broken right," according to Robert Reischauer, a former CBO director.[76]

Not everyone believed that the politics of plenty had arrived or, if it had, that it would last indefinitely. Some lawmakers suggested to their colleagues that budget surpluses stood for "BS." Another economic recession, they said, could be around the corner. "The truth is there is no surplus," exclaimed a senator, citing a national debt at the time of $5.7 trillion.[77] Nonetheless, on January 30, 2001, CBO revised its surplus projections over the next decade upward to $5.6 trillion.

THE RETURN OF DEFICITS

Given the huge projected surplus, President George W. Bush and congressional Democrats soon began to argue over what to do with the money. Although many lawmakers and pundits recognized that the ten-year projection might never materialize—because of a slowing economy, international crises, or other reasons—politicians of both parties had their own ideas on how the surplus should be spent. It was a case of fiscal projections driving policymaking, even though the money was not yet in the bank.

President Bush's top priority when he took office was a sizable tax cut. And on June 7, 2001, he signed into law the largest tax cut ($1.35 trillion) since Reagan's twenty years earlier. A little more than three months later, terrorists, attacked the United States and new demands and challenges confronted the country. The rather brief era (1998–2002) of surpluses had come to a quick end.

What happened to the surplus? It disappeared because the factors that produced it reversed themselves: Instead of defense and intelligence cutbacks, the nation was paying for military conflicts in Afghanistan and Iraq, reconstruction of those countries, and enhanced homeland security. A record ten years of uninterrupted economic growth ended and the stock market performed poorly, shrinking federal revenues. The large tax cuts pushed by the Bush administration, year after year, also contributed to the growing revenue shortfalls. Moreover, Congress's statutory fiscal constraints—spending caps and PAYGO—expired on September 30, 2002. That allowed policymakers to let the deficit increase without worrying about how to pay for tax cuts or spending hikes.

Both chambers have since restored non-statutory spending caps and PAYGO provisions. Spending caps are set in the concurrent budget resolution. Similarly, the Senate in 1993 included a pay-as-you-go provision in the budget resolution. It has been modified and extended several times and has a current expiration date of September 30, 2017. The Senate's PAYGO rule, however, applies only to legislation considered in that chamber.[78] When Democrats won control of the House in November 2006, they amended the House rulebook to include a PAYGO provision, which is still in effect today.[79] The pay-as-you-go provisions in each chamber, which can be waived, mean that lawmakers search for "pay fors" to fund their policy objectives. President Obama and congressional Democratic leaders favor enactment of a binding PAYGO law; many congressional Republicans support PAYGO for new entitlement spending but not for tax cuts.

Today, President Obama and Congress confront projected yearly deficits of more than a trillion dollars. In 2009, the administration projected that the deficit for the year would be over $1.8 trillion, "nearly quadruple the previous annual record of $454.8 billion, set last year."[80] How much is a trillion dollars? President Reagan explained it this way: "[I]f you had a stack of thousand-dollar bills in your hand only 4 inches high, you'd be a millionaire. A trillion dollars would be a stack of thousand-dollar bills 67 miles high."[81]

These record deficits are the result of the many ambitious and expensive measures to stimulate the economy and end the recession. President Obama promised that he would slash the budget deficit in half by the end of his first term. The fiscal issue is the size of the deficit when the recession ends and how, when, and by what means it will be reduced. "The overarching problem," remarked Rep. John Spratt, D-S.C., the chair of the House Budget Committee, "is how we boost the economy in the short run without worsening the deficit in the long run. I can't give you a definitive answer to that" issue.[82] The only thing that seems clear is that deficit reduction will require tough choices.

If deficits continue to rise significantly in the years ahead, the federal government faces a serious dilemma: how to fund competing priorities and commitments. As one budget analyst put it, "What we have done in the last several years is decide we can cut taxes, fight two wars, increase homeland security, expand government entitlement benefits, and leave the bill to future generations."[83] How will the government, for instance, address the looming retirement of the baby boomers? "This is a demographic time bomb that we are facing as a society," stated Senator Conrad.[84] A political consensus currently does not exist on how to deal with the impending explosion in the costs of Social Security, Medicare, and Medicaid. Some officials argue that a return to a booming economy will generate the bushels of money needed to pay for these and other priorities and that various entitlement reforms will reduce the price tag for these and other priorities. It seems doubtful that reductions in spending by themselves can stem the flow of red ink and improve the long-term fiscal outlook. Thus, the renewed concern about the dramatic hike in budget deficits. "The deficit is a hard thing to see the effects of. It's not the wolf at the door....It's termites in the woodwork, a constant drag, gnawing away at the capital stock."[85]

CONCLUSION

Today, lawmakers are preoccupied with important policy questions: an economic crisis, defense and homeland security, joblessness, energy sources and usage, and the health of various domestic social programs. Rep. Barney Frank posed a question that crystallizes the debate over these various concerns: "What is the appropriate level of public activity in our society?"[86] Democrats and Republicans tend to answer that question differently. Governing, however, means making choices. Future decisions about budgeting and national priorities will surely reflect the values, goals, and interests that result from the confrontations and accommodations inherent in America's pluralist policy-making system.

SUGGESTED READINGS

Elving, Ronald D. *Conflict and Compromise: How Congress Makes the Law.* New York: Simon and Schuster, 1995.

Hilley, John L. *The Challenge of Legislation.* Washington, D.C.: Brookings Institution Press, 2008.

Kelman, Steven. *Making Public Policy.* New York: Basic Books, Inc., 1987.

Kerwin, Cornelius M. *Rulemaking: How Government Agencies Write Laws and Make Policy.* 3d ed. Washington, D.C.: CQ Press, 2003.

Kingdon, John W. *Agendas, Alternatives, and Public Policies.* Boston: Little, Brown, 1984.

Rubin, Irene S. *Balancing the Federal Budget.* New York: Chatham House, 2003.

Schick, Allen. *The Federal Budget: Politics, Policy, Process.* Rev. ed. Washington, D.C.: Brookings Institution Press, 2007.

———. *Congress and Money: Budgeting, Spending, and Taxing.* Washington, D.C.: The Urban Institute, 1980.

"H *ard" versus "Soft" Power for National Security.* U.S. Army soldiers board a helicopter in south-central Afghanistan (top), as part of a surge against Taliban militants. Center left: The survivor from a pirate crew captured by Navy SEALS—accused of hijacking a U.S. merchant ship and taking its captain hostage—is led to a New York federal courtroom. Another use of power (center right) is the delivery of food supplies to needy countries under the State Department's foreign aid program and the Agriculture Department's P.L. 480 program, which distribute surplus farm products abroad. Lawmakers also engage in diplomacy: House Speaker Nancy Pelosi (bottom) meets with Syrian President Bashir al-Assad in Damascus in 2007.

chapter

15

Congress and National Security Policies

The "age of pirates" is back. The nation watched as the captain of a U.S. ship, the *Maersk Alabama,* was held hostage by Somali pirates, following their failed attack on the vessel itself. In a dramatic rescue, Navy SEAL sharpshooters killed the three pirates who were holding the captain hostage in a small boat launched from the *Maersk Alabama.* "We may be dealing with a 17th-century crime, but we need to bring 21st-century assets to bear" to stop the surge of pirate activity off the coast of Somalia and in other international waters, exclaimed Secretary of State Hillary Clinton.[1] Yet these pirates employ sophisticated 21st century technology in order to track and capture "target" ships and then demand millions of dollars in ransom for the return of the vessel and its crew.

It is indeed ironic that piracy has again emerged as a major international shipping problem off the coast of Africa. Presidents Thomas Jefferson and James Madison used the fledging navy and marine corps to sail to the "shores of Tripoli" and vanquish the Barbary pirates who captured U.S. frigates and held their crews hostage until the United States paid tribute to the rulers of what is now Morocco, Tunisia, Algeria, and Libya. Today, despite the status of the United States as the world's sole superpower, an armada of navy ships cannot patrol and protect all the vessels using the shipping lanes off Somalia because it is such a huge ocean area. The United States needs the assistance of other nations for anti-piracy measures to be successful. As President Obama said, "I want to be very clear that we are resolved to halt the rise of piracy in that region and to achieve that goal. We're going to have to continue to work with our [international] partners to prevent future attacks."[2] The contemporary reality is that scores of challenges lie beyond the control of any single nation. They require international cooperation and shared decision making.

International cooperation has not always marked U.S. foreign policy. Earlier generations of Americans tended to view themselves as a special people set apart from the world's conflicts. Having forsaken old world "wars and alarms," U.S. citizens—protected by two oceans—historically resolved to remain aloof from other nations' struggles. The most famous passage of President George Washington's 1796 Farewell Address counsels,

The great rule of conduct for us, in regard to foreign nations is in extending our commercial relations to have with them as little political connection as possible....'Tis our true policy to steer clear of permanent alliances, with any portion of the foreign world....Taking care to keep ourselves, by suitable establishments, on a respectable defensive posture, we may safely trust to temporary alliances for extraordinary emergencies.[3]

Although Washington's Farewell Address is dutifully read in the chambers of Congress every year on the first president's birthday, Washington's vision bears no resemblance to contemporary circumstances. As a world power today with lasting alliances spanning the globe, the United States and its foreign policies would scarcely be recognized by the nation's founders.

Formulating and implementing U.S. foreign and national security policies are not episodic activities but continual obligations. Congress and the president share in these duties just as they do in domestic and budgetary matters. Congress has broad constitutional authority to take part in foreign and domestic security decisions. Even the most decisive chief executives can find themselves constrained by active, informed, and determined policymakers on Capitol Hill.

CONSTITUTIONAL POWERS

The U.S. Constitution is, in Edward S. Corwin's classic words, "an invitation to struggle for the privilege of directing American foreign policy."[4] In other words, foreign and military powers are divided between the branches. "While the president is usually in a position to *propose,* the Senate and Congress are often in a technical position at least to *dispose.*"[5] The struggle over the proper role of each branch in shaping foreign policy involves conflict over policy as well as over process.

The President Proposes

The chief executive enjoys certain innate advantages in dealing with foreign affairs. As John Jay wrote in *The Federalist Papers* No. 64, the office's unity, its superior information sources, and its capacity for secrecy and dispatch give the president daily charge of foreign intercourse.[6] In Jay's time Congress was not in session the whole year, whereas the president was always on hand to make decisions.

The president's explicit international powers are to negotiate treaties and appoint ambassadors (powers shared with the Senate), to receive ambassadors and other emissaries, and to serve as commander in chief of the armed forces. This last-mentioned power looms large over the interbranch politics of the modern period, during which presidents have had at their disposal huge military, security, and intelligence capabilities. Presidents have claimed not only their explicit prerogatives but also others not spelled out in the Constitution. Whether they are called "implied," "inherent," or "emergency" powers, presidents increasingly invoke them in conducting foreign policy. President George W. Bush, according to GOP senator Lindsay Graham, S.C., "came up with a pretty aggressive, bordering on bizarre, theory of inherent authority that had no boundaries. As [the Bush administration] saw it, the other two branches were basically neutered in the time of war."[7]

The executive branch tends to be favored by foreign policy specia   lists, who often denigrate legislative involvement in foreign policy. Speaking to his fellow Republicans just after they ascended to power on Capitol Hill in 1995, former secretary of state James Baker cautioned the new majority "not to meddle too much" in the (then Democratic) administration's foreign policy. U.S. leadership in the world, he declared, could be sustained only "if we understand that the president has primary responsibility for the conduct of the nation's foreign policy."[8]

The president's advantages are magnified in times of warfare or crisis. It was Congress's clumsy management of affairs during the Revolutionary War that, among other things, led the founders to champion an independent, energetic executive and to designate the president as commander in chief. Authority tends to become more centralized during wars and crises, so presidential powers reach their zenith at such times. This held true during the Cold War between the United States and the Soviet Union (1947–1989) and the hot wars in Korea (1950–1953) and Vietnam (1965–1974). The same pattern was evident in the period following the terrorist attacks of September 11, 2001. Heightened security fears and the wars in Afghanistan and Iraq brought new and sometimes unprecedented assertions of executive authority. Initially at least, Congress's voice was muted.

Presidential powers usually contract and are subjected to sharper scrutiny from Capitol Hill when tensions ease or when the public tires of a prolonged conflict. Public opinion eventually came to oppose the Korean and Vietnam conflicts, a pattern that has repeated itself in the Iraq war. Divided control of the two policymaking branches spurs Congress to cast a more critical eye upon executive actions.

Perhaps the most sensible statement of the separation of powers came from Justice Robert Jackson in *Youngstown Sheet and Tube Co. v. Sawyer* (1952): that "the president might act in external affairs without congressional authority, but not that he might act contrary to an act of Congress."[9]

Congress Reacts

Congress has an impressive arsenal of explicit constitutional duties, such as the powers to declare war, to regulate foreign commerce, to raise and support military forces, and to make rules governing military forces, including for "captures on land and water" (Article I, Sec. 8). Paramount is the power of the purse: "It is within the power of Congress to determine the course of American diplomacy, by virtue of its control over expenditures by the federal government," Crabb, Antizzo, and Sarieddine write.[10]

From examining the historical record, Crabb and his colleagues identify three conditions for congressional activism in foreign and defense affairs: (1) periods of weak presidential leadership in foreign policy, (2) public groundswells of concern over America's international role, and (3) pressing domestic issues that impinge on foreign affairs. Their assessment of legislative activism in foreign affairs is pessimistic. They contend that legislative activism has been associated with "the least successful and impressive chapters in the annals of American diplomacy."[11]

Our own review of the historical record, however, yields a more positive assessment of legislative influence on foreign policy. Congress asserted itself following the Revolutionary War and at the outset of the other nineteenth-century wars. At the same time, it moved to rein in excessive presidential assertions of authority both before, during, and after those wars—an impulse that extends to the more recent wars: Korea, Vietnam, Afghanistan, and Iraq, as well as the later phases of the Cold War.

WHO SPEAKS FOR CONGRESS?

The wide-ranging subjects of foreign policy and military affairs fall within the purviews of some twenty-three congressional committees. Other House panels and Senate panels consider matters with tangential bearing on foreign and military policy.

The foreign affairs and national security panels are among the most visible on Capitol Hill. The Senate Foreign Relations Committee considers treaties and the nominations of key foreign policy officials. It normally regards itself as a working partner and adviser to the president. During the height of dispute over the Vietnam War, in the late 1960s and early 1970s, the committee became a forum for antiwar debate under the leadership of its chair, J. William Fulbright, D-Ark. (1959–1974). A later chairman, Jesse Helms, R-N.C. (1995–2001), attacked international agencies and thwarted many of the Clinton administration's diplomatic objectives. When Sen. (now Vice President) Joseph R. Biden Jr. chaired the panel, he and his Senate committee colleagues laid out alternatives to President George W. Bush's international policies.

Sen. John Kerry, D-Mass., who was elected to his fifth term in the 2008 elections, is the new chair of the panel. As a twenty-seven-year-old Vietnam veteran who turned against the war, Kerry was the first Vietnam veteran to appear before the panel. On April 22, 1971, Kerry posed a famous question: "How do you ask a man to be the last man to die for a mistake?"[12] A senator steeped in international issues, Kerry's agenda for the 111th Congress includes global warming, "the multiple crises in Africa, changes in South America, conditions in Iraq, the strategic relationship with China, the Middle East and the current state of Pakistan and Afghanistan."[13] With Obama in the White House, Senator Kerry will tend to be "a facilitator for the president," said a foreign policy scholar. "That is his style."[14]

For most of its history the House Foreign Affairs Committee worked in the shadow of its Senate counterpart. This situation changed after World War II, when foreign aid programs thrust the House—with its special powers of the purse—into virtual parity with the Senate.[15] Today the House committee addresses nearly as wide a range of issues as does the Senate committee. For example, the panel under the chairmanship of Howard Berman, D-Calif., held hearings on the foreign policy priorities of the Obama administration. It tends, however, to attract members with a more global outlook than the House as a whole. Consequently, its reports sometimes encounter skepticism on the House floor.

The Senate and House Armed Services Committees oversee the nation's military establishment. Annually, they authorize Pentagon spending for research, development, and procurement of weapons systems; construction of military facilities; and rules for civilian and uniformed personnel. The last-mentioned jurisdiction includes the Uniform Code of Military Conduct, which governs the lives of men and women in uniform and which has attracted congressional scrutiny of such diverse matters as sexual orientation, sexual harassment, treatment of enemy prisoners, overseas voting rights, and even the right of Jewish officers to wear yarmulkes while in uniform. Although global strategy or military readiness intrigues some of the committees' members, what rivets their attention is structural policymaking—issues closer to home, such as force levels, military installations, and defense contracts. Thus, constituency politics often drives military policy.

Because of their funding jurisdictions, House and Senate Appropriations subcommittees exert detailed control over foreign and defense policies. Tariffs and other trade regulations are the province of the taxing committees (House Ways and Means, Senate Finance). Committees involved with banking handle international financial and monetary policies; the commerce committees have jurisdiction over foreign commerce generally. With the creation of the Homeland Security Department, and despite the formation of homeland security committees in the House and Senate, scores of other panels assert jurisdiction linked in some way to local and national security.

The House and Senate Select Intelligence Committees were created in the late 1970s, following revelations of widespread abuses, illegalities, and misconduct on the part of intelligence agencies, particularly the Central Intelligence Agency (CIA) and the Federal Bureau of Investigation (FBI). After thirty years, however, the two oversight panels' close ties with the growing intelligence community has seemed to hamper vigorous scrutiny. The 2004 report of the 9/11 Commission (National Commission on Terrorist Attacks upon the United States) called for revitalized oversight through either a joint committee or separate House and Senate panels with authorizing and appropriating jurisdiction.[16] Neither chamber followed this advice. The House did create a select oversight panel, as noted in Chapter 7, that combined membership from the authorizing and appropriating committees. For its part, the relevant Senate committees (Appropriations and Select Intelligence) signed a memorandum of agreement "pledging greater cooperation."[17]

Congress's organization for policymaking is far from tidy. But it would be incorrect to draw any sharp contrast with the executive branch in this regard. Executive branch agencies are equally scattered: consider the long-standing coordination problems among the four military services or sixteen intelligence agencies.[18] In December 2004, the intelligence community received a major overhaul after the Intelligence Reform and Terrorism Prevention Act was enacted into law. The act created a Director of National Intelligence (DNI) who could look at the intelligence community as a whole and work to coordinate their work. However, an inspector general's report sharply criticized the DNI for "a failure to end the turf battles among America's spy agencies."[19]

The profusion of congressional power centers leads executive branch policymakers to complain that they do not know whom to consult when crises arise, that they have to testify before too many committees, and that leaks of sensitive information are inevitable with so many players. But the executive branch or their emissaries are often free to consult with as few or as many lawmakers as they choose—in some cases with only the joint party leaders, in others with chairmen and ranking members of the relevant committees. And when Congress tries to step in to influence administration policies, executive officers predictably complain about "micromanagement."

TYPES OF FOREIGN AND NATIONAL SECURITY POLICIES

Foreign policy is the total of decisions and actions governing a nation's relations with other nations and consists of national goals to be achieved and resources for achieving them. Statecraft is the art of selecting preferred outcomes and marshaling appropriate resources to attain them. As former secretary of state Henry A. Kissinger, a foreign policy pragmatist, put it, "Values are essential for defining objectives; strategy is what implements them by establishing priorities and defining timing."[20]

Defining a nation's goals is no simple matter. The subject has sparked intense conflict both between Congress and the president and within the Congress itself. Momentous congressional debates have displayed widely diverging views on subjects such as ties to England and France during the nation's early decades, American expansion abroad, tariff rates, involvement in foreign wars, approaches to combating terrorists, and U.S. involvement in nation building or forcible regime change. As for resources for meeting such goals, military strength and preparedness immediately come to mind. However, such other assets as wealth, productivity, creativity, political ideals, cultural values, and global credibility are even more potent in the long run.

In balancing national goals and national resources, policymakers confront several different types of foreign and national security policies. Structural policies involve procuring and deploying resources or personnel; strategic policies advance the nation's objectives militarily or diplomatically; and crisis policies protect the nation's safety against specific foreign or domestic threats.

STRUCTURAL POLICIES

National security programs involve millions of workers and the expenditure of billions of dollars annually. Decisions about deploying such vast resources are called structural policy decisions. Examples include choices of specific weapons systems, contracts with private suppliers, the location of military installations, sales of weapons and surplus goods to foreign countries, and trade policies that affect domestic industries and workers. Structural policymaking on foreign and defense issues is virtually the same as distributive policymaking in the domestic realm.

The last sixty years have seen a growing imbalance in the military versus nonmilitary elements of foreign policies. In fiscal year 2010, the U.S. military budget will be larger than those of the next nineteen nations of the world combined.[21] But the singular military machine of the United States is, historically speaking, a fairly recent phenomenon. After earlier wars, the United States quickly "sent the boys home" and, under congressional pressure, shrank its armed forces—though each time to somewhat higher plateaus.[22] Following World War II, however, the Cold War threat led to unprecedented levels of peacetime preparedness. By 1960, when retiring president Dwight D. Eisenhower, a career military officer, warned against the "military-industrial complex" (his speech draft said "military-industrial-congressional complex"), the new militarism was already embedded in the nation's political and economic system.

Department of Defense (DOD) spending—more than $500 billion in fiscal 2010—is the biggest discretionary portion of the federal budget. Worth noting is that by the end of 2009, the cost of the Iraq war is projected to be $694 billion, surpassing in inflation-adjusted dollars the Vietnam War ($686 billion).[23] War costs for Afghanistan are increasing with the resurgence of the Taliban. The United States spent $34 billion in 2008 in Afghanistan; the Obama administration expects to spend $47 billion in 2009, with war costs increasing as more American troops are sent to stabilize Afghanistan. As the nation's largest employer, its largest customer, and its largest procurer of equipment and services, DOD controls a huge number of structural outlays, which attract a wide swath of political interests. As a venture capitalist put it, "The military is like a Fortune No. 1 company."[24]

The State Department, in contrast, makes relatively few such decisions. For every twenty-one federal dollars spent on the military, only about one dollar goes to international affairs—including not only diplomatic representation but also military assistance, foreign development, and humanitarian aid.[25] The State Department's services and achievements are largely intangible, and in any event it spends much of its energy and money overseas. Little surprise, then, that it has few strong domestic clients and, compared to DOD, fewer champions on Capitol Hill. A surprising advocate for the State Department has been Defense Secretary Robert Gates, since typically State and Defense are rivals for resources and influence. Gates has urged Congress to provide more money for State, and stressed the importance of strengthening national security by better integrating diplomacy ("soft power") with military action ("hard power"). "We must focus our energies beyond the guns and steel of the military, beyond just our brave soldiers, sailors, marines, and airmen," Gates declared late in the

Bush administration. He envisioned a future of global conflicts that are fundamentally political in nature. "Success will be less a matter of imposing one's will and more a function of shaping [the] behavior of friends, adversaries and, most importantly, the people in between."[26]

The Congressional-Military-Industrial Complex

Defense dollars—for projects, contracts, and bases, among other things—are sought by business firms, labor unions, and local communities. The Pentagon's ties to the business community are so cozy that an estimated 40 percent of its contracts are awarded without competitive bidding, according to an independent study of some 2.2 million contracts.[27] As champions of local interests, members of Congress are naturally drawn into the process. The impulse is wholly bipartisan. (Some have even suggested that a "surveillance-industrial complex" has emerged in the post-9/11 era in which the government's interception of communications is contracted to private companies.[28])

Weapons Systems. Pentagon procurement officers anticipate congressional needs in planning and designing projects. The perfect weapons system, it is said, is one with a component manufactured in every congressional district in the nation. The Air Force's F-22 Raptor jet fighter, each costing nearly $300 million, is assembled at Georgia and Texas factories from parts made by 1,000 suppliers in forty-three states. "What it means to the company is the technology and the jobs," explained a factory manager.[29]

In a dramatic break with previous defense budgets, Defense Secretary Gates proposed major changes for the military budget for fiscal year 2010. Spending priorities would shift from big weapons programs to more funds for fighting unconventional wars, such as the battles against Al Qaeda and Taliban insurgents. Under his budget plan, which eliminated several big weapons programs, 50 percent of the Pentagon's budget would go to counter conventional threats, 10 percent to unconventional ("irregular") warfare, and 40 percent to weapons that can be used in both conventional and unconventional conflicts.[30] As one account noted:

> Defense spending traditionally reflects conventional threats such as China or perhaps Iran. But Secretary Gates's $534 billion budget recommends billions of dollars for the counterinsurgency needs of unconventional conflicts such as Iraq and Afghanistan, while making broad and controversial cuts to weapons programs such as the F-22 stealth fighter that Gates sees as part of an outdated, Cold-War mind-set.[31]

Lawmakers quickly responded to Gates' budget plan. "I will work to overturn the secretary's recommendation" regarding the F-22, declared Sen. Saxby Chambliss, R-Ga., a strong advocate of the F-22 program. The entire Connecticut congressional delegation wrote to Gates saying that stopping the F-22 program would "end jobs for 2,000 Connecticut engineers, machinists, and aerospace workers."[32] House Armed Services Chair Ike Skelton, D-Mo., said he appreciated Gates's hard work on the defense budget, but made it clear that "the buck stops with Congress, which has the critical Constitutional responsibility to decide whether to support these proposals."[33] Eliminating or reducing weapons systems is especially problematic during a recession when thousands of people are losing their jobs. Gates could nonetheless win legislative support for many of his recommendations.[34]

Even when military planners decide to phase out a weapon, lawmakers may compel them to keep the item in production. Consider the marines' V-22 Osprey, a tilt-rotor aircraft that flies like a conventional plane but takes off and lands like a helicopter. Conceived during the Cold War, the planes—which now cost over $100 million apiece—were intended to change the way the marines fight wars. But there were design problems; several planes crashed, claiming the lives of two dozen marines. Defense Secretary Dick Cheney canceled the program in 1989, judging that it was too costly; but he was overruled by fierce lobbying from Capitol Hill. The Tilt-Rotor Caucus, a group of representatives from regions where the plane is manufactured, worked with contractors to keep the project alive.[35] In 2005—twenty years after the program was conceived—DOD's Defense Acquisition Board approved full-scale production of the Osprey. "It is the only major weapons system program that was canceled and then resurrected," claimed a supporter, Rep. Curt Weldon, R-Pa. (1987–2007), then vice chair of the House Armed Services Committee.[36]

In March 2008, DOD signed a multiyear procurement contract with the Boeing Company and Bell-Textron for the manufacture and delivery of 167 V-22s.[37] So the Ospreys fly on. "It is the hardest thing to do, to take a weapon out of the budget," a Defense undersecretary noted. "It is just so easy to put one in."[38]

Lawmakers and lobbyists exploit the four services' (army, air force, navy, marines) differing priorities, which persist in the face of determined efforts at coordination by civilian managers over several presidencies, Republican and Democratic alike. The air force's projects include new jets, refueling tankers, and space weapons. The marines want the Osprey. The navy covets new aircraft carriers, and the army needs new artillery and combat vehicles.

Military Base Closures. The proliferation and geographic dispersion of military installations are another example of distributive military policymaking. L. Mendel Rivers, D-S.C., chairman of the House Armed Services Committee from 1965 to 1971, kept defense money flowing to bases in Charleston, South Carolina, campaigning on the slogan "Rivers delivers!" More recently, Sen. Trent Lott, R-Miss. (1989–2007), hailed a Pascagoula, Mississippi, firm that keeps busy building ships for the navy: "It's one of the most important shipyards in the country, and if I were not supportive of my hometown, that shipyard and the workers in that shipyard, I wouldn't deserve to be in Congress, now would I?"[39]

In the post–Cold War era, Congress tried to surmount the politically unpalatable problem of closing unneeded military installations. In 1988 it passed a law intended to insulate such decisions from congressional pressure by delegating them to bipartisan Base Realignment and Closing Commissions

(BRACs). The BRAC also aimed to eliminate pressure on lawmakers to vote for an administration's programs in exchange for keeping open military bases in their districts. As Rep. Richard Armey, R-Texas, the champion of the BRAC legislation, stated:

> The fact is, unfortunate as it is, that historically base closings have been used as a point of leverage by administrations, Democratic and Republican administrations, as political leverage over and above Members of Congress to encourage them to vote in a manner that the administration would like.[40]

From the defense secretary's recommendations, the BRAC would draw up a list of installations targeted for closure. To make the decisions hard to overturn, the list had to be accepted or rejected as a whole by the president and Congress. Base closings were also part of Congress's wider effort to balance the budget.

Five rounds of BRACs (1988, 1991, 1993, 1995, and 2005) reduced or eliminated hundreds of defense installations. Political pressures were intense. One commission chair was greeted at base entrances by parents holding children who, they said, would starve if the base closed.[41] Lawmakers from affected areas fought the closure lists and nearly succeeded in overturning them. From the Pentagon's perspective, the closures of excess infrastructure meant that the savings could be spent on higher military priorities. Communities where bases were shuttered turned their efforts to determining how lost defense jobs could be replaced by finding new uses for the military facilities (land, buildings, etc.). From the two Congresses view of lawmakers, they worked to assist their communities by, for example, providing for the cleanup of environmental contamination at these installations to enhance the potential for economic development.

Trade Politics

Another arena for distributive politics is foreign trade. Since the First Congress (1789–1791), the power to "regulate commerce with foreign nations" has been used to protect and enhance the competitive position of U.S. goods and industries, whether cotton or wheat or textiles or computer software. Until the 1930s, tariff legislation was fiercely contested on Capitol Hill by political parties and economic regions. Starting with the Reciprocal Trade Agreements Act of 1934, however, Congress began to delegate the details of tariff negotiations to the executive branch. The 1974 Trade Act is a key statute that delegates trade negotiating authority to the president, subject to Congress's ability to approve or disapprove the agreements under expedited procedures.

Protectionist impulses have not waned, however. Myriad trade interests are represented on Capitol Hill. Republicans—reflecting the business community—tend to favor lowering trade barriers at home and combating them abroad, to open world markets for U.S. goods. Democrats from areas of union strength want barriers to slow the loss of jobs to low-wage countries. Lawmakers of both parties voice concerns about specific commodities, such as steel, textiles, and farm products. Free trade finds more friends in the Senate, which overrepresents export-minded agricultural interests; the House, with its stronger representation of labor interests and heavy industry, has stronger protectionist leanings.

Most battles over trade bills call forth variations of the above lineups. In the thirteen months of negotiations leading up to the landmark 1993 North American Free Trade Agreement (NAFTA)—a trading bloc consisting of the United States, Canada, and Mexico—America's trade representative Carla A. Hills logged forty consultations with individual lawmakers and no fewer than 199 meetings with congressional groups, from the House Ways and Means and Senate Finance Committees to the Northeast-Midwest Congressional Coalition and the Senate Textile Group.[42]

When the bill implementing NAFTA reached Capitol Hill, a bipartisan effort was needed to approve it. President Clinton launched a high-profile public relations campaign, trumpeted the bill's job-creation benefits, welcomed support from Republican leaders, and cut deals to meet individual legislators' objections. Opposing were many Democrats, including the House majority leader and chief whip. In the end, only 40 percent of House Democrats supported the president, but their 102 votes along with those of 132 Republicans were enough to gain House passage. NAFTA then easily passed the Senate. The final enactment was a huge patchwork of provisions aimed at placating disparate interests.[43]

More than a decade later the modest Central American Free Trade Agreement (CAFTA), a centerpiece of President George W. Bush's trade agenda, encountered similar resistance—with many members complaining that previous administrations had failed to implement promised retraining programs for workers whose jobs went overseas.[44] The agreement was narrowly approved (the Senate vote was 54–45, the House 217–215) with scant Democratic support. Republican leaders pulled off the victory with a combination of arm-twisting and concessions to sugar growers, textile mills, and hosiery makers.

President Bush was unsuccessful in winning approval in 2008 of the Colombia free trade agreement. With Democrats in charge of Congress, a lame-duck president in the White House, and growing concern about the impact of globalization and trade agreements on their constituents, congressional Democrats led by Speaker Nancy Pelosi "broke more than three decades of precedent by changing trade rules to suspend consideration of the [Colombia trade] deal."[45] House rules trumped the legal requirements of the 1974 Trade Act setting a legislative timetable for action on the Colombia trade agreement. The 1974 law specifically recognized the constitutional authority of either chamber to make or change their own rules regardless of any statutory provisions addressing the procedural operations of the House or Senate. In this case, the House adopted a special rule from the Rules Committee that suspended the timetable for consideration of the Colombia free trade agreement.

Other foreign policy concerns create new lines of cleavage. In the debate over U.S.-China trade status, for example, representatives splintered across the political spectrum. Christian conservatives allied with liberal, pro-labor Democrats in opposing a trade deal with China because of their concerns about Beijing's persecution of Christian and other religious leaders.[46] The lure of China's vast potential market for U.S. goods vied with doubts over China's unpredictable government and its poor human rights, worker safety, and environmental records. Trade policy and negotiations, asserts Rep. Sander M. Levin, D-Mich., "now involve virtually every area of what used to be considered U.S. domestic law—from antitrust and food safety to telecommunications."[47] Separating local from global issues is difficult. As President Obama stated, "We have learned that the success of the American economy is inextricably linked to the global economy."[48]

Congress, however, confronts a dilemma in dealing with trade. Trading partners need assurances that agreements can be ratified quickly and as a package. Having delegated most decisions to the executive, lawmakers who want to review specific trade deals must struggle to get back in the game. The Trade Act of 1974, as noted above, addressed this dilemma. The president, it said, must actively consult, notify, and involve Congress as he negotiates trade agreements. These agreements take effect only after an implementing law is enacted. Such legislation would be handled under an expedited, fast-track procedure, including obligatory steps and deadlines, limits on debate, and a requirement for an up-or-down vote with no amendments.

Most presidents since 1974 have been awarded fast-track (or trade promotion) authority to negotiate trade pacts subject to up-or-down votes in both houses of Congress within ninety days. The authority lapsed during Clinton's presidency and was not renewed by the Republican-led Congress. After a vigorous lobbying effort, President Bush in 2002 won a five-year renewal of the fast-track procedure. Even so, the House vote was close—215–212 (the Senate margin was 64–34). To gain the needed House votes, numerous concessions were made, for example, to placate textile workers and citrus growers. The measure also featured a Democratic-sponsored hike in aid for workers who lost jobs to foreign competition.[49] The fast-track authority lapsed in 2007 because of heightened national concern about the loss of U.S. jobs overseas, a trend toward economic nationalism, and sharper partisanship in Congress over trade deals.

Distributive politics underlies many other foreign and defense programs. For example, P.L. 480 ("Food for Peace") dispenses agricultural surpluses to needy nations. This law's goal is to serve humanitarian purposes, but it has at times inhibited local agricultural development in Third World countries because its subsidized products undermine the ability of local farm workers to compete and sell their commodities.

The United States is also the world's largest seller of arms to developing nations. The value of all arms transfer agreements with developing nations in 2007 was over $42 billion, up from over $38 billion the year before.[50] To train military forces in 138 nations to use its weapons, the Pentagon in 2008 planned to spend nearly $90 million.[51] It is a profitable enterprise for the government and private firms that—for good or ill—affects civil and military affairs in every corner of the globe.[52]

STRATEGIC POLICIES

To protect the nation's interests, decision makers design strategic policies on spending levels for international and defense programs; total military force levels; the basic mix of military forces and weapons systems; arms sales to foreign powers; foreign trade inducements or restrictions; allocation of economic, military, and technical aid to developing nations; treaty obligations to other nations; U.S. responses to human rights abuses abroad; and its stance toward international bodies such as the United Nations (UN), the North Atlantic Treaty Organization (NATO), and world financial agencies.

Strategic policies embrace most important foreign policy questions. They engage top-level executive decision makers as well as congressional committees and midlevel executive officers. Such matters can express citizens' ideological, ethnic, racial, or economic interests.[53] Despite their obvious distributive elements, strategic issues typically involve broader themes and invoke policymakers' long-term attitudes and beliefs. The key agencies for strategic decision making include the State Department, the Office of the Secretary of Defense, the intelligence agencies, and the National Security Council—all advising the president.

The Power of the Purse

Congress uses its spending power to establish overall appropriation levels for foreign and defense purposes. Under those ceilings, priorities must be assigned among military services; among weapons systems; between uniformed personnel and military hardware; and on economic, cultural, or military aid, to name just a few of the choices. The president leads by presenting the annual budget, lobbying for the administration's priorities, and threatening to veto options deemed unacceptable. Yet if it chooses, Congress also can write its own budgets down to the smallest detail. And the omnibus character of appropriations measures places pressure on the president to accede to the outcome of legislative bargaining on expenditures. To get the 95 percent of the budget the administration wants, the president may have to swallow the 5 percent he opposes. For example, to support his ambitious post-9/11 military goals, President George W. Bush was obliged to sign military spending bills that included weapons projects he and his defense advisers had resisted.[54]

Post–Cold War Spending: Down and Up. Congress responds both to perceived levels of international tension and to shifting public views about the salience of global engagement. Following the Soviet Union's collapse, a bipartisan consensus in the Pentagon and in Congress agreed that defense funding and force levels could be gradually cut. That consensus arose either from the belief that a sizable "peace dividend" could be realized or from the hope that savings could be gained from smarter planning and trimming waste, fraud, and abuse. Downsizing the military establishment, however, is politically and economically disruptive. Defense Secretary Gates cautioned against cutting military expenditures significantly in the aftermath of the conflicts in Iraq and Afghanistan. In an address at the Naval War College, he stated:

> Every time we have come to an end of a conflict, somehow we have persuaded ourselves that the nature of mankind and the nature of the world have changed on an enduring basis and so we have dismantled our military and intelligence capabilities. My hope is that as we wind down in Iraq and whatever the level of our commitment in Afghanistan, that we not forget the basic nature of human kind has not changed.[55]

Footing the bills for combat operations poses dilemmas for Congress. How much money is needed, and how much freedom should the president have in spending it? Lyndon B. Johnson gradually deepened U.S. involvement in Vietnam, but he hesitated to ask Congress to appropriate the needed funds. Thus the first supplemental funding bill was passed in February 1966, even though Congress had signed onto the war as early as August 1964 (with the Gulf of Tonkin Resolution). Johnson's effort to hide the escalating war costs while maintaining domestic programs elevated both inflation and the federal debt.

After the September 11, 2001, attacks, Congress acted swiftly to pass a $40 billion supplemental appropriations package—one-fourth of which was under the president's near-total control. After the Afghanistan invasion Congress approved another $30 billion, again featuring flexibility. A number of lawmakers, especially on the funding committees, expressed their doubts. "All presidents want unlimited authority. In any time of conflict, there's a tendency to allow a little more leeway," said Rep. David L. Hobson, R-Ohio, an Appropriations subcommittee chair. "We have a responsibility to maintain a balance...and we're struggling with that."[56] In the years following the terrorist attacks, however, Congress approved hundreds of billions of dollars in supplemental expenditures that carried only marginal congressional adjustments. These were intended to exempt wartime spending from compliance with the annual spending caps. The Obama administration plans to reduce reliance on supplemental appropriations to fund war operations and include those costs in the Pentagon's normal budget.

The power of the purse is a blunt instrument in time of war. In the final analysis, however, no major foreign or military enterprise can be sustained unless Congress provides money and support. A president can conduct an operation for a time using existing funds and supplies, as Johnson did at first in Vietnam; but sooner or later Congress must be asked for funding. The U.S. role in South Vietnam finally ended in 1974, when Congress simply refused to provide emergency aid funds. And although Congress opened the purse strings during the first four years of the Iraq war, Democrats' initial thrust, once they regained control of Capitol Hill, was to use spending bills to define their position as opposing the war.

FIGURE 15-1   **Defence and Foreign Policy Spending as Percentage of Total Budget Outlays, 1940–2010**

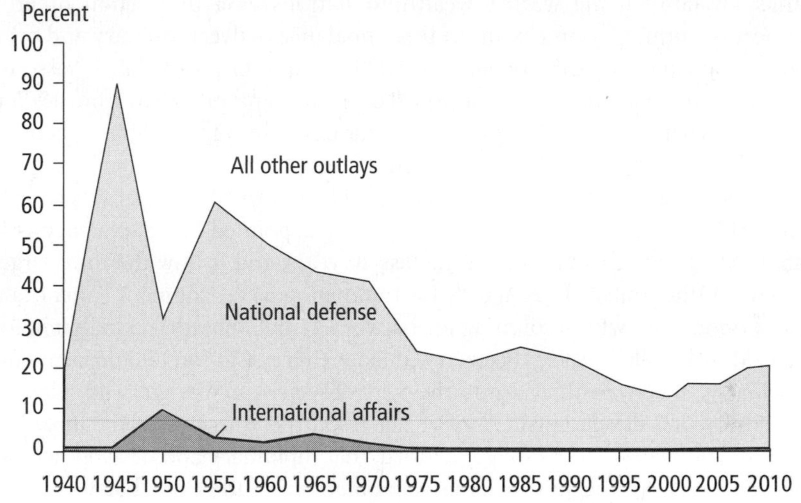

Percent

- All other outlays
- National defense
- International affairs

1940 1945 1950 1955 1960 1965 1970 1975 1980 1985 1990 1995 2000 2005 2010

Sources: Historical figures from *Budget of the United States Government, Fiscal Year 2010, Historical Tables* (Washington, D.C.: Government Printing Office, 2009), Table 3-2. Projections for 2010 are from *Budget of the United States Government, Fiscal Year 2010: Current Services Budget Authority and Outlays by Function, Category, and Programs* (Washington, D.C.: Government Printing Office, 2009), Table 24-14.

Note: Figures are fiscal year outlays, according to current statistical conventions for treating off-budget items. The total budget in billions of dollars was $9.5 in 1940, $42.6 in 1950, $92.2 in 1960, $195.6 in 1970, $590.9 in 1980, $1,253.2 in 1990, $1,825.0 in 2000, and (projected) $3,644.4 in 2010.

Spending on Diplomacy. Unlike national defense, international affairs funding represents a relatively small expenditure (see Figure 15-1). Historically, the nation's foreign operations required relatively small outlays. In the immediate post–World War II years, 1947–1951, however, programs to rebuild devastated Europe and Japan consumed as much as 16 percent of U.S. annual spending. Throughout the Cold War, the United States was a major provider of economic, military, and technical aid throughout the world.

In recent years, Department of State operations have accounted for around 1 percent of all expenditures. U.S. economic assistance to promote democracy, address poverty, and improve health and education is a fraction of that, and most of this aid goes to a handful of frontline states (Israel, Egypt, Afghanistan, and Iraq most prominently). In a pork barrel approach to foreign aid, Congress appropriated more than $30 billion—through DOD, rather than State—to rebuild Iraq. "What appeared to be a remarkably generous foreign aid package," writes T. Christian Miller, "was in fact a remarkable program of domestic handouts and corporate welfare."[57] Most of the money enriched well-placed U.S. businesses; very little reached average Iraqis.

In opinion surveys, citizens indicate only lukewarm support for foreign aid spending, and they grossly overestimate how much is actually spent. Perhaps that is the reason U.S. foreign aid, although high in pure dollar terms, ranks low among the world's wealthiest nations as a proportion of gross domestic product.[58] Some point to this imbalance between military and other aid as a weakness of U.S. foreign policy. "It's a question of balance," asserted James D. Wolfensohn, the U.S.-appointed World Bank president from 1995 to 2005. "Does it make sense to put all that money…into the military when you don't deal with the underlying causes of distress?"[59]

More recently, additional resources have been provided to various components of foreign aid. As Rep. David Price, D-N.C., pointed out, democracy assistance "has grown dramatically in the last 20 years, and is now the third largest activity of [the United States Agency for International Development], after health and economic growth, accounting for between $1 billion and $1.5 billion in foreign aid each year."[60] And as Secretary of State Hillary Clinton told departmental employees: "There are three legs to the stool of American foreign policy: defense, diplomacy, and development. And we are responsible for two of the three legs. And we will make clear, as we go forward, that diplomacy and development are essential tools in achieving the long-term objectives of the United States."

Treaties and Executive Agreements

The Constitution makes Congress an active partner with the president in a key element of strategic policy: treaties with foreign powers. Although the president initiates them, treaties are made "by and with the advice and consent of the Senate." The Senate's consent is signified by the concurrence of two-thirds of the senators present and voting. As explained by two legal scholars:

> As a matter of historical practice, the president may also make international agreements if authorized to do so by a law passed by Congress. (These are called "congressional-executive agreements; the North American Free Trade Agreement is a prominent example.) And in some narrow cases, the president may create an international agreement all by himself through his own constitutional powers. [All are] legally binding on the United States and future presidents.[61]

Congress may or may not be taken into the president's confidence when treaties and executive agreements are negotiated. To avoid a humiliation like President Woodrow Wilson's, when the Senate rejected the Treaty of Versailles after World War I, modern chief executives typically inform key senators during the negotiation process. After the pact is sent to the Senate, it faces several possible fates beyond a simple up-or-down vote.

Rarely does the Senate reject a treaty outright. It has turned down only twenty treaties since 1789. One study found that the Senate had approved without change 69 percent of those submitted to it.[62] Such was the case in March 2003, when the Senate unanimously approved a U.S.-Russian treaty requiring cuts in the two nations' arsenals of long-range missiles. Despite critics' charges that the deal was "flimsy," senators opted to send a positive signal to Russia during the run-up to the Iraq war.

The Senate may attach reservations to a treaty that, if serious enough, may oblige the president to renegotiate the document. Formal reservations are employed to change policy, according to two scholars who examined the process. "Ratification reservations can dictate how the U.S. will interpret and implement a treaty, how the U.S. will behave on unrelated foreign policy issues, and in some instances can even change the actual text of a treaty."[63] The Senate, of course, may simply decline to act at all.

The Chemical Weapons Convention, concluded in 1993 by George Bush and signed by 161 nations, illustrates the Senate's active role in ratification. Although the treaty had broad bipartisan support, a group of hawkish lawmakers argued that it was filled with loopholes and would not prevent rogue states from making and using chemical weapons. Simply to get the measure to the Senate floor required arcane negotiations with Foreign Relations Committee chairman Jesse Helms, R-N.C., the treaty's archenemy. Negotiations were spearheaded by President Bill Clinton's secretary of state, Madeleine K. Albright, and mediated by the GOP leader, Senator Lott. The administration not only agreed to twenty-eight clarifications demanded by the conservatives, but it also made other major concessions—including a State Department reorganization, UN reform, and submission of other arms control treaties to the Senate—aimed at strengthening the Senate's role in future bargaining. During the floor debate, President Clinton and his aides worked the phones, trumpeted support from such Republican luminaries as retired general Colin Powell and former senator Bob Dole, and sent a last-minute letter to Lott promising to withdraw from the treaty if it subverted U.S. interests in any way. The multifaceted offensive paid off when Lott brought in enough skeptical Republicans to ratify the treaty in April 1997.[64]

A different fate befell another major multilateral pact, the Comprehensive Test Ban Treaty (CTBT) in autumn 1999. From the moment it reached the Senate two years earlier, the pact met fierce resistance from conservatives who held that it would jeopardize the nation's nuclear superiority and weaken deterrence against would-be nuclear powers. Senate Republicans realized from private consultations that they had the votes to kill the treaty. Normally the Senate would simply have declined to act. But when pressed by President Clinton and Democratic leaders to bring the treaty to the floor, Republican leaders suddenly scheduled a flurry of hearings quickly followed by floor debate. No bargaining was evident at either stage.[65] The treaty's foes seemed bent on humiliating the president and signaling their unilateralist approach to future arms control efforts. By the time the treaty's advocates realized that they had fallen into a trap (partially of their own making), it was too late to turn back. After debate described as "nasty, brutish, and short," the treaty failed by a 48–51 vote—short of a majority, much less the required two-thirds.[66] "While there was nothing improper or illegal in their parliamentary tactics," one commentator wrote, "it was nonetheless a nasty and contemptuous way of doing business quite out of character with the [Senate's] stately, sometimes ponderous way of doing business."[67]

The hurdle of obtaining a two-thirds Senate vote has led presidents to rely increasingly on executive agreements—international accords that are not submitted to the Senate for its advice and consent. Of the more than 5,600 U.S. international accords signed between 1981 and 1996, 96 percent were executive agreements.[68] Such agreements are enforceable under international law, which regards as binding any agreement among nations. Kiki Caruson describes the agreements' subject matter:

> The vast majority of executive agreements concern routine procedural matters such as postal agreements, mutual legal assistance, cooperation in the fields of science and technology, conservation, civil aviation agreements, and other relatively non-controversial issues. But the executive agreement has also been used to address important foreign policy issues, such as security and defense matters.[69]

On security and defense matters, various lawmakers expressed dismay that President Bush kept the House and Senate in the dark about negotiations with Iraq over a Status of Forces Agreement. The agreement, for example, gave the Iraqi government considerable authority "over the operations and movements of U.S. troops."[70] Sen. James Webb, D-Va., complained that the Armed Services and Foreign Relations Committees, on which he serves, "have not been shown one word of the actual document being negotiated."[71] The administration argued that it lacked the time to consult Congress, because it had to finalize the pact "before the United Nations mandate under which U.S. troops operate expires on Dec. 31, 2008."[72] In federal court cases challenging whether such agreements should have been treaties, the justices have invoked the political questions doctrine and declined to rule on the merits. The political questions doctrine holds that the issue is best left "to the discretion and expertise of the legislative and executive branches."[73]

According to the Case-Zablocki Act of 1972, copies of all executive agreements must be transmitted to Congress within sixty days of their going into effect. From time to time a constitutional amendment to require Senate ratification of executive agreements has been proposed, but none has ever received the two-thirds vote in both chambers of Congress that would send the proposal to the states for ratification.

Other Policymaking Powers of Congress

In addition to its control of the purse strings, Congress employs an array of other techniques to shape or influence strategic policies. The most common tools of congressional policy leadership are informal advice, legislative prodding through nonbinding resolutions or policy statements, policy oversight, legislative directives or restrictions, and structural or procedural changes.[74]

Advising, Prodding. Congressional leaders and key members routinely provide the president and other executive officials with informal advice. Sometimes this advice proves decisive. In 1954 President Eisenhower dispatched Secretary of State John Foster Dulles to meet with a small bipartisan group of congressional leaders to determine whether the United States should intervene militarily in Indochina (Vietnam). The leaders unanimously declined to sponsor a resolution favoring involvement until other nations indicated their support of military action. Lacking assurances from either Congress or foreign allies, Eisenhower decided against intervening.[75]

Congress engages in legislative prodding by proposing legislation or suggesting ideas to the administration. During the 111th Congress (2009–2011), for example, congressional Democrats urged President Obama to develop an exit strategy for Afghanistan and to devise benchmarks to measure the progress of the mission. As Sen. Carl Levin, D-Mich., the chair of the Armed Services Committee, explained: "We need metrics to measure progress to report to the American people and, importantly, to hold people accountable."[76] And prodding of the White House by various lawmakers no doubt contributed to President Obama's release of four secret Department of Justice legal opinions written during the George W. Bush administration detailing the harsh interrogation techniques that could be used to extract information from terrorist suspects (interrogation policy will be discussed more fully in the subsection "Congress's War Powers in Today's World").[77]

More frequently, Congress passes resolutions that are not legally binding or enforceable. Every recent Congress has approved numerous simple or concurrent resolutions. These measures may lend support to the executive branch, advance certain policies, or signal assurances or warnings to other nations. Occasionally, nonbinding resolutions put forward fresh policy ideas; at other times they are little more than posturing. Some of both were embedded in the House resolution backing troops for the Kosovo crisis in 1999. The resolution— supported by 174 Democrats, 44 Republicans, and 1 independent—authorized the president to deploy troops with the NATO peacekeeping force, but it also instructed the president to explain to Congress an exit strategy from the area and to ensure that U.S. troops would answer only to American commanders.[78]

Oversight. Congress shapes foreign policy through oversight of the executive branch's performance. Hearings and investigations often focus on foreign policy issues. Recurrent hearings on authorizing and funding State Department and Defense Department programs offer many opportunities for lawmakers to voice their concerns, large and small. Another device is to require that certain decisions or agreements be submitted to Congress before they go into effect. Congress and its committees may also require reports from the executive that "provide not only information for oversight but also a handle for action."[79] Some six hundred foreign policy reporting requirements are embedded in current statutes.

Oversight in time of war or crisis is especially hazardous. The president resists intrusions, and lawmakers are reluctant to impede the action. "The trick is to rein in the White House but not seem unpatriotic," writes historian Bruce J. Schulman.[80]

The boldest legislative foray into wartime oversight occurred during the Civil War. As confederate guns threatened Washington, D.C., the Joint

Committee on the Conduct of the War (1861–1865), controlled by Radical Republicans, held hearings on Capitol Hill and published reports that questioned President Abraham Lincoln's war policies, criticized military operations, berated generals who failed to pursue the enemy, and exposed waste and fraud in military procurements.

During World War II, Missouri senator Harry S. Truman's Special Committee to Investigate the National Defense Program (1941–1948) uncovered profiteering, contract abuses, and shoddy workmanship in wartime projects. It saved taxpayers billions of dollars and, not incidentally, boosted the career of its chairman ("Truman Committee," its letterhead proclaimed). Senate Foreign Relations Committee hearings launched in 1966 raised doubts in the public's mind about the Vietnam War.

After the Vietnam War, Congress uncovered long-standing abuses by law enforcement and intelligence agencies. A Senate committee headed by Sen. Frank Church, D-Idaho (1957–1981), found that the FBI, CIA, and National Security Agency (NSA) had spied on politicians, protest groups, and civil rights activities; illegally opened mail; and sponsored scores of covert operations abroad. Oversight during the Cold War period had neglected these matters. As a result of the findings, Congress set up new permanent intelligence committees, required presidents to report covert operations, and in 1978 passed the Foreign Intelligence Surveillance Act (FISA, P.L. 95-511), which "squarely repudiated the idea of inherent executive power to spy on Americans without obtaining [judicial] warrants." "The United States must not adopt the tactics of the enemy," the Church committee declared, "for each time we do, each time means we use are wrong, our inner strength, the strength that makes us free, is lessened."[81]

After the burst of 1970s reforms, however, Congress reverted to a Cold War mode of complacency. Abuses reminiscent of the Vietnam era were again alleged. Presidents of both parties exercised secret and unchecked powers and evaded or resisted legislative scrutiny. Intelligence agencies during the Bush II years, for example, were found to have wiretapped U.S. citizens without warrants from the FISA-created courts. "The White House became a keen user of unilateral executive orders that bypassed Congress."[82]

In view of congressional inattention, commentators have reasoned, executive branch officials came to view Congress with contempt. Norman J. Ornstein describes a Senate Armed Services hearing in 2004 on torture in the Abu Ghraib prison—by no means a routine confrontation:

> During Sen. John McCain's [R-Ariz.] tough questioning, Secretary of Defense [Donald] Rumsfeld said that the military brass with him had prepared a thorough chart. When one of the generals said they had forgotten to bring it, Rumsfeld said, "Oh my."
>
> Could anything more clearly demonstrate the contempt this department has for Congress?…How could this happen?[83]

Ornstein blames Congress itself for this state of affairs. Executive agencies have little respect for Congress, he contends, because it has "shown no appetite to do any serious or tough oversight, to use the power of the purse or the power of pointed public hearings to put the fear of God into them."

Most observers of Congress agree that hard-hitting oversight was lacking during the recent period of GOP control of the government. Although GOP Congresses actively probed the Clinton administration's scandals, "when George Bush became president, oversight largely disappeared. From homeland security to the conduct of the war in Iraq, from the torture issue uncovered by the Abu Ghraib revelations to the performance of the IRS, Congress has mostly ignored its responsibilities."[84] When Democrats took charge of the 110th Congress, as noted in Chapter 11, they aggressively investigated the Bush administration. They have continued to exercise oversight in the 111th Congress even though their party is in charge of the executive establishment. Sen. Dianne Feinstein, D-Calif., the chair of the Select Intelligence Committee, investigated the National Security Agency (NSA) after the *New York Times* reported that the agency had intercepted the private e-mails and phone conversations of U.S. citizens, including an unidentified member of Congress (later determined to be Rep. Jane Harman, D-Calif.).[85] Members of the House Armed Services Committee are actively pursuing failures of the defense acquisition system.[86] And conservative Democrats and Republicans are closely scrutinizing President Obama's plan to close the military prison at Guantanamo Bay, Cuba.

Legislative Mandates. Congress sometimes makes foreign policy by legislative directives—to launch new programs, to authorize certain actions, or to set guidelines. A landmark enactment of the Cold War era was the Jackson-Vanik amendment to the Trade Act of 1974 (named for Sen. Henry M. "Scoop" Jackson, D-Wash., and Rep. Charles Vanik, D-Ohio). Prompted by concern over the Soviet Union's treatment of its Jewish minority, the amendment denied government credits and most-favored-nation trade status (now called "normal trade relations") to any communist country that restricted the free emigration of its citizens.

Foreign policy statutes may include explicit legislative restrictions, which perhaps are Congress's most effective weapon. Often they are embedded in authorization or appropriation bills that the president is unlikely to veto. Throughout the Reagan presidency, for example, Congress passed many limits on military aid to Central American countries. Most notable were the Boland amendments (named for House Intelligence Committee chairman Edward P. Boland, D-Mass.) attached to various bills after 1982 to forbid nonhumanitarian aid to the contra rebels in Nicaragua. The 1987 Iran-contra scandal brought to light how President Reagan and his National Security Council had circumvented this prohibition.[87]

Even the threat of passing legislation may bring about the desired result. Dissatisfied with the Reagan administration's weak "constructive engagement" policy toward South African apartheid (a brutal form of racial segregation practiced by the former government of that nation), a pro–civil rights coalition on Capitol Hill threatened to pass legislation imposing economic and other sanctions. Just before a sanctions bill was to be approved in 1985, President Reagan issued an executive order imposing limited sanctions. (The next year, over Reagan's veto, Congress enacted tougher restrictions.)

Legislation also shapes the structures and procedures through which policies are carried out. "Congress changes the structure and procedures of decision making in the executive branch in order to influence the content of policy," writes James M. Lindsay.[88] When lawmakers wanted to reform military procurement, they restructured the Defense Department to clarify and streamline the process; when they wanted more say in trade negotiations, they wrote themselves into the process with the 1974 and 1988 trade laws.

CRISIS POLICIES: THE WAR POWERS

An international crisis endangering the nation's safety, security, or vital interests pushes aside other foreign policy goals. Examples range from Japan's attack on the U.S. naval fleet in Pearl Harbor in 1941 to the Al Qaeda attacks of September 11, 2001.

Crisis policies engage decision makers at the highest levels: the president, the secretaries of state and defense, the National Security Council, and the Joint Chiefs of Staff. Congressional leaders are sometimes brought into the picture. More rarely, congressional advice is sought out and heeded—as in President Eisenhower's 1954 decision against military intervention in Indochina. Often when executive decision makers fear congressional opposition, they simply neglect to inform Capitol Hill until the planned action is under way. A failed 1980 attempt to rescue American hostages in Iran, for example, was planned in strictest secrecy, and no consultations were undertaken.

As long as a crisis lingers, policymakers keep a tight rein on information flowing upward from line officers. The attention of the media and the public is riveted on crisis events. Patriotism runs high. Citizens hasten to "rally round the flag" and support, at least initially, whatever course their leaders choose.[89]

Constitutional Powers

War powers are shared by the president and Congress. The president is the commander in chief of the military and naval forces of the United States (Article II, Section 2), but Congress has the power to declare war (Article I, Section 8). Congress has declared war only five times: the War of 1812 (1812–1814), the Mexican War (1846–1848), the Spanish-American War (1898), World War I (1917–1918), and World War II (1941–1945). In four instances, Congress readily assented to the president's call for war, acknowledging in the declaration that a state of war already existed. Only once did Congress delve into the merits of waging war, and that was in 1812, when the vote was close. In two cases—the

Mexican and Spanish-American conflicts—lawmakers later had reason to regret their haste.

More problematic than formal declarations of war are the more than 300 other instances in which U.S. military forces have been deployed abroad. (The number is uncertain because of quasi engagements involving military or intelligence advisers.)[90] The examples range from an undeclared naval war with France (1798–1800) to the invasion of Iraq (2003). Since the end of the last declared war—World War II—in 1945, numerous military interventions have taken place abroad. Some were massive and prolonged wars: Korea (1950–1953), Vietnam (1964–1975), Afghanistan (2001–), and Iraq (1991, 2003–). Still others were short-lived actions (for example, military coordination of medical and disaster relief after U.S. embassies in Kenya and Tanzania were bombed in 1998) and rescue or peacekeeping missions, some of which involved casualties (Lebanon, 1983; Somalia, 1992–1993).

Most of these interventions were authorized by the president as commander in chief on the stated grounds of protecting American lives, property, or interests abroad. Some were justified on the grounds of treaty obligations or "inherent powers" derived from a broad reading of executive prerogatives. Others were peacekeeping efforts under UN or NATO sponsorship. In virtually every armed intervention in U.S. history, constitutional questions have generated "lively disagreement among the president, Congress, and the Supreme Court, and between the central government and the states."[91]

Members of Congress, though wary of armed interventions, are reluctant to halt them: "No one actually wants to cut off funds when American troops are in harm's way," a House leadership aide explained. "The preferred stand is to let the president make the decisions and, if it goes well, praise him, and if it doesn't, criticize him," observed Lee H. Hamilton, D-Ind., former chairman of the House Foreign Affairs Committee (1993–1995) and co-chair of the 9/11 Commission and the Iraq Study Group.[92] Interventions go well if they come to a swift, successful conclusion with few American lives lost. Actions that drag on without a satisfactory resolution or that cost many lives will eventually tax lawmakers' patience. As the sense of urgency subsides, competing information appears that may challenge the president's version of the event. Congressional critics thus are emboldened to voice their reservations. This reaction occurred as the undeclared wars in Korea and Vietnam dragged on and after U.S. troops suffered casualties in Lebanon and Somalia.

The War Powers Resolution

The Johnson and Nixon administrations' conduct of the war in Vietnam left many lawmakers skeptical of presidential warmaking initiatives. In 1973 Congress passed the War Powers Resolution (WPR, P.L. 93-148) over President Nixon's veto. This law requires the president to consult with Congress before introducing U.S. troops into hostilities; report any commitment of forces to Congress within forty-eight hours; and terminate the use of forces within sixty days if Congress does not declare war, does not extend the period by law, or is unable to meet. (The president may extend the period to ninety days, if necessary.)

By the end of 2008, presidents had submitted 125 reports to Congress that troops had been deployed abroad.[93] President Bush reported on December 16 of that year, "consistent with the War Powers Resolution," that U.S. military forces were deployed to "a number of locations in the Central, Pacific, European, Southern, and Africa Command areas of operation" and were engaged in combat actions against terrorist fighters.[94] In still other cases the executive branch claimed that reports were not required because U.S. personnel were not confronting actual or imminent hostilities.

The WPR is an awkward compromise of executive and legislative authority, and presidents still intervene as they see fit. Members of Congress tend to sit on the sidelines, only later questioning presidential initiatives; but sometimes deployments are heatedly debated. President Reagan dispatched two thousand marines to Lebanon in 1982, but it was not until the troops came under hostile fire in 1983 that Congress seriously debated invoking the War Powers Resolution. Finally, a compromise was reached in which the president signed congressional legislation invoking the WPR, and Congress authorized U.S. troops to remain in Lebanon for eighteen months (P.L. 98-119). Shortly afterward, 241 marines were killed by a suicide truck bombing, raising new complaints from Congress and the public. The president subsequently withdrew the troops.

The law figured prominently in the Persian Gulf War of 1991, a brief but real war involving forces from the United States and the United Nations. A week after Iraqi troops invaded neighboring Kuwait in August 1990, President George H.W. Bush notified Congress that he had deployed troops to the region. Although the president did not consult with congressional leaders before acting, both chambers later adopted measures supporting the deployment and urging Iraqi withdrawal from Kuwait. Urged by congressional leaders, Bush later asked for a resolution supporting the use of all necessary means to implement UN resolutions demanding Iraqi withdrawal from Kuwait. After a lively, high-minded debate, both houses passed a statutory authorization of military action (P.L. 102-1) under the WPR.

Afghanistan and Iraq

Post–September 11 authorizations under the WPR found Congress in a reactive posture. Three days after the terrorist attacks, with smoke still lingering above the damaged Pentagon building, both chambers passed S.J. Res. 23, authorizing the president "to use all necessary and appropriate force against those nations, organizations, or persons he determines planned, authorized, committed, or aided the terrorist attacks." There was scant debate, and all but one member in the two chambers voted for it. The measure included the assertion that "[n]othing in this resolution supersedes any requirement of the War Powers Resolution." But, as Ivo H. Daalder and James M. Lindsay assert, "In effect, Congress declared war and left it up to the White House to decide who the enemy was."[95]

Some three weeks later, President George W. Bush notified Congress that he had launched an assault "designed to disrupt the use of Afghanistan as a terrorist base of operations." Once the operation had toppled Afghanistan's Taliban regime, however, the White House resumed its drumbeat of war threats against its preferred Mideast target: Saddam Hussein's Iraq regime, which had survived the 1991 war.

To sell the Iraq war to the American media and people, Caroline Heldman has explained, the White House framed the debate in three ways: Hussein's weapons of mass destruction (WMD) posed an imminent threat (the WMD frame); the Iraqi people should be freed from a cruel dictator (the liberation frame); and Hussein sponsored terrorist activities (the terrorism frame).[96] The WMD argument prevailed until after the fighting began and no WMDs were found; thereafter, the liberation rationale dominated the administration's rhetoric. Elite and public opinion agreed that regime change in Iraq was desirable, but it sharply divided over whether the United States should act unilaterally or work through the UN and a broad coalition of allies, as in 1991. These battles were waged more on news media talk shows and editorial pages than in the halls of Congress.

The president's advisers initially asserted that the president could launch a preemptory attack without further approval. But surveys showed that a large majority of the public—including a majority of Republicans—wanted the president to gain Congress's approval.[97] So as his father had done before the Gulf War in 1991, George W. Bush sought congressional consent.

By Gulf War standards, debate in the two chambers was muted and desultory. Sen. Chuck Hagel, R-Neb., voted for the resolution but cautioned against using the military option. "America must understand that it cannot alone win a war against terrorism," he said. "It will require allies, friends and partners."[98] Sen. Bob Graham, D-Fla., Intelligence Committee chair, opposed the resolution because Iraq posed a less urgent threat than terrorist networks: "There are many evils out there, a number of which are substantially more competent, particularly in their ability to attack America here at home, than Iraq is likely to be in the foreseeable future."[99] Sen. Robert C. Byrd, D-W.Va., railed against what he termed the president's demand for "power to launch this nation into war without provocation and without clear evidence of an imminent attack on the United States. And we are going to be foolish enough to give it to him."[100] Lopsided majorities backed the resolution: 296–133 in the House, 77–23 in the Senate. Along with almost all Republicans, many skeptical Democrats went along with the president—more than had backed his father's Gulf War resolution. Yet they accounted for almost all the opposition: 126 of 207 House Democrats and 21 of 50 Senate Democrats voted no.

The final Iraqi authorization (H. J. Res. 114) preserved no more than a fig leaf of congressional prerogative. The White House's original proposal—a blanket authorization resembling the infamous Tonkin Gulf Resolution of 1964 and the panicky post–September 11 action—was trimmed somewhat. First, the action made clear that the UN should have time to act before force was employed. Second, the president had to declare promptly that "diplomatic and other peaceful means" had failed and that U.S. action was "consistent with" continuing actions against terrorism by the nation and its allies. Finally, such action would fall under the WPR, requiring reports to Congress at least every sixty days. In March 2003 the president launched the war. Even lawmakers with misgivings signed onto resolutions of "support for the troops."

Yet as the Iraq war spiraled out of control following the fall of Saddam Hussein, it came to be seen through partisan lenses—Bush and his core supporters versus Democrats and many independents. From his detailed review of public opinion during the Bush presidency, Gary C. Jacobson concludes that Iraq opened a partisan chasm unique among recent U.S. wars: "[O]n virtually every [survey] question concerning the premises, necessity, wisdom, and effect of going to war in Iraq, partisan differences grew very large."[101] Sen. John Warner, R-Va., then chair of the Armed Services Committee, was prescient when—following a pre-war briefing for congressional leaders by President Bush and National Security Adviser Condoleezza Rice—he told one of Rice's aides: "You've got to do this and I will support you, make no mistake. But I sure hope you find weapons of mass destruction because if you don't you may have a big problem."[102]

After no weapons of mass destruction were found in Iraq, the Bush administration indeed found itself with a big problem. Public opinion turned against the war as years of sectarian conflicts and suicide bombings in that nation were highlighted in the news media. By 2008, President Bush's "surge" strategy of sending more troops to Iraq (repairing the initial error of not deploying enough troops) did improve the security environment.

The election of Barack Obama, however, brought major policy shifts from his predecessor's national security policies. On Iraq, the president announced that U.S. troops would end all combat operations by August 2010 with all American troops departing that country by the end of 2011. Obama's strategic focus shifted to shoring up a deteriorating situation in both Afghanistan and Pakistan as the renewed Taliban insurgency threatened the security and stability of both nations. Emphasizing that Iraq's future is in the hands of the Iraqi people, President Obama told marines at Camp Lejeune in North Carolina, "We have also taken into account the simple reality that America can no longer afford to see Iraq in isolation from other priorities: we face the challenge of refocusing on Afghanistan and Pakistan; of relieving the burden on our military; and of rebuilding our struggling economy—and these are challenges that we will meet."[103] Just as the war in Iraq defined President Bush's legacy, the success of Obama's presidency is linked to how well he meets the challenges outlined to the marines.

Congress's War Powers in Today's World

With each new crisis the War Powers Resolution is attacked or defended, depending on the view held of the proposed intervention. Although presidents are encouraged to pause and consult before acting, experience since 1973 shows that the WPR has not prevented them from boldly exercising military powers, including military responses to sudden threats.

Champions of executive authority, such as former vice president Cheney, think that the WPR and other post-Vietnam enactments limit executive flexibility. Recent history belies such a claim. In the case of the war powers, Louis Fisher's careful study of the historical record reveals that a combination of presidential hubris and congressional abdication has caused an "unmistakable…drift" away from Capitol Hill. "Congress had made repeated efforts since the 1970s to restore legislative prerogatives, with only moderate success," he concludes. "Presidents continue to wield military power single-handedly, agreeing only to consult with legislators and notify them of completed actions. This is not the Framers' model."[104] As James Madison wrote to Thomas Jefferson:

> The constitution supposes, what the History of all Governments demonstrate, that the Executive is the branch of power most interested in war, and most prone to it. It has accordingly with studied care vested the question of war in the Legislature.[105]

For the record, every post-1973 president has denied the WPR's legality, but few at either end of Pennsylvania Avenue are willing to risk having the Supreme Court resolve the question. Lawmakers strive vainly to be consulted. They support the action as long as it is politically feasible. If the crisis persists and the president's actions backfire, however, Congress moves in and sometimes threatens or curtails the action by refusing funds. Congress unquestionably has the constitutional authority to end wars. As Brad Berenson, who served as an attorney in the Bush White House, stated: "I am not aware of a serious dispute over whether it is constitutional for Congress to defund or otherwise terminate the war in Iraq. The big debate is over whether it is wise."[106] An outstanding issue, according to Professor Andrew Bacevich, is whether a Congress that is often too compliant will recognize that its first responsibility "is not to support the commander in chief. It is to exercise independent judgment [about committing the nation to war], an obligation that transcends party."[107]

The WPR has few outright defenders, but lawmakers are not ready to repeal or replace it. Although it diminishes Congress's constitutional power of declaring war, the WPR has some practical virtues. It accommodates the rapid use of armed force without the traditional step of formally declaring war. In the current context, declaring war may not be a viable option. "[Y]ou can't just go off and declare war when you don't know who you are declaring war against," Sen. John B. Breaux, D-La., remarked after the September 11, 2001, attacks. "It is beneath our dignity to declare war against Osama bin Laden," added Sen. Warner.[108]

The WPR gives at least a nodding respect to the framers' belief that Congress, the branch most representative of the people, is the sole source of legal and moral authority for major military enterprises. Presidents may succeed at short-lived actions without a legislative mandate and public support, but longer and more costly engagements will surely falter, as the Korean and Vietnam Wars did. For the time being, then, the enactment stands as a reminder of the ultimate need to gain congressional approval for major military deployments.

Beyond the WPR, Congress has found itself in numerous recent conflicts over the executive's wartime powers, several discussed earlier in Chapters 10 and 12. Such issues, which fell within Congress's historic powers, included information about military operations; jailing and treatment of "enemy combatants" at Guantánamo Bay, Cuba; procedures for determining the guilt or innocence of those taken prisoner; "extraordinary rendition" (abducting individuals and sending them to other countries for interrogation and possible torture); the creation of secret CIA prisons overseas; wide use of the state secrets privilege (a common law doctrine that allows the government to argue in court that cases must be dismissed because they threaten national security); and the alleged torture ("enhanced interrogation") of terrorism suspects by CIA agents. The harsh techniques—among them waterboarding, prolonged sleep deprivation, confinement in a cramped dark space—were authorized by so-called terrorist memos produced by the Office of Legal Counsel of the Department of Justice and approved by top Bush administration officials.[109]

Calls for congressional investigations or the formation of a "truth commission" to undertake a probe of the alleged abuses were met with opposition from various quarters. President Obama rebuffed calls for a truth commission, telling congressional leaders "that he wants to look forward rather than litigating the past."[110] The president wanted Congress to focus on enacting his ambitious agenda rather than investigating whether suspected Al Qaeda captives were tortured. (Worth noting is that President Obama has retained rendition as a counter-terrorism tool as well as the state secrets privilege.[111]) Some lawmakers expressed concern that a congressional investigation would heighten partisan strife. Top congressional leaders were briefed on the interrogation policies by CIA officials, but they have different recollections of what they were told. Experts have disputed whether the enhanced interrogation tactics produced credible intelligence that could not have been obtained by alternative methods.

At this juncture, it appears unlikely that Congress will create an independent commission. What is underway are investigations by congressional panels, including the Senate Intelligence Committee. Senate Majority Leader Harry Reid argued that it would be premature to create an outside entity to investigate the interrogation methods. "It would be very unwise, from my perspective, to start having commissions, boards, tribunals until we find out what the facts are, and I don't know of a better way of getting the facts than through the [Senate] Intelligence Committee," headed by Senator Feinstein.[112]

CONCLUSION

Some politicians still claim that citizens are preoccupied with domestic concerns and thus uninterested in world affairs; but that is apparently a misreading of public sentiment. Researchers have found that a strong majority of citizens endorse an active role for the United States in world affairs. The Iraq war was a prime policy concern of voters in the 2004, 2006, and 2008 elections. And although people are reluctant to use U.S. troops overseas, they support fights against international terrorism, nuclear proliferation, and drug trafficking.[113]

Several developments enhance Congress's obligations in foreign policy. First, the United States continues to exert influence in every corner of the globe: militarily, diplomatically, and culturally. Second, post–Cold War and post–Iraq war conditions, such as those at the end of the George W. Bush presidency, could lead the public to expect more legislative assertiveness in foreign affairs than was previously the case. Third, global interdependence blurs the line that once demarked domestic policy from foreign policy. Insofar as the resulting issues trespass upon traditional domestic matters, they are bound to encourage congressional intervention and influence. Finally, the question of whether the nation is able or willing to underwrite its costly international projects may lead Congress to reassess the nation's global commitments, relying more on multilateral rather than unilateral actions and policies.[114]

Members of Congress dare not abandon their interest in foreign and national security policies. As the world grows ever more interdependent, those policies impinge upon every citizen and every local community. An internationally minded electorate—sensitive to famines and plagues in Africa, deforestation in the Amazon, foreign competition for jobs and trade, and anti-Americanism and terrorism in various regions—may draw fewer distinctions between domestic and global matters than in the past.

Today's legislators genuinely care about world issues. They know that global developments touch their local constituencies, and they believe (rightly or wrongly) that they will be judged to some degree on their mastery of those subjects. "In Lyndon Johnson's age, you just had to be able to say [Soviet premier Nikita] Khrushchev," remarked Sen. Bob Kerrey, D-Neb. (1989–2001). Now, "you need to know the leaders in sixteen former Soviet Union states."

Paradoxically, the militarization of U.S. foreign policy—a disconnect between the nation's military capacity and its diplomatic resources—works to Congress's detriment. Hot (and cold) wars inevitably tend to elevate the presidency and mute legislative voices. If U.S. policy continues to be cast in military instead of diplomatic, cultural, or moral terms, the impulse on Capitol Hill will be to defer to the commander in chief and, if nothing else, to "support the troops." The following warning by former Senate Foreign Relations Committee chair Richard Lugar, R-Ind., is aimed at policymakers at both ends of Pennsylvania Avenue:

[T]he war on terrorism will not be won through attrition—particularly because military action will often breed more terrorism. To win this war, the United States must assign to economic and diplomatic capabilities the same strategic priority we assign to military capabilities. What is still missing from the American political discourse is support for the painstaking work of foreign policy and the commitment of resources to vital foreign policy objectives that lack a direct political constituency.[115]

SUGGESTED READINGS

Crabb, Cecil V., Jr., Glenn J. Antizzo, and Leila E. Sarieddine. *Congress and the Foreign Policy Process.* Baton Rouge: Louisiana State University Press, 2000.

Daalder, Ivo H., and James M. Lindsay. *America Unbound: The Bush Revolution in Foreign Policy.* New York: Wiley, 2005.

Fisher, Louis. *Constitutional Conflicts between Congress and the President.* Lawrence: University Press of Kansas, 2007.

_____. *The Constitution and 9/11.* Lawrence: University Press of Kansas, 2008.

Goldsmith, Jack. *The Terror Presidency: Law and Judgment inside the Bush Administration.* New York: W.W. Norton, 2007.

Hinckley, Barbara. *Less Than Meets the Eye: Foreign Policy Making and the Myth of the Assertive Congress.* Chicago: University of Chicago Press, 1994.

Howell, William G., and Jon C. Pevehouse. *While Dangers Gather: Congressional Checks on Presidential War Powers.* Chicago: University of Chicago Press, 2007.

Lindsay, James M. *Congress and the Politics of U.S. Foreign Policy.* Baltimore: Johns Hopkins University Press, 1994.

Rundquist, Barry S., and Thomas M. Carsey. *Congress and Defense Spending: The Distributive Politics of Military Procurements.* Norman: University of Oklahoma Press, 2002.

Citizens and Congress. Tourists in the 1930s gawk at the Capitol's elaborately decorated rooms (left). In 2008 (top right) young tourists snapped pictures during their Capitol visit when they caught sight of presidential hopeful Sen. Barack Obama. Bottom: The $621 million Capitol Visitors Center, opened in 2008, serves an estimated three million people a year, informs them about Congress's duties and achievements, guides them toward tours of the building and its chambers, offers food and restrooms, and treats them to an unusual view of the Capitol dome.

The Two Congresses and the American People

"That meeting was one of the most astounding experiences I've had in my 34 years in politics," remarked Sen. Charles E. Schumer, D-N.Y., on September 18, 2008.[1] Schumer had just emerged from a summit with then-Treasury secretary Henry M. Paulson, Jr. and Federal Reserve Chair Ben Bernanke. House and Senate leaders, along with a group of lawmakers responsible for oversight of financial markets, had assembled at 7:00 p.m. around a table in the office of House Speaker Nancy Pelosi. Seated under a portrait of Abraham Lincoln, Bernanke somberly detailed the unfolding financial crisis and warned that the entire economy "was on the brink of a heart attack."[2] Over the preceding ten days, the government had seized Fannie Mae and Freddie Mac, the investment bank Lehman Brothers had filed for bankruptcy, Merrill Lynch had been sold at a fire-sale price, and the giant insurance firm American International Group (AIG) had been pulled back from collapse by the federal government's $85 billion emergency loan. Credit markets were frozen, drying up access to credit for consumers and small businesses throughout the country. "I gulped," said Schumer. "We all realized we're not in normal times."[3]

To contain the crisis, the George W. Bush administration sought immediate congressional support for a plan that would allow the Treasury Department to buy up to $700 billion of the distressed assets weighing down the balance sheets of major financial institutions. To put this request in context, "a $700 billion expenditure...would roughly be what the country ha[d] spent so far in direct costs on the Iraq war and more than the Pentagon's yearly budget."[4] The three-page proposal asked for unfettered authority to spend these vast sums, with nothing more than semi-annual reports to Congress.

"Do you know what you are asking me to do?" said Senate Majority Leader Harry Reid, D-Nev. "It takes me 48 hours to get the Republicans to agree to flush the toilets around here."[5] The administration wanted Congress to act in a matter of days. "This is the United States Senate," said Reid. "We can't do it in that time frame."[6]

The 2008 financial crisis was so urgent that "the Capital almost had the feel of wartime."[7] Still, lawmakers understandably balked at authorizing so much taxpayer money with so little deliberation. "Just because God created the world in seven days doesn't mean we have to pass this bill in seven days," quipped Rep. Joe Barton, R-Texas.[8] Not all members were willing to trust the administration's claims of impending financial disaster. "Where have I heard this before? The Iraqis have weapons of mass destruction, and they're ready to use them," complained Rep. Gene Taylor, D-Miss. "I'm in no rush to do this." The bailout proposal was extremely unpopular with constituents, whose flood of calls into members' offices ran as much as 30–1 against.[9] The first effort to pass the bill, on September 30, went down to defeat 228–205 in the House of Representatives.[10] The House's action caused a large-scale sell-off on Wall Street, with the Dow Jones stock index plunging 7 percent in one day.

As days unfolded without a congressional consensus, opinion leaders began to speak of "financial Armageddon"[11] and a "credibility test for Congress."[12] Congress eventually acceded to the administration's $700 billion request, once lawmakers had imposed some limits on the administration of the program. Congress amended the administration's proposal in order to restrict executive compensation, mandate program oversight, and require aid to Americans in danger of losing homes to foreclosure. The amended proposal was approved by Congress and signed into law on October 3, 2008.

But in the end, Congress's efforts to assert more control over the implementation of the bailout largely foundered. In carrying out the program, the Bush administration made a quick reversal, using the funds not to buy toxic assets but to recapitalize banks. It quickly became clear that the banks could not be held accountable for their use of these funds. Treasury also refused to act on mortgage relief. A Brookings Institution report assessing Congress's response to the crisis concludes:

> Congress designed a financial package that allowed the Treasury to spend nearly $350 billion with no accountability for how the money was used, little transparency in how institutions were selected for infusions, no metrics for determining program effectiveness, and no mechanism for forcing the Treasury to comply with the terms of the law that required action to mitigate foreclosures.[13]

Congressional handling of the financial crisis was flawed in many important respects. Nevertheless, economists conceded that the action helped to stabilize the financial system and forestall further damage.[14] But crisis always poses a severe challenge for legislative assemblies. The demand for immediate action runs counter to the deliberative processes that legislatures follow. The congressional process is inherently ponderous, as different perspectives and interests are consulted and majorities are constructed.

The United States is not, as some have claimed, a "presidential nation"; it is a "separated system" marked by the ebb and flow of power among the policymaking branches of government.[15] As Speaker Newt Gingrich, R-Ga. (1995–1999), said of the nation's complex and frustrating governing arrangements:

> We have to get the country to understand that at the heart of the process of freedom is not the presidential press conference. It is the legislative process; it is the give and take of independently elected, free

people coming together to try to create a better product by the friction of their passions and the friction of their ideas.[16]

The legislative "give and take" Gingrich describes inevitably takes time. As a result, fast-moving crises—all too common in an interconnected world of complex financial and security relationships—force Congress to act quickly, often without due deliberation.

Anxious or fearful citizens need to keep in mind the American system's deliberate and fragile interplay among institutions. Citizens' ambivalence toward the popular branch of government provides yet another reminder of the dual character of Congress—the theme that has pervaded our explanations of how Congress and its members work. The two Congresses are manifest in public perceptions and assessments. Citizens evaluate Congress in Washington using different standards and expectations than they use to assess their own senators and representatives.[17] This same duality appears in media coverage: The two Congresses are covered by different sets of reporters working for different kinds of media organizations.

CONGRESS-AS-POLITICIANS

Lawmakers' working conditions and schedules are far from ideal and beg for periodic examination.[18] The hours are killing, the pay comparatively modest, the toll on family life heavy, and the psychic rewards fleeting. A 2007 *Washington Post Magazine* profile of then-freshman Rep. Joe Courtney, D-Conn., sketches his life as follows:

> Rising, going to hearings, meeting with lobbyists, fundraising, speaking on the House floor, taking more meetings, walking to the apartment, crashing, rising....The [DCCC] continues to send him reminders about his fundraising goals: *Get off the Capitol grounds; get to the phone bank; make the calls.*...Another knock. An aide pops in with a reminder: The fundraiser back home is that weekend....'It just never stops. Never.' [The congressman] says, 'You better get used to liking that.'"[19]

"Your schedule is not your own," remarked Sen. Fred Thompson, R-Tenn. (1994–2003), on announcing his retirement.[20] Rep. Joe Scarborough, R-Fla. (1995–2001), complained that "[t]he conflict between being a good congressman and full-time father has grown even greater in recent years."[21] "I'm basically single-parenting," said Representative Courtney's wife Audrey.[22]

Members' Bonds with Constituents

Despite their job pressures, elected representatives are by no means an endangered species. Diligence and attentive home styles yield dividends at the polls. If voters regard elected officials as a class as rascals, they tend to exempt their own elected representative: even in the upheaval year of 2006, only 27 percent of likely voters said their own member of Congress should not be reelected, and only 6 percent of them were actually turned out of office (see Table 3-1). When public approval of Congress stood at 14 percent in 2008,[23] most voters still believed that their own member of Congress deserved reelection.[24]

These large discrepancies between citizens' assessments of their own representatives and of Congress as an institution derive, in part, from divergent expectations. The public places different demands on individual members as compared to Congress as a whole. Legislators are judged on their service to the state or district, their communication with constituents, and their home style. From the institutional Congress, by contrast, the public expects answers to the nation's problems developed in an open and fair policy process. Put differently, Congress is viewed as a national policymaking institution, while individual legislators are seen as agents of personal or localized interests.

Lawmakers forge bonds with voters out of mutual agreement on important issues facing the constituency and the nation. The recruitment process yields representatives who reflect local views and prejudices. As Donald Manzullo, R-Ill., the former chairman of the House Small Business Committee, put it: "Members of Congress see the world through people they represent."[25] Contacts with voters during campaigns and while in office reinforce this convergence of views.

Members' high visibility in their states or districts also helps explain their strong support from constituents. Constituents receive mail from their local representatives, read about them in newspapers and magazines, and see them on television. Large numbers of citizens report having contacts with their representatives. Incumbents miss few opportunities to do favors for constituents, gestures that are usually appreciated and remembered.

Individual senators and representatives present themselves to constituents largely on their own terms, through advertising, self-promotion, and uncritical coverage by local or regional news media. Members devote countless hours to fundraising to ensure that they have the money to purchase all the paid media they need. Reflecting on the hundreds of fundraising calls he makes daily, representative Courtney said, "you could be *Abraham Lincoln*, but if you don't have the heart of a telemarketer, you're not going to make it to Congress."[26] "'Raise money early,' is probably the most oft-repeated advice" given to freshman lawmakers.[27]

Members and their staffs devote constant attention to generating publicity and local press. "I am never too busy to talk to local TV," said a prominent House member. "Period. Exclamation point."[28] A survey of House press secretaries showed virtually unanimous agreement: "We'd rather get in [the hometown paper] than on the front page of the *New York Times* any day."[29] Individual lawmakers tend to bask in the flattering light cast by their local media. Hometown reporters, especially for the electronic media, usually work on general assignment and are ill prepared to question the lawmaker in detail about issues or events. Often their primary goal is simply to get the legislator on tape or film. For politicians this is an ideal situation. They can express their views in their own words with a minimum of editing and few challenges from reporters.

Questions of Ethics

Members' personal ethics, however, are in doubt. In a 2007 survey, a mere 9 percent of respondents rated the honesty and ethical standards of Congress members as high or very high.[30] In a 2006 poll, 69 percent assessed the honesty of members of Congress as either "not so good" or "poor."[31] Assessments of local representatives' ethics and honesty were more favorable: only 30 percent of those in the same poll took such a negative view of their own representative.[32] By any accounting, the public is highly skeptical of congressional ethics.

Standards of Conduct. Public assessments of congressional ethics stand at odds with the views of most political scientists and close observers of the institution. The conventional wisdom among experts is that the vast majority of lawmakers are dedicated and ethical in their behavior. "Members of Congress behave better than people think," declares former representative Lee H. Hamilton, D-Ind. (1965–1999).[33]

Despite public distrust, lawmakers' behavior today is more transparent and less corrupt than in the past. Members' rising qualifications, broader public scrutiny, and reforms in campaign finance, disclosure, and ethics procedures have all helped curtail corruption.[34] Money used to flow freely under the table. "Back in the old days, it was a common occurrence that you walked around with envelopes of cash in your pocket" to hand out to powerful lawmakers, recalled a Washington lobbyist.[35] Today, campaign contributions and direct lobbying expenses are reported and subject to scrutiny by reporters and civic groups. Although large loopholes remain, contemporary financial abuses are rare by pre-1970s standards.

Why Ethics Questions Persist. Why, then, do citizens and commentators remain so contemptuous of lawmakers' ethics? Only 3 percent of respondents in 2006 told pollsters that members' ethical conduct had improved in recent years; a third thought ethics had declined, and 60 percent rated them as unchanged.[36]

One answer is that, unfortunately, unethical behavior persists despite the network of laws and rules intended to restrain it. In 2006 four members of Congress resigned under ethical clouds, including two sentenced to jail terms for bribery.[37] Furthermore, Congress's internal processes to police members' ethical violations fail to inspire public confidence. Members typically cringe at passing judgment on their peers. The result of this reluctance is often "a moribund ethics process."[38]

Organized interests and lobbies are no less eager than in the past to manipulate lawmakers and bend public policy to their wishes. Most notable is the recent mega-scandal centered on lobbyist Jack Abramoff, who advanced the interests of the gambling industry by means of donations, luxury trips, and favors for some half-dozen lawmakers (most, but not all, Republicans). Abramoff's schemes even went so far as to buy off conservative groups normally opposed to gambling to advance the interests of his clients. "I don't think we have had something of this scope, arrogance, and sheer venality in our lifetimes," remarked Norman J. Ornstein, long-time analyst of the Hill scene.[39] Abramoff pleaded guilty in 2006 to fraud, tax evasion, and conspiracy to bribe public officials.[40] His case reverberated into 2008, with the electoral defeat of two additional House incumbents who had been associated with Abramoff.[41]

Second, changing standards of personal behavior have cast new light upon issues of personal habits and conduct. Sexual misconduct and substance abuse, for example, are less tolerated today than they were a generation ago. Reports of adulterous affairs ended the careers of would-be Speaker Bob Livingston, R-La. (1977–1999) and Rep. Gary A. Condit, D-Calif. (1989–2003). Rep. Mark Foley, R-Fla. (1995–2006) resigned after becoming the subject of media frenzy following revelations of salacious instant messages that he sent to House pages. Foley's replacement, Rep. Tim Mahoney, D-Fla., lost his first bid for reelection in 2008 after news broke that he had "multiple" affairs while in office, and had hired one of his lovers as a congressional staffer. In June 2009, Sen. John Ensign, R-Nev., stepped down from his position as chair of the Republican Policy Committee after admitting an affair with a campaign staffer.

The public's concern with congressional corruption is fed by spasmodic but intense media focus on scandal. The media exert great enterprise and energy investigating personal indiscretions and ethical violations, regardless of how atypical of lawmakers generally such failings might be. The diligent work of law-abiding members attracts little attention, while an ethical lapse—or even rumors of one—makes headlines. As a GOP media consultant expressed it, "If I have a choice between announcing a plan to cure cancer or attacking my opponent over some crazy ethical thing, I think the ethical thing will always get coverage. So the need gets fed."[42]

In addition, the intensified regulation of public life paradoxically fuels public skepticism of congressional ethics. So many rules govern the public activities of lawmakers that they can unintentionally run afoul of them. "High-level public officials are particularly good targets for investigation," law professor Cass Sunstein explains, "if only because of the complex network of statutes that regulate their behavior."[43] Elected officials are scrutinized by the Federal Election Commission, the House and Senate ethics committees, and occasionally by the Justice Department and federal prosecutors (see Box 16-1 on congressional ethics). A number of "watchdog" groups, such as Citizens for Responsibility and Ethics in Washington and Judicial Watch, also closely monitor ethics issues and publicize the results of their investigations.

Some of these inquiries uncover real wrongdoing that warrants legal punishment or defeat at the polls. But many scandals are merely driven by political opponents of the accused. Members of Congress, challengers, and party operatives all opportunistically seize on any ethical miscue, real or manufactured, for political advantage. In the early weeks of the 110th Congress, a number of media outlets ran stories criticizing Speaker Nancy Pelosi's apparent demand for a larger jet for trips home than the one used by her predecessor. It later surfaced that the request for a larger jet came not from the Speaker herself but from the House sergeant at arms because of security concerns and the added distance (Pelosi lives in California, her predecessor in Illinois).[44] That did not, however, prevent Speaker Pelosi's detractors from using the story to push a

BOX 16-1   **Congressional Ethics**

Members of Congress are bound by the U.S. Constitution, federal laws, party provisions, and House and Senate rules and conduct codes. Although many observers criticize loopholes, the panoply of regulations is extensive.

► **Constitution.** Each chamber has the power to punish its members for "disorderly behavior" and, by a two-thirds vote, to expel a member. Members are immune from arrest during attendance at congressional sessions (except for treason, felony, or breach of peace) and "for any speech or debate in either house, they shall not be questioned in any other place" (Article I, Section 6). This latter provision protects lawmakers from any reprisals for expressing their legislative views.

► **Criminal Laws.** Federal laws make it a crime to solicit or accept a bribe; to solicit or receive "anything of value" for performing any official act or service, or for using influence in any proceeding involving the federal government; to enter into or benefit from any contracts with the government; or to commit any fraud against the United States. Lawmakers involved in the so-called Abscam affair were convicted in 1981 for violating these statutes.

► **Ethics Codes.** Adopted in 1968 and substantially tightened in 1977, 1989, 1995, 1997, and 2007, the House and Senate ethics codes apply to members and key staff aides. The codes require extensive financial disclosure; restrict members' outside earned income (to 15 percent of salaries); prohibit unofficial office accounts that many members used to supplement official allowances; impose stricter standards for using the frank for mailings; and ban lawmakers from accepting most meals and gifts from lobbyists. The House Committee on Standards of Official Conduct and the Senate Select Ethics Committee implement the codes, hear charges against members, issue advisory opinions, and recommend disciplinary actions.

► **Party Rules.** Congressional parties can discipline members who run afoul of ethics requirements. House Democratic and Republican rules require a committee leader who is indicted to step aside temporarily; a leader who is censured or convicted is automatically replaced.

► **Federal Election Campaign Act Amendments of 1974.** As amended again in 1976 and 1979, the Federal Election Campaign Act imposes extensive requirements on congressional incumbents as well as challengers. Additional rules and penalties are set in the Bipartisan Campaign Reform Act of 2002.

► **Office of Congressional Ethics.** Established by the House of Representatives in 2008, the Office of Congressional Ethics is an independent, non-partisan board of eight private citizens charged with reviewing allegations of misconduct against House members and staff and, when appropriate, referring matters to the Committee on Standards of Official Conduct.

media narrative that she was abusing the privileges of her office. In his study of the impact of what he calls "the ethics culture" on federal appointments, G. Calvin Mackenzie writes:

Instead of getting out of the way so the winners can govern, the losers begin guerrilla operations that never cease, using every weapon and every opportunity to attack, harass, embarrass, and otherwise weaken those who hold office. If you cannot beat them in an election, current practice now suggests, then do everything in your power to keep the winners from governing and implementing their policy priorities.[45]

In other words, ethics charges and countercharges are often nothing more than "politics by other means."[46] Nevertheless, the political uses of ethics charges ensure that they are continually in the public eye, undercutting perceptions of lawmakers generally.

"A Small Class of People." Do these hazards of public life deter "the best and the brightest" from seeking elective office? It is hard to answer that question. Young people, for example, show lamentably scant interest in government careers; yet their idealism often leads them to pursue other paths of public service.[47] The difficulties of balancing a parental or caregiving role with the round-the-clock demands of the lawmaker's life do appear to fall especially hard on women. Research suggests that the relentless schedule is an important reason why so few women run for political office.[48]

American democracy requires that ambitious people put themselves forward as candidates. Although open seats seem to have little shortage of claimants, many of the ablest individuals—especially in one-party areas—decide to sit on the sidelines. The unwillingness of talented, experienced politicians to challenge sitting incumbents raises the specter of unaccountability. In fact, the paucity of strong challengers is a major factor in the extremely high incumbent reelection rates. Parties frequently have great difficulty recruiting good challengers to run against officeholders. The outcomes of congressional elections almost always reveal at least a few underperforming incumbents who would have been vulnerable to defeat, had they only drawn a credible opponent who could muster the resources to mount an effective challenge.[49] Congressional elections would be more competitive if greater numbers of talented individuals were willing to enter the fray.

The rising demands and costs of congressional life probably lie beyond the reach of average men and women. Two political scientists suggest also that if "the public strongly disapproves of Congress, sitting members may decide against seeking reelection and prospective candidates may decide against running for a seat in the first place."[50] Reflecting on the multiplicity of presidential duties, Woodrow Wilson once remarked that Americans might be forced to pick their leaders from among "wise and prudent athletes—a small class of people."[51] The same might now be said of senators and representatives.

CONGRESS-AS-INSTITUTION

People expect an active and productive Congress. Opinion surveys have consistently found that people prefer that Congress play a strong, independent policymaking role. People want Congress to check the president's initiatives and to examine the president's proposals carefully.[52] They often endorse the notion of divided government: the White House controlled by one party but checked by another party controlling Capitol Hill.

Policy Success and Stalemate

Americans are often unaware of the ways that Congress affects their daily lives. Former representative Lee H. Hamilton tells the following story.

> [A] group of [young people] visiting my Indiana office told me that Congress was irrelevant. So I asked them a few questions. How had they gotten to my office? On the interstate highway, they said. Had any of them gone to the local university? Yes, they said, admitting they'd got some help from federal student loans. Did any of them have grandparents on Social Security and Medicare? Well sure, they replied, picking up on where I was headed. Their lives had been profoundly affected by Congress. They just hadn't focused on all of the connections before.[53]

Congress's response to public problems has produced many innovative policies. In an intriguing experiment, Paul C. Light of the Brookings Institution set out to identify the federal government's most influential actions over a fifty-year period.[54] A survey of historians and political scientists served to winnow a preliminary roster of 588 items to a list of fifty "greatest achievements." For the record, the top three successes were judged to be rebuilding Europe after World War II (the Marshall Plan, 1947), expanding the right to vote (Voting Rights Act of 1965), and promoting equal access to public accommodations (Civil Rights Act of 1964).

In every case Light uncovered, Congress played a vital role in the policy's inception, ratification, or implementation. Although Congress was not always the initiator, many programs associated with given presidents—for example, the Marshall Plan (Harry S. Truman) and Medicare (Lyndon Johnson)—began as proposals on Capitol Hill. "No one party, Congress, or president can be credited with any single achievement....Rather, achievement appears to be the direct product of endurance, consensus, and patience."[55]

Despite its past policy innovations, most people could compile a must-do legislative agenda that would include many items left unattended by recent Congresses. The American public is concerned that Congress fails to debate and take leadership on major policy issues. According to a recent survey, citizens are worried that Congress pays too little attention to long-term problems, such as Social Security, global warming, energy issues, and infrastructure maintenance. The survey's analyst, Paul Light, concluded: "What we found is there is tremendous demand for answers. [The citizens] may not know exactly what to do, but they're very, very worried."[56]

Recent Congresses have produced relatively few major new policy initiatives. In fact, Congress has regularly had to postpone even routine matters such as annual appropriations bills, resorting instead to passing continuing resolutions (CRs). Bills to reauthorize federal agencies and programs often lapse or are renewed without much debate. Agencies and programs are thus funded via the appropriations process without formal scrutiny and review by the appropriate authorizing committees.

A recurrent question among pundits and analysts in the early months of the Obama presidency is whether the administration has "too much on its plate" in putting forward a far-reaching agenda encompassing major changes to health care, energy, and climate change policies.[57] *New York Times* congressional reporter Carl Hulse asks whether "Congress can shake the rust from its legislative machinery and overcome the powerful inertia that has gripped it in recent years."[58] "We have been miniaturized," said Sen. Olympia J. Snowe, R-Maine, reflecting on the dearth of recent legislative achievements, "You have three talking points on a card. We are going to have to be taught and relearn the process, crack the notebooks."[59]

Assessments of the Congressional Process

Congress's institutional shortcomings are numerous and obvious. Beyond its structural and procedural complexities, the quality of its deliberations often falls short of democratic ideals.

Deliberation. Legislative assemblies are primarily designed to foster deliberation. "The assembly makes possible a deliberation in which conflicting judgments about the public good...can be examined, debated, and resolved," writes Richard Hall, "And through such a process the actions of government achieve legitimacy."[60] Recent developments have significantly undermined the quality and quantity of congressional deliberation. In order to cope with the pressures of lawmaking in a highly polarized and partisan environment, leaders of both parties tend to "short-circuit regular deliberative procedures in committee, on the floor, and in conference."[61]

The contemporary congressional process has morphed into a wide variety of highly centralized improvisations—what Barbara Sinclair has termed "unorthodox lawmaking."[62] Leaders package together disparate policies into omnibus vehicles so bulky that only a small number of staff aides and members know what provisions have been inserted or left out. Outcomes are normally predetermined, especially in the House, where majority party leaders oversee the pre-floor negotiations and craft the rules for debate. Most important measures are considered under restrictive or closed rules permitting few or no amendments.[63] Floor deliberations are then just a series of desultory recitations—public speaking in this country having become something of a lost art. Under such circumstances, lawmakers are often shocked and embarrassed by provisions they have voted into law.

Committee deliberation has been similarly weakened. Committee meetings are frequently poorly attended, with the outcomes laid out by the chairman and his majority-party colleagues. Leaders routinely bypass committee consideration altogether, bringing unreported bills directly to the floor. Staff resources for House and Senate committees were cut by more than one-third between

1979 and 2005.[64] "Committees have been marginalized in myriad ways, from central party direction to ad hoc groups to omnibus bills."[65] As committees become less consequential policymaking arenas, members have less incentive to develop policy expertise in the matters before their committees.

Even House-Senate interactions are less deliberative in character. Today's congressional leaders frequently avoid the conference process altogether, convening "pro-forma" conferences to ratify deals worked out in leadership offices or exchanging bills back and forth between the chambers. On occasion, House-Senate negotiations have even excluded minority-party conferees. Such tactics streamline the legislative process but forfeit the benefits of deliberation.

Another factor weakening congressional deliberation is Congress's frantic stop-and-go work schedule. Although earlier members did not live in the nation's capital, most of them stayed in town for weeks at a stretch, their days dominated by extended hearings or deliberations. By the mid-twentieth century, a minority of members—mostly from the eastern corridor—constituted a "Tuesday–Thursday club," spending long weekends at home. Nowadays nearly all members follow such a schedule, which often shrinks to Tuesday night-to-Thursday afternoon. And extended nonlegislative or "district work periods" surround all the major holidays. The results on Capitol Hill can be seen in declining workload numbers: fewer days in session, fewer committee and subcommittee hearings, and fewer bills introduced and processed.[66]

A blunt assessment comes from the thirty-four-year House veteran Hamilton, co-chair of the 9/11 Commission and the Iraq Study Group:

> Congress doesn't work enough at its true job. Members of Congress spend too much of their week campaigning, and not enough of it doing the hard work of governing. Building a consensus behind an approach to a national problem is tough; it takes negotiation, extended discussion, and hard study. This is impossible when you spend three days on Capitol Hill and then rush home for an extended weekend of appearances.[67]

One remedy would seem simple: longer sessions (two weeks at least) alternating with periods for constituency work or official travel. After the 2006 election, the new House leaders promised a more intensive schedule.[68] Compared to its predecessor, the 110th Congress stayed in session significantly more days and longer hours, but the difference was more notable in the first session than the second.[69] Leaders repeatedly pledge more rational scheduling, only to be thwarted by members demanding more time at home for campaigning.

Comity and Bipartisanship. A second institutional malady is the decline of interpersonal comity—the product of several converging factors, most notably the escalating cohesion within, and polarization between, the two parties. Nelson Polsby has described the contemporary period as an "era of ill feeling" in Congress.[70]

The contemporary Congress has been persuasively faulted for engaging in a "destructive form of partisanship" that prevents bipartisan give-and-take.[71]

As leaders centralize power, minority party members have less chance of being heard. "Oh, those were frustrating years," recalled former Republican leader Robert Michel of Illinois, who served in the minority for all of his thirty-eight years in the House (1957–1995):

> But...I never really felt I was out of the game or that I had no part to play. Under the rules of the House, the traditions of the House...there is a role to play for the minority....We struck a deal, we made a bargain [and worked at] bringing dissident factions together...to craft good legislation for the country. That was the joy of it![72]

Michel's successor and former staff aide, Rep. Ray LaHood, R-Ill. (now President Obama's secretary of transportation), explained that Michel "taught us by example that the House floor should be a forum for reasoned debate among colleagues equal in dignity. He came to the House every day to do the work of the people, and not to engage in ideological melodramas or political vendettas."[73]

Observing the unpredictable and not always coherent policies produced by bipartisan dealmaking in the mid-twentieth century Congress, many political scientists lamented the absence of "party government." They preferred a democratic politics in which parties would run on coherent platforms and command the leadership and unity to enact their programs into law. Key elements of the party government model have come to pass in the contemporary Congress. The parties are far more internally homogeneous; the caucuses meet regularly to decide policy; members' party-line voting presents clear alternatives to voters. Far from lifting the quality of policymaking, however, partisanship has been blamed for escalating the level of rancor and stalemate. Former representative and deputy GOP whip Mickey Edwards of Oklahoma (1977–1993) decries "partisanship in the extreme" which extends beyond policy or ideological differences:

> Instead of morphing from candidates to members of Congress on the day they are sworn in, today's legislators engage in permanent campaigning. Neither party is willing to allow the other to gain credit for an achievement that might help it in the next election, so the center aisle that divides Democrats from Republicans in the House has become a wall.[74]

Senate Roadblocks. Nowhere has the rise of partisanship created more obstacles for policymaking than in the Senate. For much of the Senate's history, filibusters were rare, employed for matters of great constituency or regional importance. Today they have become "a partisan tool."[75] The partisan filibuster—in which most or all of the Senate majority party's agenda is systematically blocked by an organized minority-party filibuster—is a recent innovation. Barbara Sinclair's research dates the organized partisan filibuster to the first two years of the Clinton presidency (the 103rd Congress, 1993–1995), in which Republican-led filibusters obstructed half of all major measures.[76]

The development of the partisan filibuster means that the Senate has evolved into an institution that has exceptional difficulty in governing. "The reality is that because of Senate rules, it takes 60 votes to order pizza, let alone to consider and vote on important pieces of legislation," quipped Rep. Jim McGovern, D-Mass.[77] "Requiring a supermajority to pass legislation that is at all controversial makes the coalition-building process much more difficult and increases a status quo–oriented system's tendency toward gridlock," writes Barbara Sinclair. "The costs of gridlock can be severe: a government that cannot act, that cannot respond satisfactorily to its citizens' demands, loses its legitimacy."[78]

Senate Democrats' large majority in the 111th Congress will allow them to push legislation through the body without Republican support, but only if they can maintain partisan unanimity. With veteran Senate Republican Arlen Specter's switch to the Democratic Party and the probable seating of Minnesota's Al Franken, the Democrats alone may be able to muster the sixty votes needed to stop a filibuster. But even within a single party, constructing 60-vote Senate majorities on controversial legislation is not easy.

Transparency. A fourth important issue is access to information about Congress. "Why focus on transparency?" ask the founders of the Sunlight Foundation, a nonpartisan group begun in 2006. "Because a major cause of voter mistrust is a feeling special interests are served by those who do their bidding in the belief they will not be detected."[79] Some aspects of the process must still be sheltered—for example, certain national security information and details of legislative bargaining—but many elements could be available or more easily searchable on electronic sites. The Sunlight Foundation's "Open House" manifesto, published in 2007, embraces such reforms as online availability of members' financial statements, lobbying expenses, "earmarks" (members' requests for constituency spending projects), senators' "holds" (halting floor debate on bills), and reports of such Hill support agencies as the Congressional Research Service (CRS).

The Perils of Reform. Reforming Congress is often touted as a solution to its organizational or procedural faults. The House and Senate themselves periodically engage in self-examination (the last broad-scale inquiry took place in 1993). Such efforts are often impeded by the two Congresses dilemma: that is, structural reforms may threaten members' electoral interests. E. Scott Adler warns, for example, that "[a]ny widespread change in the established order of policy deliberation—particularly in its centerpiece, the committee system— would create far too much uncertainty in members' electoral strategies."[80]

Congress's history nonetheless records a number of major planned innovations—affecting deliberation as well as electoral arrangements. Reformers with different and often conflicting goals—enhancing legislative power and efficiency, gaining partisan or policy advantage, or augmenting individual lawmakers' perquisites—have coalesced around significant reforms. Because of the variety of goals involved, however, the results achieved are often different from those anticipated.

In his survey of forty-two major institutional innovations of the past century, Eric Schickler explains that "preexisting institutions create constituencies for their preservation that typically force reformers with new goals to build upon, rather than dismantle, these structures."[81] An example was the series of new budget procedures piled like so many building blocks on top of the authorization-appropriations process in the 1974–1990 period. Little wonder that such reforms fall short of their sponsors' objectives. Instead of achieving stable, effective arrangements, what results is "a set of institutions that often work at cross-purposes."[82]

Media Coverage

The most open and accessible of the branches of government, Congress is covered by a large press corps containing some of the nation's most skilled journalists. As CBS News reporter Bob Schieffer notes, Capitol Hill is the best news beat in Washington.[83]

Paradoxically, however, neither reporters nor their editors are able to convey the internal subtleties or the external pressures that shape lawmaking. Moreover, the very media best suited to reporting Congress—serious daily newspapers and magazines—are suffering long-term declines in circulation. Their traditional readers are dying off. Younger-age cohorts tend to shun print media in favor of video and electronic outlets—to the extent they seek information on politics at all.[84]

In response, major mass media outlets have curtailed their coverage of Congress and national and global politics in general. Pressrooms have been downsized; most foreign bureaus have been closed. Bottom-line pressures on the media are threatening the nation's democratic processes by leaving people less informed, declared veteran TV news anchor Walter Cronkite in a recent speech at Columbia University. In today's complex world, "the need for high-quality reporting is greater than ever," he said. "It's not just the journalist's job at risk here. It's American democracy."[85]

"The market nature of reporting," writes James T. Hamilton, a Duke University political scientist, "leads to simple rules of thumb: Cover the horse race in politics; focus on the human impact of government policies; treat bad news more often than good news; and talk to your targeted audience."[86] Even prestigious daily papers and news magazines have curtailed public affairs coverage in favor of stories about celebrities, entertainment, and lifestyle issues. The first cover of *Time* magazine in 1926 portrayed former House Speaker Joseph G. Cannon, R-Ill. (1903–1911). Today, political figures—other than presidents—are rarely seen on the covers of *Time* and its competitors. "I went to a Red Sox game on Saturday, and up above home plate I couldn't help but notice the press box," observed *Washington Post* reporter William Arkin, "[there were] five, six, seven tiers of desks, filled with print, radio, television.…It dawned on me that there were more reporters covering the Sox, just one baseball team, than cover the Pentagon."[87]

The decline has been equally drastic in television (including the so-called all-news channels), where most Americans receive their news about government and politics. "Apart from technology," observes journalist Bill Moyers, "the biggest change in my thirty years in broadcasting has been the shift of content from news about government to consumer-driven information and celebrity features."[88] Radio and TV talk shows are chronic offenders. Although they spend much airtime on issues of one kind or another, their content and style are typically ill-informed, combative, and contemptuous of politicians and their work.[89]

Political news has changed in content as well as coverage. Fewer stories appear on policy issues and more on scandal, wrongdoing, or corruption. Following the canons of investigative journalism, reporters play the role of suspicious adversaries on the lookout for good guys and bad guys, winners and losers. Ethical problems, congressional pay and perquisites, campaign war chests, and foreign junkets are frequent targets of their investigations. Such stories reinforce popular negative stereotypes about Congress as an institution.

As mentioned earlier, divergent press coverage—local versus national media—widens the gap between the two Congresses' distinct images: more positive for individual members than for the institution. It is still true that "Americans love their congressmen much more than they love their Congress."[90] Individual lawmakers tend to be well known, sympathetically judged, respectfully covered by the local media, and—most important—reelected. Congress as an institution, in contrast, is covered by the national press with lots of skepticism and cynicism. In short, the two Congresses are viewed through different lenses, reported by different channels of communication, and judged by different criteria.

Citizens' Attitudes toward Congress

If individual members get respectable marks, people often seem ready to flunk Congress as a whole (see Table 16-1). The institutional Congress usually ranks well below respondents' own representatives in public esteem. Citizens' ratings of the job Congress is doing fluctuate with economic conditions, wars and crises, scandals, and waves of satisfaction or cynicism (see Figure 16-1). Approval of Congress surged briefly after it handled the Watergate affair in 1974, after the Republican takeover twenty years later, before the Clinton scandal of 1998, and in the wake of the Democrats' takeover in 2006.

After the 2001 terrorist attacks, positive appraisals of Congress soared to a historic 84 percent, double the approval level taken immediately before September 11. In Gallup polling dating back to 1974, Congress's approval had never been higher than 56 percent. But patriotic bubbles eventually burst. By 2006 an average of just 25 percent of Americans approved of the way Congress was handling its job—the worst showing in more than ten years.[91]

Although extensively reported in the media with gavel-to-gavel televised coverage of its floor proceedings on C-SPAN, Congress is not well understood by the average citizen. Partly to blame are the institution's size and complexity, not to mention the arcane twists and turns of the legislative process. "What Congress does when the subcommittee on acoustics and ventilation meets,"

TABLE 16-1 **High Approval for Members, Low Approval for Congress**	
Individual members	**Congress as an institution**
Serve constituents	Resolves national issues only with difficulty or not at all
Run against Congress	Has few defenders
Emphasize personal style and outreach to constituents	Operates as collegial body that is difficult for citizens to understand
Are covered by local media in generally positive terms	Is covered by national media, often negatively (with focus on scandals and conflicts)
Respond quickly to most constituent needs and inquiries	Moves slowly with cumbersome processes that inhibit rapid responses
Are able to highlight personal goals and accomplishments	Has many voices but none can speak clearly for Congress as a whole

Sources: Timothy E. Cook, "Legislature vs. Legislator: A Note on the Paradox of Congressional Support," *Legislative Studies Quarterly* 4 (February 1979): 43–52; Glenn R. Parker and Roger H. Davidson, "Why Do Americans Love Their Congressmen So Much More Than Their Congress?" *Legislative Studies Quarterly* 4 (February 1979): 53–61; and Richard Born, "The Shared Fortunes of Congress and Congressmen: Members May Run from Congress but They Can't Hide," *Journal of Politics* 52 (November 1990): 1223–1241.

remarks Sen. Ron Wyden, D-Ore., "is often achingly dull, which is why most Americans pay scant attention."[92]

Many citizens find more distasteful the core attributes of lawmaking: controversy, messiness, and compromise. Dissention is on display on Capitol Hill to a greater extent than in other branches of government. Although this same messiness is found in the other branches of government, it is more visible and continuous in Congress. The president speaks with one voice: Even though there is fierce competition for the president's ear, a simple statement from the president defines the administration's position. As for the judiciary, opinions are frequently divided or unclear, as judges and justices disagree about law and policy, but their decisions are usually accepted as law. By contrast, no single member, not even the institution's top leaders, speaks for Congress.

The public's ambivalence toward Congress goes far deeper than unhappiness with specific policies or disgust with scandals, if the sobering conclusions of John R. Hibbing and Elizabeth Theiss-Morse are to be believed.

> People do not wish to see uncertainty, conflicting opinions, long debate, competing interests, confusion, bargaining, and compromised, imperfect solutions. They want government to do its job quietly and efficiently, sans conflict and sans fuss. In short…they often seek a patently unrealistic form of democracy.[93]

FIGURE 16-1   **Public Assessments of the Two Congresses, 1974–2009**

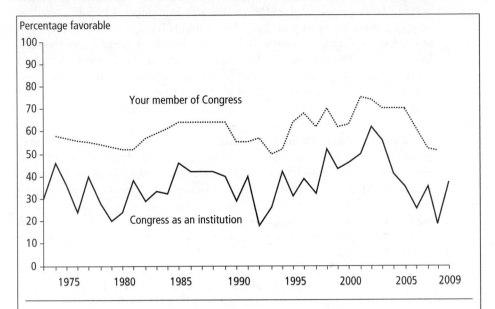

Source: Authors' interpolations of surveys of the Gallup Organization and the Harris Survey. Poll database, Roper Center for Public Opinion, University of Connecticut (www.ropercenter.uconn.edu); the Gallup Organization (www.gallup.com).

Note: The Gallup Organization's questions are "Do you approve of the way the U.S. Congress is handling its job? Do you approve or disapprove of the way the representative from your own congressional district is handling his/her job?" The Harris Survey's questions are "How would you rate the job done this past year by [Congress] [your member of Congress]—excellent, pretty good, only fair, or poor?" Responses are dichotomized as favorable ("excellent," "pretty good") or unfavorable ("only fair," "poor"). The plotted points in the figures indicate respondents having opinions who approve of or are favorable toward congressional performance.

In other words, people seem to abhor the very attributes that are the hallmarks of robust representative assemblies. As Hibbing and Theiss-Morse observe, Congress "is structured to embody what we dislike about modern democratic government, which is almost everything."[94]

TWENTY-FIRST-CENTURY CHALLENGES

The U.S. Congress is now in its third century. Survival for more than two centuries is no mean feat. Perhaps it resembles Dr. Johnson's dog (noted not for its proficiency at walking on its hind legs but for being able to do so at all). Congress has withstood repeated stress and turbulence, including a civil war, political assassinations, terrorist attacks, domestic scandals, and contentious foreign involvement. It is sobering to realize that the U.S. constitutional system is far older than most of the world's existing governments.

Global Threats and Alarms

The physical setting of the U.S. Capitol now exhibits the stepped-up security arrangements prevalent elsewhere since the September 11, 2001, terrorist attacks. Only a few short years ago, visitors and Hill personnel moved freely in and out of the Capitol and surrounding office buildings. Members of the public may still visit most Capitol Hill facilities, but they now encounter uniformed officers, metal detectors, and concrete barriers. One welcome development, however, is the long-needed Capitol Visitors' Center—constructed under the East Front—that enhances the building's safety while introducing visitors to Congress and its work.

Congressional Continuity. The possibility of future terrorist attacks forces people to think the unthinkable about the physical continuity of Congress. If the Capitol were attacked, how could the House members killed in the attack be quickly replaced? Nearly every state empowers governors to fill Senate seats temporarily, but under the Constitution House seats must be elected, which would entail time-consuming special elections. What could be done about incapacitated members? What would happen if the nation's capital were destroyed or uninhabitable?

Various constitutional amendments have been suggested to allow for the temporary appointment of House members in the event a catastrophe caused mass vacancies. A bipartisan Continuity of Government Commission recommended an amendment empowering Congress to enact legislation addressing a range of continuity questions.[95] House majorities have opposed the idea of appointing temporary members, even to fill vacancies caused by some calamity. Instead the House has passed legislation to require the states to conduct expedited special elections to fill vacancies if, for example, a terrorist attack killed large numbers of lawmakers. It also adopted at the start of the 109th Congress a provisional quorum rule that would allow the House to function if scores of members were incapacitated. The Senate, too, has introduced proposals to allow "each chamber to set terms for replacing members who die or are unable to function."[96] These modest initiatives have not satisfied reformers' concerns. "Our leaders' failure to establish a plan to ensure that our Constitution survives is irresponsible," writes Norman Ornstein. "Do we really have to wait until the nightmare scenario becomes a reality to do something?"[97]

Policy Challenges. Mere survival, though, may be the least of Congress's challenges. In a world of uncertain global challenges, Congress continues to face divisive domestic issues, such as economic crisis, energy sustainability, climate change, infrastructure renewal, economic inequality, and health care reform.

On top of these continuing domestic issues are global challenges linked to an ongoing campaign against terrorists plus war and reconstruction in Afghanistan and Iraq. Among the collateral damages inflicted by wartime conditions is the quality of deliberation—and deliberateness—essential to legislative processes. In its haste to respond to terrorist attacks, Congress gave scant attention to details of the vast grants of power it ceded to the president and the executive branch by approving, for example, open-ended military action, the problematic USA PATRIOT Act, and the 180,000-employee Homeland Security Department. "Congress has ceded its war power to the president," asserts former representative Hamilton, who sums up the institution's failures:

> The Founders explicitly gave the powers to declare and fund war to Congress. Yet Congress in recent years has rolled over and refused to take a hard look at the executive branch's war rationale and execution of plans for an end-game. Congress has failed to act as a separate and independent body, and to provide essential oversight during times of great need.[98]

Congress shied away from debate in approving the Iraq War resolution. "We have left the field," confessed Sen. Richard J. Durbin, D-Ill. "This is the largest grant of presidential authority ever given by a Congress."[99] Sen. Robert C. Byrd, D-W.Va., whose Senate career began in 1959, put it this way on the eve of the Iraq war, in an eloquent speech to an almost empty chamber:

> We stand passively mute in the Senate today, paralyzed by our own uncertainty, seemingly stunned by the sheer turmoil of events....But today we hear nothing, almost nothing, by way of debate....
> The rafters should ring. The press galleries should be filled. Senators should be at their seats listening to questions being asked about this war, questions to which the American people out there have a right to expect answers. The American people are longing for information and they are not getting it. This chamber is silent....We are truly sleepwalking through history.[100]

Congress nonetheless showed some signs of regaining its equilibrium once the initial shock waves had subsided from the terrorist attacks and the Afghanistan and Iraq wars. Issues of costs, waste and fraud, personnel deployments, war contracting, prisoners' treatment, and foreign policy implications began to be explored.

Checks and Imbalances?

The constitutional system of divided powers and competing branches does not yield a stable equilibrium. Powers ebb and flow among the branches. Crises tend to elevate the presidency, whereas more peaceful times are friendlier to congressional power. An activist bench can drive the judiciary into political thickets; at other times, the bench defers to the other branches.

Executive Hubris. Even before the September 11, 2001, attacks, members of the Bush administration tended to belittle or dismiss congressional prerogatives. The wellspring of this view came from Vice President Dick Cheney, whose most significant White House experience had taken place during Gerald R. Ford's presidency, which coincided with the zenith of a post–Vietnam War, post-Watergate congressional resurgence—a fleeting era. That experience led him to the historically dubious view that chief executives "are weaker today as an institution because of the unwise compromises" on the part of past presidents. He vowed "to pass on our offices in better shape than we found them."[101]

Through September 10, 2001, White House claims met with robust resistance on Capitol Hill. The attacks of September 11, 2001, profoundly altered the stakes and resources in the ongoing constitutional struggle. By the start of Bush's second term, the vice president could claim that "there has been over time a restoration, if you will, of the power and authority of the president."[102] If Cheney's historical analysis was flawed, his vision of the future seemed confirmed: broad, unchecked White House prerogatives, countered only by reactive, intermittent legislative involvement.

Executive branch encroachments upon legislative prerogatives are, admittedly, neither new nor confined to crisis periods. Most modern presidents have fought for broader leeway in spending appropriated funds and freedom to reorganize agencies and redeploy their personnel. President George W. Bush had precedent on his side when he used rulemaking powers to install policies Congress was unlikely to approve. Bush also was not the first president to abandon treaties without legislative consultation. Nor was he the first to issue "signing statements" to air his own interpretation of enactments.

Presidents and their appointees naturally seek to control information about what they are doing. But the Bush administration made secrecy a watchword. The White House refused to share documents with Congress, permit certain executive officials to testify before congressional committees, or otherwise cooperate with investigative hearings.[103] Staunch GOP committee chairmen Charles E. Grassley of Iowa (Senate Finance), Henry J. Hyde of Illinois (House International Relations), and F. James Sensenbrenner Jr. of Wisconsin (House Judiciary) repeatedly protested the executive's failure to provide information. (Sensenbrenner went so far as to threaten to subpoena information from the Justice Department.)[104] Similar roadblocks were encountered by later probes of intelligence failures, contracting procedures in combat zones, and treatment of detainees held secretly in Iraq, Guantánamo Bay, and elsewhere.

Despite the actions of a handful of frustrated GOP committee leaders, Congress's overall response to executive-branch stonewalling in the 2001–2007 period was not a profile in courage. Here is former representative Hamilton's sober judgment:

> A Congress that was serious about exercising its prerogatives would have administration officials on Capitol Hill every day, asking tough questions on all kinds of topics, grilling them on their policy decisions and investigating how they'd chosen to implement federal programs.... [C]ongress has long been supine in the face of presidential assertions of authority and denial of information, making the vision of government laid out by our Founders barely recognizable today.[105]

"The failure of Congress over much of the Bush administration to challenge the president's regular and far-reaching assertions of executive power was one of the main reasons we referred to the legislature as "the broken branch," write the authors of a Brookings Institution report on congressional performance.[106] Then-GOP representative Ray LaHood conceded the point: "Our party controls the levers of government. We're not about to go out and look beneath a bunch of rocks and try and cause heartburn."[107]

Loyalty to a president from the majority party (as in 2001–2007) should be no excuse for congressional timidity. Partisan loyalties did not immunize past presidents of both parties, from Franklin D. Roosevelt to Ronald Reagan to Bill Clinton, against probing oversight and sometimes fierce opposition led by their party's leaders on Capitol Hill—even in wartime. If lawmakers do not fiercely defend their prerogatives, they have only themselves to blame when executives ignore them.

In the waning years of the Bush administration after the opposition Democrats took control of Congress in the 2006 elections, committee and subcommittee chairmen began more vigorously to challenge executive-branch policies and practices. But in reining in electronic surveillance, investigations into Justice Department abuses of power, and extracting testimony from top White House officials, the new congressional leadership had only limited success in the 110th Congress.[108]

An open question is whether the Democrats' unified party control will inhibit effective oversight during the Obama administration. Democratic leaders of Congress have signaled some independence. Speaker Pelosi directed committee chairs to submit a timeline of their planned oversight hearings.[109] Senate Majority Leader Reid indicated that Vice President Joe Biden would not be welcome at Democratic senators' weekly caucus luncheons (a change from Republican senators' policy with respect to Vice President Dick Cheney). Congressional assertiveness may well crumble under the pressures of partisan and presidential politics during Democrats' unified control, just as it did in the Republican Congresses of the Bush administration.

Judicial Lawmaking. Congress at the same time faces attacks upon its powers from an activist federal judiciary, which has invalidated federal enactments in more than thirty cases since 1995. For the first time since the late 1930s, the courts challenged federal laws in such areas as interstate commerce and civil rights, often in the name of guarding states' rights. By narrow majorities, for example, the U.S. Supreme Court curbed the 1990 Americans with Disabilities Act on grounds it had not dared to apply to earlier civil rights statutes. The hoary charge of "judicial activism" continues to be flung at the federal courts, which are now overwhelmingly staffed by Republican nominees. Despite this reality, many lawmakers and outside groups continue to attack the (increasingly conservative) courts over a handful of ideologically tinged issues.

Few people, however, seem troubled by rulings regarding fundamental state and federal authority. Federal circuit court judge John T. Noonan Jr., a Reagan appointee, argues that the Supreme Court's elevation of states' rights over congressional power has "invented criteria for Congress that invaded the legislative domain."[110] Whatever the constitutional arguments, future activist courts could constrict legislative powers in much the same way that late-nineteenth-century courts gutted the Civil War constitutional amendments. As Noonan explains, "If five members of the Supreme Court are in agreement on an agenda, they are mightier than five hundred members of Congress with unmobilized or warring constituencies."[111]

Is Congress Permanently Damaged? Following the Vietnam War and the Watergate scandal, Congress valiantly tried to reclaim prerogatives that had slipped away during the Cold War period. A new equilibrium seemed to have been established; but the reform fervor was short-lived. In his detailed account of congressional initiatives, James L. Sundquist sums up that era:

> The 1970s were a period of upheaval, of change so rapid and so radical as to transform the pattern of relationships that had evolved and settled into place over the span of half a century or more. But by the end of the decade the spirit of resurgence…had waned.[112]

Although a brief period of balance between the branches ensued, Sundquist accurately predicted the coming of "a new cycle of slow decline of the Congress in favor of the president."[113]

Reflecting upon that new cycle of events, Andrew Rudalevige of Dickinson College revisits the 1970s question: "Is there a new imperial presidency?" His short answer is yes:

> [P]residents have regained freedom of unilateral action in a variety of areas, from executive privilege to war powers to covert operations to campaign spending….The default position between presidents and Congress has moved toward the presidential end of the interbranch spectrum—and irreversibly so.[114]

Is this trend irreversible? As defenders of the constitutional system, we remain cautiously hopeful of the future. Partisans of all stripes, after all, have a long-term stake in an active, robust legislative branch. Executive initiatives, however popular they may seem, demand critical review; executive programs must be overseen and evaluated.

What will the future hold? Much depends on a series of unanswered questions: Will members of Congress fulfill their constitutional duties and mount credible critiques of executive power-seeking? Will citizens reignite their interest in politics—to learn, speak, and vote in order to counteract excesses of power, whatever their source? Former representative Hamilton's assessment is on the mark. Citizens, he says,

> must understand that they need to get involved if they want our system to improve. They need to know that the nature of this relationship between the representative and the represented—and the honesty of the exchange between the two—shapes the strength of our representative democracy.[115]

Unfortunately, no advocate of the framers' constitutional design can offer confident solutions to these dilemmas. So we conclude with questions for the twenty-first century. Are the two Congresses ultimately compatible? Or are they diverging, each detrimental to the other? Whatever the size of the federal government, the burden placed on both Congresses would remain heavy by historical standards. Congress-as-institution is expected to resolve all kinds of problems, not only by processing legislation but also by monitoring programs and serving as an all-purpose watchdog. Legislators struggle to keep abreast of these demands.

Recent events are not encouraging; but the question remains whether representative democracy will in the end be a winning or losing effort. History is only mildly reassuring, and the future poses new and difficult challenges for which the margin of error may be narrower than ever before. And yet representative democracy itself is a gamble. The proposition that representation can yield wise policymaking remains a daring one. As always, it is an article of faith whose proof lies inevitably in the future.

SUGGESTED READINGS

Adler, E. Scott. *Why Congressional Reforms Fail: Reelection and the House Committee System.* Chicago: University of Chicago Press, 2002.

Binder, Sarah A., Thomas E. Mann, Norman J. Ornstein, and Molly Reynolds. *Mending the Broken Branch: Assessing the 110th Congress, Anticipating the 111th.* Brookings Institution Report, January 2009, http://www.brookings.edu/papers/2009/0108_broken_branch_binder_mann .aspx.

Bok, Derek. *The Trouble with Government.* Cambridge: Harvard University Press, 2001.

Cook, Timothy E. *Making Laws and Making News: Media Strategies in the U.S. House of Representatives.* Washington, D.C.: Brookings Institution, 1989.

Davidson, Roger H., ed. *Workways of Governance: Monitoring Our Government's Health.* Washington, D.C.: Governance Institute/Brookings Institution Press, 2003.

Hamilton, Lee H. *How Congress Works, and Why You Should Care.* Bloomington: Indiana University Press, 2004.

Hibbing, John R., and Elizabeth Theiss-Morse. *Stealth Democracy: Americans' Belief about How Government Should Work.* Cambridge: Cambridge University Press, 2002.

Mackenzie, G. Calvin, with Michael Hafken. *Scandal Proof: Do Ethics Laws Make Government Ethical?* Washington, D.C.: Brookings Institution Press, 2002.

Mann, Thomas E., and Norman J. Ornstein, *The Broken Branch: How Congress Is Failing America and How to Get It Back on Track.* New York: Oxford University Press, 2006.

Rudalevige, Andrew. *The New Imperial Presidency: Renewing Presidential Power after Watergate.* Ann Arbor: University of Michigan Press, 2005.

Wolfensberger, Donald. *Congress and the People: Deliberative Democracy on Trial.* Washington, D.C.: Woodrow Wilson Center Press, 2000.

Reference
Materials

APPENDIX A   Party Control: Presidency, Senate, House, 1901–2011

Congress	Years	President	Senate			House		
			D	R	Other	D	R	Other
57th	1901–1903	William McKinley/ Theodore Roosevelt	31	55	4	151	197	9
58th	1903–1905	T. Roosevelt	33	57	—	178	208	—
59th	1905–1907	T. Roosevelt	33	57	—	136	250	—
60th	1907–1909	T. Roosevelt	31	61	—	164	222	—
61st	1909–1911	William Howard Taft	32	61	—	172	219	—
62d	1911–1913	Taft	41	51	—	228	161	1
63d	1913–1915	Woodrow Wilson	51	44	1	291	127	17
64th	1915–1917	Wilson	56	40	—	230	196	9
65th	1917–1919	Wilson	53	42	—	216	210	6
66th	1919–1921	Wilson	47	49	—	190	240	3
67th	1921–1923	Warren G. Harding	37	59	—	131	301	1
68th	1923–1925	Calvin Coolidge	43	51	2	205	225	5
69th	1925–1927	Coolidge	39	56	1	183	247	4
70th	1927–1929	Coolidge	46	49	1	195	237	3
71st	1929–1931	Herbert Hoover	39	56	1	167	267	1
72d	1931–1933	Hoover	47	48	1	220	214	1
73d	1933–1935	Franklin D. Roosevelt	60	35	1	313	117	5
74th	1935–1937	F. D. Roosevelt	69	25	2	319	103	10
75th	1937–1939	F. D. Roosevelt	76	16	4	331	89	13
76th	1939–1941	F. D. Roosevelt	69	23	4	261	164	4
77th	1941–1943	F. D. Roosevelt	66	28	2	268	162	5
78th	1943–1945	F. D. Roosevelt	58	37	1	218	208	4
79th	1945–1947	Harry S. Truman	56	38	1	242	190	2
80th	1947–1949	Truman	45	51	—	188	245	1
81st	1949–1951	Truman	54	42	—	263	171	1
82d	1951–1953	Truman	49	47	—	234	199	1
83d	1953–1955	Dwight D. Eisenhower	47	48	1	211	221	1
84th	1955–1957	Eisenhower	48	47	1	232	203	—
85th	1957–1959	Eisenhower	49	47	—	233	200	—
86th[a]	1959–1961	Eisenhower	65	35	—	284	153	—
87th[a]	1961–1963	John F. Kennedy	65	35	—	263	174	—
88th	1963–1965	Kennedy/ Lyndon B. Johnson	67	33	—	258	177	—

Congress	Years	President	Senate D	R	Other	House D	R	Other
89th	1965–1967	Johnson	68	32	—	295	140	—
90th	1967–1969	Johnson	64	36	—	247	187	—
91st	1969–1971	Richard M. Nixon	57	43	—	243	192	—
92d	1971–1973	Nixon	54	44	2	254	180	—
93d	1973–1975	Nixon/ Gerald R. Ford	56	42	2	239	192	1
94th	1975–1977	Ford	60	37	2	291	144	—
95th	1977–1979	Jimmy Carter	61	38	1	292	143	—
96th	1979–1981	Carter	58	41	1	276	157	—
97th	1981–1983	Ronald Reagan	46	53	1	243	192	—
98th	1983–1985	Reagan	45	55	—	267	168	—
99th	1985–1987	Reagan	47	53	—	252	183	—
100th	1987–1989	Reagan	55	45	—	258	177	—
101st	1989–1991	George Bush	55	45	—	260	175	—
102d	1991–1993	Bush	57	43	—	268	166	1
103d	1993–1995	Bill Clinton	56	44	—	258	176	1
104th	1995–1997	Clinton	47	53	—	204	230	1
105th	1997–1999	Clinton	45	55	—	207	227	1
106th	1999–2001	Clinton	45	55	—	211	223	1
107th	2001–2003	George W. Bush	50	49	1	210	222	3
108th	2003–2005	Bush	48	51	1	205	229	1
109th	2005–2007	Bush	44	55	1	202	232	1
110th[b]	2007–2009	Bush	49	49	2	233	202	—
111th[c]	2009–2011	Barack Obama	58	40	2	257	178	—

☐ Republican control   ☐ Democratic control

Source: Encyclopedia of the United States Congress, ed. Donald C. Bacon, Roger H. Davidson, and Morton Keller (New York: Simon and Schuster, 1995), 1556–1558.

Note: Figures are for the beginning of the first session of each Congress and do not include vacancies, subsequent shifts, or changes in party affiliation.

[a] The House in the 86th and 87th Congress had 437 members because of an at-large representative given to both Alaska (January 3, 1959) and Hawaii (August 21, 1959) prior to redistricting in 1962.

[b] The two Senate Independents caucused with the Democrats, giving them a 51–49 majority for the purpose of organizing the chamber.

[c] For the Senate, we have counted as Democrats Arlen Specter, who shifted parties in April 2009, and Al Franken of Minnesota, who was declared winner by 312 votes but who had not been certified as of press time. Although most observers believe he will eventually be seated, his opponent's appeal to the Minnesota Supreme Court could alter the outcome.

Capitol Hill is an excellent place to obtain first-hand experience with the U.S. government. With 541 lawmakers (representatives, senators, delegates, and resident commissioners); hundreds of committees and subcommittees; scores of informal caucuses; and three congressional support agencies (the Congressional Research Service, Government Accountability Office, and Congressional Budget Office), intern opportunities abound for students interested in experiencing Congress and its members up close and personal.

Undergraduates will find useful information about landing an internship on Capitol Hill in several sources. One of the best is published under the auspices of the American Political Science Association and is titled *Studying in Washington: Academic Internships in the Nation's Capital.* Political scientist Stephen E. Frantzich discusses how to get a good internship, make the most of the experience, and find a place to live in Washington, D.C.

From our own years of "soaking and poking" around Capitol Hill, we offer five observations about getting congressional experience. First, no central clearinghouse exists for internships. Every congressional office, committee, caucus, and support agency manages its own internship program. Contact information and intern applications may be found on member and committee Web sites (www.house.gov and www.senate.gov). Many intern opportunities are available for minority students, such as through the Congressional Hispanic Caucus Institute (www.chci.org) or the minority access internship program (www.minorityaccess.org). You must be persistent, patient, and determined to find a position that will be a rewarding learning experience. Not only should you find out what duties and functions will be assigned to you as a volunteer intern (it is sometimes possible to secure paid internships), but you also need to remember that you have something useful to offer. Most congressional offices and committees are understaffed and subject to high staff turnover. Although the market for interns is competitive, congressional lawmakers, committees, and staffers want and need your talent.

Second, develop some notion as to where you would like to intern. Do research on the committee, lawmaker, support agency, or caucus that interests you. Remember that every office has its own personality. Senate offices, for instance, are often large enterprises with many staff aides, while House offices generally are smaller. Interns thus will have more opportunities for personal, day-to-day contact with House members than with senators. The best way to determine the office environment is by interviewing people who have worked in a particular office, talking with the internship coordinators at your college or university, or visiting the office yourself.

Third, target your own representative and senators. Many congressional members prefer interns from their own state or district who are likely to be familiar with the geography and concerns of that area. In addition, potential interns probably will have family and friends who are constituents of the lawmaker. Do not hesitate to use your contacts. You might also volunteer to work in a state or district office of the lawmaker. Before accepting an internship, consider your own views and ideals. If your views are conservative, working for a lawmaker who espouses liberal causes may be difficult. However, if you are tactful and open-minded, working for someone whose views differ from yours may be instructive. Because you are a student, an internship with someone who holds divergent ideological views probably will not be held against you later in landing a position.

Fourth, intern placement opportunities are plentiful. Many colleges and universities sponsor semester programs in Washington, D.C. Several schools, including the American University, Boston University, Hamilton College, the State University of New York, the University of Southern California, and the University of California run programs in Washington, D.C. Some accept students from other accredited colleges and universities. The Washington Center for Internships and Academic Seminars, in existence since 1975, has placed thousands of students from hundreds of colleges.

Finally, Congress needs and welcomes the influx of new ideas and experiences that interns bring with them. The work at times may be drudgery—answering mail and telephones, entering information into computers, and running errands—but the opportunity to learn about Congress and to pick up political smarts not easily available from textbooks is nearly without equal. You may even want to keep a private journal of your experiences: what you have done and what you have learned. In sum, a volunteer job on Capitol Hill is likely to be rewarding intellectually and in other ways that are impossible to predict.

RESOURCES

The Congressional Intern Handbook. Washington, D.C.: Congressional Management
    Foundation, 2006.
Fleishman, Sandra. "The Annual Scramble: Washington Interns Line Up for Their First
    Lesson—in Housing Supply and Demand." *Washington Post,* May 29, 2004, F1.
Frantzich, Stephen E. *Studying in Washington: Academic Internships in the Nation's Capital.*
    5th ed. Washington, D.C.: American Political Science Association, 2002.
Joyce, Amy. "Interns Seek Their Place in the Sun." *Washington Post,* July 11, 2004, F4.
Lee, Jennifer. "Crucial Unpaid Internships Increasingly Separate the Haves from the Have-
    Nots." *New York Times,* August 10, 2004, 16.
Manning, Jennifer E. "Internships, Fellowships, and Other Work Experience Opportunities in
    the Federal Government," CRS Report 98-654, January 29, 2007. Provides useful listings and
    bibliographies of internships.
Maxwell, Bruce. *Insider's Guide to Finding a Job in Washington: Contacts and Strategies to
    Build Your Career in Public Policy.* Washington, D.C.: CQ Press, 1999.
Peterson's Internships. Princeton, N.J.: Peterson's Guides. Annual.
Reeher, Grant, and Mack Mariani, eds. *The Insider's Guide to Political Internships: What to Do
    Once You're in the Door.* Boulder, Colo.: Westview Press, 2002.

Strand, Mark, Michael S. Johnson, and Jerome F. Climer, *Surviving Inside Congress* (Washington, D.C.: The Congressional Institute, 2009).

Washington Center for Internships and Academic Seminars. Address: 2301 M Street N.W., Washington, D.C. 20037. Telephone: (202) 336-7600 or (800) 486-8921. Web site: www.twc.edu/internships/index.htm.

Washington Information Directory. Washington, D.C.: Congressional Quarterly. Annual publication that provides information about governmental and nongovernmental groups as well as addresses and phone numbers for congressional offices and committees.

CHAPTER 1

1. *Congressional Record,* 110th Cong., 2d sess., September 25, 2008, H9949.
2. Thaddeus McCotter, "Opposing Paulson Plan, Outlining Alternative," Member Blog, Republican Policy Committee, September 24, 2008, www.houserepublicanpolicy.org/opposing-paulson-plan-outlining-alternative (accessed December 31, 2008).
3. Lori Montgomery, "Automakers Press High-Stakes Plea for Aid; Senators Greet CEOs' Request With Skepticism," *Washington Post,* November 19, 2008, A1.
4. David M. Herszenhorn and Bill Vlasic, "Auto Executives Face a Hard Sell on Capital Hill," *New York Times,* December 5, 2008, A1.
5. Charles L. Ballard, "An Overview of the Michigan Economy," in *Michigan at the Millennium,* ed. Charles L. Ballard, Paul N. Courant, and Douglas C. Drake (East Lansing: Michigan State University Press), 13–34.
6. Alec Friedhoff and Howard Wial, "Bearing the Brunt: Manufacturing Job Loss in the Great Lakes Region, 1995–2005," Metropolitan Economy Initiative, Number 1, The Brookings Institution, July 2006, www.brookings.edu/reports/2006/07useconomics_wial.aspx (accessed December 30, 2008).
7. Thaddeus G. McCotter, "Congressman McCotter: Defending Communities, Families and American Automobile Jobs," press release, November 20, 2008.
8. Ibid.
9. Quoted in David M. Herszenhorn, "About Those Charges of Bailout Bias," *New York Times,* December 7, 2008, WK3.
10. Thaddeus G. McCotter, "Now, Seize Freedom!" *The American Spectator,* November 5, 2008.
11. Stephen Dinan and Ralph Z. Hallow, "At 'Rock Bottom' GOP Choosing Leaders," *Washington Times,* November 6, 2008, A1.
12. Quoted in Stephen Dinan, "Republican Rips Bush for Caving on Principles: Sees Congress Leadership Purge," *Washington Times,* October 30, 2008, A1.
13. Paul S. Herrnson, *Congressional Elections: Campaigning at Home and in Washington,* 5th ed. (Washington, D.C.: CQ Press, 2008), 272.
14. Sam Rayburn, *Speak, Mr. Speaker,* ed. H. G. Dulaney and Edward Hake Phillips (Bonham, Texas: Sam Rayburn Foundation, 1978), 263–264. Rayburn was Speaker from 1940 to 1947, 1949 to 1953, and 1955 to 1961.
15. U.S. Congress, House Committee on Administrative Review, *Administrative Management and Legislative Management,* 2 vols., H. Doc. 95–232, 95th Cong., 1st sess., September 28, 1977, 2: 18–19.
16. Frank E. Smith, *Congressman from Mississippi* (New York: Random House, 1964), 127.
17. David R. Mayhew, *Congress: The Electoral Connection* (New Haven: Yale University Press, 1974), 16.
18. Alan Abramowitz, "A Comparison of Voting for U.S. Senator and Representative in 1978," *American Political Science Review* 74 (September 1980): 633–640; Richard F. Fenno Jr., *The United States Senate: A Bicameral Perspective* (Washington, D.C.: American Enterprise Institute, 1982), 29ff; and Frances E. Lee and Bruce I. Oppenheimer, *Sizing Up the Senate: The Unequal Consequences of Equal Representation* (Chicago: University of Chicago Press, 1999), 111–113.

19. U.S. Congress, Joint Committee on the Organization of Congress, *Organization of the Congress, Final Report,* 2 vols., H. Rep. 103–14, 103d Cong., 1st sess., December 1993, 2: 275–287. See also Table 5-2 in this book.

20. Glenn R. Parker and Roger H. Davidson, "Why Do Americans Love Their Congressmen So Much More Than Their Congress?" *Legislative Studies Quarterly* 4 (February 1979): 53–61; Kelly D. Patterson and David B. Magleby, "Public Support for Congress," *Public Opinion Quarterly* 56 (winter 1992): 539–540; and Randall B. Ripley, Samuel C. Patterson, Lynn M. Mauer, and Stephen V. Quinlan, "Constituents' Evaluations of U.S. House Members," *American Politics Quarterly* 20 (October 1992): 442–456.

21. On how the public's perceptions of the policy process affect Congress's institutional image, see John R. Hibbing and Elizabeth Theiss Morse, *Congress As Public Enemy: Public Attitudes Toward American Political Institutions* (New York: Cambridge University Press, 1995).

22. Alexander Hamilton, James Madison, and John Jay, *The Federalist Papers,* No. 51, ed. Clinton Rossiter, (New York: Mentor, 1961), 322.

23. *The Federalist Papers,* No. 52, 327.

24. Edmund Burke, "Speech to Electors at Bristol," in *Burke's Politics,* ed. Ross J. S. Hoffman and Paul Levack (New York: Knopf, 1949), 116.

25. Burke, "Speech to Electors at Bristol."

26. Quoted in *Roll Call,* September 9, 1993, 16.

27. *U.S. Term Limits v. Thornton,* 115 S. Ct. 1842 (1995).

28. Quoted in Mark Carl Rom, "Why Not Assume That Public Officials Seek to Promote the Public Interest?" *Public Affairs Report* 37 (July 1996): 12.

29. For an accessible discussion of different voting systems, see Douglas J. Amy, *Behind the Ballot Box: A Citizen's Guide to Voting Systems* (Westport, CT: Praeger, 2000), 65.

30. For an analysis of members facing this representational difficulty, see Richard F. Fenno, Jr., *Home Style: House Members in Their Districts* (Boston: Little, Brown, 1978), especially pages 91–99 and 102–114.

31. Fenno, *Home Style: House Members in Their Districts,* 168.

32. Matt Taibbi, "The Worst Congress Ever: How Our National Legislature Has Become a Stable of Thieves and Perverts—in Five Easy Steps," *Rolling Stone,* November 2, 2006, 46.

33. Woodrow Wilson, *Congressional Government* (1885; reprint, Baltimore: Johns Hopkins University Press, 1981), 210.

34. Thomas E. Mann and Norman J. Ornstein, *The Broken Branch: How Congress is Failing America and How to Get it Back on Track* (New York: Oxford University Press, 2006), 141–191.

CHAPTER 2

1. Joseph J. Ellis, *His Excellency George Washington* (New York: Alfred A. Knopf, 2006), 184–186.

2. Alvin M. Josephy Jr., *On the Hill: A History of the American Congress* (New York: Simon and Schuster, 1980), 41–48.

3. Charles A. Beard and John P. Lewis, "Representative Government in Evolution," *American Political Science Review* (April 1932): 223–240.

4. Jack P. Green, ed., *Great Britain and the American Colonies, 1606–1763* (New York: Harper TorchBooks, 1970), xxxix.

5. Edmund C. Burnett, *Continental Congress* (New York: Norton, 1964).

6. *Congressional Quarterly's Guide to Congress,* 5th ed., vol. I (Washington, D.C.: CQ Press, 2000), 9.

7. Burnett, *Continental Congress,* 171. When quoting the Constitution in this volume, the authors use modern capitalization.

8. Jack N. Rakove, *The Beginnings of National Politics: An Interpretive History of the Continental Congress* (New York: Knopf, 1979), 43.

9. Charles C. Thach Jr., *The Creation of the Presidency, 1775–1789: A Study in Constitutional History* (Baltimore: Johns Hopkins University Press, 1969), 34.

10. James Sterling Young, "America's First Hundred Days," *Miller Center Journal* 1 (winter 1994): 57.

11. On the Framers' general consensus on the need for a stronger national government, see Lance Banning, "The Constitutional Convention," in *The Framing and Ratification of the Constitution,* ed. Leonard W. Levy and Dennis J. Mahoney (New York: Macmillan, 1987); and John P. Roche, "The Founding Fathers: A Reform Caucus in Action," *American Political Science Review* 55 (1961): 799–816.

12. John Locke, *Two Tracts on Government,* ed. Philip Abrams (New York: Cambridge University Press, 1967), 374.

13. Alexander Hamilton, James Madison, and John Jay, *The Federalist Papers,* No. 48, ed. Clinton Rossiter (New York: Mentor, 1961), 308.

14. Joseph Story, *Commentaries on the Constitution of the United States,* 5th ed., vol. 1 (Boston: Little, Brown, 1905), 396. For Justice Robert Jackson's comments, see *Youngstown Sheet and Tube Co. v. Sawyer,* 343 U.S. 579, 635 (1952).

15. Mark A. Peterson, "The Three Branches of Government: Powers, Relationships and Checks" in *A Republic Divided,* eds. The Annenberg Democracy Project (New York: Oxford University Press, 2007), 105.

16. *Nixon v. United States,* 506 U.S. 224 (1993).

17. *The Federalist Papers,* No. 65, 396.

18. Emily Field, Van Tassel, and Paul Finkelman, *Impeachable Offenses: A Documentary History from 1787 to the Present* (Washington, D.C.: Congressional Quarterly, 1999).

19. Patrick O'Connor, "Hastert Tells President Bush FBI Raid Was Unconstitutional," *The Hill,* May 24, 2006, 8.

20. *In re Search of the Rayburn House Office Bldg., Room 2113, Washington, DC, 20515* 432 F. Supp. 2d 100, 113 (D.D.C. 2006).

21. *U.S. v. Rayburn House Office Bldg., Room 2113, Washington, DC, 20515,* 497 F.3d 654 (D.C. Cir. 2007).

22. *U.S. v. Rayburn House Office Bldg., Room 2113, Washington, DC, 20515,* cert. denied, 128 S. Ct. 1738 (2008).

23. *Marbury v. Madison,* 1 Cranch 137 (1803).

24. *The Constitution of the United States of America: Analysis and Interpretation,* S. Doc. 92–80, 92d Cong., 2d sess., 1973, 1597–1619. Recent figures are courtesy of Kenneth Thomas, Legislative Attorney in the American Law Division, Congressional Research Service.

25. Figures cited in this paragraph are from: J. Mitchell Pickerill, "Congressional Responses to Judicial Review." in *Congress and the Constitution,* eds. Neal Devins and Keith E. Whittington (Durham and London: Duke University Press, 2005), 159.

26. William N. Eskridge Jr., "Overriding Supreme Court Statutory Interpretation Decisions," *Yale Law Journal* 101 (November 1991): 331–455. See also R. Shep Melnick, *Between the Lines: Interpreting Welfare Rights* (Washington, D.C.: Brookings Institution, 1994).

27. *Ledbetter v. Goodyear Tire & Rubber Co.,* 550 U.S. 618 (2007).

28. *Dred Scott v. Sandford,* 60 U.S. 393 (1856).

29. *Immigration and Naturalization Service v. Chadha,* 463 U.S. 919 (1983).

30. Louis Fisher, *Constitutional Dialogues: Interpretation as Political Process* (Princeton: Princeton University Press, 1988), 275.

31. Quoted in Charles Warren, *The Making of the Constitution* (Boston: Little, Brown, 1928), 162.

32. Quoted in Charles Warren, *The Supreme Court in United States History* (Boston: Little, Brown, 1919), 195.

33. Wendy J. Schiller, "Building Careers and Courting Constituents: U.S. Senate Representation: 1889–1924," *Studies in American Political Development* 20 (fall 2006): 185–197.

34. See Charles Stewart III, "Responsiveness in the Upper Chamber: The Constitution and the Institutional Development of the Senate," in *The Constitution and American Political Development,* ed. Peter F. Nardulli (Urbana: University of Illinois Press, 1992), 63–96; and Gregory J. Wawro and Eric Schickler, *Filibuster: Obstruction and Lawmaking in the U.S. Senate* (Princeton: Princeton University Press, 2006).

35. Joel H. Silbey, *The Partisan Imperative: The Dynamics of American Politics Before the Civil War* (New York: Oxford University Press).

36. Sarah A. Binder, *Minority Rights, Majority Rule* (New York: Cambridge University Press, 1997), 49.

37. Norman J. Ornstein, Thomas E. Mann, and Michael J. Malbin, *Vital Statistics on Congress, 2001–2002* (Washington, D.C.: American Enterprise Institute Press, 2002), 126–127.

38. See Jefferson's Manual, Section XI; House, *Rules of the House of Representatives,* H. Doc. 105–358, 105th Cong., 2d sess., 1999, 145–148.

39. Nelson W. Polsby, "The Institutionalization of the House of Representatives," *American Political Science Review* 62 (March 1968): 146–147

40. Norman J. Ornstein, Thomas E. Mann, and Michael J. Malbin, *Vital Statistics on Congress, 2001–2002* (Washington, D.C.: American Enterprise Institute Press, 2002), 149.

41. Eric Schickler, "Institutional Development of Congress," in *The Legislative Branch,* ed. Paul J. Quirk and Sarah A. Binder (New York: Oxford University Press), 40. Ornstein, Mann, and Malbin, *Vital Statistics on Congress,* 149.

42. George B. Galloway, *History of the House of Representatives* (New York: Crowell, 1961), 67.

43. Joseph Cooper and Cheryl D. Young, "Bill Introduction in the Nineteenth Century: A Study of Institutional Change," *Legislative Studies Quarterly* 14: 67–105.

44. Barbara Sinclair, *Unorthodox Lawmaking: New Legislative Processes in the U.S. Congress* (Washington, D.C.: CQ Press, 2005).

45. Andrew J. Taylor, "Size, Power, and Electoral Determinants: Exogenous Determinants of Legislative Procedural Choice," *Legislative Studies Quarterly* 31 (August 2006): 338.

46. Eric Schickler, "Institutional Development of Congress," 40.

47. Roger H. Davidson and Walter J. Oleszek, *Congress Against Itself* (Bloomington: Indiana University Press, 1977), 14; cited in Eric Schickler *Disjointed Pluralism: Institutional Innovation and the Development of the U.S. Congress* (Princeton: Princeton University Press, 2001), 142.

48. Quoted in Schickler, *Disjointed Pluralism,* 142.

49. James L. Sundquist, *The Decline and Resurgence of Congress* (Washington, D.C.: Brookings Institution Press, 1982).

50. Julian E. Zelizer, *On Capitol Hill: The Struggle to Reform Congress and Its Consequences, 1948-2000* (New York: Cambridge University Press, 2004), 153.

51. Roy Swanstrom, *The United States Senate, 1787–1801,* S. Doc. 99–19, 99th Cong., 1st sess., 1985, 283.

52. Gary W. Cox and Mathew McCubbins, *Setting the Agenda: Responsible Party Government in the U.S. House of Representatives* (Cambridge, U.K.: Cambridge University Press, 2005).

53. Sarah A. Binder, *Minority Rights, Majority Rule,* 17.

54. Ibid., 84.
55. David R. Mayhew, *Congress: The Electoral Connection* (New Haven: Yale University Press, 1974), 95.
56. See David W. Rohde, *Parties and Leaders in the Postreform House* (Chicago: University of Chicago Press, 1991); and Nelson W. Polsby, *How Congress Evolves: Social Bases of Institutional Change* (New York: Oxford University Press, 2004).
57. See Sarah A. Binder and Steven S. Smith, *Politics or Principle? Filibustering in the United States Senate* (Washington, D.C.: Brookings Institution Press, 1997), Gregory J. Wawro and Eric Schickler, *Filibuster: Obstruction and Lawmaking in the U.S. Senate* (Princeton: Princeton University Press, 2006), and Sarah A. Binder, Anthony J. Madonna, and Steven S. Smith, "Going Nuclear, Senate Style," *Perspectives on Politics* 5(4): 729–740
58. Schickler, *Disjointed Pluralism,* 13.
59. Ibid., 141–146.
60. Ibid., 213–217.
61. Ibid., 267.
62. Ibid., 267.
63. James Sterling Young, *The Washington Community, 1800–1828* (New York: Harcourt Brace Jovanovich, 1966), 89.
64. Noble Cunningham Jr., ed., *Circular Letters of Congressmen, 1789–1839,* 3 vols. (Chapel Hill: University of North Carolina Press, 1978) 57.
65. Swanstrom, *The United States Senate,* 80.
66. Mildred Amer, *Average Years of Service for Members of the Senate and the House of Representatives, First–109th Congresses,* Congressional Research Service Report RL32648, November 9, 2005. Earlier studies include: Nelson W. Polsby, "The Institutionalization of the House of Representatives," *American Political Science Review* 62 (March 1968): 146–147; and Randall B. Ripley, *Power in the Senate* (New York: St. Martin's, 1969), 42–43.
67. Peter Swenson, "The Influence of Recruitment on the Structure of Power in the U.S. House, 1870–1940," *Legislative Studies Quarterly* 7 (February 1982): 7–36.
68. Ripley, *Power in the Senate,* 43–44.
69. David W. Brady, "After the Big Bang: House Battles Focused on Committee Issues," *Public Affairs Report* 32 (March 1991): 8. See also Samuel Kernell, "Toward Understanding the Nineteenth Century Congressional Career Patterns: Ambition, Competition, and Rotation," *American Journal of Political Science* 21 (November 1977): 669–693; and Nelson W. Polsby, Miriam Gallagher, and Barry S. Rundquist, "The Growth of the Seniority System in the U.S. House of Representatives," *American Political Science Review* 63 (September 1969): 794.
70. Joe Martin as told to Robert J. Donovan, *My First Fifty Years in Politics* (New York: McGraw-Hill, 1960), 49–50.
71. Martin, *My First Fifty Years,* 49.
72. U.S. Congress, House Commission on Administrative Review, *Administrative Reorganization and Legislative Management,* 2 vols., H. Doc. 95–232, 95th Cong., 1st sess., September 28, 1977, 2:17; and U.S. Congress, Senate Commission on the Operation of the Senate, *Senators: Offices, Ethics, and Pressures,* 94th Cong., 2d sess., 1977, Committee Print, xi.
73. Cunningham, *Circular Letters of Congressmen.*
74. Quoted in Galloway, *History of the House,* 122.
75. Quoted in Anthony Champagne, "John Nance Garner," in *Masters of the House: Congressional Leaders over Two Centuries,* ed. Roger H. Davidson, Susan Webb Hammond, and Raymond W. Smock (Boulder, Colo.: Westview Press, 1998), 148.
76. Martin, *My First Fifty Years,* 101.

77. Elaine K. Swift, *The Making of an American Senate* (Ann Arbor: University of Michigan Press, 1996), 5.

78. David C. King, *Turf Wars: How Congressional Committees Claim Jurisdiction* (Chicago: University of Chicago Press, 1997).

CHAPTER 3

1. David Wasserman, "Double-Digit Response?" *National Journal*, July 26, 2008, 31.

2. Under the Seventeenth Amendment to the U.S. Constitution, "When vacancies happen in the representation of any State in the Senate, the executive authority of such State shall issue writs of election to fill such vacancies: Provided, That the legislature of any State may empower the executive thereof to make temporary appointments until the people fill the vacancies as the legislature may direct." See Thomas H. Neale, "Filling U.S. Senate Vacancies: Perspectives and Contemporary Developments," *Congressional Research Service Report* R40421, March 10, 2009.

3. David Kesmodel and Douglas Belkin, "Burris Predicts Senators Will Relent, Let Him Serve," *Wall Street Journal*, January 2, 2009, A3.

4. Brian Bakst, "Franken Is Ahead as Recount For Minnesota Seat Ends," *Washington Post*, January 4, 2009, A2. See Chris Cillizza and Paul Kane, "Franken Looks Like a Winner, but Not Quite a Senator," *Washington Post*, January 5, 2009, A3.

5. Adam Nossiter, "History and Amazement In House Race Outcome," *New York Times*, December 8, 2008, A18.

6. In addition to the delegate from the Northern Mariana Islands, there are four other delegates who have two-year terms and represent the Virgin Islands, Guam, American Samoa, and the District of Columbia. There is also a Resident Commissioner from Puerto Rico, who is elected to a four-year term. To date, all are nonvoting members of the House of Representatives. However, the delegates have the same privileges on the standing committees as other lawmakers.

7. *U.S. Term Limits v. Thornton*, 514 U.S. 779 (1995).

8. Sara Hatch, "Must House Members Be Homegrown to Win?" *Roll Call*, May 10, 2006, 11.

9. Arend Lijphart, *Democracies: Patterns of Majoritarian and Consensus Government in Twenty-one Countries* (New Haven: Yale University Press, 1984), 174.

10. See Gary C. Jacobson, *The Politics of Congressional Elections*, 7th ed. (New York: Pearson Education, Inc., 2009), 16.

11. See Daniel H. Pink, "Givers and Takers," *New York Times*, January 30, 2004, A21.

12. Quoted in Judith Havemann, "Moynihan Poses Questions of Balance," *Washington Post*, August 14, 1995, A15.

13. John D. Griffin, "Senate Apportionment as a Source of Political Inequality," *Legislative Studies Quarterly* 31 (August 2006): 425.

14. This method is only one of several mathematical formulas that could be employed. Another, the major fractions method, was used from 1911 until 1940. The methods yield slightly different results. For example, in 1992 Montana faced the prospect of losing its second House seat. The state challenged the apportionment formula in the courts but was rejected by the Supreme Court, which found no conclusive answer to the question of "what is the better measure of inequality." *Department of Commerce v. Montana*, 503 U.S. 442 (1992). See Linda Greenhouse, "Supreme Court Upholds Method Used in Apportionment of House," *New York Times*, April 1, 1992, B8.

15. Carl Bialik, "Bad Math = Mad Politics," *Wall Street Journal*, April 25, 2008, A10.

16. In 1960, the size of the House was temporarily increased from 435 to 437 members to accommodate the admission of Alaska and Hawaii as states. Three years later the House

reverted back to 435 following the 1960 census. The 110th House, on April 19, 2007, voted to grant full voting rights to the Delegate from the District of Columbia (overwhelmingly Democratic in registration) and to add a House seat to Utah, a GOP state. The Delegate can vote in committees and in a House forum called the Committee of the Whole (see Chapter 8), but not in the full House. The legislation (H.R. 1905) failed to pass Congress but if it had been signed into law, the size of the House would permanently increase to 437.

17. *Guide to Congress,* Vol. II, (Washington, D.C.: CQ Press, 2000), 898.

18. Clark Bensen, "The Political Impact of Katrina: Apportionment in 2010," POLIDATA Press Release, December 22, 2006, 2.

19. Haya El Nasser, "For 2010 Census, the Counting Gets Tougher," *USA Today,* October 8, 2008, 1A.

20. Kathleen Hunter, "Minority Lawmakers to Ask Leadership to Address U.S. Census Undercounts," *CQ Today,* October 29, 2007, 6.

21. Sandy Hume, "GOP Fears 2000 Census Plan Will Overestimate Minorities," *The Hill,* May 7, 1997, 1.

22. Jim Snyder, "Census Bureau Finds It Can't Count Americans Abroad," *The Hill,* March 30, 2006, 17.

23. Charles Mahtesian, "Dollars and Census," *Government Executive,* December 2007, 50.

24. June Kronholz, "Strength in Newcomers' Numbers," *Wall Street Journal,* April 23, 2007, A4.

25. Ibid., A4.

26. The six states are: Arizona, Hawaii, Idaho, Indiana, Montana, New Jersey, and Washington. Iowa has a unique process, in which the legislature's professional nonpartisan legislative staff conducts the congressional line-drawing.

27. Juliet Eilperin, "The Gerrymander That Ate America," Slate, an on-line journal, April 17, 2006. Quoted from her book, *Fight Club Politics: How Partisanship Is Poisoning the House of Representatives* (Lanham, Md.: Rowman & Littlefield, 2006).

28. *Growe v. Emerson,* 507 U.S. 25 (1993). See Susan B. Glasser, "Supreme Court Voids Minnesota Redistricting," *Roll Call,* February 25, 1993, 1.

29. The classic study is still Gordon E. Baker, *The Reapportionment Revolution: Representation, Political Power, and the Supreme Court* (New York: Random House, 1966).

30. In 2001 Georgia Democrats produced a state legislature redistricting plan testing the notion that a population deviation of plus-or-minus 5 percent would be acceptable at the state level. A circuit court panel invalidated the scheme and eventually drew its own plan, which was ultimately affirmed by the Supreme Court. See *Larios v. Cox,* 300 F. Supp. 2d 1320 (N.D. Ga. 2004).

31. Alan Ehrenhalt, "Redistricting and the Erosion of Community," *Governing,* June 1992, 10.

32. Charles Backstrom, Samuel Krislov, and Leonard Robins, "Desperately Seeking Standards: The Court's Frustrating Attempts to Limit Political Gerrymandering," *Political Science and Politics,* July 2006, 411.

33. Quoted in David G. Savage and Scott Gold, "Justices Order Review of Texas' Political Map," *Los Angeles Times,* October 19, 2004, A10.

34. 548 U.S. 399 (2006). This complex case raised no less than four separate issues: (1) whether a state could engage in mid-decade redistricting; (2) whether Texas's partisan gerrymandering violated the "equal protection clause"; (3) whether the plan's breakup of a racially diverse Dallas district violated the voting rights of black voters; and (4) whether the plan violated the rights of Latino voters in southern Texas districts. See Charles Lane and Dan Baltz, "Justices Affirm GOP Map for Texas," *Washington Post,* June 29, 2006, A1.

35. *Davis v. Bandemer,* 478 U.S. 109 (1986).

36. *Vieth v. Jubelirer,* 541 U.S. Ct. 267 (2004).

37. Gregory L. Giroux, "High Court Draws No Bright Lines To Limit Political Gerrymandering," *CQ Weekly,* May 1, 2004, 1019.

38. James A. Gardner, "A Post-*Vieth* Strategy for Litigating Partisan Gerrymandering Claims," *Election Law Journal,* November 4, 2004, 643.

39. *Congressional Record,* July 29, 2008, H7285.

40. Nolan McCarty, Keith T. Poole, and Howard Rosenthal, "Does Gerrymandering Cause Polarization?" *WWS [Woodrow Wilson School] News,* summer 2007, 13.

41. Rhodes Cook, "Do the Math, and the Result Is: Not Much of a Contest," *Washington Post,* October 6, 2002, B3.

42. Charles Backstrom, Samuel Krislov, and Leonard Robins, "Desperately Seeking Standards: The Court's Frustrating Attempts to Limit Political Gerrymandering," *PS: Political Science & Politics* (July 2006): 409.

43. Steven Hill, "Schwarzenegger versus Gerrymander," *New York Times,* February 19, 2005, A29. See also Steve Lawrence, "Experts Question Redistricting Plan," *Santa Barbara News-Press,* February 20, 2005, A7.

44. Bruce Oppenheimer's and Alan Abramowitz's recent findings are reported by Bill Bishop, "You Can't Compete With Voters' Feet," *Washington Post,* May 15, 2005, B2. Also see Bill Bishop, *The Big Sort: Why the Clustering of Like-Minded America Is Tearing Us Apart* (Boston: Houghton Mifflin, 2008).

45. Alan Abramowitz, Brad Alexander, and Matthew Gunning, "Don't Blame Redistricting for Uncompetitive Elections," *PS: Political Science & Politics* (January 2006): 87–90. In the same forum, see also Thomas L. Brunell's essay, "Rethinking Redistricting: How Drawing Uncompetitive Districts Eliminates Gerrymanders, Enhances Representation, and Improves Attitudes toward Congress," 77–85.

46. Dean E. Murphy, "Who Should Redistrict?" *New York Times* Magazine, October 23, 2005, 24, 26–28.

47. Charles S. Bullock, "Affirmative Action Districts: In Whose Faces Will They Blow Up?," *Campaigns and Elections* (April 1995): 23.

48. David Lublin, *The Paradox of Representation: Racial Gerrymandering and Minority Interests in Congress* (Princeton: Princeton University Press, 1997).

49. Lani Guinier, "What Color Is Your Gerrymander?" *Washington Post,* March 27, 1994, C3.

50. Abigail M. Thernstrom, "A Republican–Civil Rights Conspiracy," *Washington Post,* September 23, 1991, A11. See also Abigail M. Thernstrom, *Whose Votes Count? Affirmative Action and Minority Voting Rights* (Cambridge: Harvard University Press, 1987).

51. *Shaw v. Reno,* 509 U.S. 630 (1993).

52. Ehrenhalt, "Redistricting and the Erosion of Community," 10.

53. Carol M. Swain, "The Voting Rights Act: Some Unintended Consequences," *Brookings Review* 10 (winter 1992): 51. See also Lublin, *The Paradox of Representation.*

54. Alexander Bolton, "Dems Seek To 'Unpack' Minority Districts," *The Hill,* May 9, 2001, 4.

55. Ibid.

56. *Gomillion v. Lightfoot,* 364 U.S. 339 (1960).

57. *Shaw v. Reno.*

58. *Miller v. Johnson,* 515 U.S. 900 (1995).

59. Research by Charles S. Bullock and Richard E. Dunn, cited in Adam Clymer, "Shaping the New Math of Racial Redistricting," *New York Times,* July 15, 2001, D16.

60. *Easley v. Cromartie,* 532 U.S. 234 (2001). The decision was described by Linda Greenhouse in "Court Gives Wiggle Room to Racially Drawn Districts," *New York Times,* May 18, 1999, A12; and in "Justices Reconsider Race and Redistricting," *New York Times,* November 28, 2000, A25.

61. Linda Greenhouse, "Justices Permit Race as a Factor in Redistricting," *New York Times,* April 19, 2001, A1, A16.

62. David T. Canon, "Representing Racial and Ethnic Minorities," in Paul J. Quirk and Sarah A. Binder, eds., *The Legislative Branch* (New York: Oxford University Press, 2005), 191.

63. Mara Caputo and Ragan Narash, "Despite Series of Court Rulings, State Officials Are Left Guessing," *CQ Weekly*, August 11, 2001, 1970.

64. Louis Sandy Maisel, *From Obscurity to Oblivion: Running in the Congressional Primary* (Knoxville: University of Tennessee Press, 1982), 34.

65. Quoted in Jon Margolis, "The Disappearing Candidates," *American Prospect* 11 (January 31, 2000): 32.

66. Alan Ehrenhalt, *The United States of Ambition* (New York: Random House, 1991), 17.

67. The four Capitol Hill campaign committees are the National Republican Senatorial Committee (NRSC), the Democratic Senatorial Campaign Committee (DSCC), the National Republican Congressional Committee (NRCC), and the Democratic Congressional Campaign Committee (DCCC). See Paul S. Herrnson, *Congressional Elections: Campaigning at Home and in Washington,* 4th ed. (Washington, D.C.: CQ Press, 2004), 90–94.

68. Edward Walsh, "To Every Campaign, There Is a Recruiting Season," *Washington Post,* November 12, 1985, A1.

69. Alice A. Love, "Small Business Group Helps Grow Its Own Grassroots Candidates at Meeting Next Week," *Roll Call,* October 16, 1995, 22.

70. Valerie Richardson, "Name Change Latest Quirk in Race for Senate," *Washington Times,* September 30, 2008, B1.

71. David T. Canon, *Actors, Athletes, and Astronauts: Political Amateurs in the United States Congress* (Chicago: University of Chicago Press, 1990), 2–3, 25–31.

72. Maisel, *From Obscurity to Oblivion,* 23.

73. Michael Janofsky, "Two Congressional Candidates Know They'll Lose, But It's Still Fun," *New York Times,* October 31, 1992, 27.

74. Maisel, *From Obscurity to Oblivion,* 23.

75. William Claiborne, "In Neb., a Gridiron Hero Scores in Political Arena," *Washington Post,* June 14, 2000, A3.

76. This conceptualization is a combination of insights derived from a broad-based, pioneering study of House candidate recruitment by a team of scholars: Cherie D. Maestas, Sara Fulton, L. Sandy Maisel, and Walter J. Stone, "When to Risk It? Institutions, Ambitions, and the Decision to Run for the U.S. House," *American Political Science Review* 100 (May 2006): 195–208; and Stone and Maisel, "The Not-So-Simple Calculus of Winning: U.S. House Candidates' Nomination and General Election Prospects," *Journal of Politics* 65 (November 2003): 951–977.

77. The seminal work on strategic politician theory is Gary C. Jacobson and Samuel Kernell, *Strategy and Choice in Congressional Elections,* 2d ed. (New Haven: Yale University Press, 1983).

78. Shira Toeplitz, "Ohio's Limits Tip Races," *Roll Call,* November 20, 2008, 15.

79. Jacobson and Kernell, *Strategy and Choice in Congressional Elections,* chapter 3.

80. L. Sandy Maisel, Cherie Maestas, and Walter J. Stone, "The Party Role in Congressional Competition," in *The Parties Respond,* ed. Paul S. Herrnson (Boulder, Colo.: Westview Press, 2002), 129.

81. Linda L. Fowler and Robert D. McClure, *Political Ambition: Who Decides to Run for Congress* (New Haven: Yale University Press, 1989).

82. Quoted in Burt Solomon, "A Daunting Task: Running for House," *National Journal,* March 21, 1992, 712.

83. Maisel, Maestas, and Stone, "The Party Role in Congressional Competition," 129.

84. Cited in Robin Toner, "Willing Contenders at a Premium in Fierce Fight to Rule Congress," *New York Times,* January 3, 2000, A14.

85. Quoted in Sheryl Gay Stolberg, "Wooed for Congress, Fewer Will Say, 'I Do,'" *New York Times,* October 14, 2003, A22.

86. Gary C. Jacobson, *The Politics of Congressional Elections,* 6th ed. (New York: Pearson Longman, 2004), 23.

87. Frances E. Lee and Bruce I. Oppenheimer, *Sizing Up the Senate: The Unequal Consequences of Equal Representation* (Chicago: University of Chicago Press, 1999), 95.

88. On the first view mentioned in this paragraph, see Morris P. Fiorina, *Congress: Keystone of the Washington Establishment,* 2d ed. (New Haven: Yale University Press, 1989); and Bruce Cain, John Ferejohn, and Morris Fiorina, *The Personal Vote: Constituency Service and Electoral Independence* (Cambridge: Harvard University Press, 1987), especially chapters 6–7. For more on the second view, see Glenn R. Parker and Roger H. Davidson, "Why Do Americans Love Their Congressmen So Much More Than Their Congress?" *Legislative Studies Quarterly* 4 (February 1979): 53–61. On the question of whether incumbents' resources are directly tied to votes, see John R. Johannes, *To Serve the People: Congress and Constituency Service* (Lincoln: University of Nebraska Press, 1984), especially chapter 8.

89. Jacobson, *Politics of Congressional Elections,* 38.

90. Gary C. Jacobson, *The Politics of Congressional Elections,* 7th ed. (New York: Pearson Education, Inc., 2009), 19.

91. *California Democratic Party v. Jones,* 530 U.S. 567 (2000).

92. Harvey L. Schantz, "Contested and Uncontested Primaries for the U.S. House," *Legislative Studies Quarterly* 5 (November 1980): 559. The linkage between interparty and intraparty competition is sometimes referred to as Key's Law. See V. O. Key Jr., *Parties, Politics, and Pressure Groups,* 5th ed. (New York: Crowell, 1964), 438, 447.

93. Maisel, Gibson, and Ivry, "The Continuing Importance of the Rules of the Game," 162–164.

94. Maisel, Maestas, and Stone, "The Party Role in Congressional Competition," 130 ff.

95. Ibid., 132.

96. Erin McPike, "With Muscle, Not Endorsements, DCCC Getting Its Way," *National Journal*'s CongressDailyAM, May 23, 2008, 12.

97. Ibid.

98. Rosalind S. Helderman, William Van, and Ovetta Wiggins, "Rare Dual Losses in Md. Put Incumbents on Notice," *Washington Post,* February 14, 2008, B1.

99. Raymond Hernandez. "Democrat Carrying Anti-Abortion Banner Put More Congressional Races in Play," *New York Times,* October 26, 2008, 26. See Greg Hitt, "The New Southern Strategy, Democrats Tap Conservative Candidates in GOP Bastions," *Wall Street Journal,* August 7, 2008, A1.

100. Richard A. Oppel Jr., "Despite Big Issues, Primaries Prompted Only 17% to Vote," *New York Times,* September 28, 2002, A12.

101. Austin Ranney, "Parties in State Politics," in *Politics in the American States,* eds. Herbert Jacob and Kenneth Vines (Boston: Little, Brown, 1976), 61–99.

102. John F. Bibby, "State Party Organizations," in *The Parties Respond,* 3d ed., eds. L. Sandy Maisel (Boulder, Colo.: Westview Press, 1998), 20.

103. Herrnson, *Congressional Elections,* 159.

104. Figures cited in this chapter for the 2007–2008 cycle are derived from the Web site of the Center for Responsive Politics, available at *www.opensecrets.org.* In addition, they are taken from reports issued by the Campaign Finance Institute in Washington, D.C.

105. Norman J. Ornstein, Thomas E. Mann, and Michael J. Malbin, *Vital Statistics in Congress, 1999–2000* (Washington, D.C.: American Enterprise Institute, 2000): 87–88.

106. Gary C. Jacobson, "Money in the 1980 and 1982 Congressional Elections," in *Money and Politics in the United States,* ed. Michael J. Malbin (Chatham, N.J.: Chatham House, 1984), 58.

107. Christopher Buchanan, "Candidates' Campaign Costs for Congressional Contests Have Gone Up at a Fast Pace," *Congressional Quarterly Weekly Report,* September 29, 1979, 2154–2155.

108. Jacobson, "Money in the 1980 and 1982 Congressional Elections," 57.

109. Gary C. Jacobson, *The Politics of Congressional Elections,* 7th ed. (New York, Pearson Education, 2009), 47.

110. Jennifer Haberkorn, "Money Walks, Talks and Wins Elections," *Washington Times,* November 13, 2008, A7.

111. Quoted in Andy Plattner, "The High Cost of Holding—and Keeping—Public Office," *U.S. News and World Report,* June 22, 1997, 30.

112. See Thomas Romer and James M. Snyder Jr., "An Empirical Investigation of the Dynamics of PAC Contributions," *American Journal of Political Science* 38 (1994): 745–769.

113. Tom Hamburger, Dan Morain, and Robin Fields, "Hsu Thrived in 'Bundling' System," *Los Angeles Times,* September 14, 2007, online version.

114. Matthew Murray, "Senators Differ on Easing Coordinated Spending Limits," *Roll Call,* April 19, 2007, 3.

115. See John Bresnahan, "Dems to Members: Pay Up For '08," *Politico,* June 19, 2008, 19; Steven T. Dennis, and Lauren Whittington, "Chairmen Sing Dues Blues," *Roll Call,* April 21, 2008, 16; and Jared Allen and Mike Soraghan, "Harman, Jackson Cut Large Checks to DCCC," *The Hill,* October 29, 2008, 6. For a GOP perspective, see Patrick O'Connor, "Boehner Gives GOP Kick In the Cash," *Politico,* February 27, 2008, 1. The lead sentence of this article has House GOP Leader John Boehner exhorting his colleagues to get off their "dead asses" and contribute to the campaign committee. In addition, see Lauren W. Whittington, "GOP Targets Member Giving," *Roll Call,* June 16, 2008, 1.

116. Case studies of political action committees are found in Robert Biersack, Paul S. Herrnson, and Clyde Wilcox, *Risky Business? PAC Decisionmaking and Congressional Elections* (Armonk, N.Y.: M.E. Sharpe, 1994).

117. Quoted in Sam Youngman, "Sununu Wins Club for Growth Backing in '08 Bid," *The Hill,* February 27, 2007, 19.

118. Mary Ann Ackers and Paul Kane, "Anti-Sack PAC," *Washington Post,* May 8, 2008, A21.

119. Alexander Bolton, "Clinton Helped with $15M," *The Hill,* February 7, 2007, 1.

120. Quoted in Jonathan D. Salant, "Business PACs Pick Their Cause," *Congressional Quarterly Weekly Report,* May 6, 1995, 1234.

121. *Congressional Quarterly Almanac,* 1976 (Washington, D.C.: Congressional Quarterly, Inc., 1976), 459–471.

122. Quoted in Diana F. Dwyer and Victoria A. Farrar-Myers, *Legislative Labyrinth: Congress and Campaign Finance Reform* (Washington, D.C.: CQ Press, 2001), 233.

123. Scott Turow, "The High Court's 20-Year-Old Mistake," *New York Times,* October 12, 1997, E15.

124. E.J. Dionne Jr., "Politics as Public Auction," *Washington Post,* June 19, 1998, A25.

125. Gary C. Jacobson, *Money in Congressional Elections* (New Haven: Yale University Press, 1980).

126. Brody Mullins, "Georgia Runoff Exposes Gaps in Finance Law," *Wall Street Journal,* November 19, 2008, A3. See Michael Luo and Griff Palmer, "Laws Let Donors Surpass Regular Campaign Limits," *New York Times,* October 21, 2008, A1.

127. Quoted in Dan Balz, "In Long Battle, Small Victories Add Up," *Washington Post,* March 21, 2002, A1.

128. *McConnell v. Federal Election Commission,* 540 U.S. 93 (2003). See Linda Greenhouse, "Justices, in a 5-to-4 Decision, Back Campaign Finance Law That Curbs Contributions," *New York Times,* December 11, 2003, A1; and David G. Savage, "High Court Upholds Most of Campaign Finance Law," *Los Angeles Times,* December 11, 2003, Al.

129. See John Samples, *The Fallacy of Campaign Finance Reform* (Chicago: University of Chicago Press, 2006).

130. Linda Greenhouse and David D. Kirkpatrick, "Justices Loosen Ad Restrictions In Campaign Law," *New York Times,* June 26, 2007, A1.

131. Matthew Mosk and Robert Barners, "High Court Deals Blow To Campaign Finance Law," *Washington Post,* June 27, 2008, A4.

132. Kenneth P. Doyle, "BCRA 'Millionaires' Amendment Struck; Ruling Says Hill Cannot 'Level' Campaigns," *Daily Report for Executives,* June 27, 2008, A-13.

133. Quoted in Glen Justice, "In New Landscape of Campaign Finance, Big Donations Flow to Groups, Not Parties," *New York Times,* December 11, 2003, A25.

134. Quoted in Joe Hadfield, "More Than Survive, Parties Thrive under New Campaign Finance Rules," *Campaigns and Elections* 26 (April 2005): 22–24.

135. Mark Wegner, "Democrats Propose Public Financing For House Races," *National Journal*'s CongressDailyPM, June 29, 2007, 7.

136. Editorial, *USA Today,* December 10, 2007, 12A. Another editorial headline on the same day and page, which reflected the newspaper's position, endorsed public financing: "5 Reasons for Public Financing."

137. William Schneider, "The Obama Model," *National Journal,* June 14, 2008, 64.

138. Norman Ornstein, "Obama's Fundraising Success May Herald A Whole New Model," *Roll Call,* June 30, 2008, 8.

139. Chuck Alston, "A Field Guide to Election Spending Limits," *CQ Weekly,* May 22, 1990, 1621–1626.

CHAPTER 4

1. Shaila Dewan, "A Republican Incumbent Finds a Once-Safe Race Less So," *New York Times,* October 16, 2008, 19.

2. Jack Betts, "How Dole Missed her Chance to Land Safely," *Charlotte Observer,* October 21, 2008, A11.

3. "Obama's Earnest Army," *The Economist,* October 23, 2008.

4. Mark Binker, "Aggressive Campaign Puts Hagan in Senate," *News & Record,* November 6, 2008, A1.

5. Jim Morrill, "High-energy Hagan was Dynamo in Community," *News & Observer,* October 5, 2008, A1.

6. Rob Christensen, "Dole's Manner Masks Mettle," *News & Observer,* September 28, 2008, A1.

7. Ibid.

8. Sean Mussenden and James Romoser, "N.C. Time and Issue in Dole Race," *Winston-Salem Journal,* September 28, 2008.

9. Ibid.

10. Bob Benenson, "Election 2008: Muscling Up the Majorities," *CQ Weekly Report,* October 27, 2008, 2866.

11. The full text of the ad is quoted in Robert G. Kaiser, "In Senate Battlegrounds, Fusillades of TV Ads," *Washington Post,* October 28, 2008, A1.

12. See Richard G. Niemi, Lynda W. Powell, and Patricia L. Bickell, "The Effects of Congruity between Community and District on Salience of U.S. House Candidates," *Legislative Studies Quarterly* 11 (May 1986): 187–201; and Dena Levy and Peverill Squire, "Television Markets

and the Competitiveness of U.S. House Elections," *Legislative Studies Quarterly* 25 (May 2000): 313–325.

13. Theodore E. Jackson Jr., "Brand Marketing in Today's Cluttered Political Marketplace," *Campaigns and Elections* 24 (April 2003): 30.

14. Quoted material in this paragraph is from Allison Stevens, "House Candidates in Maryland Striving to Hone Their Messages," *The Hill,* May 8, 2002, 31–32.

15. Quoted in Robin Toner, "In a Cynical Election Season, the Ads Tell an Angry Tale," *New York Times,* October 24, 1994, A1.

16. Chris Cillizza, "Playing It Safe in Carolina," *Roll Call,* October 28, 2004, 1.

17. Parke Skelton, quoted in Mary Clare Jalonick, "How to 'Primary' an Incumbent," *Campaigns and Elections* 22 (May 2001): 35.

18. Robin Toner, "In Final Rounds, Both Sides Whip Out Bare-Knuckle Ads," *New York Times,* October 21, 1996, B7.

19. Statistics on spending in the 2007–2008 electoral cycle are found in "A First Look at Money in the House and Senate Elections," The Campaign Finance Institute, www.cfinst.org/pr/prRelease.aspx?ReleaseID=215 (accessed February 8, 2009).

20. Carl Hulse and Adam Nagourney, "Specter Switches Parties: More Heft for Democrats," *New York Times*, April 29, 2009, A1; Kathleen Hunder and Bart Jansen, "Specter's Defection Has Consequences for Balance of Power on Committees," *CQ Today*, April 30, 2009, 8, 12.

21. Lynn Sweet, "Durbin Launches Fundraising Blitz for 2008 Re-Elect Campaign," Sweet Column Blog, *Chicago Sun Times,* February 8, 2007, http://blogs.suntimes.com/sweet/2007/02/sweet_column_durbin_launchs_fu.html (accessed February 8, 2009).

22. "Democratic Senatorial Campaign Committee: Top Contributors," Center for Responsive Politics, www.opensecrets.org.

23. Gary C. Jacobson, *The Politics of Congressional Elections*, 6th ed. (New York: Pearson Longman, 2004), 98.

24. Thomas B. Edsall, "In Tight Races, Early Cash Means Staying Competitive," *Washington Post,* July 14, 1998, A6.

25. Gary C. Jacobson, "The Effects of Campaign Spending on Congressional Elections," *American Political Science Review* 72 (June 1978): 469–491.

26. "Total Congressional Campaign Spending," *New York Times,* November 6, 2002, B2.

27. Quoted in Herbert E. Alexander and Brian A. Haggarty, "Misinformation on Media Money," *Public Opinion* 11 (May–June 1988): 7.

28. Edie N. Goldberg and Michael W. Traugott, *Campaigning for Congress* (Washington, D.C.: CQ Press, 1984), 93.

29. Craig Karmin, "Campaign Funds Used for Private Expenses," *The Hill,* September 6, 1995, 1.

30. Reported in: Aaron Blake, "Consultants Account for Half of Campaign Spending, Study Finds," *The Hill*, September 28, 2006, 27.

31. Pew Research Center for the People and the Press, "Internet Now Major Source of Campaign News" news release, October 31, 2008, http://pewresearch.org/pubs/1017/internet-now-major-source-of-campaign-news (accessed February 8, 2009).

32. University of Southern California, Annenberg School of Communications, Norman Lear Center, "Local TV News Largely Ignores Local Political Races," press release, February 15, 2005.

33. Eamon Javers, "Advertisers Brace for an Election-Year Squeeze," *Business Week,* February 25, 2008, 24.

34. Adam Serwer, "How Tom Perriello Showed Virgil Goode The Door," *The American Prospect,* November 14, 2008, Web only content, www.prospect.org/cs/articles?article=how_tom_perriello_showed_virgil_goode_the_door.

35. Burdett A. Loomis, "Kansas's Third District: 'Pros from Dover' Set Up Shop," in *The Battle for Congress,* ed. James A. Thurber (Washington, D.C.: Brookings Institution, 1999), 148.

36. Michael Barone and Grant Ujifusa, *The Almanac of American Politics, 1996* (Washington, D.C.: National Journal, 1995), 1445–1446.

37. David T. Canon, "The Wisconsin Second District: History in the Making," in *The Battle for Congress,* ed. James A. Thurber, 230.

38. Larry J. Sabato and Glenn R. Simpson, *Dirty Little Secrets: The Persistence of Corruption in American Politics* (New York: Times Books, 1996), 156.

39. Quoted in Janet Hook, "Negative Ads a Positive in GOP Strategy," *Los Angeles Times,* September 26, 2006, A10.

40. *Ibid.*

41. Stephen Ansolabehere and Shanto Iyengar, *Going Negative: How Attack Ads Shrink and Polarize the Electorate* (New York: Free Press, 1996), 128.

42. Quoted in David S. Broder, "Death by Negative Ads," *Washington Post,* November 3, 2002, B7.

43. Richard R. Lau and Gerald M. Pomper, "Effects of Negative Campaigning on Turnout in U.S. Senate Elections, 1988–1998," *Journal of Politics* 63 (August 2001): 817.

44. Lisa Zagaroli, "'Godless' Ads Stoke Political Fire," *News & Observer,* November 1, 2008.

45. Rob Christenson, "Dole's 'Godless' Ad Held as Last Resort," *News & Observer,* November 9, 2008, A1.

46. Frank Newport, "State of the States: Importance of Religion," Gallup press release, January 28, 2009, www.gallup.com/poll/114022/State-States-Importance-Religion.aspx (accessed February 11, 2009).

47. *Ibid.*

48. Mark Binker, "Inflammatory Ad Alters Race's Tone," *News & Record,* October 30, 2008, A1.

49. Lisa Zagaroli, "Hagan Takes Action on Dole Ad," *Charlotte Observer,* October 31, 2008, A1.

50. Rob Christenson, "Dole's 'Godless' Ad," A1.

51. *Ibid.*

52. See Howard Kurtz, "Hearing 'Foul,' Stations Pull Political Ads," *Washington Post,* September 20, 2002, A14.

53. Norman J. Ornstein, "Should Liars Be Seated? It's Not Up to Congress," *Roll Call,* May 17, 1993, 12.

54. General Social Surveys (1972–2004), cited in Martin P. Wattenburg, *Is Voting for Young People?* (New York: Pearson Longman, 2007), 12–16.

55. Pew Research Center for the People and the Press, "Internet Now Major Source of Campaign News" news release, October 31, 2008, http://pewresearch.org/pubs/1017/internet-now-major-source-of-campaign-news (accessed February 9, 2009).

56. The source for material in this paragraph is Dan Morain, "Undercover Campaigning on the Web," *Los Angeles Times* (March 21, 2007), A11.

57. Quoted in Adam Nagourney, "Politicians Turn to Alternatives to TV Advertising," *New York Times,* October 5, 2002, A1.

58. Merle Miller, *Lyndon: An Oral Biography* (New York: Putnam, 1980), 120.

59. David S. Broder, "Shoe Leather Politicking," *Washington Post,* June 13, 2001, A29.

60. Joseph Gershtenson, "Mobilization Strategies of the Democrats and Republicans, 1956–2000," *Political Research Quarterly* 56 (September 2003): 293–308; David Wegel, "The Political Bull's-Eye: Persuading the Right People with Microtargeting," *Campaigns & Elections* 27 (February 2006): 20–24.

61. Donald P. Green and Alan S. Gerber, *Get Out the Vote!* (Washington, D.C.: Brookings Institution Press, 2004), 40.

62. Dan Glickman, as told to Amy Zipkin, "Landing the Job He Wanted," *New York Times,* April 17, 2005, C10.

63. Paul Houston, "TV and High Tech Send Campaign Costs Soaring," *Los Angeles Times,* October 2, 1986, 121.

64. Jamie Stiehm, "Ben and Jerry's State Offers a Choice of Three Flavors," *The Hill,* November 22, 1995, 26.

65. Glenn R. Simpson, "In Rhode Island, Everyone Goes to Bristol Parade," *Roll Call,* July 9, 1990, 1; and Glenn R. Simpson, "Judging from July 4th Bristol Parade in R.I., Chafee Looks Well-Positioned for November," *Roll Call,* July 11, 1994, 21.

66. Ron Faucheux, "Candidate Canvassing," *Campaigns and Elections* (May 1997): 43.

67. Canon, "The Wisconsin Second Congressional District," 229–232.

68. Green and Gerber, *Get Out the Vote!* 93–96.

69. Leslie Wayne, "Democrats Take Page from their Rival's Playbook," *New York Times,* November 1, 2008, A15.

70. David M. Halbfinger, "Improved Ground Game Is Seen as Important Factor in G.O.P. Victories," *New York Times,* November 10, 2002, A24.

71. Peter Wallsten and Tom Hamburger, "Two Parties Far Apart in Turnover Tactics Too," *Los Angeles Times,* November 6, 2006, A1.

72. Wayne, "Democrats Take Page From Their Rival's Playbook," A15.

73. Alec MacGillis, "Obama Campaign Relying Heavily on Ground Effort," *Washington Post,* October 12, 2008, A4.

74. Adam Doster, "Expand the Vote: The Obama Campaign's Voter Registration Drive Could Radically Alter the Electoral map this Fall," *In These Times,* July 2008, 20.

75. Matthew Mosk, "In Final Stretch, McCain to Pour Money Into TV Ads," *Washington Post,* October 31, 2008, A3.

76. Jonathan E. Kaplan, "Large Voter Turnout Was Key to GOP Victory," *The Hill,* November 7, 2002, 17.

77. Emily Cadei and Karoun Demirjian, "Labor's High Hopes Matched by Money," *CQ Weekly Report,* September 29, 2008, 2556-2558.

78. Alec MacGillis, "For the Republican Base, Palin Pick is Energizing," *Washington Post,* September 8, 2008, A1.

79. *McConnell v. Federal Election Commission,* 540 U.S. 93 (2003).

80. Louis Jacobson, "Fighting the Political 'Ground War,'" *National Journal,* October 12, 2002, 2983–2985.

81. From the report on the activities of the National Federation of Independent Business/Save America's Free Enterprise Trust produced by CampaignMoney.org, a nonpartisan Web site that draws on Federal Election Commission disclosures, www.campaignmoney.com/political/committees/national-federation-of-independent-business-save-americas-free-enterprise-trust-101105.asp?cycle=08.

82. Quoted in David S. Broder and Thomas B. Edsall, "Amid Election Apathy, Parties Bet on Core Voters," *Washington Post,* September 7, 1998, A12.

83. Thomas Edsall, "Issues Coalitions Take On Political Party Functions," *Washington Post,* August 9, 1996, A1.

84. Jerome Armstrong and Markos Moulitsas Zúnigo, *Crashing the Gate: Netroots, Grassroots, and the Rise of People Powered Politics* (White River Junction, Vt: Chelsea Green Publishing, 2006).

85. Center for Responsive Politics, "527s: Advocacy Group Spending in the 2008 Elections," December 3, 2008, http://www.opensecrets.org/527s/index.php (accessed February 9, 2009).

86. Curtis Gans, "African Americans, Fear, and Youth Propel Turnout to Highest Level Since 1960," Center for the Study of the American Electorate, American University, December 17, 2008, http://www.american.edu/ia/cdem/csae/pdfs/2008pdfoffinaledited.pdf (accessed February 12, 2009).

87. M. Margaret Conway, "Political Participation in Midterm Congressional Elections," *American Politics Quarterly* 9 (April 1981): 221–244.

88. International turnout figures from Institute for Social Research, University of Michigan, reported in Pippa Norris, *Electoral Engineering: Voting Rules and Political Behavior* (Cambridge, United Kingdom: Cambridge University Press, 2004). A sensible review of the question is found in Martin P. Wattenberg, *Where Have All the Voters Gone?* (Cambridge: Harvard University Press, 2002).

89. Pew Research Center for the People and the Press, "Who Votes, Who Doesn't, and Why," October 18, 2006, 4.

90. Scott Keeter, Juliana Horowitz, and Alec Tyson, "Young Voters in the 2008 Election," Report by the Pew Research Center for the People and the Press, November 12, 2008, http://pewresearch.org/pubs/1031/young-voters-in-the-2008-election (accessed February 9, 2009).

91. Ibid.

92. Data on the results of the act are distressingly incomplete. See Raymond E. Wolfinger and Jonathan Hoffman, "Registering and Voting with Motor Voter," *P.S.* 34 (March 2001): 85–92.

93. B. Drummond Ayres Jr., "Easier Voter Registration Doesn't Raise Participation," *New York Times,* December 3, 1995, 22. Registration data are from the Committee for the Study of the American Electorate, news release, November 6, 1998.

94. Pew Research Center, "Who Votes, Who Doesn't, and Why," October 18, 2006, 1.

95. Nina Totenberg, "Supreme Court Weighs Voter ID Requirements," *Morning Edition,* January 9, 2008, http://www.npr.org/templates/story/story.php?storyId=17942818 (accessed February 9, 2009).

96. Joseph D. Rich, "Playing Politics with Justice," *Los Angeles Times,* March 29, 2007, A23. Rich is former chief (1999–2005) of the voting section in the Department of Justice's civil rights division.

97. *Crawford* v. *Marion County Election Board,* 553 U.S. ___ (2008).

98. See Eric Lipton and Ian Urbina, "In 5-Year Effort, Scant Evidence of Voter Fraud," *New York Times,* April 12, 2007, A1, A15.

99. Richard Morin and Claudia Deane, "As Turnout Falls, Apathy Emerges as Driving Force," *Washington Post,* November 4, 2000, A1. Michael Waldman and Justin Levin, "The Myth of Voter Fraud," *Washington Post,* March 29, 2007, A19.

100. Samuel L. Popkin and Michael P. McDonald, "Turnout's Not as Bad as You Think," *Washington Post,* November 5, 2000, B1.

101. Sidney Verba, Kay Lehman Schlozman, and Henry E. Brady, *Voice and Equality: Civic Voluntarism in American Politics* (Cambridge: Harvard University Press, 1995).

102. Samuel L. Popkin, *The Reasoning Voter* (Chicago: University of Chicago Press, 1994), 7.

103. Exit polls (November 2, 2004, and November 7, 2006). Reported in *New York Times,* November 9, 2006, P7. *Los Angeles Times* and by Ronald Brownstein, "Democrats' Losses Go Far Beyond One Defeat," *Los Angeles Times,* November 4, 2004, A1, 17.

104. Alec MacGillis and Jon Cohen, "A Vote Decided by Big Turnout and Big Discontent With GOP," *Washington Post,* November 5, 2008, A5.

105. Quoted in Richard Morin and Claudia Deane, "How Independent Are Independents?" *Washington Post,* August 2, 2002, A1.

106. Gary C. Jacobson, *The Politics of Congressional Elections,* 5th edition (New York: Addison, Wesley, Longman, 2001), 108.

107. Martin P. Wattenberg, *The Rise of Candidate-Centered Politics* (Cambridge: Harvard University Press, 1991), 36–39.

108. See Bernard Grofman, William Koetzle, Michael P. McDonald, and Thomas L. Brunell, "A New Look at Split-Ticket Outcomes for House and President: The Comparative Midpoints Model," *Journal of Politics* 62 (February 2000): 34–50.

109. Cited in Jeffrey McMurray, "Conservative Southern Dems Disappearing," *Washington Post*, April 25, 2005, A1.

110. Gary C. Jacobson, *The Politics of Congressional Elections,* 6th edition (New York: Pearson, Longman, 2004), 163.

111. Jacobson, *The Politics of Congressional Elections,* 6th ed., 162.

112. Angus Campbell, "Surge and Decline: A Study of Electoral Change," in *Elections and the Political Order,* ed. Angus Campbell, Phillip E. Converse, Warren E. Miller, and Donald E. Stokes (New York: Wiley, 1966), 40–62; and Raymond E. Wolfinger, Steven J. Rosenstone, and Richard A. McIntosh, "Presidential and Congressional Voters Compared," *American Politics Quarterly* 9 (April 1981): 245–255.

113. Eric M. Uslaner and M. Margaret Conway, "The Responsible Electorate: Watergate, the Economy, and Vote Choice in 1974," *American Political Science Review* 79 (September 1985): 788–803; and Samuel Kernell, "Presidential Popularity and Negative Voting: An Alternative Explanation of the Midterm Congressional Decline of the President's Party," *American Political Science Review* 71 (March 1977): 44–46.

114. Pew Research Center, "Democrats Hold Solid Lead; Strong Anti-Incumbent, Anti-Bush Mood," September 14, 2006, 1. Bush's approval score is from *Washington Post*-ABC News Poll, November 5, 2006.

115. Quoted in Dale Russakoff, "In Tight Arkansas Senate Race, Family Matters," *Washington Post,* August 3, 2002, A1.

116. Jacobson, *The Politics of Congressional Elections,* 6th ed., 26.

117. Ibid., 27–28.

118. Gary C. Jacobson, "Incumbents' Advantages in the 1978 U.S. Congressional Elections," *Legislative Studies Quarterly* 6 (May 1981): 198.

119. National Elections Studies, 1980–2002, summarized in Jacobson, *The Politics of Congressional Elections,* 122–125. Thomas E. Mann and Raymond E. Wolfinger, "Candidates and Parties in Congressional Elections," *American Political Science Review* 74 (September 1980): 623.

120. Lydia Saad, "Congressional Approval Hits Record-Low 14%," Gallup, Inc., News Release, http://www.gallup.com/poll/108856/Congressional-Approval-Hits-RecordLow-14.aspx (accessed February 13, 2009).

121. Jeffrey M. Jones, "Voters Not Strongly Backing Incumbents for Congress," Gallup, Inc., News Release, http://www.gallup.com/poll/109267/Voters-Strongly-Backing-Incumbents-Congress.aspx (accessed February 13, 2009).

122. David R. Mayhew, *Congress: The Electoral Connection,* 2d ed. (New Haven: Yale University Press, 2004).

123. Michael J. Robinson, "Three Faces of Congressional Media," in *The New Congress,* ed. Thomas E. Mann and Norman J. Ornstein (Washington, D.C.: American Enterprise Institute, 1981), 91.

124. Frances E. Lee and Bruce I. Oppenheimer, *Sizing Up the Senate: The Unequal Consequences of Equal Representation* (Chicago: University of Chicago Press, 1999), chap. 4.

125. Owen G. Abbe, Jay Goodliffe, Paul S. Herrnson, and Kelly D. Patterson, "Agenda Setting in Congressional Elections: The Impact of Issues and Campaigns on Voting Behavior," *Political Research Quarterly* 56 (December 2003): 419.

126. John B. Bader, *Taking the Initiative: Leadership Agendas in Congress and the "Contract with America"* (Washington, D.C.: Georgetown University Press, 1996).

127. Quoted in Judy Newman, "Do Women Vote for Women?" *Public Perspective* 7 (February–March 1996): 10.

128. Kaufmann, Karen M. and John R. Petrocik. "The Changing Politics of American Men: Understanding the Sources of the Gender Gap." *American Journal of Political Science* 43 (July 1999): 864-887.

129. Quoted in Barbara Vobejda, "Fragmentation of Society Formidable Challenge to Candidates, Report Says," *Washington Post*, March 7, 1996, A15.

130. Jennifer E. Duffy, "In Senate, GOP Braces for Cold November," *National Journal*, August 2, 2008 and "Senate GOP About to Downsize Again," *National Journal*, November 1, 2008.

131. Richard E. Cohen, "Rolling. . . . and Reeling," *National Journal*, May 24, 2008.

132. Competitiveness classifications are drawn from *CQ Weekly Report*'s 2008 pre-election analyses in the October 27, 2008 issue.

133. Paul Kane, "Democrats Press Battle For 60 Seats In Senate" *Washington Post*, August 28, 2008, A31.

134. For a discussion of these reversals, see Gary Miller and Norman Schofield, "Activists and Partisan Realignment in the United States," *American Political Science Review* 97 (May 2003): 245-260.

135. Jacobson, *The Politics of Congressional Elections*, 6th ed., 249-253.

136. Delegates to the parties' national conventions were analyzed in a classic study by Herbert McCloskey, Paul Hoffman, and Rosemary O'Hara, "Issue Conflict and Consensus among Party Leaders and Followers," *American Political Science Review* 54 (1950): 406–427.

137. The "middlingness" of the citizenry is vigorously argued in Morris P. Fiorina, with Samuel J. Abrams and Jeremy C. Pope, *Culture War? The Myth of a Polarized America* (New York: Pearson-Longman, 2005).

138. Pew Research Center for the People and the Press, "The 2004 Political Landscape: Evenly Divided and Increasingly Polarized," survey report, November 5, 2003, www.people-press .org/reports/.

139. David W. Brady, "Electoral Realignments in the U.S. House of Representatives," in *Congress and Policy Change*, ed. Gerald C. Wright Jr., Leroy N. Reiselbach, and Lawrence C. Dodd (New York: Agathon Press, 1986), 46–69.

140. These numbers include the senators appointed to replace Senators taking executive branch positions (Obama, Biden, Clinton, and Salazar) and three House members to be elected, at this writing, in special elections to replace Representatives Emanuel, Solis, and Gillibrand.

141. Warren E. Miller and Donald E. Stokes, "Constituency Influence in Congress," *American Political Science Review* 57 (March 1963): 45–57.

142. Tracy Sulkin, *Issue Politics in Congress* (New York: Cambridge University Press, 2005, 2.

143. Ibid., 177.

CHAPTER 5

1. "Baucus Says He Will Lead Health-Care Overhaul," *The Associated Press State and Local Wire*, October 18, 2008.

2. Ezra Klein, "The Sleeper of the Senate," *The American Prospect*, November 6, 2008, 23.

3. Staff of Congressional Quarterly, *CQ's Politics in America 2008: The 110th Congress*, ed. Jackie Koszczuk and Martha Angle (Washington DC: CQ Press), 597.

4. John K. Inglehart, "The New Medicare Prescription-Drug Benefit—A Pure Power Play," *New England Journal of Medicine* 350 (8, 2004): 826–833.

5. Michael Barone with Richard E. Cohen, *The Almanac of American Politics 2008* (Washington, D.C.: National Journal, 2008).

6. Quoted in Klein, *The American Prospect,* 23.

7. Max Baucus, "Economic Development," Official Senate Web site, http://baucus.senate.gov/issues/development.cfm?view=priorities (accessed February 21, 2009).

8. *CQ's Politics in America 2008: The 110th Congress,* 598.

9. "High Plains Grifters: A Misguided Senate Plan Repackages Agricultural Welfare as Disaster Relief," Editorial, *Washington Post,* October 28, 2007, B6.

10. Rachel Van Dongen, "110th Senate Committees: Finance," *Congressional Quarterly Weekly Report,* November 13, 2006, 3029.

11. Amy Goldstein, "Hill Supports Medicare Boost to Rural Areas," *Washington Post,* October 20, 2003, A1.

12. Max Baucus, "A National Leader With Montana Values," Official Senate Web site, http://baucus.senate.gov/about/values.cfn (accessed February 18, 2009).

13. Matt Gouras, "Kelleher Says He Can Beat Baucus," *The Associate Press State and Local Wire,* September 4, 2008.

14. Mary Clare Jalonick, "Montana's Five-Term Senator Faces Light Challenge," *The Associated Press State and Local Wire,* October 5, 2008.

15. Roger H. Davidson, *The Role of the Congressman* (Indianapolis: Bobbs-Merrill, 1969), 199.

16. Rob Hotakainen, "A Millionaire's Club on Capitol Hill," *Philadelphia Inquirer,* October 28, 2008.

17. John Stuart Mill, *Considerations on Representative Government* (London, Longmans, Green and Co., 1967 [1861]), quoted in Lisa Schwindt-Bayer and William Mishler, "An Integrated Model of Women's Representation," *Journal of Politics* 67 (2, 2005): 413.

18. Hannah Finichel Pitkin, *The Concept of Representation* (Berkeley: University of California Press, 1967), 166.

19. Susan Welch and John R. Hibbing, "Hispanic Representation in the U.S. Congress," *Social Science Quarterly* 64 (June 1984): 328–335; and Charles Tien and Dena Levy, "Asian-American and Hispanic Representation in the U.S. House of Representatives" (paper presented at the Midwest Political Science Association, Chicago, April 1998).

20. See David Canon, *Race, Redistricting, and Representation: The Unintended Consequences of Black Majority Districts* (Chicago: University of Chicago Press, 1999); Brinck Kerr and Will Miller, "Latino Representation, It's Direct and Indirect," *American Journal of Political Science* 41(3, 1997): 1066–1071; Michele L. Swers, *The Difference Women Make* (Chicago: University of Chicago, 2002); and Sue Thomas, *How Women Legislate* (New York: Oxford University Press, 1994).

21. See Claudine Gay, "Spirals of Trust? The Effect of Descriptive Representation on the Relationship between Citizens and Their Government," *American Journal of Political Science* 46 (4, 2002): 717–732; John D. Griffin and Michael Keane, "Descriptive Representation and the Composition of African American Turnout," *American Journal of Political Science* 50 (4, 2006): 998–1012; and Katherine Tate, "The Political Representation of Blacks in Congress: Does Race Matter?" *Legislative Studies Quarterly* 26 (4, 2001): 623–638.

22. Data on characteristics of members are found in Mildred L. Amer and Jennifer E. Manning, *Membership of the 110th Congress: A Profile,* Congressional Research Service Report, No. R40086, January 30, 2009.

23. Alan Ehrenhalt, *The United States of Ambition: Politicians, Power, and the Pursuit of Office* (New York: Times Books, 1992), 16.

24. Nate Silver, "Daddy, Where do Senators Come From?" *Five Thirty Eight: Politics Done Right,* January 9, 2009, http://www.fivethirtyeight.com/2009/01/daddy-where-do-senators-come-from.html (accessed February 3, 2009).

25. William T. Bianco, "Last Post for 'The Greatest Generation': The Policy Implications of the Decline of Military Experience in the U.S. Congress," *Legislative Studies Quarterly* 30 (February 2005): 85–102.

26. Betsy Rothstein, "Congresswomen Press Women's Health Issues," *The Hill*, February 24, 1999, 19; and Maureen Dowd, "Growing Sorority in Congress Edges into the Ol' Boys' Club," *New York Times,* March 5, 1993, A1, A18.

27. Kerry L. Haynie, "African Americans and the New Politics of Inclusion: A Representational Dilemma?" In *Congress Reconsidered,* 8th edition, ed. Lawrence C. Dodd and Bruce I. Oppenheimer (Washington, DC: CQ Press, 2005).

28. Thomas L. Brunell, Christopher J. Anderson, and Rachel K. Cremona, "Descriptive Representation, District Demography, and Attitudes Toward Congress Among African Americans," *Legislative Studies Quarterly* 33 (2, 2008): 223–242.

29. Katherine Tate, "The Political Representation of Blacks in Congress: Does Race Matter?" *Legislative Studies Quarterly* 26 (November 2001): 631.

30. Janet M. Box-Steffensmeier, David C. Kimball, Scott R. Meinke, and Katherine Tate, "The Effects of Political Representation on the Electoral Advantages of Incumbents," *Political Research Quarterly* 56 (September 2003): 264.

31. See David T. Canon, *Race, Redistricting, and Representation;* and Kerry L. Haynie, *African American Legislators in the American States* (New York: Columbia University Press, 2001).

32. Katrina L. Gamble, "Black Political Representation: An Examination of Legislative Activity Within U.S. House Committees," *Legislative Studies Quarterly* 32 (2007): 421–448.

33. See the discussion in Charles Cameron, David Epstein, and Sharyn O'Halloran, "Do Majority-Minority Districts Maximize Substantive Black Representation in Congress?" *American Political Science Review* 90 (1996): 794–812.

34. L. Marvin Overby and Kenneth Cosgrove, cited in Carol Swain, "The Future of Black Representation," *American Prospect* 23 (fall 1995): 81.

35. Carol M. Swain, *Black Faces, Black Interests: The Representation of African Americans in Congress* (Cambridge: Harvard University Press, 1993).

36. Inter-Parliamentary Union, "Women in National Parliaments," www.ipu.org/wmn-e/classif .htm.

37. The pioneering study of this subject is Irwin N. Gertzog, *Congressional Women: Their Recruitment, Treatment, and Behavior* (New York: Praeger, 1984). Two more recent studies are Barbara C. Burrell, *A Woman's Place Is in the House* (Ann Arbor: University of Michigan Press, 1994); and Richard Logan Fox, *Gender Dynamics in Congressional Elections* (Thousand Oaks, Calif.: Sage Publications, 1997).

38. Quoted in Sheryl Gay Stolberg, "Working Mothers Swaying Senate Debate, as Senators," *New York Times,* June 7, 2003, A3.

39. Jamie Stiehm, "In Senate, Sisterhood Can Override Party," *The Hill*, November 22, 1995, 16.

40. Arturo Vega and Juanita Firestone, "The Effects of Gender on Congressional Behavior and the Substantive Representation of Women," *Legislative Studies Quarterly* 20 (May 1995): 213–222.

41. Quoted in Richard E. Cohen, "Member Moms," *National Journal*, April 7, 2007, 16.

42. Quoted in Cohen, *National Journal,* 19.

43. Quoted in Lyndsey Layton, "Mom's in the House, With Kids at Home: For Congresswomen With Young Children, a Tough Balance," *Washington Post*, July 19, 2007, A01.

44. Kirk Victor, "Still an Old Boys' Club?" *National Journal* 37 (March 12, 2005): 750, 752.

45. See Kathleen Dolan, *Voting for Women: How the Public Evaluates Women Candidates* (Boulder, CO: Westview, 2004) and Leonie Huddy and Nayda Terkildsen, "Gender

Stereotypes and the Perception of Male and Female Candidates," *American Journal of Political Science* 37 (1993): 119–147.

46. Michele Swers, "Building a Reputation on National Security: The Impact of Stereotypes Related to Gender and Military Experience," *Legislative Studies Quarterly* 32 (4, 2007): 559–595.

47. Amy Cavanaugh, "Polis Becomes 3rd Openly Gay Member of Congress," *Washington Blade,* November 5, 2008.

48. Donald P. Haider-Markel, Mark R. Joslyn, and Chad J. Kniss, "Minority Group Interests and Political Representation: Gay Elected Officials in the Policy Process." *Journal of Politics* 62 (2000): 568–577.

49. Quoted in Erika Niedowski, "Four Walk Out of the Closet and toward the House," *CQ Weekly,* April 25, 1998, 1051.

50. Pew Forum on Religion and Public Life, *U.S. Religious Landscapes Survey,* Report, February 2008, http://religions.pewforum.org/reports.

51. Brett Lieberman and Rebecca Spence, "Record Number of Jews Slated for Next U.S. Congress," *Haaretz.com,* November 20, 2008, www.haaretz.com/hasen/spages/1039304.html.

52. Amer, *Membership of the 110th Congress,* 2.

53. *Ibid.,* 4–5. For tenure figures, see Table 2-1.

54. Charles S. Bullock and Burdett A. Loomis, "The Changing Congressional Career," in *Congress Reconsidered,* 3d ed., ed. Lawrence C. Dodd and Bruce I. Oppenheimer (Washington, D.C.: CQ Press, 1985), 66–69, 80–82.

55. Jennifer Wolak, "Strategic Retirements: The Influence of Public Preferences on Voluntary Departures from Congress," *Legislative Studies Quarterly* 32 (May 2007): 285–308.

56. Arend Lijphart, *Democracies: Patterns of Majoritarian and Consensus Government in Twenty-One Countries* (New Haven: Yale University Press, 1984); David Samuels and Richard Snyder, "The Value of a Vote: Malapportionment in Comparative Perspective," *British Journal of Political Science* 31 (2001): 651–671.

57. Frances E. Lee and Bruce I. Oppenheimer, *Sizing Up the Senate: The Unequal Consequences of Equal Representation* (Chicago: University of Chicago Press, 1999), 20–23. See also Robert A. Dahl, *A Preface to Democratic Theory* (New Haven: Yale University Press, 1956).

58. John D. Griffin, "Senate Apportionment as a Source of Political Inequality," *Legislative Studies Quarterly* 31 (3, 2006): 405–432).

59. Bruce I. Oppenheimer, "The Representational Experience: The Effect of State Population on Senator-Constituency Linkages," *American Journal of Political Science* 40 (1996): 1280–1299.

60. Stephen Ansolabehere, James M. Snyder, Jr., and Michael Ting, "Bargaining in Bicameral Legislatures: When and Why Does Malapportionment Matter?" *American Political Science Review* 97 (2003): 471.

61. Frances E. Lee, "Representation and Public Policy: The Consequences of Senate Apportionment for the Geographic Distribution of Federal Funds," *Journal of Politics* 60 (1998): 34–64. See also Stephen Ansolabehere, Alan Gerber, and James M. Snyder, Jr., "Equal Votes: Equal Money: Court-Ordered Redistricting and the Distribution of Public Expenditures in the American States," *American Politial Science Review* 96 (2002): 767–777; Cary M. Atlas, Thomas W. Gilligan, Robert J. Hendershott, and Mark A. Zupan, "Slicing the Federal Government Net Spending Pie: Who Wins, Who Loses, and Why," *American Economic Review* 85 (1995): 624–629.

62. Robert Weissberg, "Collective vs. Dyadic Representation in Congress," *American Political Science Review* 72 (2, 1978): 535–547.

63. Jane Mansbridge, "Rethinking Representation," *American Political Science Review* 97 (November 2003): 515–528.

64. Barry C. Burden, *Personal Roots of Representation* (Princeton: Princeton University Press, 2007).

65. Richard F. Fenno Jr., *The Making of a Senator: Dan Quayle* (Washington, D.C.: CQ Press, 1989), 119.

66. Quoted in Adam Nagourney, "Upbeat Schumer Battles Polls, Low Turnouts, and His Image," *New York Times,* May 16, 1998, A14.

67. Frank E. Smith, *Congressman from Mississippi* (New York: Pantheon, 1964), 129–130.

68. Donald R. Matthews, *U.S. Senators and Their World* (Chapel Hill: University of North Carolina Press, 1960), chap. 5; and Ross K. Baker, *House and Senate,* 3d ed. (New York: Norton, 2001), chap. 2.

69. Barbara Sinclair, *The Transformation of the U.S. Senate* (Baltimore: Johns Hopkins University Press, 1989).

70. Herbert B. Asher, "The Learning of Legislative Norms," *American Political Science Review* 67 (June 1973): 499–513.

71. Quoted from an interview with Jake Tapper, "Retiring, Not Shy," *New York Times Magazine,* September 1, 2002, 25.

72. Quoted in Thomas E. Cavanagh, "The Two Arenas of Congress," in *The House at Work,* ed. Joseph Cooper and G. Calvin Mackenzie (Austin: University of Texas Press, 1981), 65.

73. Quoted in *New York Times,* August 14, 1980, B9.

74. Box-Steffensmeier, et al., 266.

75. Kenneth M. Bickers and Robert M. Stein, "The Electoral Dynamics of the Federal Pork Barrel," *American Journal of Political Science* 40 (November 1996): 1300–1326.

76. Robert M. Stein and Kenneth M. Bickers, "Congressional Elections and the Pork Barrel," *Journal of Politics* 56 (May 1994): 377–399.

77. Damon Chappie, "The New Look of Pork in the 104th," *Roll Call,* January 22, 1996, B19.

78. Quoted in Louis Jacobson, "For Arkansas, No Abundance of Clout," *National Journal,* February 20, 1999, 475.

79. Quoted in Scott MacKay, "Chafee's New Book is Tough on Pro-War Democrats, Republicans, President Bush," *Providence Journal,* January 27, 2008.

80. Eric S. Heberlig, "Congressional Parties, Fundraising, and Committee Ambition," *Political Research Quarterly* 56 (2, 2003): 151–161.

81. Anne H. Bedlington, and Michael J. Malbin, "The Party as Extended Network: Members Giving to Each Other and to their Parties," in *Life After Reform,* ed. Michael J. Malbin (Lanham, MD: Rowman & Littlefield, 2003), 121–140.

82. Marian Currinder, *Money in the House: Campaign Funds and Congressional Party Politics* (Boulder, CO: Westview Press, 2009), 5.

83. Davidson, *The Role of the Congressman,* 98; Senate Commission on the Operation of the Senate, *Toward a Modern Senate,* S. Doc. 94–278, 94th Cong., 2d sess., committee print, 1997, 27; and House Commission on Administrative Review, *Final Report,* 2 vols., H. Doc. 95–272, 95th Cong., 1st sess., December 31, 1977, 2:874–875.

84. Joint Committee on the Organization of Congress, *Organization of Congress, Final Report,* H. Rept. 103–413, 103d Congress, 1st sess., December 1993, 2:231–232.

85. Quoted in Lyndsey Layton, "Capitol's Newcomers Try a Little Openness," *Washington Post,* February 4, 2007, A6. Then House freshman, now Sen. Kirsten Gillibrand, D-N.Y., identifies the lobbyists she meets and the issues discussed. See Raymond Hernandez, "The Frantic First Days of One of the Members of the Democratic Class of '06," *New York Times,* February 20, 2007, C14.

86. Ross A. Webber, "U.S. Senators: See How They Run," *Wharton Magazine* (winter 1980–1981): 38.

87. Quoted in Cohen, *National Journal,* 17, 21.

88. Senate Commission on the Operation of the Senate, *Toward a Modern Senate.*

89. Quoted in Lindsay Sobel, "Former Lawmakers Find Trade Association Gold," *The Hill,* November 26, 1997, 14.

90. Webber, "U.S. Senators," 37.

91. Center for Responsive Politics, *Congressional Operations: Congress Speaks—A Survey of the 100th Congress* (Washington, D.C.: Center for Responsive Politics, 1988), 47–49.

92. Quoted in *Washington Post,* October 18, 1994, B3.

93. Center for Responsive Politics, *Congressional Operations,* 62–64.

94. Thomas Mann and Norman Ornstein, "Our Do-Nothing Congress," *Los Angeles Times,* September 27, 2006, B13.

95. Quoted in Lyndsey Layton, "Culture Shock on Capitol Hill: House to Work Five Days a Week," *Washington Post,* December 6, 2006, A1.

96. Joint Committee on the Organization of Congress, *Organization of Congress,* 2: 281–287.

97. Quoted in Vernon Louviere, "For Retiring Congressmen, Enough Is Enough," *Nation's Business,* May 1980, 32.

98. John R. Hibbing, *Congressional Careers: Contours of Life in the U.S. House of Representatives* (Chapel Hill: University of North Carolina Press, 1991), 117 (italics in original).

99. Hibbing, *Congressional Careers,* 126, 128.

100. Gerard Padro I Miquel and James M. Snyder, Jr., "Legislative Effectiveness and Legislative Careers," *Legislative Studies Quarterly* 31 (August 2006): 348.

101. Ibid.

102. Gary W. Cox and William C. Terry, "Legislative Productivity in the 93rd–105th Congresses," *Legislative Studies Quarterly* 33 (4, 2008): 613.

103. William H. Riker, *The Theory of Political Coalitions* (New Haven: Yale University Press, 1962), 24–38.

104. Pitkin, *The Concept of Representation,* 166.

105. Steven Kull, *Expecting More Say: The American Public on Its Role in Government Decisionmaking* (Washington, D.C.: Center on Policy Attitudes, 1999), 13–14.

106. Henry J. Hyde, "Advice to Freshmen: 'There Are Things Worth Losing For,'" *Roll Call,* December 3, 1990, 5.

107. Quoted in Jamie Stiehm, "Ex-Rep Mike Synar, Who Fought Lobbyists, Succumbs to Brain Tumor," *The Hill,* January 10, 1996, 5.

108. J. Tobin Grant and Thomas J. Rudolph, "The Job of Representation in Congress: Public Expectations and Representative Approval," *Legislative Studies Quarterly* 29 (August 2004): 442.

109. Thomas E. Cavanagh, "The Calculus of Representation: A Congressional Perspective," *Western Political Quarterly* 35 (March 1982): 120–129.

110. John W. Kingdon, *Congressmen's Voting Decisions,* 3d ed. (Ann Arbor: University of Michigan Press, 1989), 47–54.

111. Lawrence N. Hansen, *Our Turn: Politicians Talk about Themselves, Politics, the Public, the Press, and Reform,* part 2 (Washington, D.C.: Centel Public Accountability Project, 1992), 9.

112. Richard F. Fenno Jr., *Home Style: House Members in Their Districts* (New York: Pearson Longman, 2003), 1.

113. See the discussion of senators' varied constituencies in Frances E. Lee and Bruce I. Oppenheimer, *Sizing Up the Senate* (Chicago: University of Chicago Press, 1999), chap. 3.

114. Congressional Quarterly, *Congressional Districts in the 2000s* (Washington, D.C.: CQ Press. 2003), 1027–1028.

115. Fenno, *Home Style,* 4–8.

116. John F. Bibby and Thomas M. Holbrook, "Parties and Elections," in *Politics in the American States: A Comparative Analysis,* 7th ed., ed. Virginia Gray, Russell L. Hanson, and Herbert Jacob (Washington, D.C.: CQ Press, 1999), 66–112. See also Thomas L. Brunell, *Redistricting and Representation: Why Competitive Elections are Bad for America* (New York: Routledge, 2008).

117. James L. Payne, "The Personal Electoral Advantage of House Incumbents, 1936–1976," *American Politics Quarterly* 8 (October 1980): 465–482; and Robert S. Erikson, "Is There Such a Thing as a Safe Seat?" *Polity* 8 (summer 1976): 623–632.

118. Thomas E. Mann, *Unsafe at Any Margin: Interpreting Congressional Elections* (Washington, D.C.: American Enterprise Institute, 1978).

119. Fenno, *Home Style,* 8–27.

120. Thomas P. O'Neill Jr., with William Novak, *Man of the House* (New York: St. Martin's, 1987), 25.

121. Nancy Bocskor, "Fundraising Lessons Candidates Can Learn from Tom Sawyer … and Other Great American Salesmen," *Campaigns and Elections* 24 (April 2003): 33.

122. Richard F. Fenno Jr., *Senators on the Campaign Trail* (Norman: University of Oklahoma Press, 1996), 131–132.

123. David E. Price, *The Congressional Experience,* 3d ed. (Boulder, Colo.: Westview Press, 2004), 10.

124. Fenno, *Home Style,* 153.

125. Ibid., 56.

126. Anthony Champagne, *Congressman Sam Rayburn* (New Brunswick: Rutgers University Press, 1984), 28.

127. Kingdon, *Congressmen's Voting Decisions.*

128. Fenno, *Home Style,* 153.

129. Quoted in David S. Cloud, "Lawmaker Returns Home, A Hawk Turned War Foe," *New York Times,* November 22, 2005, A12.

130. Rhodes Cook, "The Safe and the Vulnerable: A Look Behind the Numbers," *Congressional Quarterly Weekly Report,* January 9, 1982, 35–38.

131. Fenno, *Home Style,* 36, 209; and Myers, "Millions of Miles from Home," *The Hill,* June 14, 1995, 8.

132. Quoted in Jim Wright, *You and Your Congressman* (New York: Coward-McCann, 1965), 35.

133. Betsy Rothstein, "Hey, Congressman! Someone Is Blocking My Driveway!" *The Hill,* June 9, 2004, 18–19.

134. John R. Johannes, *To Serve the People: Congress and Constituency Service* (Lincoln: University of Nebraska Press, 1984), chap. 5.

135. House Commission on Administrative Review, *Final Report,* 1:655; and Janet Breslin, "Constituent Service," in U.S. Senate, Senate Commission on the Operation of the Senate, *Senators: Offices, Ethics, and Pressures,* 94th Cong., 2d sess., committee print, 1977, 21.

136. Lee and Oppenheimer, *Sizing Up the Senate,* 56.

137. Ibid., 58.

138. Warren E. Miller, Donald R. Kinder, Steven J. Rosenstone, and the National Election Studies, *American National Election Study, 1990: Post–Election Survey,* 2d ed. (Ann Arbor, Mich.: Inter–University Consortium for Political and Social Research, January 1992), 166–170.

139. Ida A. Brudnick, *Congressional Salaries and Allowances,* Congressional Research Service Report No. RL30064, October 1, 2008. See also Congressional Management Foundation, *1999 Senate Staff Employment Study* (Washington, D.C.: Congressional Management Foundation, 1999), 82ff; and Congressional Management Foundation, *2000 House Staff Employment Study* (Washington, D.C.: Congressional Management Foundation, 2000), 48–49.

140. Congressional Management Foundation, *1999 Senate Staff Employment Study,* 88–89; and Congressional Management Foundation, *2000 House Staff Employment Study,* 1–2.

141. Amy Keller, "Senate Salaries Lag Behind," *Roll Call,* September 5, 2002, 1, 34; and Congressional Management Foundation, *2000 House Staff Employment Study,* 34–35.

142. Cited in C. Simon Davidson, "Congressional Office Off-Limits for Members' Campaigns," *Roll Call,* April 16, 2007, 8.

143. Richard Simon, Chuck Neubauer, and Rone Tempest, "Political Payrolls Include Families," *Los Angeles Times,* April 14, 2005, A1.

144. Quoted in Charles R. Babcock, "Frankly, an Election-Year Avalanche," *Washington Post,* September 19, 1988, A19.

145. John Pontius, *Congressional Official Mail Costs,* Congressional Research Service Report No. RS20671, March 24, 2003, 5.

146. Quoted in David Burnham, "Congress's Computer Subsidy," *New York Times Magazine,* November 2, 1980, 98.

147. U.S. Congress, Committee on Administration, *Campaign Reform and Election Integrity Act of 1999* H. Rept. 106–295, 106th Congress, 1st sess., 22.

148. Pew Research Center, "Key News Audiences now Blend Online and Traditional Sources," Survey Report, August 17, 2008, http://pewresearch.org/pubs/928/key-news-audiences-now-blend-online-and-traditional-sources (accessed February 28, 2009).

149. Brian Wingfield, "The Latest Initiative in Congress: Blogging," *New York Times,* February 24, 2005, E4.

150. E. Scott Adler, Chariti E. Gent, and Cary B. Overmeyer, "The Home Style Homepage: Legislator Use of the World Wide Web for Constituency Contact" *Legislative Studies Quarterly* 23 (November 1998): 585–595.

151. Dana Milbank, "A Tale of 140 Characters, Plus the Ones in Congress," *Washington Post,* February 25, 2009, A3.

152. Charles Bosley, "Senate Communications with the Public," in U.S. Senate, Commission on the Operation of the Senate, *Senate Communications with the Public,* 94th Cong., 2d sess., 1977, 17.

153. For descriptions of the studios, see Michael J. Robinson, "Three Faces of Congressional Media," in *The New Congress,* ed. Thomas E. Mann and Norman J. Ornstein (Washington, D.C.: American Enterprise Institute, 1981), 62–63; and Martin Tolchin, "TV Studio Serves Congress," *New York Times,* March 7, 1984, C22.

154. Tolchin, "TV Studio Serves Congress."

155. R. Douglas Arnold, *Congress, the Press, and Political Accountability* (Princeton: Princeton University Press, 2004).

156. Brian F. Schaffner, "Local News Coverage and the Incumbency Advantage in the U.S. House," *Legislative Studies Quarterly* 31 (November 2006): 491–511.

157. Robinson, "Three Faces of Congressional Media," 80–81.

158. Peter Clarke and Susan H. Evans, *Covering Campaigns: Journalism in Congressional Elections* (Stanford: Stanford University Press, 1983). See also Charles M. Tidmarch and Brad S. Karp, "The Missing Beat: Press Coverage of Congressional Elections in Eight Metropolitan Areas," *Congress and the Presidency* 10 (spring 1983): 47–61.

159. Brian J. Fogarty, "The Strategy of the Story: Media Monitoring Legislative Activity," *Legislative Studies Quarterly* 33 (August 2008): 445-469.

160. Robinson, "Three Faces of Congressional Media," 84.

161. Cokie Roberts, "Leadership and the Media in the 101st Congress," in *Leading Congress: New Styles, New Strategies,* ed. John J. Kornacki (Washington, D.C.: CQ Press, 1990), 94.

162. Markus Prior, "The Incumbent in the Living Room: The Rise of Television and the Incumbency Advantage in U.S. House Elections," *Journal of Politics* 68 (August 2006): 657–673.

163. Bob Benenson and Jonathan Allen, "It's Looking Like Blue Skies All Over Again," *Congressional Quarterly Weekly Report,* November 26, 2007, 3541.

164. Fenno, *Home Style,* 99.

CHAPTER 6

1. Katherine Skiba, "Nancy Pelosi's House: After Her Historic First Term as Speaker, Tough Challenges Ahead," *U.S. News and World Report,* January 5, 2009, http://www.usnews .com/articles/news/politics/2009/01/05/nancy-pelosis-house-after-her-historic-first-term-as-speaker-tough-challenges-ahead.html.

2. Ibid.

3. Don Wolfensberger, "Early Organization of New Congress Has Roots in Reform Era," *Roll Call,* November 10, 2008.

4. John Bresnahan, "Van Hollen to Lead DCCC," *Politico,* November 10, 2008.

5. Ibid.

6. The vote on the issue in the Steering Committee was 25–22 in favor of Waxman. The vote among the whole Democratic caucus was 137–122 for Waxman. See Alan K. Ota, "Leadership Battles Break Out in House," *Congressional Quarterly Weekly Report,* November 10, 2008, 2998; and Edward Epstein, "Upset Is Not First Shock to the Seniority System," *Congressional Quarterly Weekly Report,* November 24, 2008, 3150.

7. Tory Newmyer and Paul Singer, "Dingell-Waxman Brouhaha Awaits," *Roll Call,* November 6, 2008.

8. Patrick O'Connor and John Bresnahan, "Hoyer Steps in Waxman-Dingell Fight," *Politico,* November 12, 2008.

9. Mike Soraghan, "Despite Differences, Pelosi Praises Dingell's Service," *The Hill,* February 10, 2009.

10. Molly K. Hooper, "Pelosi's Power Move Leaves House Republicans Fuming," *The Hill,* January 5, 2009.

11. Edward Epstein, "Upset is Not First Shock to the Seniority System," *Congressional Quarterly Weekly Report,* November 24, 2008, 3150.

12. Quoted in Richard E. Cohen, "Pelosi vs. Bush," *National Journal,* May 12, 2007.

13. *Wall Street Journal,* January 30, 1985, 5.

14. The seminal work on the collective action problem is Mancur Olson, *The Logic of Collective Action, Public Goods, and the Theory of Groups* (Cambridge: Harvard University Press, 1965).

15. Barbara Sinclair, *Legislators, Leaders, and Lawmaking* (Baltimore: Johns Hopkins University Press, 1995), 9.

16. Quoted in Carl Hulse, "Hastert, the Reticent Speaker, Suddenly Has Plenty to Say," *New York Times,* May 24, 2004, A17.

17. Quoted in Kerry Kantin, "Rep. Rob Portman," *The Hill,* April 10, 2002, 12.

18. Michael Teitelbaum, "You're Off to a Great Start, but Can You Keep It Up," *CQ Today,* February 2, 2007, 1.

19. See Graeme Browning, "The Steward," *National Journal,* August 5, 1995, 2004–2007.

20. Quoted in *U.S. News and World Report,* October 13, 1950, 30.

21. See, for example, Barbara Sinclair, *Majority Leadership in the U.S. House* (Baltimore: Johns Hopkins University Press, 1983).

22. Quoted in John M. Barry, *The Ambition and the Power: The Fall of Jim Wright* (New York: Viking Penguin, 1989), 4.

23. Tom Kenworthy, "House GOP Signals It's in a Fighting Mood," *Washington Post,* December 26, 1988, A8.
24. Quoted in Barry, *The Ambition and the Power,* 6.
25. A.B. Stoddard, "Rejuvenated Gingrich Mounts Media Offensive," *The Hill,* July 10, 1996, 24.
26. Newt Gingrich, *Lessons Learned the Hard Way* (New York: HarperCollins, 1998), 37.
27. David Rogers, "Gingrich's New Style as Speaker Has a Few Hitches," *Wall Street Journal,* June 2, 1997, A24.
28. Randall Strahan, *Leading Representatives: The Agency of Leaders in the Politics of the U.S. House* (Baltimore: John Hopkins University Press, 2007), 165.
29. Ibid., 165–176.
30. Peter King, "Why I Oppose Newt," *Weekly Standard,* March 31, 1997, 23.
31. See, for example, Ceci Connolly, David Broder, and Dan Balz, "GOP's House Divided," *Washington Post,* July 28, 1997, A1; Sandy Hume, "Gingrich Foils Coup by Deputies," *The Hill,* July 16, 1997, 1; and Jackie Koszczuk, "Party Stalwarts Will Determine Gingrich's Long-Term Survival," *CQ Weekly Report,* July 26, 1997, 1751–1755.
32. Quoted in Sheryl Gay Stolberg, "Quietly, But Firmly, Hastert Asserts His Power," *New York Times,* January 3, 2005, A14.
33. Quoted in Robert Pear, Pam Belluck, and Lizette Alvarez, "Humble Man at the Helm: John Dennis Hastert," *New York Times,* January 7, 1999, A20.
34. Quoted in Kathy Kiely, "'Listener' of the House Takes Reins," *USA Today,* June 8, 2001, 11A.
35. Quoted in Eric Pianin and Helen Dewar, "GOP Leaders on Hill Find Unity Elusive," *Washington Post,* September 30, 2000, A10.
36. Ceci Connolly and Juliet Eilperin, "Hastert Steps Up to Leading Role," *Washington Post,* January 5, 1999, A4.
37. Quoted in The Cannon Centenary Conference: "The Changing Nature of the Speakership," House Document No. 108-204 (Washington, D.C.: Government Printing Office, 2004), 62.
38. Ben Pershing, "Smith Spars with Leaders," *Roll Call,* March 26, 2003, 13.
39. Quoted in Daniel Parks and Andrew Taylor, "House GOP Discord Prompts Fiscal Showdown," *CQ Daily Monitor,* September 13, 2002, 2.
40. Quoted in Karen Breslau, Eleanor Clift, and Daren Briscoe, "Rolling With Pelosi," *Newsweek,* October 23, 2006, 45.
41. Lois Ramano, "The Woman Who Would Be Speaker," *Washington Post,* October 21, 2006, A6.
42. Ibid.
43. Mark Leibovich, "Among His Official Duties, Keeping on Top of the 100-Hour Clock," *New York Times,* January 10, 2007, A18.
44. Carl Hulse, "Frustrated G.O.P. Tries to Drive Wedge Between Obama and Pelosi," *New York Times,* March 1, 2009, A1.
45. Quoted in Sasha Issenberg, "GOP Makes Pelosi Focus in Stimulus Fight," *Boston Globe,* February 11, 2009, A12.
46. Quoted in Richard E. Cohen, "GOP's Dilemma: Substance Versus Spin," *National Journal,* March 7, 2009.
47. Quoted in Hulse, "Frustrated G.O.P. Tries to Drive Wedge."
48. Rep. Jack Kingston, "When Is 100 Hours Not 100 Hours? When You're a Democrat," *The Examiner,* January 19, 2007, 18.
49. Richard E. Cohen and Brian Friel, "Chairman Rising In The Democratic Congress," *National Journal,* January 24, 2009.
50. Ibid.
51. Sarah A. Binder, Thomas E. Mann, Norman J. Ornstein, and Molly Reynolds, *Mending the Broken Branch: Assessing the 110th Congress, Anticipating the 111th,* Brookings Institution

Report, January 2009, www.brookings.edu/papers/2009/0108_broken_branch_binder_mann.aspx.

52. John Aldrich and David Rohde, "The Logic of Conditional Party Government: Revisiting the Electoral Connection," in *Congress Reconsidered,* 7th ed., ed. Lawrence Dodd and Bruce Oppenheimer (Washington, D.C.: CQ Press, 2001), 275–276.

53. See "The House in Sam Rayburn's Time" in Nelson W. Polsby, *How Congress Evolves: Social Bases of Institutional Change* (New York: Oxford University Press, 2003).

54. Randall Strahan, *Leading Representatives,* xii.

55. See, for example, Ronald M. Peters Jr., *The American Speakership: The Office in Historical Perspective,* 2d ed. (Baltimore: Johns Hopkins University Press, 1997); and D.B. Hardeman and Donald C. Bacon, *Rayburn: A Biography* (Austin, Texas: Texas Monthly Press, 1987).

56. Quoted in Randall Strahan and Daniel J. Palazzolo, "The Gingrich Effect," *Political Science Quarterly* (2004): 107.

57. Quoted in Jonathan Kaplan, "Hastert, DeLay: Political Pros Get Along to Go Along," *The Hill,* July 22, 2003, 8.

58. Jonathan Weisman, "In Backing Murtha, Pelosi Draws Fire," *Washington Post,* November 14, 2006, A1; and Karen Tumulty and Perry Bacon Jr., "Did Nancy Pelosi Get the Message?" *Time,* November 27, 2006, 31–34.

59. The Eshoo and Kind quotes are from Jonathan Kaplan, "Emanuel Cites Progress in Dem Decision-Making," *The Hill,* February 14, 2007, 4.

60. Sometimes exceptions are made to the general norm that top party leaders do not chair committees. During the 107th Congress (2001–2003), Majority Leader Dick Armey, R-Texas, chaired the Select Committee on Homeland Security, which reported the bill signed into law by President Bush creating the Department of Homeland Security.

61. Christopher Madison, "Message Bearer," *National Journal,* December 1, 1990, 2906.

62. Floyd M. Riddick, *Congressional Procedure* (Boston: Chapman and Grimes, 1941), 345–346.

63. Quoted in Richard E. Cohen, "GOP's Dilemma: Substance Versus Spin," *National Journal,* March 7, 2009.

64. See Charles O. Jones, *The Minority Party in Congress* (Boston: Little, Brown, 1970), 23.

65. Quoted in Jennifer Yachnin, "No 'Sharp Elbows' For Whip Clyburn," *Roll Call,* December 11, 2006, 36. Also see Richard Cohen, "A Different Kind of Whip," *National Journal,* January 20, 2007, 42–44.

66. Jonathan Kaplan, "New GOP Whip, Roy Blunt Offers Different Style," *The Hill,* November 20, 2002, 4.

67. Quoted in Jackie Kucinich, "For Cantor, Message is the Medium," *Roll Call,* January 12, 2009.

68. Ibid.

69. Quoted in Jackie Kucinich and Anna Palmer, "House GOP Bulks Up Outreach Operation," *Roll Call,* January 7, 2009.

70. Quoted in Jackie Kucinich, "For Cantor, Message is the Medium."

71. Alan K. Ota, "New Team Repackages the Right's Thinking," *Congressional Quarterly Weekly Report,* February 17, 2009.

72. Quoted in Alec MacGillis and Perry Bacon Jr., "GOP Sees Positives in Negative Stand; Leaders Seize on Spending Issue," *Washington Post,* February 9, 2009, A1.

73. Woodrow Wilson, *Congressional Government* (Boston: Houghton Mifflin, 1885), 223.

74. David J. Rothman, *Politics and Power: The United States Senate, 1869–1901* (Cambridge: Harvard University Press, 1966), 5–7.

75. Margaret Munk, "Origin and Development of the Party Floor Leadership in the United States Senate," *Capital Studies* 2 (winter 1974): 23–41; and Richard A. Baker and Roger H.

Davidson, eds., *First among Equals: Outstanding Senate Leaders of the Twentieth Century* (Washington, D.C.: Congressional Quarterly, 1991).

76. See Robert Caro, *Master of the Senate* (New York: Random House, 2002).

77. Rowland Evans and Robert Novak, *Lyndon B. Johnson: The Exercise of Power* (New York: New American Library, 1966), 104.

78. See John G. Stewart, "Two Strategies of Leadership: Johnson and Mansfield," in *Congressional Behavior,* ed. Nelson W. Polsby (New York: Random House, 1971), 61–92; William S. White, *Citadel: The Story of the United States Senate* (New York: Harper and Bros., 1956); Joseph S. Clark, *The Senate Establishment* (New York: Hill and Wang, 1963); and Randall B. Ripley, *Power in the Senate* (New York: St. Martin's, 1969).

79. U.S. Congress, *Congressional Record,* daily ed., 96th Cong., 2d sess., April 18, 1980, S3294.

80. David S. Broder, "Don't Bet on Bipartisan Niceties," *Washington Post,* January 1, 2003, A19.

81. Quoted in Kathy Kiely and Wendy Koch, "Committee Shaped by Party Ties," *USA Today,* October 5, 1998, 2A.

82. Shawn Zeller, "2008 Vote Studies: Party Unity—Parties Dig In Deep on a Fractured Hill," *Congressional Quarterly Weekly Report,* December 15, 2008, 3332; Isiah Poole, "Party Unity Vote Study: Votes Echo Electoral Theme," *CQ Weekly,* December 11, 2004, 2906.

83. Kirk Victor, "Deconstructing Daschle," *National Journal,* June 1, 2002, 610.

84. U.S. Congress, *Congressional Record,* daily ed., 107th Cong., 1st sess., June 6, 2001, S5844.

85. Dave Boyer, "Lott Rails on Radio against Jeffords' 'Coup of One,'" *Washington Times,* May 31, 2001, A1.

86. Quoted in Kirk Victor, "Bill Frist, In His Own Words," *National Journal,* January 4, 2003, 37.

87. Quoted in William Welch, "In Reid, Bush Faces A Tenacious Force in the Senate," *USA Today,* December 12, 2006, 13A.

88. Quoted in Kirk Victor, "Getting To 60," *National Journal,* January 13, 2007, 37.

89. Kate Ackley and John Stanton, "Reid Keeps a Short List Of Trusted Confidants," *Roll Call,* January 22, 2007, B-16.

90. Karen Tumulty, "Inside Man," *Time,* January 22, 2007, 29.

91. Shawn Zeller, "2008 Vote Studies, 3332.

92. Quoted in Tumulty, "Inside Man."

93. Quoted in Erin Billings, "McConnell Takes The Inside Track," *Roll Call,* January 31, 2007, 18.

94. Quoted in Carl Hulse, "Senate G.O.P. Leader Adapts to an Unexpected Role," *New York Times,* November 30, 2006, A20.

95. Kirk Victor, "Short on Surprises," *National Journal,* October 28, 2006, 37.

96. Quoted in Jill Zuckman, "Dick Durbin's Passion Ignites Foes' Ire," *Chicago Tribune,* June 17, 2005, online edition.

97. Massimo Calabresi and Perry Bacon Jr., "Jon Kyl: The Operator," *Time,* April 14, 2006.

98. Quoted in Erin P. Billings, "Kyl Faces First Test on Stimulus," *Roll Call,* February 4, 2008.

99. Susan Davis, "'Draft Cantor' Move Pondered," *Roll Call,* November 14, 2006, 18.

100. *New York Times,* December 6, 1988, B13.

101. Barbara Sinclair, *Majority Leadership in the U.S. House* (Baltimore: Johns Hopkins University Press, 1983).

102. U.S. Congress, *Congressional Record,* daily ed., 98th Cong., 1st sess., November 15, 1983, H9856.

103. Quoted in Thomas B. Rosenstiel and Edith Stanley, "For Gingrich, It's 'Mr. Speaker!'" *Los Angeles Times,* November 9, 1994, A2.

104. U.S. Congress, *Congressional Record,* daily ed., 94th Cong., 1st sess., January 26, 1973, S2301.

105. Quoted in Christopher Madison, "The Heir Presumptive," *National Journal,* April 29, 1989, 1036.

106. Sidney Waldman, "Majority Leadership in the House of Representatives," *Political Science Quarterly* 95 (fall 1980): 377.

107. Kirk Victor, "Reid's Smooth Start," *National Journal,* December 9, 2006, 47.

108. Neil MacNeil, *Dirksen: Portrait of a Public Man* (New York: World, 1970), 168–169.

109. Mark Preston, "Daschle May Write Book Chronicling His Times as Leader," *Roll Call Daily Issue E-newsletter,* May 20, 2002, 3.

110. *New York Times,* June 7, 1984, B16.

111. Noelle Straub and Melanie Fonder, "GOP Shifts Strategy for New Minority Status," *The Hill,* July 18, 2001, 6.

112. Mark Preston, "Lott Showcases Senators Facing Re-election," *Roll Call,* March 15, 2001, 3.

113. Stephen Gettinger, "Potential Senate Leaders Flex Money Muscles," *Congressional Quarterly Weekly Report,* October 8, 1988, 2776.

114. Eric Heberlig, Marc Hetherington, and Bruce Larson, "The Price of Leadership: Campaign Money and the Polarization of Congressional Parties," *Journal of Politics* 68 (2006): 992–1005.

115. Susan Crabtree, "Edgy GOP Lawmakers Plot Public Relations Strategy," *CQ Today,* January 31, 2005, 6.

116. Sinclair, *Majority Leadership in the U.S. House,* 96–97.

117. Erin Billings, "Pelosi Revamps the Steering Committee," *Roll Call,* March 13, 2003, 3.

118. Sen. Byron Dorgan, "Senate's DPC Role Expands as It Begins New Decade," *Roll Call,* January 30, 2007, 4.

119. Quoted in Fred Barnes, "Raging Representatives," *New Republic,* June 3, 1985, 9.

120. Jim Hoagland, "The Price of Polarization," *Washington Post,* May 5, 2005, A25.

121. Gail Russell Chaddock, "Obama Wins His Economic Stimulus Package, But Without the Bipartisanship He Sought," *Christian Science Monitor,* February 14, 2009.

122. Erin Billings, "All Together Now, Senate," *Roll Call,* January 4, 2007, 1.

123. Shailagh Murray and Jonathan Weisman, "Iraq Resolution Typifies Rift in Senate," *Washington Post,* February 11, 2007, A3.

124. Lyndsey Layton, "In Majority, Democrats Run Hill Much as GOP Did," *Washington Post,* February 18, 2007, A4.

125. Sean M. Theriault, *Party Polarization in Congress* (New York: Cambridge University Press, 2008).

126. Quoted in Elizabeth Shogren, "Will Welfare Go Way of Health Reform?" *Los Angeles Times,* August 10, 1995, A18.

127. See V. O. Key Jr., *Politics, Parties, and Pressure Groups,* 5th ed. (New York: Crowell, 1964); and Austin Ranney and Willmoore Kendall, *Democracy and the American Party System* (New York: Harcourt Brace, 1956).

128. See Harold Stanley and Richard Niemi, *Vital Statistics on American Politics, 2001–2002* (Washington, D.C.: CQ Press, 2001), 38–39.

129. Quoted in Jackie Kucinich and Anna Palmer, "House GOP Bulks Up Outreach Operation," *Roll Call,* January 7, 2009.

130. U.S. Congress, *Congressional Record,* daily ed., 104th Cong., 1st sess., October 11, 1995, E1926. Rep. Lee Hamilton, D-Ind., who made the comment, strongly opposed the overuse of omnibus bills.

131. Lee H. Hamilton with Jordan Tama, *A Creative Tension: The Foreign Policy Roles of the President and Congress* (Washington, D.C.: Woodrow Wilson Center Press, 2002), 33.

132. Nick Anderson, "In Shift, GOP Proposes Easing Immigration Rules," *Los Angeles Times,* October 26, 2000, A6.

133. Quoted in Erin Billings, "GOP Senators Stressing Reform," *Roll Call*, January 24, 2007, 25.

134. Quoted in Richard E. Cohen, "Byrd of West Virginia: A New Job, a New Image," *National Journal*, August 20, 1977, 1294.

135. For an essential guide about members of Congress and their districts, see Jackie Koszczuk and Martha Angle, eds. *CQ's Politics in America, 2008: The 110th Congress* (Washington, D.C.: CQ Press, 2007).

CHAPTER 7

1. *Washington Post,* May 14, 1987, A23.

2. U.S. Congress, *Congressional Record,* daily ed., 100th Cong., 1st sess., June 25, 1987, H5564.

3. Woodrow Wilson coined the term "little legislatures" in *Congressional Government* (Boston: Houghton Mifflin, 1885), 79.

4. Peter Cohn, "Lawmakers Back Off from Quick Acton on Bonus Tax," *National Journal's CongressDailyPM,* March 23, 2009, 1.

5. Quoted in *New York Times,* July 11, 1988, A14.

6. See, for example, Kenneth A. Shepsle and Barry R. Weingast, "The Institutional Foundations of Committee Power," *American Political Science Review* 81 (March 1987): 85–104.

7. See Keith Krehbiel, *Information and Legislative Organization* (Ann Arbor: University of Michigan Press, 1991); and Bruce Bimber, "Information as a Factor in Congressional Politics," *Legislative Studies Quarterly* (1991): 585–606.

8. Gary W. Cox and Mathew D. McCubbins, *Setting the Agenda: Responsible Party Government in the U.S. House of Representatives* (New York: Cambridge University Press, 2005), 18–19.

9. Mark S. Hurwitz, Roger J. Moiles, and David W. Rohde, "Distributive and Partisan Issues in Agriculture Policy in the 104th House," *American Political Science Review* 95 (December 2001), 911–922.

10. John W. Ellwood, "The Great Exception: The Congressional Budget Process in an Age of Decentralization," in *Congress Reconsidered,* 3d ed., ed. Lawrence C. Dodd and Bruce I. Oppenheimer (Washington, D.C.: CQ Press, 1985), 329. For the classic discussion of committee and member roles, see Richard F. Fenno Jr., *Congressmen in Committees* (Boston: Little, Brown, 1973).

11. Roy Swanstrom, *The United States Senate, 1787–1801,* S. Doc. 87–64, 87th Cong., 1st sess., 1962, 224.

12. Lauros G. McConachie, *Congressional Committees* (New York: Crowell, 1898), 124.

13. DeAlva Stanwood Alexander, *History and Procedure of the House of Representatives* (Boston: Houghton Mifflin, 1916), 228; George H. Haynes, *The Senate of the United States: Its History and Practice,* vol. 1 (Boston: Houghton Mifflin, 1938), 272; and Ralph V. Harlow, *The History of Legislative Methods in the Period before 1825* (New Haven: Yale University Press, 1917), 157–158.

14. *Cannon's Procedures in the House of Representatives,* H. Doc. 80–122, 80th Cong., 1st sess., 1959, 83.

15. Quoted in *Wall Street Journal,* May 3, 1979, 1.

16. Molly K. Hooper, "House Democrats Plan to Shrink Appropriations," *CQ Today,* December 10, 2008, p. 4.

17. *Congressional Record,* January 9, 2009, H143.

18. Edward Epstein, "Boehner Decries Party Ratios on Two Committees," *CQ Today,* January 13, 2009, 10.

19. *Congressional Record,* January 15, 2009, S590.

20. Carl Hulse and Adam Nagourney, "Specter Switches Parties: More Heft for Democrats," *New York Times,* April 29, 2009, A1; Kathleen Hunter and Bart Jansen, "Specter's Defection Has Consequences for Balance of Power on Committees," *CQ Today,* April 30, 2009, 8, 12.

21. Jessica Brady, "Waxman Reduces Number of Subcommittees; Lineup Set," *National Journal's CongressDailyPM,* December 12, 2006, 10.

22. Leora Falk, "Waxman Announces Subcommittee Shuffle; Chairmanships Await Decision From Markey," *Daily Report for Executives,* January 8, 2009, A-17.

23. U.S. Congress, *Congressional Record,* daily ed., 104th Cong., 1st sess., January 4, 1995, H33.

24. Erin Billings, "Pelosi Seeks Rules Change," *Roll Call,* March 22, 2004, 16. See also Erin Billings, "Pelosi to Prevail on Rule," *Roll Call,* March 31, 2004, 1; and Susan Ferrechio, "House Democrats Give Pelosi Authority to Name 'Exclusive' Panel Ranking Members," *CQ Today,* April 1, 2004, 14.

25. Bart Jansen, "Leiberman Decision Could Have an Impact on Other Chairmanships," *CQ Today,* November 19, 2008, 8.

26. Catharine Richert, "Enforcing Little-Used Senate Rule May Ruffle Feathers," *CQ Today,* November 20, 2008, 7. As of February 2009, Majority Leader Reid was still working to implement the two gavel rule.

27. Martin Kady, "Select Homeland Security," *CQ Weekly,* January 11, 2003, 95.

28. Charles L. Clapp, *The Congressman: His Job as He Sees It* (Washington, D.C.: Brookings Institution, 1963), 245.

29. Lawrence D. Longley and Walter J. Oleszek, *Bicameral Politics: Conference Committees in Congress* (New Haven: Yale University Press, 1989), 196.

30. Keith Krehbiel, Kenneth A. Shepsle, and Barry R. Weingast, "Why Are Congressional Committees Powerful?" *American Political Science Review* 81 (September 1987): 935.

31. Roderick Kiewiet and Mathew McCubbins, *The Logic of Delegation: Congressional Parties and the Appropriations Process* (Chicago: University of Chicago Press, 1991).

32. Don Wolfensberger, "Have House-Senate Conferences Gone The Way of the Dodo?" *Roll Call,* April 28, 2008, 8.

33. William Wan, "New Lawmaker Vows to Reflect 1st District Views," *Washington Post,* January 3, 2009, B2.

34. James Bornemeier, "Berman Accepts Seat on House Ethics Panel," *Los Angeles Times,* February 5, 1997, B1; and *CQ Daily Monitor,* December 11, 1999, 1.

35. Alan K. Ota, "Pelosi Picks Lofgren to Chair Ethics Committee," *CQ Today,* January 21, 2009, 21.

36. Sonni Efron and Janet Hook, "Lugar Now the Man in the Middle," *Los Angeles Times,* December 23, 2002, A7. See Shailagh Murray, "Foreign Relations at Center Stage," *Washington Post,* March 28, 2007, A13.

37. Fenno, *Congressmen in Committees.* See also Heinz Eulau, "Legislative Committee Assignments," *Legislative Studies Quarterly* 9 (November 1984): 587–633.

38. Christopher J. Deering and Steven S. Smith, *Committees in Congress,* 3d ed. (Washington, D.C.: CQ Press, 1997), 61–62, 78.

39. Quoted in Nancy Roman, "Freshman Nets Prized Panel by Seeking Leader's Support," *Washington Times,* December 3, 1996, A4. See also Greg Hitt, "Ways and Means: An Illinois Republican Staged Hard Campaign for Key House Panel," *Wall Street Journal,* January 3, 1997, A1.

40. Michael Barone and Richard E. Cohen, *The Almanac of American Politics, 2006* (Washington, D.C.: National Journal, 2005), 59.

41. Office of Rep. Jennifer Dunn, R-Wash., Washington, D.C.

42. Shirley Chisholm, *Unbought and Unbossed* (Boston: Houghton Mifflin, 1970), 84, 86.

43. *Congressional Record,* January 21, 2009, S729.

44. Quoted in Ethan Wallison, "Freshman Democrats Get Panel Waivers," *Roll Call,* June 21, 1999, 20.

45. Andrew Beadle, "First Lady's Résumé Won't Impress Seniority System," *CQ Daily Monitor,* November 20, 2000, 9.

46. Quoted in Peter Kaplan and David Mark, "With Election Day Over, the Campaigns Begin in the House," *CQ Daily Monitor,* November 20, 2000, 3.

47. Jim VandeHei, "Would-Be Chairmen Hit Money Trail," *Roll Call,* July 12, 1999, 1.

48. Susan Davis and Jennifer Yachnin, "Both Parties Set to Hand Out Top Committee Slots," *Roll Call,* December 4, 2006.

49. Josephine Hearn, "Dems Scramble for Committee Spoils," *The Hill,* November 29, 2006, 3.

50. *Congressional Record,* January 6, 2009, H10.

51. Jonathan Weisman, "Rank Would Guide Pelosi As She Chose Chairmen," *Washington Post,* October 21, 2006, A6.

52. *Congressional Record,* March 8, 2007, H2309–H2321.

53. "Lawmakers Reach Deal On Climate Committee," *Washington Post,* February 7, 2007, A15. See Juliet Eilperin and Michael Grunwald, "Internal Rifts Cloud Democrats' Opportunity on Warming," *Washington Post,* January 23, 2007, A1.

54. Paul Gigot, "Mack Uses Knife on Old Senate Order," *Wall Street Journal,* July 14, 1995, A12.

55. Michele Swers, *The Difference Women Make: The Policy Impact of Women in Congress* (Chicago: University of Chicago Press, 2002), 89.

56. Margaret Kriz, "Gavels Turn Green," *National Journal,* November 18, 2006, 62.

57. Tom LoBianco, "Waxman's Ascent Marks 'Sea Change' in House," *Washington Times,* November 21, 2008, A6. See Coral Davenport, "Waxman Claims a Premier Gavel," *CQ Weekly,* November 24, 2008, 3148–3150.

58. Dan Friedman and Christian Bourge, "Dems See Much At Stake In Choosing Waxman or Dingell," *National Journal's CongressDailyAM,* November 20, 2008, 9. Barney Frank, the chair of the House Financial Services Committee who voted for Dingell, offered this observation soon after the contest. "I thought Henry was making a great mistake. One of the advantages we have today is that we appear to be much less ideologically driven than the Republicans. I think there is a danger of what will look like liberal overreach. We need all the moderates to pass legislation, even at two hundred and fifty-seven. If Dingell and Waxman were running ab initio, I'd vote for Waxman. But I do think there should be some burden of proof before you throw out a chairman." See Jeffrey Tobin, "Barney's Great Adventure," *The New Yorker,* January 12, 2009, 43.

59. Quoted in *Washington Post,* November 20, 1983, A9.

60. Amy Fagan, "Thomas Takes Reins on Social Security," *Washington Times,* February 6, 2005, A3.

61. Alan Ota, "Détente on Ways and Means—At Least for Now," *CQ Today,* February 12, 2007, 1.

62. Quoted in John Maggs, "The Imperative of Compromise," *National Journal,* January 27, 2007, 50.

63. See David C. King, *Turf Wars: How Congressional Committees Claim Jurisdiction* (Chicago: University of Chicago Press, 1997).

64. David C. King, *Turf Wars* 12.

65. Patrick Yoest and Colby Itkowitz, "Jurisdictional Disputes Could Hinder Quick Conference on September 11 Measure," *CQ Today,* July 19, 2007, 15.

66. John Baughman, *Common Ground: Committee Politics in the U.S. House of Representatives* (Stanford, Calif.: Stanford University Press, 2006), 213.

67. See, for example, the jurisdictional memorandum of understanding between the chairs of the House Committees on Homeland Security and Transportation and Infrastructure inserted in the *Congressional Record,* January 4, 2007, H15–H16.

68. Catharine Richert, "Senate GOP Seeks to Shore Up Influence Through Committee Assignments," *CQ Today,* January 26, 2009, 2.

69. Quoted in Bob Pool, "Survivors Take Stock of Gains against Cancer," *Los Angeles Times,* May 30, 1997, B1.

70. Ralph Vartabedian, "Senate Panel Is Ready to Take IRS to Task," *Los Angeles Times,* September 22, 1997, A1.

71. Dana Milbank, "Auto Execs Fly Corporate Jets to D.C., Tin Cups in Hand," *Washington Post,* November 20, 2008, A3.

72. Darlene Superville, "Congressional Panels Seek 'Real People'," *Los Angeles Times,* March 25, 2007, online version.

73. Seth Stern, "Conscious of 2010 Election, Specter May Get Tough During Holder Hearing," *CQ Today,* January 15, 2009, 9. Importantly, Senator Specter's tough questions highlighted his long-standing concern that attorney generals must maintain their independence from presidents in rendering legal opinions and judgments. Senator Specter voted to confirm Holder for attorney general.

74. Elizabeth Brotherton, "Webcasting Goes Mainstream Among House Committees," *Roll Call,* March 7, 2007, 3.

75. Sean Piccoli, "Hill Samples 'Third Wave,'" *Washington Times,* June 13, 1995, A8.

76. Warren Leary, "When Astronauts Brief Congress, A Little Levity Goes a Long Way," *New York Times,* June 15, 2005, A16.

77. U.S. Congress, *Congressional Record,* daily ed., 107th Cong., 2d sess., July 16, 2002, S6849.

78. Quoted in Fawn Johnson, "Leahy: No Immigration Markup Until Bush Commits Support," *National Journal's CongressDailyAM,* March 14, 2007, 12.

79. Quoted in *Washington Post,* November 25, 1985, A4. See also Richard L. Hall, *Participation in Congress* (New Haven: Yale University Press, 1997).

80. Quoted in "CQ Midday Update Email," December 14, 2004, 1.

81. Eric Redman, *The Dance of Legislation* (New York: Simon and Schuster, 1973), 140.

82. Hugh Heclo, "Issue Networks in the Executive Establishment," in *The New American Political System,* ed. Anthony King (Washington, D.C.: American Enterprise Institute, 1978), 87–124. See also David E. Price, "Policy Making in Congressional Committees: The Impact of 'Environmental Factors,'"*American Political Science Review* (Fall 1978): 548–574.

83. Norris Cotton, *In the Senate* (New York: Dodd, Mead, 1978), 65.

84. *2004 House Staff Employment Study: Guide for the 109th Congress,* produced for the chief administrative officer, U.S. House of Representatives (Washington, D.C.: Congressional Management Foundation, 2004), 3. The Congressional Management Foundation is a private, nonpartisan group.

85. *Washington Post,* March 20, 1977, E9.

86. David Whiteman, *Communication in Congress: Members, Staff, and the Search for Information* (Lawrence: University Press of Kansas, 1995).

87. Siobhan Gorman and Richard Cohen, "Hurtling toward an Intelligence Overhaul," *National Journal,* September 18, 2004, 2808.

88. Quoted in *Washington Post,* November 20, 1983, A13.

89. Josephine Hearn, "House Staffers Follow Bosses' Footsteps On the Campaign Trail," *The Hill,* October 18, 2006, 4.

90. See Roger H. Davidson and Walter J. Oleszek, *Congress Against Itself* (Bloomington, Ind.: Indiana University Press, 1977); Judith Parris, "The Senate Reorganizes Its Committees, 1977," *Political Science Quarterly,* 94 (summer 1979), 319–337; and Roger H. Davidson, "Two Roads of Change: House and Senate Committee Reorganization," in Lawrence C. Dodd and

Bruce I. Oppenheimer, eds., *Congress Reconsidered,* 2d ed. (Washington, D.C.: CQ Press, 1981), 107–133.

91. Quoted in Andrew Taylor, "Security Plan Changes Committee Name, Little Else," *CQ Today,* October 8, 2004, 1.

92. Ibid., 4.

93. At the start of the 111th Congress (2009–2011), the House amended its rules to clarify the oversight responsibilities of the Homeland Security Committee. Specifically, the rules change authorized the panel to conduct continuing oversight of all governmental programs, activities, and agencies related to homeland security that fall within its primary jurisdiction.

94. U.S. Congress, *Congressional Record,* daily ed., 109th Cong., 1st sess., January 4, 2005, H25–H26.

95. Quoted in Davidson and Oleszek, *Congress against Itself,* 263.

96. E. Scott Adler, *Why Congressional Reforms Fail* (Chicago: University of Chicago Press, 2002), 11.

97. Richard Cohen and Marilyn Serfina, "Taxing Times," *National Journal,* December 23, 2000, 3961.

98. David Firestone, "G.O.P.'s 'Cardinals of Spending' Are Reined In by House Leaders," *New York Times,* December 2, 2002, A16.

99. Alexander Bolton, "House GOP Puts Taylor On Warning," *The Hill,* February 15, 2005, 1.

100. Quoted in Josephine Hearn, "Pelosi Riles Old Guard Chairmen," *The Politico,* January 23, 2007, 4.

101. David Herszenhorn, "Fuel Bill Shows House Speaker's Muscle," *New York Times,* December 2, 2007, E22.

102. Richard E. Cohen and Brian Friel, "Chairmen Rising," *National Journal,* January 24, 2009, 24.

103. Jared Allen, "Panel Chairmen Fighting Mad Over Snubs by Pelosi," *The Hill,* January 16, 2009, 1, 10.

104. Quoted in Kirk Victor, "Getting To 60," *National Journal,* January 13, 2007, 38.

105. David Nather, "Daschle's Soft Touch Lost in Tough Senate Arena," *CQ Weekly,* July 20, 2002, 1922.

106. Noelle Straub, "Senate Finance Panel Faces July 15 Deadline," *The Hill,* July 3, 2002, 6.

107. Susan Davis, "Pelosi, Boehner Name Eight Members to Ethics Task Force," *Roll Call,* February 1, 2007, 3.

108. "Sen. McConnell Names Senate Republican Health Reform Team," *Daily Report for Executives,* January 13, 2009, A-4.

109. See Barbara Sinclair, *Unorthodox Lawmaking: New Legislative Processes in the U.S. Congress* 3d ed. (Washington, D.C.: CQ Press, 2007), 118–122.

110. *Congressional Record,* January 27, 2009, H533.

111. *Congressional Record,* January 15, 2009, H330.

112. *Congressional Record,* February 14, 2004, S1496.

113. Nather, "Daschle's Soft Touch Lost in Tough Senate Arena," 1922.

114. *Committee Structure,* hearings before the Joint Committee on the Organization of Congress (Washington, D.C.: U.S. Government Printing Office, 1993), 779.

115. Curt Suplee, "The Science Chairman's Unpredictable Approach," *Washington Post,* October 15, 1991, A21.

CHAPTER 8

1. *Constitution, Jefferson's Manual, and Rules of the House of Representatives,* H. Doc. 107-284, 108th Cong., 2003, 127–128. The rules of the Senate are contained in *Senate Manual,* S. Doc. 107-1, 107th Cong., 2002.

2. Donald R. Matthews, *U.S. Senators and Their World* (Chapel Hill: University of North Carolina Press, 1960), chapter 5.

3. *Congressional Record,* March 31, 2008, S2234.

4. *Wall Street Journal,* October 2, 1987, 1.

5. Quoted in John Solomon, "Family Crisis Shifts Politics," *USA Today,* August 16, 2001, 15A.

6. See Mark Leibovich, "Democrat, Republican and a Bond of Addiction," *New York Times,* September 19, 2006, A1. The bill was entitled the "Paul Wellstone and Pete Domenici Mental Health Parity and Addiction Equity Act of 2008." Senator Wellstone, D-Minn., who perished in an airplane crash, and Domenici, R-N.M., had immediate family members who suffered from mental illness. Senator Domenici retired at the end of the 110th Congress. He called the measure his most important legacy after thirty-six years of continuous Senate service.

7. *National Journal,* April 10, 1982, 632.

8. Quoted in Julie Rovner, "Senate Committee Approves Health Warnings on Alcohol," *Congressional Quarterly Weekly Report,* May 24, 1986, 1175.

9. Woodrow Wilson, *Congressional Government* (Boston: Houghton Mifflin, 1885), 320.

10. Theodore Sorensen, *Kennedy* (New York: Harper and Row, 1965), 184.

11. *Wall Street Journal,* June 2, 1988, 56.

12. U.S. Congress, *Congressional Record,* daily ed., 95th Cong., 1st sess., May 17, 1977, E3076.

13. Peter Baker, "White House Finds 'Fast Track' Too Slippery," *Washington Post,* September 14, 1997, A4. See also U.S. Congress, *Congressional Record,* daily ed., 105th Cong., 2d sess., September 29, 1998, S11133; U.S. Congress, *Congressional Record,* daily ed., 106th Cong., 1st sess., January 25, 1999, S979; and Ceci Connolly, "Consultant Offers GOP a Language for the Future," *Washington Post,* September 4, 1997, A1.

14. Lisa Lerer, "Senate Embraces Sanders' Pay Cap," *Politico,* February 9, 2009, 1.

15. For information on the drafting process, see Lawrence E. Filson, *The Legislative Drafter's Desk Reference* (Washington, D.C.: Congressional Quarterly, 1992).

16. *CQ Monitor,* July 24, 1998, 5.

17. Lawrence J. Haas, "Unauthorized Action," *National Journal,* January 2, 1988, 20.

18. T. R. Reid, *Congressional Odyssey: The Saga of a Senate Bill* (San Francisco: W. H. Freeman, 1980), 17.

19. Paul Singer, "More Bills, More Lawyers for Leg. Offices," *Roll Call,* March 28, 2007, 22.

20. Carroll J. Doherty, "Lots of Inertia, Little Lawmaking as Election '98 Approaches," *CQ Weekly,* July 18, 1998, 1925.

21. Quoted in Margaret Kriz, "Still Charging," *National Journal,* December 6, 1997, 2462.

22. Donald R. Wolfensberger, "Suspended Partisanship in the House: How Most Laws Are Really Made" (paper prepared for the 2002 annual meeting of the American Political Science Association, Boston, Mass., August 29–September 1, 2002), 11.

23. Martin Gold, et al., *The Book on Congress* (Washington, D.C.: Big Eagle Publishing, 1992), 124.

24. *Congressional Record,* February 28, 2007, H1986.

25. U.S. Congress, *Congressional Record,* daily ed., 109th Cong., 1st sess., January 4, 2005, H34.

26. Quoted in Jonathan Salant, "Under Open Rules, Discord Rules," *Congressional Quarterly Weekly Report,* January 28, 1995, 277.

27. *National Journal,* January 21, 1995, 183.
28. Lizette Alvarez, "Campaign Finance Measure Soundly Rejected by House," *New York Times,* June 18, 1998, A26.
29. Stanley Bach and Steven S. Smith, *Managing Uncertainty in the House of Representatives: Adaptation and Innovation in Special Rules* (Washington, D.C.: Brookings Institution, 1988), 87.
30. *Congressional Record,* December 7, 2006, J8896.
31. *Congressional Record,* May 14, 2008, H3824.
32. Ibid.
33. Quoted in S. A. Miller, "Democrats Hedge On Bipartisan Pledge," *Washington Times,* January 25, 2007, A9.
34. Tory Newmyer, "Pelosi Vows a Return to Regular Order," *Roll Call,* February 5, 2009, online edition. See Christian Bourge, "Pelosi Tells Dems Chamber Will Return To Regular Order," National Journal's *CongressDailyAM,* February 6, 2009, 8 and David Sands, "Calls for 'Regular Order' Grow Louder," *Washington Times,* February 10, 2009, B1.
35. Mary Lynn F. Jones, "The Republican Railroad," *American Prospect,* April 2003, 16.
36. Lindsay Sobel, "Democrats Weight Discharge Petition Barrage," *The Hill,* July 1, 1998, 2.
37. David Sands, "Short Session Likely Partisan," *Washington Times,* September 10, 2008, A13.
38. Alexander Bolton, "House Leaders Tighten Grip, Anger Centrists," *The Hill,* January 15, 2003, 23.
39. Susan Ferrechio, "Parliamentary Smackdown? Rules Change Effort Could Bring—Gasp!—Stalling Motions," *CQ Today,* April 2, 2007, 1.
40. Information courtesy of Richard Beth, specialist in legislative process, Congressional Research Service, Library of Congress.
41. Quoted in Jennifer Yachnin, "Hoyer: House to Work Monday–Friday in 110th," *Roll Call,* December 6, 2006, 1.
42. Jennifer Bendery, "House Democrats Plan 137 Days of Voting Next Year," *Roll Call,* December 5, 2008, online edition.
43. Arie Dekker, "A Redhead In An Ocean of Gray Hair," *The Hill,* July 8, 2008, 23. Real debate between the majority and minority is sometimes scheduled during a nonlegislative period called "special orders" at the end of the day. Members can reserve up to one hour during the special order period to debate specific legislative topics. July 14, 2008, was one of those times. The Speaker and minority leader agreed to combine two special orders "so that both sides can participate in the debate about energy policy." See *Congressional Record,* July 14, 2008, H6456.
44. *National Journal's CongressDaily/PM,* January 13, 1995, 4.
45. Robert S. Walker, "Why House Republicans Need a Watchdog," *Roll Call,* January 19, 1987, 10.
46. John F. Bibby, ed., *Congress off the Record* (Washington, D.C.: American Enterprise Institute, 1983), 23.
47. Martin Kady II, "SCHIP Vote Haunts Republican Losers," *Politico,* November 12, 2008, 15.
48. For an excellent analysis of the motion to recommit, see Megan S. Lynch, *The Motion to Recommit in the House of Representatives: Effects, Recent Trends, and Options for Change,* CRS Report RL34757, November 20, 2008.
49. Kathleen Hunter, "GOP Continues to Vex Democrats on Procedure," *CQ Today,* November 7, 2007, 30.
50. Sen. J. Bennett Johnston, D-La. (1972–1997), quoted in *New York Times,* November 22, 1985, B8.

51. Quoted in "Democrats to Forgo Control in Brief Edge," *Washington Times,* November 29, 2000, A4.

52. David Rogers, "The Senate's Moment," *Politico,* June 15, 2008, 6.

53. Carl Hulse, "With Flurry of Deals, And Eye on Calendar, Congress Clears Decks," *New York Times*, June 21, 2008, A14.

54. U.S. Congress, *Congressional Record,* daily ed., 101st Cong., 2d sess., July 20, 1990, S10183.

55. Susan F. Rasky, "With Few Bills Passed or Ready for Action, Congress Seems Sluggish," *New York Times,* May 14, 1989, 24.

56. John Felton, "Senate's Climate of Partisanship Yields...An Agreement of Unusual Complexity," *Congressional Quarterly Weekly Report*, Aug. 16, 1986, 1878.

57. U.S. Congress, *Congressional Record,* daily ed., 98th Cong., 2d sess., January 27, 1984, S328–S329.

58. Walter J. Oleszek, *Congressional Procedures and the Policy Process,* 7th ed. (Washington, D.C.: CQ Press, 2007), 245–250. See also Lewis A. Froman Jr., *The Congressional Process* (Boston: Little, Brown, 1967); and Terry Sullivan, *Procedural Structure: Success and Influence in Congress* (New York: Praeger, 1984).

59. Elizabeth Drew, *Senator* (New York: Simon and Schuster, 1979), 158.

60. U.S. Congress, *Congressional Record,* daily ed., 97th Cong., 2d sess., May 20, 1982, S5648.

61. Mary Dalrymple, "Democrats Say They Are Unified in Opposition Platform," *CQ Today,* January 29, 2002, 5.

62. Gail Russell Chaddock, "Limits on Filibusters Are Already Pervasive," *Christian Science Monitor,* May 24, 2005, 2.

63. U.S. Congress, *Congressional Record,* daily ed., 107th Cong., 2d sess., April 17, 2002, S2850.

64. Helen Dewar, "'Hold' Likely for IRS Pick, Daschle Says," *Washington Post,* October 30, 1997, A11.

65. See comments by Alan Cranston of California, then Senate Democratic whip, in *New York Times,* July 17, 1986, A3.

66. Quoted in Sean Piccoli, "Byrd Still Senate Caesar Despite GOP Takeover," *Washington Times,* February 14, 1995, A11.

67. U.S. Congress, *Operations of the Congress: Testimony of House and Senate Leaders,* hearing before the Joint Committee on the Organization of Congress (Washington, D.C.: U.S. Government Printing Office, 1993), 50.

68. Doug Obey, "Alaska," *The Hill,* July 10, 1996, 27.

69. See Barbara Sinclair, *Party Wars: Polarization and the Politics of National Policy Making* (Norman, Okla.: University of Oklahoma Press, 2006).

70. Testimony of Steven S. Smith, University of Minnesota, before the Joint Committee on the Organization of Congress, 103d Cong., 1st sess., May 20, 1993, 14.

71. Richard Cohen, *National Journal,* July 28, 2001, 2396.

72. Carl Hulse and Robert Pear, "Feeling Left Out on Major Bills, Democrats Turn to Stalling Others," *New York Times,* May 3, 2004, A8.

73. See Walter J. Oleszek, *Whither the Role of Conference Committees: An Analysis,* CRS Report RL34611, August 12, 2008.

74. U.S. Congress, *Congressional Record,* daily ed., 106th Cong., 2d sess., October 13, 2000, S10520.

75. Jonathan Allen and John Cochran, "The Might of the Right," *CQ Weekly,* November 8, 2003, 2762.

76. Barbara Sinclair, *Unorthodox Lawmaking: New Legislative Processes in the U.S. Congress,* 3d ed. (Washington, D.C.: CQ Press, 2007).

77. Barber B. Conable, "Weaving Webs: Lobbying by Charities," *Tax Notes,* November 10, 1975, 27–28.

CHAPTER 9

1. David M. Herszenhorn, "In Senate, Republicans Block Spending Measure," *New York Times,* March 6, 2009, A16.
2. Quoted in ibid.
3. Humberto Sanchez and Christian Bourge, "Reid Sees Senate Action on Omnibus by March 6 Deadline," *Congress Daily PM,* February 24, 2009.
4. Gail Russell Chaddock, "Omnibus Bill's Hidden Item: A Democratic Rift," *Christian Science Monitor,* March 12, 2009.
5. Robert Pear, "House Passes Spending Bill, and Critics Are Quick to Point Out Pork," *New York Times,* February 26, 2009, A20.
6. Evan Bayh, "Deficits and Fiscal Credibility," *Wall Street Journal,* March 4, 2009.
7. Dan Friedman and Humberto Sanchez, "GOP Senators Say Attacks on Omnibus Bill Are Paying Off," *Congress Daily PM,* March 4, 2009.
8. Shailagh Murray, "Democrats Stung By Dissenters: Unity on Agenda Eludes Party Leaders," *Washington Post,* March 10, 2009, A1.
9. Quoted in Jill Smallen and Jason Dick, "The Week on the Hill: Obama Signs Omnibus Package," *National Journal,* March 14, 2009.
10. Dan Friedman, "Despite Threat, Appointed Senators Hold Firm Against Vitter," *Congress Daily AM,* March 11, 2009.
11. Quoted in ibid.
12. Quoted in ibid.
13. Quoted in Emily Pierce, "Omnibus' Fate Not Accompli," *Roll Call,* March 5, 2009.
14. Quoted in ibid.
15. Emily Pierce, "Menendez Feels the Heat; Senators Fume Over Omnibus," *Roll Call,* March 11, 2009.
16. Quoted in Carl Hulse, "Their Ranks Bolstered, and With Big Issues Ahead, Democrats Stumble," *New York Times,* March 7, 2009, A11.
17. Quoted in ibid.
18. Quoted in ibid.
19. Paul Kane and Scott Wilson, "Obama Signs Spending Bill, Vowing to Battle Earmarks," *Washington Post,* March 12, 2009, A01.
20. Richard L. Hall, *Participation in Congress* (New Haven: Yale University Press, 1996), 27–30.
21. Lauren Whittington, "Obscure Caucus: Members Allergic to the Spotlight Find a Home," *Roll Call,* September 10, 2007. The listing omits senators: "[S]enators are by definition not obscure, although there are several who seem to strive for it." To be listed in the Obscure Caucus, House members must have served at least two full terms.
22. Quoted in *The Hill,* November 15, 2000, 16.
23. David Price, *Who Makes the Laws?* (Cambridge, Mass.: Schenkman Publishing, 1972), 297; and David E. Price, *The Congressional Experience,* 3d ed. (Boulder, Colo.: Westview Press, 2004), chapter 6.
24. Quoted in Bernard Asbell, *The Senate Nobody Knows* (Garden City, N.Y.: Doubleday, 1978), 210.
25. Richard F. Fenno Jr., "Observation, Context, and Sequence in the Study of Politics," *American Political Science Review* 80 (March 1976): 3–15.
26. Lindsay Sobel, "Early Fast-Track Support Cost Members Leverage," *The Hill,* November 12, 1997, 33.
27. Quoted in Betsy Rothstein, "GOP Leaders Must Cope with Pesky Chafee and Jeffords," *The Hill,* May 16, 2001, 28.

28. Quoted in Joel Havemann, "Last-Minute Swap Let Spending Bill Through," *Los Angeles Times,* December 24, 2005, A14.

29. Cited in Philippe Shepnick, "Moynihan Is Champion Bill Writer," *The Hill,* March 10, 1999, 6.

30. Rick K. Wilson and Cheryl D. Young, "Cosponsorship in the U.S. Congress," *Legislative Studies Quarterly* 22 (February 1997): 25–43.

31. Jacob R. Straus, "Dear Colleague Letters in the House of Representatives: The Tracking of Internal House Communications," Paper presented at the annual meeting of the Midwest Political Science Association, Chicago, IL, April 2–5, 2009, Figure 1.

32. Richard F. Fenno Jr., *The Making of a Senator: Dan Quayle* (Washington, D.C.: CQ Press, 1989), 43–45.

33. T. R. Reid, *Congressional Odyssey: The Saga of a Senate Bill* (San Francisco: W. H. Freeman, 1980), 15.

34. Hall, *Participation in Congress,* 139; see also 119.

35. Ibid., 126–127.

36. Ibid., 102.

37. Gary Mucchiaroni and Paul J. Quirk, *Deliberative Choices: Debating Public Policy in Congress* (Chicago: University of Chicago Press, 2006), 197.

38. Ibid., 194–195.

39. Helen Fessenden and Carolyn Skorneck, "GOP Rebellion on Nature of Iraq Funds Augurs Further Grief for White House," *Congressional Quarterly Weekly Report,* October 25, 2003, 2652.

40. A University of Pennsylvania National Annenberg Election Survey released on January 8, 2004, reported that 53 percent of respondents wanted to spend less or no money at all rebuilding Iraq. Only 9 percent wanted to spend more.

41. Carolyn Skorneck, "Iraq Supplemental Will Pass, But Many Say Well is Going Dry," *Congressional Quarterly Weekly Report,* September 27, 2003, 2369.

42. Mary Beth Sheridan and Hamil R. Harris, "D.C. Voting Measure Clears the Senate: Added Gun Language Might Pose a Problem," *Washington Post,* February 27, 2009, A1.

43. U.S. Congress, *Congressional Record,* daily ed., 103d Cong., 1st sess., June 23, 1993, H3941–3973.

44. John D. Wilkerson, "'Killer' Amendments in Congress," *American Political Science Review* 93 (September 1999): 535–552.

45. Quoted in Peter Gosselin, "Paulson Will Have No Peer Under Bailout Deal," *Los Angeles Times,* September 29, 2008, online edition.

46. Quoted in Krissah Williams Thompson, "Those Up for Reelection Have Explaining to Do," *Washington Post,* October 1, 2008, A10.

47. John Cranford, "Present and Counted," *CQ Weekly,* January 1, 2007, 54–55.

48. John B. Gilmour, *Strategic Disagreement* (Pittsburgh: University of Pittsburgh Press, 1995), 41.

49. Quoted in Ramesh Ponnuru, "Division on the Right," *National Review,* November 21, 2003.

50. David C. King and Richard J. Zeckhauser, "Congressional Vote Options," *Legislative Studies Quarterly* 28 (August 2003): 400–401.

51. Quoted in Eric Schmitt, "House Votes to Bar Religious Abuse Abroad," *New York Times,* May 15, 1998, A1.

52. Albert R. Hunt, "Balanced-Budget Measure Is Likely to Pass Senate Next Week, Faces Battle in House," *Wall Street Journal,* July 30, 1982, 2.

53. Norman J. Ornstein, Thomas E. Mann, and Michael J. Malbin, *Vital Statistics on Congress, 2008* (Washington, D.C.: The Brookings Institution, 2008), 148–149.

54. The most recent figures on party unity votes and scores are found in *CQ Weekly,* December 15, 2008, 3337; and February 16, 2009, 335.

55. For an authoritative analysis of the decline and resurgence of congressional partisanship, see David W. Rohde, *Parties and Leaders in the Postreform House* (Chicago: University of Chicago Press, 1991), especially 3–11.

56. For an extended analysis of partisan interests as a source of party cohesion and conflict, see Frances E. Lee, *Beyond Ideology: Politics, Principles, and Partisanship in the U.S. Senate* (Chicago: University of Chicago Press, 2009).

57. Gary C. Jacobson, *The Politics of Congressional Elections,* 7th ed. (New York: Pearson Longman, 2009), 135–144.

58. Quoted in Randall B. Ripley, *Party Leaders in the House of Representatives* (Washington, DC: The Brookings Institution, 1967), 144.

59. John Breaux, "Congress's Lost Art of Compromise," *Roll Call,* April 19, 2005, 17.

60. Bart Jansen, "GOP Looks for Ways to Regroup After Losses," *CQ Today,* May 6, 2008.

61. Erin P. Billings and Mark Preston, "Democrats Look for Expert Help; Message Gurus Asked for Input," *Roll Call,* February 17, 2005.

62. Quoted in ibid.

63. Gary W. Cox and Mathew D. McCubbins, *Setting the Agenda: Responsible Party Government in the U.S. House of Representatives* (New York: Cambridge University Press, 2005), 18.

64. See John W. Kingdon, *Congressmen's Voting Decisions* (New York: Harper and Row, 1981) and Ripley, *Party Leaders in the House of Representatives,* 139–159.

65. Donald R. Matthews and James A. Stimson. *Yeas and Nays: Normal Decisionmaking in the U.S. House of Representatives* (New York: John Wiley & Sons, 1975), 95.

66. Quoted in Morton Kondracke, "Who's Running the House? GOP Freshmen or Newt?" *Roll Call,* December 18, 1995, 5.

67. See Gary W. Cox and Mathew D. McCubbins, *Legislative Leviathan: Party Government in the House* (Berkeley: University of California Press, 1993); Gary W. Cox and Keith T. Poole, "On Measuring Partisanship in Roll-Call Voting: The U.S. House of Representatives, 1877–1999," *American Journal of Political Science* 46(3): 477–489; and Sean M. Theriault, "Procedural Polarization in the US Congress" (paper presented at the 2006 Midwest Political Science Association, Chicago, Ill.).

68. Garry Young and Vicky Wilkins, "Vote Switchers and Party Influence in the U.S. House," *Legislative Studies Quarterly* 32 (February 2007): 59–77.

69. See Lee, *Beyond Ideology,* Chapter 6.

70. *Congressional Record,* June 23, 1987, S8438.

71. Rohde, "Electoral Forces," 28.

72. Helmut Norpoth, "Explaining Party Cohesion in Congress: The Case of Shared Policy Attitudes," *American Political Science Review* 70 (December 1976): 1171.

73. David Frum, "Republicans Face Fraught Choice Between Two Roads to Revival," *National Post,* November 5, 2008.

74. Alan K. Ota, "New Team Repackages the Right's Thinking," *CQ Weekly,* February 17, 2009.

75. For discussion of the "creative class," see Richard Florida, "The Rise of the Creative Class," *Washington Monthly,* May 2002. For extended treatment of these different sources of electoral support for the Democratic Party, see John B. Judis and Ruy Teixeira, *The Emerging Democratic Majority* (New York: Simon and Schuster, 2004).

76. Brian Friel and Richard E. Cohen, "The Congressional Jigsaw: Needy Democratic Moderates," *National Journal,* February 28, 2009.

77. John F. Manley, "The Conservative Coalition in Congress," *American Behavioral Scientist* 17 (December 1973): 223–247; Barbara Sinclair, *Congressional Realignment: 1925–1978* (Austin: University of Texas Press, 1982); and Mack C. Shelley, *The Permanent Majority: The Conservative Coalition in the United States Congress* (University: University of Alabama Press, 1983).

78. Stephen Gettinger, "R.I.P. to a Conservative Force," *CQ Weekly,* January 9, 1999, 82–83.

79. Sarah A. Binder, "The Disappearing Political Center," *Brookings Review* 15 (fall 1996): 36–39. An extended analysis of the problem and its results is found in Sarah A. Binder, *Stalemate: Causes and Consequences of Legislative Gridlock* (Washington, D.C.: Brookings Institution Press, 2003).

80. Keith T. Poole and Howard Rosenthal, "Patterns of Congressional Voting," *American Journal of Political Science* 35 (February 1991), 228–278; and Keith T. Poole and Howard Rosenthal, *Congress: A Political-Economic History of Roll-Call Voting* (New York: Oxford University Press, 1997). See Ornstein, Mann, and Malbin, *Vital Statistics on Congress,* 160–161.

81. Using different measures of similar data, the same point is made in Morris P. Fiorina, with Samuel J. Adams and Jeremy C. Pope, *Culture War? The Myth of a Polarized America,* 2d ed. (New York, Pearson Longman, 2006), 16–21 and Fig. 2-2.

82. Sean M. Theriault, "The Case of the Vanishing Moderates: Party Polarization in the Modern Congress" (paper presented at the 2003 annual meeting of the Western Political Science Association, Denver, Colo.), Figure 1. Ideology scores from similar years (1969–1970 and 1999–2000) yield virtually the same results. Binder, *Stalemate,* 23–26.

83. Quoted by E. J. Dionne Jr., "The Real Pelosi," *Washington Post,* April 9, 2009, A17.

84. Binder, "The Disappearing Political Center," 37. Binder defines centrists as those members who are closer to the ideological midpoint between the two parties than to the ideological center of their own party.

85. These estimates are based on the Prof. Keith Poole's DW-NOMINATE scores for senators and House members provided on his Web site, http://voteview.com/dwnomin.htm.

86. Binder, *Stalemate,* 69.

87. David W. Rohde, "Electoral Forces, Political Agendas, and Partisanship in the House and Senate," in *The Postreform Congress,* ed. Roger H. Davidson (New York: St. Martin's, 1992), especially 34–40.

88. Jeffrey M. Stonecash, Mark D. Brewer, and Mack Mariani, *Diverging Parties* (Boulder, Co.: Westview Press, 2002).

89. Data on party loyalty in roll-call voting in the 110th Congress is drawn from CQ's annual vote study *CQ Weekly,* December 15, 2008, 3339–3341.

90. Quoted in Eve Fairbanks, "Extremely Moderate," *Los Angeles Times,* April 15, 2007, M4.

91. R. Douglas Arnold, *The Logic of Congressional Action* (New Haven: Yale University Press, 1990).

92. Ibid., 68.

93. Ibid., 84.

94. It is worth noting that recent presidents have taken stands on fewer issues. See Ornstein, Mann, and Malbin, *Vital Statistics on Congress,* 144–145.

95. It must be noted that presidents take positions on legislative matters with an eye to polishing their record. Lyndon Johnson's success rate was boosted by his habit of sending up messages supporting measures he already knew would pass. George W. Bush's record owes much to his strategy of focusing on a few core initiatives.

96. Jill Barshay, "Popularity Not Required," *CQ Weekly,* January 1, 2007, 44–53.

97. Sen. James M. Jeffords, R-Vt., statement, Burlington, Vermont, May 24, 2001. See Jeffords's Web site at senate.gov/Jeffords.

98. Clea Benson, "Presidential Support: The Power of No," *CQ Weekly,* December 15, 2008, 132.

99. David Nather, "Clinton's Floor Vote Victories Yielded Few Accomplishments," *CQ Weekly,* January 6, 2001, 52ff.

100. Roger H. Davidson, *The Role of the Congressman* (Indianapolis: Bobbs-Merrill, 1969), 22–23.

101. Robert L. Peabody, "Organization Theory and Legislative Behavior: Bargaining, Hierarchy, and Change in the U.S. House of Representatives" (paper presented at the 1963 annual meeting of the American Political Science Association, New York).

102. Carl J. Friedrich, *Constitutional Government and Democracy,* 4th ed. (Waltham, Mass.: Blaisdell Publishing, 1967), 269–270.

103. Quoted in Ben Pershing, "Boehlert Holding Bush's Feet to Fire," *Roll Call,* April 30, 2001, 28.

104. Quoted in Mark Preston, "Chafee Remembered as War Hero, Political Giant," *Roll Call,* October 28, 1999, 36.

105. John W. Kingdon, *Congressmen's Voting Decisions,* 3d ed. (Ann Arbor: University of Michigan Press, 1989).

106. Quoted in John F. Bibby, ed., *Congress Off the Record* (Washington, D.C.: American Enterprise Institute, 1983), 22.

107. Quoted in Claudia Dreifus, "Exit Reasonable Right," *New York Times Magazine,* June 2, 1996, 26.

108. Edward J. Derwinski, "The Art of Negotiation within the Congress," in *International Negotiation: Art and Science,* ed. Diane B. Bendahmane and John W. McDonald Jr. (Washington, D.C.: U.S. Department of State, Foreign Service Institute, 1984), 11.

109. Lizette Alvarez, "In Slap at GOP Leadership, House Stops Move to Deny Food Stamps to Immigrants," *New York Times,* May 23, 1998, A9. For background, see John Ferejohn, "Logrolling in an Institutional Context: A Case Study of Food Stamp Legislation," in *Congress and Policy Change,* ed. Gerald C. Wright Jr., Leroy N. Rieselbach, and Lawrence C. Dodd (New York: Agathon Press, 1986), 223–253.

110. Elliott Abrams, "Unforgettable Scoop Jackson," *Reader's Digest,* February 1985. Quotation cited in U.S. Congress, *Congressional Record,* daily ed., 99th Cong., 1st sess., February 20, 1985, E478.

111. Quoted in David E. Rosenbaum, "The Favors of Rostenkowski: Tax Revision's Quid Pro Quo," *New York Times,* November 27, 1985, B6.

112. Steve Waldman, *The Bill* (New York: Viking, 1994), 94–95.

113. Quoted in John Sawyer, "Prescription Drug Vote Came Down to Emerson, Push for Reimportation; Missouri Republican Believes Measure Could Save Billions in Drug Costs," *St. Louis Post-Dispatch,* June 29, 2003, A5.

114. Ibid.

115. Lynn Sweet, "House OKs Foreign Drug Imports," *Chicago Sun-Times,* July 26, 2003, 3.

116. Dan Morgan, "Sugar Industry Expands Influence: Donations Spread Beyond Farm Areas," *Washington Post,* November 3, 2007, A1.

117. Quotes from Jonathan Allen, "Effective House Leadership Makes the Most of Majority," *CQ Weekly,* March 29, 2003, 751.

118. Quoted in Kirk Victor, "Kennedy the Pragmatist," *National Journal,* December 8, 2001, 3791.

119. John B. Gilmour, *Strategic Disagreement: Stalemate in American Politics* (Pittsburgh: University of Pittsburgh Press, 1995), 4.

120. Gary W. Cox and Jonathan N. Katz, "Gerrymandering Roll Calls in Congress, 1879–2000," *American Journal of Political Science* 51 (January 2007): 117.

121. See William H. Riker, *The Theory of Political Coalitions* (New Haven: Yale University Press, 1962), 32. Theorists define legislative bargaining situations formally as *n*-person, zero-sum games in which side payments are permitted. That is, a sizable number of participants are involved; when some participants win, others must lose; and participants can trade items outside the substantive issues under consideration.

122. John G. Stewart, "Two Strategies of Leadership: Johnson and Mansfield," in *Congressional Behavior,* ed. Nelson W. Polsby (New York: Random House, 1971), 67.

123. Russell Hardin, "Hollow Victory: The Minimum Winning Coalition," *American Political Science Review* 79 (December 1976): 1202–1214.

124. Breaux, "Congress's Lost Art of Compromise," 17.

125. Binder, *Stalemate,* 127.

126. Robert J. Dole, remarks to the Senate, March 29, 2000, quoted in *The Hill,* April 5, 2000, 32.

127. Clinton T. Brass, "Shutdown of the Federal Government: Causes, Processes, and Effects," Congressional Research Service Report RL34680, September 23, 2008. Note that "shutdowns" also include "funding gaps" that occur when there is a lag between the expiration of a continuing resolution (CR) and the enactment of a new one. In the absence of a CR, agencies begin their shutdown, even if it is only for a few days.

CHAPTER 10

1. Aaron Blake, "Republicans Are Wagering Heavily On Stimulus As Major Issue in 2010," *The Hill,* February 12, 2009, 12. See Jackie Kucinich, "Republicans Ramp Up Fiscal Crisis Criticism," *Roll Call,* March 12, 2009, 3.

2. Jonathan Weisman and Naftali Bendavid, "Obama Turns Up Heat, Slams GOP Ideas," *Wall Street Journal,* February 6, 2009, A4.

3. Bob Cusack, J. Taylor Rushing, and Hugo Gurdon, "I Don't Work for Obama," *The Hill,* January 7, 2009, 1.

4. *Congressional Record,* January 14, 2009, H268–H281.

5. Ross K. Baker, "Democrats, Not So Fast," *USA Today,* June 19, 2008, 11A.

6. Jim VandeHei and Mike Allen, "Lesson: Communication is More Than Eloquence," *Politico,* March 20, 2009, 7.

7. Kara Rowland, "Democrat Hits Farm Proposal As Misguided," *Washington Times,* March 10, 2009, A6. See Jackie Calmes and Carl Hulse, "Obama's Budget Faces Challenge By Party Barons," *New York Times,* March 10, 2009, A1.

8. See Stephen Wayne, *The Legislative Presidency* (New York: Harper and Row, 1978).

9. Charles O. Jones, *Separate but Equal Branches: Congress and the Presidency* (Chatham, N.J.: Chatham House, 1995), 138–157.

10. Michael Nelson, "Evaluating the President," in *The Presidency and the Political System,* 7th ed., ed. Michael Nelson (Washington, D.C.: CQ Press, 2003), 21.

11. See Norman J. Ornstein, "Theories of the Presidency," in *Encyclopedia of the American Presidency,* vol. 4, ed. Leonard Levy and Louis Fisher (New York: Simon and Schuster, 1994), 1458–1462.

12. Richard E. Neustadt, *Presidential Power* (New York: John Wiley, 1960), 23.

13. Ibid., 16.

14. Leonard D. White, *The Federalists* (New York: Macmillan, 1948), 55.

15. Leonard D. White, *The Jeffersonians* (New York: Macmillan, 1951), 35.

16. John A. Farrell, *Tip O'Neill and the Democratic Century* (Boston: Little, Brown, 2001), 553.

17. Paul C. Light, *The President's Agenda* (Baltimore: Johns Hopkins University Press, 1982), 230–231.

18. Frank James, "Congressional Budget Office Sees More Red Ink in Obama Budget," *Los Angeles Times,* March 20, 2009, online edition.

19. Janet Hook, "Obama Budget Faces New Hurdles," *Los Angeles Times,* March 20, 2009, online edition.

20. George E. Condon, Jr., "Can Congress Keep Up?" *CongressDailyAM,* March 13, 2009, 5.

21. Lyndon B. Johnson, *The Vantage Point* (New York: Popular Library, 1971), 448.

22. Jack Valenti, "Some Advice on the Care and Feeding of Congressional Egos," *Los Angeles Times,* April 23, 1978, 3.

23. Richard Berke, "Courting Congress Nonstop, Clinton Looks for an Alliance," *New York Times,* March 8, 1993, A1.

24. Roy P. Basler, ed., *The Collected Works of Abraham Lincoln,* vol. 3 (New Brunswick: Rutgers University Press, 1953), 27.

25. Samuel Kernell, *Going Public: New Strategies of Presidential Leadership,* 3d ed. (Washington, D.C.: CQ Press, 1997), 2. Also see James Ceaser and others, "The Rise of the Rhetorical Presidency," *Presidential Studies Quarterly* 21 (spring 1981): 158–171.

26. Richard M. Pious, *The American Presidency* (New York: Basic Books, 1979), 194. See also George C. Edwards III, *The Public Presidency* (New York: St. Martin's, 1983).

27. Farrell, *Tip O'Neill and the Democratic Century,* 553.

28. *Wall Street Journal,* December 4, 1987, 8D.

29. Tom Rosenstiel and James Gerstenzang, "Bush Team Rejects Public Relations Techniques of Reagan White House," *Los Angeles Times,* April 30, 1989, 1.

30. George Hager, "For GOP, a New Song—Same Ending," *Congressional Quarterly Weekly Report,* June 14, 1997, 1406.

31. Paul Bedard, "Living, Dying by the Polls," *Washington Times,* April 30, 1993, A1.

32. David S. Broder, "The Reticent President," *Washington Post,* April 22, 2001, B7. See also Mike Allen, "Bush on Stage: Deft or Just Lacking Depth?" *Washington Post,* February 19, 2001, A8–A9.

33. Ibid., A20.

34. Susan Page, "Bush's Job-Approval Rating Stuck Below 40%," *USA Today,* April 9, 2007, 8A.

35. Martin Kady II, "Reid Maps Confrontational Agenda," *CQ Today,* April 10, 2007, 6.

36. James Oliphant, "Bush Never Recovered From Response to Katrina, Former Aides Say," *Los Angeles Times,* January 2, 2009, online edition.

37. Quoted in Jeff Eller, "It's Time to Rewrite the Bully Pulpit," *Politico,* November 18, 2008, 29.

38. Peter Baker, "President Sticks to the Script, With a Little Help," *New York Times,* March 6, 2009, A16. President Obama uses a teleprompter regularly for both major addresses and routine announcements.

39. Christi Parsona and Mark Z. Barabak, "Obama To Sit Down with Leno on The Tonight Show," *Los Angeles Times,* March 17, 2009, online edition.

40. Jonathan Martin, "Obama Wants Filter-Free News," *Politico,* March 24, 2009, 17.

41. Sheryl Gay Stolberg, "Obama Makes History in Live Internet Video Chat," *New York Times,* March 27, 2009, A15.

42. Lois Romano, "08 Campaign Guru Focuses On Grass Roots," *Washington Post,* January 13, 2009, A13. Also see Chris Cillizza, "Obama Enlists Campaign Army In Budget Fight," *Washington Post,* March 16, 2009, A1.

43. Helene Cooper and Carl Hulse, "Obama's Efforts on Budget Echoes Fall Campaign," *New York Times,* March 18, 2009, A14.

44. See, for example, Richard P. Nathan, *The Administrative Presidency* (New York: John Wiley, 1983); and Robert R. Durant, *The Administrative Presidency Revisited* (Albany: State University of New York Press, 1992).

45. William G. Howell and David E. Lewis, "Agencies by Presidential Design," *Journal of Politics,* November 2002, 1096.

46. Ibid., 1100.

47. William G. Howell, *Power without Persuasion: The Politics of Direct Presidential Action* (Princeton: Princeton University Press, 2003). The Obama administration has abandoned the term "enemy combatant" for those held at Guantánamo Bay, Cuba. See David Savage,

"No More 'Enemy Combatants' at Guantánamo Bay," *Los Angeles Times*, March 14, 2009, online edition.

48. See Kenneth Mayer, *With the Stroke of a Pen: Executive Orders and Presidential Power* (Princeton: Princeton University Press, 2001).

49. Elizabeth Shogren, "President Plans Blitz of Executive Orders Soon," *Los Angeles Times*, July 5, 1998, A11.

50. Dana Milbank and Ellen Nakashima, "Bush Team Has 'Right' Credentials," *Washington Post*, March 25, 2001, A1.

51. Linda Feldmann, "Faith-Based Initiatives Quietly Lunge Forward," *Christian Science Monitor*, February 6, 2003, 2.

52. Gregg Carlstrom, "Midnight Rule-Making Bonanza," *Federal Times*, November 3, 2008, 19.

53. Cindy Skrzycki, "Democrats Eye Bush Midnight Regulations," *Washington Post*, November 11, 2009, D3.

54. Ceci Connolly and R. Jeffrey Smith, "Obama Positioned to Quickly Reverse Bush Actions," *Washington Post*, November 9, 2008, A16.

55. Andrew Noyes, "Obama's FOIA Directive Brings Praise, Bit of Skepticism," National Journal's *CongressDailyAM*, January 22, 2009, 8. Also see Dan Eggen and Michael D. Shear, "The Effort to Roll Back Bush Policies Continues," *Washington Post*, January 27, 2009, A4.

56. Stephen Skowronek, *The Politics Presidents Make: Leadership from John Adams to George Bush* (Cambridge: Harvard University Press, 1993).

57. Stephen Skowronek, "Presidential Leadership in Political Time," in *The Presidency and the Political System*, 7th ed., ed. Michael Nelson (Washington, D.C.: CQ Press, 2003), 112.

58. Skowronek, *The Politics Presidents Make*, 8.

59. Cited by Gerald F. Seib, "In Crisis, Opportunity for Obama," *Wall Street Journal*, November 21, 2008.

60. Skowronek, *The Politics Presidents Make*, 23.

61. Aaron Wildavsky, "The Two Presidencies," in *The Beleaguered Presidency*, ed. Aaron Wildavsky (Brunswick, N.J.: Transaction Publishers, 1991), 29. Wildavsky's article originally appeared in the December 1966 issue of *Transaction* magazine.

62. Aaron Wildavsky, "The Two Presidencies Thesis Revisited at a Time of Political Dissensus," in Wildavsky, *The Beleaguered Presidency*, 47–65.

63. Dan Balz, "Bush Lays out Ambitious Plan for Long Term," *Washington Post*, May 6, 2001, A10.

64. Ronald Brownstein, "Strategies Shift as Bush Drops in Polls," *Los Angeles Times*, July 5, 2001, A9.

65. Ronald Brownstein, "Bush Is a Surprise Hard Liner," *Los Angeles Times*, March 2, 2003, A14.

66. John Harwood and Jeanne Cummings, "Bush's Approval Rating Slips to 50%, a 5-Year Presidential Low," *Wall Street Journal*, June 28, 2001, A18.

67. Ron Faucheux, "Presidential Popularity: A History of Highs and Lows," *CQ Daily Monitor*, February 7, 2002, 14.

68. Lynne Duke, "No I-Told-You-Sos," *Washington Post*, February 4, 2007, D1.

69. Editorial, "Bush's Big Regret," *Los Angeles Times*, December 4, 2008, online edition.

70. Greg Miller, "Global Economic Crisis Called Biggest U.S. Security Threat," *Los Angeles Times*, February 13, 2009, online edition.

71. Woodrow Wilson, *Congressional Government* (Boston: Houghton Mifflin, 1885), 52.

72. Kevin R. Kosar, *Regular Vetoes and Pocket Vetoes: An Overview*, CRS Report RS22188, January 26, 2009, 1.

73. Alexis Simendinger, "The Veto-Free Zone," *National Journal*, December 17, 2005, 3888.

74. Ethan Wallison, "Can President Bush Stay Veto-Free for Four More Years?" *Roll Call,* January 24, 2005, 10.
75. Jill Barshay, "Popularity Not Required," *CQ Weekly,* January 1, 2007, 45.
76. Sheryl Gay Stolbert, "First Bush Veto Maintains Limits on Stem Cell Use," *New York Times,* July 20, 2006, A1.
77. Clea Benson, "The Power of No," *CQ Weekly,* January 14, 2008, 133.
78. Mike Allen, "Bush Signs Corporate Reforms into Law," *Washington Post,* July 31, 2002, A4. Also see Elizabeth Bumiller, "When Bush Picks up a Pen, He Drops Names," *New York Times,* December 2, 2002, A16.
79. Stephen Dinan, "Bloggers Will Join Bush in Bill-Signing Ceremony," *Washington Times,* September 26, 2006, A4.
80. See, for example, *The Hill,* December 19, 2007, 1, and *Washington Times,* December 19, 2007, A10 for photo coverage.
81. *Los Angeles Times,* March 18, 1988, part I, 4.
82. See T. J. Halstead, *Presidential Signing Statements: Constitutional and Institutional Implications,* CRS Report RL33667, April 13, 2007.
83. Ibid., 9.
84. Charles Savage, "Bush Challenges Hundreds of Laws; President Cites Powers of His Office," *Boston Globe,* April 30, 2006, A1. See Phillip J. Cooper, "George W. Bush, Edgar Allen Poe, and the Use and Abuse of Presidential Signing Statements," *Presidential Studies Quarterly,* September 2005, 515–532.
85. Dan Friedman, "On the Other Hand," *National Journal,* March 28, 2009, 54.
86. Michael D. Shear, "Obama Pledges to Limit Use of Signing Statements," *Washington Post,* March 10, 2009, A4.
87. Charlie Savage, "Obama Says He Can Ignore Some Parts of Spending Bill," *New York Times,* March 12, 2009, A18.
88. David Nather, "Grassley Blows Whistle on Obama For Signing Statement," *CQ Today,* March 16, 2009, 10.
89. Aaron Lorenzo, "Obama Review of Past Signing Statements Does Not Signal End of Presidential Practice," *Daily Report for Executives,* March 10, 2009, A-25.
90. *Congressional Record,* October 2, 2008, E2197.
91. Louis Fisher, "The Pocket Veto: Its Current Status," CRS Report RL30909, March 30, 2001, summary.
92. Erika Niedowski, "GOP to Skirt Line-Item Veto," *The Hill,* February 12, 1997, 24.
93. John Broder, "Clinton Vetoes Eight Projects, Two in States of Leadership," *New York Times,* October 18, 1997, A10.
94. Helen Dewar and Joan Biskupic, "Line-Item Vote Struck Down: Backers Push for Alternative," *Washington Post,* June 26, 1998, A1.
95. *Congressional Record,* March 4, 2009, S2771.
96. Neustadt, *Presidential Power,* 187.
97. Glenn Thrush, "With the 111th, The Age of Pelosi Dawns," *Politico,* January 6, 2009, 16.
98. Keith Koffler and Steven T. Dennis, "Obama Seeks Allies," *Roll Call,* March 12, 2009, 29.
99. Johnson, *The Vantage Point,* 448.
100. George C. Edwards III, *At the Margins* (New Haven: Yale University Press, 1989).
101. See Joseph P. Harris, *The Advice and Consent of the Senate* (Berkeley: University of California Press, 1953); and G. Calvin Mackenzie, *The Politics of Presidential Appointments* (New York: Free Press, 1981).
102. James MacGregor Burns, *Presidential Government* (Boston: Houghton Mifflin, 1966), 284.

103. See, for example, Stephen J. Wayne, "Great Expectations: What People Want from Presidents," in *Rethinking the Presidency,* ed. Thomas E. Cronin (Boston: Little, Brown, 1982), 185–199.

104. Dean Scott, "Next President Likely to Have Limited Chance For Passage of Emission Caps, Senator Says," *Daily Report for Executives,* August 4, 2008, A-15.

105. Arthur M. Schlesinger Jr. and Alfred De Grazia, *Congress and the Presidency: Their Role in Modern Times* (Washington, D.C.: American Enterprise Institute, 1967), 1.

106. Wilson, *Congressional Government;* and Burns, *Presidential Government.*

107. See Joseph S. Clark, *Congress: The Sapless Branch* (New York: Harper and Row, 1964); and Arthur Schlesinger Jr., *The Imperial Presidency* (Boston: Houghton Mifflin, 1973).

108. David Mayhew, *Divided We Govern* (New Haven: Yale University Press, 1991), 198.

109. J. William Fulbright, "The Legislator as Educator," *Foreign Affairs,* spring 1979, 726.

CHAPTER 11

1. David S. Broder, "So, Now Bigger Is Better?" *Washington Post,* January 12, 2003, B1.

2. Neil King Jr. and John D. Stoll, "Government Forces Out Wagoner at GM," *Wall Street Journal,* March 30, 2009, A1.

3. Janet Hook, "Obama's Budget Is the End Of An Era," *Los Angeles Times,* February 27, 2009, online edition.

4. Donald F. Kettl, "Heading for Disaster," *Government Executive,* February 2009, 22.

5. Quoted in E. J. Dionne Jr., "Back from the Dead: Neoprogressivism in the 90s," *American Prospect* (September–October 1996): 25.

6. Jonathan Walters, "Preempting Washington," *Governing,* September 2004, 12.

7. *Congressional Record,* November 5, 1997, S11737.

8. Richard E. Neustadt, "Politicians and Bureaucrats," in *The Congress and America's Future,* 2d ed., ed. David B. Truman (Englewood Cliffs, N.J.: Prentice-Hall, 1973), 199. See also Louis Fisher, *The Politics of Shared Power: Congress and the Executive,* 3d ed. (Washington, D.C.: CQ Press, 1993).

9. See Harold Relyea, "Executive Branch Reorganization and Management Initiatives: A Brief Overview," Congressional Research Service Report RL33441, May 30, 2006.

10. U.S. Congress, *Congressional Record,* daily ed., 109th Cong., 1st sess., February 15, 2005, S1437.

11. Keith Koffler, "Confirmation Wars Could Be Thing of the Past," *Roll Call,* November 21, 2008, 10.

12. Steven V. Roberts, "In Confirmation Process, Hearings Offer a Stage," *New York Times,* February 8, 1989, B7.

13. See Al Kamen, "Recess Appointments Granted to 'Swift Boat' Donor, 2 Other Nominees," *Washington Post,* April 5, 2007, A6.

14. Kathleen Hunter, "Senators Maintain Vigil Against Recess Appointments," *CQ Today,* December 12, 2008, 1.

15. See Henry Hogue, *Temporarily Filling Presidentially Appointed, Senate-Confirmed Positions,* CRS Report RS21412, January 25, 2008.

16. See, for example, Will Englund, "Czar Wars," *National Journal,* February 14, 2009, 16–24.

17. S. A. Miller, "Democrats Use Omnibus To Eviscerate Bush Policies," *Washington Times,* February 26, 2009, A17.

18. Bruce Ackerman, "A Role for Congress to Reclaim," *Washington Post,* March 11, 2009, A15.

19. Ibid.; William Schneider, "New Rules for the Game of Politics," *National Journal,* April 1, 1989, 830.

20. See Dennis Thompson, *Ethics in Congress* (Washington, D.C.: Brookings Institution, 1995).

21. Anne Kornblut and Michael Shear, "Obama Says He Erred in Nominations," *Washington Post,* February 4, 2009, A1.

22. Edward Luce and Krishna Guha, "Appointments Bottleneck at Treasury Tightens," *Financial Times,* March 19, 2009, 4.

23. Philip Rucker, "Potential Obama Appointees Face Extensive Vetting," *Washington Post,* November 18, 2008, A12.

24. Nancy Kassebaum Baker and Franklin Raines, "Uncle Sam Wants a Few Good Appointees," *Los Angeles Times,* April 5, 2001, A17. Baker and Raines were co-chairs of the Presidential Appointee Initiative Advisory Board, which was a project of the Brookings Institution. Its basic goal was to propose improvements in the presidential appointment process.

25. G. Calvin Mackenzie, "Hung Out to Dry," *Washington Post,* April 1, 2001, B5.

26. Paul Light, "The Glacial Pace of Presidential Appointments," *Wall Street Journal,* April 4, 2001, A20.

27. Al Kamen, "Confirmation Delays Hobble Administration," *Washington Post,* May 20, 2001, A1. See also Laurence McQuillan, "Complex Process Slows Hiring," *USA Today,* May 30, 2001, 10A.

28. Bart Jansen, "Despite Significant Vacancies, Obama Outpaces Bush in Nominations," *CQ Today,* March 30, 2009, 3.

29. Light, "The Glacial Pace of Presidential Appointments," A20.

30. See *United States Government Policy and Supporting Positions,* Senate Committee on Homeland Security and Governmental Affairs (Senate Print 110-36), November 12, 2008, Appendix No. 1, 197. This report is informally known as the "Plum Book" for its plum-colored title page. There is another privately published report called *The Prune Book* that identifies what are alleged to be the most difficult jobs in government. See John H. Trattner, *The Prune Book, Top Management Challenges for Presidential Appointees* (Washington, D.C.: Brookings Institution Press, 2005).

31. Paul C. Light, *Thickening Government* (Washington, D.C.: Brookings Institution and Governance Institute, 1995), esp. 111–116.

32. Paul C. Light, "Big Bureaucracy," *Washington Times,* May 10, 2001, A17.

33. Christopher Lee, "Agencies Getting Heavier on Top," *Washington Times,* July 23, 2004, A27.

34. Stephen Barr, "Title Creep Reported at Agencies," *Washington Post,* March 8, 1999, A17.

35. Paul C. Light, *A Government Ill Executed* (Cambridge, Mass.: Harvard University Press, 2008), 53.

36. Lee, "Agencies Getting Heavier on Top," A27.

37. G. Calvin Mackenzie, ed., *Innocent until Nominated* (Washington, D.C.: Brookings Institution Press, 2001), 30.

38. Doyle McManus and Robert Shogun, "Acrid Tone Reflects Long-Term Trend for Nominations," *Los Angeles Times,* March 9, 1997, A6.

39. Peter Grier, "Why Senate Roughs Up Some Cabinet Nominees," *Christian Science Monitor,* March 19, 1997, 3.

40. John Stanton, "GOP Ponders Filibuster," *Roll Call,* April 1, 2009, 14. Also see Neil A. Lewis, "In Senate Judiciary Wars, G.O.P. Struggles With Role," *New York Times,* April 1, 2009, A18.

41. David M. Cohen, "Amateur Government," *Journal of Public Administration Research and Theory* (October 1998): 451.

42. Stephen Barr, "Plum Book Counts Political Jobs in Executive, Legislative Branches," *Washington Post,* December 15, 2004, B2.

43. See Henry Hogue, "Statutory Qualifications for Executive Branch Positions," Congressional Research Service Report RL33886, February 20, 2007.

44. U.S. Congress, *Congressional Record,* daily ed., 106th Cong., 1st sess., January 19, 1999, S554.

45. U.S. Congress, *Congressional Record,* daily ed., 105th Cong., 1st sess., September 12, 1996, S10367.

46. Shankar Vedantam, "Who Are the Better Managers—Political Appointees or Career Bureaucrats?" *Washington Post,* November 24, 2008, A6.

47. Alyssa Rosenberg, "Minding the Hatch Act," *Government Executive,* October 2008, 76.

48. Bart Jansen, "Details of the Lobbying Rules Law," *CQ Weekly,* September 17, 2007, 2693.

49. Ellen Nakashima, "Pentagon Hires Out More Than In," *Washington Post,* April 3, 2001, A19.

50. Nakashima, "Pentagon Hires Out More Than In."

51. Paul C. Light, "The True Size of Government," *Government Executive,* January 1999, 20. See Light, *The True Size of Government* (Washington, D.C.: The Brookings Institution Press, 1990). Periodically, Professor Light updates the number of contract workers. In his August 2006 revision, he compares the number of contract workers in 1999 (6,968,000) to 2005 (10,526,000), a 51.1 percent increase.

52. Rand L. Allen and John R. Prairie, "Now You Have to Tell the Government," *Legal Times,* January 9, 2009, 22.

53. Bernard Wysocki Jr., "Is U.S. Government 'Outsourcing Its Brain'?" *Wall Street Journal,* March 30, 2007, A1.

54. U.S. Congress, *Congressional Record,* daily ed., 96th Cong., 2d sess., July 1, 1980, E3320.

55. Cornelius Kerwin, *Rulemaking: How Government Agencies Write Law and Make Policy,* 2d ed. (Washington, D.C.: CQ Press, 1999), 8–9. See also Jeffrey Lubbers, *A Guide to Federal Agency Rulemaking,* 3d ed. (Chicago: ABA Publishing, 1998).

56. Vicki Kemper, "Draft Rules for Medicare Law Unveiled," *Los Angeles Times,* July 27, 2004, A1. For the length of the law, see U.S. Congress, *Congressional Record,* daily ed., 108th Cong., 1st sess., December 8, 2003, H12750.

57. Ed Rogers and Lanny Griffith, "What-You-Know Washington," *The Hill,* April 25, 2007, 22.

58. Adam Satariano, "Hershey Seeks a Great American Trans-Fat Bar," *Washington Times,* April 26, 2006, A1.

59. U.S. Congress, *Congressional Record,* daily ed., 100th Cong., 1st sess., July 29, 1987, S10850.

60. Robert Barnes and Juliet Eilperin, "High Court Faults EPA Inaction on Emissions," *Washington Post,* April 3, 2007, A1.

61. Robert C. Cook, "Supreme Court Allows EPA to Consider Cost to Utilities in Cooling Water Rules," *Daily Report for Executives,* April 2,2009, A-27. Also see Robert Barnes, "EPA Can Weigh Cost-Benefits in Environmental Action, Court Says," *Washington Post,* April 2, 2009, A6.

62. Matthew Wald, "Court Voids a Bush Move on Energy," *New York Times,* January 14, 2004, A12.

63. Cyril Zaneski, "Escape Artist," *Government Executive,* March 2001, 29.

64. Amy Goldstein, "Regulators Ordered to Leave Work Unfinished," *Washington Post,* January 21, 2009, A2.

65. Ralph Lindeman, "Advocate Groups Want Reduced OIRA Role In OMB's Regulatory Review Revision Process," *Daily Report for Executives,* April 2, 2009, A-13.

66. Rebecca Adams, "Regulating the Rule-Makers: John Graham at OIRA," *CQ Weekly,* February 23, 2002, 520.

67. Ralph Lindeman, "House Panels Seeks Ways to Curb Impact of Executive Order on Regulatory Activity," *Daily Report for Executives,* April 27, 2007, A-39.

68. Ralph Lindeman, "White House Revokes 2007 Bush Order Concerning OMB Regulatory Review Process," *Daily Report forExecutives,* February 4, 2009, A-10.

69. Frank Ackerman, Lisa Heinzerling, James K. Hammitt, and Milton C. Weinstein, "Balancing Lives against Lucre," *Los Angeles Times,* February 25, 2004, A17. Ackerman and Heinzerling are economists, and Hammitt and Weinstein are risk analysis experts.

70. Charlie Savage, "Democrats Look for Ways to Undo Late Bush-Era Rules by Agencies," *New York Times,* January 12, 2009, A10. See Curtis W. Copeland and Richard S. Beth, *Congressional Review Act: Disapproval of Rules in a Subsequent Session of Congress,* CRS Report RL34633, September 3, 2008.

71. Mary Clare Jalonick, "Bipartisan Senate Effort Forces Vote on Easing Canadian Beef Import Restrictions," *CQ Today,* March 3, 2005, 13.

72. Stephen Labaton, "Agencies Postpone Issuing New Rules as Election Nears," *New York Times,* September 27, 2004, A21.

73. U.S. Congress, *Congressional Record,* daily ed., 104th Cong., 1st sess., July 11, 1995, S9705.

74. U.S. Congress, *Congressional Record,* daily ed., 104th Cong., 1st sess., July 11, 1995, S9697.

75. Morris P. Fiorina, *Congress: Keystone of the Washington Establishment* (New Haven: Yale University Press, 1977), 48.

76. R. Douglas Arnold, "The Local Roots of Domestic Policy," in *The New Congress,* ed. Thomas E. Mann and Norman J. Ornstein (Washington, D.C.: American Enterprise Institute, 1981), 284.

77. *CQ Monitor,* July 15, 1998, 5; and Donald L. Barlett and James B. Steele, "Special Report: Corporate Welfare," *Time,* November 16, 1998, 79–93.

78. Joseph S. Clark, *Congress: The Sapless Branch* (New York: Harper and Row, 1964), 63–64.

79. David B. Frohnmayer, "The Separation of Powers: An Essay on the Vitality of a Constitutional Idea," *Oregon Law Review* (spring 1973): 330.

80. David B. Truman, *The Governmental Process,* rev. ed. (New York: Knopf, 1971), 439.

81. Woodrow Wilson, *Congressional Government* (Boston: Houghton Mifflin, 1885), 297.

82. *Washington Times,* December 29, 1986, A1; and David Rogers, "Sen. Lott Becomes GOP's New Standard-bearer, But His Style Will Be Tested in the Next Congress," *Wall Street Journal,* November 15, 1996, A16.

83. Woodrow Wilson, *Congressional Government* (Boston: Houghton Mifflin, 1885), 303.

84. Rochelle Stanfield, "Plotting Every Move," *National Journal,* March 26, 1988, 796.

85. *Watkins v. United States,* 354 U.S. 178 (1957). See also James Hamilton, *The Power to Probe* (New York: Vantage Books, 1976).

86. William S. Cohen and George J. Mitchell, *Men of Zeal: A Candid Inside Story of the Iran-Contra Hearings* (New York: Viking Penguin, 1988), 305.

87. *Immigration and Naturalization Service v. Chadha,* 462 U.S. 919 (1983).

88. Louis Fisher, in *Extensions,* Carl Albert Congressional Research and Studies Center newsletter (spring 1984): 2.

89. John R. Johannes, "Study and Recommend: Statutory Reporting Requirements as a Technique of Legislative Initiative—A Research Note," *Western Political Quarterly* (December 1976): 589–596.

90. Guy Gugliotta, "Reporting on a Practice That's Ripe for Reform," *Washington Post,* February 11, 1997, A19.

91. Walter Pincus, "Congress Cracks Down on Overdue CIA Reports," *Washington Post,* December 1, 2002, A5.

92. Cindy Skrzycki, "The Regulators," *Washington Post,* January 8, 1999, F7. See also *CQ Monitor,* March 25, 1996, 7.

93. Michael W. Kirst, *Government without Passing Laws* (Chapel Hill: University of North Carolina Press, 1969).

94. Joseph A. Davis, "War Declared Over Report-Language Issue," *Congressional Quarterly Weekly Report,* June 25, 1988, 1752–1753; and David Rapp, "OMB's Miller Backs Away from Report-Language Battle," *Congressional Quarterly Weekly Report,* July 9, 1988, 1928.

95. Edward Pound, "Q&A With Earl Devaney," *National Journal,* March 14, 2009, Inside Washington.

96. R. Jeffrey Smith, "Initiative On Worker Safety Gets Poor Marks," *Washington Post,* April 2, 2009, A6.

97. Otto Kreisher, "Pentagon IG Details Waste In Military Contractor Spending," *CongressDailyAM,* February 27, 2009, 8.

98. Steven Holmes, "Amendment Would Strip a Top Official of His Powers," *New York Times,* October 6, 2000, A20.

99. Greta Wodele, "DHS Facing Appropriators' Wrath for Missing Deadlines," *CongressDaily/PM,* February 17, 2005, 2.

100. Slade Gorton and Larry Craig, "Congress's Call to Accounting," *Washington Post,* July 27, 1998, A23.

101. U.S. Congress, *Congressional Record,* daily ed., 95th Cong., 1st sess., April 30, 1975, E2080.

102. See Peter Baker, *The Breach: Inside the Impeachment and Trial of William Jefferson Clinton* (New York: Scribner's, 2000).

103. Frank Bowman, "He's Impeachable, You Know," *New York Times,* May 3, 2007, A25.

104. Stuart Taylor Jr., "Congress Should Censure Gonzales," *National Journal,* May 5, 2007, 17.

105. Dan Eggen and Amy Goldstein, "No-Confidence Vote Sought on Gonzales," *Washington Post,* May 18, 2007, A3, and David Johnston and Neil Lewis, "Senate Democrats Plan a Resolution on Gonzales," *New York Times,* May 18, 2007, A16.

106. See Joel D. Aberbach, *Keeping a Watchful Eye: The Politics of Congressional Oversight* (Washington, D.C.: Brookings Institution, 1990); and James Q. Wilson, *Bureaucracy: What Governmental Agencies Do and Why They Do It* (New York: Basic Books, 1991).

107. Richard Cohen, "King of Oversight," *Government Executive,* September 1988, 17.

108. David Nather, "Congress as Watchdog: Asleep on the Job?" *CQ Weekly,* May 22, 2004, 1190.

109. Ronald Brownstein, "Treating Oversight as an Afterthought Has Its Costs," *Los Angeles Times,* November 19, 2006.

110. Joel D. Aberbach, "The Congressional Committee Intelligence System: Information, Oversight, and Change," *Congress and the Presidency* 14 (spring 1987): 51–76; and Mathew McCubbins and Thomas Schwartz, "Congressional Oversight Overlooked: Police Patrol versus Fire Alarm," *American Journal of Political Science* (February 1984): 165–177.

111. Bill Myers, " 'Google Your Government' Database Bill Signed into Law," *Examiner,* September 29, 2006, 17.

112. Louis Fisher, "Micromanagement by Congress: Reality and Mythology" (paper presented at a conference sponsored by the American Enterprise Institute, Washington, D.C., April 8–9, 1988), 8. See also David S. Broder and Stephen Barr, "Hill's Micromanagement of Cabinet Blurs Separation of Powers," *Washington Post,* July 25, 1993, A1.

CHAPTER 12

1. Alexis de Tocqueville, *Democracy in America* (New York: American Library, 1956), 72.

2. Quoted in Cliff Sloan and David McKean, "Why *Marbury v. Madison* Still Matters," *Newsweek,* March 2, 2009, 49.

3. Richard L. Pacelle Jr., *The Role of the Supreme Court in American Politics: The Least Dangerous Branch?* (Boulder, Colo.: Westview Press, 2001).

4. Alexander Bickel, *The Least Dangerous Branch* (Indianapolis, Ind.: Bobbs-Merrill, 1962), 1.

5. See Dexter Perkins and Glyndon Van Deusen, *The United States of America: A History,* vol. II (New York: Macmillan, 1962), 560–566.

6. 119 Stat. 44 (February 18, 2005).

7. Thomas E. Willging and Emery G. Lee III, *The Impact of the Class Action Fairness Act of 2005 on the Federal Courts: Third Interim Report to the Judicial Conference Advisory Committee on Civil Rules* (Washington, D.C.: Federal Judicial Center, 2007).

8. Joan Biskupic, "Justices Defer to Congress' Power to Extend Copyright," *USA Today,* January 16, 2003, 4A.

9. Jamin Raskin, "Courts v. Citizens," *American Prospect* 14 (March 2003): A25.

10. Colton C. Campbell and John F. Stack Jr., "Diverging Perspectives on Lawmaking: The Delicate Balance between Congress and the Court," in *Congress Confronts the Court,* ed. Colton C. Campbell and John F. Stack Jr. (Lanham, Md.: Rowman and Littlefield, 2001), 2.

11. Charles Gardner Geyh, *When Courts and Congress Collide: The Struggle for Control of America's Judicial System* (Ann Arbor: University of Michigan Press, 2006), 229.

12. Linda Greenhouse, "High Court Faces Moment of Truth in Federalism Cases," *New York Times,* March 28, 1999, 3.

13. Louis Fisher, *American Constitutional Law,* 6th ed. (Durham, N.C.: Carolina Academic Press, 2005), 355.

14. Louis Fisher, "The Law: Litigating the War Power with *Campbell v. Clinton,*" *Presidential Studies Quarterly* (September 2000): 568.

15. The two quotations on standing are from Jay Shampansky, "Congressional Standing to Sue: An Overview," Congressional Research Service Report RL30280, June 19, 2001, 2, 3.

16. The U.S. Supreme Court majority contended, in this and similar rulings, that the Eleventh Amendment granted states "sovereign immunity" from legal suits. But the amendment's plain language protects states only from suits by citizens of other states or foreign nations, not those from its own citizens. Moreover, it is hard to escape the supposition that, whatever the protections afforded by the Eleventh Amendment (ratified in 1798), they were superseded—at least in the realm of civil rights—by the Fourteenth Amendment (ratified in 1868), which not only nationalized basic civil rights but also expressly granted Congress the power of enforcement. For a detailed critique of the Court's activism in such cases, see John T. Noonan Jr., *Narrowing the Nation's Power: The Supreme Court Sides with the States* (Berkeley: University of California Press, 2002).

17. Quotes from the opinions of Chief Justice William H. Rehnquist and Justice Stephen G. Breyer are drawn from "Excerpts from Supreme Court Opinions on Limits of Disabilities Act," *New York Times,* February 22, 2001, A21.

18. Linda Greenhouse, "Will the Court Reassert National Authority?" *New York Times,* September 30, 2001, E14.

19. See Louis Fisher, *The Constitution and 9/11* (Lawrence, Kan.: University Press of Kansas, 2008).

20. Quoted in Linda Greenhouse, "The Imperial Presidency vs. the Imperial Judiciary," *New York Times,* September 8, 2002, E5.

21. Charles Lane, "Justices Back Detainee Access to U.S. Courts," *Washington Post,* June 29, 2004, A1.

22. Josh White, "Guantánamo Detainees Lose Appeal," *Washington Post,* February 21, 2007, A1. See Louis Fisher, *Military Tribunals and Presidential Power* (Lawrence: University Press of Kansas, 2005), and "Today's Debate: Civil Liberties," *USA Today,* May 11, 2007, 14A.

23. *Congressional Record,* February 13, 2009, S2333. The comment of Sen. Arlen Spector is quoted.

24. David G. Savage, "Solicitor General Nominee Says 'Enemy Combatants' Can Be Held Without Trial," *Los Angeles Times,* February 11, 2009, online edition.

25. Charlie Savage, "Judge Rules Some Prisoners at Bagram Have Right to Habeas Corpus," *New York Times,* April 3, 2009, A10. Moreover, lawyers for more than a dozen Chinese Muslims, held at Guantánamo Bay without charge for more than seven years, have asked the Supreme Court to order their release. See Carol J. Williams, "Supreme Court Is Urged to Order Uighurs' Release Into U.S.," *Los Angeles Times,* April 7, 2009, online edition.

26. See, for example, House debate on the Lilly Ledbetter case, *Congressional Record,* January 9, 2009, H113–H138.

27. The Court's decision was denounced in many quarters. In addition, soon after Justice Kennedy wrote the majority decision, which also stated that there was no federal law applying the death penalty to a child rapist, he was immediately proven wrong. As Sen. David Vitter, R-La., and others pointed out, when Congress passed the National Defense Authorization Act in 2006 amending the Uniform Code of Military Justice, it provided the death penalty for child rape. *Congressional Record,* September 18, 2008, S8990. On January 6, 2009, Senator Vitter introduced a resolution (S. Res. 4) expressing "the sense of the Senate that the Supreme Court of the United States erroneously decided *Kennedy v. Louisiana,* and that the Eighth Amendment to the Constitution of the United States allows the imposition of the death penalty for the rape of a child." To date, the Senate has taken no action on Vitter's proposal.

28. See Robert A. Katzmann, ed., *Judges and Legislators* (Washington, D.C.: Brookings Institution, 1988); and Robert A. Katzmann, *Courts and Congress* (Washington, D.C.: Brookings Institution Press, 1997).

29. *New York Times,* May 12, 1983, B8.

30. David Rogers and Monica Langley, "Bush Set to Sign Landmark Bill on Class Actions," *Wall Street Journal,* February 18, 2005, A7.

31. Dan Eggen, "Record Shows Senators' 'Debate' That Wasn't," *Washington Post,* March 29, 2006, A6.

32. Emily Bazelon, "Invisible Men: Did Lindsay Graham and Jon Kyl Mislead the Supreme Court?" *Slate,* March 27, 2006.

33. Eggen, "Record Shows Senators' 'Debate' That Wasn't," A6.

34. See, for example, Antonin Scalia, *A Matter of Interpretation* (Princeton: Princeton University Press, 1997).

35. Quoted in Jonathan Kaplan, "High Court to Congress: Say What You Mean," *The Hill,* February 5, 2003, 21.

36. Ruth Marcus, "Lawmakers Override High Court," *Washington Post,* October 31, 1991, A1.

37. U.S. Congress, *Congressional Record,* daily ed., 102d Cong., 1st sess., October 29, 1991, S15324-15325.

38. Quoted in Joan Biskupic, "Scalia Sees No Justice in Trying to Judge Intent of Congress on a Law," *Washington Post,* May 11, 1993, A4.

39. Kaplan, "High Court to Congress," 21.

40. Joan Biskupic and Elder Witt, *Guide to the U.S. Supreme Court,* 3d ed., vol. II (Washington, D.C.: CQ Press, 1997), 720.

41. William H. Rehnquist, *Grand Inquests: The Historic Impeachment of Justice Samuel Chase and President Andrew Johnson* (New York: William Morrow, 1992), 132.

42. Quoted in Stephen Dinan, "DeLay Threatens to Curb Courts' Jurisdiction," *Washington Times,* March 6, 2003, A4.

43. Sandra Day O'Connor, "The Threat to Judicial Independence," *Wall Street Journal,* September 27, 2006, A18.

44. Russell R. Wheeler and Robert A. Katzmann, "A Primer on Interbranch Relations," *The Georgetown Law Journal,* April 2007, 1172.

45. Rehnquist, *Grand Inquests*, 114.

46. See Pamela A. MacLean, "Little Public Airing of Abusive Judges," *National Law Journal,* February 25, 2008, 18.

47. Louis Fisher, "Congressional Checks on the Judiciary," *CRS Report for Congress,* 97–497, April 29, 1997, 4.

48. *Congressional Record,* January 13, 2009, H179-H182.

49. Biskupic and Witt, *Guide to the U.S. Supreme Court,* 717.

50. Ibid., 718.

51. Carol Leonning, "New Rules for Judges Are Weaker, Critics Say," *Washington Post,* December 17, 2004, A31; David Von Drehle, "Scalia Rejects Pleas for Recusal in Cheney Case," *Washington Post,* February 12, 2004, A35; and Eileen Sullivan, "Courts Order Review of Judges' Security," *Federal Times,* March 21, 2005, 12.

52. Tony Mauro, "Kennedy Talks Tough on Salaries, Cameras," *Legal Times,* February 19, 2007, 14.

53. Robert Barnes, "A Renewed Call to Televise High Court," *Washington Post,* February 12, 2007, A15. See Senator Specter's remarks in the *Congressional Record,* January 29, 2007, S1257-S1262; and February 13, 2009, S2332-S2336.

54. Seth Stern, "A Career as Federal Judge Isn't What It Used to Be," *Christian Science Monitor,* January 22, 2002, 1.

55. American Bar Association, *Federal Judicial Pay, an Update on the Urgent Need for Action,* May 2003, 4.

56. Mark Sherman, "Big Money Depletes Judges' Ranks," *Washington Times,* December 30, 2008, B3. Also see Adam Liptak, "The State of Courts, And a Plea For a Raise," *New York Times,* January 1, 2009, A13.

57. Greenhouse, "Chief Justice Advocates Higher Pay for Judiciary," A14. See Editorial, "There Oughta Be a Law," *USA Today,* January 9, 2007, 12A.

58. Adam Liptak, "On the Subject of Judicial Salaries, a Sharp Difference of Opinion," *New York Times,* January 20, 2009, A14.

59. See Fisher, *American Constitutional Law,* 1072.

60. Jennifer Dlouhy, "Congress Reluctant to Change Constitution," *CQ Today,* February 11, 2003, 9.

61. Norman Ornstein, "To Break the Stalemate, Give Judges Less than Life," *Washington Post,* November 28, 2004, B3.

62. Tony Mauro, "Profs Pitch Plan for Limits on Supreme Court Service," *Legal Times,* January 3, 2005, 1. Also see Robert Barnes, "Legal Experts Propose Limiting Justices' Powers, Terms," *Washington Post,* February 23, 2009, A15.

63. From 1952 to 2001, the Standing Committee on Federal Judiciary of the American Bar Association (ABA) was consulted by every president with respect to judicial candidates prior to their formal nomination. President George W. Bush curtailed the ABA's role in providing evaluations of prospective judicial candidates. However, the ABA still provides its evaluations to the Senate and the administration after the candidates' names have been made public. See Amy Goldstein, "Bush Curtails ABA Role in Selecting U.S. Judges," *Washington Post,* March 23, 2001, A1.

64. Terri L. Peretti, "Where Have All the Politicians Gone? Recruiting for the Modern Supreme Court," *Judicature,* November–December 2007, 120. Also see Paul A. Sracic, "Politician on Court Isn't a Bad Thing," *USA Today,* March 30, 2005, 13A.

65. Dennis Steven Rutkus and Lorraine H. Tong, "The Chief Justice of the United States: Responsibilities of the Office and Process for Appointment," Congressional Research Service Report RL32831, September 12, 2005, 26. Every one of the six summary points draws heavily on this report by the CRS scholars.

66. Alpheus Thomas Mason, *Harlan Fiske Stone: Pillar of the Law* (New York: Viking, 1959), ch. 12.

67. Rutkus and Tong, "The Chief Justice of the United States," 30.

68. Ibid., 37.

69. Ibid., 34.

70. Brannon Denning, "The 'Blue Slip': Enforcing the Norms of the Judicial Confirmation Process," *William and Mary Bill of Rights Journal* 10 (December 2001): 92.

71. "GOP Move Would Help Nominees," *Washington Post,* January 24, 2003, A25.

72. Keith Perine, "Leahy Plans to Maintain 'Blue Slip' Policy," *CQ Today,* March 12, 2009, 17.

73. Stephen Dinan, "Strategy Shift on Nominations," *Washington Times,* March 17, 2009, B3.

74. Quoted in Keith Perine, "As Judiciary Battles Loom, Leahy Revives Senate 'Blue Slip' Tradition," *CQ Today,* January 4, 2007, 3.

75. Michael J. Gerhardt, "Here's What Less Experience Gets You," *Washington Post,* March 2, 2003, B1, B4.

76. Jess Bravin, "Barack Obama: The Present Is Prologue," *Wall Street Journal,* October 7, 2008, A22. President Obama's first judicial nomination was naming federal district judge David Hamilton to the U.S. Court of Appeals for the Seventh Circuit. Hamilton was cited by the White House as the prototype for Obama's judicial nominees. However, Hamilton was quickly criticized by conservative groups as being too liberal and out of the judicial mainstream. See Michael Fletcher, "Obama Names Judge to Appeals Court," *Washington Post,* March 18, 2009, A4.

77. Ralph Neas, "United States Needs More Discussion of Judicial Philosophy," *Roll Call,* May 9, 2002, 10.

78. Richard Baker, "Senate Historical Minute," *The Hill,* October 2, 2002, 12.

79. Many Senate Republicans today dispute whether a real filibuster was conducted on Abe Fortas's nomination. "So that was not a real filibuster," stated Sen. Orrin G. Hatch, R-Utah. U.S. Congress, *Congressional Record,* daily ed., 109th Cong., 1st sess., March 1, 2005, S1834. See Charles Babington, "Filibuster Precedent? Democrats Point to '68 and Fortas," *Washington Post,* March 18, 2005, A3.

80. Ronald Brownstein, "To End Battle over Judicial Picks, Each Side Must Lay Down Arms," *Los Angeles Times,* February 21, 2005, A8.

81. Helen Dewar, "Polarized Politics, Confirmation Chaos," *Washington Post,* May 11, 2003, A5.

82. James Robertson, "A Cure for What Ails the Judiciary," *Washington Post,* May 27, 2003, A19.

83. Linda Greenhouse, "Case of the Dwindling Docket Mystifies the Supreme Court," *New York Times,* December 7, 2006, A1.

84. Warren Richey, "Conservatives Near Lock on U.S. Courts," *Christian Science Monitor,* April 14, 2005, 10.

85. Elizabeth Palmer, "Appellate Courts at Center of Fight for Control of Judiciary," *CQ Weekly,* February 23, 2002, 534.

86. Palmer, "Appellate Courts at Center of Fight for Control of Judiciary."

87. Neil A. Lewis, "In Senate Judiciary Wars, G.O.P. Struggles With Role," *New York Times,* April 1, 2009, A18.

88. Sarah Binder, "Advice and Consent for Judicial Nominations: Can the President and Senate Do Better?" A paper prepared for delivery at "Presidential Nominations and the Senate Confirmation Process," Woodrow Wilson International Center for Scholars, Washington, D.C., March 16, 2009, 10–11.

89. Ronald Brownstein, "To End Battle over Judicial Picks, Each Side Must Lay Down Arms," *Los Angeles Times,* February 21, 2005, A8.

90. *Congressional Record,* April 15, 2008, S3012.

91. Binder, "Advice and Consent for Judicial Nominations," 16.

92. Neil A. Lewis, "New Democratic Majority Throws Bush's Judicial Nominations Into Uncertainty," *New York Times,* November 12, 2006, 22.

93. R. Jeffrey Smith, "Judge's Fate Could Turn on 1994 Case," *Washington Post,* May 27, 2003, A8.

94. E. J. Dionne Jr., "They Started It," *Washington Post,* February 21, 2003, A27.

95. Richey, "Conservatives Near Lock on U.S. Courts," 1. See Keith Perine, "House Republicans' Plan to Split 9th Circuit Court Is Adopted; No More Action Expected in 108th," *CQ Weekly,* October 9, 2004, 2375.

96. Stuart Taylor, Jr., "In the Balance," *National Journal,* July 26, 2008, 27. Also see Charlie Savage, "Appeals Courts Pushed To Right By Bush Choices," *New York Times,* October 29, 2008, A1; and R. Jeffrey Smith, "The Politics of the Federal Bench," *Washington Post,* December 8, 2008, A1.

97. Dahlia Lithwick, "Court Nomination Fights—Enough!" *Los Angeles Times,* March 8, 2009, online edition.

98. Louis Fisher, "Congressional Checks on the Judiciary," in *Congress Confronts the Court,* ed. Colton C. Campbell and John F. Stack Jr. (Lanham, Md.: Rowman and Littlefield, 2001), 35.

CHAPTER 13

1. Robert Pear, "Doctors Press Senate to Undo Medicare Cuts," *New York Times,* July 7, 2008, A1.

2. See, for example, Marc Kaufman and Rob Stein, "Record Share of Economy Spent on Health Care," *Washington Post,* January 10, 2006, A1.

3. Jeffrey Young, "Medicare Bill More than Just a 'Doc Fix,'" *The Hill,* July 16, 2008, 14.

4. Pear, "Doctors Press Senate," A1.

5. Michael Abramowitz and Paul Kane, "Congress Easily Overrides Medicare Veto," *Washington Post,* July 16, 2008, A2.

6. Pear, "Doctors Press Senate," A1.

7. Lauren W. Whittington and Steven T. Dennis, "Republicans Jump Ship; Boehner Can't Hold Line on Vote," *Roll Call,* June 26, 2008.

8. Ibid.

9. Jeffrey Young, "House Democratic Leaders Score Stunning Victory on Medicare Bill," *The Hill,* June 25, 2008, 3.

10. Michael Abramowitz and Paul Kane, "Congress Easily Overrides Medicare Veto," A2.

11. Ibid.

12. Ibid.

13. See John R. Hibbing and Elizabeth Theiss-Morse, *Congress as Public Enemy: Public Attitudes Toward American Political Institutions* (New York: Cambridge University Press, 1995).

14. See the discussion of the various interests that obtained concessions in the legislation provided by Jeffrey Young, "Medicare Bill More Than Just a 'Doc Fix,'" *The Hill,* July 16, 2008, 14.

15. Data are from James A. Thurber, American University.

16. Jim Drinkard, "Drugmakers Go Further to Sway Congress," *USA Today,* April 26, 2005, 2B.

17. Shawn Zeller, "K Street Remains an Easy Street in Hard Times," 995.

18. Alex Knott, "Six Lobby Shops on the Fast Track," *CQ Weekly,* October 8, 2007, 2901.

19. Shawn Zeller, "K Street Remains an Easy Street in Hard Times," *CQ Weekly,* April 21, 2008, 995.

20. Ibid.

21. Ibid.

22. Brody Mullins and Elizabeth Williamson, "Lobbyists Raise Stimulus Price Tag," *Wall Street Journal,* February 3, 2009.

23. Shawn Zeller, "K Street Remains an Easy Street in Hard Times," 995.

24. Alexis de Tocqueville, *Democracy in America,* ed. Phillips Bradley (New York: Knopf, 1951), 119. See also Richard A. Smith, "Interest Group Influence in the U.S. Congress," *Legislative Studies Quarterly* 20 (February 1995): 89–139.

25. Helmut K. Anheier, *Nonprofit Associations: Theory, Management and Policy* (New York: Routledge, 2005), 76–77.

26. Janny Scott, "Medicine's Big Dose of Politics," *Los Angeles Times,* September 25, 1991, A15.

27. Robert Putnam, "The Strange Disappearance of Civic America," *Amercian Prospect,* Winter 1996, 35.

28. Quoted in Suzi Parker, "Civic Clubs: Elks, Lions May Go Way of the Dodo," *Christian Science Monitor,* August 24, 1998, 1.

29. Seth Stern, "No More Bowling Alone," *Christian Science Monitor,* September 4, 2003, 17.

30. Everett Carll Ladd, "The American Way—Civic Engagement—Thrives," *Christian Science Monitor,* March 1, 1999, 9. See Theda Skocpol, *Diminished Democracy: From Membership to Management in American Civic Life* (Norman: University of Oklahoma Press, 2003). Professor Skocpol argues that the decline of broad membership organizations such as the Elks or Moose, which encouraged civic and political participation, occurred in part because many middle-class citizens chose to rely on professionally run advocacy groups to speak on their behalf.

31. Ladd, "The American Way."

32. Mancur Olson Jr., *The Logic of Collective Action: Public Goods and the Theory of Groups* (Cambridge, Mass.: Harvard University Press, 1965).

33. Kay L. Schlozman and John T. Tierney, *Organized Interests and American Democracy* (New York: Harper and Row, 1986).

34. E. E. Schattschneider, *The Semi-Sovereign People* (New York: Holt, Rinehart and Winston, 1960), 35.

35. Kristina C. Miler, "The View from the Hill: Legislative Perceptions of the District," *Legislative Studies Quarterly* 32 (November 2007): 597–628.

36. Sidney Verba, Kay Lehman Schlozman, and Henry Brady, "The Big Tilt: Participatory Inequality in America," *American Prospect,* May/June 1997, 78.

37. Elise D. Garcia, "Money in Politics," *Common Cause,* February 1981, 11.

38. Jeffrey H. Birnbaum, "Lobbyists: Why the Bad Rap?" *American Enterprise,* November/December 1992, 74. See also Jeffrey H. Birnbaum, *The Lobbyists* (New York: Times Books, 1992).

39. Norman J. Ornstein and Shirley Elder, *Interest Groups, Lobbying, and Policymaking* (Washington, D.C.: Congressional Quarterly, 1978), 224.

40. Tory Newmyer, "Majority Formalizes K St. Ties," *Roll Call,* February 15, 2007, 23.

41. Alexander Bolton, "Dems Enlist Help to Push Their Agenda," *The Hill,* February 14, 2007, 1.

42. Jeffrey Birnbaum, "The Thursday Group," *Time,* March 27, 1995, 30–31.

43. Emily Pierce, "GOP Taps Thune to Get Cozy with K St.," *Roll Call,* January 22, 2009.

44. Quoted in Hedrick Smith, *The Power Game* (New York: Random House, 1988), 232.

45. Quoted in Alan K. Ota, "Democratic Foot in Revolving Door," *CQ Weekly,* June 25, 2007, 1900.

46. Ronald J. Hrebenar and Ruth K. Scott, *Interest Group Politics in America* (Englewood Cliffs, N.J.: Prentice-Hall, 1982), 63.

47. "The 195 Former Members Who Are Lobbying," *CQ Weekly,* June 25, 2007, 1901.

48. Jonathan D. Salant, "Obama's Spending Spurs Former U.S. Lawmakers to Join Lobbyists," *Bloomberg.com,* April 9, 2009.

49. Chris Frates, "Hill Experience Gives Lobbyists a Leg Up," *Politico,* May 17, 2007, 10.

50. See, for example, David Ottaway and Dan Morgan, "Former Top U.S. Aides Seek Caspian Gusher," *Washington Post,* July 6, 1997, A1; and Chuck Neubauer and Ted Rohrlich, "Capitalizing on a Politician's Clout," *Los Angeles Times,* December 19, 2004, A1.

51. Mark Preston, "Ex-GOP Senators Get Special Access," *Roll Call,* April 3, 2003, 1, 24.

52. Quoted in Alan K. Ota, "Democratic Foot in the Revolving Door," *CQ Weekly,* June 25, 2007, 1900.

53. Peter Whoriskey and William Branigin, "Abramoff Is Sentenced for Casino Boat Fraud," *Washington Post,* March 30, 2006, A1.

54. Editorial, "Scandal? What Scandal? Congress Ducks Ethics Reform," *USA Today,* September 6, 2006, 12A.

55. Sarah Pekkanen, "How Lobbyists Are Changing the Lobbying Game," *The Hill,* February 12, 1997, 21.

56. *CongressDaily/PM,* May 30, 1997, 6.

57. Quoted in Sam Walker, "Who's in and Who's out among Capitol Lobbyists," *Christian Science Monitor,* November 8, 1995, 3.

58. Quoted in *CongressDaily/PM,* March 15, 2002, 8.

59. Bertram J. Levine, *The Art of Lobbying: Building Trust and Selling Policy* (Washington, DC: CQ Press, 2008).

60. *New York Times,* January 20, 1981, B3.

61. Adam Graham-Silverman, "Travel Decreases as Ethics Rules Complicate Privately Funded Trips," *CQ Weekly,* December 1, 2008, 3178.

62. John Cochran and Martin Kady II, "The New Laws of the Lobby," *CQ Press,* February 26, 2007, 594.

63. Eliza Newlin Carney and Bara Vaida, "Shifting Ground," *National Journal,* March 31, 2007, 27.

64. Quoted in John Cochran and Martin Kady II, "The New Laws of the Lobby," *CQ Press,* February 26, 2007, 594.

65. David Kirkpatrick, "Congress Finds Ways of Avoiding Lobbyist Limit," *New York Times,* February 11, 2007, 1.

66. Ibid.

67. Quoted in Editorial, "Wasn't There an Election Last November?" *Examiner,* March 9, 2007, 18.

68. Carol Matlack, "Getting around the Rules," *National Journal,* May 12, 1990, 1139.

69. Eliza Newlin Carney, "Charitable Chicanery," *National Journal,* June 24, 2006, 20.

70. John Breaux, "Effective Coalitions for Coalitions," *The Hill,* March 21, 2007, 18.

71. Dan Eggen, "Investments Can Yield More on K Street, Study Indicates," *Washington Post,* April 12, 2009, A8.

72. Ernest Wittenberg, "How Lobbying Helps Make Democracy Work," *Vital Speeches of the Day,* November 1, 1982, 47.

73. Robert Pear, "In Divide Over Health Care Overhaul, 2 Major Unions Withdraw From a Coalition," *New York Times,* March 7, 2009, A12.

74. Jeff Patch, "Farm Bill Renewal Sows Fresh Alliances on Subsidies," *Politico,* May 8, 2007, www.politico.com.

75. Martin Kady II, "Keeping Grass-Roots Lobbying Under Wraps," *CQ Weekly,* March 26, 2007, 877.

76. Shawn Zeller, "SEIU Spreads Its Wings, Ruffles Some Feathers," *CQ Weekly,* May 12, 2008, 1233.

77. John T. Tierney and Kay Lehman Schlozman, "Congress and Organized Interests," in *Congressional Politics,* ed. Christopher J. Deering (Chicago: Dorsey, 1989), 212.

78. *Washington Star,* December 31, 1980, C2.

79. Kady II "Keeping Grass-Roots Lobbying under Wraps," 877.
80. Ibid.
81. Juliet Eilperin, "Police Track Down Telecom Telegraphs," *Roll Call,* August 7, 1995, 1.
82. Lisa Caruso, "Turf Battle," *National Journal,* March 31, 2007, 34.
83. Cited in Jack Maskell, "Grassroots Lobbying: Constitutionality of Disclosure Requirements," CRS Report RL33794, January 12, 2007, 3. Also see, for example, John Cochran, "A New Medium for the Message," *CQ Weekly,* March 13, 2006, 652–658, and Kady, "Keeping Grass-Roots Lobbying under Wraps," 877–878.
84. Alison Mitchell, "A New Form of Lobbying Puts Public Face on Private Interest," *New York Times,* September 30, 1998, A14. See also Ken Kollman, *Outside Lobbying: Public Opinion and Interest Group Strategies* (Princeton: Princeton University Press, 1998).
85. Sara Fritz and Dan Morain, "Stealth Lobby Drives Fuel-Additive War," *Los Angeles Times,* June 16, 1997, A6.
86. Mitchell, "A New Form of Lobbying Puts Public Face on Private Interest."
87. Kevin Bogardus, "Act Now on Lobbying Reform, Watchdogs Tell the House," *The Hill,* April 17, 2007, 18.
88. "Trends in Grassroots Lobbying: Consultant Q&A," *Campaigns and Elections,* February 1999, 22.
89. *New York Times,* January 24, 1980, A16.
90. Quoted in Jeffrey Birnbaum, "Advocacy Groups Blur Media Lines," *Washington Post,* December 6, 2004, A1.
91. Ibid., A7.
92. Jeffrey Birnbaum, "The Forces That Set the Agenda," *Washington Post,* April 24, 2005, B5.
93. Paul S. Herrnson, "Party Organizations, Party-Connected Committees, Party Allies, and the Financing of Federal Elections," *Journal of Politics* (November 2009, forthcoming).
94. Juliet Eilperin and Dan Morgan, "Something Borrowed, Something Blue," *Washington Post,* March 9, 2001, A16.
95. Brody Mullins, "Growing Role for Lobbyists: Raising Funds for Lawmakers," *Wall Street Journal,* January 27, 2006, A1.
96. Philip M. Stern, "The Tin Cup Congress," *Washington Monthly,* May 1988, 24.
97. U.S. Congress, *Congressional Record,* daily ed., 100th Cong., 1st sess., August 5, 1987, S11292.
98. "Fundamentals of Fund-raising," *Washington Post,* December 5, 1990, A23.
99. Jack Maskell, "Lobbying Law and Ethics Rules Changes in the 110th Congress," *Congressional Research Service Report,* September 18, 2007.
100. Kimberley A. Strassel, "Chafee vs. Laffey: A Populist Conservative Challenges the Senate's Most Liberal Republican," *Wall Street Journal,* August 17, 2006.
101. Matthew Continetti, *The K Street Gang* (New York: Doubleday, 2006). Also see Carrie Sheffield, "Norquist Seeks Trademark on 'K Street Project' Name," *The Hill,* April 12, 2006, 1.
102. *Congressional Record,* January 4, 2007, H32.
103. Quoted in David S. Broder and Amy Goldstein, "AARP Decision Followed a Long GOP Courtship," *Washington Post,* November 20, 2003, A1.
104. Quoted in Sara Fritz, "AARP Supports Deal on Medicare," *St. Petersburg Times,* November 18, 2003, 1A.
105. John Brinkley, "Members of Congress Perform under Judging Eyes of Lobbyists," *Washington Times,* March 16, 1994, A16. See John Cochran, "Interest Groups Make Sure Lawmakers Know the 'Score,'" *CQ Weekly,* April 19, 2003, 924–929.

106. Bill Whalen, "Rating Lawmakers' Politics by Looking into Their Eyes," *Insight,* October 20, 1986, 21. See Cochran, "Interest Groups Make Sure Lawmakers Know the 'Score.'"
107. *New York Times,* May 13, 1986, A24.
108. *CQ Monitor,* April 13, 1998, 4.
109. "Environment," *CongressDailyPM,* February 21, 2006, 10.
110. Hibbing and Theiss-Morse, *Congress as Public Enemy,* 63–65.
111. Frank R. Baumgartner and Beth L. Leech, *Basic Interests: The Importance of Groups in Politics and in Political Science* (Princeton: Princeton University Press, 1998), 13.
112. Leslie Wayne, "Lobbyists' Gift to Politicians Reap Benefits, Study Shows," *New York Times,* January 23, 1997, B11.
113. Jim Drinkard, "Report: Interests Are Running Congress," *USA Today,* September 10, 1998, 7A.
114. Janet M. Gretzke, "PACs and the Congressional Supermarket: The Currency is Complex," *American Journal of Political Science* 33 (1989): 1–24, Lawrence S. Rothenberg, *Linking Citizens to Government: Interest Group Politics at Common Cause* (New York: Cambridge University Press, 1992); and John R. Wright, "Contributions, Lobbying, and Committee Voting in the U.S. House of Representatives," *American Political Science Review* 84 (1990): 417–438.
115. See the labor union profile at the Center for Responsive Politics, www.opensecrets.org/industries/indus.php?ind=P.
116. See the oil and gas industry's profile at the Center for Responsive Politics, www.opensecrets.org/industries/indus.php?ind=E01.
117. Richard L. Hall and Frank W. Wayman, "Buying Time: Moneyed Interests and the Mobilization of Bias in Congressional Committees," *American Political Science Review* 84 (September, 1990): 800. See also their review of the literature on patterns in campaign contributions on 799–800.
118. Paul S. Herrnson, *Congressional Elections: Campaigning at Home and in Washington,* 5th ed. (Washington, D.C.: CQ Press, 2008), 167–168.
119. Quoted in Claudia Dreifus, "And Then There Was Frank," *New York Times Magazine,* February 4, 1996, 25.
120. Don Van Natta Jr., "$250,000 Buys Donors 'Best Access to Congress,'" *New York Times,* January 27, 1997, A1.
121. See Richard A. Smith, "Advocacy, Interpretation, and Influence in the U.S. Congress," *American Political Science Review* 78 (1, 1984): 44–63 and Hall and Wayman, *American Political Science Review.*
122. Marie Hojnacki and David C. Kimball, "Organized Interests and the Decision of Whom to Lobby in Congress," *American Political Science Review,* December 1998, 775–790.
123. *Washington Star,* May 22, 1978, A1.
124. Elizabeth Brotherton, "A Recycled Idea," *Roll Call,* June 13, 2006, 3.
125. Richard L. Hall and Alan V. Deardorff, "Lobbying as Legislative Subsidy," *American Political Science Review,* February 2006, 69–84.
126. *Wall Street Journal,* October 5, 1987, 54.
127. Thomas Hale Boggs Jr., "All Interests Are Special," *New York Times,* February 16, 1993, A17.
128. Mary Lynn Jones, "Survey Says Lobbyists Find Information Rules the Hill," *The Hill,* November 18, 1998, 8. See also Allan J. Cigler and Burdett Loomis, *Interest Group Politics,* 5th ed. (Washington, D.C.: CQ Press, 1998).
129. Kirk Victor, "New Kids on the Block," *National Journal,* October 31, 1987, 2727.
130. Alexander Bolton, "House Partisan Conflict Roils Enron Reform," *The Hill,* February 27, 2002, 7.

131. William Luneburg and Thomas Susman, *The Lobbying Manual*, 3d ed. (Washington, D.C.: American Bar Association, 2005), 7.

132. U.S. Congress, *Organization of the Congress*, H. Rept. 1675, 79th Cong., 2d sess., 1946, 26.

133. Francesca Contiguaglia, "GAO Finds That Lobbyist Registration Has Soared," *Roll Call*, May 14, 1998, 14.

134. Jeffrey H. Birnbaum, "The Road to Riches Is Called K Street," *Washington Post*, June 22, 2005, A1.

135. Sam Fulwood, "Lobbying Reform Passes House on Unanimous Vote," *Los Angeles Times*, November 30, 1995, A9.

136. Alex Knott, *Special Report: Industry of Influence Nets Almost $13 Billion* (Washington, D.C.: Center for Public Integrity, 2005), 1–4.

137. Lee Hamilton, "Lobbying Murkiness Undermines Our Trust in Congress," Center on Congress at Indiana University, April 11, 2005, 2, http://congress.indiana.edu.

138. Deirdre Shesgreen, "Shining a Dim Light," *Legal Times*, December 21 and 28, 1998, 26, 27.

139. Quoted in Mark Wegner, "Lobbying Reforms Readied in House," *National Journal*, May 19, 2007, 47.

140. See Ken Silverstein, "Oil Adds Sheen to Kazakh Regime," *Los Angeles Times*, May 12, 2004, A1.

141. Ibid.

142. See Adam Hochschild, "Into the Light from the Heart of Darkness," *Los Angeles Times*, December 6, 1998, M1; and Katharine Seeyle, "National Rifle Association Is Turning to World Stage to Fight Gun Control," *New York Times*, April 2, 1997, A12.

143. Alan Ohnsman and Gopal Ratnam, "Toyota to Boost Lobbying Efforts as U. S. Operations Expand," *Examiner*, March 7, 2007, 21.

144. Edgar Lane, *Lobbying and the Law* (Berkeley: University of California Press, 1964), 18.

CHAPTER 14

1. The oft-stated quotation continues to say, "Omitted, all the voyage of their life is bound in shallows and miseries."

2. Naftali Bendavid, "Blueprint Finds Support, Unease on Capitol Hill," *Wall Street Journal*, February 27, 2009, A10.

3. Peter Grier, "Bailout Tab: $3 Trillion So Far," *Christian Science Monitor*, March 31, 2009, online edition.

4. Humberto Sanchez, "Budget Experts See Crunch on Spending, Initiatives Ahead," National Journal's *CongressDailyPM*, October 8, 2008, 4.

5. Gerald F. Seib, "Obama Puts All His Chips on Table," *Wall Street Journal*, March 27, 2009, A2.

6. Janet Hook, "Obama's Budget Is the End of an Era," *Los Angeles Times*, February 27, 2009, online edition.

7. Ibid.

8. See David Easton, *The Political System* (New York: Knopf, 1963); Harold D. Lasswell, *Politics: Who Gets What, When, How* (New York: Meridian Books, 1958); and Randall B. Ripley and Grace A. Franklin, *Congress, the Bureaucracy, and Public Policy*, 5th ed. (Pacific Grove, Calif.: Brooks/Cole, 1991).

9. Theodore R. Marmor, *The Politics of Medicare* (Chicago: Aldine Publishing, 1973).

10. John W. Kingdon, *Agendas, Alternatives, and Public Policies* (Boston: Little, Brown, 1984), 3.

11. Ibid., 17–19.

12. Quoted in Sheryl Gay Stolberg, "The Revolution That Wasn't," *New York Times*, February 13, 2005, E16.

13. Kingdon, *Agendas, Alternatives, and Public Policies,* chap. 2.
14. Fareed Zakaria, "Free at Last," *Newsweek,* April 13, 2009, 42.
15. Steven Chu, "Pulling the Plug on Oil," *Newsweek,* April 13, 2009, 44.
16. Nelson W. Polsby, "Strengthening Congress in National Policymaking," *Yale Review* (Summer 1970): 481–497.
17. James L. Sundquist, *Politics and Policy: The Eisenhower, Kennedy, and Johnson Years* (Washington, D.C.: Brookings Institution Press, 1968).
18. Elizabeth Wehr, "Numerous Factors Favoring Good Relationship between Reagan and New Congress," *Congressional Quarterly Weekly Report,* January 24, 1981, 173.
19. Kingdon, *Agendas, Alternatives, and Public Policies,* 148–149.
20. American Enterprise Institute, *The State of the Congress: Tomorrow's Challenges?* (Washington, D.C.: American Enterprise Institute, 1981), 8.
21. Theodore Lowi, "American Business, Public Policy, Case Studies, and Political Theory," *World Politics,* July 1964, 677–715; Theodore Lowi, "Four Systems of Policy, Politics, and Choice," *Public Administration Review,* July-August 1972, 298–310; Samuel P. Huntington, *The Common Defense* (New York: Columbia University Press, 1961); and Ripley and Franklin, *Congress, the Bureaucracy, and Public Policy.*
22. *Wall Street Journal,* May 13, 1988, R17.
23. Mary Russell, "'Park-Barrel Bill' Clears House Panel," *Washington Post,* June 22, 1978, A3.
24. *Congressional Record,* February 9, 2006, S980.
25. John Solomon and Jeffrey Birnbaum, "In the Democratic Congress, Pork Still Gets Served," *Washington Post,* May 24, 2007, A1.
26. "A Helping of Pork," *Washington Post,* March 15, 2009, A17.
27. Stephen Dinan, "Temptation of Pork Changes Minds on Capitol Hill," *Washington Times,* February 23, 2009, A1.
28. See, for example, Margaret Kriz, "Heavy Breathing," *National Journal,* January 4, 1997, 8–12.
29. Joby Warrick, "White House Taking a Hands-on Role in Writing New Clean Air Standards," *Washington Post,* May 22, 1997, A10.
30. Ricardo Alonso-Zaldivar, "Overhauling U.S. Health System Could Cost $1.5 Trillion," *Christian Science Monitor,* March 19, 2009, 2.
31. Donald Lambro, "Steady GOP Rebound Strategy," *Washington Times,* June 7, 2001, A17.
32. Benjamin I. Page, "Cooling the Legislative Tea," in *American Politics and Public Policy,* ed. Walter Dean Burnham and Martha Wagner Weinberg (Cambridge: MIT Press, 1978), 171–187.
33. Judy Sarasohn, "Money for Lat. 40 N, Long. 73 W," *Congressional Quarterly Weekly Report,* May 12, 1979, 916.
34. Paula Drummond, "Unfunded Mandates Bill Becomes Law," *Kansas Government Journal,* May 1995, 122.
35. "Don't Just Do Something, Sit There," *Economist,* December 23, 1995–January 5, 1996, 11–12.
36. Barber Conable, "Government Is Working," *Roll Call,* April 19, 1984, 3. Congress has initiated change many times. A classic example is the 37th Congress (1861–1863), which drafted "the blueprint for modern America" by enacting measures to finance the Civil War, build the transcontinental railroad, eradicate slavery, promote the land-grant college movement, provide settlers with homestead land, and create the Department of Agriculture. See James M. McPherson, *Battle Cry of Freedom: The Civil War Era* (New York: Ballantine, 1988), 452.
37. *Congressional Record,* September 22, 2008, S9173.

38. Robert Luce, *Legislative Problems* (Boston: Houghton Mifflin, 1935), 426. See also Louis Fisher, "The Authorization-Appropriation Process in Congress: Formal Rules and Informal Practices," *Catholic University Law Review* (Fall 1979): 51–105; and Richard F. Fenno Jr., *The Power of the Purse* (Boston: Little, Brown, 1966).

39. Richard Munson, *The Cardinals of Capitol Hill* (New York: Grove Press, 1993), 6.

40. See Louis Fisher, "Annual Authorizations: Durable Roadblocks to Biennial Budgeting," *Public Budgeting and Finance* (Spring 1983): 23–40.

41. Quoted in Alan Ota, "Spending Bills May Be Democrats' Plan B," *CQ Today,* April 27, 2007, 8.

42. U.S. Congress, *Congressional Record,* daily ed., 109th Cong., 1st sess., May 10, 2005, S4847.

43. See Elana Shor and Jackie Kucinich, "GOP Plots Blue-Slip Attack," *The Hill,* May 30, 2007, 1.

44. See Robert Keith, *Duration of Continuing Resolutions in Recent Years,* CRS Report RL32614, March 9, 2009.

45. Erik Eckholm, "Payments to the Retired Loom Ever Larger," *New York Times,* August 30, 1992, E1, E4.

46. Jason DeParle, "U.S. Welfare System Dies as State Programs Emerge," *New York Times,* June 30. 1997, A1.

47. Quoted in Jonathan Weisman and Michael Fletcher, "GOP May Be Splintering on Social Security," *Washington Post,* April 27, 2005, A4.

48. Michael D. Shear, "Obama Pledges Entitlement Reform," *Washington Post,* January 16, 2009, A1.

49. Robert Bixby, Stuart Butler, Isabel Sawhill, "Entitlement Reform Options," *Washington Times,* November 18, 2008, A19, and Robert Pear,"Recession Erodes 2 Largest Funds in U.S. Safety Net," *New York Times,* May 13, 2009, A1.

50. U.S. Congress, *Congressional Record,* 109th Cong., 1st sess., February 28, 2005, S1784.

51. Andrew Taylor, "Weighing Nip, Tuck vs. Total Makeover," *CQ Weekly,* April 4, 2005, 843.

52. Dennis Cauchon, "Rethinking Social Security," *USA Today,* March 18, 2005, 4A.

53. David Clarke, "Annual Report Projects Earlier Shortfalls for Social Security and Medicare," *CQ Today,* May 13, 2009, 3.

54. David R. Francis, "Social Security: A Contrarian View," *Christian Science Monitor,* February 26, 2007, 17.

55. David Cook, "Rising Healthcare Costs Pose Fundamental Risk to U.S.," *Christian Science Monitor,* September 18, 2007, online edition.

56. Ceci Connolly and Mike Allen, "Medicare Drug Benefit May Cost $1.2 Trillion," *Washington Post,* February 9, 2005, A1.

57. William Welch, "Medicare: The Next Riddle for the Ages," *USA Today,* March 17, 2005, 10A.

58. Quoted in Julie Rovner, "The Real Budget Buster," National Journal's *CongressDaily/AM,* April 5, 2001, 5.

59. Donald Kettl, "Looking for a Real Crisis: Try Medicaid," *Governing,* April 2005, 20.

60. Matthew Miller, "The Big Federal Freeze," *New York Times Magazine,* October 15, 2000, 94.

61. Quoted in Gail Russell Chaddock, "Off-Radar Tax Breaks Draw New Scrutiny," *Christian Science Monitor,* March 9, 2005, 11.

62. David Clarke, "The 2 Percent Dissolution," *CQ Weekly,* May 28, 2007, 1576–1583.

63. U.S. Congress, *Congressional Record,* daily ed., 106th Cong., 2d sess., March 2, 2000, S1050.

64. Mark Preston, "'Vote-a-Rama' Keeps Wearing Senate Down," *Roll Call,* March 26, 2003, 1.

65. U.S. Congress, *Congressional Record,* daily ed., 107th Cong., 1st sess., February 15, 2001, S1532.

66. John Ellwood, "Budget Control in a Redistributive Environment," in *Making Economic Policy in Congress,* ed. Allen Schick (Washington, D.C.: American Enterprise Institute, 1983), 93. Data on the number of times reconciliation has been employed were provided by budget expert Robert Keith, Congressional Research Service.

67. "Senate parliamentarians have ruled that a congressional budget resolution can spawn up to three reconciliation bills—one for spending, one for taxes, and one for raising the debt limit. But if a reconciliation measure combines two or more elements, such as tax law changes and spending, that single bill counts for both." See Paul Krawzak and Chuck Conlon, "If Reconciliation Is a Problem, Try Procrastination Instead," *CQ Today*, March 19, 2009, 11.

68. Jonathan Nicholson, "Budget Chairmen Both Leery of Using Reconciliation for Cap-and-Trade Legislation," *Daily Report for Executives*, March 18, 2009, A-24.

69. Testimony of Sen. Robert C. Byrd, Senate Budget Committee, *Senate Procedures for Consideration of the Budget Resolution/Reconciliation*, February 12, 2009, 3.

70. Manu Raju and Jonathan Martin, "GOP Warns About Budget Hardball," *Politico*, March 24, 2009, 15.

71. David Clarke and Paul Krawzak, "Negotiators Face Post-Recess Quandary on How Aggressively to Move," *CQ Today*, April 3, 2009, 3.

72. Emily Pierce. "Up Next: More Partisan Fights," *Politico*, April 13, 2009, 17.

73. David Rosenbaum, "Democratic Filibuster Hopes Fade," *New York Times*, November 18, 2002, A15; and David Baumann, "The Octopus That Might Eat Congress," *National Journal*, May 14, 2005, 1470–1475.

74. Peter Cohn, "Hill Veteran Sees Pitfalls in Using Budget Reconciliation," National Journal's *CongressDailyPM*, March 6, 2009, 3.

75. William Dauster, "Budget Process Issues for 1993," *Journal of Law and Politics* 9 (1992): 26.

76. Quoted in *Ibid.*, 27.

77. U.S. Congress, *Congressional Record*, daily ed., 107th Cong., 1st sess., January 4, 2001, S19.

78. Bill Heniff, Jr., *Budget Enforcement Procedures: Pay-As-you-Go (PAYGO) Rule*, CRS Report RL31943, December 6, 2007.

79. Robert Keith, *The House's "Pay-As-You-Go" (PAYGO) Rule in the 110th Congress: A Brief Overview*, CRS Report RL33850.

80. Martin Crutsinger, "Deficit Nears $1 Trillion, Sets Record," *Washington Post*, April 11, 2009, A6.

81. John Maggs, "The Trillion-Dollar Deficit," *National Journal*, November 1, 2008, 34.

82. Jonathan Nicholson, "Economic Crisis Will Upstage Budget Deficit in '09, but Red Ink Shadow Will Loom Large," *Daily Report for Executives*, January 6, 2009, C-1.

83. Gail Russell Chaddock, "GOP's Family Feud Over Spending," *Christian Science Monitor*, May 22, 2006, 10.

84. U.S. Congress, *Congressional Record*, daily ed., 107th Cong., 2d sess., June 20, 2002, S5810.

85. Sue Kirchhoff, "Deficit Warnings Increase in Urgency," *USA Today*, February 27, 2003, 5B.

86. U.S. Congress, *Congressional Record*, daily ed., 107th Cong., 2d sess., July 16, 2002, H4749.

CHAPTER 15

1. Jim Michaels and Ken Dillanian, "U.S. to Target Pirates' Assets in Effort to Thwart Attacks," *USA Today*, April 16, 2009, 1A.

2. Martha Raddatz, Kirit Radia, and Lee Ferran, "American Ship Survives Somali Pirates Hijack Attempt," *ABC News*, April 15, 2009 (online report).

3. Quoted in Samuel Eliot Morison, *The Oxford History of the American People* (New York: Oxford University Press, 1965), 346.

4. Edward S. Corwin, *The President: Office and Powers, 1787–1957*, 4th ed. (New York: New York University Press, 1957), 171. See also Cecil V. Crabb Jr. and Pat M. Holt, *Invitation to Struggle: Congress, the President, and Foreign Policy*, 4th ed. (Washington, D.C.: CQ Press, 1992).

5. Corwin, *The President*, 171; italics are in the original.

6. Alexander Hamilton, James Madison, and John Jay, *The Federalist Papers*, ed. Clinton Rossiter (New York: Mentor Books, 1961), 391–393.

7. Jonathan Mahler, "After the Imperial Presidency," *New York Times Magazine,* November 9, 2008, 45.

8. Testimony before the House International Relations Committee, January 12, 1995. Reported by Maureen Dowd, *New York Times,* January 13, 1995, A1.

9. *Youngstown Sheet and Tube Co. v. Sawyer,* 343 U.S. 636 (1952).

10. Cecil V. Crabb Jr., Glenn J. Antizzo, and Leila E. Sarieddine, *Congress and the Foreign Policy Process* (Baton Rouge: Louisiana State University Press, 2000), 4.

11. Ibid., 163.

12. Bryan Bender, "Kerry Poised to Cap Long Journey," *Boston Globe,* November 20, 2008, online edition.

13. Carl Hulse, "Kerry Aims To Make a Mark as a Senate Chairman," *New York Times,* January 13, 2009, online edition.

14. Bender, "Kerry Poised to Cap Long Journey."

15. Holbert N. Carroll, *The House of Representatives and Foreign Affairs,* rev. ed. (Boston: Little, Brown, 1966), 20.

16. National Commission on Terrorist Attacks upon the United States, *The 9/11 Report* (New York: St. Martin's Paperbacks, 2004), 596–599.

17. *Congressional Record,* September 23, 2008, S9268.

18. By law, the sixteen intelligence agencies are: the CIA; the State Department's Bureau of Intelligence and Research; the Defense Intelligence Agency; the National Security Agency; the National Reconnaissance Office; the National Geospatial-Intelligence Agency; the FBI; Army Intelligence; Navy Intelligence; Air Force Intelligence; Marine Corps Intelligence; the Department of Homeland Security; Coast Guard; Treasury Department; Energy Department; and Drug Enforcement Agency. See Richard A. Best, Jr., *Intelligence Issues for Congress,* CRS Report RL33539, January 9, 2009.

19. Mark Mazzetti, "Report Faults Spy Chief for Inaction on Turf Wars," *New York Times,* April 2, 2009, A15.

20. Henry A. Kissinger, "Implementing Bush's Vision," *Washington Post,* May 16, 2005, A17.

21. Information provided by CRS defense expert Pat Towell.

22. Christopher J. Deering, "Congress, the President, and Military Policy," in *Congress and the Presidency: Invitation to Struggle,* ed. Roger H. Davidson, *The Annals* 499 (September 1988): 136–147.

23. Julian E. Barnes, "Cost of Iraq War Will Surpass Vietnam's By Year's End," *Los Angeles Times,* April 11, 2009, online edition.

24. Quoted in Matt Richtel, "Trade Investors Cull Start-Ups for Pentagon," *New York Times,* May 7, 2007, C8.

25. *Budget of the United States Government, Fiscal Year 2006,* Historical Tables (Washington, D.C.: Government Printing Office, 2005), Table 3.2.

26. Thomas Shanker, "Defense Secretary Urges More Spending for U.S. Diplomacy," *New York Times,* November 27, 2007, A6.

27. Leslie Wayne, "Pentagon Spends without Bids, a Study Finds," *New York Times,* September 30, 2004, C1.

28. Christopher Dickey, "The Surveillance-Industrial Complex," *New York Times Book Review,* January 11, 2009, 11.

29. Tim Smart, "Getting the F-22 off the Ground," *Washington Post,* April 20, 1998, 12; and Tim Weiner, "Air Superiority at $258 Million a Pop," *New York Times,* October 27, 2004, C1.

30. Julian E. Barnes, "Pentagon Chief Takes Aim at Big Weapons Systems," *Los Angeles Times,* April 7, 2009, online edition.

31. Gordon Lubold, "Gates Axes Some Costly Weapons, Emphasizes 'Irregular' Warfare," *Christian Science Monitor,* April 6, 2009, online edition.

32. Both quotes are from William Matthews and John T. Bennett, "Outlook for Gates' Plan Good, Despite Opposition," *Federal Times,* April 13, 2009, 8.

33. Press Release, "Skelton Statement on Defense Budget Proposals," House Armed Services Committee, April 6, 2009.

34. Julian E. Barnes, "Gates Defuses the Defense Budget Battle," *Los Angeles Times,* April 25, 2009, online edition.

35. Tim Weiner, "For Military Plane in Crash, a History of Political Conflict," *New York Times,* April 11, 2000, A1.

36. Quoted in Roxana Tiron, "Marines, Weldon Score Victory on Osprey," *The Hill,* October 6, 2005, 16.

37. Christopher Bolkcom, *V-22 Osprey Tilt-Rotor Aircraft,* CRS Report RL31384, January 2, 2009, 11.

38. Quoted in Vernon Loeb, "Weapon Systems Die Hard, Especially on Capitol Hill," *Washington Post,* May 6, 2002, A4.

39. Quoted in Kevin Sack, "For the South, GOP Secures Defense Bounty," *New York Times,* November 18, 1997, A1.

40. *Congressional Record,* July 7, 1988, 17072.

41. Karl Viox, "It's Closing Time for Base Commission," *Washington Post,* December 29, 1995, A21. Scholars regard this as an intriguing example of blame-avoidance politics. See, for example, Christopher J. Deering, "Congress, the President, and Automatic Government: The Case of Military Base Closures," in *Rivals for Power: Presidential-Congressional Relations,* ed. James A. Thurber (Washington, D.C.: CQ Press, 1996).

42. *Congressional Record,* daily ed., 102d Cong., 2d sess., August 6, 1992, H7701–7703.

43. Keith Bradsher, "NAFTA: Something to Offend Everyone," *New York Times,* November 14, 1993. See also I. M. Destler, "Protecting Congress or Protecting Trade?" *Foreign Policy* 62 (Spring 1986): 96–107.

44. Elizabeth Becker, "Free Trade Pact Faces Trouble in Congress," *New York Times,* May 10, 2005, C1.

45. Patrick O'Connor and Martin Kady II, "Dems Finally Seize Rules Advantage on Trade," *Politico,* April 15, 2008, 1.

46. John E. Yang, "House Backs Clinton on China Trade Privileges," *Washington Post,* June 25, 1997, A1.

47. Sander Levin, "Derailing a Consensus on Trade," *Washington Post,* December 5, 2001, A29.

48. Barack Obama, "Making the World Work Again," *Los Angeles Times,* March 24, 2009, online edition.

49. Richard Simon and Nancy Cleeland, "Senate OKs Fast-Track Trade Bill," *Los Angeles Times,* August 2, 2002, A1.

50. Richard F. Grimmett, *Conventional Arms Transfers to Developing Nations, 2000–2007,* CRS Report RL34723, October 23, 2008.

51. Frida Berrigan, "Arms Pusher to the World," *Los Angeles Times,* May 21, 2007, A17.

52. Leslie Wayne, "Foreign Sales by U.S. Arms Makers Doubled in a Year," *New York Times,* November 11, 2006, B3.

53. Charles McC. Mathias Jr., "Ethnic Groups and Foreign Policy," *Foreign Affairs* 59 (Summer 1981): 975–998.

54. Leslie Wayne, "So Much for the Plan to Scrap Old Weapons," *New York Times,* December 22, 2002, D1.

55. Megan Scully, "Gates Warns against Big Cuts in Future Defense Spending," National Journal's *CongressDailyPM,* April 17, 2009, 4.

56. Joseph J. Schatz, "Has Congress Given Bush Too Free a Spending Hand?" *CQ Weekly,* April 12, 2002, 859.

57. T. Christian Miller, *Blood Money: Wasted Billions, Lost Lives, and Corporate Greed in Iraq* (New York: Little, Brown, 2006).

58. Robin Wright, "Don't Just Fund the War, Shell Out for Peace," *Washington Post,* March 10, 2002, B5; and Stephen Kinzer, "Why They Don't Know Us," *New York Times,* November 11, 2001, D5.

59. Elizabeth Becker, "Chief Urges World Bank to Pick Leader More Carefully," *New York Times,* May 25, 2005, C5.

60. David Price, "Global Democracy Promotion: Seven Lessons for the New Administration," *Washington Quarterly,* January 2009, 165.

61. Justin Florence and Matthew Gerke, "Pen Him In," *Legal Times,* February 4, 2008, 51.

62. Loch Johnson and James M. McCormick, "Foreign Policy by Executive Fiat," *Foreign Policy* 28 (Fall 1977): 118–124.

63. David Auerswald and Forrest Maltzman, "Shaping Foreign Policy through Ratification: The Senate and Treaties," paper delivered at an American Political Science Association meeting, Boston, Mass., August 2002, 6.

64. Thomas W. Lippman and Peter Baker, "Bipartisanship, but at a Price," *Washington Post,* April 25, 1997, A1.

65. Roger H. Davidson, "Senate Floor Deliberation: A Preliminary Inquiry," in *The Contentious Senate,* ed. Colton C. Campbell and Nicol C. Rae (Lanham, Md.: Rowman and Littlefield, 2001), 22–29.

66. David Silverberg, "Nasty, Brutish and Short: The CTBT Debates," *The Hill,* December 8, 1999, 16.

67. Ibid.

68. Kiki Caruson, "International Agreement-Making and the Executive-Legislative Relationship," *Presidential Research Group Report* 25 (Fall 2002): 22.

69. Ibid., 21.

70. Josh Rogin, "Iraq Agreement Including Withdrawal Timeline Proceeds without Congress," *CQ Today,* November 18, 2008, 9.

71. *Congressional Record,* September 9, 2008, S8156.

72. "Delahunt Slaps Administration for Secrecy on Iraq Agreement," National Journal's *CongressDailyAM,* November 20, 2008, 6.

73. Jeanne J. Grimmett, *Why Certain Trade Agreements Are Approved as Congressional-Executive Agreements Rather Than as Treaties,* CRS Report 97-896, February 17, 2009, 5.

74. This section draws upon the invaluable summary of congressional policy initiation in Ellen C. Collier, *Foreign Policy Roles of the President and Congress,* Congressional Research Service Report No. 93-20F, January 6, 1993, 11–17.

75. The classic account of this incident is Chalmers M. Roberts, "The Day We Didn't Go to War," *The Reporter,* September 14, 1954, 31–35.

76. Alexander Bolton, "Dems Want Clearer Benchmarks from Obama on Afghanistan," *The Hill,* April 15, 2009, 3.

77. Mark Mazzetti amd Scott Shane, "Memos Spell Out Brutal C.I.A. Mode of Interrogation," *New York Times,* April 17, 2009, A1.

78. Alison Mitchell, "In Vote Clinton Sought to Avoid, House Backs a Force for Kosovo," *New York Times,* March 12, 1999, A1.

79. Ellen C. Collier, "Foreign Policy by Reporting Requirement," *Washington Quarterly* 11 (Winter 1988): 75.

80. Bruce J. Schulman, "Congress' Wartime Quandary," *Los Angeles Times,* April 27, 2003, M2.

81. Cited in Frederick A. O. Schwarz Jr. and Aziz Huq, "Where's Congress in This Power Play?" *Washington Post,* April 1, 2007, B1.

82. Ibid.

83. Norman J. Ornstein, "Abu Ghraib Hearings Put Dismissal of Congress on Display," *Roll Call,* May 12, 2004.

84. Thomas E. Mann and Norman J. Ornstein, *The Broken Branch* (New York: Oxford University Press, 2006), 151–152.

85. Eric Lichtblau and James Risen, "Recent Wiretapping's Scale Exceeded Law, Officials Say," *New York Times,* April 16, 2009, A1. Also see David M. Herszenhorn, "Pelosi Tells of a Briefing by Officials on Colleague," *New York Times,* April 23, 2009, A16.

86. Steve Vogel, "Hill Panel to Begin Review of Defense Acquisition System," *Washington Post,* March 9, 2009, A13.

87. Richard Sobel, "Contra Aid Fundamentals: Exploring the Intricacies and the Issues," *Political Science Quarterly* 110 (Summer 1995): 287–306.

88. James M. Lindsay, "Congress, Foreign Policy, and the New Institutionalism," *International Studies Quarterly* 38 (June 1994): 281–304.

89. An early, influential analysis of this phenomenon is John E. Mueller, *War, Presidents, and Public Opinion* (New York: Wiley, 1973), 208–213.

90. Richard F. Grimmett, *Instances of Use of United States Armed Forces Abroad, 1798–2006,* Congressional Research Service Report RL32170, January 8, 2007.

91. Harold M. Hyman, *Quiet Past and Stormy Present: War Powers in American History* (Washington, D.C.: American Historical Association Bicentennial Essays on the Constitution, 1986).

92. Quotes from Helen Dewar, "Congress's Reaction to TV Coverage Shows Ambivalence on Foreign Policy," *Washington Post,* October 9, 1993, A14; and Dewar, "Clinton, Congress at Brink of Foreign Policy Dispute," A1.

93. Richard F. Grimmett, *War Powers Resolution: Presidential Compliance,* Congressional Research Service Report RL33532, February 2, 2009.

94. Ibid., 1.

95. Ivo H. Daalder and James M. Lindsay, *America Unbound: The Bush Revolution in Foreign Policy* (New York: Wiley), 90.

96. Caroline Heldman, "Presidential Persuasion and Press Coverage of the War in Iraq," in *Understanding the Presidency,* 4th ed., ed. James P. Pfiffner and Roger H. Davidson (New York: Pearson Longman, 2007), 199–200.

97. Gary C. Jacobson, *A Divider, not a Uniter* (New York: Pearson Longman, 2007), 108.

98. *Congressional Record,* daily ed., 107th Cong., 2d sess., October 9, 2002, S10175.

99. Ibid., S10161.

100. *Congressional Record,* daily ed., 107th Cong., 2d sess., October 10, 2002, S10247.

101. Jacobson, *A Divider, not a Uniter,* 147.

102. Quote by Bob Woodward, *Plan of Attack* (New York: Simon and Schuster, 2004), 309.

103. "Obama's Speech at Camp Lejeune, N.C.," *New York Times,* February 27, 2009, online edition.

104. Louis Fisher, *Presidential War Power,* 2d ed., revised (Lawrence: University Press of Kansas, 2004), 261.

105. Quoted in Dahlia Lithwick, "Wrestling Over War Powers," *Newsweek,* July 21, 2008, 18.

106. Michael Abramowitz, "Bush, Congress Could Face Confrontation on Issue of War Powers," *Washington Post,* February 16, 2007, A5.

107. Andrew J. Bacevich, "War Powers in the Age of Terror," *New York Times,* October 31, 2005, A21.

108. Both these quotes are from "Congress Backs Bush on Emergency Aid," *International Herald-Tribune,* September 15, 2001, 5.

109. Mark Mazzetti and Scott Shane, "Memos Spell Out Brutal C.I.A. Mode of Interrogation," *New York Times,* April 17, 2009, A1.

110. Shailagh Murray and Paul Kane, "Obama Rejects Truth Panel," *Washington Post,* April 24, 2009, A6.

111. Greg Miller, "Obama Preserves Renditions as Counter-Terrorism Tool," *Los Angeles Times,* February 1, 2009, online edition; and editorial, "New Team, Old Position," *Washington Post,* February 14, 2009, A18.

112. Alexander Bolton, "Leaders Balk at Setting Up Panel," *The Hill,* April 24, 2009, 8. Also see, for example, Ali Soufan, "My Tortured Decision," *New York Times,* April 23, 2009, A25; Kara Rowland, "Top Legislators Knew of Interrogations," *Washington Times,* April 23, 2009, A1; Dan Eggen, "Cheney Requests Release of 2 CIA Reports on Interrogations," *Washington Post,* April 25, 2009, A4; Scott Shane, "Interrogations' Effectiveness May Prove Elusive," *New York Times,* April 23, 2009, A14; Dan Balz and Perry Bacon Jr., "Congress Debates Fresh Investigations of Interrogations," *Washington Post,* April 23, 2009, A1; Michael Hayden and Michael B. Mukasey, "The President Ties His Own Hands on Terror," *Wall Street Journal,* April 17, 2009, A13; and Mark Danner, "U.S. Torture: Voices from the Black Sites," *New York Review of Books,* April 9, 2009, 69–77.

113. John E. Reilly, *Public Opinion and Foreign Policy* (Chicago: Chicago Council on Foreign Relations, April 25, 1999).

114. James M. Lindsay, "Congress and Foreign Policy: Why the Hill Matters," *Political Science Quarterly* 107 (Winter 1992–1993): 626–627.

115. Richard G. Lugar, "Beating Terror," *Washington Post,* January 27, 2003, A19.

CHAPTER 16

1. Quoted in Carl Hulse and David M. Herszenhorn, "Behind Closed Doors, Warnings of Calamity," *New York Times,* September 20, 2008, C5.

2. Jonathan Weisman, David Cho, and Paul Kane, "With No Plan B, House Reluctantly Passes Politically Risky Measure," *Washington Post,* October 4, 2008, A1.

3. Quoted in ibid.

4. David M. Herszenhorn, "Administration Is Seeking $700 Billion for Wall Street in Possible Record Bailout," *New York Times,* September 21, 2008, A1.

5. Quoted in Hulse and Herszenhorn, "Behind Closed Doors," C5.

6. Quoted in Joe Nocera, "36 Hours of Alarm and Action as Crisis Spread," *New York Times,* October 2, 2008, A1.

7. Jackie Calmes, "Dazed Capital Feels Its Way, Eyes on Nov. 4," *Washington Post,* September 20, 2008, A1.

8. Quoted in Lori Montgomery, Paul Kane, and Neil Irwin, "Bailout Proposal Meets Bipartisan Outrage; Lawmakers Balk as Officials Press Case for Quick Action," *Washington Post,* September 24, 2008, A1.

9. David M. Herszenhorn, "Word Reaches Congress: As the Market Goes Down, So Goes the Electorate," *New York Times,* October 2, 2008, C10.

10. Jonathan Weisman, "House Rejects Financial Rescue, Sending Stocks Plummeting," *Washington Post,* September 30, 2008, A1.

11. Editorial, "Bailout Breakdown," *New York Times,* September 25, 2008, A18.

12. David S. Broder, "Credibility Test for Congress," September 25, 2008, A19.

13. Sarah A. Binder, Thomas E. Mann, Norman J. Ornstein, and Molly Reynolds. *Mending the Broken Branch: Assessing the 110th Congress, Anticipating the 111th.* Brookings Institution Report, January 2009, www.brookings.edu/papers/2009/0108_broken_branch_binder_ mann.aspx, 33.

14. Steven Pearlstein, "Unfairly Rewarding Greedy Bankers, and Why It Works," *Washington Post,* January 14, 2009, D1.

15. See Charles O. Jones, *The Presidency in a Separated System* (Washington, D.C.: Brookings Institution, 1994).

16. U.S. Congress, *Congressional Record,* daily ed., 105th Cong., 1st sess., May 21, 1997, H3072.

17. Glenn R. Parker and Roger H. Davidson, "Why Do Americans Love Their Congressmen So Much More Than Their Congress?" *Legislative Studies Quarterly* 4 (February 1979): 53–61.

18. See Roger H. Davidson, "The House of Representatives: Managing Legislative Complexity," in *Workways of Governance: Monitoring Our Government's Health,* ed. Roger H. Davidson (Washington, D.C.: Governance Institute and Brookings Institution Press, 2003), 24–46; and Sarah A. Binder, "The Senate: Does It Deliberate? Can It Act?" in *Workways of Governance,* ed. Roger H. Davidson, 47–64.

19. Michael Leahy, "House Rules: Freshman Congressman Joe Courtney, Elected by a Margin of 83 Votes, Is Learning that the First Requirement of Power is Self-Preservation," *Washington Post Magazine,* June 10, 2007, W12.

20. Quoted in Mary Lynn F. Jones, "Family Concerns Prompt Early Hill Retirements," *The Hill,* March 20, 2002, 12.

21. Quoted in ibid.

22. Quoted in Leahy, *Washington Post Magazine,* W12.

23. Lydia Saad, "Congressional Approval Hits Record-Low 14%," Gallup, Inc., News Release, www.gallup.com/poll/108856/Congressional-Approval-Hits-RecordLow-14.aspx.

24. Jeffrey M. Jones, "Voters Not Strongly Backing Incumbents for Congress," Gallup, Inc., News Release, www.gallup.com/poll/109267/Voters-Strongly-Backing-Incumbents-Congress.aspx.

25. Quoted by Jonathan Kaplan, "Not on Speaking Terms," *The Hill,* June 3, 2004, 8.

26. Quoted in Leahy, *Washington Post Magazine,* W12.

27. Greg Giroux, "Big Early Money for Democrats Defending 'Frontline,'" *CQ Today,* April 16, 2009.

28. Bob Benenson, "Savvy 'Stars' Making Local TV a Potent Tool," *Congressional Quarterly Weekly Report,* July 18, 1987, 1551–1555.

29. Timothy Cook, *Making Laws and Making News: Media Strategies in the U.S. House of Representatives* (Washington, D.C.: Brookings Institution, 1989), 82–83.

30. Survey by the Gallup Organization, November 30–December 2, 2007. Retrieved from the Gallup Brain Databank.

31. Survey by ABC News/Washington Post, October 5–October 8, 2006. Retrieved from the iPOLL Databank, Roper Center for Public Opinion Research, University of Connecticut.

32. Ibid.

33. Lee H. Hamilton, "Ten Things I Wish Political Scientists Would Teach about Congress," Pi Sigma Alpha Lecture, American Political Science Association, August 31, 2000, 7. See also Hamilton's thoughtful book, *How Congress Works and Why You Should Care* (Bloomington: Indiana University Press, 2004).

34. Norman J. Ornstein, "Prosecutors Must End Their Big Game Hunt of Politicians," *Roll Call,* April 26, 1993, 16.

35. Quoted in T. R. Goldman, "The Influence Industry's Senior Class," *Legal Times,* June 16, 1997, 4.

36. Survey by NBC News, Wall Street Journal, and Hart and McInturff Research Companies, June 9–June 12, 2006. Retrieved from the iPOLL Databank, The Roper Center for Public Opinion Research, University of Connecticut.

37. Jack Tripper, Avery Miller, and Katie Hinman, "The 2006 Election: The Year of the Scandal," October 6, 2006, *ABCNews.com.*

38. Norman J. Ornstein, "Lax Ethics Enforcement Created Culture of Carelessness in House," *Roll Call,* May 11, 2005, 6.

39. Norman J. Ornstein, "The Abramoff Saga: The Worst Hill Scandal in Our Lifetime?" *Roll Call,* October 19, 2005, 5–6.

40. Susan Schmidt and James V. Grimaldi, "Abramoff Pleads Guilty to 3 Counts," *Washington Post,* January 4, 2006, A1.

41. Both Tom Feeney, R-Fla., and John T. Doolittle, R-Calif., had been asked repeatedly to account for their contacts with Abramoff, and both were defeated in 2008.

42. Ronald Brownstein and Alan Miller, "In Politics, Investigation Has Become a Way of Life," *Los Angeles Times,* September 8, 1998, A9.

43. Cass R. Sunstein, "Unchecked and Unbalanced," *American Prospect* 38 (May–June 1998): 23.

44. Edward Epstein, "GOP Makes Much Ado about the Size of Pelosi's Plane; the House Speaker Has Had the Use of a Government Jet since the September 11 Attacks," *San Francisco Chronicle,* February 8, 2007, A3.

45. G. Calvin Mackenzie with Michael Hafken, *Scandal Proof: Do Ethics Laws Make Government Ethical?* (Washington, D.C.: Brookings Institution Press, 2002), 158.

46. Benjamin Ginsberg and Martin Shefter, *Politics by Other Means: Politicians, Prosecutors, and the Press from Watergate to Whitewater,* 3rd ed. (New York: W.W. Norton & Company, 2002).

47. Paul C. Light, "Measuring the Health of the Public Service," in *Workways of Governance: Monitoring the Government's Health,* ed. Roger H. Davidson, 96–97.

48. Jennifer L. Lawless and Richard Logan Fox, *It Takes a Candidate: Why Women Don't Run For Office* (New York: Cambridge University Press, 2005).

49. Gary C. Jacobson, "The Misallocation of Resources in House Campaigns," *Congress Reconsidered,* 5th edition, ed. Lawrence C. Dodd and Bruce I. Oppenheimer. (Washington, D.C.: CQ Press, 1993), 153–182.

50. John Hibbing and Christopher Larimer, "What the American Public Wants Congress to Be," in *Congress Reconsidered,* 8th ed., ed. Lawrence C. Dodd and Bruce I. Oppenheimer (Washington, D.C.: CQ Press, 2005), 55.

51. Woodrow Wilson, *Constitutional Government in the United States* (New York: Columbia University Press, 1908), 79–80.

52. Diane Hollern Harvey, "Who Should Govern? Public Preferences for Congressional and Presidential Power," Ph.D. dissertation, University of Maryland, 1998.

53. Hamilton, "Ten Things I Wish Political Scientists Would Teach about Congress," 3.

54. Paul C. Light, *Government's Greatest Achievements: From Civil Rights to Homeland Security* (Washington, D.C.: Brookings Institution Press, 2002).

55. Ibid., 63.

56. Devlin Barrett, "Most in U.S. Say Congress Short-Sighted," *Washington Post,* September 29, 2006.

57. Media Matters for America, "Full Plate-itude: Media Repeat Charge That Obama Has Taken On Too Much," March 12, 2009, http://mediamatters.org/items/200903120022.

58. Carl Hulse, "Policy Agenda Poses Test for Rusty Legislative Machinery," *New York Times,* April 5, 2009.

59. Quoted in ibid.

60. Richard Hall, *Participation in Congress* (New Haven: Yale University Press, 1996), 2.

61. Binder et al., *Mending the Broken Branch,* 7.

62. Barbara Sinclair, *Unorthodox Lawmaking: New Legislative Processes in the U.S. Congress,* 3rd ed. (Washington, D.C.: CQ Press, 2007).

63. Ibid.
64. Norman J. Ornstein, Thomas E. Mann, and Michael J. Malbin, *Vital Statistics on Congress, 2008* (Washington, DC: Brookings Institution Press, 2008), 110.
65. Thomas E. Mann and Norman J. Ornstein, *The Broken Branch: How Congress Is Failing America and How to Get It Back on Track* (New York: Oxford University Press, 2006), 216.
66. See Norman J. Ornstein, "Part-Time Congress," *Washington Post,* March 7, 2006, A17.
67. Lee Hamilton, "We Can't Wait Much Longer to Fix Congress," *Comments on Congress,* December 15, 2005.
68. Jim Abrams, "Democrats Vow 5-Day Workweek…Sort Of," Associated Press, January 15, 2007.
69. Binder et al., *Mending the Broken Branch,* 7.
70. Nelson W. Polsby, *How Congress Evolves: Social Bases of Institutional Change* (New York: Oxford University Press, 2004), 130–137.
71. Binder et al., *Mending the Broken Branch,* 7.
72. Quoted by David S. Broder, "Role Models, Now More than Ever," *Washington Post,* July 13, 2003, B7.
73. Ibid.
74. Mickey Edwards, "Wanted: A Congress with a Backbone," *Los Angeles Times,* August 29, 2006, B13.
75. Sinclair, *Unorthodox Lawmaking,* 127.
76. Ibid.
77. *Congressional Record,* December 17, 2007, H15508.
78. Sinclair, *Unorthodox Lawmaking,* 282.
79. Elizabeth Brotherton, "Sunlight to Unveil 'Open House' Proposal," *Roll Call,* May 8, 2007, 3.
80. E. Scott Adler, *Why Congressional Reforms Fail: Reelection and the House Committee System* (Chicago: University of Chicago Press, 2002), 11.
81. Eric Schickler, *Disjointed Pluralism: Institutional Innovation and the Development of the U.S. Congress* (Princeton: Princeton University Press, 2001), 268.
82. Ibid., 267.
83. Bob Schieffer, *This Just In: What I Couldn't Tell You on TV* (New York: Putnam, 2003).
84. See Martin P. Wattenburg, *Is Voting for Young People?* 2d ed. (New York: Pearson Longman, 2007), esp. chaps. 1–2.
85. Quoted by Pamela Constable, "Demise of the Foreign Correspondent," *Washington Post,* February 18, 2007, B1.
86. James T. Hamilton, *All the News That's Fit to Sell* (Princeton: Princeton University Press, 2004).
87. William Arkin, "If Only War Reporting Were More Like Sports Reporting," The *Washington Post*'s Early Warning Blog, May 22, 2007, http://blog.washingtonpost.com/earlywarning/.
88. Bill Moyers, "Journalism and Democracy," *Nation,* May 7, 2001, 12.
89. Media critic Neal Gabler's commentaries are especially incisive. See "The Media Bias Myth," *Los Angeles Times,* December 22, 2002, M1.
90. Parker and Davidson, "Why Do Americans Love Their Congressmen So Much More Than Their Congress?"
91. Gallup Poll News Service, www.galluppoll.com; Isaiah Poole, "Congress Confronts Skeptical Public," *CQ Today,* May 31, 2005, 17.
92. Quoted by Sheryl Gay Stolbert, "The Dangers of Political Theater," *New York Times,* March 27, 2005, D3.
93. John R. Hibbing and Elizabeth Theiss-Morse, *Congress as Public Enemy* (Cambridge: Cambridge University Press, 1995), 147.

94. Ibid., 158.
95. Christopher Lee, "An Amendment to Be Recommended on Continuity of Congress," *Washington Post,* May 25, 2003, A11.
96. Ibid.
97. Norman Ornstein, "Government in Denial; No Branch Is Prepared for a Decapitating Strike," *Washington Post,* July 12, 2007, A23.
98. Hamilton, "We Can't Wait Much Longer to Fix Congress."
99. Quoted in Kirk Victor, "Congress in Eclipse," *National Journal,* April 5, 2003, 1067.
100. U.S. Congress, *Congressional Record,* daily ed., 107th Congress, 2d sess., February 12, 2002, S2268, S2271.
101. Quoted in Victor, "Congress in Eclipse," 1068.
102. Bob Woodward, "Cheney Upholds Power of the Presidency," *Washington Post,* January 20, 2005, A7.
103. Quoted in Victor, "Congress in Eclipse," 1068.
104. Ibid., 1069.
105. Lee Hamilton, "Congress Should Use Its Muscle," *Comments on Congress,* August 9, 2006, 2.
106. Binder et al., *Mending the Broken Branch,* 13.
107. David Nather, "Congress as Watchdog: Asleep on the Job?" *CQ Weekly,* May 22, 2004, 1190.
108. Binder et al., *Mending the Broken Branch.*
109. Don Wolfensberger, "Fiscal Oversight Directive a Welcome Breath of Spring Air," *Roll Call,* March 2, 2009, 6.
110. John T. Noonan Jr., *Narrowing the Nation's Power* (Berkeley: University of California Press, 2002), 11.
111. Ibid., 139.
112. James L. Sundquist, *The Decline and Resurgence of Congress* (Washington, D.C.: Brookings Institution, 1981), 482–483.
113. Ibid., 483.
114. Andrew Rudalevige, *The New Imperial Presidency: Renewing Presidential Power after Watergate* (Ann Arbor: University of Michigan Press, 2005), 261.
115. Hamilton, "Ten Things I Wish Political Scientists Would Teach about Congress," 10.

Index

Boxes, figures, tables, and notes are indicated by b, f, t, and n following the page number. Appendix page numbers start with A, and note page numbers start with N.

Photo Credits

Frontispiece, page iv: AP Images (bottom); GEORGE TAMES/The *New York Times* (center left); Library of Congress (top left; top right).

Chapter 1, page xxx: AP Images (top right; center); Office of Representative Thaddeus McCotter (top left; bottom).

Chapter 2, page 10: Library of Congress (top; center); ROD LAMKEY JR./The *Washington Times*/ Landov (bottom).

Chapter 3, page 38: AFP/Getty Images (top right); AP Images (center left; bottom).

Chapter 4, page 86: AP Images (top right; center left); Getty Images (top left); KEVIN MOLONEY/ The *New York Times* (bottom).

Chapter 5, page 124: AP Images (all).

Chapter 6, page 156: Getty Images (bottom); KEVIN DIETSCH/UPI/Landov (center); MANDEL NGAN/AFP/Getty Images (top).

Chapter 7, page 198: AP Images (top left; top right); Getty Images (center); Scott Ferrell/ *Congressional Quarterly* (bottom).

Chapter 8, page 236: Scott Ferrell/*Congressional Quarterly.*

Chapter 9, page 270: AP Images (bottom left); League of Conservation Voters (bottom right); Scott Ferrell/*Congressional Quarterly* (top left; center right); Reuters/Landov (center left).

Chapter 10, page 300: AFP/Getty Images (bottom left; bottom right); Getty Images (top).

Chapter 11, page 332: AFP/Getty Images (center); Getty Images (top; bottom).

Chapter 12, page 360: AFP/Getty Images (center; bottom); Getty Images (top).

Chapter 13, page 388: AFP/Getty Images (bottom right); AP Images (top; bottom left).

Chapter 14, page 414: Getty Images (bottom); NIKKI KAHN/The *Washington Post* (top); Scott Ferrell/*Congressional Quarterly* (center).

Chapter 15, page 446: Agence France Presse (center right); AP Images (bottom); ERIC THAYER/ Reuters (center left); Getty Images (top).

Chapter 16, page 478: Getty Images (bottom); Scott Ferrell/*Congressional Quarterly* (top right); Time & Life Pictures/Getty Images (top left).

CQ Press, a division of SAGE, is a leading publisher of books, directories, periodicals, and electronic products on American government and politics, with an expanding list in international affairs, history, and journalism. CQ Press consistently ranks among the top commercial publishers in terms of quality, as evidenced by the numerous awards its products have won over the years. CQ Press owes its existence to Nelson Poynter, former publisher of the *St. Petersburg Times,* and his wife Henrietta, with whom he founded Congressional Quarterly in 1945. Poynter established CQ with the mission of promoting democracy through education and in 1975 founded the Modern Media Institute, renamed The Poynter Institute for Media Studies after his death. The Poynter Institute (*www.poynter.org*) is a nonprofit organization dedicated to training journalists and media leaders.

In 2008, CQ Press was acquired by SAGE, a leading international publisher of journals, books, and electronic media for academic, educational, and professional markets. Since 1965, SAGE has helped inform and educate a global community of scholars, practitioners, researchers, and students spanning a wide range of subject areas, including business, humanities, social sciences, and science, technology, and medicine. A privately owned corporation, SAGE has offices in Los Angeles, London, New Delhi, and Singapore, in addition to the Washington DC office of CQ Press.

CONGRESSIONAL TIME LINE: **1789–1932**

	1790		1810		1830		1850
Size of House of Representatives	65	142	186	213	242	232	237
Size of Senate	26	34	36	48	48	52	62

Parties	Federalist Era (1789–1800)	Jeffersonian Era (1800–1828)	Jacksonian Era (1828–1856)	GOP formed (1856)

Presidents

"Doughfaces" (Fillmore, Pierce, Buchanan) (1849–1861)

"Jeffersonians"

Washington (1789–1797)	Jefferson (1801–1809)	Madison, Monroe (1809–1825)	Jackson (1829–1837)	Polk (1845–1849)

Internal

Capitol burned by British (1814)   Restored Capitol (1818–1826)   Printed election ballots (1829)

Capitol cornerstone (1793)

Speaker Henry Clay (1811)

Senate oratory (Webster, Clay, Calhoun) (1830s, 1840s)

Procedural rules, standing committees (1790s)   Congressional Nominating Caucus (1804–1828)   Committees control legislation (1820s)

Congress convenes; Ways and Means Committee (1789)   Jefferson's *Manual* (1801)   Unlimited debate in Senate (1828)

Major Laws/ Investigations

Louisiana Purchase (1803)   Rivers and Harbors Act (1823)

Judicial review *Marbury v. Madison* (1803)   *McCulloch v. Maryland* (1819)   *Dred Scott v. Sandford* (1857)

Judiciary Act (1789)   Slave importation halted (1807)

St. Clair investigation (1792)

Alien and Sedition Acts (1798)   Missouri Compromise (1820)   Compromise of 1850

Bill of Rights (1791)

Wars and Alarms

Barbary pirates (1801–1805)

War of 1812 (1812–1814)   Mexican War (1846–1848)

1790	1810	1830	1850